ARTS&
CRAFTS

COMPLETE ILLUSTRATED LIBRARY
OF

ARTS&
CRAFTS

MODERN PROMOTIONS
A Division of Unisystems Inc., New York, New York 10022

Contents

Introduction

The **Complete Illustrated Library of Arts and Crafts** is designed for the beginner interested in becoming involved in crafts. Because of the renewed interest in creative handicrafts, this volume describes 26 different types of crafts — all contained in a single source. This volume could not cover all possible crafts, so the articles are limited to those of current popularity and to those which involve a minimum of expense.

Each article is divided into six main categories. The **Historical Introduction** describes the origin and development of the craft, its spread through various cultures, as well as famous people who have been associated with the craft. The **Common Terms** section defines terms, items, or names as they relate to the individual craft. **Basic Equipment and Supplies** lists the tools and materials needed. The section under **Basic Procedures** provides start-to-finish procedures for handicraft projects. Each article also contains three to five projects based on the supplies and procedures discussed. **For Additional Reading** lists other references for those who wish to increase their knowledge of a particular craft.

The **Complete Illustrated Library of Arts and Crafts** is intended not only to inspire the budding craftsman, but to provide new ideas, techniques and whole new areas of creative handicrafts for the experienced craftsman to explore. The fun-to-do projects in this comprehensive book will be a source of enjoyment and relaxation for the entire family.

Batik

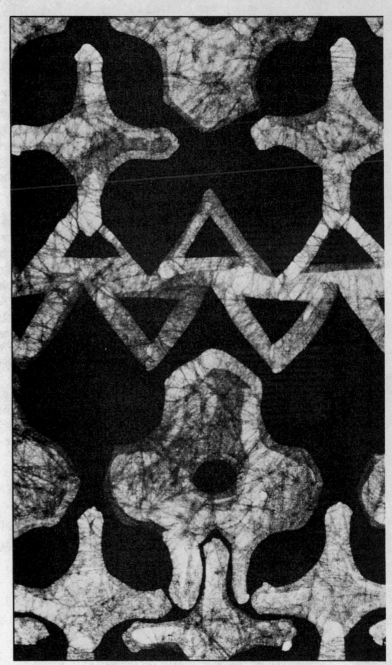

Batik, an ancient craft newly revived, results in the creation of beautiful and decorative fabrics through the use of resist substances and dyes.

Throughout civilization, mankind has been interested in self-adornment. One manifestation of this interest is fabric decoration, which has played a significant part in the history of various peoples. Wall paintings and tablets have told the story of cloth dyeing and embellishment. Indeed, archaeological evidence of this craft dates as far back as 5000 years.

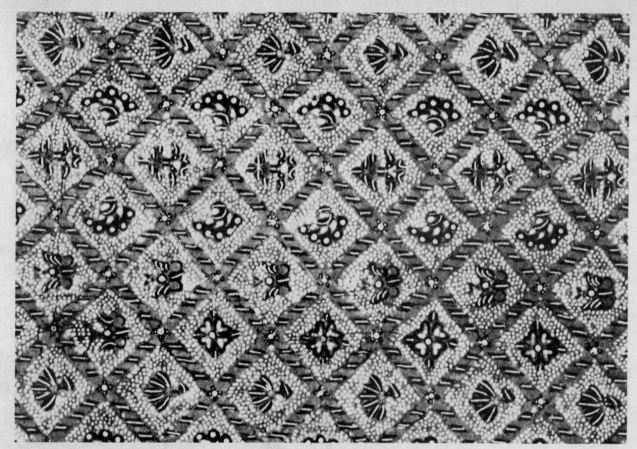

Figure 2. Archaeological evidence indicates that the ancient art of batik was widespread among various cultures throughout the world. This traditional Indonesian batik illustrates the skill achieved by early craftsmen. (Collection, Mr. and Mrs. Edward Holcomb.)

Although the discoverers or originators of the batik process remain unknown, fragments of decorated fabrics which have been resist dyed have been found in many places in the world. In Roman writings, wax, flour paste, clay resists, and dyeing have been described in historical accounts. It is assumed that the techniques were brought to Egypt from India, because tools and blocks for fabric decoration dating from 3000 B. C. have been found in India. And it was trade with India which also introduced wax resists to Indonesia and Java, where the world's finest batiks are still produced. (In Javanese, *tik* means light dots or points against a darker background.)

Ancient and highly prized decorated fabrics are

Figure 1. The batik process utilizes wax resists and dyes to print designs on cloth. Stencils were used to create the unusual patterns shown on the cotton batiste fabric (opposite).

also attributed to China and Japan, while African history shows that the first decorated textiles were probably painted with fingers, sticks, twigs, or simple brushes; designs were printed with resist pastes and dyed on cloth. Pre-Hispanic Peruvians also used hand stamps, stencils, and rollers to print designs on cloth, while dyes were painted. Many fabric fragments found have been dyed in one color.

Batik has been defined as writing with wax, writing with light against dark, or writing with little bits or little dots. The art is called writing because of the tool, called a *tjanting*, which is used in the application of hot wax to cloth. A tjanting is a pen-shaped tool with a brass or copper receptacle for holding hot wax and a spout for its application. The wax is drawn on the cloth and the cloth is then dyed, the original color of the cloth being retained only under the wax.

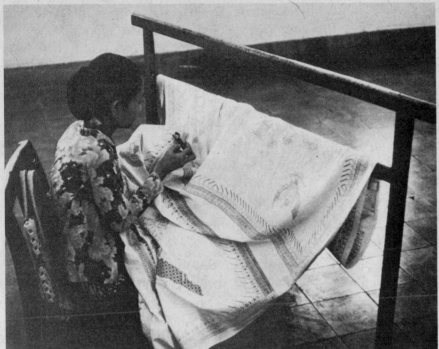

Figure 3. A Javanese batik artist (left) applies wax with a tjanting, the traditional tool of batik. (Photo, courtesy of Alice Holcomb.) Historically, batik was used for self-adornment as well as decorative purposes. The silk scarf from India (below, left) and the dress from Malaysia demonstrate the versatility of this craft. (Silk scarf from the collection of Dr. and Mrs. Jack Arends; dress from the collection of Mr. and Mrs. Edward Holcomb.)

Batik is a fabric-dyeing process in which a resist substance is applied to the cloth wherever color is to be reserved. Waxes, resins, and starch pastes can be used as resists. Decorative design patterns are produced through use of resists and dyes on cloth and paper.

Recently, artists and craftsmen have been reviving several of these techniques. In Java, the old traditional methods are still used; however, there and elsewhere in the world, new ideas and processes are being tried. Presently, there are hundreds of craftsmen working and experimenting with batik.

Contemporary methods and inexpensive materials are available to all who are eager to learn. The idea of painting designs on cloth with waxes and immersing the cloth into dyes to create images is, indeed, like magic.

Common Terms Used In Batik

Acid Dyes: a group of dyes for silk and woolens requiring acetic acid as an assistant.

Assistant: a chemical that allows dye to work with fabric.

Batik: a process of fabric decoration in which waxes, resins, and flour pastes are used as resists on cloth before dyeing.

Cold Dyeing: a process of coloring fabric in a dye solution of about 100° Fahrenheit.

Crackle: thin web-like lines caused by cracking wax in fabric before dyeing.

Direct Dyes: that group of dyes with an affinity for cotton, linen, and viscose rayon.

Dye Bath: the liquid containing dyestuff, assistants, and water in which cloth is immersed and colored.

Dye Paste: a thick mixture in which dyestuffs, assistants, chemicals, and thickening agent are combined and used for painting and printing on cloth.

Dyes and Dyestuffs: chemicals that can be put into solution and become basically transparent liquids for coloring cloth.

Fastness: the ability of a dye on cloth to retain its intensity and depth of color after being subjected to washing, boiling, sun, and light.

Fiber Reactive Dyes: a fairly new group of dyes, invented in 1956 in England. These work in a cool water solution with salt and washing soda assistants and react with cotton, linen, and silk fibers.

Finishing: the completion process that includes the washing, rinsing, drying, and ironing of a decorated fabric.

Fixation: the process by which dye color is set in fabric.

Ground Color: the original color of cloth before dyeing.

Hot Dyeing: the process of dyeing cloth in a color bath that has been heated to 140° Fahrenheit or higher.

Household Dyes: a combination of several groups of dyestuffs that can be used for natural and synthetic fabrics.

Immersion Dyeing: the process of placing a fabric into a solution of dyes for coloring fibers.

Mercerizing Process: the treatment of cotton with caustic soda to increase its affinity for dyes; mercerized cottons should not be washed before dyeing.

Overdyeing: the process of dyeing color over color.

Paste (To Paste): the mixing of dyestuff with a small amount of cold water before dissolving in hot water prior to dyeing cloth.

Repeat: a unit of design used repeatedly in the decoration of a single fabric.

Resist: the process of applying a substance for the purpose of keeping an area of cloth free from dyes.

Salt: common or plain salt (sodium chloride) used as a chemical assistant for fabric dyeing; it is not mixed with iodine as is iodized salt.

Sizing: the stiffener applied to a fabric to give it body.

Solvent: the liquid used to dissolve the remainder of waxes in fabric.

Stamping: a method of creating designs on fabric by pressing objects or blocks into a substance and onto cloth.

Steaming: the process for setting colors in fabric through moist heat.

Stencil: a thin paper, film, or metal cut or perforated to allow a design to form on the surface underneath when resists or dye pastes are applied.

Synthetic Fibers: man-made fibers produced through chemical synthesis.

Thickener: a gel-like substance made with starch or gum and added to dyes for direct application to cloth.

Viscose Rayon: a manufactured fiber that can be dyed with the same dyes used for linen and cotton.

Washing Soda: a chemical substance used as a fixing agent that causes a reaction between fiber reactive dyes and fabric.

Wet Out: the dampening of fabric with water before immersing in a dye.

Basic Equipment And Supplies

The materials used for batik are readily available in most communities. Many of the materials and supplies can be purchased in grocery, drug, variety, department, and hardware stores. Some equipment is available in the home. The following is a basic list: (1) an appliance for heating wax, such as an electric skillet, fryer, hot plate, or double boiler; (2) a table or other large working surface; and (3) a frame (stretcher, embroidery hoop, or other type of frame used to hold cloth).

Basic supplies include: (1) fabric (about three yards of 100% cotton—especially muslin—is excellent for the beginner); (2) wax (one to two pounds of paraffin and some beeswax, available in grocery stores and candle shops, among others); (3) household or fiber reactive dyes (the former are available in drug and variety stores and the latter can be bought from batik craft suppliers)

of the following colors: lemon yellow, yellow, scarlet, magenta red, blue, and turquoise—brown and black are optional; (4) cleaning fluid; (5) contact paper; and (6) common salt, soap, and vinegar.

TOOLS AND OBJECTS

1. Brushes. One wide bristle brush, one narrow bristle brush, and one pointed brush for application of waxes and dyes. Natural bristle brushes of various widths can be purchased at hardware stores or artist supply shops. Flat paint brushes in one-half inch, one-inch and three-inch widths are adequate for most surface application in batik work. One tapered brush or flat brush with bristles cut diagonally could be used for small areas. Japanese bamboo brushes, which are pointed, can be used for application of wax in fine details.

2. Tjanting. A *tjanting* is a drawing tool for holding hot wax and is used for designing line

Figure 4. A wide assortment of tools (left) may be used to create intersting batik patterns. After drawing the design with a crayon, a pencil, or charcoal, wax is applied to the design with a tjanting or a brush. Designs may also be applied to the fabric with woodblocks, metal stamps, or cookie cutters. Both household and fiber-reactive dyes (right) provide the batik artist with a variety of colors.

patterns; available at craft shops handling batik supplies.

3. Stamps and blocks used for printing designs with hot wax on fabric. Such objects include cookie cutters, metal tools, or cardboard tubes.

OTHER EQUIPMENT AND SUPPLIES

In addition to the basic items already mentioned, other equipment supplies needed are: (1) rubber gloves; (2) an electric iron; (3) large plastic or enamel dishpans (pans should be large enough to immerse fabric in dyebath); (4) measuring spoons and cups; (5) wooden spoons, dowels, or paint sticks for stirring dyes; (6) jars, preferably with wide mouths; (7) scissors; (8) cardboard scraps to be used for making printing blocks; (9) newspaper; (10) plastic bags and plastic wrap; and (11) crayons, pencil, charcoal, or ball-point pen for drawing design on fabric.

Figure 5. Many of the basic supplies for batik are found in the household. The equipment shown here includes washing soda, soap flakes, an iron, spray starch, salt, dish pans, paper towels, an appliance for heating wax, measuring cups and spoons, rubber gloves, newspapers, and fabric.

Basic Procedures

The batik process is basically a resist method of producing images and designs on cloth or paper: designs are planned, the cloth is washed, hot wax is applied to it, and the cloth is dyed. The areas covered with wax resist the dyes and remain the color of the cloth. Unwaxed areas are the dyed color. Batiks can be planned for one-, two-, or three-color sequences—some designers use as many as 20 colors. After the last dye application, the wax is removed and the cloth is finished.

Batik is fun and satisfying but the process is a time-consuming one that requires patience on the part of the beginner. Designs need to be drawn carefully so the eventual placement of waxes and dyes is clear.

FABRIC

Very fine, 100% cottons are best for batik. Because most new fabrics are treated with sizing, preparation of the cloth requires washing, pre-shrinking, rinsing, and pressing. A thin starch solution or spray starch will help in pressing fabric smooth and in keeping the hot wax from spreading into the fabric.

The exciting part of doing batiks lies in the production of original designs. Beginners should try to create design ideas which might be derived from nature or man-made environments; from people and animals; or from geometric and free shapes. Design patterns can, of course, be drawn repeatedly on the fabric.

The design should be drawn on the fabric with crayon, pencil, charcoal, or ball-point pen. When drawing on paper, the artist usually draws dark lines and shapes against a light background. However, in drawing a design for a batik, the dots, lines, and shapes are drawn in wax and remain light against a dark (dyed) background. The hot wax drawing should penetrate the cloth. This is done by having the cloth stretched tightly on a frame, stretcher, or embroidery hoop.

Stretching or Holding the Fabric

The cloth should be stretched tightly so that waxing tools can glide freely, allowing the hot wax to penetrate easily.

Stretch the cloth evenly on a frame, tacking it at corners—the position of the fabric being waxed can be changed as often as necessary. Keeping the fabric free of the working surface is advantageous and the stretcher frame permits this both for waxing and for painting dyes onto the cloth. Some craftsmen also like to have fabric on a frame when using a stamping process. Regular batik frames are available at batik supply stores.

There are some things about stretching the fabric which should be kept in mind. Large frames are cumbersome and heavy, a definite disadvantage. Tacking of lightweight cotton or silk may leave marks on the cloth, so some artists pin fabric to a chair and hold cloth stretched tightly in one hand while waxing with brush or tjanting with the other hand. One might also place bricks, rocks, or other weighted objects on the end of the cloth and hold the section to be waxed tightly in one hand. Some artists let the fabric lie flat on waxed paper or foil that has been placed on the working surface; after the waxing, the fabric is gently pulled away from the surface.

WAX

Paraffin, the most inexpensive wax for batik, produces a crackle or vein-like webbing in the design pattern. Because using paraffin alone can result in the wax not clinging to or penetrating the cloth, a small portion of beeswax should be combined with the paraffin. Beeswax may be more difficult to obtain. Some art supply companies sell a batik wax which is a combination of beeswax and paraffin—an ideal wax contains equal amounts of each. A cake wax, product #2305, much like beeswax but less expensive, is produced by Mobil Oil Company. Other petroleum companies have similar products.

Applying Hot Wax

The simplest way to apply wax to the fabric is with a brush while the wax is hot. A double boiler or a saucepan set in a pan of water can be used for melting wax, either on the stove or on a hot plate. If using a can of wax, place it in a pan with three or four inches of water that is heated at a low boil. Never place a can of wax directly on the burner.

When the wax reaches a temperature of about 240° Fahrenheit, it can be brushed on the fabric.

The temperature is correct if the wax goes through the cloth and looks quite clear. If the wax is not hot enough, it only coats the fabric and is opaque. When this happens the fabric should be rewaxed with hot wax in the same areas on the under side. Wax is too hot when it starts to smoke. The wax pot should never be left unattended and baking soda should be kept handy to smother a flame. *Never* use water on or near hot wax. The table on which fabric is to be waxed should be heavily covered with newspaper and should be within reach of the hot wax.

The brush is immersed in the hot wax and should be allowed to heat up a bit. When picking up the hot wax on the brush, wipe the excess wax against the edge of the pan to prevent any dripping. Apply the wax to the design on the area of fabric that is to be kept free of dye.

Large areas that are to be waxed should be outlined with a small brush first. Then the larger space inside the outline can be filled in with a wider brush. Apply the wax by brushing in towards the middle of the space from the outline.

Decorative Processes

Design outlines should be kept open and free of wax. The wax can be applied about one-eighth to one-fourth inch from the lines. To prevent wax from spreading over the line, water can be painted on the outline. This wets the cloth and

Figure 6. The most common method of applying hot wax to a design is with a brush. Broad areas may be quickly and easily covered. The fabric should be raised to allow the wax to penetrate the cloth.

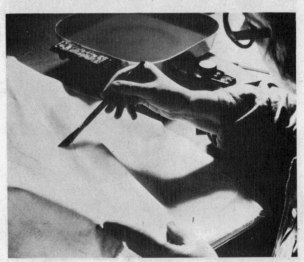

resists the wax. When the outlines of the design are consistently kept free of waxing, subsequent dyeing will create dark lines around the shapes and patterns of the batik fabric.

Brushes should be cared for between waxings. While they should not be left to cool and harden in the wax, they do not need to be cleaned each time they are used. When placed in hot wax for a few minutes, wax-coated brushes will soften and can be used again for waxing.

For centuries, as mentioned earlier, the Javanese have used a tool called a tjanting for wax writing in dots and lines. Using a tjanting is optional for the beginner—as with any other new skill, it requires practice. It is held very much like a pencil, and hot wax is picked up in the brass or copper cup and permitted to flow through the spout, thus creating a delicate linear drawing. To prevent accidental drippings of hot wax, always hold a piece of cloth or a padded paper under the tjanting when carrying it to the work surface from the stove or burner. Covering areas of designs not to be waxed with newspaper is always helpful. Designs created with the tjanting have identifiable characteristics. The fabric, penetrated just as it is with brush work, usually has fine patterns of swirls, spirals, dots, and lines.

The simplest, most inexpensive stamping tools can be made from cardboard or the cardboard tubing which comes inside paper towel rolls. Cut the tubing or cardboard in about two-inch lengths. Fold and shape into a block or form in a lengthwise direction, with the ends retaining the cut surface. The block can be bound tightly with tape. Both ends of the block must be flat and can be used for stamping hot wax onto the cloth.

The contemporary batik artist also can devise many metal stamps for designing fabric. The hardware and kitchenware departments of stores contain hundreds of such items. All kinds and shapes of cookie and doughnut cutters, and such kitchen tools as apple cutters, potato mashers, canape cutters, patty shell makers, etc., can be used. Metal tools, nuts, bolts, washers, pipes, and boxes are among other objects found in the hardware store that are excellent. Other objects might include metal parts of toys, corks, or cans which can be cut, bent, and shaped. Imagination is very important in visualizing how a variety of objects can become tools for batik designs. It is important to keep experimenting.

Because metals are excellent conductors of heat, small metal objects such as cutters should be glued on wood or pressed into cork, the latter to be used as handles. Small sections of dowel rods attached to the metal objects also work effectively.

Figure 7. With practice, the tjanting (below left) may be used to apply wax for linear designs. Imaginative patterns are easily stamped by dipping printing blocks (right) into hot wax.

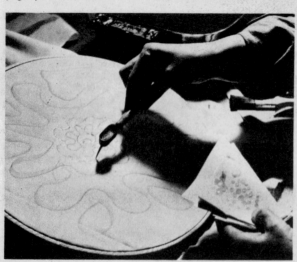

Pipe cleaners can also be formed into simple designs. An extra pipe cleaner can be tied into the form and twisted into a handle. Printing blocks made of pipe cleaners are effective because the covering holds the wax while the thin wire retains the heat.

The temperature of the wax for stamping can be a little lower than the temperature for brush and tjanting work. If the wax is too hot, it will spread too much as the block is stamped onto the fabric. One way of helping to avoid this is to place a piece of foam rubber on the bottom of the wax pan—wax should just cover the surface. The printing block can be pressed onto the foam pad to pick up the wax and then stamped onto the cloth. The hot wax will penetrate the cloth so that a better resist occurs when the fabric is immersed into the dye bath.

Stencils can be cut in simple, geometric designs from commercial stencil paper or from a waxy tagboard. One way to apply stencil decorations to fabric is by placing a stencil on the cloth and drawing around the shapes lightly with pencil. Move the stencil and repeat until the fabric is covered with the designs. Then carefully brush hot wax within the shapes to create repeat patterns. Several stencil designs can be drawn on one fabric piece.

Self-adhesive stencils can be made from plastic preparations such as contact paper. After the designs and their placement are planned, the paper backing can be peeled off and the stencils adhered to the cloth. Hot wax is brushed carefully over the stencils. After the waxing is completed, the stencils can be pulled away, one at a time, and attached to a plastic surface to be saved for later use. In fact, contact stencils can be used about fifty times before they deteriorate. After the stencils are put away, check the waxed areas on the cloth. If the wax has penetrated the cloth, apply hot wax to those areas of the fabric which need retouching. The fabric is then ready for dyeing.

The creative craftsman may wish to combine various waxing techniques: brush and tjanting; brush and stencil; stencil and tjanting; stencil and block; or block, brush, stencil, and tjanting. Other interesting effects can be created by drawing lines into the wax before final dyeing. This can be achieved by scratching into the wax with a sharpened dowel, a bamboo skewer, or an orange stick. The process is called *sqrafitto*.

Wax can be removed from the cloth by ironing the fabric between newspapers. Old newspapers should be layered on a large work surface, an old pattern-cutting board, or on the floor. Layer the paper approximately one-half inch in thickness. Place the fabric on the newspaper padding, put more sheets of newspaper on top of fabric, and then iron with dry heat. After ironing, pull out one newspaper sheet from under and over the fabric and repeat the process. When wax no longer stains the newspapers, the fabric is ironed suffi-

Figure 8. Stencils may be used to make repeated patterns on the fabric. After the design is cut from stencil paper, place the sheet on the material and brush hot wax within the open shapes. Continue waxing the stenciled areas until the desired effect is achieved.

Figure 9. To prepare a dye bath using household dyes, begin by pouring the powder into a mixing cup (above). Then, add enough water (above right) and stir to make a paste (opposite.).

ciently and will be stiff. There will always be a residue of wax in the fabric.

DYES

There are many kinds of dyes available to the batik craftsman. For the beginner, there are enough household dyes, direct dyes, and fiber reactive dyes to choose from to achieve excellent and successful results. Basic colors for developing a wide color range are lemon yellow, scarlet, and ultramarine blue. Other colors that would add to color exploration are magenta red, deep yellow, turquoise, brown, and black.

Household Dyes

Household dyes (Rit, Putnam, Cushing, Tintex) are available at grocery, drug, variety, and department stores. They are basically multipurpose dyes, usually a combination of dyestuffs that react with an assortment of fabrics. The dyes are effective on cotton, silk, linen, and wool as well as on viscose rayon, which is a man-made fiber. They are easy to use and fairly inexpensive.

These dyes can be used for direct brushing by preparing a more concentrated solution. Most household dyes come in powder form. Disregard

directions for soaking. One teaspoon of the dye, made into paste with cold water and then mixed with two cups of boiling hot water and three tablespoons of salt, is of sufficient strength for direct painting on fabric. The dye bath should be a colored clear liquid to which one more pint of cool water should be added. Remember that areas to be dyed should be drawn in with wax to keep one dye area from running into another. When working with immersion of fabrics in dye baths,

Figure 10. A dye bath is made by diluting a concentrated dye solution in a large dishpan of hot water (above). The transparent liquid can be intensified in color by dissolving table salt in the mixture (below). It is a good idea to wear rubber gloves when working with dyestuffs.

always wear rubber gloves and a cover-up such as a rubber apron. Dyes can be removed from hands with household bleach solution.

Dyes usually work best when they are very hot because they will be faster and more fadeproof.

However, in batik work hot dyes are impractical because the wax designs on the cloth would be obliterated. Therefore, even though the dyes for wax batik should be prepared hot, when the fabric is finally immersed in the dye bath, the mixture should be cool.

The fabric should be immersed in the dye for 45 minutes to an hour. If more dye is needed, follow the same proportions for each additional quart required. Also, if darker or more intense colors are desired, add one-half cup of plain salt to the dye bath—be sure the salt is thoroughly dissolved.

After the fabric has been in the dye bath about an hour, take the cloth out of the dye, rinse in cold water, and let it dry. The fabric can be laid on layers of newspapers or on a drying rack. Do not hang it in direct sunlight or put it in a dryer because the wax will melt. After the fabric is dry, rinse it in cold water until all excess dye has been removed and the water runs clear. The fabric can then be dried again.

For additional dyeing, wax can be applied to the cloth again by repeating the dyeing process. Start with light colors for the first dyeing and go to darker colors. Household dyes are not light-fast or washable and should be dry cleaned, a process which preserves the dye color.

Direct Dyes

Direct dyes (Aljo, Dick Blick, Craftool, Fezan) are available in art stores, craft supply shops, and batik supply resources. These dyes work best at high temperatures: the dye can be mixed with water as hot as it can be from the faucet. Because direct dyes should be cool to the touch when used for batik, twice the amount of dye powder should be mixed to a paste. Usually two to three heaping teaspoons will be sufficient for about one pound or three yards of fabric. After the dye has been made into a paste, hot water is added to yield one-half gallon of dye bath, to which three heaping tablespoons of plain salt should be added before the fabric is immersed. Fabric should be left in dye bath for 40 minutes to an hour. For brush painting on fabric, a concentrated solution can be used. Make a paste of one teaspoon of dye and a little water. Add one pint of hot water from the faucet and three tablespoons of salt. Brush on the fabric and let dry.

After the fabric is taken from the dye bath, it should be rinsed in cold water until the water runs clear. Because direct dyes are not light-fast or washable, dry cleaning is again recommended.

Fabric dyed with direct dyes and with household dyes should be steamed for a little more color fastness.

Fiber Reactive Dyes

Fiber reactive dyes (Dylon, Hi-Dye, Fibrec, ICI Organics, Pylam), which react with and affect fibers, work very well in cool dye baths. The colors are bright to brilliant, light-fast and can be washed—fabrics do not have to be dry cleaned. Moreover, because they mix well, only a few basic colors are needed to create an adequate range. These dyes are effective on cotton, linen, silk, and viscose rayon; they are not effective on polyesters, dacrons, acetates, or other man-made fabrics.

Fiber reactive dyes can be purchased with packages of fixitive and with paste activators. The user needs only to follow directions on the packages. For the beginning batik artist, buying just what is needed is a logical way to proceed. If the craft is continued, then it is wise to buy larger quantities of dyes.

A dye bath with fiber reactive or Procion dyes can be prepared by making a paste of one teaspoon of dye powder with a little cold water. Two pints of very hot water (from the faucet) should be added and six tablespoons of salt also dissolved in the solution. Finally, two tablespoons of washing soda (e.g., Sal Soda) should be dissolved in a little warm water and added to the dye bath.

After the cloth is put into the dye bath it should be moved about constantly for a half-hour. If the fabric is not covered by the dye, increase the amount of dye powder, water, salt, and soda according to formula.

There is also a long-method fiber-reactive dyeing procedure, explained here for one pound of cloth (about three yards), which is done as follows:

1. Dissolve 1 or 2 teaspoons of dye in 1 cup of hot water (140° F).

2. Add the dye solution to 2 gallons of warm water (100° F).

3. Place the clean cloth in the dye bath for 10 to 15 minutes. (All cloth should have been washed before dyeing except for mercerized cotton, which need not be washed.)

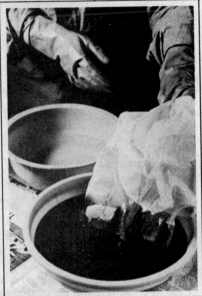

4. Add 2 tablespoons of plain salt every 5 minutes for 15 minutes. Then leave fabric in bath for 20 minutes more. (Stir fabric in bath occasionally.)

5. Dissolve 3 tablespoons of washing soda in 2 ounces of water and add to dye bath. Stir occasionally for 1 hour.

6. Rinse the dyed cloth in warm water and soap (Lux or Ivory).

7. Rinse well until water runs clear. Let the fabric dry.

Always wear rubber gloves. Pans for dyes should be plastic, enamel, or stainless steel—do not use copper, aluminum, or galvanized metal.

In order to brush dye directly on cloth, mix two teaspoons of dye powder (pasted in water), one pint of hot tap water, six tablespoons of plain salt, and two tablespoons of washing soda (dissolved in warm water). This solution will be active for about five or six hours. The fabric should be allowed to dry in a warm humid place for a day or two, or ironed for five minutes between paper towels with a steam iron.

COLOR

The one-color process is an excellent way for the beginner to start batik. In using one color at a time, there can be dramatic contrasts of dye color to the white or light background color—trying a dark or intense color will bring the designs out even more. An experiment for the beginner follows.

Begin by waxing out all areas that are to remain the original color of the fabric. Then, wet the fabric and immerse in a red dye bath. Rinse the fabric and let dry.

Once this process is mastered, plan a design using the following four-color dye bath process. Wax areas that are to remain the original color of the fabric, wet the fabric, and immerse it in a yellow dye bath, following dye directions previously given. Rinse and dry. Next, wax out areas to remain yellow and rewax white if necessary. Wet

Figure 11. Waxed cloth is immersed in cold water (top) before it is placed in a dye bath (center). The fabric should be removed from the dye bath in about an hour (bottom).

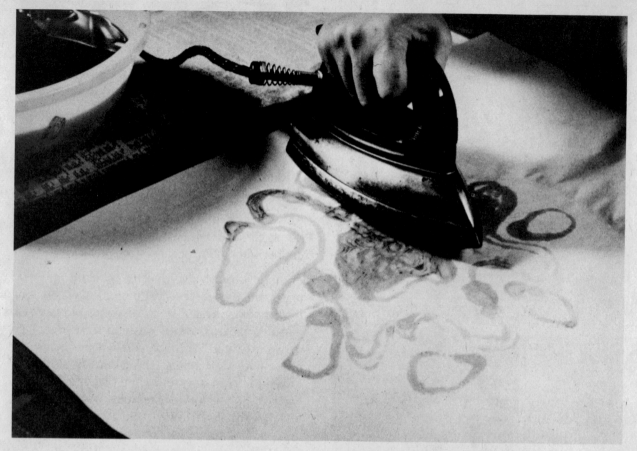

Figure 12. When the batik cloth is dry, place it on a thick padding of newspapers and iron the fabric until all the wax has been removed from the finished piece.

the fabric in plain water and then put into a red dye (unwaxed yellow areas will become orange). Follow the dyeing procedure then rinse and dry. Now wax areas that are to remain orange, wet the fabric, and immerse it in a brown dye. Rinse and dry. Wax out any area to be left brown and rewax other areas if necessary. Wet the fabric and finally put it into a dark-blue or black dye. Follow dyeing procedures, then rinse and dry. Iron out wax between newspapers until the fabric is as free of wax as possible (there will still be dark wax outlines left). Dry clean to remove all remaining wax.

Because dyes are transparent, one needs to think about color and experiment with it. Remember that red over yellow produces orange; blue over yellow produces green; and blue over red produces violet. It is always a good idea to have some small pieces of fabric available as test pieces and to keep a record of successful combinations. In this way one accumulates information and acquires an expertise in working with dye colors.

Projects You Can Do

As mentioned above, the beginner in batik work should start work simply with one- and two-color designs. Concentration can then be on design and craftsmanship. Learning to work with the application of hot wax, the dyeing of fabrics, and the removal of wax are basic to all batik work. Planning a good design and careful procedure will result in success and satisfaction.

BRUSH BATIK PANEL (ONE DYE BATH)

1. Wash piece of white cotton cloth, rinse, dry, and iron.

2. Place several layers of newspapers on working surface.

3. Heat paraffin or batik wax in an old electric skillet or double boiler to 240° F.

4. While wax is heating, draw design on cloth with pencil or artist's charcoal.

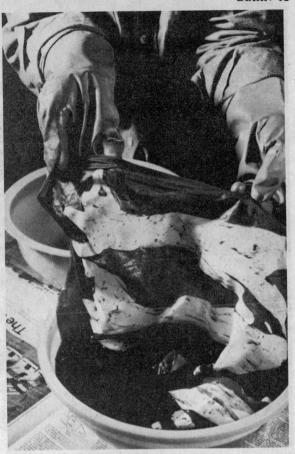

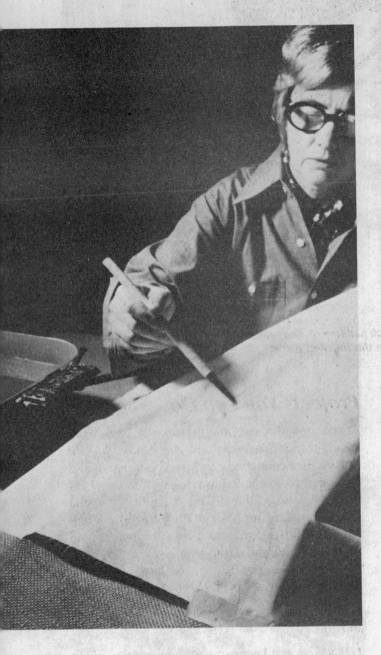

Figure 13. Hot wax is brushed on the design (left), and the waxed cloth is immersed into a dye bath (above). The waxed areas on the finished batik (below) remain white.

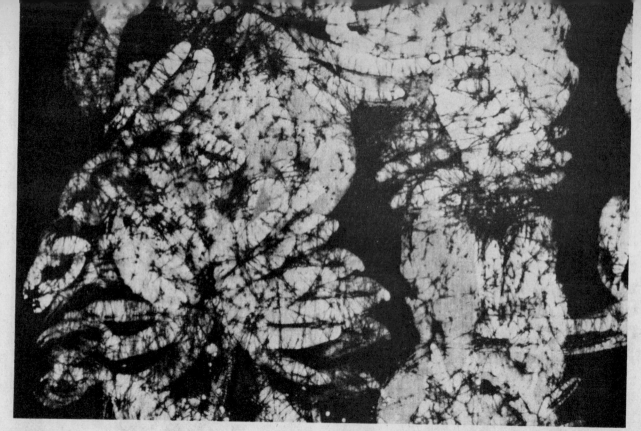

5. When wax is hot enough to penetrate cloth, apply it with a brush to areas which are to remain white.

6. After wax is applied let it cool on cloth.

7. Make a paste of one color of dye and pour mixture into a plastic or enameled pan. Add water and three tablespoons of salt to make dye bath and stir well.

8. Wet the waxed cloth with cold water.

9. Immerse wet waxed cloth in dye bath. Remember to use rubber gloves. Leave in dye for 30 minutes to an hour.

10. Remove cloth from dye and rinse in cold water until it runs clear.

11. Let cloth air dry (place on newspapers on floor or hang on line).

12. Place several layers of old newspapers, newsprint, or paper toweling under batik cloth and also over cloth.

13. Iron out wax. Keep removing wax-laden papers and adding fresh papers until all wax is out of cloth.

14. Finish cloth by dry cleaning.

15. Finished batik can be tacked over stretchers and framed as an art work.

Figure 14. Dramatic effects can be achieved with one color dye baths. The brush batik above has bold designs which dominate the background color. The brushed patterns on the batik below make the solid background an important aspect of the design.

WAX PRINTED BATIK FABRIC (ONE DYE BATH)

1. Wash two or three yard lengths of white cotton cloth, rinse, dry, and iron.

2. Prepare working surface with newspapers.

Figure 15. After preparing the fabric and organizing a work area, dip printing object in hot wax and stamp material (below). The finished batik cloth (opposite) has many decorative uses.

TJANTING BATIK (ONE DYE BATH)

1. Wash piece of white cotton cloth, rinse, dry, and iron.

2. Place several layers of newspapers on working surface.

Figure 16. The cup of a tjanting tool picks up wax which has been heated in an old electric skillet.

3. Heat paraffin or batik wax in electric skillet or double boiler to 240° F.

4. When wax is hot enough to penetrate cloth, use block, stamp, or other object to pick up wax and apply to fabric in overall design. Wax should be maintained at even heat so that the block or stamp prints the wax design evenly on cloth.

5. After design is applied to whole length of cloth, let it cool.

6. Follow steps 6 through 14 as described for previous project.

7. Fabric can be used for skirts, dresses, pillows, or wall hangings.

Figure 17. Wax flows through a spout in the receptacle of the tjanting (above). By following the drawn patterns, this batik technique produces unusual linear designs (below and opposite).

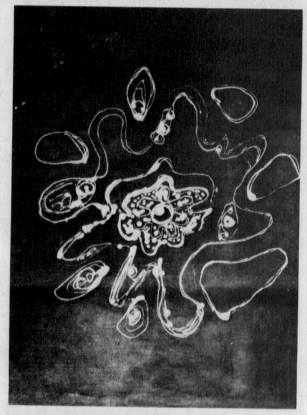

pick up wax with tjanting. Carry over to cloth and follow drawn lines with flow of hot wax. Put dots of hot wax in some of the wax outlined shapes or areas.

6. Follow steps 6 through 14 for first project.

7. Tjanting batik can be matted and framed under glass.

BATIK WALLHANGING (TWO OR THREE DYE BATHS)

1. Wash piece of white cotton cloth, rinse, dry, and iron.

2. Place several layers of newspapers on working surface.

3. Heat paraffin or batik wax in an old electric skillet or double boiler to 240° F.

4. While wax is heating, draw design on cloth with pencil or artist's charcoal.

5. When wax is hot enough to penetrate cloth, apply it with a brush to areas which are to remain white.

6. After wax is applied let it cool on cloth.

3. Heat paraffin or batik wax in an old electric skillet or double boiler to 240° F.

4. While wax is heating, draw design on cloth with pencil or artist's charcoal.

5. When wax is hot enough to penetrate the cloth,

Figure 18. Multicolored wallhangings require several dye baths. Brush wax on the portion which is to remain white and immerse the fabric in the lightest dye bath first (top left). Dry the fabric and repeat the waxing process, covering only those areas that are to remain the initial color. Then, place the cloth in a second, darker dye bath (bottom left). Three dye baths were used to produce the color variations in this piece (below).

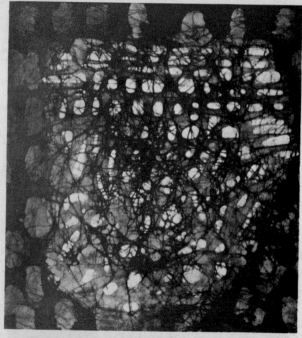

7. Make a paste of a light-colored dye, pour mixture into plastic or enameled pan, and add water to make dye bath. Stir well.

8. Follow steps 8 through 11 for first project.

9. Wax areas of design to remain first light color. Repeat steps 7 and 8 for each additional color. The second dye should be darker than the first and the final color should be the darkest. Example: first color, yellow; second color, red; third color, blue.

10. Put cloth between newspapers and iron out wax. Use as many clean newspapers as needed until all wax is removed.

11. Finish cloth by dry cleaning.

12. Batik can be hemmed on all raw edges. Casings can be sewed at top and bottom. Curtain or dowel rods can be put through casings for hanging batik as a decorative wall hanging.

For Additional Reading

Belfer, Nancy, **Designing in Batik and Tie Dye,** Davis, 1972.

Johnston, Meda, and Kaufman, Glen, **Design on Fabric,** Reinhold, 1967.

Keller, Ila, **Batik: The Art and Craft,** Tuttle, 1966.

Krevitsky, Nik, **Batik: Art and Craft,** Reinhold, 1964.

Meilach, Dona Z., **Contemporary Batik and Tie-Dye,** Crown, 1973.

Nea, Sara, **Batik,** Reinhold, 1970.

Figure 19. Once the batik method is learned, cloth design becomes a uniquely personal form of artistic expression (opposite page).

Crafting With Gourds

Of all the ecological materials that have been used by craftsmen, the gourd is one of the most versatile and beautiful.

Throughout recorded history artists have selected simple natural materials from their environment to create beautiful pieces of art. Depending on geographical location, craftsmen have utilized stones, sand, mud, animal skins, feathers, bones, and many other earth-related items.

Indians in the northwestern part of North America, where trees were lush and abundant, turned out massive pieces of wood sculpture. Indians in the southwestern United States became expert potters, utilizing the natural clay of their environment to make pots of incredible beauty. These were fired in open pits and then colored with pastes made from other kinds of earth. Eskimos in Canada made objects for both utility and beauty from soapstone native to their area. The skin boxes, shields, and shelters of the Plains Indians would have been just as useful without decoration, yet they were elaborately embellished with paints, feathers, beads, and porcupine quills. It is interesting to note that when people had no need for shields, boxes, or shelters, they used their decorative talents on their bodies. The Nubian tribes of Africa, for instance, developed an elaborate system of body decoration.

One of the most durable environmental materials which has been used for craft purposes is the gourd. Gourds in perfect condition have been found in Egyptian tombs dating as far back as 3500 B.C. and, symbols representing gourd cultivation have been found in almost every primitive society.

The variety inherent in the gourd is amazing. The fruits of this plant vary in size from that of an orange to some twice the size of a pumpkin. Because of the hard outer shell and hollow interior,

Figure 1. The techniques of incising and relief are beautifully illustrated on this contemporary gourd by Peter Nzuki, Nairobi, Kenya. (Courtesy, The Field Museum of Natural History, Chicago.)

gourds have been utilized for containers of all kinds. In the islands of the South Sea, 36 different uses have been documented for the gourd, including ladles, dippers, bowls, strainers, funnels, carrying-baskets, and musical instruments. They were decorated with feathers or paint, and some were encased in baskets woven from the vines of the "ieie" plant.

The Japanese grew a bottle-shaped variety of gourd in which they stored wine. These were highly polished and many of them were decorated with floral patterns. Chinese craftsmen used a tiny variety of gourd to make cages for pet crickets. The gourds were decorated as they grew.

A two-part carved mold was placed over the gourd about midway in its growth. As it grew, the pattern became incised on the skin of the gourd. Examples of these cages can be seen at the Peabody Museum in Salem, Massachusetts.

All over Africa gourds were turned into useful objects decorated with a variety of materials. The simplest was a gourd stained with millet leaves or dyes made from earth pigments. More elaborately decorated gourds were created by cutting, scraping, or engraving techniques. Hats were even made from gourds by cutting them in half and decorating them with cowrie shells.

Both colonial and frontier Americans found many uses for the gourd. Today, interest in their growth and use is once again growing rapidly. Craftsmen turn gourds into containers for display materials. They are used to show off arrangements of wild flowers and for table centerpieces. They are also used for holiday decorations such as Easter eggs and Christmas ornaments. And, as a result of a resurgence of interest in old time music, people are shaping gourds into copies of the once-popular gourd fiddle and banjo.

Figure 2. The Japanese stored wine in bottle-shaped gourds which were specially grown for this purpose (left). (Courtesy, The Peabody Museum, Salem.) Africans made useful hats by cutting gourds in half (right). (Courtesy, Smithsonian Institution Photo No. 72-3652A.)

Common Terms Used In Crafting With Gourds

Gourds once grew wild. But, even after years of cultivation, their promiscuous breeding habits still result in new, curious shapes with each growing season. Gourds not only mate indiscriminately with most other gourds, they are also happy to join families with cucumbers, squash and pumpkins. Hence, there are several dozen basic shapes plus all the different variations as a result of cross breeding. This gives the artist an almost unlimited choice of shapes from which to choose his craft material.

Within this mixture of shapes and sizes, two basic types emerge which relate to craft work. One type consists of the small colorful green, yellow, warted, and striped varieties that are seen in many supermarkets in the fall. These are called "ornamentals" and, with few exceptions, are not suited for craft work. Their deep colors and waxy natural sheen will look beautiful for several months. But, with age, they have a tendency to develop a terrible kind of acne on the skin. This discourages any kind of craft work.

The other main type of gourd is called a "hardshell." These are much larger and will age with a smooth, wood-like hard shell that lasts for many years. Hardshells grow in such a wide variety of shapes and sizes that it is not practical to describe each. But, a few of the most popular ones are listed below by their common or "country names" as a reference for purchasing gourds or seeds by mail.

Apple and Pear Gourds: shaped like the fruits for which they are named, these gourds are quite small — no more than 3" to 4" in diameter. They are most often used as decorations. Those with stable bottoms can be cleaned out, lacquered, and made into unusual wine cups.

Baseball Bat Gourd: a spectacular gourd which grows to lengths of 3 feet or more and measures 15" to 30" in circumference at its widest part. The smallest ones are sometimes made into percussion instruments by scoring a section across the middle of the body. Larger ones are left uncut and become decorative objects.

Bird House Gourd: the term applied to almost any gourd which looks like it could be turned into a home for a bird. It is actually used for that purpose and hung out in early spring.

Bottle or Vase Gourd: a gourd with a rounded bowl-shaped bottom and an extended neck that is sometimes narrow and sometimes thick. These

Figure 3. The breeding habits of gourds have produced an almost unlimited variety of shapes and sizes. Selection for craft purposes depends partly on the proposed function of the gourd.

gourds are often manipulated during their growth by tying parts of the neck with strips of soft cloth. Generally, their bowl is 6" to 20" in diameter and the neck ranges from 8" to 20" in length.

Club Gourd: a gourd with an extremely long neck that gradually widens into an elongated bowl. These are often covered with welts and warts about the size of a thumb tip. The combination of long neck and bowl-bottom makes them useful for fashioning gourd fiddles or banjos.

Dipper Gourd: a gourd with a long and slender neck which, if allowed to hang free as it grows, will have a perfectly straight neck. Sometimes the gourd reaches a length of 2 to 4 feet. If it grows on the ground, the neck twists and curves into interesting shapes. One type of dipper gourd has a short handle only 5" to 6" long.

Powder Horn Gourd: this is a medium-sized gourd with a short neck which curves gently into the bowl. Once, this gourd was actually used as a powder horn by hunters on the frontier. Powder horns make interesting animal shapes.

Basic Equipment And Supplies

Because gourds are so inherently handsome and adaptable, they are fun to work with. The exterior of the gourd is smooth and wood-like, making it easy to paint, stain, dye, cut, drill, or glue. In some instances, it can even be sewn with threads made of grasses or wire. Gourds, quite inexpensive to buy, can be grown by the home gardener. They require nothing more than sun and a little space to climb. Their unpredictable shape is an asset because one is tempted to elaborate on the ideas the body of the gourd suggests: some look like birds, others like fish, and still others like natural baskets. Primitive craftsmen painted gourds with coloring materials from the earth or from plants. They also used cutting tools that were no doubt made from stone or bone. Today, the commercial colors and craft tools that are available should be used. But, these should not overpower the simplicity of the gourd itself.

Following is a list of equipment and supplies needed for making the simple projects which are described later in this article.

COPING SAW

This saw should have a 1/8" removable blade. These blades come in 4" to 6" lengths and are easily removed from the frame. The blade is then fitted with a handle by winding all but 3" with tape. Because of their flexibility, they are particularly helpful when a gourd is to be cut in half and then fitted back together. A wood saw would remove too much of the gourd.

HALF-ROUND WOOD FILE

After a gourd is sawed, the cut surface needs to be smoothed. One side of this file is flat and the other has a gentle curve. This makes it adaptable for both curved and straight surfaces. The file cuts quickly and takes off jagged or splintered edges.

CRAFT KNIVES

There are many different kinds of craft knives suitable for cutting. Because gourds are easy to carve, only two different blades are needed: one to give sharp edges to figures; the other for piercing and

 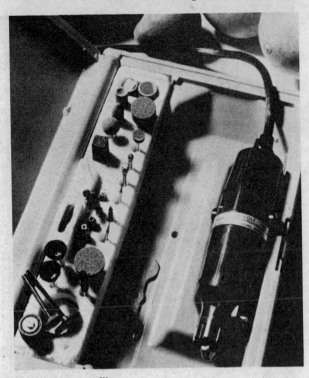

Figure 4. Equipment needed for crafting with gourds (left) includes a saw, file, knives, sandpaper, detergent, and a scrubber. Other materials required are wax, stain, lacquer, and felt tip markers. An electric craft tool (right) may be purchased as part of a "set" with all of the necessary attachments.

making holes or for outlining and then removing small sections of skin. A 5" aluminum handle with a tapered razor-sharp blade is a good choice for the former operation. This blade can also be used to score and cut away unwanted portions of gourds. The blade for the latter operation should be tapered and about 1/8" wide. A kitchen paring knife can be substituted for either knife if it is very sharp and has a thin blade.

FELT-TIP MARKING PENS

Sets of felt-tip markers (permanent colors) can be found in most craft and stationery stores. They are also available from those mail-order firms that sell to craftsmen in Indian Arts. Non-toxic, instant dry pens are best for these projects. They come with fine tips and write on any surface. A few broad-tip felt markers will also come in handy and can be used to cover broad areas. Though the colors are brilliant, they are translucent and the shadings of the gourd skin can still be seen through the color of the marker.

FOAM WOOD STAIN

This is used to add depth and color to designs. It is rubbed into cuts and marks in the skin, then rubbed away. The stain stays in the cracks but

rubs away from the skin. Wood stain also is used to deepen the overall color of the gourd.

METALLIC WAXES

Waxes with a metallic base are fairly new. They are creamy, semihard, and available in tubes or small glass containers. Originally designed to use as an aid to antiquing wood and metal, they are especially suited to the task of applying color to a gourd. There are a large number of colors available which can be used as highlights or to cover the whole gourd.

LIGHTWEIGHT ELECTRIC CRAFT TOOL

This is a compact motorized tool weighing less than a pound. It comes as part of a "set" which contains all the attachments necessary for making the projects in this article. Other attachments are available for the craftsman who wishes to work with other kinds of raw materials or to perform a wide variety of other skills.

These motorized tools are available from hardware stores and from general household mail-order catalogues. At this writing, their cost is in the $25.00 to $35.00 price range. More powerful models are also made, but their price is double

Figure 5. Gourds are available in a great variety of shapes, sizes, and colors. There is a plentiful market stock of gourds during the fall season, and they may be purchased through suppliers year-round.

that of the lightweight model. The more expensive motor is mounted on a stand instead of being held in the hand and the attachments fit a flexible shaft. Because the mounted model is less tiring to use, it might be worth the investment for anyone planning to do an extensive amount of this kind of craft work.

GOURDS

Gourds grow abundantly and can be found in many markets beginning in September. Supermarkets, farmers' markets, and county fairs all display them through the early part of winter. After that time, gourds can be purchased from people who grow them as a hobby and from commercial growers. A list of hobbyists who have gourds for sale is available from the American Gourd Society, Box 274, Mt. Gilead, Ohio 43338. A large number can be purchased at one time because gourds do not deteriorate with age. Only usage will wear them out.

OTHER SUPPLIES

In addition to the items described above, other materials also needed for gourd projects are: (1) several sheets of medium-coarse sandpaper to smooth edges or rough spots on the skin; (2) de-

tergent and a metal pot-scrubber for cleaning the surface of the gourd; and (3) one can of clear spray lacquer to give a final protective coat to projects and to add a sheen.

Basic Procedures

Because gourds are so attractive to begin with, the craftsman will find working with their varied sizes and shapes quite satisfying. They become dry, light, and airy as they age. On the vine, gourds can weigh from a few ounces to over 80 pounds. The skin turns golden with flecks of white, yellow, pale brown, and patches of darker brown. When the skin is scored and parts removed, a pearly white underskin is exposed. This contrast in color is dramatized when areas of outer skin are scraped away in an engraving technique.

In the course of working with gourds, it is possible to cut, glue, saw, dye, paint, and drill them — almost any process that can be applied to wood. Decorating can be as simple as applying a coat of colored wax in a few minutes time — or, it can become a task of several weeks.

PREPARING GOURDS

Gourds that are purchased fresh in the fall must go through a drying process before they can be used in craft projects. This requires no work or equipment—only patience.

The gourds should be brought into the house and laid out to dry on newspapers. They can also be hung by the stems if they are not too heavy. Choose a dry spot in the basement or storage room. An attic is also a satisfactory location, provided the temperature does not go down to freezing. The fruit needs to be turned occasionally to make sure the entire surface is exposed to the air. Do not be alarmed if after several weeks the gourds begin to mold and look grim and tired. They are not suffering from a terminal illness; they are only passing through a natural cycle in the drying process. Mold will not hurt gourds —it may look ugly, but it is harmless. In fact, mold is responsible for the beautiful mottled rings of color which are later seen on the skin.

If a gourd actually caves in or parts of it collapse into a soft ungainly mush, nothing can be done to save it. These gourds have not matured enough on the vines.

To determine when gourds are dry, tap them with a fingernail as one would tap a table top. When dry, they will give off a sharp crack instead of a thump. Depending on the size and the drying conditions, it takes from one to three months for gourds to dry. Small, apple-sized ones will be ready long before Christmas. Larger bowls may not be dry until January or February.

When dry, gourds need to be washed and scrubbed to remove the thin outer layer of skin. As they bob around in the water, the rough moldy material begins to disappear and smooth golden skin appears. To make the job easier, soak the gourds overnight. Because they are hollow and will float, they need to be weighted down to keep them submerged. Put a bit of detergent in the water to help loosen the skin. A metal pot-scrubber, such as the ones used to scour pots and pans, is useful for cleaning the skin. Heavy collections of debris or scar tissue can be removed with the side of a knife, but care should be taken not to damage the skin. After the gourds are clean, they are set aside to dry.

Some projects described here call for the gourd to be cut open. The hollow, ivory-colored interior contains clumps of seeds attached to glossy layers of membrane. These should be removed and may be put aside in a dry place for planting them in the spring. The interior can then be smoothed with the back of a spoon.

PLANNING THE DESIGN

Every project described later in this article includes a photograph which can be used as a design guide for the project. However, one may want to create an original design. If so, suggestions may be in order. Gourds do not come in perfect shapes. Some may have flattened areas, warts, or knobs. There may even be, in some of the larger models, areas where the skin has split and holes have opened up. These "flaws" are to be taken advantage of — not scorned — as they can be incorporated into the design. African craftsmen repair gourds that have cracked by stitching them together with copper or brass wire. The stitching then becomes a decoration rather than a patch.

Anything done to gourds should be in harmony with their shape. Do not impose a rigid design.

Colors should only enhance, not obliterate or overpower the natural shadings. One should work out a design on paper first; the, apply it to the gourd with a pencil. Go over the whole gourd in pencil before beginning to work. Do not depend on luck to match up lines which disappear around a curve. Pencil lines can easily be erased and adjusted — corrections are not possible if a knife or a marker is used.

USING THE WAXES

A double layer of soft cloth covering the end of the finger makes a good applicator for soft waxes. A small amount is rubbed directly onto the skin of the gourd. Several thin coats can be applied to get the desired effect. Allow each coat to dry for a few minutes. When wax is dry it can be buffed to a soft glow with another soft cloth. When markers are being used over the wax, these are applied after the surface has been buffed. If wax becomes hard in the container, it can be thinned with a drop of turpentine. It also can be thinned considerably and then applied with a brush if this seems desirable.

MARKERS

The purpose of these almost transparent colors is to give a stained-glass effect to the gourd. Two kinds of markers are used: the fine-tipped ones can fill in a small areas and outline the designs; the broad ones are used to cover large areas. The skin should be completely dry before color is applied. Fine lines should be filled in first and allowed to dry before another color is applied. One color can be added over another if the first color proves unsatisfactory, or if a deeper color is wanted. Keep a spare gourd on the side for testing colors and combinations of colors.

The broad areas are covered more smoothly if broad-tipped pens are used. The colors flow freely at about the consistency of watercolors. They can be wiped off if a mistake is made, but this must be done very quickly.

DRILLING

Though gourds are sturdy, they are also hollow and care needs to be taken not to put too much pressure on one spot. To drill a hole with an electric drill, choose the smallest cutting attachment

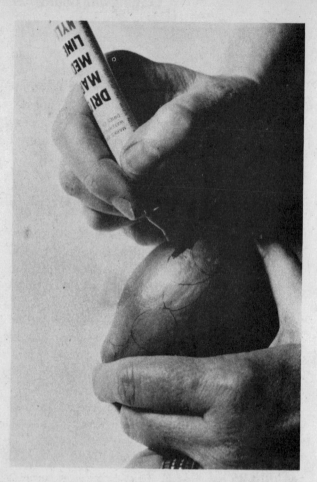

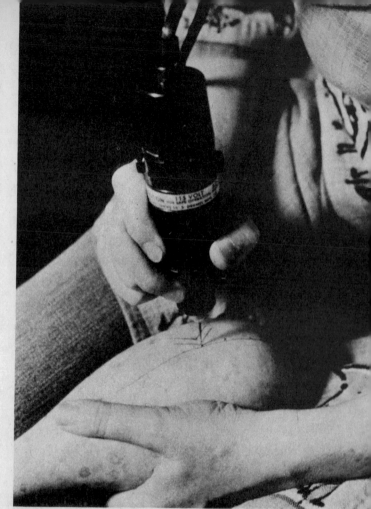

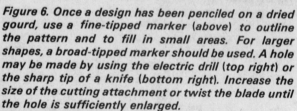

Figure 6. Once a design has been penciled on a dried gourd, use a fine-tipped marker (above) to outline the pattern and to fill in small areas. For larger shapes, a broad-tipped marker should be used. A hole may be made by using the electric drill (top right) or the sharp tip of a knife (bottom right). Increase the size of the cutting attachment or twist the blade until the hole is sufficiently enlarged.

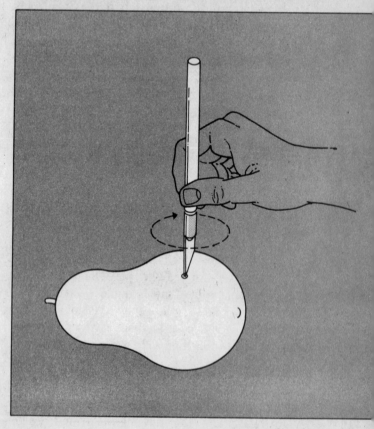

first. After drilling with that, enlarge the hole with the next largest attachment. First, mark the spot to be drilled with a pencil; then, lay the gourd across the legs while drilling. Because a gourd is round, it is difficult to control if placed on a work bench or table.

It is possible to make a hole without an electric tool by using the sharp tip of a knife. Hold the gourd steady, insert just the tip of the knife, and twist it until it pierces the skin. Continue to twist the blade until the hole is enlarged to the proper size.

SAWING

To begin sawing, a hole large enough to admit the blade is first made by the above method. The saw blade is then inserted into the hole. The blade should be held as if it were a feather and the sawing should be done with long, slow, even strokes. It is not necessary to apply pressure. If the body of the gourd is accidentally cracked during this process, it can be glued back together with ordinary white glue.

USE OF THE KNIFE

To begin a long cut, such as one needed to separate the neck of the gourd from the bowl, use the craft knife with the wider blade. Insert the tip of the knife and then go around the pencil line once, just scoring the line. Repeat this process several times until the inside is reached. Care should be taken not to use too much pressure. It is better to go over the line many times rather than risk cracking the gourd.

To make purely decorative cuts, such as those needed to remove triangular-shaped pieces, use the narrow-bladed knife. Holding the gourd in one hand, insert the tip of the knife and score along the triangular-shaped pencil line. Go over the line several times, being careful not to cut all the way through. Only the top layer of skin is to be

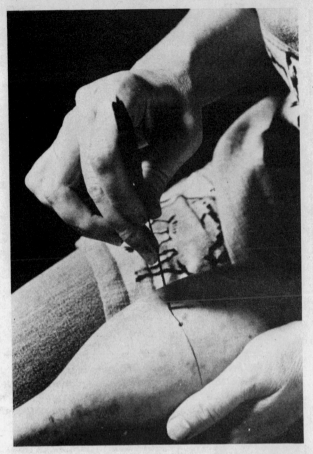

Figure 7. A hole must be made in a gourd before a saw blade can be inserted. All sawing should be done with long, slow, even strokes to avoid damaging the gourd. If breakage does occur, the gourd may be repaired with glue.

Figure 8. Before beginning the cut to remove the neck of the gourd, draw a line where the cut will be made. Insert the knife and follow the line several times until the inside is reached.

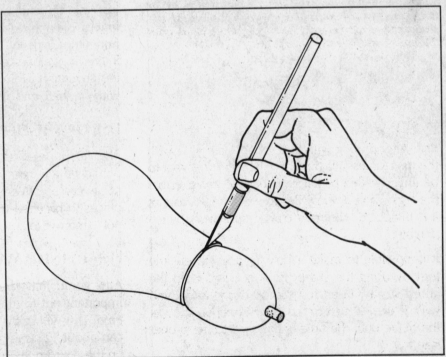

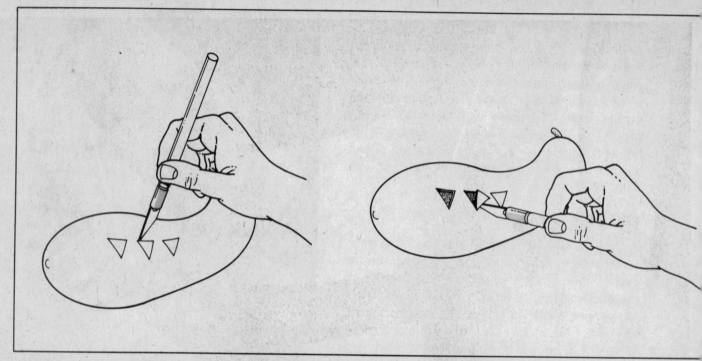

Figure 9. The narrow blade craft knife is used to cut decorative shapes. Score the design on the top layer so that all lines are joined (top left) and insert the blade under the skin to remove unwanted sections (top right). To smooth the cut surfaces, use a half-round wood file (below). When filing two pieces that are to be joined together, do not remove too much of the surface.

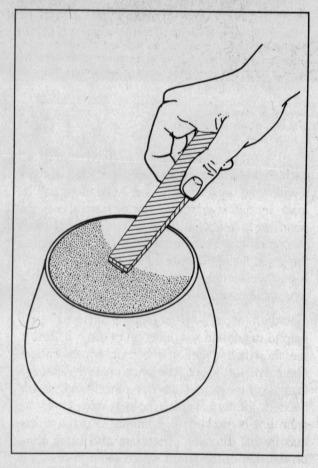

removed. When all the lines are cut and joined, insert the tip of the blade just under the skin and pry out the unwanted portion.

A variety of decorative lines can be made with just the tip end of the knives. Kitchen paring knives often have blades that are wider on the noncutting side of the blade. These produce an interesting elongated triangle. A running stitch design can be formed by just pricking the skin with the sharp end of any small knife.

USE OF THE FILE

The file is used in one direction only, just as would be the case with wood. Heavy pressure is not necessary. When smoothing the edges of two pieces to be fitted together, care should be taken not to remove too much surface.

FINAL FINISH WITH LACQUER

After gourds have been decorated with color, it is important not to apply too much lacquer at one time. This will cause colors to run. Hold the spray can about 12" away and let the spray float down on the gourd rather than reach it directly. Moving

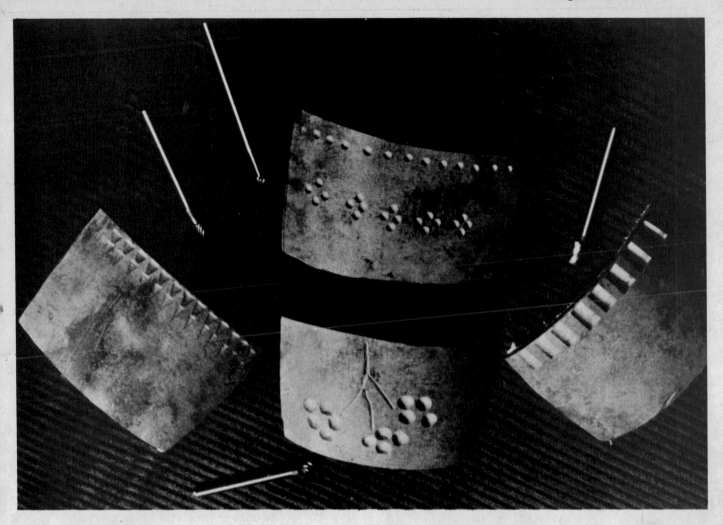

Figure 10. The electric craft tool is used to create a wide variety of decorative effects on the surface of the gourd. The tool comes with bits in a number of sizes; the smallest bit is used to make simple lines. A large bit is used for making broad strokes and carving massive designs.

around the gourd, let each thin coat dry before applying the next. Five or six coats may be necessary to completely cover the surface. It is better to take time with this step rather than risk having the colors run together. Spraying is best done in an open area. As with all materials from pressurized cans, it is wise to work where there is plenty of air to minimize the danger of inhaling too much of the material.

USE OF THE ELECTRIC CRAFT TOOL

The craft tool will come equipped with its own set of instructions for general usage. The directions which follow here are those which relate specifically to its use with gourds. Remember that this is a high speed tool which will cut very quickly. Before using it, practice on one or two gourds. Try

each of the attachments to see what kind of mark it will make. Also check to see if variations can be made by holding it to the side or from above. Experiment to see what kinds of patterns can result by combining two different lines or dots. Because the gourd has no straight edges, it is better to hold it on the lap rather than trying to secure it to a work table or bench.

Gourds have an imperceptible grain which will help to determine the direction of the cut. Test to see in which direction the tool moves easiest. There will be more resistance in one direction (against the grain) than the other; and, if not heeded, the tool will not hold steady. Once the grain line is established, continue to make all the cuts in that direction. There are also small areas on the skin of the gourd which seem to resist the tool altogether. Simply move the tool away a fraction of an inch and set it down in a new area.

To make a simple fine line, the smallest of the cutting tools is used. Holding the gourd on the lap, steady it with one hand. The tool is held to the side with the tip just touching the cutting line. A broader line is made in the same fashion, but with the next largest tool.

To drill a hole, use the smallest of the cutting tools. The tool is held like a pencil and approaches the place marked for the hole from above. If a larger hole is needed, the same hole can be enlarged by the next largest cutting tool.

To scrape away areas, leaving a raised design behind, use short clean strokes with the small cutting tool. The tool is held to the side so there is good control. It is better to cut right up to the pencilled design in short strokes rather than try to outline it with the tool first. If a razor-clean outline of a design is desired, it can be outlined first with the craft knife.

Projects You Can Do

Gourds can be altered to such a degree that their former identity as a living plant can be lost completely. The projects in this article, however, have been designed primarily in the hope that the gourd's identity will still be apparent — that its natural form, color, and spirit dominate the finished product.

The projects which follow are meant to be copied or to be used simply as a take-off point for original ideas. The simplest ones to execute are described first. None of them, however, is complicated or requires great skill.

SMALL DECORATED SPHERES

1. Select six small apple- or pear-shaped gourds that have been cleaned and dried. Have ready a

Figure 11. Short clean strokes are used to carve a raised design with a small cutting tool (left). Small gourds, colored with metallic wax, are displayed in a basket (below).

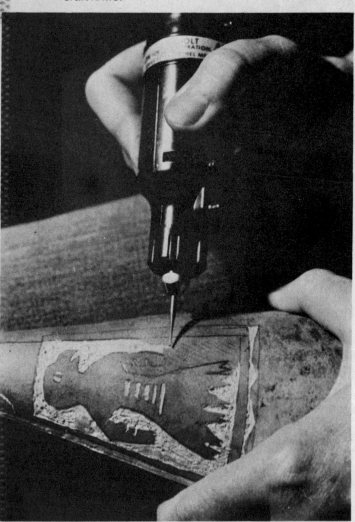

selection of metallic waxes of assorted colors, a selection of felt-tipped marking pens, a can of spray lacquer, and one soft dry cloth.

2. Using the soft cloth, apply a small amount of wax at a time until the gourd is covered with a base color.

3. Allow the base color to dry for five minutes; buff so the color takes on a soft sheen.

4. Following the illustration as a guide, use a pencil to apply the design to the sphere. Taking advantage of the wax's color and sheen, try for a design with much open space.

5. Fill in or outline the design with markers, letting each color dry before applying the next.

6. When the sphere is completely dry, spray it with four thin coats of lacquer.

These spheres can be displayed in a nest as though they were eggs, or they can be hung as Christmas tree decorations if a small hole is drilled in each end and a thread run through for hanging. These last for many years and make excellent gifts.

HANGING PLANTER

1. Select one bird house gourd with a bowl measuring approximately 6" in diameter. Supplies needed are a coping saw blade, a knife or electric craft tool, felt-tip markers, file, sandpaper, lacquer, and a 20-inch cord for hanging the planter.

2. Cut the top, unwanted portion off the gourd. Mark the cutting line with a pencil 5" from the bottom of the gourd. There should be an "ear" on each side of the gourd to allow for the hole which will hold the hanging cord.

3. Following the sawing procedure as described previously, saw away the top portion. (The discarded top can be used for practicing designs or to try out color combinations.)

4. Pry off the top of the gourd, clean out the seeds and membrane, and file the rim free of rough spots. Sandpaper to further smooth the edge.

5. Drill one hole in each "ear."

6. Decorate the gourd with markers and with the tip of a small knife.

7. Apply four thin coats of spray lacquer. Allow to dry. Tie cord through holes for hanging.

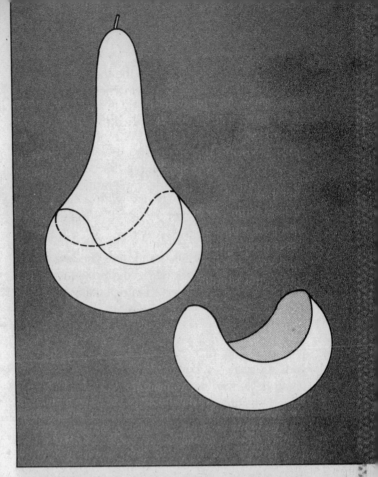

Figure 12. Gourds make unusual containers for hanging plants. Measure from the bottom of the bowl to mark cutting line, saw away the top section, and clean out the inside (above). The plant should be put in a clay pot and surrounded with moss before it is placed in the gourd (below).

The plant which goes into the planter should be planted in a clay pot before being put into the gourd. Surround the clay pot with moss to absorb excess moisture and to enhance the beauty of the planter.

BOWL WITH FITTED LID

1. Select a bird house gourd with a bowl 6" in diameter. Also needed are a set of markers, two craft knives, and spray lacquer.

2. Mark the cutting line for the lid. The line should be drawn at the point where the bowl just begins its inward curve toward the neck. After a straight line is drawn around the bowl, mark another line 1/2" directly below it and join the two lines with a zigzag mark.

3. Cut off the lid with the saw. Before trying to lift it off, go along the cutting line with a knife to be sure all the edges are free and clear. Pry off the top and remove the seeds.

4. Decorate the gourd with the markers. The one shown here is red with brown, green, and orange accent lines. The overall color of red is applied first to the bottom of the bowl, after which a green line is drawn 1-1/2" up from the bottom. This is followed by a 1/4" strip of brown. Draw one final thin line of green above the brown. Cover the lid of the gourd with red and brown. Draw a thin accent line of green at the base of the neck and a thick line of green to accent the zigzag edge of the lid.

5. Using a craft knife, cut a triangular design into the top green stripe at the bottom of the bowl. Then, with the same knife, cut ascending decorative lines on four sides of the bowl.

6. Put the lid on the bowl and make an indention with the knife on the lid just above each ascending line. This acts as an aid for repositioning the lid after it has been removed.

Figure 13. A zigzag pattern (below) is easily made by drawing two equidistant lines around the bowl and connecting them with smaller lines. The pattern is then cut and the seeds removed. The finished bowl (left) is not only an attractive object, but also serves a utilitarian purpose.

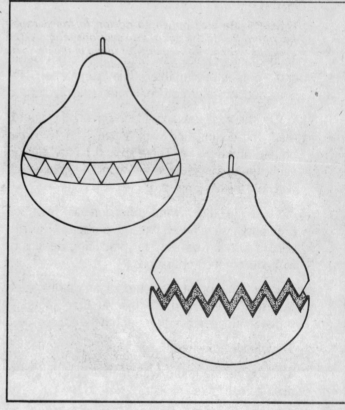

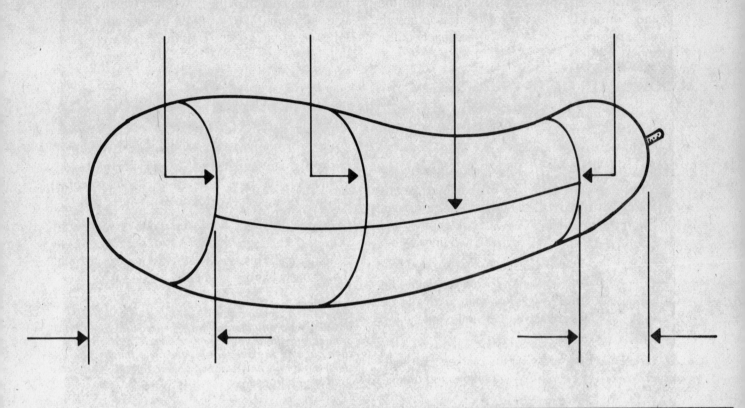

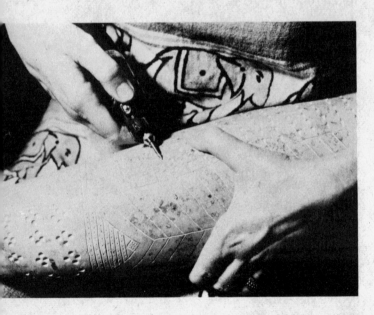

Figure 14. Before applying a design to the baseball bat gourd divide the gourd into sections (above). The sections will serve as a guide for filling in the intricate details of the planned design (below).

LARGE DECORATED GOURD

1. Select a clean, dry baseball gourd. Also needed are the electric craft tool, a can of foam-wood stain (fruitwood stain is used here), and a spray can of lacquer.

2. Decide on a design. It is not necessary to duplicate the design illustrated here, although it might be helpful to use the larger blocks as a starting point and then fill in as desired. Block out the general areas of the design by starting at the bottom of the gourd. Draw one line, 2" up from the bottom, all the way around the gourd. Draw a similar line 2" down from the top. From this point draw one line straight down from the top to the bottom of the gourd. Though the line is straight, it will have a slight curve to it to match the curve of the gourd. One more line can be drawn around the circumference about one-third of the way down. These four lines can serve as base lines for filling in the rest of the design.

3. Using the electric tool, cut all the major lines first. Then fill in with the holes, flowers, and other decorative cuts.

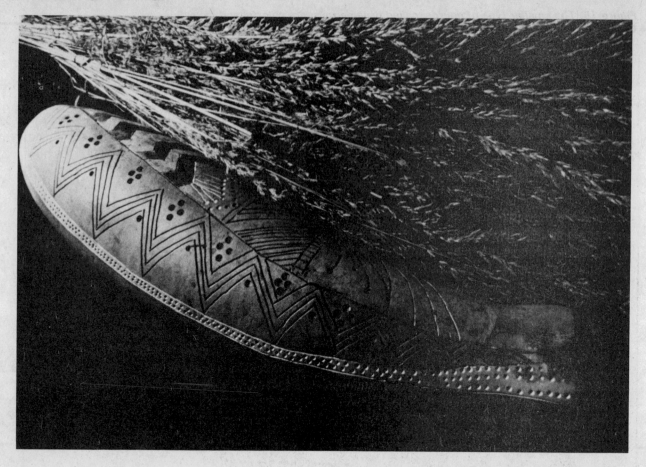

4. Covering a small area at a time, apply foam to the gourd. Allow it to soak into the cuts. Rub the surface color away immediately — color should remain only in the cuts.

5. When the gourd is thoroughly dry, spray it with four thin coats of lacquer.

GROWING GOURDS

Although it is possible to purchase gourds for craft projects, they are quite easily grown. The vines are prolific climbers and can be used as a natural decorative screen for porches, patios, and fences. Not only will home-grown gourds provide abundant raw material for craft work, but it is fun to watch the bright-yellow, white, or orange blossoms turn into bowls, dippers, bottles, or other handy containers.

Shaping the Gourds

People have found some very dramatic ways to shape gourds while they are growing. Any shaping has to be done while the gourds are still young enough to feel soft. It is possible, for in-

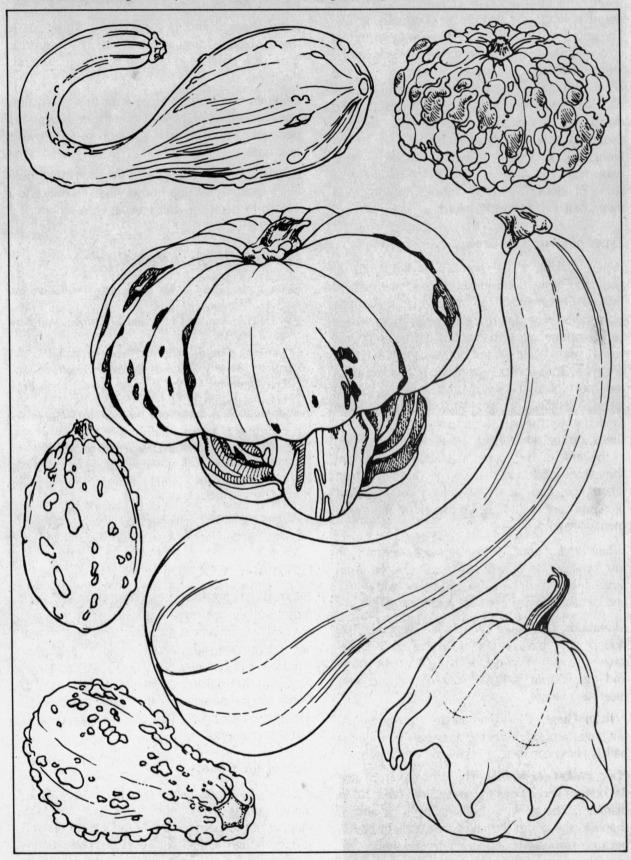

Figure 15. The smaller type of gourds, called ornamentals, are colorful and have beautiful natural designs. They are available in a wide range of shapes and sizes.

stance, to tie a knot in the long neck of a dipper gourd. This must be done on a hot day, when the gourd is limp, and it must be done very gently. The gourd will then continue to grow to its normal size with the knot in its neck. Or the neck can be lengthened by tying a bag of sand around the bowl and gradually adding more sand to the bag each day. However, there is a risk involved when doing this to the gourds. But because there is usually a good supply available, it's fun to try. Elongated or cylindrical gourds can be given a wasp waist by wrapping them in the middle with strips of cloth. The cloth should not bind too tightly or it will cut into the gourd.

Types of Gourds to Grow

When making a decision about the kinds of gourds to grow, don't just buy a package marked "Mixed Ornamentals" or "Mixed, Large Variety, Hardshells." The difference between these two is very pronounced. Ornamentals are those gourds which look beautiful for one season, and then decay. Melons and pumpkins are in this group, as are most of the small and beautifully shaped green, yellow, orange, striped, warted, and twisted gourds usually seen in the autumn. Hardshells, on the other hand, are the ones described in this article. They grow in large, rounded, and sometimes grotesque shapes. They are pale green when ripe, then age to a golden yellow. Their blossoms are white, while those of the ornamental are golden.

When buying gourd seeds, be more specific than just buying the mixed packages. Choose from those listed earlier in this article or widen the choice by considering one of the following.

Mammoth. This gourd can reach a weight of 100 pounds and have a circumference of 50". Because the body is more pear-shaped than round and the bottom is flat, it can be utilized very nicely as a basket.

African Giant. This is similar to the Mammoth, but larger around. It has the appearance of a large ball that has been flattened at the top and bottom.

Hard Basket (or Kettle). This grows with a nice flat bottom and a bowl that measures about 20" in diameter. The neck is short, giving a pyramidal shape to the gourd. It makes an excellent basket because it grows with an extremely hard shell.

Knob. This is a bowl-shaped gourd with a slender neck topped by a knob.

Baby Dipper. This is a miniature dipper, as its name suggests, and is great fun for children to grow. It is possible to buy seeds for miniature bottles, too.

Penguin. The body and neck of this gourd flow into each other, and the stem at the end suggests a penguin's bill. This is a variation of the Powder Horn gourd.

Eel. This is a very long, slender gourd that looks like a snake as it hangs from a vine. It is only 2 to 3 inches in diameter, but can attain a length of 3 feet.

For Additional Reading

Bailey, L. H., **The Garden of Gourds,** The Gourd Society of America, 1958.

Gardi, Rene, **African Crafts and Craftsmen,** Van Nostrand, 1970.

Organ, John, **Gourds,** Faber and Faber, London, 1963.

Plummer, Beverly, "Gourds Become Ornaments and Entertainments for the Eye and Hand," **Earth Presents,** Atheneum, 1973.

Publications and Bulletin of the American Gourd Society, Box 274, Mt. Gilead, Ohio 43338.

Trowell, Margaret, **African Design,** Praeger, 1960.

Silk-Screen Printing

A contemporary printing process done on silk represents an ancient Oriental technique of graphic expression.

Silk-screen printing is a direct outgrowth of the common stencil as used by ancient Chinese and Japanese artists. People of the Fiji Islands used to make stencils by cutting perforations in huge banana leaves and then applying vegetable dyes through these openings onto bark cloth. About 500 A.D., the teachings of Buddha were spread by decorating walls with stenciled images of religious dogmas.

The Japanese adapted stenciling to their own uses for decorating the backgrounds of ceremonial robes and kimonos. They cut their stencils with skill, patience, and fine detail from specially treated mulberry tree paper that was water-proofed by oil, making it impervious to dyes. The sheet was coated with glue and stuck on a card-board frame, then a brush was used to press color through the stencil and onto fabric. The Oriental artists used as many as five colors in combination to print their designs. This Japanese process is undoubtedly the origin of silk-screen printing.

During the Middle Ages stencils were used for decorating playing cards, murals, and wall hangings. In the sixteenth and seventeenth centuries, the art of stenciling spread through Europe, reaching its height of appeal in Germany and France where it became an established art. It was used in conjunction with woodblock and brush painting for religious pictures and illuminated manuscripts. During the seventeenth century in England, the stencil was used to apply an adhesive to wallpaper, after which a flock dust was sprinkled over the sticky paper to produce flocked wallpaper. A Frenchman, Jean Papillon, used a stencil roller to print the first wallpapers in the eighteenth century. Early stencils, made from oil paper, were being used in America by 1787 to decorate on wallpaper, furniture, and directly onto walls with designs of the federal eagle, vines, flowers, and fruit.

Figure 1. A paper stencil, glue, and maskoid were used in the printing of this original serigraph, "Ribbonscape," by Dorothea Bilder (opposite). It is a fine example of the varied possibilities of modern silk-screening.

In 1907, Samuel Simon of Manchester, England, received a patent to manufacture a screen using a silk fabric. Then, in 1923 John Pilsworth of San Francisco developed a multicolor method of printing called Selectasine. This method, which consisted of using the screen to print multicolor work, was used to produce the great variety of commercial signs that sprung up all over America and Europe. The silk-screen technique continued to develop not only for printing posters and for general advertising, but for decorating such items as furniture, lamp shades, tablecloths, rugs, book jackets, and scarves.

The process was considered only of commerical value until 1938, when a group of artists convened to study the artistic possibilities of the techniques. Inspired by Anthony Velonis, the group received permission from the Works Progress Administration of New York City for a silk-screen art project. This experiment ultimately produced original prints of such high caliber that they were shown in exhibitions and museums. The artists' works received much praise and proved that the ancient process of stenciling had tremendous possibilities for contemporary fine art prints.

Carl Zigrosser, an art critic and writer on the subject of graphic arts, coined the word "serigraph" for this new fine art printing technique. The serigraph (derived from the Greek word *serikos* meaning silk) came to be recognized in the United States on a level with engraving and lithography. Largely responsible for promoting this new print form as a fine art was the National Serigraph Society in New York. Certainly, as a result of this recognition, more and more artists have become and continue to be aware of the silk-screen process as a means of creative expression.

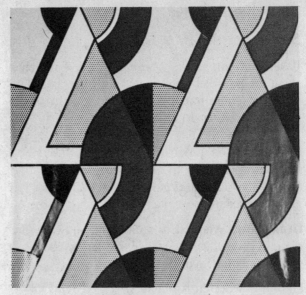

Figure 2. Silk-screen printing is believed to have originated with the Japanese process of stenciling. Ceremonial garments were designed by utilizing detailed stenciling techniques. The Japanese No Robe (below), dated 1800, was worn for theatrical performances. Oriental motifs found graphic expression in the early hand-cut Japanese stencil (below right). Contemporary artists have adapted this technique to produce modern designs such as the wrapping paper (opposite) created by Roy Lichtenstein. (Courtesy, The Art Institute of Chicago for two bottom pictures.)

Common Terms Used In Silk-Screen Printing

Base: that part of the printing table on which a sheet of paper to be printed is placed and to which a screen frame is hinged; can be made of masonite, plywood, or baseboard.

Block-Out: the process for covering or coating the meshes around the design to be printed; to control the open and closed areas of the design, glue or paper are most often used for this purpose.

Draw-Direct Method: the drawing of the design directly onto the silk, usually by using Vaseline, grease, or litho crayons.

Frame: a wooden structure stretched with fabric that constitutes the screen. For a screen larger than 16 inches by 20 inches, 2-inch by 2-inch lengths of wood are used; 1-inch by 2-inch lengths can be used for smaller screens. A cardboard box, shoe box, or shirt box can be used by children for a simple frame. Frames with silk already stretched over them may be purchased commercially.

Hinges: hardware that allows the screen to be lowered or raised.

Lock-In: a method for setting the screen in place for printing by placing a corner of the screen in the right-hand corner made with two C-clamps and wood attached to the edge of a table; used when baseboard and hinges are not used.

Padding: a base made by stacking newspaper and placing a clean sheet of any unprinted paper on top of the stack, which is then attached to a table top with masking tape.

Pin Holes: tiny holes not covered by block-out and through which ink leaks. Check for these by holding the screen up to the light after the glue is dry. Then, using a small brush, dab glue on any pin holes and wait for them to dry before printing. These holes also can be covered with masking tape.

Prop: a piece of wood, old brush handle, or paint stick attached to the side of a screen frame to hold it off the baseboard.

Puddle: ink poured from a jar into the well or border of the screen at the uppermost section of the frame.

Pull: the action of printing or squeegeeing the puddled ink down from the top and across the silk.

Registration: the accurate positioning of each sheet of paper so that each color will occupy the same position or place in relation to every other color on every sheet of paper.

Registration Tabs: brown paper tape squares folded and taped in three places on the baseboard as a guide to insuring that the various colors fall properly onto each sheet of paper.

Resist: a substance, such as an oil-based ink, applied to keep an area free from dyes; does not affect a glue block-out.

Screen Clogs: any buildup of glue or dried ink that clogs pores of the silk.

Silk: the fabric that is stretched over the frame, usually with a mesh count of 10, 12, or 14, and costing anywhere from $4 to $8 a yard.

Solvents: substances used for cleaning oil-based inks from the silk; if tempera paints are used, the screen is cleaned with water.

Squeegee Angle: the 55- or 65-degree angle at which the squeegee is held as it is being pulled or pushed across the screen: enables a tight close contact between the ink and silk, forcing color through the fine mesh.

Stencil: a paper design that determines through which parts of the screen there will be a passage of ink.

Wash-Out: the process of cleaning the screen after each printing.

Basic Equipment And Supplies

Silk-screen printing, as a graphic art process, has unlimited possibilities. The work can be done at home and there is no need for the assistance of other individuals. All supplies and equipment—such as inks, silk, squeegees, transparent base, bamboo pens, litho crayons—may be purchased or ordered at art supply stores. Any form of wood may be obtained at a nearby lumber yard. Following is information about the various supplies needed.

Figure 3. Materials used for silk-screen printing are readily available and may be purchased at any art supply store.

BAMBOO PEN

This Japanese pen, or reed pen as it is also called, is used for drawing with maskoid (see below) directly on the silk. Pens with metal points tear fibers and should be avoided.

BRUSHES

Inexpensive, small brushes should be used for the application of glue. A scrub brush three inches by one inch, which is made of natural fiber and has a wooden handle, should be used to wash out ink from the silk.

CRAYONS

Because crayons are used to fill in fibers of the silk, the softest, greasiest type to draw with is suggested. Oil crayons or grease-litho crayons are best.

DRYING RACK

By simply spreading the print or paper directly on the floor (covering the floor first with an old sheet, newspaper, or large sheets of cardboard), one has an adequate drying rack. A clothes line and clothes pins are preferable.

ERASER

Use a natural rubber square for removing maskoid (see below).

FABRIC

Silk, preferably with a mesh count of 10, 12, or 14, can be purchased at any art supply store carrying silk-screen supplies. Organdy or nylon may also be used. When considering how much fabric to buy, be sure to add, for stapling purposes, two inches to the measurement of all four sides.

GLASS JARS

These are necessary for the storage of inks and should preferably be four to eight ounces in size, with large mouths and metal lids.

GLUE

Used for the block-out procedure, two-thirds parts glue should be mixed with one-third part water in a glass jar. It is both wise and economical to purchase glue in large quantities.

INK

Oil-based ink sold expressly for stencil or silk-screen printing is available in pint or quart cans. To begin, buy white, black, raw umber, red, yellow, and cobalt blue. The raw umber can be used for dulling the intense colors. (Tempera or poster paints can be used for simpler screening methods.)

MASKOID

Used as a block-out and insoluble in water, this glue-like substance may be removed with a natural rubber eraser or with mineral spirits.

MAT BOARD

Stiff cardboard, cut in 2-inch squares, used to spread glue or to remove excess ink from screen after printing.

PAPER
Contact Paper

This is adhesive-backed paper that can be cut to the required shape and applied to the back of the screen as a block-out.

Newspaper

This is used for padding and also for the wash-out of ink from silk.

Newsprint

This may be used as a block-out or for experimenting with colors and shapes.

Paper Towels

These are used for the wash-out process and are handy for general clean-up processes.

Printing

Any relatively smooth surfaced paper may be used for printing, such as drawing paper, heavy rice paper, index paper, manila paper, cover stock, card stock, or oak tag. Watercolor and charcoal paper have a definite grain or tooth that is not very desirable.

Q-TIPS

When saturated with water or a solvent, a Q-Tip will dislodge glue or ink from a clogged area.

SANDPAPERS

After constructing the frame, use sandpaper to smooth any rough edges.

SHELLACS

The brown water tape (see below) for covering the silk where staples or tacks are used is given two coats of shellac to protect them from water, inks, and solvents.

SOLVENTS

Mineral spirits or any paint thinner are acceptable solvents. The fumes of the former are less toxic and both are less expensive than turpentine. Alcohol should never be used.

SQUEEGEE

A rubber blade with a wooden handle that is used to force ink through the silk. A squeegee should be long enough to cover the width of the silk on the frame. Squeegees are easy to clean and should be kept clean because caked inks will eventually rot the rubber and cause poor contact with the silk. The blade can be sharpened, if it gets dull, by rubbing it over a long sandpaper board. A wooden ruler or a tongue depressor can also be used as a squeegee.

Figure 4. There should be ample work space on top of a large, sturdy table in order to accommodate all the silk-screening supplies and equipment.

SPOON (METAL)

Used for mixing ink and for applying and removing it from the frame. Ink also may be removed from the frame with a rubber spatula.

STAPLES

These are used to attach the silk to the wooden frame. Carpet tacks and a hammer may be used instead.

TABLE

Preferably, this should be an old workbench-type table. If new, be sure to cover it with plastic cloth or newspaper to protect the surface.

TAPES

Brown Water Tape

This is used to make registration tabs and to cover the silk in areas where staples or tacks are to be used.

Masking Tape

This can be used as a quick block-out.

TRANSPARENT BASES

Commercially manufactured, this substance is used to thin down colors for transparencies or glazing. It is sold where inks are purchased. Note: It is always useful to have at least a tablespoon of transparent base in every color used. This keeps the color opaque and allows the ink to be washed out of the silk more easily and quickly.

WOOD

Used for baseboards; the wood—preferably pine or fir—may be purchased at any lumber yard.

VASELINE

Sometimes used as a block-out, Vaseline creates an interesting effect.

Basic Procedures

The technical considerations in silk-screen printing are limitless—the process is particularly adaptable to flat-patterned or painting-like effects through a build-up of various successive colors. By tightly stretching a piece of finely woven fabric such as silk, organdy, or nylon over a wooden frame, the basic piece of equipment is ready for use. Printing and the making of stencils can be done in a number of ways until the desired image is completed.

Prepare the mesh of the silk by sealing with glue or covering with a crayon those areas not to be printed. Cover the entire surface of the screen with glue, let the glue dry, and then, using mineral spirits, wash out the meshes where any previous design was applied.

MAKING THE FRAME

Using two-inch by two-inch strips of pine or fir, nail or glue together two lengths and two widths to form a rectangle. The corners can be butted together or mitered. It is most important that the frame be rigid and that corners join at right angles. Any poor construction will make for poor registration and distortion of the stencil. Remember, the function of the frame is as a support for the silk and as a basin for the ink. After the frame is nailed and glued together, use joiners or angles for reinforcement of the corners. Using sandpaper, remove any rough or splintered edges. The frame is now ready for the silk to be stretched over it.

STRETCHING THE FABRIC

It is advisable to use silk, as opposed to organdy or nylon, because silk produces sharper and clearer printed images. The higher the mesh count, the finer the mesh and the clearer the the print. The number 12 mesh is of a medium fine quality and recommended for all work.

Measure the size of the frame and cut the silk two inches larger than the frame to allow for stapling or tacking. Place the frame on a flat surface and then place the silk directly and evenly onto the frame. Using a staple gun or carpet tacks and a hammer, stretch the silk as follows. Place a tack or staple in the middle of each length, keeping the fabric taut by gripping it firmly. Then place staples alternately on the opposite sides of each center staple, doing this on all four sides of the frame and continuing to pull the fabric tightly. Tack or staple until within one inch of the corners of the frame, then fold under the remaining silk to form a folded

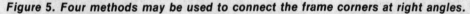

Figure 5. Four methods may be used to connect the frame corners at right angles.

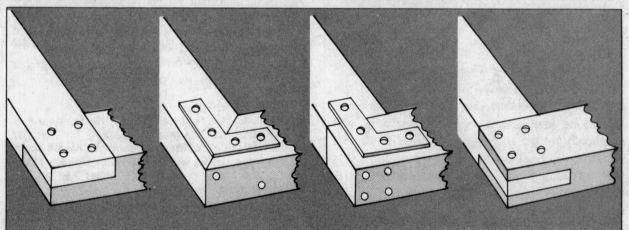

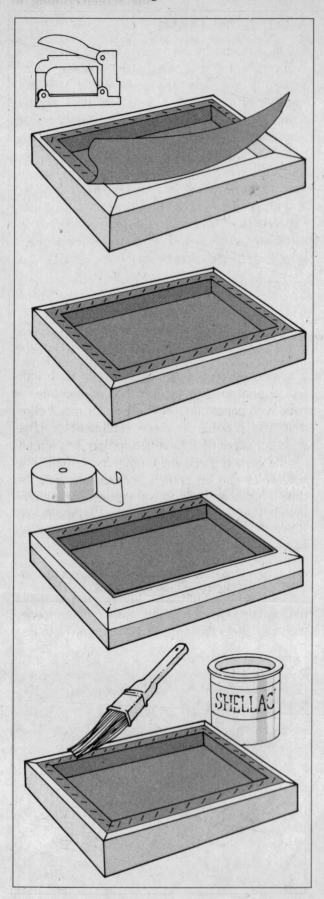

corner, pull it tightly, and staple or tack the fabric in place. The stretched fabric should be "tight as a drum." Trim off any excess silk that extends beyond the frame.

Now cut four strips of brown water tape. Each strip should correspond to the lengths of the sides of the frame. Use these strips to cover the tacks or staples and to hold the silk in place. Turn the frame over, with the basin side up, and cut four more brown paper strips. Fold the paper tape in half lengthwise and seal the four inside edges of the frame by pasting the paper strips so that half of the tape goes on the silk and the other half goes on the wood frame. This will prevent the ink from seeping through the frame during printing and will also reinforce the silk.

The brown taped areas of both sides of the frame should be shellacked to make them waterproof; the shellacked areas will also make it easier to remove the paint from the tape and wood. Be sure to extend the shellac one-half inch or so into the screen (fabric) on all four sides. This will assure an area for holding the paint during printing.

Finally, wash the silk with detergent and a rag or sponge to remove the fabric sizing. If the silk ever develops a hole or is torn, take a piece of masking tape and attach it to the silk, covering the area on the back of the screen. This tape must be removed and replaced for each color. If the tear covers a large area, the silk has to be restretched.

PREPARING THE BASEBOARD

This flat board, upon which the screen rests, should be two or more inches larger (on all four sides) than the frame and about one-half inch thick. The baseboard allows for a flat, level area on which to print and on which the entire frame and wood can be easily stored. (An alternative to making a baseboard and hinging it to the frame, is to lock the screen in place with C-clamps, making a permanent set-up on a table. Tape newspaper padding to the table as a support for printing.)

Figure 6. To stretch the fabric, cut the material two inches wider than the frame and staple the material with a staple gun (a). After the fabric has been stapled (b), cover the staples with brown water tape (c). Then, shellac the taped portions and about half of the adjoining screen on all four sides (d). The finished screen should be washed before the first print is made.

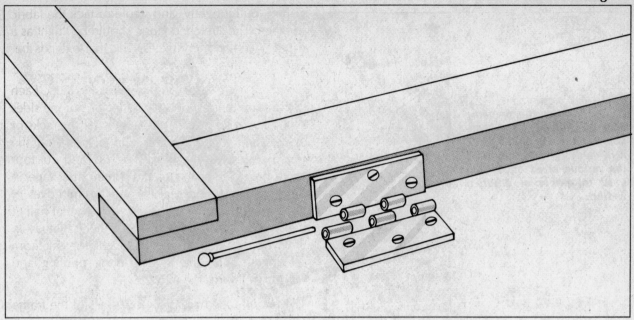

Figure 7. The frame is attached to the baseboard with two sets of slip pin hinges.

HINGING

The purpose of hinging the frame to the base-board is to allow for a more portable arrangement for painting. Two sets of 2½-inch or 3-inch slip pin hinges should be attached to a long side of the frame. Center the frame on the baseboard with the silk side down. Use ¾-inch flat-head screws and fasten the hinges—one side to the baseboard and the other side to the frame. The frame can now be lowered or raised easily. Be sure the slip pins are oiled for easy removal.

PREPARING A PROP

This is nothing more than a leg stand used to support the screen at approximately a 40- or 45-degree angle from the baseboard, making it easier to remove the printed sheet and to insert and register a clean sheet of paper. A wood, metal, plastic, or formica wedge—four to seven inches in length—can be nailed or screwed into the side of the screen frame about eight inches from the hinged end to serve as a prop.

DRYING PRINTS

The time for drying a color or print varies, based on the mixture of ink used as well as its build-up. Inks mixed with transparent base will dry faster, but a humid climate as well as a rainy day often will slow down the drying process. Drying time may vary anywhere from ten minutes to two hours—most prints dry in 20 to 30 minutes.

The simplest drying method is to clip each individual print to a strong wire line, clothesline, or rope with paper clips, clothespins, or metal clips. It is also possible to place cardboard or large sheets of paper on the workshop floor and simply set the printed sheets there until dry. Usually, the next color can be printed immediately after the screen has been washed and the next stencil prepared. This is because the first color usually has dried during the time that it takes to prepare the next stencil.

Figure 8. A prop is used to support the screen at a 40- or 45-degree angle from the baseboard.

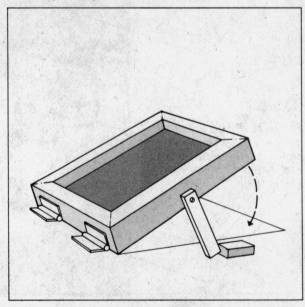

Figure 9. After the prepared screen is hinged to the base-board and raised on the prop, it is ready for printing. Note the various sized squeegees used for prints of different widths.

REGISTERING THE DESIGN

The registration of each sheet is to insure that the design is lined up properly—especially when one is working with various stencils and colors. There are a few methods for registering prints, but the following one is extremely accurate as well as convenient.

First of all, make sure the paper is cut with straight edges and that each sheet is equal in width and length. Registration tabs can be made from brown water tape. Cut the tape into three small strips, two inches by two inches, and fold them in half. Then, on each folded strip, fold each half back to the center fold, creating an accordian-type fold. Wet or lick the center of the fold and glue the top half of the strip together. When attaching the tabs to the baseboard, have handy the sketch, design, or sheet of paper on which you will be printing. Align the sketch or paper under the screen and lightly tape it down. One half of the registration tab is placed under the paper and then the center portion (the part that has been taped together) is

Figure 10. Prints are dried most easily by attaching a clothespin to each corner and hanging them on a strong wire.

Figure 11. Registration tabs are cut and folded, then glued together in the center.

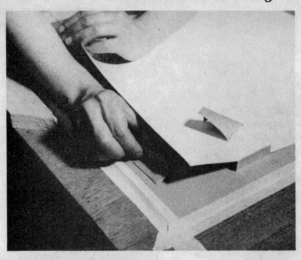

Figure 12. Position tabs so that paper edges fit tightly against the register folds.

Figure 13. When the tabs are secured and the printing paper is aligned, uniform prints can be made. Place the paper on the baseboard so that the edge of the paper rests against the edge of the inside tab fold. Tape the paper to the baseboard and attach the tabs in place.

Figure 14. Fold the center portion of the tab over the paper to firmly hold it in place.

folded over the paper. Now tape down the other half of the tab to the baseboard, lift the corner of the paper, and tape the over end of the tab down. It is a good idea to wet the tape just before setting it under the paper because then it glues itself to the baseboard.

Place two of the tabs at either the top or bottom of the sketch and the remaining tab on one of the sides. These hold the paper in place during printing and insure that each sheet of paper aligns properly to a design of several colors. When working with a free or spontaneous design or print, it is also helpful to mark with an "X" the top of the paper to avoid confusion with the bottom.

Figure 15. The print appears on the paper in the desired position. Keep register marks in place for multiple printings.

Figure 16. After mixing the inks (left), a transparent base is added (right).

PREPARING THE INK

The amount of ink used depends on the number of prints being made. The ink should be the consistency of heavy cream. Ink that is left over may be easily stored in glass jars for at least a year. When using ink straight from a can or when mixing colors, always use at least a tablespoon of transparent base; this will thin the ink as well as facilitate the wash-out. Ink also can be thinned with mineral spirits. An ink supply usually needs replennishing after printing ten prints.

PREPARING THE PAPER

The kind of paper used is based on personal preference as well as what works best with a particular design. Remember that the paper should be cut to allow for a two- or three-inch margin extending beyond the design. This margin can later be cut away, but it allows for fingerprints, matting, and easier handling in general. The paper should always be prepared before printing: determine and cut the necessary number of sheets.

PULLING A PRINT

After positioning the printing paper, make sure the registration tabs are secure and accurate. Assuming the screen to be used has a stencil or glue block-out on it, place the screen down and puddle some ink in the well at the top of the frame. Spread the ink across the top of the frame from one side to the other along the tape, so that it is evenly distributed. Take the squeegee and, holding it at about a 55- or 65-degree angle, pull it very firmly across the silk towards you. Then, at the same angle, push the squeegee firmly back to the top of the frame. Leave the squeegee resting against the top of the frame or set it next to the frame on a cookie sheet, board, or waxed paper. It is better to use more ink than not enough. Also, try to keep all of the ink on one side of the squeegee; this helps to produce a cleaner, more even color.

Now lift the screen, prop it up, remove the printed paper, and set it somewhere to dry. Take another sheet of paper and continue the process. When all of the prints of the first color (or only color) have

Figure 17. After the paper is securely aligned and the screen is placed down, puddle the ink from jar into the well at the top of the frame.

Figure 18. Spread the ink with a metal spoon along the tape from side to side across the uppermost section of the frame.

Figure 19. Position the squeegee in the ink-filled well and take a firm grip on the handle to insure even coating of the screen's surface.

Figure 20. Pull the squeegee at about a 55-to 65-degree angle toward you, forcing the ink through the silk onto the printing paper.

been made, remove the remaining or excess ink with a spoon or rubber spatula and place the ink in a clean glass jar for further use. This procedure, after a wash-out, is repeated for the remaining colors. Finished prints should be stored in flat, dry areas.

WASH-OUT

It is necessary to do a wash-out before each new color is applied. This means cleaning the screen, squeegee, spoon, and anything else that is covered with ink. The screen need not be removed from the hinges. Sheets of newspaper can be spead between the underneath side of the screen and the baseboard and mineral spirits (or another such solvent) sprinkled over the silk and tapes. Use paper towels to wipe the ink from the silk as well as from the tapes, and to wipe off the squeegee, spoon, and other materials. It will be necessary to wash out the silk two, three, or even four

times in order to cleanse it thoroughly. Change the newspapers each time. The amount of ink left on the towels shows whether the silk is clean. (Note: After two wash-outs, prop up the screen and rub it with mineral spirits and paper towels on both sides. This will knock out the ink from the pores of the silk and prevent the ink from clogging.)

If, after four wash-outs, ink still seems to be clogged in an area, use a small-bristle scrub brush with a wooden handle and, sprinkling mineral spirits on the silk, lightly scrub the silk on both sides. Some people will always do this to assure a thorough cleaning. To tell if an area is clogged, remove the hinge pins and hold the screen up to the light. The clogged ink is easily seen. If the silk is clogged, continue to use the brush and mineral spirits. Do not be concerned if ink appears to be lodged in the fibers even though the paper towels

Figure 21. Before applying additional colors, all the equipment should be cleaned. Begin by placing the excess puddled ink in a glass jar.

Figure 22. Place newspapers beneath the screen and, using a paper towel, wash out any inked portions with a solvent such as mineral spirits.

Figure 23. For ink-clogged areas, it may be necessary to use a small brush to lightly scrub the surface (above). Unhinge the frame and thoroughly clean both sides with mineral spirits (right).

are without ink. Many colors stain or dye the fibers and a faint trace of color is almost always evident. Repeat these procedures after each color printing.

Projects You Can Do

Successful silk-screen printing depends on the ink being forced through the silk and onto the paper underneath to be printed, producing the desired image. The stencil and block-out must be soluble in water, since oil-based ink is most often used.

There are several methods and materials which can be used for both the stencil and block-out methods. Three of these stencil processes—glue block-out, paper stencil, and direct drawing with oil crayons and Vaseline—will be described here, step-by-step. These processes are all direct, spontaneous, easy, and inexpensive. They use very

basic skills which can produce exciting and versatile items, resulting in finished prints, posters, cards, or announcements.

Cut-film stencils or photo silk-screen processes are not described here because both of these necessitate more expensive materials, a greater variety of solvents, and complicated techniques. Each of the processes discussed here, on the other

Figure 24. A glass jar is used to mix two-thirds parts glue to one-third part water (a) for the glue block-out. This mixture is applied to the raised screen with a brush (b) or with Q-Tips (c), depending upon the effect desired in the finished print. A portable hair dryer may be used to speed the drying process (d). The dried screen is then positioned on the baseboard for printing.

hand, is simple and direct and can be used separately or combined in any number of ways. Always remember to precut the paper before printing and to determine at the beginning how many sheets will be printed.

GLUE BLOCK-OUT STENCIL
In a jar, mix two-thirds parts glue and one-third part water. This will be used for the block-out to create a textural drawn spontaneous image for the first color.

1. Remove the hinge pins and either hold the screen up with one hand or, as mentioned earlier, prop it up with two strips of wood or jar lids. This will allow the frame to dry from both sides. Have newspaper underneath to catch any dripping of glue.

2. Spatter on glue with a brush, letting it drip or flow and dotting it on the silk with Q-Tips or fingertips to create a free flowing image. Make no attempt at this point to control the image—it will become more organized later.

3. Allow the glue to dry. To speed up the drying time, a portable hair dryer or the nozzle of a vacuum cleaner can be used.

4. Before the glue has set or dried completely, added textures may be created by pressing into wet areas of glue with crumpled waxed paper, aluminum foil, or crushed paper towels. Use paper towels to wipe off any excess glue that accumulates on the tapes.

5. When the glue is completely dry, place the screen in position on the baseboard. Now take a sheet of inexpensive paper, such as newsprint, and place it under the silk.

6. Mix ink, puddle it, and print two or three experimental proofs in a desired first color.

7. After noting the image, place the proofs to dry, register the actual paper to be used, and begin printing, following the instructions described above. The glue is the block-out—the untouched silk will be left open, letting the color pass through.

8. After printing all sheets of paper, follow instructions for the wash-out. However, the same glue block-out can be used again, before removing it from the silk, by using either of the following two methods:

a. Place the printed sheet with the first color on it back under the screen frame, but shift the paper slightly out of the registration tabs. Use a new color and print each sheet a second time, making sure each is lined up properly in its new position. Use new registration tabs if desired. This process creates an interesting double image.

b. Reversing the printed sheet from top to bottom, overprint the first two colors with a third color. The same glue block-out acts as a resist, and can create interesting effects by being used with three different colors.

9. When the glue block-out possibilities have been exhausted and all the ink has been thoroughly washed out of the silk, take the screen and remove the glue by using plenty of warm to hot water. This can be done in a sink, bathtub, shower stall, utility tub, or with a garden hose out of doors, depending upon the size of the screen.

10. Wipe the excess water from the silk, using paper towels and rubbing from both sides.

11. Hold the screen up to the light to check for any clogged areas. If necessary, repeat the water wash-out and use a scrub brush on the silk to dislodge any remaining glue. Ink will sometimes collect around glued edges and the silk may also be washed out with mineral spirits after it has dried following the water wash-out.

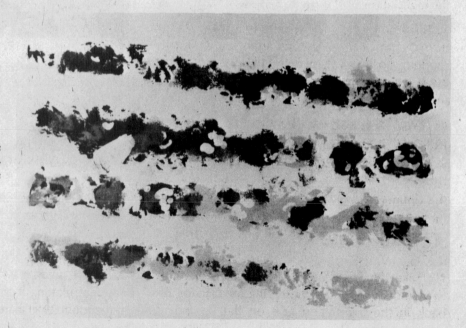

Figure 25. The glue, acting as a block-out, creates a delicate textural image on this finished print.

1. Create a paper stencil by cutting or tearing newsprint paper. The torn edge gives a soft effect compared to a crisp, cut edge. Newsprint—not newspaper—should be used because it is not absorbent, it is less expensive, and it may be used as a block-out for printing approximately 30 prints. This particular project utilizes abstract geometric forms. Of course, the design is up to the individual.

2. After the design is complete, cut out the shapes with scissors or with an X-acto knife. Save the cut-out pieces for the second color.

3. With masking tape, tape the cut newsprint stencil to the frame on the underneath side of the silk. The newsprint stencil must cover or extend onto the taped areas of the frame.

4. Put the frame back in the hinges, prop up the screen, place the paper in the registration tabs, lower the screen, puddle the ink, and print all the sheets of paper. Remember to pull a few experimental newsprint proofs first to check both the image and the color.

5. After printing, remove the excess ink, remove the paper stencil (carefully if it is to be saved), and wash out the silk with mineral spirits.

6. Return the screen to the baseboard and place one of the already printed sheets under the silk in the registration tabs.

7. Take the pieces of newsprint that were cut out from the previous stencil and arrange them in any random position or directly upon the colored areas which were created by the first stencil. Mix the second color of ink.

8. Lower the screen, puddle the ink, and squeegee across the silk. The cut-out sections will adhere to the underneath side of the silk as the squeegee is drawn across.

9. Continue printing all of the paper. Then remove the cut-out stencil shapes, remove the excess paint, and wash out the silk with mineral spirits.

10. Take the first printed sheet, which now has two colors on it, from the drying area. Place this back in the registration tabs on the baseboard,

Figure 26. Newsprint may be used for paper stencils. A design is drawn on the newsprint, then cut out with an X-acto knife (above). Masking tape is used to hold the cut newsprint to the frame (below).

and place one of the newsprint proofs on top of the printed sheet.

11. Take a clean sheet of newsprint and tear some random or drawn shapes out of it. The ragged, soft edge will give a new dimension to the print. Mix the ink, making it transparent this time by using three-fourths transparent base to one-fourth ink.

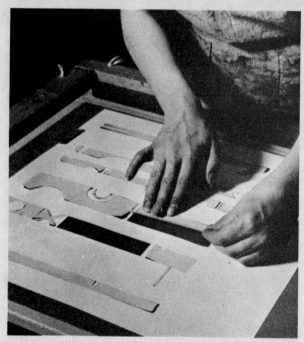

Figure 27. When the newsprint sheets have been pulled, the screen is cleaned. The cut-out pieces of stencil are re-positioned on the registered print (above). The printing process is repeated, using a second color (below).

Figure 28. The printing process has "glued" the cut shapes to the silk (above), resulting in a second paper stencil. An additional printing with torn shapes placed on the printed newsprint produced a three-colored print (below).

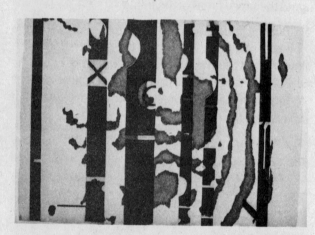

12. Place the torn shapes on the printed newsprint sheet, arranged as desired. Lower the screen, puddle the ink, and pull the squeegee across the silk, to which the torn shapes will again adhere. By taking a proof on the newsprint, the arrangement of shapes and the transparent color can be tested.

13. If the results are desirable, lower the screen, puddle the ink, squeegee across the silk two or three times, lift the screen, remove the proof sheet, and set it aside to dry.

14. Register the print paper in the tabs, lower the screen, continue printing all sheets of paper, and set them aside to dry.

15. Remove the excess ink, remove the paper stencil block-out, and wash out the screen with mineral spirits.

It is possible to continue overlaying and building a print of numerous colors and shapes. A stencil also may be created by cutting shapes out of contact paper. The sticky side of the contact paper will dissolve with the mineral spirits during the wash-out.

DIRECT DRAWING

Oil crayons, grease crayons or pencils, and Vaseline can be dissolved by mineral spirits. These materials yield soft paint-like qualities.

1. Take a clean screen and prop it up. Using oil or grease crayons, draw on the silk, pressing firmly so as to fill in the mesh that *will* print.

2. Coat the silk evenly with glue, using a small piece of matt board to spread the glue over the entire screen.

3. After the glue has dried, check the silk for pin holes by holding the screen up to the light. If there are pin holes in many areas, coat the entire screen with glue a second time. If the pin holes are in only a few places, dab the screen with glue. Wait for this second coat to dry and wipe the excess glue from the tape wells.

4. Now wash out the oil crayon drawing with mineral spirits and paper towels. The glue will work as a block-out and the crayon drawing will print as the image.

5. Put the screen back in the hinges, place a sheet of newsprint for proofing under the screen, mix the ink, puddle the ink, and squeegee it across the screen. Remove the print.

6. If ink is coming through some pin holes that were not part of the original drawing, do one of two things. Either take masking tape and block-out the pin holes with small strips of tape, or leave the pin holes alone—they will plug up with ink or add to the image.

7. Register the print paper, lower the screen, and print. After printing all the sheets of paper, set them aside to dry, remove the excess ink, and wash out the silk with mineral spirits.

8. Wash out the glue, using hot water and possibly a scrub brush, rubbing on both sides to unclog stubborn glue. It may be necessary to do a wash-out with mineral spirits after the glue wash-out, as ink has a tendency to collect on the edges of glued areas.

9. Prop up the clean screen and, using the fingertips, smear Vaseline on the silk in any desired manner.

10. Spread glue over the entire silk and wait for it

Figure 29. To create the third project (a), the soft edges of the first color (b) are drawn with crayons. A Vaseline smear (c) adds a transparent look to the second color. The third color is a combination of a glue resist and pressed aluminum foil (d).

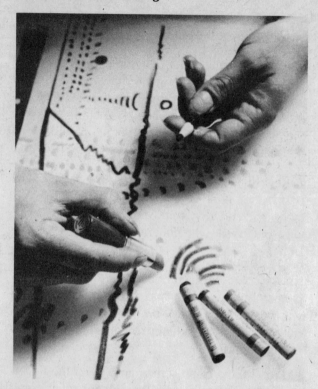

Figure 30. Paint-like qualities are achieved by drawing directly on the screen with lipstick as well as with oil and grease crayons.

to dry. The Vaseline will create a very soft, cloudy area. Wipe excess glue from the tape wells.

11. When the glue is dry, wash out the Vaseline with mineral spirits, replace the screen, and place the newsprint proof sheet under the screen.

12. Mix and puddle the ink, then print the image on the newsprint proof. After checking the proof sheet, place the sheet with the first color printed on it in the proper position. Make sure to check the registration tabs and remember which is the top of your printed sheet.

13. Print the Vaseline-smeared image on all the sheets. This will create an interesting effect over the previously drawn image. After printing each sheet, set it aside to dry. Remove the excess ink and wash out the screen with mineral spirits. Again, the glue block-out must be washed out with hot water and possibly a scrub brush.

14. For the third color, prop up the screen again and spread mineral spirits all over the silk. Make sure there is newspaper under the screen frame. (This is an example of a mineral spirit and glue resist.)

15. Before the mineral spirits dry on the silk, spread glue over the entire screen, using a piece of matt board. Wipe off excess glue along the taped wells with paper towels and let dry.

16. There is nothing to wash out at this point. Merely position the screen frame, position the newsprint proof sheet under the silk, mix the ink, puddle the ink, and squeegee the third color across the screen. If the third color is transparent, the underneath colors will show.

17. After printing the proof, register the printed sheet (now with two colors on it) in the tabs, lower the screen, and continue printing until all sheets have the new images upon them. Set the prints aside to dry.

18. Remove excess ink from the screen frame and do a wash-out. Wash out the glue resist with hot water and a brush if necessary. Again, rub both sides of the silk.

This direct drawing process can be continued any number of times, repeating with oil crayon to build areas, as well as with Vaseline or the glue-resist method. Another idea is to draw directly with lipstick. Because it is oil-based, lipstick can be used the same way grease pencil, oil crayon, or Vaseline is used.

For Additional Reading

Auvil, Kenneth W., **Serigraphy: Silk Screen Techniques for the Artist,** Prentice-Hall, 1965.

Biezeleisen, J. I., and Cohn, Max A., **Silk Screen Techniques,** Dover, 1958.

Caza, Michael, **Silk Screen Printing,** Van Nostrand, 1974.

Chieffo, Clifford I., **Silk Screen as a Fine Art,** Van Nostrand, 1967.

Schwalbach, Mathilda V. and James A., **Screen Process Printing,** Van Nostrand, 1970.

Shoklu, Harry, **Artist's Manual for Silk Screen Print Making,** Tudor, 1960.

Relief Printing

Although one of the oldest forms of printing, relief printing offers the twentieth-century craftsman a simple, effective, hand-printing method.

The development of the relief printing process can be traced back to the first century A. D., when the Chinese cut designs in stones or wood and pressed the images into wax tablets to create a signature. Eventually, they realized that these wax seals could be dipped in ink and would reproduce when pressed onto cloth. In the sixth century, the Egyptians are known to have used this printing process on fabric. Simultaneously, the Chinese were printing on blocks and transferring the work to paper.

Early relief printing was done with stamps, similar in size to present-day rubber stamps and therefore limiting the size of the created impression. It was not until the eighth century that the first full pages of type were printed. This was done by the Japanese, who discovered that a design could be transferred by rubbing the back of paper with a tool known as a baren, a stiff pad made by wrapping a large bamboo leaf around a coil of bamboo

rope. The first printed picture was done by the artist Wang Chieh in the ninth century and is presently in the British Museum in London.

In Europe, relief printing also began with the use of seals and extended to textile printing in the sixth century. These early examples were primarily decorative patterns; pictorial images did not begin to appear until the late fourteenth and early fifteenth centuries. These, however, were still printed on cloth. During the fifteenth century, paper became available to the Europeans. With Johann Gutenberg's invention of the printing press and movable type, the need for woodcuts as decoration and illustration in books became immense.

After the invention of the press, block printing expanded greatly. Early woodcuts were mostly concerned with religious subjects. They were used on holy cards and devotional pictures for private prayer. Woodcuts of patron saints were

Figure 1. The woodcut "Riders on the Four Horses from the Apocalypse" was created by the German artist Albrecht Durer. The fine detailing on this print can be seen in a close-up of the angel (opposite).

even sewn inside travelers' clothing or pasted inside lids of trunks. However, the majority of the early religious prints were made by monks who sold them to travelers as mementos.

As time went on, people began to purchase prints merely for enjoyment. Middle class merchants in Europe could not afford original paintings or sculptures by famous artists, so they bought the less expensive prints made by the same artists. It is because a print is a relatively inexpensive piece of art that woodcuts and relief printing have continued to flourish since the Middle Ages.

The first of the great woodcut artists was Albrecht Durer (1471-1528), a German who used woodcut printing to its full potential. His work, ranging from religious subjects to everyday themes to fantasy, was linear in character and always in black and white.

Color printing with wood blocks was developed in Japan and began with the Ekiyo-E school of art

in 1680 (Ekiyo-E means pictures of the floating world, or everyday life). The first Ekiyo-E prints were done in black and white and hand-colored with red watercolor paint after the print was dry. As more colors of ink were invented, blocks of wood were cut for particular colors. Thus the art of color printing began to be highly developed and prints were done in as many as 10 or 12 colors.

By 1880, this process was so common in Japan that dinnerware exported to Europe was wrapped in this kind of paper. In fact, these prints became collector's items and their style became very influential in Europe. Color came to be used even more in European artistry and certainly the brightly colored linoleum and woodblock prints of today are directly related to the first Japanese color prints. Indeed, some of the world's greatest artists, including Picasso, Matisse, Gauguin, and Winslow Homer, have employed relief printing methods, widely used by contemporary artists.

Figure 2. The woodcut "Lovers in the Snow" (left) is the work of the Japanese artist Harunobu. (Courtesy, Honolulu Academy of Arts, Honolulu, Hawaii.)

Figure 3. "The Buxheim St. Christopher" (above) is a medieval woodcut portraying a religious scene. (Courtesy, The John Rylands University Library, Manchester, England.)

Common Terms Used In

Relief Printing

Bite: slang term referring to etching (see below).

Block: general term referring to surface being printed.

Caustic: strong base used for etching linoleum.

Collagraph: block made by adding materials to a surface.

Edition: a group of identical prints.

Etching: the chemical removal of material from a surface.

Fixed Sheet System: a registration system in which the sheet remains in a fixed position until all colors are printed on it.

Found Object: any object not created by the craftsman.

Kento: Japanese registration system involving an L-shaped notch and a long notch at opposite corners of the block.

Lost Block: color printing method that involves the destruction of part of the image after each printing.

Printmaking: the process and practice of making multiple original works of art.

Proof: trial impression made of a block.

Registration: proper arrangement of colors and shapes printed from separate blocks onto the same page.

Relief Printing: surface printing, or the printing of images from a surface which has a design cut into it.

Figure 4. "Seated Wo-man, after Cranach" (1958), by Pablo Picasso. (Collection, The Museum of Modern Art, New York.)

Resist: any material which will prevent a caustic from etching a surface.

Rice Paper: a variety of thin, tough handmade papers produced in Japan from plant fibers.

Rolling Up: the application of ink with a roller to the block.

Split Fountain: a method of rolling up several colors on one roller in a rainbow effect.

Woodcut: print made from a wooden block.

Basic Equipment And Supplies

Relief printing is, perhaps, one of the most popular current art forms. It is simple, inexpensive, and gives immediate results. Most of the equipment and materials listed below can be found at local hardware stores, lumber yards, or arts and crafts stores. For items not usually available locally, specific sources are given.

TOOLS

1. Baren. A Japanese hand-printing tool made of a hemp coil covered with a banana leaf. The American variety is usually a smooth block of wood.

2. Bench hook. A board with a block attached to the top surface at the back and another at the bottom surface at the front. It is used to hold the block steady while cutting.

3. Brayers. Small rollers of varying hardness used to apply ink to the block.

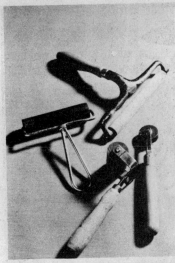

Figure 5. Supplies for relief printing include brayers (left), barens (above), and an electric drill with attachments (right).

4. Brushes. Various sizes used to apply wax, shellac, varnish, and other liquid materials.

5. C-clamp. A clamp used to hold the block to the table while cutting.

6. Drill bits. Small drilling and grinding tools which are attached to an electric drill to create various textures on the block.

7. Electric drill. Any one of the various makes of power drills.

8. Gouges. Cutting tools available in a variety of styles; used to cut images into the block.

9. Grinding bits. Small circular file-like bits used in an electric drill for texture and removal of surface area.

10. Knives. Any type with a straight edge and long handle; used to outline the forms on a block.

11. L-stop. An L-shaped piece of wood clamped to a table to hold the block in place while cutting.

12. Mat knife. A knife with a large handle and a small replaceable blade.

13. Propane torch. A simple torch used to burn a surface and melt wax.

14. Putty knife. A small spatula with a wide flat blade used to spread modeling paste.

15. Spatula.

16. Wire brush.

17. Wooden spoon.

18. X-acto knife. A small pen-like knife used for delicate cutting.

SUPPLIES

1. Burnt plate oil. Used with ink to alter its consistency and transparency.

2. Clothes lines. The simplest method for drying wet prints.

3. Fabric.

4. Glass. A sheet of glass is used on which to roll up ink because it is very smooth and easy to clean.

5. Glue. White craft glue is used to glue objects to the collagraph. Lepage's glue is used to paste the design to the block.

6. Gouache. A water-soluble paint often used as ink.

7. Ink.

8. Linoleum. Only true linoleum which is usually gray or Indian red in color can be used. Most decorative floor coverings are not true linoleum.

9. Linseed oil. Used with an oil-based ink to change the consistency and degree of color.

10. Masonite. A compressed wood-like substance made from sawdust and used as a base for collagraphs.

11. Mat board. A decorative cardboard usually used in framing.

12. Mineral spirits. A solvent for wax and ink.

13. Modeling paste. A non-brittle, plaster-like substance useful for textures in collagraphs.

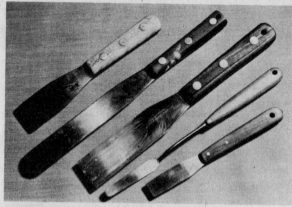

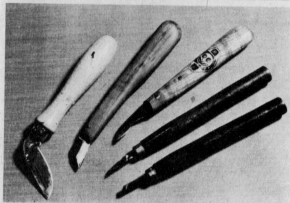

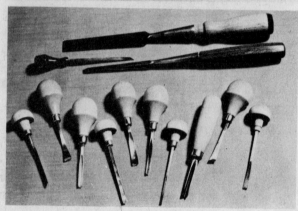

Figure 6. Other important supplies include putty knives and spatulas (top), knives (center), and gouges (bottom). All are available in a variety of sizes.

14. Oven cleaner. An easily available caustic used in etching linoleum.

15. Paint thinner. Used as a solvent for oil-based paints.

16. Plastic wood. A wood-like filler used to correct mistakes on a block.

17. Plywood. Layered wood useful as a block.

18. Poster board. Compressed cardboard that is useful in collagraphs.

19. Rag paper. Good paper for heavy and coarse printing.

20. Rice paper. Good paper for more delicate prints, although available in various thicknesses. Cost ranges from $0.10 to $1.00 per sheet.

21. Shellac. Used to seal and protect the block from ink and turpentine.

22. Sodium hydroxide. Used to etch linoleum.

23. Tempera. A water-based paint often used as ink.

24. Varnish. Used as a resist in etching linoleum.

25. Wax. Paraffin wax is used as a resist in etching linoleum.

26. Wood. A variety of woods are used for block printing. Cherry and poplar are best; pine is available in larger sizes, is inexpensive, and easy to use.

Basic Procedures

There are several basic approaches to relief printing — woodcut printing, linoleum printing, collagraphs, and the use of found objects. With all these methods, however, there is one similarity: the print is taken from the raised surface of the blocks. The only difference in the various methods is the way the print is created — either by cutting into the block with a gouge or by adding onto the block with glue. All the procedures are simple and basic and can be used in various combinations to create literally hundreds of different effects.

Figure 7. This drawing illustrates the "mountain and valley" effect in relief printing. As the brayer is rolled over the block, it inks only the mountains and not the valleys.

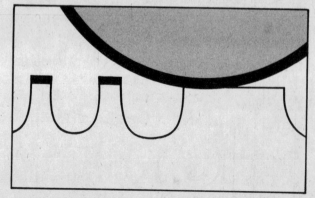

The following discussion deals first with the differences in creating blocks in various materials. It is followed by a general discussion of procedures for registration and printing used in all media of relief printing.

THE LINOLEUM BLOCK

The simplest method of relief printing is linoleum printing because linoleum is soft and easy to cut, yet rigid enough to print from.

Designing the Image

The first step in making any print is to decide upon its design. Do a drawing first on paper rather than on the block itself. Changes and variations in design can be made easily on paper — once the block is cut it is difficult, if not impossible, to change the design. After the design is finished, it can be transferred on to the block in one of several ways: (1) redraw the design on the block with a felt-tip pen; (2) place carbon paper on top of the block, place the design on top of the carbon, and trace over it; (3) glue the design to the block with a water-soluble glue. Any of these methods works well, and once the design is secured onto the block, the cutting may begin.

Arranging Bench Supports

Before cutting the image, it is best to construct a simple bench hook or L-stop to prevent the block from moving while printing (see "Basic Equipment"). The block may also be clamped to the table with a C-clamp.

It is usually easiest to work on a block at the corner of a table because the cutting can be done from two directions without having to move the block. When working from the corner, however, use an L-stop or C-clamp and not a bench hook, for the latter only offers support while carving in one direction. The time spent arranging these supports is saved many times over while cutting. The height of the table should be roughly that of a kitchen counter, as cutting is always done from a standing position.

Cutting the Block

The cutting of linoleum has several advantages over wood. The first, as stated before, is the relative softness of the material; second, linoleum does not split. Remember while cutting that the amount of resistance or pressure varies with the depth of the cut. Often while pushing hard, the gouge will slip when it reaches another cut-out area. To avoid this, ease the pressure. The gouge will also slip if the angle of the gouge is not consistent and allowed to decrease towards the surface. Because of this tendency to slip (even among experienced cutters), the cutting should *always* be done away from the cutter and the opposite hand should never be in front of the gouge at any distance.

Keep in mind that what is removed will remain white on the print. The choice of gouges to be used depends on the area to be removed. Small areas are removed with small U-shaped or V-shaped gouges. Larger areas are removed with flat gouges or large U-shaped gouges. In cutting an

Figure 8. Use a bench-hook (left) or an L-stop (right) to hold the block securely on the table.

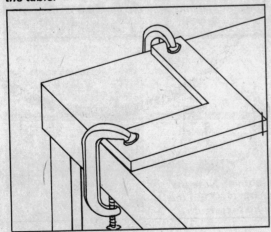 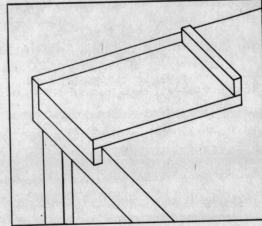

area of line, the angle of the cut should slope away from the image, and the cut should be wider at the base than it is on the surface. This gives the area or line greater support and strength. It is not necessary to cut away all the linoleum — the depth of a cut should never exceed one-eighth of an inch.

Several times during cutting it is good idea to make a trial impression to see how the image is developing. What is removed cannot be replaced, so when in doubt, experiment with a proof.

Etching

Another method of preparing a linoleum block (without cutting) is to use a caustic solution to etch the image into the surface. The results are striking and much different from those derived by cutting the block. The procedure involves using sodium hydroxide, which dissolves linoleum, and a wax that resists the action of the caustic in other areas.

Transfer the design either by painting melted wax on the areas which are to remain as surface or by covering the entire surface with wax and scraping away those areas which are to be removed. The wax serves as a resist and keeps the caustic from affecting those areas that remain as surface areas.

The next step is to etch the linoleum. The most practical and available source of caustic is oven cleaner. The variety in a jar is preferable to a spray because, with brush application, more control is possible. The caustic is simply painted liberally over the entire block and allowed to stand. The depth of the bite depends upon the time involved: a light bite takes two to three hours; a medium bite, four to six hours; a deep bite, twelve hours. Since the strength of the caustic is diminished by time, it should be washed off and replaced every few hours. It is advisable to wear gloves.

By controlling the depth of the bite in various areas, many effects can be achieved. If one area is covered with wax and an adjoining area is etched for two hours, the resulting image, when a print is taken, will be a black area and a gray area with a thin white line between. Lightly bitten areas will print as gray areas of grainy dots while deeply bitten areas will not print at all because they are too deep to pick up ink. (If fine white lines are required, a quick-drying varnish instead of wax can be used as a resist, scratched into with a needle, and etched for several hours. This will give remarkable results.) After the image has been bitten sufficiently, remove the block to the sink and scrub with soap, water, and a small scrub brush until no more particles appear. Then melt off the wax with a propane torch and wash with

Figure 9. Scrape the linoleum block to remove appropriate areas (above). Note the difference in the effects obtained by varying the time that the caustic is left on the block (above center and above right). Another means of introducing texture on a linoleum block is to etch thin lines with a fine needle (right).

mineral spirits to remove the wax residue. Various experimentation in this area will create a variety of effects.

Miscellaneous Techniques

Aside from the two methods mentioned above, a variety of other methods can be used. Essentially any mark that can be made into the surface of the linoleum will make a representative mark on the print. What would happen if screening were placed on the block and pounded with a hammer? What about a heavy wire brush or an electric drill with a variety of bits? Sandpaper, pounded or rubbed, creates an image. The possibilities are only as limited as the imagination of the craftsman.

THE WOODCUT

The main advantage of using wood for the block is that the surface is hard and capable of holding more detail. It also has, depending on the variety, natural wood grain texture. Wood is easily repaired if some area is accidentally removed and is adaptable to a variety of techniques for creating images.

There are many varieties of wood which may be used. As mentioned earlier, the best are probably cherry or poplar. They are harder than pine but not nearly as hard or brittle as maple or oak. Both have relatively smooth grains and cut easily and evenly with a minimum of splitting and splintering. Pine, which is inexpensive, is available at almost any lumber yard and often is glued together in planks as wide as 20 inches (if a large print is planned). Clear pine is soft and easy to work. It is very good for rough, textural approaches, such as scratching or denting, as well as for finer more detailed images. Pine is often the beginner's favorite.

Various kinds of plywood are very handy for large prints and, because of its layered construction, the removal of excess material is simplified. One simply cuts through the first layer and peels it off. The type chosen depends upon the surface desired.

Figure 10. "Bay of Cancer" (below) is a color linoleum cut by the author, Charles Guerin. Also shown is one of the three blocks used to make the print (left).

Fiture 11. Many craftsmen like to experiment by printing the grain of wood. These three examples show the variety of effects that can be obtained with wood. Brushing the wood with a wire brush intensifies the grain and adds interest to the print.

Cutting the Woodcut

Cutting a woodblock is somewhat different from cutting linoleum because wood has a tendency to split, especially when cut against the grain. To avoid unwanted splitting, cut around the form with an X-acto knife or mat knife. Then, if a split occurs while clearing an area with a gouge, it will be stopped when it reaches the perimeter of one of the permanent areas. If a split does occur in an important area, simply apply white craft glue to the piece, replace it, and weight it down for approximately an hour. Plastic wood can also be used. When dry, sand lightly and the repair will go unnoticed.

Texture

With many craftsmen, wood is chosen for its grain. When printing grain, there are several methods, depending upon the boldness desired. A very light and subtle grain effect is produced simply by printing the wood surface. To achieve a slightly more vivid reproduction, brush the surface with a wire brush several times. This removes the softer wood fibers, leaving the harder ones in relief. If still more relief is desired, lightly burn the surface with a propane torch before brushing with the wire brush. Grainy wood can be obtained from old weathered barns or fences.

Since wood dents easily, it is possible to create many images, designs, and patterns by hammering hard objects into the wood, such as tacks, pins, staples, punches, washers, or screws.

Besides pounding, punching, or denting the surface, scratching, scraping, and buffing also create textures. There are a variety of grinding and scraping bits designed to fit an electric drill which make the work fairly simple and which create new and unique textures at the same time. In working with wood, it should be remembered that almost anything can be used as a tool.

THE COLLAGRAPH OR THE BUILT UP BLOCK

All the methods previously described involved the cutting or scraping away of material. With the collagraph, the craftsman creates the surface by adding materials and has the advantage of using various textures and shapes. In the easiest collagraph method, shapes made from poster board (compressed cardboard) or mat board are glued with white craft glue to masonite. It is advisable when using any kind of paper or cardboard that the finished block be given a coat of shellac to seal the surface and to prevent it from absorbing ink or turpentine during clean-up.

With the collagraph, virtually any flat object can be mounted to the block to create images. Fabric is frequently used because there is such a large variety of textures. It is often wise to glue the fabric to illustration board (*i.e.,* poster board or mat board) with Elmer's glue and then cut and

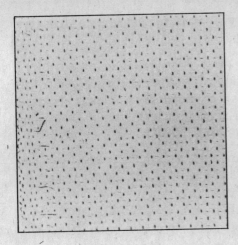
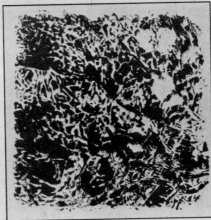

Figure 12. Interesting effects may be achieved in colla-graphs by experimenting with a variety of textures. Proofs are shown for two: screening (far left) and tinfoil (left).

mount the shape to the masonite block. Again, shellac should be used to seal the surface.

Another versatile material is modeling paste. This is a mixture of acrylic and powdered marble that dries hard like plaster yet is not breakable. Begin with a sheet of masonite. On the rough side, using a spatula or putty knife, smooth on a layer of modeling paste about one-eighth inch thick. While the paste is wet, the surface texture can be altered with the fingers or a hard tool. It may also be altered by pressing in a texture with such items as leaves or twigs, grass, lace, keys, or coins. After the paste is dry, coat it with shellac and allow it to dry before proofing. Once dry it is possible to go back into the surface with a knife or gouge and remove areas or create lines. Remember to coat the surface again with shellac because turpentine and paint thinners will weaken the paste.

Figure 13. An interesting texture can be created by printing mat board (below). Modeling paste can be used to create a textured effect on a block, too (below right).

It should be remembered that many of these various methods can be used together on the same block or separately, depending on the imagination of the craftsman.

FOUND OBJECTS

Found object printing is often very fascinating because one never knows what to expect. Almost anything that has a relief or a textured surface can be printed: bricks, manhole covers, saw blades, ends of logs, concrete, coins, or keys. Found objects allow for maximum use of the imagination and experimentation.

COLOR PRINTING

Color printing can be approached in several ways. The first is to make a separate block for each color and print them on the same page by registering the page to each block (see "Registration" below). This method permits a variety of effects because each block can be unique. The

combination of various color blocks on the same page is interesting because the results cannot be completely planned and each new impression is different.

Another method of color printing is the lost block technique, a process which ultimately destroys the block's entire surface by the time the last image is completed. Although this sounds somewhat complex, it is really quite simple.

1. Choose the order in which the colors will be printed—usually light to dark.

2. Cut away those areas which are to remain white, and print the first color.

3. Cut away the areas which are to remain the first color and print the next darkest color.

4. Cut away those areas which are to remain the latter color and print the next darkest color. This procedure is continued until the last color is printed; it has the advantage of many colors being printed with only one block.

A third method of color printing is to ink separate areas of the same block with different colors, either for the same impression or for different impressions. Still another very simple, yet very dramatic method is called the split fountain. This method involves rolling up two or more colors on

Figure 14. Printing found objects can yield offbeat effects. Examples shown are a shirt (right), coins (below), a board (bottom), and leaves (bottom right).

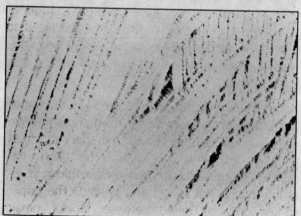

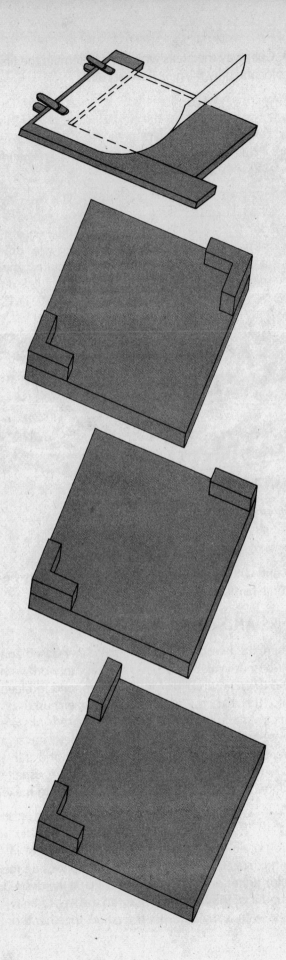

Figure 15. Registration systems include (from top) the fixed-sheet type and a variety of Kento types. In the fixed-sheet system, clothespins hold the paper to the block. All three Kento systems shown use notches and stops to hold the paper. Two L-shaped, or Kento, notches may be used. Or, one L-shaped notch can be placed diagonally opposite a long flat notch. Still another variation involves placing the L-shaped notch and the long notch on the same side of the rectangular block.

the same roller at the same time and letting them blend together. The roller, however, must be larger than the area to be covered because the ink is always rolled in the same direction. If the colors were not rolled this way, they would completely mix and defeat the purpose.

REGISTRATION

Registration refers to any method used to align the paper and the block to assure proper positioning of the image on the paper in relation to a previously printed color. One technique, a Japanese method called *kento*, involves cutting the image into a block that is about two inches larger than the image. This will allow for a two-inch border. At one corner an L-shaped notch is cut, and at the opposite corner a flat notch is cut. On each block of a color print, these notches are positioned in exactly the same place. When printing, one corner of the paper is placed in the L-shaped notch or *kento* and the opposite edge is butted up against the long notch. The impression is then made. There are other variations on this system: if each piece of paper is the same size, two *kentos* at opposite corners can be used; or the long notch can be placed on the same side as the *kento*.

One disadvantage of the *kento* system is that it is only practical where a larger piece of wood is available; it cannot be used with an image that covers the entire block. On the other hand, the *kento* method should always be used for the lost block method.

When printing an image which covers the entire block, the best system is the fixed sheet system. Here, an L-stop is used with the sheet attached with two clips to one end. With this system the paper is raised and each consecutive block is inserted against the L-stop and printed. The paper should only be raised between blocks, never

Figure 16. This is a famous woodcut by the Japanese artist Hokusai, "Fuji Seen in the Distance Below a Great Breaking Wave of the Sea." (Courtesy, The Art Institute of Chicago.)

removed, for this destroys the registration. It is not possible to use this system with the lost block techniques because all colors are printed in order.

PAPER FOR RELIEF PRINTING

The choice of paper for relief printing is important because the printing process involves vigorous rubbing on the back of the paper. The paper most frequently used is handmade Japanese rice paper. This comes in various sizes, textures, colors, and degrees of thickness and absorbency. In choosing paper, keep in mind the nature of the print and the block. If the print is smooth and delicate, use a thin paper with a smooth surface.

One hundred percent rag papers, either hand-made or machine made, are especially useful when printing many colors. They are heavier than rice paper and hold more ink without becoming heavy. They are also extremely durable. Experi-

ment with papers until their various effects become familiar.

INKS AND OILS

There are two basic kinds of ink: water-based and oil-based. Water-based inks are easy to work with and to clean up. They do, however, tend to bleed into the paper and work best when used on slightly dampened rice paper. Oil-based inks are more commonly used because they have a greater versatility in terms of thickness and transparency. These are thick inks which are usually thinned with linseed oil or burnt plate oil to make them less heavy on the paper, more transparent, and more durable.

It is possible and desirable with either type of ink to mix special colors rather than simply using the color right from the can or tube. Place the desired amount of ink from each can on a sheet of heavy glass with a spatula. Mix the colors together thor-

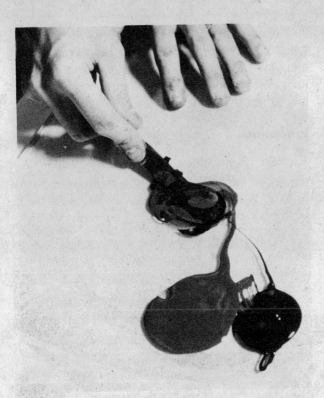

Figure 17. Ink colors can be mixed and blended as desired. Place the inks on a clean surface as shown; then mix thoroughly with a spatula. Experiment with various proportions of basic colors.

Figure 18. All materials should be neatly laid out and organized before printing is begun. Be certain that the work surface and the block are free of dust or scraps that could mar the print.

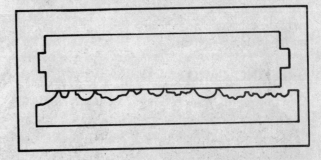

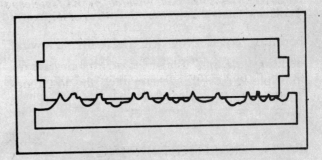

Figure 19. The hard roller (top) hits only the very top of the raised surface on the block. By contrast the soft roller hits both the top and the depressions.

oughly with the desired amount of oil before rolling out the color on the glass. This will insure a smooth and uniform color. The exact consistency of the ink will depend on the desired effect. Test print the ink before beginning to print.

HAND PRINTING

Before beginning, make sure that the table and block are completely free of dust and wood chips. Have the paper handy and a clothes line set up for drying the prints.

The quality of the print will depend upon two things: the choice of the roller or brayer and the choice of the baren (see "Tools"). Make experimental proofs with a soft roller, a hard roller, and one with each baren. Compare these proofs and decide which tools give the desired effect. Clean and put away those not in use to avoid using them accidentally.

PRINTING

The actual printing is done by placing the paper over the inked block. Be careful not to smudge the paper as it is laid down. Once in position, begin

rubbing the block with the wooden spoon or baren. To obtain a uniform print, use the same movement over the entire area, or begin at one corner and rub each area until the image begins to appear on the back of the paper. (More can be seen on rice paper than on 100% rag paper.) Once the image appears uniform, the printing is finished. If the paper used is particularly fragile or if several colors are to be printed, place another piece of smooth paper over the first sheet before beginning to rub. This will protect the print from the friction of the baren. Once printed, gently pull the paper off the block to avoid tearing, and hang it up to dry. Repeat for the next print. If printing a multicolored print, lift the paper, remove the block, insert the next block, and begin printing. Remove paper only when all colors are printed.

It is possible to get various effects by placing some texture over the back of the paper, covering with a second sheet, and rubbing. The ink on the block will pick up that texture.

Projects You Can Do

The projects described here will allow use of the lost block method of linoleum printing, printing of a black and white woodcut, and making of a collagraph. Choose whichever is desirable — it would be a good idea to read through each one and then decide which to try.

GREETING CARD

Greeting cards can be made by using the lost block method of linoleum printing. Before beginning, however, review the procedures for the lost block method as described in the section on Color Printing.

Tools and Materials

For this project, you will need the following items: (1) blank greeting cards, which can be ordered through any small commercial printer (a wide variety of stocks are available); (2) one linoleum block that is somewhat larger in size than the blank cards; (3) one inexpensive set of gouges; (4) one brayer; (5) a small sheet of glass or a cookie tray on which to roll the ink; (6) a spatula; (7) a wooden spoon; and (8) several colors of ink, either oil- or water-based.

Procedures

1. Begin by creating a full color drawing of the design for the greeting card on a blank card. Keep in mind that the image as well as any words will be in reverse to print correctly.

2. Position the card with the drawing face down on the block and mark the position of the *kento* as well as the boundaries of the card.

3. Within the traced boundaries on the block, draw in the design in full color with felt-tip pens.

4. Cut away everything outside the boundaries of the image except for the registration grooves.

5. Within the image, cut away those areas which are to remain white.

6. Mix the lightest color of those to be used, roll it onto the glass, and then onto the block. Make sure the entire surface has a thin uniform film of ink.

7. Place the appropriate corner of the blank card into the *kento* and up against the straight notch. Be careful not to smudge the paper when laying it down.

8. With the wooden spoon, rub the back of the card until the image begins to be visible from the back of the sheet.

Figure 20. A small, basic collection of materials is needed for printing greeting cards. A modest set of gouges and a frosting spatula may be used to keep down costs.

Figure 21. Begin the greeting card project by making a drawing of the design (above left). Carefully cut away the image on the block (left). Rub the baren over the paper and block (above center). After printing, clean block carefully (above right). The finished greeting card (below) is handsome and cheerful.

9. Carefully remove the sheet and examine the results. If they are satisfactory, hang the card on a clothes lines to dry and repeat steps 7 and 8 until the desired number of cards have been printed. Always print a few extra to allow for errors — five or six extra should do for a three- or four-color print.

10. Clean off the ink from the block with a rag moistened with mineral spirits. Try not to remove the drawing.

11. Cut away those areas which are to remain the color previously printed.

12. Mix up the next darker color and apply it to the block.

13. Repeat steps 7 through 12 for each additional color desired. Sometimes it is advisable to let each color dry before proceeding, but it is not absolutely necessary.

14. Let cards dry thoroughly.

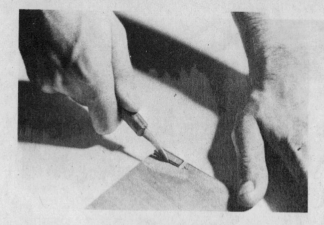

Figure 22. Cutting of the block should begin at the outside edge (above left). When the basic design has been cut away, use a gouge to clean up rough areas that should not print (above). Ink is rolled out onto a glass, then transferred from the glass to the block (left). Rub the baren over the paper carefully and evenly to avoid smudging the image (below).

BLACK AND WHITE WOODCUT

Materials and Tools

To do this project, you will need: (1) 15 sheets of medium-weight rice paper; (2) a one-inch thick block of wood of the desired size; (3) pencils, black felt-tip pen, and drawing paper; (4) carbon paper; (5) mat knife; (6) one X-acto knife; (7) a set of fine, good quality gouges; (8) a baren or flat wooden spoon; (9) one tube or can of black oil-based ink; (10) one quart of mineral spirits; (11) a small clothes line; and (12) one brayer or roller about six inches long and two inches in diameter.

Procedures

1. Create the design, keeping in mind the size of the block and of the paper.

2. After the drawing is completed, place a piece of carbon paper between the block and the drawing and trace the image from the back of the sheet onto the block.

3. Remove the drawing paper and carbon paper and fill in the black areas of the drawing with a felt-tip pen. Once completed, this drawing on the block will look exactly like the finished print in reverse.

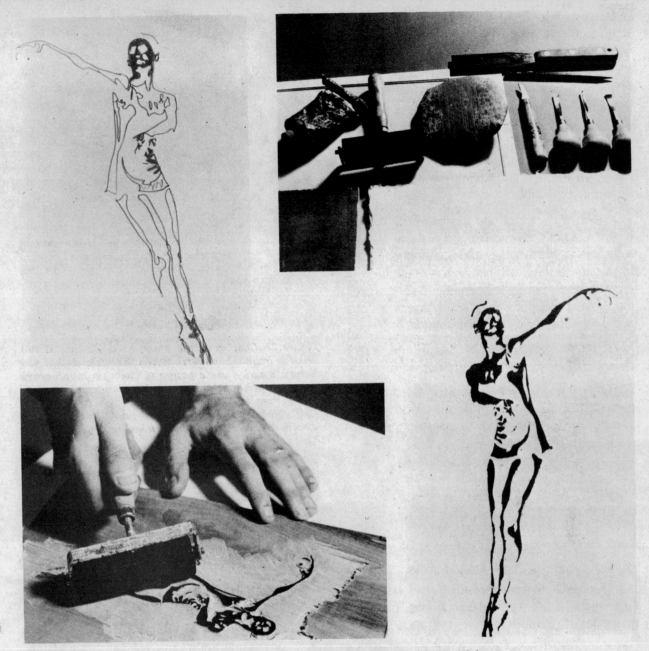

Figure 23. A drawing of the subject was made for the woodcut (top left). Some of the tools needed for the project are shown (top right). The artist carefully inks the block, preparatory to the printing process (bottom left). The finished print is neat and professional looking (bottom right).

4. Using a mat knife and an X-acto knife for intricate areas, cut around the perimeter of the drawing to prevent the wood from splitting in the wrong places. The angle of the cut should always slope away from the area to be printed.

5. With gouges of appropriate size, clear those areas of the design not to be printed.

6. Clear away all debris on the table as well as on the block in preparation for taking a proof.

7. Roll out a thin layer (it should look like velvet while rolling out) of black ink onto a sheet of glass and then apply it evenly to the block. Recharge the roller with ink several times to assure an even layer of ink.

8. While holding a sheet of paper at opposite corners, gently lay it onto the block. Be careful not to move the paper once it is down. In the case of a black and white print, registration methods are not needed because only one printing is involved.

9. Gently but firmly rub the back of the paper with a baren or wooden spoon while holding the paper firm with the opposite hand. Rub evenly until the image begins to appear from the back of the paper. To insure a good print, rub as evenly and uniformly as possible.

10. Remove the proof and examine it. If the impression is not dark enough, the pressure was not sufficient or not enough ink was applied. If the impression is thick and heavy, too much ink was used. If there appears to be light and dark strokes, the rubbing was not even. If the image is uniform and a crisp black, the impression is good.

11. If the impression was not good, repeat steps 8 through 10, using a new sheet of paper.

12. Once a good proof is achieved, repeat steps 8 through 10 on all sheets of paper. Compare each print to the first good proof to maintain a uniform quality.

13. Hang prints to dry.

MAKING AND PRINTING A COLLAGRAPH

Tools and Materials

The following items are needed for this project: (1) 15 sheets of medium-weight rice paper or lightweight 100% rag paper; (2) one piece of masonite; (3) various textures to apply to the

Figure 24. Materials for a collagraph should be assembled before the work is begun. They include scraps of fabric, modeling paste, a spatula, and one or two brayers.

Figure 25. Begin the collagraph by experimenting with different arrangements of the textured objects on a ''dry run'' basis. Complete the design in this way before applying modeling paste.

block such as fabrics, leaves, grass, wire, string, or small found objects; (4) various thick materials to build up the relief — e.g., mat board, illustration board, wood veneer; (5) modeling paste; (6) white craft glue; (7) spatula or putty knife; (8) shellac; (9) an X-acto knife and a mat knife; (10) scissors; (11) various tubes of colored ink; (12) one soft brayer and one hard brayer; (13) linseed or burnt plate oil (optional); (14) a sheet of glass; and (15) a clothes line.

Procedures

1. Begin by doing a rough drawing or by arranging various bits and shapes of cardboard, fabric, buttons, and any other planned articles.

2. Once the design has been decided upon, begin applying the shapes to the masonite block with white craft glue.

3. Also consider applying a layer of modeling paste and then applying the textures. Note that the paste has its own texture. Continue to use the tools and materials as freely and as imaginatively as possible. To make linear patterns, cut into the dry paste and textures. Remember, the surface is what will print.

4. Once the collagraph is thoroughly dry, apply two coats of shellac, three hours apart. Let these dry.

5. In printing, there are various approaches to color: using one color only, applying different colors to various sections of the block and printing as many times as desired, starting with

Figure 26. Four proofs taken from the same block illustrate the subtle differences obtainable in printing. The craftsman should experiment with proofing to insure interesting results.

the finished collagraph block and following the lost block technique described in the first project, or trying various combinations and approaches.

6. The soft brayer will apply ink to more surface than the hard brayer. Decide which to use by experimenting.

7. If printing more than once on the same sheet of paper, use the fixed sheet system of registration. (Note: This will not work with the lost block technique unless the sheet is fixed to the L-stop in the same place each time it is printed.)

8. Make several proofs to decide what is desir-

able. More than one edition can be made from the same block.

9. Run the edition, taking notes on the process so it can be repeated for each print.

10. Hang and dry.

For Additional Reading

Heller, Jules, **Printmaking Today,** Holt, 1972.

Ross, John, and Romano, Clare, **The Complete Printmaker,** Free Press, 1972.

Rothenstein, Michael, **Relief Printing,** Watson-Guptill, 1970.

Mask Making

The ancient art of mask making is still a means of magically transforming oneself into another being for parties, plays, and holidays.

The rich tradition of mask art can be historically traced through the cultures of every continent: Europe, Asia, Africa, and the Americas. Best known perhaps are the tragic and comic masks of ancient Greek harvest festivals and of the plays during the times of Aristotle. Because Greek amphitheatres were extremely large and the costumes either uniformly alike or nonexistent, the extra large masks were a great help in showing the identity of each character. Furthermore, these masks helped to portray women, since female roles were acted by men.

New identities were given African tribesmen by huge masks which fit down over their shoulders. The masks made them appear superhuman or animal-like and helped them in their invocations to evil demons which seemed to cause illness and bad times. The masks were also used to summon up extra strength with which to meet the enemy in battle, or to thank the gods for showing favors.

Certainly, there were more uses for masks than the giant tasks just mentioned. For centuries, much fun has been derived from simply covering part of one's face at masked balls and at such well-known festivals as Mardi Gras and the Beaux Arts Balls. In palace life of the sixteenth-century French kings, many coy flirtations were carried on by dancing courtesans camouflaged only by small bejeweled eyemasks.

In American folklore, Batman and Robin stepped out of everyday commonness to become — behind their masks — comic book heroes. For years, Emmett Kelly and other circus clowns wore masks when portraying the foibles of people. If they poked fun without their masks, they might very well be considered offensive. By covering their original identities, they each become Everyman, and everyone is able to laugh together at their satire.

Another type of mask is represented by such well-known black-faced minstrels as the late Al Jolson and by such white-faced pantomimists as Marcel Marceau. Those entertainers who wear make-up applied directly to their faces are following a tradition that started when prehistoric man smeared berry juice on his face to emphasize the exaggerated shadows thrown by campfires. He became more angry or horrible-looking to ward off evil

Figure 1. This Senufo mask from the Ivory Coast (opposite) is an excellent example of the artistic expression that can be achieved in mask making. (Courtesy, The Museum of Primitive Art, New York.)

spirits in the surrounding darkness, or to add more excitement in relating the day's hunting adventures. And as early as the seventh century, the Japanese ceremonial dances of Bugaku used direct facial make-up as well as masks to convey religious meanings.

A mask, of course, is not necessarily applied to the face. Indeed, totem poles are a series of carvings resembling the carved masks worn by Alaskan Indians and those of the Pacific Northwest; the Kachina dolls made by Indians of the Southwest have a similar heritage. The totem, doll, and mask all served the same functions of warding off evil and of appeasing ancestors who had departed from this life. Surely, during the age of armor, the helmeted knight whose face shield was mask-like in its engraved design evoked more fear from those he confronted than a knight wearing an unadorned and purely functional armor piece.

The function of a mask also may be purely utilitarian. For example, the goalie in a hockey game is protected by his mask. And the faces of today's astronauts are always hidden from view as they perform their complicated missions in space.

At one time masks were molded directly from the faces of dead heroes, and then applied to the statuary figures that honored them. Or, they were done in wax, such as those created by the Toussard family and housed today in the Wax Museum in London. As a positive version of the death masks, contemporary potters often take life masks and use the ceramic faces as decoration for plaques and vases.

The masks of today, which are done for whatever special occasions, might well be shown off as part of a wall hanging, attached to the side of a show-off wastepaper basket, or teasingly propped up among the potted plants in one's house. Perhaps such light-hearted fantasy will add humor to today's often over-burdened, logical mind.

Figure 2. Pericles, leader of the ancient Greeks, wears a mask-like helmet. Armor masks have been an essential part of warfare throughout history. (Courtesy, Vatican Museum; photo, Alinari.)

Common Terms Used In Mask Making

Armature: the underlying material that gives the mask its structure and stiffness. Such structures may be balloons, wire frames, etc. Often, they give temporary support while the surface material is drying or hardening.

Contrast: marked differences in the surface or shape of a mask which provide strong and dramatic effect.

Embossing: the process of pressing a pattern or texture into a semistiff material, such as leather or tooling metal foil.

Enrichment: any decorations with colors, textures, and shapes that enhance the basic design.

Foil (Tooling): a special gauge (thickness) of metal which will hold both its shape and embossed textures without being too heavy to use for mask making. The common metals used are copper and aluminum, and the gauge most often used is number 32.

Harmony: the design quality of all basic parts being alike in some way, such as having similar or related colors.

Motif: the main idea in a pattern or a shape that is used repeatedly, with or without variations, to give a unified effect to the design.

Pattern: repeated shapes in surface decoration; also a model or template for making things.

Planes: surfaces that are basically flat; when two planes meet, the armature or surface must be reinforced at that angle.

Repoussee: designs made by embossing lines or punching small holes through a material in decorative patterns.

Repetition: using alike things repeatedly to achieve a special total effect; for example, using repeated straight lines to create stripes.

Symmetry: a design configuration in which patterns on both sides of a center axis are exactly alike.

Basic Equipment And Supplies

Materials used in several other crafts may also be used in mask making. However, weight, permanence, and safety must be taken into account. Beware of sharp edges or ends and of substances requiring solvents that might irritate the skin or lungs. Look for materials which will convey ideas in unusual or whimsical ways.

Tools and materials for four types of masks will be described later. However, there are certain common items which fall into specific categories, as listed below.

TOOLS

1. **For Attaching:** Needles, thread, yarn, fabric glue, modeling paste, casein glue, wheat paste, masking tape, string.

2. **For Cutting:** Scissors and a utility or mat knife.

3. **For Measuring:** Tape measure, ruler, string.

4. **For Marking:** Oil crayons, eye make-up, lipstick, tempera paint.

MATERIALS

1. **Items From Nature:** Shells, bones, feathers, bark, grass, leaves, husks.

2. **Fibers and Fabrics:** Yarn, string, cloth, rope, nylon stockings, thread.

3. **Papers:** Cardboard, newspaper, magazines, paper bags, wrapping paper.

4. **Metals:** Foil, wire, coat hanger.

Figure 3. Masks have been used to conceal the individual and, thus, protect his identity. An African dance mask (above) hides a tribesman during funeral rites. (Courtesy, The Seattle Art Museum.) In New Guinea, a ceremonial mask (top right) is a means of disguise in rituals. (Courtesy, The British Museum.) Even the astronauts (below) wore mask-like visors to protect their faces on lunar landings. (Courtesy, NASA.) A wax effigy (bottom right) preserves the image of Lord Nelson. (Courtesy, Madame Tussaud's, London.)

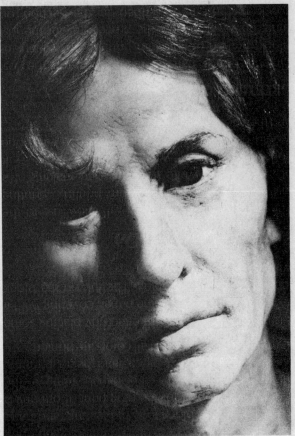

Basic Procedures

The first part of a mask-making project is primarily psychological: it sets the stage for the final product.

First, carefully consider the mask's purpose and the mood it is to convey. Second, read the following directions thoroughly to get a feeling of what is to be accomplished. Third, assemble all the necessary materials and set aside a place for working so the mask can be made without clean-up interruptions.

In considering the mood and purpose of a mask, remember these basic guidelines: happy ideas are conveyed by lines and shapes that curve up; violence, anger, and hatred are typified by angular and straight lines; and sadness is shown by drooping shapes and lines. These line variations represent a kind of symbolic language people have learned through the ages, and the so-called reading of them is quite uniform and immediate. Make use of this while planning a mask.

Partially hidden faces are teasing; completely hooded figures are fearsome. Unnatural propor-

tions are usually comical; and painted faces are very mysterious because the face is human but unrecognizable.

Extreme contrasts in texture, made by applying several different materials, are more dramatic and often more frightening. Color changes and color contrasts might also be dramatic; while the use of harmonious, closely related colors can result in gentle and quite elegant effects.

In designing a mask, one might choose a picture to copy or do an original design. If doing an original design, it is fun to go to a large mirror and make faces. Find the expression needed for the purpose of the mask and, while holding the head very still, draw the reflected image on the mirror with lipstick or an oil crayon. Trace all the main lines and features of the facial expression. Then press a piece of typing paper or paper towel to the mirror and rub the back of the paper vigorously. Be careful not to slide the paper while rubbing, as this will smear the image. The drawn image will transfer to the paper. It may be somewhat smaller than expected because of the distance from

Figure 4. Line variations are used to convey the mood of a mask. Depression (left) and happiness (right) are portrayed on two sides of this four-sided mask titled "All My Faces" by Hede von Nagel. (Courtesy, Hede von Nagel.)

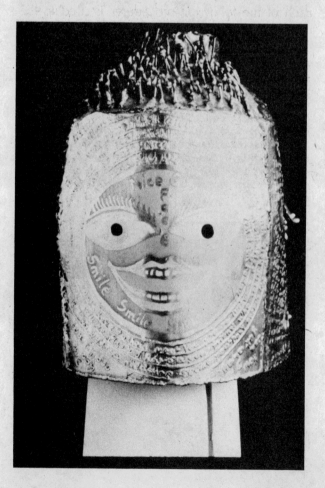

which it was traced, but it will provide a basic form and distinguishing lines. This is a quick way for beginning a design.

Next, read through the procedural steps that follow to get an overview of the approach. Read the part about setting up the armature very carefully. It is the key to the functional success of the total project. These procedural steps are involved in the making of four separate types of masks:

1. Rigid paper masks — made with papier-mâché cardboard, and wheat paste).

2. Metal foil mask with tooling — made with foil which is embossed and cut.

3. Soft fabric mask — a hood enriched with appliquéd design and pattern.

4. Cosmetic painted mask — an application of the mask directly to the face with cosmetics and stage make-up.

PROCEDURES FOR BEGINNING ALL MASKS

Each of the following procedures is used in the making of one or more of the four types of masks described above.

Key Measurements for the Masks or Armatures

Make all of the following measurements *loosely*, otherwise heat and lack of air circulation may make the wearer uncomfortable.

1. Measure around the edge of the face — from in front of the ears, following the hairline, and under the jaw. (Use this method to make masks 1, 2, or 3.)

2. Measure around the head — above the ears, and across the fullest part of the skull. (Use this method to make masks 1, 2, or 3.)

3. Measure the face vertically to locate the placement of eyes, nostrils, mouth, etc. (Use this method to make masks 1, 2, or 3.)

4. Measure from the top of the head to the desired bottom length of the hood. (Use this method to make mask 3.)

Figure 5. Loose measurements should be taken to insure a comfortably fitted mask. Begin by measuring around the outline of the face (A); then, measure around the head at its fullest part (B). Vertical measurements for placement of the features are taken (C), and the length of the mask is determined (D).

A

B

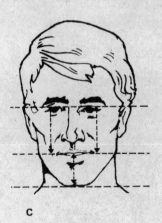

C

D

Making the Armature

1. Use wire (approximately 10-12 gauge thickness) or coat hangers cleaned with steel wool to make the major planes of the form. Each change of surface direction may need the support of additional wire at its edge. (Use this method to make masks 1 or 2.)

2. Attach the wires to each other by tightly bending the ends of one around the other with pliers. (Use this method for masks 1 or 2.)

3. If the mask is only frontal, and is not held in place by a top piece, attach rag strips above the ears. Test whether it will stay on the face throughout its development. The rag strips can be replaced later by a more finished elastic band.

4. For a hood or any other mask covering the top of the skull, an old wig stand would provide excellent support while working on the mask.

5. Use large to medium balloons as support for fabric and paper masks. But double tie them so no air leaks out midway through the project.

6. After a bit of hunting in attics and garages, one may discover that some armatures are "ready-made." For instance, a wire armature for a mask with a long, animal "snoot" might come directly from an old lampshade.

Projects You Can Do

The projects discussed here are simple and inexpensive to do. The important thing to keep in mind is that mask making is fun: the work is enjoyable and creative, and the results are quickly seen.

Remember the basic areas of consideration before undertaking a mask-making project: What is the mask's purpose and mood? Have instructions been read carefully? Are all of the necessary materials assembled?

RIGID PAPER ANIMAL HEAD

This mask will humorously portray an animal, using a basic and inexpensive form of sculpture. Some distortion, upcurved lines, and happy colors will be used to achieve humorous results. For a temporary armature, paper "sausages" will be made from paper bags and newspaper wrapped together with masking tape.

Tools and Materials

The tools and materials needed for attaching, cutting, measuring, and marking are masking tape, string, wheat paste or wallpaper paste, casein glue, scissors, utility or mat knife or single-edged razor blade, sandpaper, measuring tape, tempera

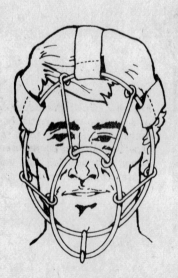 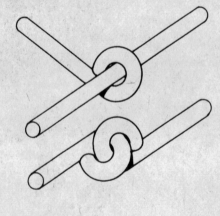

Figure 6. Wire imparts structure and stiffness to a mask. The ends of the wire must be tightly joined to support the form (right). An old lampshade is an ideal armature for constructing animal-head masks (left).

or acrylic paints, felt-tip markers, and art brushes in two or three sizes — approximately 2, 5, and 8.

Also needed are buckets for paste and water, pans for paints, and oil of cloves or wintergreen to preserve the paste during the time the mask is being worked on.

The working medium will mostly be two-inch strips of newspaper applied over several brown paper bags.

Procedures

1. Prepare the work area with two or three layers of newspaper and assemble the materials.

2. Tear two-inch strips of newspaper, stockpiling at least ten pages for this project. Because newspaper has a grain and will tear more easily one way than another, it is generally best to tear from top to bottom.

3. Stir the wheat paste or wallpaper paste in a mixing bowl, using lukewarm water. Stir constantly to avoid lumps. The final consistency should be somewhat like pea soup: not so watery that it is transparent and not so thick that a spoon would stand upright in it. Stir a teaspoon of oil of cloves or wintergreen into the mixture if you wish to keep it for several days. The oil will retard spoiling for a short time.

4. Bunch, roll, or bag some shapes that will make up the parts of the mask you wish to make. Run masking tape around them to hold them in shape. Stuff paper bags with dry, loosely crumpled newspaper to make the form desired, then tape the end of the bag shut so the newspaper cannot fall out while the paste strips are being applied.

5. Choose one large shopping bag or grocery bag that will fit over the head. This will become the primary armature — that is, several layers of newspaper laminated with wheat paste will, when dry, become a cardboard shell upon which to build the character of the mask. Stuff the bag full of crumpled newspaper and tape it shut. The taped end will eventually become the opening of the mask; the bottom of the bag will become the top of the mask.

6. Now begin to apply the newspaper strips to the armature by dragging them through the wheat paste so that they are wet on both sides, and then by laying them across the bag's surface. Crisscross the strips so that they overlap constantly, and apply no less than three complete layers. Then let the form dry, being sure to support the wet sculptural forms while they are drying. Wet paper is heavy and soft, and is very apt to sag and harden into an unwanted shape. Use crumpled newspaper sheets, boxes, or whatever else ingenuity suggests for support. The drying process often takes a day or more.

7. Be satisfied with creating only the basic shell on the first session. Three layers of thin newspa-

Figure 7. Stuff the paper bag with crumpled newspaper to make the desired form and tape the bottom so the newspaper will not fall out while paste strips are applied.

per, when pasted together, become the stuff that cardboard is made of and are quite as durable. The shell, when dry, can be added to, cut, and otherwise modified as desired.

8. Taking the cue from the humorous animal kingdom, tape a small, sausage-like roll of newspaper to the base to make a nose or snout of a pig. Attach tighter rolls to form all of the other shapes of an animal face: cheeks, nostrils, mouth, and eyebrows. Try to be creative. It is not important whether or not the face looks real; rather, it should look imaginative or funny.

9. One very useful shape in such sculpture is the cone. Cut a circle, and then cut a line from the edge into the center. When the two cut edges are overlapped slightly, a concave-convex cone is formed. It can be used for eyes, for cheeks, a chin, or any number of possibilities.

10. Combine the previous step with another idea. Laminate about four layers of newspaper sheets with paste between each layer. While still wet,

cut the material with scissors to form such shapes as the cone. The result will be a shape that has been formed with scissor precision, but which will dry into cardboard-like stiffness later.

11. Every object or shape applied to the base or to another form must be "bandaged" into place by using tiny strips of paper dipped in paste; and finally, by postage stamp sized pieces to make smooth but durable "welds." Failure to do this could result in some parts dropping off when they dry, and it may also present a very difficult surface to paint because of its roughness. Avoid both problems by smoothly applying the bandages, and by graduating from large to tiny paper strips.

12. To try the mask on for size, cut the tapes on the opening of the bag and remove all of the newspaper stuffing. The three-to-five-layer shell will not collapse, but will serve as the light, rigid structure upon which all further decoration is to be applied.

13. Place the mask on the person to be wearing it

Figure 8. The base for the pig's nose (below) is easily made by forming a cone with a circle cut from a paper bag. The other forms for the pig's facial features (right) are cut and shaped in a similar manner.

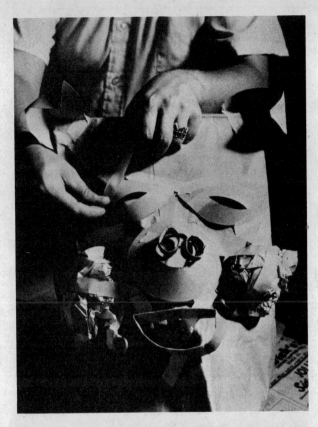

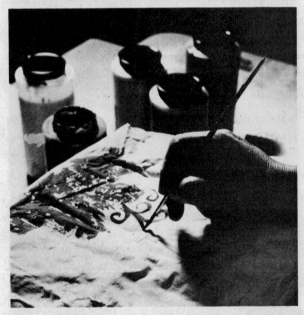

Figure 9. Use masking tape to attach the cut-out forms to the base (above). Newspaper strips that have been dipped in paste are stuck on the bag (top right). After the paper has dried, brush the surface with tempera paints (bottom right).

and find the precise eye level, so the eye holes may be marked. Take the mask off and cut small holes. Try the mask on again and check for accuracy of the holes. Then make them larger. Remember that the farther away the eye holes are from the wearer's eyes, the larger they must be for good vision as well as safety. **Never cut the eye holes or mouth hole while the mask is being worn.**

14. Do not build any area up with paper and paste to more than a half-inch thickness before allowing it to dry. Thicker areas may not dry.

15. Try the dry mask on and check its weight. If it needs to be lighter, consider cutting open some of the "sausage" areas that were filled with dry crumpled paper for initial support. Pull out the stuffing and patch the surface with more paper bandages. The result will be a series of air pocket shells that will be very strong but quite light.

16. When the modeled areas are finished and dry, assemble the paints and brushes. Tempera

paint comes in a powder or as a premixed liquid and is water soluble. The newer acrylic paints are water soluble initially, but harden into a colorful plastic over a short period of time. The latter plastic coating will give the mask a shine and dust-proof durability that could be achieved from tempera only by adding a coat of shellac or clear lacquer.

17. Prepare the surface for painting. If there are rough spots, sandpaper them.

Figure 10. The finished mask is an imaginative representation of a pig.

18. Draw the desired basic features on the mask: curving mouth, nostrils, eyelids, eyelashes, and so forth.

19. Using a brush, paint the biggest or solid blocks of color first. Then go on to the edges, lines, and details after the first color has dried.

20. Create texture for manes or whiskers by sewing yarn into the mask surface with a heavy-duty tapestry needle. If desired, dip the yarn into casein glue first to provide it with stiffness and a plastic-like durability.

21. Finally, give the mask the mirror test. Put it on and stand some 15 or 20 feet away from the mirror. Decide from the view if the desired effect has been achieved. The whole project will have been worthwhile if the magic of visual transformation occurs.

METAL FOIL MASK FOR TOOLING

The metal foil mask is as old as man's ability to hammer precious metals into sheets which would glitter in the sunlight and cast the sunbeams back at his audience.

Tools and Materials

Working with metal calls for a few specialized tools and much improvisation. Necessary tools are metal shears or old scissors, nails of various sizes, steelwool, liver of sulphur (obtainable at craft shops or drug stores — sometimes known as potassium sulfide), ballpeen hammer (or any hammer with one round end), ballpoint pen, string, and straightedge ruler.

The metal foil to be used is very thin (number 32 gauge), but very strong. Copper is preferred because it is easily colored chemically and allows for dramatic highlighting. Aluminum foil is acceptable because it has some of the physical characteristics needed in brightness, toughness, and accessibility. Both are easily impressed or embossed, and will hold the shapes forced into the surfaces.

Procedures

1. Begin by cutting a paper pattern the size of the face — a curved sheet should reach from one ear across the face to the other ear. After measuring around the head (above the ears and across the fullest part of the skull) and across the face from ear to ear, add at least one extra inch for a border "hem." The metal will be sharp, and a half-inch border should be turned down on all sides. Crease the metal first, by pressing a ball-point pen into the metal while drawing it along a straight-edge ruler. Then fold the border over and firmly press the edges closed.

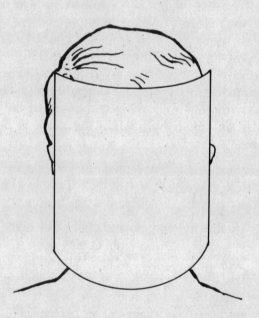

Figure 11. The first step in making a metal mask is to construct a paper pattern the size of the face. The mask should be large enough to reach from ear to ear.

Figure 12. After basic measurements have been made, add at least 1" on the metal for a border hem (A). Using the pattern as a guide, draw the eyes and mouth onto the metal and cut out (B). Cut a U-shape for the nose (C) and fold (D).

2. Now prepare to cut a face into the metal by first drawing the shapes directly onto the metal sheet with a felt-tip pen. Use the paper pattern to locate the eyes and nose and to determine how large the eye and mouth holes should be. Then transfer the shapes to the metal, and cut out the three holes with metal shears.

3. Create a nose (first on the paper, then on the metal) by cutting down from one eyebrow, around the bottom of the nose, and up to the other eyebrow in a U-shaped form. This nose can then be bent out to conform to whatever shape is most interesting on the whole face.

4. Embossing is done by pressing a ball-point pen or a blunt, rounded nail against the metal. Increase the opportunity for the metal to stretch, both by pressing against the sheet (only when it is supported by a thick pad of soft newspapers) and by pressing from both sides by turning the metal over several times while working it. Use the embossing to create lines under and over the eyes, and over the eyebrows. Cut out or emboss the cheekbones, also.

5. When all of the shapes and textures are completed in the mask, cut holes for attachment of an elastic strap to extend from ear to ear behind the head.

6. For all practical purposes the aluminum mask will be finished at this point. But if you are working in copper, prepare to color the metal as a final step. First steelwool the entire surface to make sure that it is clean (do not worry about making it shiny at this point).

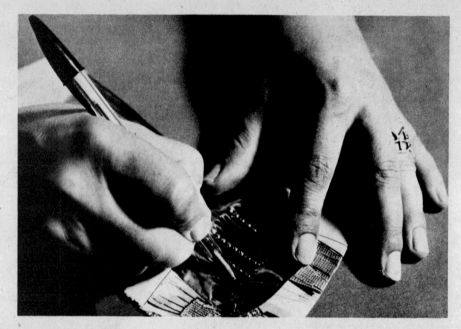

Figure 13. A ball-point pen is used to emboss a mask design on metal foil (right). After potassium sulfide has been painted on the surface, burnish the surface lightly with steel wool (below).

Figure 14. After the metal has been embossed, cut two holes near each ear, and attach an elastic strap. The strap is worn behind the head to hold the mask in position.

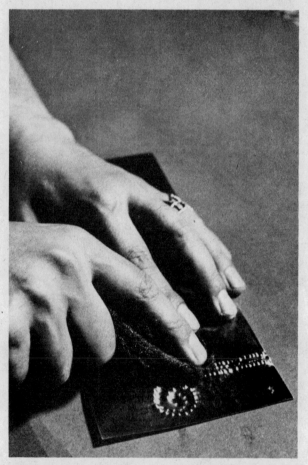

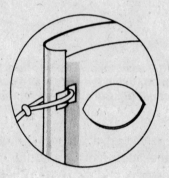

plenty of ventilation: the sulphur fumes are not dangerous but are unpleasant. Cap the container immediately after using it.

8. Upon application of the liver of sulphur, the copper will immediately turn black. When it is dry, rub it carefully with fine steel wool. The result should be one of high contrast in color. Do not try to remove all of the black. Merely brush off the top surfaces, which will turn brightly copper-colored in beautiful contrast to the dark sulphur-coated contour areas.

7. In a small tin can (about one cup), dissolve a tiny pebble of liver of sulphur (about the size of a pea) in boiling water. Then brush on the liquid with a small paint brush, covering the entire outside surface. Be sure that the working area has

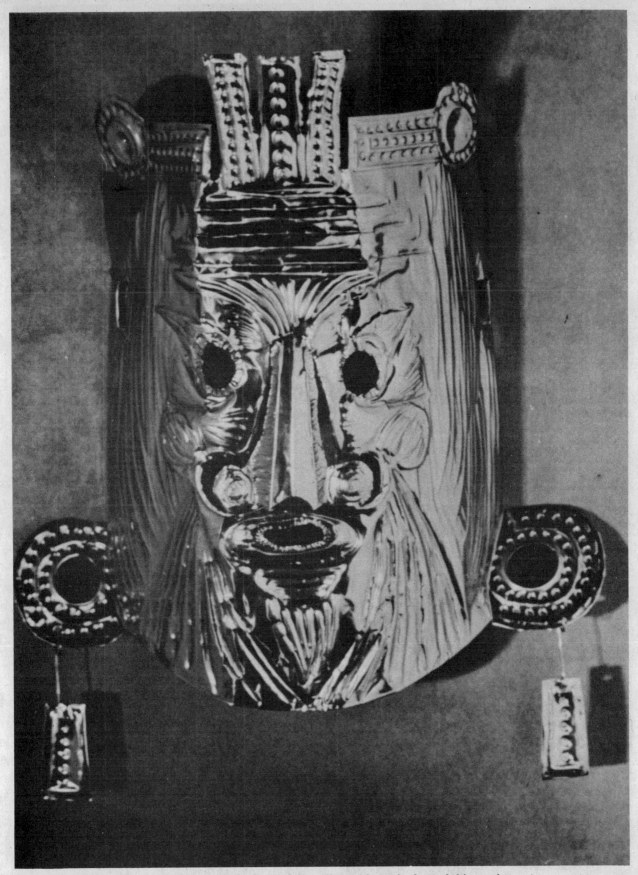

Figure 15. An interesting effect is created when light is reflected from the face of this mask.

SOFT FABRIC HOOD

This hood is not for distorting features, nor for the effects of comedy or fear. Rather, the mood hoped for is one of elegant intrigue. Hiding all facial features except the eyes creates a mood of intrigue; emphasizing the design quality of harmony helps to develop elegance.

Harmony can be used either by duplicating the lines of the hood in a costume's lines, or by matching the main color of a mask to that of a costume — using several similar colors. Very little textural contrast is used, so harmony is not disturbed.

This hooded mask is going to be combined with the cosmetic mask, so harmony is again in play by using the curves of eye and eyebrow shape as secondary mask shapes. No possibility for setting the mood of a mask should be overlooked.

Figure 16. An intriguing hooded mask can be designed using felt remnants, paint, glue, scissors, and a measuring tape. Old buttons and yarn could be used for additional decoration.

Tools and Materials

Necessary tools include fabric glue (flexible), pins and needles, tapestry needle, scissors, measuring tape, string, and tailor's chalk. This mask will be made from felt remnants, yarn and floss remnants, and some medium-sheer, lightweight fabric, such as batiste or dacron and cotton blend.

Procedures

In addition to the suggestions for measuring described in the section "Basic Procedures," the following measurements should be included:

1. Add 8 inches to the line around the fullest part of the skull and across the bridge of the nose, to provide for seams and for air circulation. For example, if the measurement is exactly 16 inches, add 8 inches more, providing a safe total of 24 inches of fabric.

2. Divide the total girth established in the pre-

Figure 17. The fabric is divided into four equal parts (A). An arc, cut from folded paper, serves as a pattern (B). The material is then cut, and the two side panels are sewn to the back panel (C).

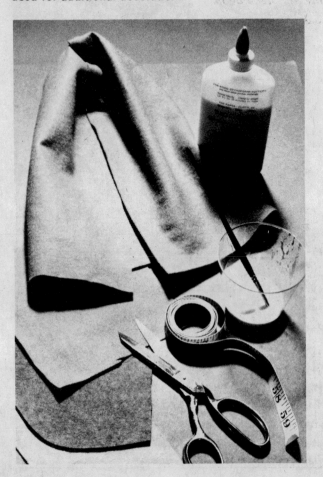

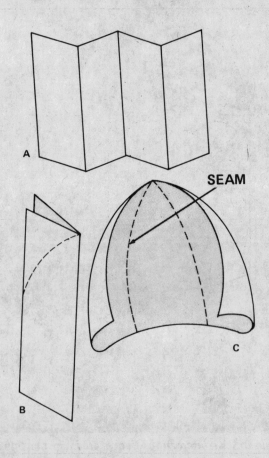

vious step by 4, creating four panels representing the sides of the hood.

3. To the length obtained by measuring from the top of the head to wherever the bottom of the hood is desired, add 2 inches. This dimension is the length of each hood panel. Cut out only three sides of the hood. Cut a piece of paper to match the size of one of the hood sides. Fold it in half lengthwise, and cut an arc at the top. Use this as a pattern for cutting curves on all sides.

4. Sew three sides together, leaving the front open to develop the face of the mask. Decorate the sides with strips of felt and lengths of yarn. These can either be glued or sewn onto the fabric. Strips with slight variations of color and texture could be used for enrichment. To find the curve motif to use for the facial design of the mask, trace with lipstick or oil crayon on the mirror as described earlier. The eyebrow curve can also be turned

upside down for use as the bottom of each eye-hole and for the bottom curve of the nose shape.

5. Measure vertically up and down the face to locate the placement of eyes, nostrils, and mouth. On the fourth piece of vertical material, mark the position of the eyes and nose and the curves below them. This piece of fabric will become the pattern for the features of the mask. It will be called the Face Base.

6. Using short lengths of string and yarn, measure from slightly above the eyebrows to the point on the cheekbones where the bottom mask curve seems to fall.

7. Using yarn as a guide on the fabric, shape a length of the yarn into the curve of the eyebrow. Trace the line of yarn with tailor's chalk. Then, repeat the curve upside down to complete the drawing of the eye shape.

Figure 18. Make a pattern to show placement of facial features. Mark and cut the shapes for the eyes (A). Draw a curve at the nose to indicate where the fabric is to be cut; fold pattern in half lengthwise and cut along curve (B). The cut-out mask (C) is now ready for decoration.

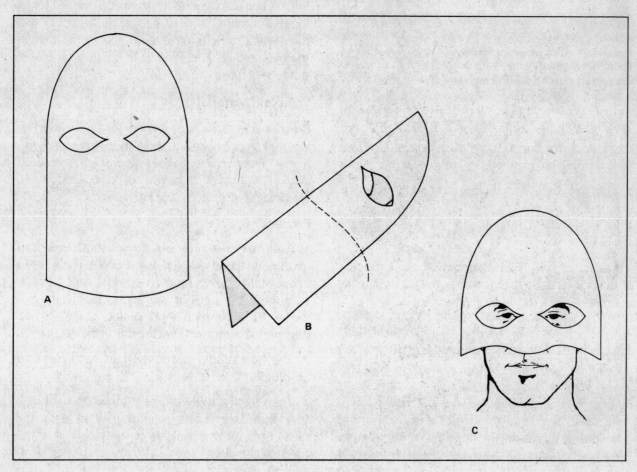

Figure 19. Four pieces of felt were sewn together to form this hooded mask. Variations of color and shape are added to the face to create an aura of mystery.

8. Connect the upper and lower curves with slightly arching vertical lines. Cut out the eye shapes — making the eyeholes large will allow for intriguing use of cosmetics later.

9. Fold the mask front in half and cut off the piece of mask material at the nose, starting with the nose curve and continuing to the outer edges of the mask.

10. Lay this cotton lining down on felt remnants and cut out several felt shapes by following the eyeholes and nose line up into the forehead.

11. Glue the pieces for nose and forehead onto the Face Base with fabric cement.

12. If the mouth and chin are to be covered, cut a piece of medium-sheer, lightweight fabric, following the curve below the nose for the top edge, and make the length half of the top-to-bottom measure of the hood side to allow for hemming. Sew it to the bottom of the curve at the nose line.

13. Turn the face and hood inside out, and stitch the side seams together to complete the hood shape.

14. Hand stitch extra decoration on the front of the hood if it seems desirable after having tried on the mask. Try to keep the enrichment features in the center and above the eyes to continue the effect of intrigue.

15. Because the eyebrow line was the basis for all curves on the mask front, emphasize the eyes and eyebrows with make-up when wearing the mask. Use colors which harmonize with the hood. Don't shy away from colors that you might usually shun — let imagination beneath the mask provide the sense of fantasy.

COSMETIC PAINTED FACES

Painting the mask directly onto the face has great possibilities because it combines the hint of reality with whatever fantasy one wishes to evoke. Combining the painted face with some disguise for the rest of the head multiplies the effect of mystery or comedy by obscuring more of the reality. Occasionally lining up the edges of the design with the person's facial muscles or features will also help make the design come alive as the person talks. The effect is one that is unique to this type of mask.

Tools and Materials

Brushes and pads are needed for application of the make-up. Make-up and other accessories include: cream base or petroleum jelly, colored cosmetics, lipstick, eyebrow pencils, eyeshadow, tempera paint, and a wig or headpiece.

Procedures

1. Assemble materials, but do not start more than two hours ahead of the masked event. It is wise to allow at least one hour to work. If not familiar with the procedures, it is a good idea for the beginner to experiment and perfect them several days ahead of time and not the day of the event.

2. The hair should be pulled back and the face absolutely clean.

3. Then lightly apply a cream make-up base or a very thin layer of petroleum jelly to ease the clean-up later and to protect the face if it is not used to cosmetics.

4. Cover the entire face with the lightest possible tone of make-up or the darkest — the idea is to create a contrast with the natural skin color. Pancake make-up applied with a natural sponge and water is best because it is easy to apply and lasts for a long period of time.

5. Cover the eyebrows, too, and the outer edge of the lips if these shapes are not in harmony with the intended design.

6. Now begin designing the mask. Lipstick, eyebrow pencil, and eyeshadow are locally available in every possible shade. Even nontoxic tempera paint will not harm a face when prepared in the way described, if the skin is healthy. Stage make-up works especially well when the wearer will be seen mainly from a distance. Three sources of professional stage make-up are:

Stagecraft Industries, 615 Bradford, Redwood City, California 94063

Bob Kelly, 151 West 46th Street, New York, New York 10036

New York Costume Company, Inc., 10 West Hubbard, Chicago, Illinois 60610

7. To find innovative patterns to use as a mask, one can have another person project a slide with a symmetrical image, such as a butterfly, a flower, or a bird with outstretched wings, onto one's own face, after which the other person can then trace the image onto the face with eyebrow pencil, stick eyeshadow, lipstick, and so forth. The design may be outlined or filled in with sequins or colored with eyeshadow crayons. Adhere sequins to the skin with an adhesive such as used with false eyelashes, or with a dab of clear nail polish applied to back of sequins and pressed onto the design area. Do not use felt-tip pens or food coloring, as they will stain the skin.

8. To top off the masking efforts, cover the hair to further conceal identity. Consider making wigs of old, clean nylons cut in strips and glued or sewn to an elastic band that hides under a hat or at the edge of the mask. Wigs that have lost their cap elasticity can be worn as is, or cut and colored with food coloring. Old shower caps or women's heavy net caps for holding hair rollers in place can be used with string, yarn, ribbon, or braid sewn on.

When making the mask, consider extending the forehead (binding material over the top of the head, then teasing or back-coming the hair that sticks out from under the band). Also, a strip of knit fabric from 1 to 2 inches wide and from 2½ to 3½ feet long can be twisted around the head and secured with an old pin or brooch to create a mysterious effect.

In planning the mask, remember to coordinate the costume so that it enhances the illusion being created. All aspects of both the mask and the costume should harmonize. The main thing is to use your imagination.

For Additional Reading

Baranski, Matthew, **Mask Making,** Davis, 1966.
Grater, Michael, **Paper Faces,** Taplinger, 1968.
Laliberte, Norman, and Mogelon, Alex, **Masks, Face Coverings, and Headgear,** Van Nostrand, 1973.
Shapiro, David, "Faces and Masks and Auxiliary Deceptions," **Craft Horizons,** 30: 36-45 (Dec. 1970).

Terrariums

Terrariums, once the province of Victorian parlors, are enjoying a resurgence of popularity. These lilliputian gardens under glass provide delightful green vistas throughout the bleakest months of winter.

Perhaps the first recorded instance of plants being grown in sealed containers comes from the ancient Phoenician and Greek cultures. During the festival of Adonis, the slain lover of Aphrodite, the youth's death was mourned and then his resurrection celebrated. Quick-flowering plants were sealed in earthenware pots, baskets, or small glass bottles and carefully tended during the eight-day festival. These so-called "Gardens of Adonis" were used to celebrate the perpetual cycle of seasons. At the end of the celebration, the containers of plants, which had begun to fade, were thrown into the Aegean Sea, along with images of Adonis. This represented the completed seasonal cycle of death to life to death again.

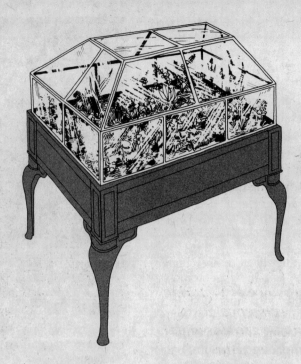

Figure 2. The Wardian case was the original terrarium. Initially, the cases were used for transporting plants from one country to another.

Further interest in raising plants in small, closed environments for scientific and decorative purposes did not actually evidence itself until the early nineteenth century. As so often happens, the basic principle of growing plants under glass was discovered quite by accident. A London surgeon, Dr. Nathaniel Ward, was an avid student of natural history. During the summer of 1829, while pursuing the careful study of the sphinx moth, he obtained a chrysalis and partially buried it in a small amount of moist garden soil which he placed in a bottle and sealed with a metal lid. Intent upon studying the moth as it emerged from the pupa state, he was astounded, some days later, to discover a small fern and one species of grass growing from the clump of dirt. With the moth completely forgotten, Dr. Ward continued his daily observations of the growing plants and began experimenting with other glass containers and a wide variety of plants. The original terrarium lasted four years, the plants dying eventually only after the lid rusted away, allowing rainwater to seep in and collect in the bottom of the jar.

Figure 1. Terrariums can be used as the focal point in a room. This floor terrarium, consisting of a covered arrangement of ferns and orchids, can be planted professionally or in the home.

In 1832, Ward attempted a daring experiment. Filling two large, glazed cases with ferns and grasses, he sent them by ship to Sydney, Australia, a journey of eight months. Lashed to the deck, the compartments were exposed to all extremes of weather and temperature, yet the plants survived the trip. Upon their arrival in Sydney, the cases were filled again, this time with Australian plants, and shipped back to England, around the Cape of Good Hope; again the plants arrived safely. Ward continued his studies, eventually raising over 100 species of ferns normally considered too delicate for cultivation in the polluted air of nineteenth-century London. In 1842, he finally published his research in a study entitled "On the Growth of Plants in Closely Glazed Cases."

By mid-century, Wardian cases, as they became known, were traveling around the world. The profitable Indian tea industry was started when 20,000 young tea plants were shipped to the Himalayas from Shanghai. The Samoan and Fiji Islands received banana trees from China, and Brazilian rubber trees were packed off to Ceylon. Flowering plants and ferns were shipped between Europe and America, and one London nursery reported using over 500 Wardian cases in a seven-year period. The Royal Botanical Gardens in England imported more plants in 15 years than in the previous 100.

Wardian cases as ornamental decoration became very fashionable during the Victorian age. Lavishly designed with many glass panels, a span or domed roof, and special compartments for heating built into the bases, the cases were described by one nineteenth-century author as ". . . elegant and pleasing additions to the most tasteful and elaborately furnished drawing room . . . some being extremely light and graceful and most beautifully finished, with delicate enamel and gilding."

As homes became centrally heated and better insulated, it was possible to grow plants without the glass cases; and by the mid-1920s interest in terrariums had faded. However, in recent years, ecological concerns for saving the environment have brought the contemporary terrarium back into the home, providing once again a small portion of the natural world for man's enjoyment.

Common Terms Used In Planting Terrariums

Charcoal: small amounts of crushed horticultural charcoal, an important feature of the terrarium soil, are generally mixed with drainage material (pebbles) as well as with soil. Charcoal adds porosity and acts as a sweetener by absorbing soil impurities and rank odors.

Environment: inside a terrarium, the sum of conditions consisting of available water, humidity, space, temperature, light, atmosphere, and the more subtle effects each plant has on the others.

Epiphyte: a plant, such as an orchid, which normally does not grow in soil; usually found in a wild state growing from branches or crotches in trees, deriving most of its nourishment from the air.

Etiolation: the stretching of plant cells caused by insufficient light, resulting in weak and drooping stems.

Featherock: a form of unusually lightweight, gray stone that makes an attractive, natural-looking addition to a terrarium landscape.

Habitat: the conditions necessary for the survival of a particular plant or group of plants; a terrarium

Figure 3. Natural habitats may be recreated in miniature landscapes. Insectivorous plants such as the Venus Fly-Trap are used to duplicate surroundings found in boggy areas.

can be designed to achieve a variety of habitats, including woodland, tropical, marsh or bog, desert, or aquatic.

Humus: that material which forms the organic portion of soil.

Insectivorous Plants: unusual plants having evolved with a variety of structures enabling them to trap insects, the digestion of which is necessary for the plants to survive in boggy areas, where the supply of nitrates and phosphates is insufficient.

Lichen: a nonflowering slow-growing plant that resembles moss but is actually composed of a fungus and an alga.

Photosynthesis: the process by which special cells in a green plant manufacture nutrients by using energy from the sun and carbon dioxide in the air, giving off water and oxygen as by-products.

Porosity: the state of the soil necessary to prevent sogginess; often achieved by adding sand or vermiculite to topsoil or humus.

Sheet Moss: thin layers of moss in large sheets.

Soil pH: the acid or alkaline condition of soil; easily measured with a special kit obtained at garden supply shops.

Species: those groups of biological organisms that have similar or identical characteristics and that can reproduce amongst themselves but not with individuals of another group.

Terrarium: a miniature greenhouse in which the humidity and temperature can be easily controlled and in which a wide variety of small plants may be raised as long as they all thrive on the same conditions of moisture, light, and temperature.

Vermiculite: a mica by-product expanded by heat into a spongy, resilient material which, in the form of tiny particles, is often added to soil to make it more porous.

Basic Equipment And Supplies

Because terrariums are enjoying a tremendous resurgence of popularity, it is no problem to find a wide selection of containers and plants offered for sale. Appropriate glass containers may be found at local department stores, hardware stores, and grocery stores as well as at florists and nurseries. Many varieties of small common plants are sold in general merchandise stores. An excellent source for hard-to-find wild plants, including insectivorous plants and wild orchids, is Arthur Eames Allgrove, North Wilmington, Massachusetts. This mail-order firm ships plants during the fall and winter months and the material arrives well packaged and healthy. Miniature tropical orchids are sold by Hausermann, Inc., P. O. Box 363, Elmhurst, Illinois.

Containers

Modern terrariums are copied directly after the Victorian Wardian cases. The only basic of sufficient light for healthy plant growth. Often the loveliest bottles are made of tinted glass, and one is tempted to make terrariums from them. However, unless the color is quite muted, the light intensity is reduced and the colored glass tends to transmit its own hue while absorbing other colors in the spectrum. This may cause abnormal growth or stunting in the plants.

Nearly any clear glass or plastic container will do. Various sizes of round, octagonal, and rectangular fish aquariums make pleasing terrariums. Bottles of all sizes and shapes are readily available, including candy jars, large goblets, decanters, gallon-sized mayonnaise jars, apothecary jars, canning jars, large bottles, cider jugs, wide-

mouthed juice and water pitchers, crystal beer mugs, flower vases, scientific laboratory glassware, domes, and bell jars.

The size of the terrarium container is optional. A single, tiny fern set among a few pebbles can look quite charming in a dainty antique perfume bottle, while a fifty-gallon fish tank would be magnificent housing a complete woodland or jungle scene in miniature. In general, the size of the plants should be in keeping with the scale of the container.

Antique Containers

For a more unusual terrarium, search through antique shops for old curio cabinets. Made with glass sides and a hinged lid set in an oak or mahogany framework, these small cabinets were originally used to display jewelry, china, or collections of miniatures. The cases can be found in a variety of sizes and shapes and make distinc-

Figure 4. When choosing a container, the primary concern is to select one made of clear glass or plastic. The size and shape are optional but should be in proportion to the plants.

Figure 5. One way of displaying a terrarium is to hang it from the ceiling. The design of the container enhances the overall effect of plant arrangements. (Courtesy, Stained Glass City, Chicago.)

tive terrariums after a sealant is applied to help regulate the environment. Other antique glass containers such as candy, tobacco, apothecary and spice jars, decanters, covered dishes, stemmed goblets, and glass teapots may all be transformed into striking gardens under glass.

Hanging Containers

Not all terrariums must be set on a surface; they can hang from walls or a ceiling in a variety of ways. Some manufacturers are producing glass bottles with a long neck for hanging and a side opening for ease in planting. Any other bottle or reasonably light container may be hung by using wire, twine, macraméd cords, or leather thongs.

Figure 6. Terrarium containers made of acrylic plastic are available in a variety of shapes and sizes. (Courtesy, Microscapes, Inc., Chicago.)

Commercial Terrarium Containers

A number of acrylic plastic containers made specifically for terrariums are on the market. These come in a variety of shapes, including rounded or flattened domes of all sizes, containers resembling small pagodas or temples, and even ordinary bottles. Most are made with two halves for ease of planting and may or may not contain an opening in the top half. Some plastic containers are cube-shaped or rectangular with a removable base. One company makes a very large plastic globe 20 inches in diameter which rests on a plastic stand, the entire structure measuring three feet in height. Another specialty shops. These are flat on the wall side, rounded on the remaining surface, and again come in a variety of sizes. Some are designed to fit into a corner (with two flat sides and one curved) or structured to hang on an outside corner.

Handmade Containers

A terrarium container can easily be handmade by using ordinary window glass, masking tape, and cement sealant. Decide upon the size and shape, measure carefully, and have the glass cut by a glazier. Clean and dry each piece of glass, then tape the four sides together with the tape on the

TERRARIUM POTTING MATERIAL

The material going into a terrarium before the plants are added is as important as the plants themselves in assuring the success of a terrarium. The potting material must provide proper nutrition, drainage, support, and room for growth as well as add to the total design and attractiveness of the finished product.

Moss Lining

The first material to put into a terrarium is a layer of moss. If possible, this should be a thin sheet of living moss that has been gently tugged loose from the forest floor or a damp river bank. Often it will continue to grow within the terrarium. If fresh moss is not available, sheet moss obtained from a florist is acceptable when it has been soaked in water and well drained.

Figure 7. This terrarium is hung directly against the wall. Its planting of ferns and a zebra plant is brightened by a chrysanthemum blossom. (Courtesy, Microscapes, Inc., Chicago.)

inside. Join the sides to the bottom with tape and seal all inside seams with the sealant. Immediately wipe off excess sealant with a clean rag. If necessary, a razor blade may be used to scrape off remaining sealant after it hardens. Allow the seams to dry for 48 hours before planting, and either buff all sharp glass edges or cover them with decorative tape to prevent cuts.

Lids for Containers

Opinions differ on the virtues of sealing a terrarium, although the very term signifies a closed environment. If sealed, the moisture and humidity remain constant and the plants are protected against dust, molds, and household type fungi. An open terrarium is suitable for many plants but must be more carefully watched to prevent excessive drying.

Any number of materials can be used to cover a terrarium opening. The various plastic wraps make unobtrusive seals; but such decorative objects as old perfume bottle stoppers, candy or soap dish lids, crystal dessert dishes, pieces of driftwood, rocks, shells, and large clay or wooden beads can also be used. Corks of all sizes are available at hardware stores, and one can always get glass cut to fit over the larger openings.

Figure 8. Careful attention must be given to the selection of plants and potting materials. A proper combination of moss, pebbles, charcoal, and special formulated soil will insure a successful terrarium.

Drainage Layer

Providing adequate drainage inside a sealed terrarium is of particular importance. Too much moisture trapped around the root area will quickly lead to rot. For the smallest terrariums, the layer of moss is sufficient; larger containers, however, require a layer of pebbles or broken clay potsherds in addition to the moss.

Charcoal

Small pieces of horticultural or activated charcoal, sprinkled liberally among the drainage pebbles, serve several purposes. They aid in drainage and absorb excess moisture and soil impurities, keeping the soil "sweet" and free of mold and decay.

Soil

A general-purpose potting soil obtained from a plant supply store is recommended over soil dug from a garden or woodland. In the first place, the potting soil will be properly formulated, containing a mixture of humus, peat, sand, or vermiculite, and will provide enough nutrients for the average terrarium. Secondly, the soil is sterile and, unlike garden soil, will not contain mold or fungus spores or any "mystery" seeds that may sprout after the terrarium has been planted and sealed.

If soil from the garden or forest is to be used, care must be taken to see that it is well mixed with sand or vermiculite to provide porosity. Vermiculite can be purchased at garden supply centers. If sand is used, it must never be ocean beach sand because the salt contained in such sand is toxic to plants and no amount of washing can remove it. A general formula of one part loam (topsoil), one part humus (leaf mold), and one part sand should be followed when mixing one's own terrarium soil.

Decorative Materials

Sand, pebbles, rocks or featherock, and pieces of wood all lend an air of naturalness to a terrarium scene. In larger containers the rocks can be used as "boulders" to help bank and hold soil, producing several levels or "hills and valleys" in the landscape. Interesting pieces of driftwood or branches are effective as part of the total design

but are prone to mold after a time. Occasionally, it helps to wash and then sterilize all outside materials by placing them in a warm oven (200 degrees) for several hours.

PLANTING TOOLS

Some types of terrariums require more planting tools than others. When the opening is large enough, one's own hand is often the only tool needed and the most reliable. Invention is the rule with small containers and narrow-necked bottles.

Household Tools

Anything around the house that is suitable can be used. Items useful for planting a narrow-necked bottle might be a chopstick, dowel rod, coat hanger, pencil, ruler, tongs, long tweezers, or pieces of an old bamboo fishing pole. A long cardboard tube left over from fancy wrapping paper or a kitchen funnel can be helpful in directing the flow of pebbles, charcoal, and soil into a long-necked bottle. A baby bottle brush might be used to clean

Figure 9. Although commercial tools are available, adequate planting utensils may be found around the household. Spoons may be used for planting, hooks for arranging, and basters for watering.

the inside walls of a bottle garden after planting. A turkey baster or a small spray-type bottle make fine tools for adding water to the finished terrarium.

Commercial Tools

Occasionally, one can find a hand tool called "Flexible Finger" or "Astro Finger" for sale. This device has a grabbing mechanism that aids in planting bottles. Plants can be placed carefully and rocks, twigs, or wood accents added more easily. Also, this tool can help with pruning out dead or unattractive vegetation or cutting back any vigorous growers.

WATER

Distilled water is highly recommended for all terrariums. Water from the faucet usually contains chlorine, fluoride, salts, and other chemicals that may be harmful to plants. Do not use water from a water softener.

PLANTS

The proper choice of plants depends upon many factors, including size and shape of the container, whether it is to be left open or sealed, and the amount of light available to the plants. The basic rule is to pick plants requiring similar growing conditions while keeping in mind the total scale of the entire planting.

House Plants

Most so-called house plants are originally from the tropics and many will thrive in a terrarium. A wonderful variety of small plants are readily available in any number of stores and greenhouses.

Native Plants

A walk in a nearby woodland will turn up an interesting assortment of mosses, lichens, ferns, and small flowering plants that will add charm to a terrarium setting. Rare or unusual plants such as wild orchids should never be picked, and plants must never be taken from local, state, or national parks. Perhaps the best method of obtaining wild plants is to purchase them from mail-order firms, as mentioned earlier, or from a nursery which handles unusual plants for the wildflower garden.

Figure 10. Native plants add charm to a terrarium. A selaginella (bottom right) provides ground cover, ferns (top right) enhance fullness and height, and partridge berries (below) add color to the arrangement.

Basic Procedures

Terrariums are fun to plant and a continuing source of pleasure afterward. Inexpensive to make and easy to maintain, these gardens under glass are a perfect hobby the year around for all ages, including the very young and very old. Terrariums can bring a special joy to the bedridden or confined person.

Limited only by the size of the container and one's imagination, the miniature landscape may be designed to resemble many habitats found in nature. A damp forest floor, ferny ravine, or mossy rock outcropping is achieved by using native ferns, mosses, lichens, and small flowering woodland plants. Insectivorous plants create the effect of a swampy bog, while various house plants can be chosen to create a rank jungle scene or an open meadow.

Plants can survive in a closed environment when provided with a continuing source of light and sufficient moisture before sealing. Respiration is a complex series of chemical reactions in a plant, but basically the process takes in oxygen from the air and releases carbon dioxide. A second process, photosynthesis, is the manufacture of food by a plant, utilizing sunlight and carbon dioxide and giving off oxygen and water. So, in simple terms, a plant recycles its own oxygen, carbon dioxide, and water; and when all conditions are stable, plants tightly closed up in a bottle or other container can continue to live indefinitely.

ASSEMBLING MATERIALS

The first step in making a terrarium is to assemble all the materials: container, plants, soil, pebbles, charcoal, sheet moss, decorative rocks or wood, and any necessary tools. Choose a well-lighted work area and an unhurried time of day or evening in order to avoid being rushed.

THE FIRST LAYER

The glass or plastic container should be absolutely clean and dry before beginning (it is much easier to clean before planting than afterwards). A thin layer of sheet moss goes into the container first, upside down with the green mossy side against the surface. One of the purposes of the moss is to hide the soil, so arrange it as a bowl to hold and disguise the potting materials, letting it come up the sides one-fourth to one-third the height of the container. Determine in advance how the plantings are to lie: whether the terrarium is to have a single level or whether it is to resemble a hilly terrain and have slopes, dips, or rocky outcroppings. The mossy foundation may need to rise higher in one portion than in another. If the terrarium is to have a front and back, the moss may be lower in front and higher in back.

THE SECOND LAYER

Sprinkle the moss with a small amount of crushed charcoal and add the drainage layer of pebbles or rocks. Plan for one-half inch of pebbles per one inch of soil. It is not generally necessary to have a drainage layer deeper than two inches, even for the largest terrariums. Again, add a scattering of charcoal.

THE THIRD LAYER

Next, the soil is put in, taking care to keep the sides of the container clean. The soil is more easily handled if somewhat damp — wipe off smudges on the glass as they occur. Before placing the larger rocks, driftwood, and plants, review the design for the terrarium. Are there enough plants for the container? Are there too many? Now that the soil is in, are some plants going to be too tall? Is there too much soil? Remember, for the most pleasing effect, the moss liner and all potting material should not exceed one-third the height of the container. If changes are necessary, now is the time to make them.

CHOOSING THE PLANTS

Plants should be chosen carefully for variety in height, color, texture, and form. Use tall and medium-sized plants as well as tiny low plants that cover the ground. Leaves may be big, small, broad, narrow, smooth, or hairy, with leaf margins entire, toothed, or greatly dissected and lacy.

Consider the possible colors: some leaves are deep green, some nearly yellow-green, and others variegated white and green or green on the top surface and another color underneath. Plants may stand upright, grow in dense tufts, sprawl along the ground, or may be viny.

After reviewing the selected plants, any rocks needed for banking the soil or for a more natural-istic appearance in the terrarium should be care-fully placed. Partially bury each rock or rock grouping if a ledge effect is desired.

PLACING THE PLANTS

Start with the tallest plants or the ones to be put in the back of the terrarium. Generally, a plant can be loosened from its pot by tapping gently on a hard surface, or by using a hammer. Occasion-ally, however, one must break the pot in order to free the plant. Remove a plant from its pot imme-diately before transferring it to the terrarium to avoid exposing the roots to drying conditions. Gently loosen the dirt of the root ball and place in the container. Position the plant at a soil depth equal to that of the plant when potted or when growing in its natural condition. Press the soil firmly around each plant.

Keep in mind the basic elements of good design as well as the basic needs of each plant. Avoid symmetry. Put the tallest or most showy plant to the left or right of center and try to have one or more particular points of interest within the de-sign — whether brightly colored leaves, berries, or an attractive rock. Watch out for the tangled mass look. Moderation in numbers is a good rule of thumb. Each plant needs space in which to grow, so it is better to have too few plants than too many.

FINISHING THE TERRARIUM

The addition of mosses, lichens, pebbles, rocks, driftwood, or other accessory objects to hide any exposed soil is the final step in completing the design. In addition to improving the appearance of the finished terrarium, such coverings help reduce the rate of evaporation in an open con-tainer. If the terrarium is large enough, a reflecting pool may be added: use anything that will hold a few drops or more of water such as a jar lid, trans-parent ash tray, coaster, soap dish, saucer, or a small bowl or pan. Bury the pool in soil and hide the rim with moss and rocks.

ADDING THE INITIAL WATER

When everything is firmly in place, the terrarium should be watered sparingly and carefully. Sprinkle water evenly over the entire planted sur-face, stopping as soon as water seeps through the moss liner on the bottom of the container. Too little water is more easily remedied than too much.

The terrarium can now be sealed, if desired (see *Lids for Containers* under "Basic Equipment and Supplies"), and placed in spot while the plants recover from being transplanted. After a few days, the terrarium may be moved to its permanent lo-cation, in indirect or filtered sunlight or under ar-tificial light.

MAKING A BOTTLE GARDEN

Making a terrarium out of a narrow-necked bottle requires a few tricks and special tools. A straight-ened coat hanger with a small hook on the end along with one or more long rods or sticks for dig-ging, poking, and probing are sufficient; but a commercially made "mechanical finger," as de-scribed in the section "Basic Equipment and Sup-plies," may be handy.

Adding Potting Material

Follow the general procedure for planting a ter-rarium as described previously. The moss liner may be lowered into the bottle in pieces or dis-pensed with entirely. (The moss is not necessary for healthy plant growth. Its main purpose in both terrariums and bottle gardens is to make the plant-ings more attractive by hiding the soil.) A funnel or rolled newspaper or a long cardboard tube is helpful in directing the flow of drainage pebbles, charcoal, and soil. Using a stick or dowel rod to mound and firm the dirt, prepare depressions for each plant before placing the first one.

Placing the Plants

To be certain each plant will fit through the bottle neck, make a circle with the thumb and forefinger the size of the bottle opening and draw the leafy portion of each plant through. The dirt ball around the roots can be gently washed away in a pan of lukewarm water or under a faucet. Plant immediately after removing the soil.

Lower each plant in the crook of the coat hanger and place inside the bottle; spread the roots if possible and cover with soil, firming gently. After all plants are situated embellish the bare areas with moss pieces, decorative gravel, or whatever other accessories will go through the bottle neck.

Finishing the Bottle Garden

Clean the inside of the bottle with a bent bottle brush or a piece of sponge attached to a coat hanger. Water well by trickling water slowly over the entire surface with a funnel taped to a drinking straw or narrow tubing. Carefully avoid dislodging any plants. Seal with a cork or lid and follow the general directions given below for maintaining a sealed terrarium.

MAINTENANCE

Terrariums require some attention beyond admiring glances from time to time. Proper watering and sufficient light are necessary for satisfactory plant growth. Insufficient or excessive moisture and light will cause problems.

Water

An open terrarium needs water when the plants look wilted, the moss appears dry, or the soil feels dry about one inch below the surface. A closed terrarium needs additional water if condensation fails to appear on the inside of the glass surface for several hours each day. Remember to use distilled water, rainwater, or melted snow.

Light

Most terrariums require either bright indirect light or filtered sunlight. Never put a closed case containing plants in direct sunshine. The heat of the light will be trapped inside and will cook the plants in a short time. If the light source is not sufficient, the plants will stretch toward the light and grow leggy and stringy. When light always comes from one direction, all the plants will grow toward it, so a container on a window sill should be turned occasionally for more uniform growth.

When natural light is not available or is insufficient, artificial light should be used. This can be in the form of fluorescent light, mercury vapor bulbs, or incandescent lighting. When artificial light is the only source of illumination, color-corrected fluorescent light tubes mounted directly over the terrarium are the best solution. Such tubes produce the full color spectrum necessary for plant growth and do not cast the characteristic purple glow. The length of the light fixture, the number of bulbs, and the distance between the light and the plants are all factors in determining the actual amount of illumination received by the plants. Increasing the length or number of the bulbs or reducing the distance from bulbs to terrarium increases the light intensity. One needs to experiment. The length of time the artificial light remains on should approximate natural sunlight. Plants need a normal period of darkness in each 24-hour period, as do most other living organisms.

Problems

Probably the trickiest problem common to terrariums is mold. The damp, slightly warm, humid conditions of the terrarium are ideal for the rapid spread of mold; and once this spreading starts, it is difficult to stop. Sometimes overwatering will cause mold to develop and an extended drying out period will clear up the problem. Care must be taken to check an opened terrarium regularly during the airing out process so that over-drying does not occur. A narrow-necked bottle may be left to dry longer than an open fish bowl. When mold first appears on an individual plant or piece of wood, it is best to remove the molding item before the fungus engulfs the entire terrarium. Sometimes a piece of facial tissue tucked into the neck of a bottle garden helps to dry out the bottle faster by absorbing the moisture inside the bottle.

If the mold takes over in spite of precautions, the only remedy is to discard the entire planting, scrub the container well with hot, soapy water, and let it stand in the sunshine for a few days. Then, begin again with all fresh material.

Other problems can be caused by inadequate drainage or the wrong soil pH for the particular plants involved. When stunted growth, abnormal growth, or lack or growth occurs, it is wise to start over.

Terrariums usually need a minimum of care and may survive for years. Often, however, some plants will grow luxuriantly at the expense of others, eventually crowding them out. After a time, any carefully scaled landscape may develop into an unruly, tangled mass. Whenever necessary, one can carefully clean up and remodel a terrarium by removing dead or dying plants, adding new soil and moss, and pruning back the more vigorous growers.

Projects You Can Do

Probably the ideal terrarium project for the beginner is one utilizing a wide-mouthed bottle, open fish bowl, tank, brandy snifter, or one of the commercial plastic terrarium containers, and a variety of house plants. These containers are easily handled because of the large openings and offer a wide variety of design possibilities incorporating rocks, driftwood, and so forth. House plants, already accustomed to growing inside the home, will thrive with the least amount of care and are most likely to reward the terrarium enthusiast with luxuriant growth.

After experimenting successfully with one or more simple terrariums, a choice among more unusual containers and plants can be made. Planting a bottle garden looks far more difficult than it actually is. The finished effect is even more dramatic once the plants in the bottle garden reach a good size. Having become an enthusiast, the terrarium zealot will find it difficult to look at any clear glass container without mentally planting something in it.

TROPICAL PLANTS IN A SIMPLE CONTAINER

The following chart lists a variety of tropical plants suitable for the sealed or opened terrarium. Many plants that are large when mature are slow growers and quite satisfactory as terrarium material while in the juvenile state. The important life requirements are listed for each plant. It is important to remember that only plants which have

Figure 11. These small covered terrariums were prepared with tropical plants. Small rocks have been added to give a natural appearance to the planned environments.

similar preferences for light, temperature and humidity should be grouped together in the same container. These characteristics are also given on the accompanying chart. For assembling the terrarium, follow the general steps as outlined in the section "Basic Procedures."

WILD PLANTS IN A TERRARIUM

A terrarium of wild plants may be particularly fascinating but should not be attempted until one has gained some expertise in raising plants under

Figure 12. Wild plants may be gathered directly from their natural habitat and transplanted.

glass. Small woodland plants can either be transplanted from nature or purchased commercially. When moving plants from the wild, however, a few rules should be observed. (1) A number of plants are protected by law in various states and are not to be disturbed unless facing immediate destruction through roadbuilding or some other construction projects. (2) Take only a small portion of any one type of plant from a single site and repair any damage to surrounding vegetation by replacing loose dirt and leaves. (3) Gather only plants which are found abundantly and carry them home in sealed plastic bags with the root balls wrapped in damp paper towels or moss. (4) If traveling some distance by car, do not leave the plants in the hot trunk. (5) Place the material in a terrarium as soon as possible.

Wild plant terrariums should be kept in bright, filtered sunlight with the temperature on the cool side (50 to 70 degrees). Many spring wildflowers will bloom in terrariums but should be transplanted outside again in the late spring or after blooming. The chart on page 202 lists a number of wild plants suitable for terrariums. Follow the basic directions for assembling a terrarium.

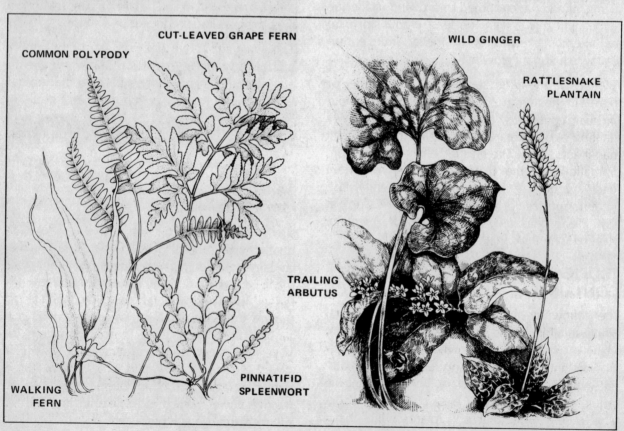

COMMON POLYPODY
CUT-LEAVED GRAPE FERN
WILD GINGER
RATTLESNAKE PLANTAIN
TRAILING ARBUTUS
PINNATIFID SPLEENWORT
WALKING FERN

INSECTIVOROUS PLANTS IN A TERRARIUM

Some of the most curious and interesting members of the plant world are the insectivorous plants. These small, exotically shaped and brightly colored plant oddities have evolved the means to capture insects and derive from the bodies of their victims some degree of nutrition. Animal-trapping plants have aroused particular interest and speculation among scientists as well as the layman. Science fiction writers have capitalized on this fascination by going one step further and creating vicious man-eating plants. However, the small carnivorous plants are quite harmless to all except the unwary insect and are attractive to observe in their natural habitat or in the specialized terrarium.

Special Requirements

Insectivorous plants are found naturally in cedar swamps or sphagnum (mossy) bogs and thus make a striking addition to a woodland or bog terrarium. They require an extremely high humidity and a soil that is constantly moist but not waterlogged. They also prefer direct sunshine for a portion of the day, but care must be taken to allow ventilation during those hours. At all other times the terrarium must be sealed. Shredded sphagnum moss should be used as the growing medium for the insectivorous plants. In the absence of moss, sand or vermiculite may be tried. A damp, swampy area can be designed in the front portion of the terrarium and a retaining wall constructed of stones or a hidden layer of aluminum foil incorporated to keep the regular potting soil away from the roots of the insectivorous plants. One may also protect the plant by placing it in a clay pot of sphagnum and sinking the pot in the terrarium soil so that the rim is hidden by moss or stones.

Insectivorous plants may be hand fed sparingly about every two months. Small bugs, flies, or minute pieces of hamburger can be offered by using tweezers. Any excess food will quickly rot, forming bacteria harmful to the plants, so care must be taken to remove any food particles accidentally dropped during the feeding process.

When constructing the terrarium, follow the general steps as outlined in the section on "Basic Procedures," but choose a container that can be sealed. The following plants are recommended for a terrarium of insectivorous plants.

Venus Fly Trap (*Dionaea muscipula*)

The Venus Fly Trap is the best known of the insectivorous plants and one of the most interesting. It develops from an underground bulb, producing light-green, slender leaves that terminate in two hinged lobes set along the margins with hairlike bristles. This structure is the insect trap. It produces a slightly sweet nectar and is shaded a brilliant red, with both features designed to guarantee close examination by insects. When the insect alights on the leaf, the lobes snap shut in a fraction of a second, trapping and crushing the victim. Digestive juices are secreted by the plant and the leaves remain closed until the insect is absorbed.

The Venus Fly Trap may produce only a few traps or as many as twelve. Generally, the older the bulb, the larger and more numerous the traps. Under terrarium conditions the plant may flower, producing small, undistinguished white blossoms on the end of a long, upright stem. If the flower stalk is removed before maturing, the energy of the plant goes into producing larger traps.

This plant regularly undergoes a normal growth and rest cycle. The traps turn black and eventually all the top growth dies back to the ground. During this dormancy period the plant should be kept moist, in a cool place, and in filtered light. Six to eight weeks later, new growth should appear.

Northern Pitcher Plant (*Sarracenia purpurea*)

The Northern Pitcher Plant is another interesting insectivorous plant. The leaves are juglike, forming rounded, hollow tubes, generally half-filled with rainwater and digestive enzymes. The lip and hood on each leaf are covered with sharp, downward-facing bristles. Once an insect has landed on the leaf, there is no return from the water trap. The leaves are attractively shaded in green, red, and yellow and turn a bright red in winter, resembling boiled lobster claws. An attractive flower, which looks like an inverted red tulip on a long stem, is produced.

TABLE OF TROPICAL PLANTS

Name of Tropical Plant	Non-Flowering	Light Low	Med	Bright	Nighttime Temperature (F) 40–50°	50–60°	60°+	Terrarium Sealed	Open
Achimenes - Magic Flower			X				X		X
Acorus - Japanese Sweet Flag	X		X				X	X	
Aglaonema - Chinese Evergreen	X	X					X	X	
Allophytum - Mexican Foxglove			X			X		X	
Anthurium - Flaming Flower			X				X	X	
Aphelandra			X				X		X
Ardisia			X			X			X
Beaucarnea - Mexican Bottle Plant	X		X			X			X
Begonia			X			X		X	
Buxus - Boxwood	X		X			X		X	
Caladium	X		X				X	X	
Calathea - Peacock Plant	X		X				X	X	
Calceolaria - Pocketbook Plant			X		X				X
Callisia - Stripped Inch Plant	X		X		X				X
Capsicum - Ornamental Pepper				X			X		X
Ceropegia - Rosary Vine	X		X			X			X
Chamaedorea - Parlor Palm	X	X					X	X	
Chlorophytum - Spider Plant			X			X		X	
Crassandra				X		X			X
Cryptanthus - Earth Star			X				X		X
Cuphea - Cigar Plant				X		X			X
Cyclamen			X		X				X
Cyperus - Umbrella Plant	X			X	X			X	
Dichorisandra - Seersucker Plant	X		X				X		X
Dracaena - Dragon Tree	X	X					X	X	
Episcia - Flame Violet			X				X	X	
Euonymus - Wintercreeper	X	X			X			X	
Euphorbia - Corncob Euphorbia	X			X		X			X
Exacum - Arabian Violet			X				X		X
Fatshedera - Tree Ivy	X			X	X				X
Felicia - Blue Marguerite				X		X			X
Ferns	X		X			X		X	
Ficus - Weeping Fig	X		X				X	X	
Fittonia - Silver-Nerved Fittonia	X		X				X	X	
Gazania - Treasure Flower				X		X			X
Gloxinera - Rosebells			X				X		X
Hedera - English Ivy	X		X		X			X	
Heliotropium				X		X			X

TABLE OF TROPICAL PLANTS

Name of Tropical Plant	Non-Flowering	Light			Nighttime Temperature (F)			Terrarium	
		Low	Med	Bright	40–50°	50–60°	60°+	Sealed	Open
Hypoestes	X		X				X		X
Impatiens - Patient Lucy				X		X			X
Jacobinia				X			X		X
Kalanchoe				X		X			X
Lachenalia - Cape Cowslip				X	X				X
Lobularia - Sweet Alyssum				X		X			X
Maranta - Prayer Plant	X		X				X		X
Nicotiana - Flowering Tobacco				X		X			X
Osmanthus - Holly Osmanthus			X		X				X
Oxalis				X		X			X
Pedilanthus - Devil's Backbone	X		X			X			X
Peperomia	X		X				X		X
Philodendron	X	X				X		X	
Pilea - Aluminum Plant	X		X				X		X
Plectranthus - White-Edged Swedish Ivy	X		X			X			X
Podocarpus - Chinese Podocarpus	X		X			X		X	
Primula - Primrose			X		X				X
Rosa - Miniature Rose			X			X			X
Rosmarinus - Rosemary			X			X			X
Saintpaulia - African Violet			X				X		X
Sansevieria - Mother-In-Law Tongue	X	X				X			X
Saxifraga - Strawberry Geranium			X			X			X
Schizocentron - Spanish Shawl		X				X			X
Scilla - Siberian Squill			X			X			X
Scindapsus - Devil's Ivy	X	X					X		X
Setcreasea - Purple Heart	X			X		X			X
Sinningia - Gloxinia			X				X		X
Smithiantha - Templebells			X				X		X
Solanum - Jerusalem Cherry				X		X			X
Spathiphyllum - Mauna Loa		X					X		X
Streptocarpus - Cap Primrose			X				X	X	
Syngonium - Arrowhead Vine	X	X					X	X	
Tetranema - Mexican Foxglove		X				X			X
Tradescantia - Wandering Jew			X			X		X	
Zebrina - Four-Colored Wandering Jew			X			X		X	

TABLE OF WILD PLANTS

Name of Wild Plants	Non-Flowering	Height In Inches	General Description
Anemone quinquefolia Wood Anemone		3—6	Flowers small, 5-petalled with yellow center; leaves 3-lobed
Anemonella thalictroides Rue Anemone		4—6	Leaves delicate green, rounded, lobed; flower white
Arisaema triphyllum Jack-in-the-Pulpit		6—8	Leaves 3-lobed; flowers shaped like hooded pulpit, green and red
Asarum canadense Wild Ginger		4—6	Leaves elevated on stalks, kidney shaped; flower hugs ground, bell-like, deep maroon
Chimaphila sp. Pipsissewa, Prince's Pine		6—10	Leaves attractive, green; flowers white
Claytonia virginia Spring Beauty		4—6	Leaves long, narrow; flowers pink-white, on long arching stem
Coptis groenlandica Goldthread		3—4	Leaves dainty, clover-like; flowers tiny, white
Cornus canadensis Bunchberry		3—5	Flowers large, white, 4-petalled
Dicentra canadensis Squirrel Corn		6—10	Leaves deeply dissected, lacy; flowers white, several on stalk
Dicentra cucullaria Dutchman's Britches		6—12	Leaves lacy, gray-green; flowers white, resemble inverted pantaloons.
Dodecatheon meadia Shooting Star		6—12	Leaves strap-shaped; flowers star-like, on long stem, white, pink, or lavender
Epigea repens Trailing Arbutus		6—10	Leaves leathery, evergreen; waxen flowers of creamy white; acid soil
Equisetum sp. Horsetails	X	6—12	Grass-like, stiff; stems joined, smooth or with whorls of needle-like branches
Erythronium sp. Dog-Tooth Violet		5—8	Leaves 2, mottled green, maroon; flower like dangling lily, white or yellow
Ferns	X	3—12	Many, wild ferns are small enough for terrariums.
Fragaria virginiana Wild Strawberry		4—6	Typical strawberry leaves, forms new plants on tips of runners; white flowers.
Gautheria procumbens Checkerberry		2—4	Leaves shiny, aromatic; clusters of berries in fall
Goodyera pubescens Rattlesnake Plantain		2—4	Member of orchid family; leaves unusually attractive, green with white veins
Hepatica sp. Liverleaf		3—4	Leaves liver-shaped, maroon; flowers pink-purple or white

TABLE OF WILD PLANTS

Name of Wild Plant	Non-Flowering	Height In Inches	General Description
Juniperus virginiana Juniper	X	1–6	Seedling tree
Lichens	X	1–3	Tiny, gray-green scale-like leaves, interesting
Liverworts	X	½–1	Leaves flat, scale-like, form low-lying mats, interesting
Lycopodium lucidulum Club Moss	X	2–5	Leaves deep green, tiny scale-like, many branches.
Lysimachia nummularia Moneywort		6–15	Leaves round; flowers bright yellow; a low vine.
Mitchella repens Partridge Berry		6–15	Creeping vine, leaves small, round; bright red berries in fall.
Mosses	X	1–6	Many species — various textures, colors, sizes; good groundcover
Myosotis laxa Forget-Me-Not		6–15	Flowers tiny, sky-blue with yellow centers.
Oxalis sp. Wood Sorrel		4–8	Leaves clover-like, 3-leaflets, fold at night; flowers white, yellow, pink, red
Pinus sp. Pine	X	1–6	Seedling tree
Pyrola elliptica Wintergreen		6–8	Leaves dark green, stiff
Selaginella sp.	X	1	Dense mat, hugs ground; leaves delicate, lacy, deep green
Taxus canadensis Yew	X	1–6	Seedling tree.
Tiarella cordifolia Foam Flower		6–8	Leaves heart-shaped; spikes of white flowers
Trillium sp.		6–15	Leaves 3-lobed, mottled green and red; flower white or deep maroon
Tsuga canadensis Eastern Hemlock	X	1–6	Seedling tree
Uvularia sessilifolia Bellwort		6–10	Flowers drooping, bell-like, yellow
Viola sp. Violet		3–12	Many species; colors from white, cream to blue, violet

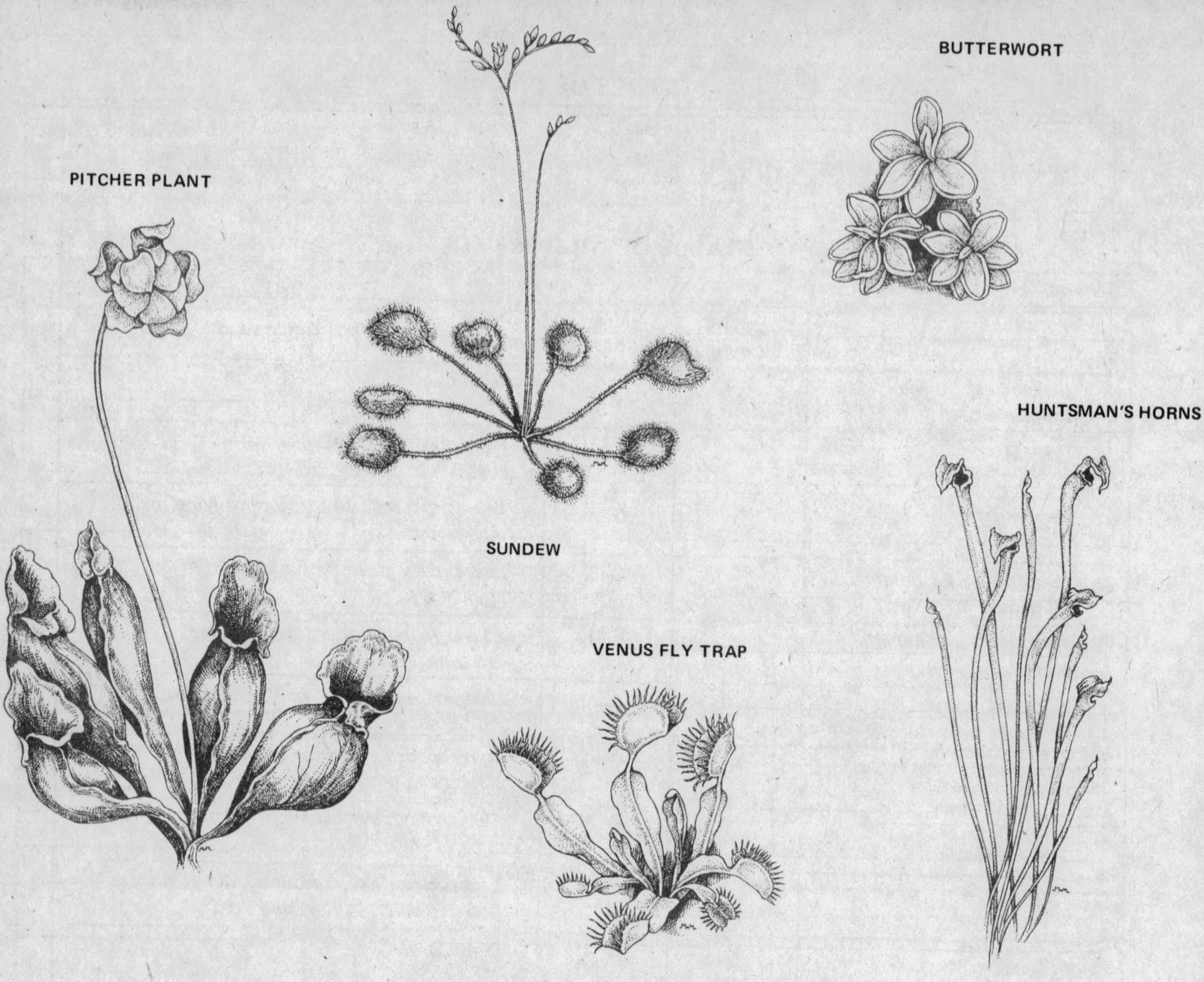

PITCHER PLANT

BUTTERWORT

SUNDEW

HUNTSMAN'S HORNS

VENUS FLY TRAP

Figure 13. Insectivorous plants are an unusual addition to a terrarium.

Huntsman's Horn (*Sarracenia flaval*)

Somewhat less striking than the Pitcher Plant, but related to it, is the Huntsman's Horn. This plant produces long, narrow, hollow leaves that entrap insects in the same manner as the Pitcher Plant. A beautiful but foul-smelling yellow flower occasionally appears among the slender horns.

Other Insectivorous Plants

Flypaper-type traps are utilized by two other insect-eating plants, the Sundue (*Drosera* species) and Butterwort (*Pinguicula vulgarisis*). The tiny Sundue lures the insect to its doom with slender leaves stretched upright and covered with sticky, glistening red hairs. When an insect touches the leaf, it is caught by the secretions and can not tear its way free before the tentacles close over it.

The Butterwort presents a similar trap, offering shiny, buttery leaf surfaces to the passing insect. The insect lands in the leaf, becomes mired in the sticky surface, and the leaf margins slowly fold over it in a deadly embrace.

ORCHIDS IN A TERRARIUM

Growing miniature orchids in a terrarium is an exciting challenge for the expert gardener. Orchids are found in the tropical and temperate zones of the world and are either terrestrial or epiphytic in habit. There may be over 30,000 different kinds of orchids with scarcely half of these identified as to species. Hundreds of miniature orchids are offered for sale by orchid growers.

TABLE OF ORCHIDS

Name of Orchid	Flower Color	Blooming Time	Height in Inches
Crastrochillas bellinas	Cream Brown	Spring	3-5
Dendrobium arachnites		Spring	
Epidendrum bractescens		Spring	
Epidendrum paleaceum	Yellow	Spring	6-8
Ionopsis paniculata	Blush Lavender	Spring	4-10
Laelia pumila	Rose Purple	Fall Winter	8
Lockhartia oersderii	Yellow Red		
Lockhartia pallida	Creamy Yellow		
Maxillaria fredrickstahlii	Pale Yellow		3-4
Miltonia cindy Kane Waterfall	Violet-Purple	Spring	6-12
Miltonia snohomish	White Violet	Spring	6-12
Miltonia woodlands Suzii x M. roezii	White	Spring	6-12
Mystacidium distichum		Summer	9
Neofinetia falcata	White		3-6
Notylia bicolor	Green White		
Odontoglossum krameri	Violet	Winter	4-8
Odontoglossum rossii	White Rose Brown	Winter	6
Odontonia dubutante x Oncidium maculatum	White Maroon	Spring	8-12
Oncidium cheirophorum	Yellow	Fall	4-8
Oncidium iridifolium	Yellow Red	Summer	3
Oncidium pulchellum	Blush Lavender	Spring	10-12
Oncidium tetrapetalum	White Brown	Summer	3-6
Oncidium triquetrum	Yellow White Brown	Winter Spring	3-5
Ornithocephalus bicornis	Green White	Winter	2

Name of Orchid	Flower Color	Blooming Time	Height in Inches
Ornithocephalus cohleariformis	Green White		
Ornithocephalus iridifolius	Green White	Spring	3
Paphiopedilum bellatulum	Cream Maroon		10
Paphiopedilum concolor	Yellow Violet	Fall	6
Paphiopedilum fairieanum	White Purple	Fall Winter	6
Phalaenopsis equestris	White Rose		8
Phalaenopsis intermedia	White	Spring	10-12
Phalaenopsis lueddomammiona	Violet Maroon	Spring	6-12
Phalaenopsis parishii	White Brown		
Physosiphon tubatus	Orange	Winter Spring Summer	6-8
Pleurothallis aribuloides	Red		
Pleurothallis fulgens	Red		
Pleurothallis grobyi	Yellow Crimson		
Pleurothallis leptotifolia	Purple Green		
Pleurothallis minuthallis	Green Brown		
Pleurothallis picta	Orange		2
Sophronitis coccinea	Orange Red	Winter	3-6
Sophronitis grandiflora	Red		
Sophronitis violacea	Lavender		
Trichoccentrum pfavii	White Brown		
Vanda cristata	Pink Brown	Spring	8-12
Vanda samperiana x Abco curvifolia	Orange	Spring	6-10
Warmingia eugenii	Cream Brown	Spring	10-12

Before beginning an orchid terrarium, one should be familiar with the general rules of orchid culture. Species differ as to light, temperature, and water requirements, and it is of utmost importance to group plants that require similar growing conditions in the same container. Unlike other terrarium plants, orchids must be grown in special material — generally osmunda (ferny) fiber or redwood bark — and fed regularly with orchid fertilizer. Care, too, must be taken when watering. Some plants like to be kept evenly moist while others prefer to dry out between waterings. All will quickly die with too much water or poor drainage. Orchid terrariums can never be sealed as these exotic plants need circulating air.

Some miniature orchids will do better than others under terrarium conditions, and the entire subject could use more research and experimentation. The chart on page 117 lists miniature orchids that may do well in a terrarium. Species marked with an asterisk (*) are recommended by Hausermann, Inc., an orchid nursery near Chicago. Complete success is not guaranteed.

For Additional Reading

Ashberry, Anne, **Bottle Gardens and Fern Cases,** Bonanza Books, 1964.

Baur, Robert C., **Gardens in Glass Containers,** Hearthside Press, 1970.

Budlong, Ware, **Indoor Gardens,** Hawthorn, 1967.

Elbert, Virginia and George B., **Fun With Terrarium Gardening,** Crown, 1973.

Evan, Charles M., **The Terrarium Book,** Random House, 1973.

Grubman, Barbara Joan, **Introduction to Terrariums,** Nash, 1972.

Lewis, Glen, "Terrariums, the World of Nature," **Outdoor World,** 1973.

Wolff, Wendy, **Terrariums and Other Nice Things,** James E. Gick, 1972.

Figure 14. Miltonia Snohomish (top) Miltonia Cindy (center), and Phalaenopsis Lueddomammiona (bottom) are just a few of the species recommended for growing orchids in a terrarium.

String and Wire Art

The artistic discipline of creating geometric designs with string and wire is a relatively new creative phenomenon.

Although man has been using string and wire for centuries, it was
only recently that these items have been used to create the kinds of art
objects to be discussed here. Primitive man used string
for weaving, wrapping, and holding objects; wire
and string have also been used since early
times to create beautiful sounds on
musical instruments.

Figure 2. The Brooklyn Bridge, designed by John Roebling in the 19th century, is famed as a feat of engineering but also deserves recognition as a work of art. (Courtesy, Paul Popper Ltd.)

All of the designs in this new art form have one thing in common: they are rooted in geometry. Some designs emphasize the geometric form itself, while others combine forms to create the impression of some object — for example, a butterfly, a flower, a bridge, or the sun. The designs are generally flat, two-dimensional shapes, constructed of colorful strings or threads stretched back and forth around nails.

Of course, it is also possible to work with string and wire in a three-dimensional way. Many modern sculptors have been experimenting with this new concept. The work of the Russian constructivist, Naum Gabo, is an excellent example. Gabo used string in his sculptural work to stress space, time, and "dynamic rhythm." He wanted to open up solid volumes to show the stress tensions inherent therein. Gabo denied that volume was an adequate expression of space and saw his work as a germinating point for architecture of the future.

Figure 1. Henry Moore's sculpture "Bird Basket" (opposite), 1939, uses string to emphasize the massive hollows of the basic hardwood structure. (Courtesy, Henry Moore.)

Another artist who experimented with string in his work is the British sculptor, Henry Moore. Moore's work is basically concerned with volumes and mass. He used stringed areas to help delineate the hollows and holes incorporated into the solid forms. Barbara Hepworth, another British sculptor, used string much in the same manner.

The principle behind stringed design work can also be seen in architectural structures. John Roebling's Brooklyn Bridge is a perfect example. In combination with the heavy stone masonry, the steel suspension cables are delicate but structurally strong. Besides being a practical object, the Brooklyn Bridge has often been called a work of art. The George Washington Bridge in New York and the Golden Gate Bridge in San Francisco are also excellent examples of cable work that inspire string designs. In fact, from spider webs to power lines, such geometric artistic designs can be seen everywhere.

The basis of string design work comes from geometric principles. For years, high school and college teachers have used stringed two- and three-

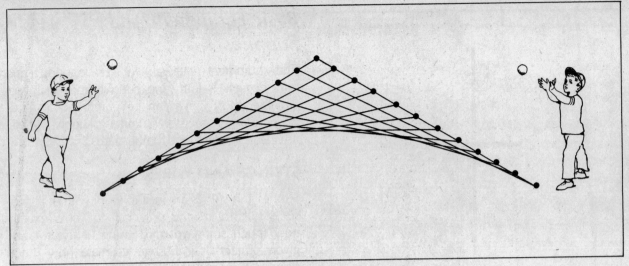

Figure 3. In this design, lines are set along points to form a parabolic curve.

Figure 4. The sculpture "Winged Figure," by artist Barbara Hepworth, was commissioned for the John Lewis department store in London. This work is a prime example of wire art in sculpture.

dimensional designs to illustrate certain mathematical ideas, such as the parabola, which involves the making of curves with straight lines. This principle is also used to illustrate the flight of an object, such as a baseball.

There are a variety of basic geometric forms used to create stringed designs: the circle, triangle, square, rectangle, and ellipse are a few common examples. Certainly part of the appeal of string and wire design work is the modern, futuristic look that can be achieved with clean geometric forms and colorful, crossing lines.

In recent years string design work has been called "symmography." As Lois Kreischer in her book *String Art: Symmography* explains: "The word symmography is derived from 'symmetry' and the suffix '-graphy.' Together they describe a linear representation in which proportion, balance, and harmony are used to create the proper relationship of rays of yarn to one another, thus producing an aesthetically pleasing picture."

Common Terms Used In String and Wire Art

Axis: any lengthwise central line, real or imaginary, around which parts of a body are symmetrically (proportionally) arranged.

Diagonal: the line that crosses a square or rectangle from opposite angles (corners).

Grid: a pattern of horizontal and vertical lines crossing each other at 90° angles.

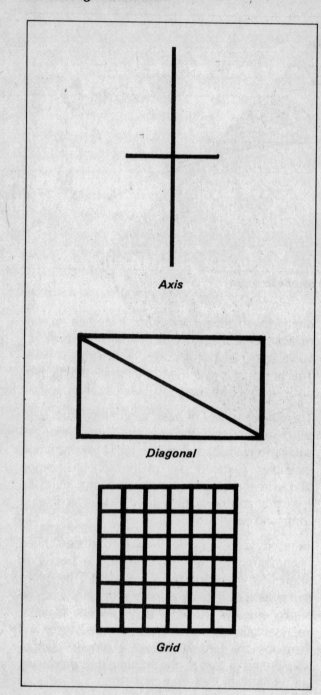

Axis

Diagonal

Grid

Mat Board: thick cardboard, which comes in colors; and used by artists to mat pictures for framing.

Mandala: a Hindu or Budhist symbol used for meditation; a design in which a circle encloses a square.

Parabolic Curve: a curve formed from only straight lines.

Symmography: a term used for string designing.

Basic Equipment And Supplies

The equipment necessary for creating string and wire designs is fairly inexpensive and easily accessible. Most items can be purchased at hardware stores, retail stores, knitting supply outlets, artist supply stores, and lumber yards.

STRINGS AND WIRES

Strong, thin strings are best to work with. It is possible, but not always practical, to know exactly how much string you are going to use for any given project. It is best to estimate how much string will be needed so that extra string is available in case something goes wrong. It is also best to purchase your strings, threads, and yarns at a store where a complete stock is always maintained. The kinds of fiber materials that may be used for almost any project are described below.

String

Any kind of colorful strong string is appropriate. One of the best is crochet string, which comes in an assortment of vivid colors and is strong and durable. It is generally better not to use especially hairy or slippery strings and cords, like jute and fine silk, because these materials are difficult to manage. However, the decision on what string to use ultimately depends on the desired effect. One may be striving for a very earthy look, or for a delicate and fragile motif. The type of room in which the finished design will be placed also has an effect, as does the size of nails or tacks being used. Crochet string works very well with the size tacks suggested below.

Thread

Mercerized cotton thread is also good for string art. It has the desirable characteristics of being thin and strong and is also available in many colors.

Yarn

Yarns can also be used effectively, especially orlon acrylic or four-ply knitting worsted. Because yarn thins out when it is pulled tight, the thickness of the yarns in the finished product will look different from the thickness in the skeins. Be careful of yarns that unravel easily, or that tear

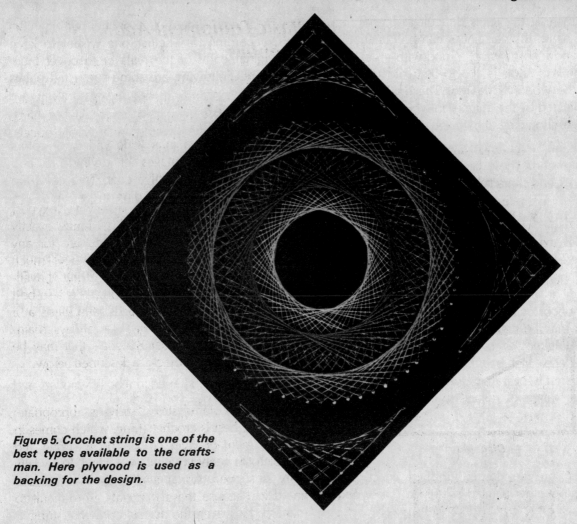

Figure 5. Crochet string is one of the best types available to the craftsman. Here plywood is used as a backing for the design.

when pressure is applied to them. For special effects, experiment with very fluffy yarns, like mohair and Icelandic mountain sheep's wool.

Wire

Wire is generally more expensive than string. The most commonly used wire for design is galvanized steel wire, copper, brass, and aluminum wires are also available. These latter allow for different color effects, but are more expensive than steel. Wire comes in different gauges, a few of which are practical for general wire art: gauges 30 to 18 are recommended. Gauge 30 wire is 0.0140 inch in diameter and gauge 18 is 0.0475. A pound of 30-gauge wire yields 1913 feet of working wire. Wire can be purchased in small or medium-sized spools but that is the most expensive way to buy it. Purchasing it by the pound is much more economical.

NAILS AND TACKS

The kind, color, and size of nail or tack is, of course, a matter of personal preference. There is only one necessary characteristic: it must have a small head to prevent the string, thread, yarn or wire from slipping off. A nail also needs to be long enough to carry the required layers of material, which sometimes can be quite thick. The best size nail to use for the first project is a 1 inch or 7/8 inch nail with a small head. Later, as proficiency increases, experiment with all kinds of tacks, hooks, pins, and even thin dowels of wood.

WOODS

To create background for the design, the nails or tacks are pounded into a piece of wood. The least expensive and most readily obtainable is indoor plywood. It is generally best to use 1/2-inch plywood. Anything thicker is difficult to frame and heavy to hang; thinner pieces can be penetrated by nails and tend to warp. Wood with an excessive number of knots is also to be avoided. Paint or stain the wood as desired. The final product will be affected by the manner in which the wood is cut: edges should be smooth and even.

Once again, experiment with varieties and shapes of wood. These can lend interesting textures, colors, and characteristics to each project.

CARDBOARD AND MAT BOARD

Not all designs have to be worked on wood with nails. Interesting effects can also be achieved by stringing thread, yarn, string, and wire through cardboard or mat board. Almost any kind of sturdy, noncorrugated cardboard is usable, although it may be necessary to glue together two or three thicknesses of cardboard to create a sturdy surface. Mat board can be purchased at any artist supply or framing store and is available in a large range of colors. It is usually sturdy enough to use as is.

PAINTS AND STAINS

Depending on the desired finished effect, the wood can be either painted or stained. The wood may be painted either before or after putting in the nails, according to whether one wishes to keep the original color of the nails or to cover them with paint. Following are some suggested paints and stains.

Acrylic

Acrylic paints come in a wide variety of colors and have the advantages of drying fast and leaving a durable, attractive coat. Two coats are sometimes necessary, depending on the color.

Housepaint

Both water-based and oil-based housepaints are a practical possibility for covering wooden backgrounds. These often have the advantage of matching the accessories in one's home and of already being on hand.

Spray Paint.

Spray paints can be used on both wooden and cardboard surfaces.

Stain

There are a variety of stains from which to choose. Wire designs look especially good on stained wood.

Figure 6. This attractive, carefully planned geometric design, deceptively simple to make, uses crochet string on a background of stained plywood.

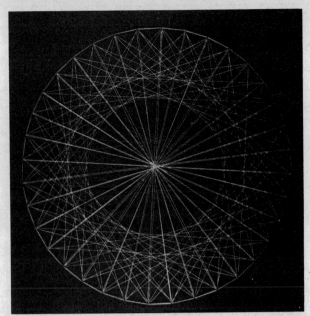

Figure 7. Cloth can be stretched over the wood used as a basic background for string art. Burlap was used in this example. The cloth is stretched tight and glued or tacked to the back of the wood.

FABRIC

Some craftsmen prefer a fabric background instead of paints or stain. There are a number of interesting possibilities: Colored burlap, velvet, velveteen, corduroy, and terrycloth make fine backgrounds. Solid colors are best because they allow the string design to be prominent. The material can be stretched over the wood and either glued or tacked to the back. Be careful that the edges do not wrinkle or bulge.

MISCELLANEOUS ITEMS

Other materials that are needed include hammer, scissors, masking tape, yarn needle, crochet hook, sandpaper, pencils, ruler or yardstick, eraser, compass, protractor, T-square, brushes, and paper designs. Also, some basic knowledge about parabolic curves and other shapes made from straight lines is required.

CREATING PARABOLIC CURVES

This technique can be practiced by first using paper and pencil and then transferring the ideas to cardboard and wood. There is some difference in technique between stringing a cardboard with holes punched in it and stringing a piece of wood with tacks in it. Both will be explained for the diagram shown, which represents a 90° angle. On each axis, X and Y, there are five points — the zero is shared and five is an arbitrary number. There could be 100 or more points if desired. Start with cardboard. Lightly draw a right angle on the board. Place the points an equal distance from each other on both axes. Using the point of a compass, punch through the cardboard at each point, including zero. Now take a single strand of crochet string and thread a yarn needle that will fit through the holes. Tie a large knot at one end of the string. Starting the threaded needle from the back side of the cardboard, proceed as follows:

1. Up through 1 on X.

2. Down through 4 on Y.

3. Up through 3 on Y.

4. Down through 2 on X.

5. Up through 3 on X.

6. Down through 2 on Y.

7. Up through 1 on Y.

8. Down through 4 on X.

9. Up through 0.

10. Down through 4 on Y.

11. Up through 4 on X.

12. Down through 0 and, keeping the string tight, tie a knot in it at the rear of the cardboard behind 0.

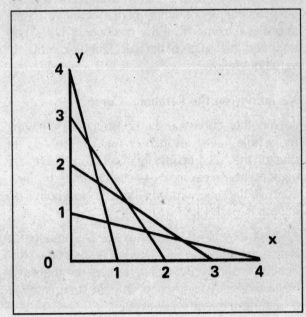

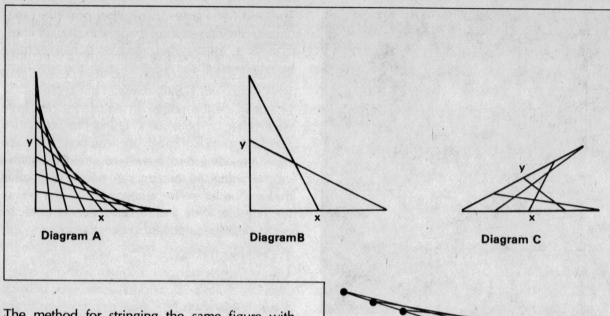

The method for stringing the same figure with tacks on wood is as follows:

1. Tie the string to tack 4 on X.

2. From 4X go to 1Y and, keeping the string tight, wrap it around 1Y once.

3. From 1Y go to 3X, wrap, then back to 2Y, then to 2X.

4. From 2X go to 3Y, and then to 1X.

5. Finally carry the string to 4Y and then go from 4Y to 0 and back to 4X. Tie the string off.

Make sure that the knot is strong. Clip the string close to the knot and put a small drop of any clear drying glue on to prevent unraveling. This is the basic technique for simple parabolic curves. Variations will come from the position of holes and nails and the length of the axis. Some examples of variations follow.

Variations on the Parabolic Curve

A smoother curve can be constructed by having more holes/nails per inch or foot on the axis. In one of the accompanying illustrations there are eight points on each axis — each point is 1/4 inch apart. In the other drawing there are two points on each axis, each 1 inch apart.

Another way to change the curve is to reduce or widen the angle, as illustrated. It is sometimes difficult to work with wide angles because the string has a tendency to lay unevenly. In such cases, a thin string or thread will work best.

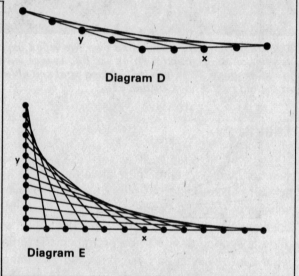

Figure 8. Diagrams A and B show that use of more nails produces a smoother curve; C and D demonstrate that changing the 90° angle changes the curve; E stretches out the curve by lengthening one axis.

Also illustrated is still another way to vary the shape of a parabolic curve. Axis Y is twice the length of axis X. Each has the same number of points; however, the points on axis Y are twice as far apart as the points on axis X. This creates a less regular, but more dramatic curve — one that suggests flight and motion. The curve could be made even steeper by making the Y axis four times the length of the X axis. Of course, it is also possible to make the X axis longer than the Y axis. In either case, there always should be the same number of points on each axis. More variations on the curve can be achieved by widening or reducing the size of the angle between the axes and simultaneously lengthening one of the axes.

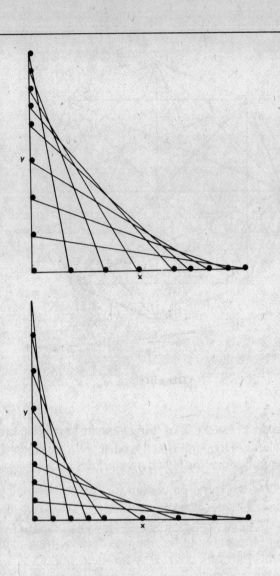

The next two figures show other possible variations on the curved form made with straight lines. In the first, the last four points on both axes have been placed closer together than the first four. This creates a curve that tends to flatten out in the center. This can be more exaggerated by placing the end points even closer together, while spreading the points near zero farther apart.

The opposite effect has been created in the second figure by putting the points near zero closer together, while spreading the end points farther apart. This curve tends to bend in closer to zero. It too could be more exaggerated, depending on the desired effect.

This technique can be combined with the others mentioned above to produce some very unusual curves. Before trying a new design, experiment with ruler, pencil, and paper to get the overall effect of the new idea.

Of course, open angled shapes can be combined to create squares, rectangles, triangles, and parallelograms. The accompanying diagrams illustrate the design possibilities inherent in these shapes.

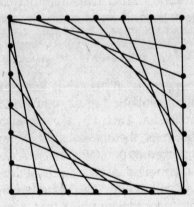
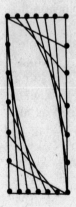
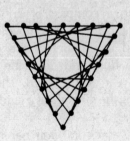

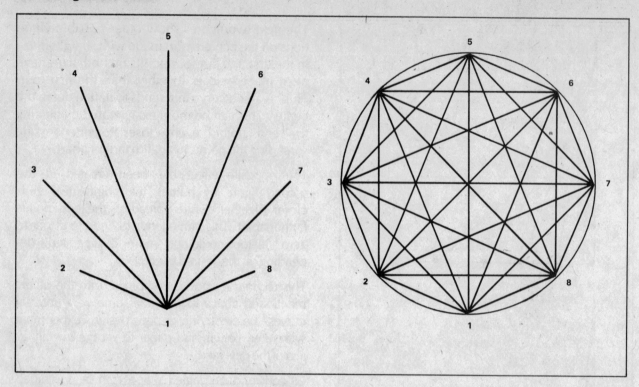

CIRCULAR FORMS

There are a number of techniques for creating unusual designs with circles. The first one to be demonstrated is especially effective on colorful cardboard with crochet string. Cut a square of cardboard and locate its center by lightly drawing diagonals from opposite corners. Where these lines cross is the center of both the square and the circle. Use a compass to draw a circle of the desired size. Place an even number of points on the circumference of the circle. Punch a hole at each point with a compass or another sharp-pointed instrument. Thread the needle with a colored string and tie a knot at the end of the string. Choose a hole and draw the needle through it from the rear of the board. Then proceed as follows, using the diagram as a guide:

1. Down 2, back up 1 from behind.

2. Down 3, back up 1 from behind.

3. Down 4, back up 1 from behind.

4. Down 5, back up 1 from behind.

5. Down 6, back up 1 from behind.

6. Down 7, back up 1 from behind.

7. Down 8, tie a knot behind 8.

Tie on a new piece of string if the first runs out, but make sure the knot is at the back of the cardboard. Carefully erase the light diagonal lines.

Follow the same procedure for each new starting point. Notice that previous strings will have already filled certain lines, so that with each new point there should be one less hole to string than at the previous point. The finished product gives the impression of rays radiating from each point. Experiment with this technique by not filling a certain number of holes. This also yields an interesting result.

The next technique is an excellent one to use with tacks on either stained or painted wood. Necessary supplies are a pencil, a piece of paper the size of the wood, a compass, masking tape, and a ruler. Tape the paper over the wooden shape. Using the compass, draw a circle at the center of the board. Subdivide the circumference of the circle into a prime number, that is, a number which is evenly divisible only by 1 and itself — e.g.: 1, 2, 3, 5, 7, 11, 13, 17, 19, 23. By using such a number of points, each colored layer in the design can be laid with one continuous string.

Take the circumference of the circle and divide it by the chosen prime number. Set the compass at

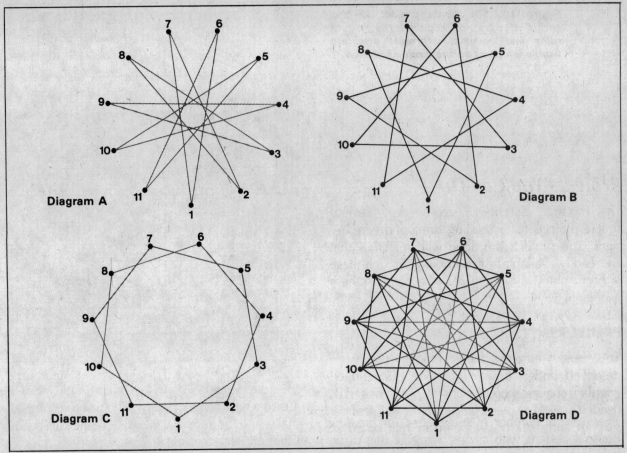

Figure 9. A design based on circles of different sizes is achieved by skipping tacks while stringing. Skip four tacks (A) to create the first circle, then three (B), then one (C); and finally string the border (D).

that amount and mark it off along the circle. Don't expect perfect results with the first effort — adjust and remark as necessary.

Having marked the prime number of points, hammer a nail into each point. Try to keep the nails at equal height above the wood. Once the nails are in place, remove the paper (carefully if keeping the pattern). The effect achieved with the stringing technique varies with the number of tacks skipped while stringing. The bottom layer of string should be the one that closes in the most; it can be any color desired. In the illustration the string was tied on nail 1 and then carried to 7, wrapped once and carried to 2. This pattern of skipping four tacks between connections was carried out until each tack had a string coming to it and going from it. When a large number of tacks is skipped, the finished circle will be small. Take care to keep the string taut from nail to nail. It is also a good idea to wrap the string once around each nail to help secure the finished design.

The next layer of the design can be a second color. This time the string starts at nail 1 and goes to nail 8, wraps once, and goes to nail 4, then to 11, 7, 3, and so on. In this layer the string skips three nails between each connection. Notice that the circle created here is larger than the one created by skipping four nails.

In the next figure, the string starts at nail 1 and goes to 10, wraps once, goes to 8, 6, 4, and so on until each nail is filled. In this case the string is skipping one nail and the resulting circle is very large. This is the third layer of the design.

To finish the design as illustrated, a final layer of string is attached from nail to nail, which creates an edge. There are many possibilities for this circular technique. The more nails on the circumference of the circle, the smoother the inner circles will look. Also, the number of colored layers used depends upon the number of nails.

Once all the strings are laid, the lines can be straightened so that the inner circles are even.

Figure 10. The circle project in this series of diagrams requires the use of ruler and compass. Threads originate from each point on the circle as shown.

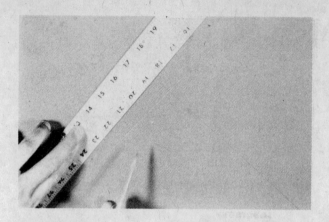

Projects You Can Do

This section describes, step-by-step, several simple projects for interesting string and wire designs. The projects are done with materials that are readily available. After working through these projects, one will be prepared to expand on them in original ways.

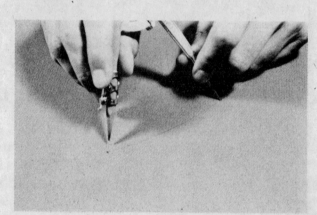

PROJECT I

This project employs the techniques that were described under "Basic Procedures" for stringed circular shapes on cardboard. The materials needed are: (1) a square piece (from 1 to 3 feet per side) of fairly sturdy cardboard or mat board of any color (for practice use a piece of shirt cardboard with wrapping string); (2) two colors of crochet string to contrast with the color of the board; (3) a compass; (4) a ruler; and (5) a yarn needle.

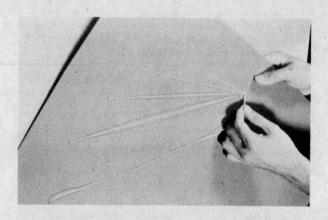

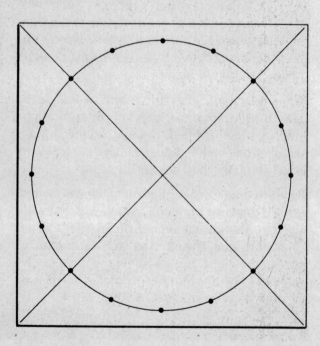

rear of the board. From that point bring the needle to the next hole and through. The needle then comes back to the original point of insertion before going to each of the other points on the circle. When the needle has been brought through the last empty hole, tie the string off at the back of the board.

Now move to a hole next to the one used as the starting point for the previous stringing. Change the color of the string and repeat the process. The first hole strung is the center point for seven holes — the companion color will be at each end of the set of seven.

The design created with this project is one of a circle in the process of being drawn. This is accomplished by leaving the other nine holes half empty. It is also possible to create a series of circles in various stages of development either on different colored boards or by adding different colored strings with each new hole.

Find the center of the square piece of board by lightly drawing two diagonals from opposite corners. With the point of the compass at the center (where the diagonals cross), draw a large circle. Do not go to the very edge of the square, but leave 1 or 2 inches between the circumference of the circle and the edge of the cardboard.

Now, with the compass or using the ruler, mark off 16 points on the circumference of the circle. These points should be equidistant from each other. Then, take the point of the compass and punch a hole in each point from the *front of the board to the back*. Lightly erase the diagonal and circle lines.

Next, pick a point at which to start stringing. This is an important step because every hole is not going to be fully strung. If the finished board is to be hung as a square, choose a point that is the nearest to the middle of one of the edges. If it is to be hung as a diamond shape, then use a hole that is nearest one of the corners. Thread the needle and tie a large knot at the end of the piece of string. Put the needle through the hole from the

Figure 11. Many pleasing variations can be obtained using the basic circle pattern. In this example, seven of the points are completed and the others are not — suggesting a fan shape.

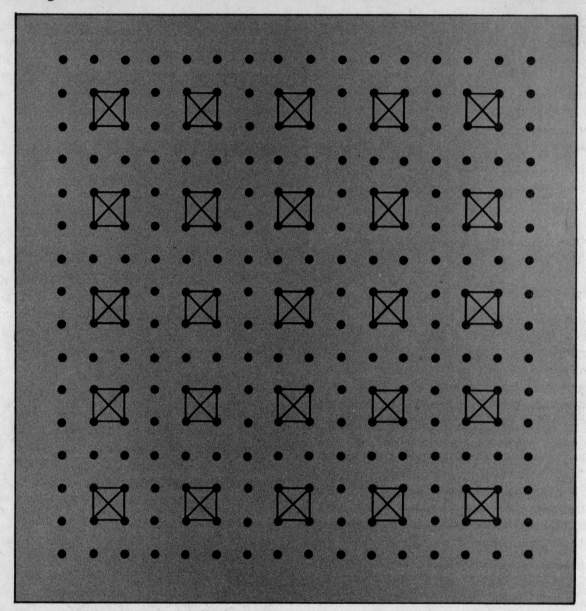

PROJECT II

This project is somewhat more complicated than the first. It is called the "Coptic Cross" because it is reminiscent of the shape of the crosses used in Ethiopia by the Coptic Church. Needed are: (1) a piece of 18″ x 18″ plywood (the corners can be curved or right angles); (2) 3/4-inch tacks with small heads; (3) a can of flat black spray paint; (4) four colors of crochet string; (5) a small spool of metallic thread (gold or silver); (6) a hammer; (7) scissors; and (8) a yardstick.

Work on the smooth side of the wood and avoid a side that has any knots or irregularities. With the yardstick, draw a line 1½ inches in from the four edges of the wood. There should be an equal margin on all sides, leaving a 15-inch square in the center of the board. Now take a pencil and mark off every inch on the drawn line. Connect the dots on lines opposite each other with a light pencil line — the result will look like a piece of graph paper. Once the grid is completed, hammer in a tack at every spot where two lines meet. This requires exactly 256 tacks. Do not hammer the tacks in completely, but be sure they are sturdy. Now look at the upper right hand corner of the grid. Count left four tacks and then down four. Then go back right four and up four to the original point. This will delineate a small square with four tacks within it. Hammer the inside tacks in farther than the surrounding ones. Now look at the grid. There should be 25 such squares each with a small square comprised of four tacks inside of each. Hammer down the four tacks inside each of these 25 small squares.

Once all the tacks have been hammered in, the board can be spray painted. To apply, read the directions on the can. It is usually best to spray a number of light coats. Let dry and then begin to string the tacks.

Stringing the Tacks

The first tacks to string are the 25 very small 4-tack squares that were hammered lower than the others. String these with the metallic thread. Start at one corner, go to the next, wrap around, and continue until a small square is strung. Then string the diagonals, producing a small square with a cross in it. This can be done with only two small knots. Use a drop of clear drying glue on these knots. When all the small squares are completed, turn the board so that it is in a diamond shape. It is now time to string the four large corner squares: the top and bottom squares should be the same color; the 2 side squares should be the same color also but different from the top and bottom.

To delineate the top and bottom squares, do the following. From the top nail count down seven nails in both directions. At the last nail on each side, turn a 90° angle and count over seven nails. This marks out a square with seven nails per side. The nails will be strung so that the curve goes from the top nail to the bottom one (see diagram). Follow the same procedure for stringing that was shown for stringing the first figure illustrated in the section "Creating Parabolic Curves" — the only difference is that there are now seven nails. After stringing one side of the square, string the other.

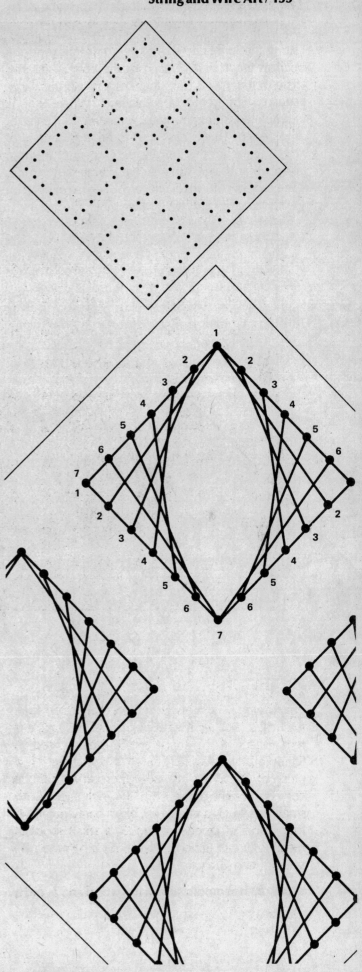

After the four corner squares are completed, string the large center square. To do this, find the nail at the center of each of the corner squares. These four nails are the corners of the large square. String the large square. When that is completed, string the small square in the center of the design. This is easy to do: the four corners of this square are the four inside corners of the top, bottom, and side squares that are already strung. The project is finished and can be framed or not.

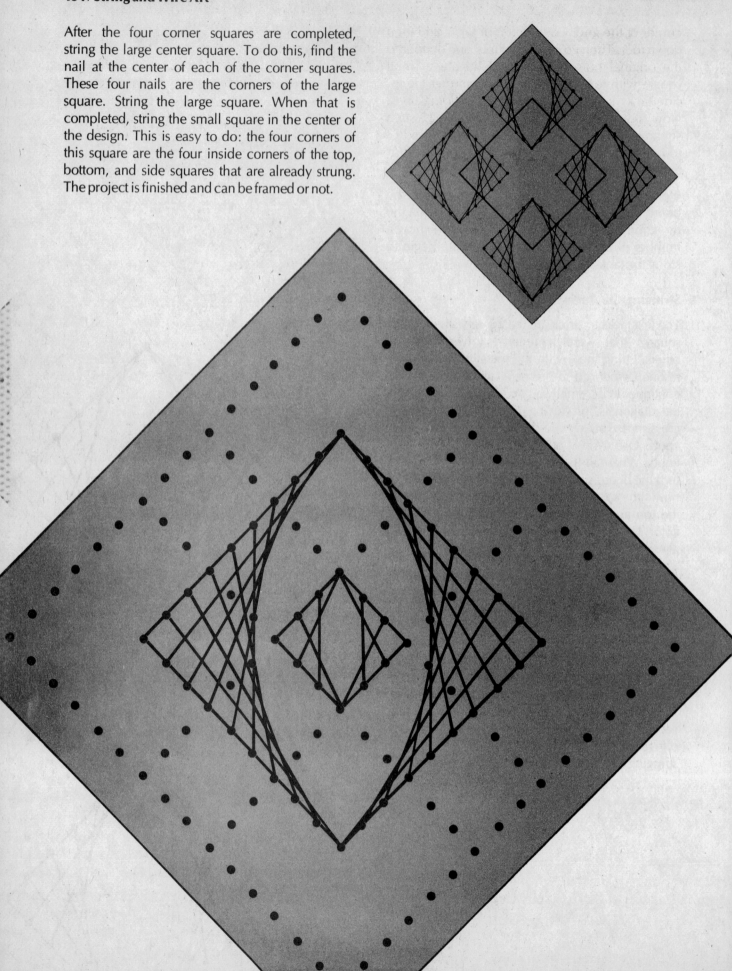

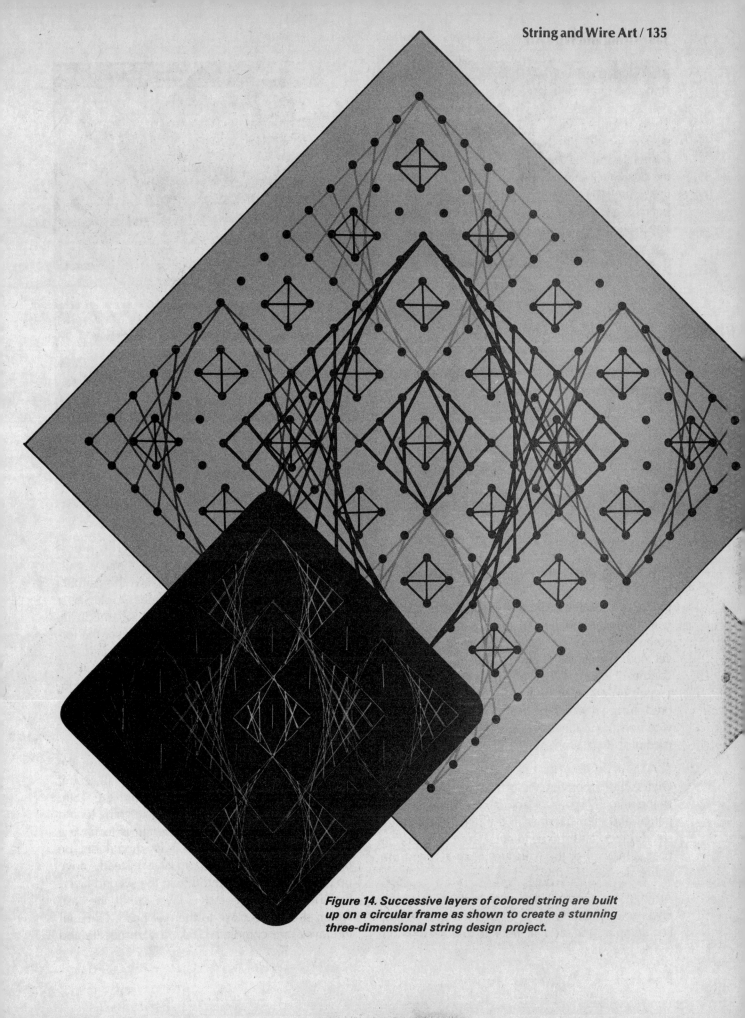

Figure 14. *Successive layers of colored string are built up on a circular frame as shown to create a stunning three-dimensional string design project.*

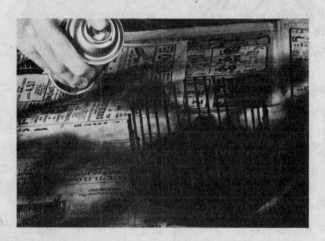
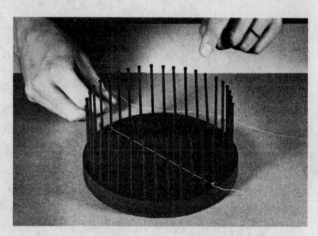

PROJECT III

This project provides a sense of the depth possibilities of string design. Needed are: (1) a circular piece of wood 6½ inches in diameter; (2) 37 nails, 3 inches in length; (3) between 13 to 18 colors of mercerized cotton thread (it is wise to get colors that are close in color (lightness and darkness) value and of an interesting chromatic range); (4) a can of spray paint (if using light-colored strings, it would be best to get dark paint, and vice versa); (5) clear drying glue or some acrylic medium; (6) a brush; and (7) a pencil, compass, and ruler.

Divide the circumference of the circular wooden shape into 37 parts. Mark off the spots with a pencil and then hammer in the nails so that they stand erect and perpendicular to the wooden base. Once all of the nails are in, spray paint the entire piece and let dry.

Arrange the threads in a preferred color order. Each color thread will be a layer on the design. For stringing the design, refer to the section on stringing a circular design with tacks. This procedure is similar. To determine how many nails must be skipped in each layer; use the formula $(X-1) \div 2$. To find the number of nails to skip over in the bottom layer, subtract 1 from 37 and divide by 2: $(37-1) \div 2 = 18$. For the next layer the formula is the same except that 3 is subtracted: $(37-3) \div 2 = 17$. For the third layer, subtract 5 from 37 and divide by 2: $(37-5) \div 2 = 16$; for the fourth, $(37-7) \div 2 = 15$; and so on. This simple formula can be used with any amount of nails on other circular designs.

Now begin stringing. Choose a nail and tie the first color to it. Starting with the next nail, count 18 nails and wrap the thread around the 18th. Continue until each nail has a thread going to and coming from it. Because this design is to have a depth dimension, the next layer should not be directly on top of the bottom one. Instead, move up a little on the nail and thread the second layer. Do this for all successive layers until the last, which should lie close to the nail head. Once all the layers are completed, take a yarn needle and

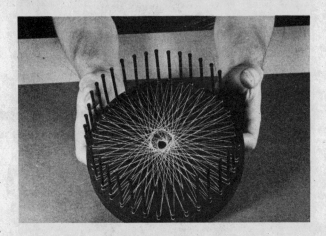

adjust them. Make sure that each layer is even and equidistant from each other.

Once all the thread is in place, take some clear drying glue or acrylic medium and lightly brush it on the threads covering the nails. This will prevent the threads from slipping and falling down.

For Additional Reading

Carelson, Jim, "Space Looms: Thread in Three Dimensions," **Creative Crafts,** June 1974, Vol. 4, No. 3

Jansen, Mark, **The Art of Geometric Thread Design,** Open Door Company, 1972.

Kreischer, Lois, **String Art: Symmography — Three Dimensional Design with Yarn Without Knotting or Knitting,** Crown, 1971.

Open Door Company, **The Art of Thread Design,** Open Door.

Saeger, Glen, **String Things You Can Create,** Little Craft Book Series, 1973.

Sharpton, Robert, "Symmography: String Pictures," **Creative Crafts,** Aug., 1972, Vol. 3 No. 4.

Wasserman, Burt, "String A Design," **Arts and Activities Yearbook,** 1967.

Plaster Crafts

Plaster is an inexpensive, readily available, and versatile material which may be carved, modeled, or cast in a wide variety of personally innovative as well as traditional ways.

Although there are several different kinds of plaster, most people refer to all plaster as "plaster of Paris." Plaster is associated with the capital of France because gypsum — the soft, white, mineral rock from which plaster is made — was mined commercially in the Montmartre section of Paris in the 1770s. The fine quality plaster made from this gypsum was widely used in making elaborate ceilings, moldings, and other interior architectural details, as well as for making reproductions of original stone or bronze sculptures. The popularity of these Parisian art products resulted in a permanent linkage of the words "plaster" and "Paris."

The use of plaster for sculpture and crafts did not originate in Paris, however. Plaster was known to the ancient Egyptians as early as 2500 B.C. and was used as a base for mural painting, original sculpture, casting, and molding. Despite the comparative softness and impermanence of plaster, many evidences of Egyptian plaster arts have survived in the tightly sealed tombs of the Egyptian nobility.

Although the elegance of marble and bronze sculpture comes quickly to mind when thinking of classical Greece, plaster was also in common use as a sculptural material as early as the time of Phidias (475-30 B.C.). The first-century Roman historian, Pliny, reported that such famous Greek sculptors as Lysistratus and Arcesilaus modelled both idealized and portrait sculptures using direct additive plaster techniques. Although only a few small statuettes have survived from ancient Greek times, it appears, from Pliny's writing, that the Greeks placed a surprisingly high value on plaster statuary and frequently erected large victory and commemorative statues in connection with their athletic games.

There is also evidence to support the theory that, prior to the Roman era, the Etruscans cast many of their terra cotta statuettes in plaster molds. Thus, ancient Rome abounded in plaster reproductions of antique Greek sculpture. While only the wealthy and powerful Romans could possess original Greek marbles and bronzes, those Romans of lesser means contented themselves with plaster reproductions.

During the Italian Renaissance, plaster again emerged as a sculptural medium. The noted sculptor Verrocchio (1435-88) made plaster casts of heads, hands, feet, and other anatomical features, retaining them as references for later works. Plaster "life masks" and "death masks" were cast directly on the faces of both living and dead individuals. Such masks have been an inexpensive means of accurate sculptural portraiture from the Renaissance to the present.

Many contemporary artists and craftsmen use plaster both as a means to an end and as a medium for their finished products. Scores of modern sculptors, in the development of their works and concepts, depend heavily on this unique white powder which turns to soft stone when water is added.

Figure 1. This finished sand casting (opposite) was made by an 11-year-old child. The sand remaining in the plaster gives the plaque a pleasant textured finish, and the design is highly personal.

Figure 2. This abstract plaster scultpure by French artist Jean Arp, called Human Concretion, *shows the possibilities of this art medium. (Collection, the Museum of Modern Art, New York, gift of the Advisory Committee.)*

Realizing, however, that the foregoing paragraphs scarcely scratch the surface of the history of plaster crafts, the reader should bear three things in mind. First, plaster has at least a 3500-year history as an art medium. Second, plaster usage throughout history has often been unfairly associated with inferior taste and lack of originality. Third, it is a versatile and inexpensive material which offers the artist/craftsman a wide range for creativity, after mastering only a few basic, manipulative techniques.

Figure 3. Plaster craft was known to the Egyptians more than 4,000 years ago. This death mask of Amenhotep III dates from the New Kingdom, about 1370 B.C. (Courtesy, Staatliche Museum, Berlin.)

Common Terms Used In Plaster Crafts

Armature: the inner support or skeleton of a modelled sculpture. Armatures may be of any material, but flexible wire is best for plaster.

Batch: a given quantity of a water and plaster mixture which is used for a specific task during the short period of time prior to its setting.

Casting Plaster: a plaster which is slightly harder and more dense than plaster of Paris; contains glue-size or other surface hardeners.

Dehydration: the heating of pulverized gypsum to a temperature of 350° F. Dehydration eliminates most water, leaving the resulting powder in a water-seeking or so-called "thirsty" state.

Gypsum: the single basic ingredient of plaster, gypsum is a soft, white mineral rock found in large deposits throughout the world.

Hydration: the setting process during which water is absorbed by the "thirsty" plaster particles.

Mold: the negative design, matrix, or impressed surface into which plaster is poured.

Molding Plaster: a soft plaster, commonly called plaster of Paris. It is pure dehydrated gypsum without surface hardening additives.

Patina: the final surface treatment of the plaster work. Patinas may be paint, stains, paste wax, shoe polish, spray lacquers, or any other coating applied for color, sheen, or surface sealing.

Plaster of Paris: a term used interchangeably with molding plaster.

Rasp: a coarse-toothed metal file used for shaping and smoothing set plaster.

Reinforcement: thin strips of gauze, burlap, or other open mesh fabric used in plaster to build up and strengthen the form.

Setting: the hardening of the liquid plaster mix. The batch sets when water is restored to the dehydrated gypsum powder. During the setting process, the gypsum particles realign themselves into long, thin crystals, forming a new rocky substance nearly identical to the original gypsum. Heat is spontaneously generated as some of the water recombines chemically with the dehydrated gypsum.

Slurry: a fluid mixture of plaster and water.

Stirring: the mixing of plaster and water either with a spoon or with the hands. During the stirring process, all air bubbles should be removed from the batch and the water evenly distributed throughout the mix.

Surform: a tool which has characteristics of both a carpenter's plane and a rasp; used for shaping and smoothing set plaster.

Basic Equipment And Supplies

Most of the basic equipment and supplies for plaster crafts may be purchased in the local hardware store, lumberyard, or building supply center. In all likelihood, most of the necessary tools and equipment are already in the kitchen, garage, or basement. As proficiency and enthusiasm for working in plaster increase, then it is time to invest in a few special tools and to set up a special work area. In the meantime, be inventive about tools and equipment, and avoid spending a lot of money. If the items listed below are ac-

quired, one can undertake each of the three basic plaster-working techniques: casting, carving, and "additive" or built-up sculpture.

ARMATURE WIRE

Any wire which is flexible enough to bend with minimal assistance from a pair of pliers is acceptable for armature building. Soft aluminum wire (1/8" diameter) is ideal because it is fairly inexpensive, flexible, and does not rust from contact with the wet plaster. Soft copper wire is also good, but it is expensive. Coat hanger wire is usable, but difficult to bend and will rust. Unless a small piece of sculpture is planned, avoid "stove-pipe wire" because it is too flexible to support the weight of the wet plaster.

The purpose of the armature wire is not only to provide support for the plaster and reinforcement, but also to lend tensile strength to the otherwise brittle plaster sculpture. It is this inner skeleton of the piece which helps to prevent breakage. Many varieties of wire are available in the hardware store. Experiment with various gauges and varieties before buying in quantity.

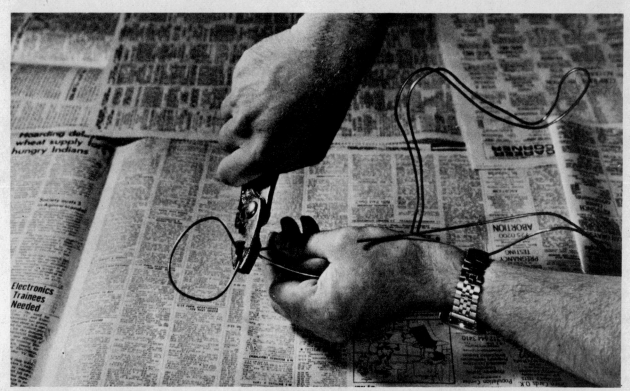

Figure 4. Use soft aluminum or copper wire when building an armature, avoiding "stove pipe" or coat hanger wire, which will rust. Fasten ends securely by hand or with pliers.

BOWLS

Flexible plastic bowls are best for mixing plaster. Depending upon the size of the work, bowls as small as cereal bowls or bowls and basins with a capacity of several quarts may be used. Glass, ceramic, or metal bowls are usable, but difficult to clean if plaster dries on their sides. Flexible plastic allows for cracking and knocking out dried plaster. Plastic cups and margarine containers are handy throw-away mixing bowls for small jobs.

CASTING BASE

A firm base is necessary when reliefs are cast on soft clay slabs. It is possible, but not desirable, to work directly on a countertop or table. Look for a portable board, approximately 2' x 2' and 1" thick. An old pastry board or a scrap of heavy plastic countertop would be quite adequate.

CLAY

Natural clays, such as those used in ceramic sculpture and pottery, are best for casting plaster reliefs. These clays are commonly available in 50-pound moist lots, usually comprised of two 25-pound plastic bags, at a total cost of approximately $7.00. Natural clay will harden as its water content evaporates and, therefore, must be stored in a plastic bag or air-tight container when not in use. Clay may be purchased at art supply stores as well as at hobby, ceramic supply, or ceramic hobby centers.

Some plaster craftsmen prefer to use oil-based or synthetic modelling clay. It is more expensive but does not dry out between projects, is quite adequate for small casting jobs, and is available in the dime store. Both natural and oil-based clays are reusable and should be kept clean and free of plaster scraps.

FOUND OBJECTS

These are the infinitely varied and indescribable objects which are found in desk drawers, sewing baskets, toy chests, and on window sills over the kitchen sink. These are the things which are interesting for personal reasons and which are firm enough to be pressed into soft clay, yielding shallow impressions or molds into which liquid plaster may be poured.

Figure 5. Children of all ages love to experiment with patterns on clay.

Figure 6. Creating design with clay and a stick.

Figure 7. An 11-year-old carefully rolls her clay.

KNIVES

Paring knives, spatulas, putty knives, or tableware are all acceptable. Wash and dry them between uses to avoid build-up of plaster.

PATINAS

Although plaster has its own pristine, white beauty and the surface of a piece does not necessarily have to be sealed, it is soft and chalky and will rub off on clothing or anything else. For color or surface sealing, experiment with spray enamels, oil or acrylic paint, paste wax, shoe polish, or other substances. Do not apply patinas until the plaster is bone dry.

PLASTER

For first attempts, go to the hardware store and purchase a five-pound box of plaster of Paris. If involvement with plaster develops into a major interest, buy the 100-pound sack of molding plaster at a building supply center. As with most things, the unit price of plaster sharply decreases as the bulk amount increases. Keep plaster in a dry place because it is always "thirsty" and will absorb water even from the air, becoming lumpy and of little or no value.

PLASTIC WRAP

Plastic bags, including garbage bags, cleaners' bags, and frozen-food bags, are useful for keeping clay moist, protecting working surfaces, and retaining moisture in cast plaster blocks between carving sessions.

REINFORCEMENT

The reinforcement strips, dipped in wet plaster, are wrapped around the armature wire to build up the sculptural forms. Surgical gauze is a good reinforcement fabric for small works. It is available in rolls of various widths at all drug and first-aid counters. Burlap, cut in strips of various widths and lengths, is used for reinforcement in larger sculptures. Use old burlap sacks or purchase it by the yard at a fabric store.

Rolls of gauze already impregnated with dry plaster of Paris are available commercially in art and hobby centers. Strips of this material, cut in desired lengths, are merely dipped in water and applied as needed to build up sculptural forms. The material is excellent and easily used by a beginner, but it is rather expensive. Because it is convenient and not messy, many craftsmen feel it is worth the expense.

RINSE BUCKET

A large rinse bucket is absolutely essential. Use a mop bucket, a strong wastebasket, a dishpan, or a baby's bathtub. Rinse mixing bowls, tools, and hands before plaster sets on them. The plaster will settle to the bottom of the rinse water and may be thrown away after the water has been poured off. Never rinse plaster down the drain. It settles out and solidifies in sink traps and will eventually clog the plumbing.

An ordinary baker's rolling pin is useful for rolling clay into one-inch thick slabs used for casting plaster reliefs.

SAND

Any clean, coarse sand may be used for sand-casting with plaster. Very fine, "smooth" sand is less satisfactory because it does not hold its shape well in forming molds. Sand from a child's sandbox may be used or it may be purchased from a building supply company. Because only a bucketful is necessary, the cost is nominal. The sand may be reused.

SCRAPING TOOLS

In addition to the knives already mentioned, a variety of scraping and filing tools are useful for carving plaster blocks, texturing moist plaster surfaces, and smoothing dried sculptural forms. The advanced craftsman will want to acquire special plaster sculpture rasps at an art supply center, but these are not essential for the beginner. Be inventive. Use old hack-saw blades or three-inch sections of a broken wood-saw blade. A useful scraping tool can be made by bending the top of a tin can in half. This provides a semi-circular scraping tool with a smooth side that is in contact with the hand. When improvising scrapers from cut or broken metal, file down all nonfunctional sharp edges or cover them with adhesive tape.

SPOONS

A strong plastic mixing spoon is recommended. Others may be used, but these work best for stirring plaster, scraping the bowl, and spreading the slurry into a mold.

WOODEN STRIPS

Wooden strips — 3/4 inch thick, 3 inches wide, and in lengths varying from 12 to 30 inches — are used for building the box-like enclosures in which the plaster reliefs are cast. Use either plain boards or strips of plywood. Sand the rough edges and apply a coat of shellac or varnish to avoid water absorption and warping. The strips used to form the opposite sides of the box should be exactly equal in length. These strips are reusable as they are tied together or wedged in place with lumps of wet clay, rather than joined by nailing.

Basic Procedures

The basic procedures for working in plaster are governed by a few simple facts concerning the essential characteristics of the material. The craftsman should know how to mix the plaster, understand the setting process, and learn how to manipulate the material in its various stages of hardness. The rules are easy to learn; the medium is inexpensive and safe; and a satisfying end-product may be produced in a relatively short time.

HOW THE MATERIAL WORKS

Plaster is powdered, dehydrated gypsum. In its dehydrated state, plaster will absorb water up to approximately 20% of its weight. Normally, plaster and water are mixed in a 2:3 ratio — i.e., three parts of plaster to two parts of water (for example, three pounds of plaster would be added to two pounds of water). In a 2:3 ratio, 80% of the water used to mix the slurry merely provides a temporary surrounding or suspension fluid for the gypsum particles. Suspended in the fluid, these gypsum particles can again form into interlacing, needle-like crystals, thus reconstituting the original grainless, rocky substance. This 80% "free" water eventually evaporates, while 20% of the water is permanently combined with the gypsum. When more water is used, the interlacing crystals form farther apart, yielding a less dense and softer plaster. When less water is used, the crystals form closer together, yielding a denser, harder plaster. More water slows up the setting process, while less water accelerates the setting process.

THE MIXING AND STIRRING PROCESS

There is no point in trying to guess or prescribe the exact amount of plaster to be mixed for a given project. The craftsman, himself, must estimate the volume of plaster needed for his own project and select a mixing bowl which will hold about twice that amount. This allows room for stirring without spilling over the sides.

Weighing the Water and Plastic

Fill the mixing bowl to approximately 1/3 of its capacity with water. Weigh the water on the kitchen or bathroom scale, allowing for the weight of the bowl. Then, weigh out 1½ times that amount of plaster (e.g., one pound of water to 1½ pounds of plaster). Keep hands, container, and plaster dry until ready to begin the stirring process. Eventually one becomes so familiar with the look and feel of plaster that the weighing step can be skipped. Until then, use the scales.

Adding the Plaster

Sprinkle the plaster by hand into the water. Air bubbles will rise as the plaster sinks, and by the time all of the plaster has been added, one or more little islands or peaks of plaster will rise above the surface of the water. Keep hands dry while sprinkling the plaster.

Stirring

When all of the plaster has been added, begin to stir it thoroughly until all air has been released and the water evenly distributed. A strong plastic spoon is a good stirring tool. However, the hand is a better and more sensitive one because it can feel inconsistencies in texture. Scrape the bowl and pinch out lumps. Stirring is the first step in the setting process.

THE SETTING PROCESS

This process involves the absorption of water by the dehydrated gypsum particles, the formation of crystals, and the eventual hardening of the substance. Whether casting on clay or sand, casting a block for carving, or building a sculpture on an armature, the plaster will become increasingly rigid as each minute elapses. For all practical purposes, complete hardness is achieved in 20 to

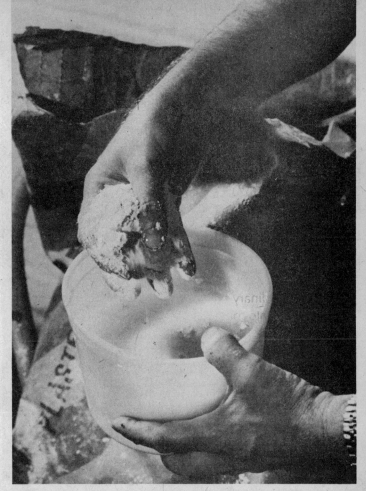

Figure 8. Sprinkle dry plaster into water.

25 minutes when the mix is a 2:3 ratio. As plaster sets, it loses its shiny, watery surface and generates a considerable amount of spontaneous heat. The larger the plaster mass, the more observable the heat will be. A one-quart milk carton full of plaster will be hot to the touch in a few minutes. Although plaster is considered fully set and ready to handle in 20 or 25 minutes, it continues to gain compressive strength as it dries out. Fully dry plaster has nearly twice the strength of wet plaster.

When casting a plaster block or plaque, do not disturb the wet plaster until it is fully set. On the other hand, when building up or modelling reinforced plaster sculpture, feel free to move, scrape, and smooth the plaster with tools or fingers as long as the setting process permits. The reinforcement will prevent breakage.

CASTING ON CLAY

Decorative wall plaques may be made by impressing designs or found objects into rectangular slabs of moist clay and pouring plaster into the

Figure 9. Peaks form as the bowl fills.

Figure 10. Stir carefully with a plastic spoon or, better, mix thoroughly with hands.

resulting mold. Follow the procedures outlined below.

Rolling the Slab

On newspaper, cardboard, or heavy cloth, roll out a thick slab of moist clay. For plaques of less than 12 inches long, a clay slab of one inch in thickness is ideal. Increase the thickness of the slab as the size of the plaque is increased. Strive for uniform thickness so that the plaster may be poured on a nearly level surface.

Impressing the Design

Create a design or a representational (realistic) picture by pressing objects into the clay. Press straight downward to avoid angular undercuts in the mold and pull the objects out of the clay carefully to avoid damage to the resulting impressions. Draw lines and details boldly with a pencil or sharp stick.

Building the Wooden Enclosure

Place the impressed slab on a firm surface. With the three-inch wooden strips, build a dam-like enclosure around the slab, wedging the strips in place with wads of soft clay. If the strips are placed in direct contact with the clay slab, the plaque will have the same dimensions as the slab. If the enclosure is constructed with about a 1/2 inch space on all sides between itself and the clay, a ready-made frame will be cast with the plaque. During the setting process, the plaster will adhere to the wooden strips. However, the bond is easily broken by a light tap with a hammer.

Pouring and Spreading

Do not mix the slurry until the slab is impressed and the wooden strips have been positioned firmly to form the casting enclosure. When the mix has been thoroughly stirred, but before it has shown any signs of setting, apply a thin layer (about 1/4 inch) over the clay. An initial thin layer will permit small air bubbles caught in the details of the mold to escape. If an air bubble seems trapped, pat the liquid plaster gently with the finger tips, being careful not to damage the mold.

Figure 11. A selection of materials for clay casting a decorative plaque.

Figure 12. Moist clay is rolled to form a thick slab of uniform thickness.

Figure 13. Objects are pressed straight down into the clay, then carefully removed.

Figure 14. The slab is enclosed with wood strips.

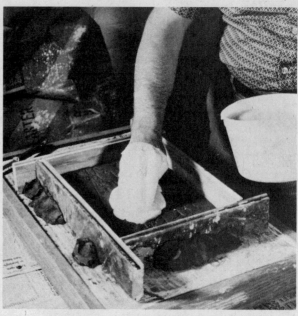

Figure 15. A thin layer of mix is then applied.

Figure 16. A thicker layer of slurry follows.

Figure 17. A hanging wire is embedded in the mix.

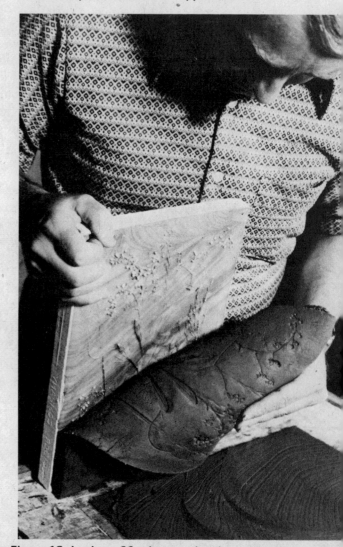

Figure 18. In about 30 minutes, the clay peels off.

Next, pour or spoon on the remainder of the slurry until the thickness of the plaster layer is at least 1/2 inch. Larger plaques require a greater thickness of plaster, but avoid making the piece too thick because the plaque may be too heavy for hanging. While the plaster is still soft, it is possible to embed some wire in the plaque near the top center, leaving a loop of wire exposed as a hanging fixture. Or, if the piece is very large, embed a layer of burlap in the plaster about halfway in the thickness for purposes of reinforcement.

Removing the Clay

Wait at least 30 minutes before trying to remove the clay from the plaque. Then, remove the wooden strips and loosen the whole clay and plaster mass from the casting base. Rest the piece carefully on a table, clay side up, and gently loosen and lift the clay from the plaster. The clay mold may lift off in one piece or it may tear. In either case, the mold is usable only once. Separate any plaster scraps from the clay and return the clay to a plastic bag to keep it soft for future casting. Traces of clay may be stuck to the plaque. These are removed by gently washing when the plaster is fully set.

SAND CASTING

Sand casting is similar in principle to casting on clay, but it is easier, quicker, and, perhaps, more fun. Pack two or three inches of clean, moist sand in the bottom of a plastic pan or a cardboard box. (A shoe box is quite suitable for this purpose.) Impress a design, pour the slurry, and embed some hanging wire. When the plaster is fully set, loosen by gently bending the plastic pan or by peeling away the wet cardboard. Brush off loose sand with a soft brush, but leave the sandy surface which is embedded in the plaster.

Sand casting will not reproduce minute details as clay casting will. Accept this limitation and have fun making quick, bold designs.

CASTING A BLOCK

Plaster sculpture may be carved from a cast block using the same general principles involved in carving wood, stone, or even soap. It handles easier than wood or stone and is not much harder

Figure 19. Moist sand is readied for sand casting.

Figure 22. Pencil drawing creates additional design.

Figure 20. The sand is impressed with a coffee can.

Figure 21. Wooden forms make design impressions.

Figure 23. Plaster is then smoothed over the mold.

Figure 24. The remaining plaster is poured.

Figure 25. The sand is removed from the cast with a brush, leaving sandy surface embedded in plaster.

than soap. The plaster should be cast in a container from which it can be removed easily. Cardboard milk cartons are particularly useful for casting a block because they come in many sizes, hold liquid without losing their shape, and are easily peeled away from the hardened block.

Select the appropriate size milk container, cutting off the top for ease in filling. Stir the slurry until it begins to thicken slightly. Otherwise, the plaster particles will settle to the bottom of the container, forming a harder, more dense plaster at the bottom with a puddle of water on top. Pour the slurry into the container. It is wise to have a small extra container handy to hold any extra plaster which may have been mixed.

If you wish to add color to the plaster, stir in any water-soluble paint or dye while mixing the slurry. Do not use acrylic, latex, or any oil-based paint. If desired, add texture to the slurry while mixing by adding sand, coffee grounds, or vermiculite. The addition of a tablespoonful of any of these, plus a teaspoon of brown tempera (poster paint) per cup of plaster will result in a block which will resemble rough-grained stone when carved. Experiment with colors and textures while casting a block for carving.

CARVING FROM THE BLOCK

Carving or "subtractive" sculpture may seem a bit formidable for the beginner. When part of a block is chipped or scraped away, it cannot be restored. Many carvers like to make pencil sketches of the finished form and mark guidelines on the block. Others prefer to dig right in, allowing forms to suggest themselves as the carving takes place.

Begin carving as soon as the block is removed from the mold. Damp plaster is more easily carved and less brittle than dry plaster. Any small knife with a short, sharp blade will suffice for plaster carving. Dig, chip, or scrape away the forms. Large areas of unwanted plaster may be removed with a coping saw, but do not attempt to chip away large chunks with a knife or chisel — this might split the block. Turn the block constantly, examining all angles for compositional interest. If more than one carving session is necessary, wrap the piece in plastic to preserve moistness. Otherwise, the block will become too hard and brittle for easy carving.

Figure 26. Drawing the design on a cast plaster block provides the artist with guidelines in creating a plaster sculpture.

Figure 27. An ordinary kitchen paring knife is used to trim away the unnecessary plaster carefully.

Figure 28. Different tools, such as the surform, can give the piece an attractive variety of surface textures.

Figure 29. A deep depression is cut into the moist plaster block as the carved design begins to take shape.

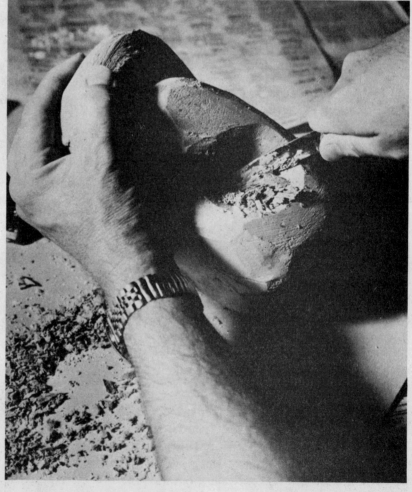

Carved pieces may be left roughly textured, smoothed to a satiny surface, or planed to have contrasting areas of roughness and smoothness.

BUILDING AN ARMATURE

Building an armature is essentially a matter of cutting, bending, and firmly twisting wire to form a sculptural composition and provide the inner support for a piece. The armature remains permanently embedded in the sculpture. The wire must be firm enough to support the wet plaster, yet flexible enough to bend into the desired shapes. Each piece of wire used must be firmly twisted and joined at all points of contact. A combination of thick and thin wires is sometimes desirable, with the thicker wire determining the large structural lines and the thinner wire providing secondary lines and details. Remember that the quality of the final sculptural forms will depend in large measure upon a well-designed armature. Examine the sculptural lines from every angle to assure a strong composition.

BUILDING ON THE ARMATURE

When building up sculptural forms on an armature, add the plaster-soaked reinforcement strips with thought and care. Start with gauze or burlap strips of 1-inch widths and no longer than 6 inches. Dip strips in wet plaster, dragging them over the rim of the bowl to remove dripping plaster. Wrap carefully around wire forms, building up the thickness of the wire gradually and uniformly. If the wire starts to sag slightly under the weight of the plaster, stop for a few minutes until the plaster sets and gives reciprocal strength to the wire. Mix only small batches of plaster at a time. If the sculpture is less than 12 inches high, work with batches of one pint or less. When the first layers of plaster and reinforcement begin to harden (or if they have become entirely dry between work sessions), successive layers will set quite rapidly and the piece will no longer be in danger of collapse.

When the piece has almost reached its full thickness, discontinue using reinforcement strips and apply pure plaster with a small knife or fingers. The top layers of plaster must be mixed with more water if the under layers have dried out to the point where they will absorb water from the new plaster. In such cases, the new layer of plaster sets almost as soon as it is applied, indicating that more water is necessary. Top layers may be modelled with the fingers or a small knife to achieve desired surface forms and textures.

SURFACING THE PLASTER FORMS

Plaster may be filed with a rasp, scraped with a knife, or sanded to complete smoothness. On the other hand, very attractive surfaces may be achieved by applying wet plaster with fingers or brushes, or even by dripping wet plaster over the piece.

When building up patinas, experiment with various methods of surfacing. Smooth sculpture may be enhanced by applying an even coating of color and sheen. Rough pieces may be enhanced by rubbing patinas into the crevices and buffing them off raised areas. Surface the sculpture in a way that is personally pleasing.

Figure 30. Tools needed for building wire armature.

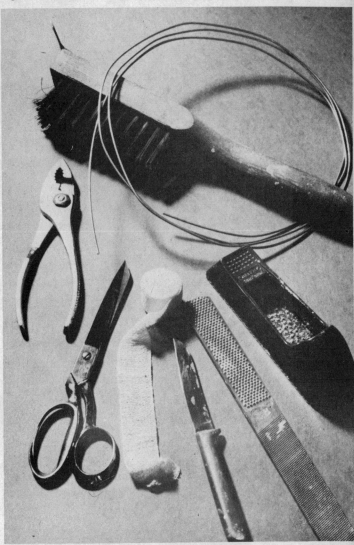

Figure 31. Wire is bent and twisted into the shape the artist desires.

Figure 32. Gauze or burlap strips dipped in wet plaster are wrapped around the wire form.

Figure 33. The surface is scraped with a rasp or knife to achieve the desired finish.

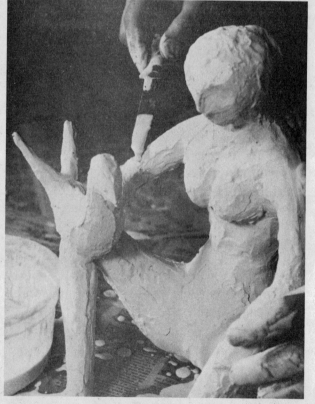

Figure 34. An interesting surface texture is obtained by dripping plaster from a knife.

Projects You Can Do

Now that you have acquainted yourself with this brief history of plaster, its tools and equipment, and the basic procedures of the craft, it is time to think about undertaking a project. The following projects should be thought of as suggestions, not as rules and regulations that must be observed. Copy them if desired, but do not underestimate your imagination or ability for original invention. If the directions and illustrations suggest other ideas and variations of the projects, trust intuition. The worst that can happen is temporary failure, but remember that plaster is inexpensive and creative thoughts are rare. One can always try again.

SEATED GIRL: REINFORCED PLASTER ON ARMATURE

This project is approximately 10 inches high. A seated figure is used because it provides several points of contact with the horizontal surface on which it is built. The beginner will encounter few problems of stability and balance with a seated figure as opposed to a standing figure. A small bird is added for a whimsical effect.

The materials used are as follows: approximately 12 feet of 18-gauge wire; 2 rolls of 1-inch surgical gauze; and about 5 pounds of plaster. (The actual amount of plaster in the sculpture is less than 5 pounds, but a certain amount of plaster is always wasted — even when mixing only small batches.) Working time for the project should consist of two sessions of approximately 90 minutes each. The surface plaster is applied with a paring knife and fingers and should be deliberately left roughly textured for interest.

When doing this project, feel free to vary details. The seated figure could be a boy instead of a girl. The secondary subject matter need not be a bird. Consider various other points of individuality which could be added: try distorting the figure, exaggerating fatness or thinness, increasing or decreasing the size of the head, or making amusing facial features.

CLAY CASTING: BOTANICAL FORMS

This project is approximately 10 x 12 inches and roughly 3/4 inch in depth. Collect three or four kinds of small branches, firm-stemmed weeds, or distinctive seed pods. One need not be limited to the botanical forms shown in the illustration. Choose specimens which are easily available and which are personally interesting.

Roll out a slab of clay, soft enough to take an impression but firm enough not to stick to the botan-

Figure 35. This decorative plaster wall plaque is a clay casting, the finished product of the process illustrated on pages 344-345.

ical specimens. Make the slab larger than 10 x 12 inches and trim to size. Read the instructions on impressing and casting on clay under "Basic Procedures." Proceed as directed. When the plaster plaque has been removed, use a rasp or surform to clean up and smooth off rough edges.

For a variation on the project, substitute either items from a child's toy chest or cooking gadgets from the kitchen drawer. Smooth metal or plastic items used to make impressions will stick less if dusted with talcum powder.

SAND CASTING: A SUNBURST

This project is an irregular shape, about 12 inches in the largest dimension. Fill a rectangular plastic pan with clean sand to a depth of about 3 inches. Add enough water so that the sand is firm enough to make an impression — about the degree of moistness necessary for making sand castles.

Find a small pan or tin can which is approximately 5 inches in diameter, and impress a circle to a depth of about 1/2 inch. This will comprise the main form for the sunburst. Impress eyes and other features, augmenting impressed shapes with lines drawn with a pencil or sharp stick. Add rays around the face with a thin triangular object. Extend the rays by drawing wavy lines outward to achieve a pleasant free design. Cast as described in the section on "Basic Procedures."

Figure 36. The detailed steps in the author's creation of this sand casting of a cheerful sunburst are shown on pages 149-150.

ABSTRACT SCULPTURE: CARVED PLASTERS

Cast a plaster block in a 1/2 gallon milk container. Try to visualize in which areas of the block to carve deep holes and what the general outlines and curves will be when viewed from each of the four sides. Draw a design on the sides and start to remove that part of the block which is not needed. Use a rasp or a surform to round off corners, and a paring knife to chip and scrape away little bits of plaster in concave areas. In this piece, a tablespoon of brown tempera and 1/2 cup of sand can be added to the slurry for the effect of simulated stone. Blue watercolor can be brushed into the concave areas to increase the impression of cool shadows. To poise the piece at the proper angle, bore a hole 1/4 inch in diameter into the plaster and into the wooden base. Then insert a 1/4 inch dowel to a depth of approximately two inches and set with white glue.

For Additional Reading

Chaney, Charles, and Skee, Stanley, **Plaster Mold and Model Making,** Van Nostrand Reinhold, 1973.

Cowley, David, **Working With Clay and Plaster,** Watson-Guptill, 1973.

Meilach, Dona Z., **Creating With Plaster,** Reilly and Lee, 1966.

Miller, Richard McDermott, **Figure Sculpture in Wax and Plaster,** Watson-Guptill, 1971.

Figure 37. *This attractive abstract sculpture was carved from a plaster block by the author.*

Plastic Crafts

Because of its stability and versatility, plastic has become a new and revolutionary art medium.

The first true plastic form was discovered in 1909 by a chemist, Leo H. Baekeland. His material, called Bakelite, could be molded into a shape and become a solid composition when heated and compressed. Since 1909, much progress has been made in the study and manufacturing of plastic. However, not until after World War II was there a great increase in the production and use of plastics as substitutes for products made from natural resources. In many cases the plastic substitutes were better suited for a particular purpose than the original natural materials.

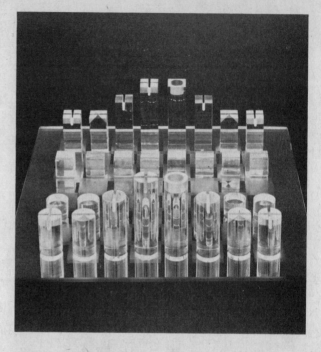

Figure 1. This stunning contemporary chess set, called "Urban Gambit," was designed by Robert A. Propper and made with plastic resins. (Courtesy, Robert A. Propper.)

Today, the science of plastics has merged with the fine arts to create an endless variety of art forms. Transparency, reflection, distortion, refraction, diminution, and magnification are all characteristics of plastics which allow the contemporary artist many expressive possibilities. Indeed, many established artists consider plastics a suitable medium for capturing their expressions. One such artist is David Weinrib of New York, who has said, "One of the primary advantages in the use of plastics for sculpture is that one can work directly with colored material. Plastic, in its immediate response to heat and pressure, opens for me the possibilities of greater and greater moldability and a fluidity which I want to bring to my forms as they move through space." Carolyn Kriegman has designed sculptural body ornaments in plastics to obtain light, color, and transparent qualities. Ted Hallman, who has experimented with synthetics in combination with his weaving, has used plastics for their transparent and luminous color qualities. Even for the arts and crafts enthusiast, plastics provide a new dimension of creativity in the home. The curious craftsman will surely enjoy the simple, basic techniques of plastic craft and will be fascinated with the results.

Common Terms Used In Plastic Crafts

Acetone: a solvent for cleaning uncured polyester resin.

Acrylic: a synthetic resin, formed into rods, sheets, or tubes under heat (acrylic rods are 1/16" to 12" in diameter; acrylic tubes, 1/4" to 18" in diameter; and acrylic sheets, 3/64" to 4" thick).

Casting: the method of pouring liquid resin (thermosetting) into a mold to form an object.

Casting Resin: a thermosetting plastic, either of flexible or rigid polyester resin.

Catalyst: in plastics, a substance mixed with polyester resin to cause a chemical reaction within the plastic for the process of curing.

Cementing: a process of bonding two pieces of plastic by adhesives or solvents.

Cure: the hardening process which occurs when a catalyst has been added to liquid polyester resin to make it a solid.

Edge Lighting: because acrylic has the ability to transmit light from one end to another, when an unpolished edge of an acrylic sheet is placed on a light box, light is filtered through the sheet.

Embedding: a process of laminating materials or casting objects in resin.

Epoxy: a thermosetting plastic, used as an adhesive.

Fillers: inert materials added to resin to make it stronger or paste-like.

Gel: a stage during the curing process of resin when it becomes gelatin-like.

Lamination: a process of impregnating absorbent materials within resin to build up layers.

Light Box: a structure containing a light which is transferred through an acrylic art form.

Shelf Life: the amount of time a plastic can be stored before it becomes unusable.

Thermoplastic: a plastic that becomes soft when heated and hard when cooled.

Thermosetting plastic: a plastic which, after a chemical reaction, assumes a solid state.

Translucent: a partially transparent quality; light can pass through but objects cannot be clearly distinguished when viewed through a translucent substance.

Transparent: the ability of a substance to transmit light so that objects are clearly visible when viewed through the substance.

V-Support: a rectangular board, with a V-shape cut at one end; it is clamped to a work table with the V-cut end extending from the table's surface.

Welt: the change which occurs in an acrylic surface when it is heated over a strip heater.

Basic Equipment And Supplies

Plastic craft supplies can be purchased at hardware stores, craft and hobby shops, and plastic manufacturers and distributors. Many items are also found in the home. Of the following materials, not all are necessary for particular projects but are included here for easy reference: (1) acetone; (2) acrylic plastic; (3) an aluminum cooking sheet for fusing polyester mosaics and pellets; (4) asbestos, a fireproof material on which acrylic can be heated in the oven; (5) a small pointed tool

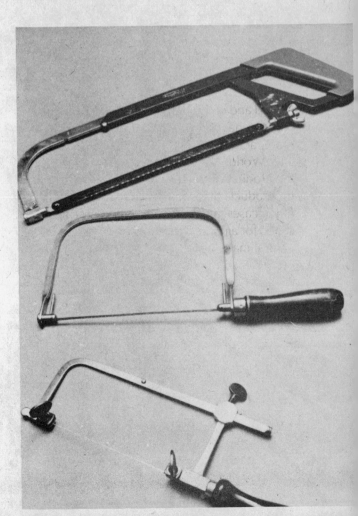

for making holes; (6) a candle for polishing polystyrene mosaics and pellets with the flame; (7) catalyst; (8) cellophane for use as a separator when embedding polyester resin and fabric; (9) a clamp to secure plastic when cutting, drilling, or filing; (10) epoxy; (11) an eyedropper for measuring catalyst; (12) fabric for use in the resin-embedding method; (13) files for smoothing plastic; (14) a fine-grain abrasive powder to be used with water for polishing acrylic; (15) a flat edge, such as a piece of wood or spatula, for smoothing resin when embedding material; (16) a grease pencil for marking acrylic surfaces; (17) a hand drill for drilling holes; (18) handsaws, such as hack, back, straight, coping, and jeweler's saws, to cut plastic; (19) a pliable plastic container for mixing resin and catalyst; (20) a mold, purchased ready-made, for casting resin forms; (21) polyester coloring, in liquid, powder, or paste form, for adding to polyester resin; (22) polyester resin, a thermosetting plastic for casting and laminating; (23) polystyrene mosaic, a thermoplastic that fuses under heat; (24) polystyrene pellets, another thermoplastic that fuses under heat; (25) a respirator with a chemical filter to be worn when working with polyester resin for long periods of time or when using large amounts of resin; (26) a ruler for measuring and to serve as a good straight edge when marking layouts; (27) sandpaper, medium to fine grit, for smoothing polystyrene plastic; (28) a spatula to remove fused polystyrene mosaics and pellets from cooking sheet; (29) #00 steel wool for the polishing of acrylic; (30) a stirring stick for mixing polyester resin and catalyst; (31) a strip heater for bending acrylic; (32) tile clippers for cutting polystyrene mosaic tiles (substitutes are nippers and nail clippers); (33) tweezers for forming polystyrene mosaics; (34) a vise; (35) a V-support; (36) wet or dry sandpaper to use with water for smoothing a plastic surface; and (37) wire for connecting fused sheets of polystyrene mosaic tiles and pellets.

Plastics are a new and exciting medium for the craftsman. Their physical properties permit endless creative possibilities for functional and aesthetic art forms. Moreover, the craftsman should find the learning of plastic art form techniques a stimulating and enjoyable experience.

Within the family of plastics, there are two basic types that will be dealt with here: thermoplastic and thermosetting plastic. A thermoplastic substance becomes soft when heated and hard when cooled. It is shaped when heated after which the new shape is retained by cooling. However, although the process of heating, shaping, and cooling may be done repeatedly, the plastic will eventually become lifeless. Thermosetting plastic is a liquid that becomes a solid when it goes through a chemical change. Once it is a solid, it is a permanent form.

WORKING WITH THERMOPLASTICS

A thermoplastic substance is hard and rigid. Two basic types, fusible and acrylic, will be discussed here.

Figure 2. A variety of hand saws can be used to cut plastic; three are shown (opposite), and many more are available. A good selection of files (left) is needed to smooth the edges and the surface of the plastic.

Figure 3. Polymosaic tiles are fused together in a basic pattern of 16 tiles arranged as a square. After the tiles are fused together (below), the square can be cut or shaped into various objects.

Fusible Thermoplastic

Fusible thermoplastic, better known as polystyrene, is very common in industry. It is easy to work with and ideal for the beginning craftsman. Because it has an indefinite shelf life, it will not change with time. Tools for working with this type of plastic are utensils commonly found in the home. Although there are two types of fusible thermoplastics, polystyrene mosaics and polystyrene pellets, only the former will be discussed here.

Polystyrene mosaics are 3/4" tiles which can be purchased at craft stores. They are available in a wide range of opaque, transparent, and translucent colors. Fused tiles (fused together when heated in an oven) can be made into jewelry, flowers, mobiles, and many other attractive designs. The process of fusing polymosaic tiles is easy.

1. Create a design with 16 tiles but use only three colors. Arrange the design in a square.

2. Preheat oven to 350° F.

3. Place the created arrangement of mosaic tiles on a clean, scratchless, aluminum cooking sheet and put it in the oven. Make sure the oven temperature does not exceed 400° F or the tiles will decompose.

4. The tiles can stay in the oven between 45 to 60 minutes. The exact amount of time determines the texture that the mosaic design will have. For a rough surface, the plastic should stay in the oven for a shorter period of time so there is only partial melting of the mosaics. A smoother surface is achieved by a longer duration of heat; the tiles will melt down and make the surface more even.

5. Be attentive to the tiles in the oven: check them for any air caught between the tiles; this will cause a gap. If this happens, use a spatula to gently push the tiles together.

6. When the surface texture is at the desirable consistency, remove the tray from the oven. Let the design cool before removing from the tray.

This completes the basic procedure of fusing mosaic tiles. The craftsman can now experiment with the finished design by shaping, cutting, sanding and polishing, and puncturing.

Figure 4. To shape polymosaic tiles, place the large square over a metal object of the shape desired. The tiles should be warm when placed over the metal.

Shaping

When the design has been removed from the oven and while it is cooling, the craftsman can shape it into a creative form. Using a protective covering for the hands, lift the design from the cooking sheet with a spatula and shape into the desired form. Then, place it in cool water. The plastic can also be shaped by putting it over or into a form — such as a metal or glass cup, bowl, or bottle — and then allowed to cool.

It is also quite simple to shape a single tile into a bead form. Heat a tile until it becomes soft and moldable, then place a metal rod, such as a knitting needle, diagonally across the center of the tile. Using tweezers, fold one corner of the tile over the needle and adhere it to the opposite side. Roll the metal rod back and forth, making the bead symmetrical.

Figure 5. To make a bead from a tile, heat the tile until flexible, grasp with a tweezers, and fold over a thin metal rod (such as a knitting needle). Then roll the rod around to make the bead symmetrical.

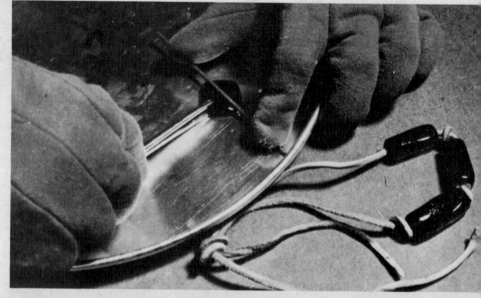

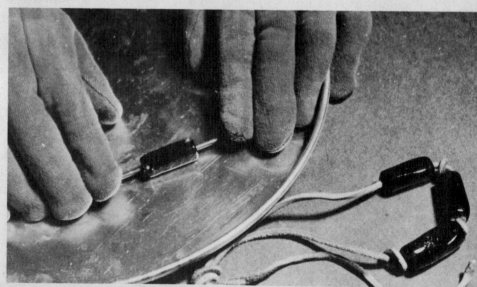

Figure 6. Tile clippers can be used to cut a single plastic tile into small pieces of various sizes and shapes. With practice, the craftsman can cut pieces at the angle desired.

Figure 7. To polish a sheet of polymosaic tiles, move the sheet rapidly over a flame. A deft touch and a careful eye are needed to avoid scorching the tiles during this procedure.

Cutting

A single tile can be cut with tile clippers, nippers, or nail clippers. A fused tile design can also be cut with a handsaw.

Sanding and Polishing

Polymosaics can be hand-sanded with regular sandpaper. Start with a medium-grit paper and work to a fine-grit paper. Areas that have been sanded, however, will become dull. To restore the brilliance, move the plastic rapidly and carefully over a candle flame — charring will occur if the plastic is held too close to the flame.

Puncturing

It is possible to connect separate fused design forms to create linked panels for such items as a room divider, window hanging, or — on a smaller scale — jewelry. To make the holes, heat a metal awl or other sharp metal instrument (stick a cork on one end if the implement does not have a handle) over a flame and push it through the plastic. During this flexible stage, wire can be permanently embedded in the plastic. After inserting the wire, let the plastic cool. A wire can also be permanently embedded in cool plastic by heating the wire first and then inserting it into the plastic.

Figure 8. To make a small hole in a tile or a mosaic, heat a metal awl over a flame and push it through the plastic. It may be necessary to push and twist the awl to open a larger hole.

Figure 9. To embed a wire in cool plastic, heat the wire and push it into the plastic with pliers. A glove should be worn — a necessary safety precaution with hot metals.

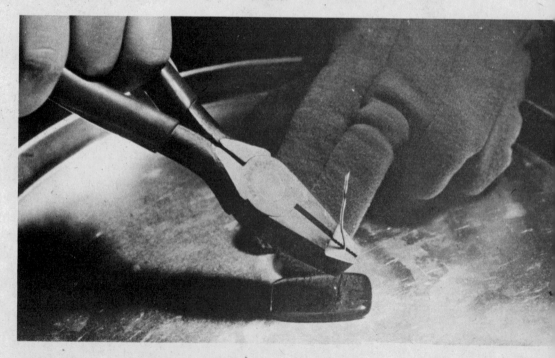

Acrylic Thermoplastic

An acrylic thermoplastic can be shaped while hot and will retain its shape when cooled. When reheated, however, the plastic will assume its original shape. Acrylic can be purchased in tube, rod, block, or sheet forms — the last being the most commonly used — and is available in various patterns and textures as well as mirrored, opaque, and transparent colors. It has an indefinite shelf life but will corrode if exposed to acetone, benzene, ketones, lacquer, turpentine, and other similar solutions. It may be sawed, drilled, carved, and sanded by metal and woodworking tools. Shaping and cementing are also possible. There are two methods used in working with acrylic design forms — (1) working with acrylic in its natural state and (2) by heat-forming — only the latter will be discussed here.

Acrylic is moldable when heated between 250° F and 340° F. When soft and flexible, its shape can be altered and retained after it is allowed to cool. If reheated, however, the new form will be lost, as the plastic will assume its original shape. As mentioned earlier, the heating, shaping, and cooling process can be repeated several times on one piece of plastic before it loses its workability. Acrylic can be heated and shaped in two ways: (1) to heat a large area, a kitchen oven is used; (2) to bend a straight line, a strip heater is needed.

Figure 10. A variety of tools can be used on an acrylic sheet, including a jewelry saw (below, left), a hand drill (below, right), a file (opposite, top), a wet-sanding device (opposite, lower left), and a carving needle (opposite, lower right).

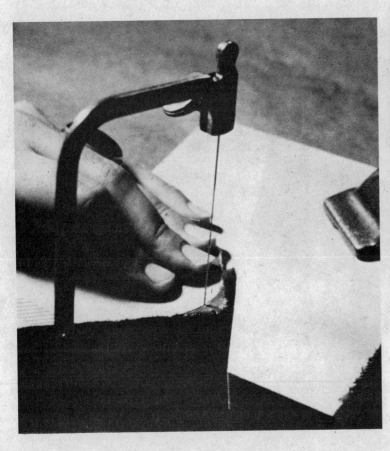

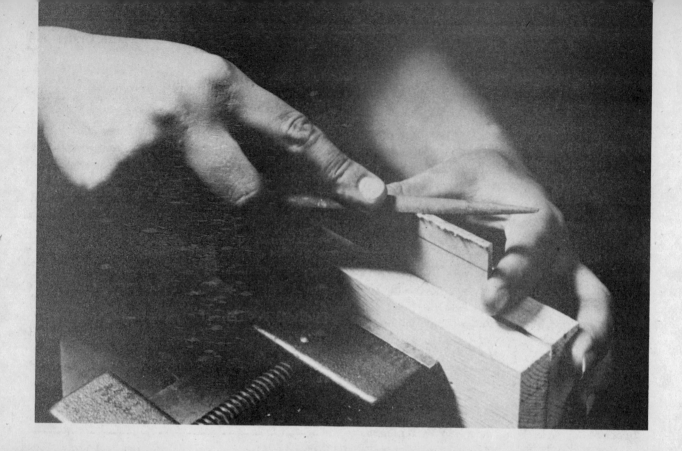

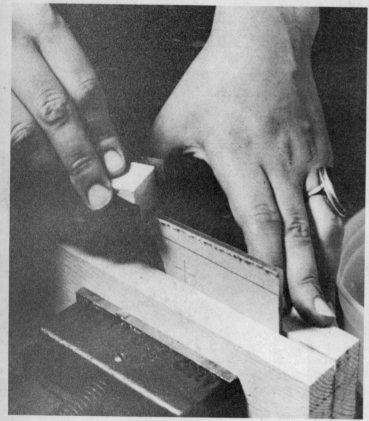

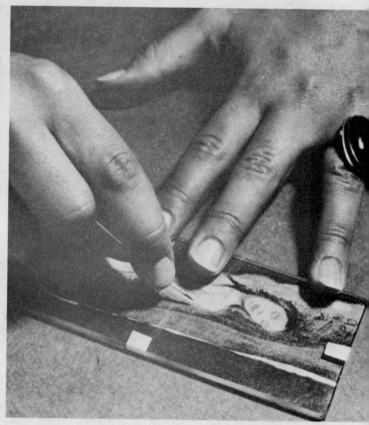

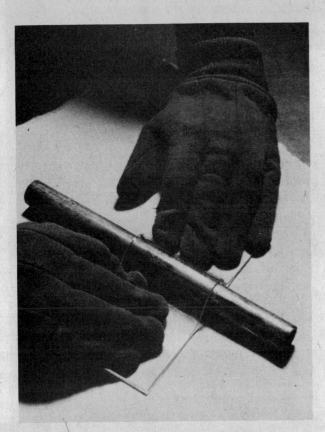

Shaping in an Oven

When heating acrylic plastic in an oven, always use asbestos. Do not leave the flexible acrylic unattended. When the plastic is soft, remove it from the oven with protective gloves and shape the acrylic by hand (still using protective gloves) or place it over a form. The new shape must be kept in place until the plastic has cooled completely. Spring clamps can be used to secure the shape while cooling, but remove them before the plastic is completely cooled to prevent a marred surface.

Shaping With a Strip Heater

Acrylic can be bent with accuracy by using a strip heater, which can be purchased or easily constructed. Materials needed for constructing a strip heater are: (1) 1/2" plywood, 6" x 42"; (2) two 1/4" plywood strips, 2-5/8" x 36"; (3) two heavy-duty aluminum foil sheets, 6" x 36"; (4) two asbestos

Figure 11. Wear protective gloves to mold a sheet of acrylic. The sheet is heated in an oven, then placed over a form of the desired shape and size (above). After the acrylic cools, the new shape is fixed.

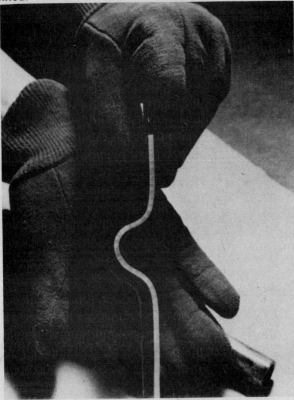

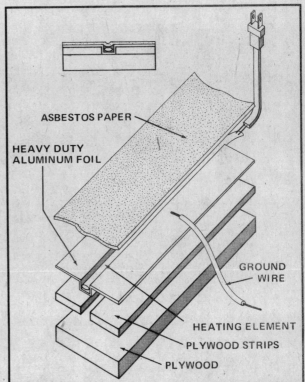

ASBESTOS PAPER

HEAVY DUTY
ALUMINUM FOIL

GROUND
WIRE

HEATING ELEMENT

PLYWOOD STRIPS

PLYWOOD

papers, 6-1/4" x 36"; (5) staples; (6) ground wire and screw; (7) hammer and nails; and (8) a Briskeat RH-36 heating element, 1/2" x 36", wired with a two-prong plug and used in a 110-volt outlet (this item can be purchased from hardware stores or from the Briscoe Manufacturing Co., Columbus, Ohio 43216.)

Nail one of the two 1/4″ plywood strips to each side of the 1/2″ plywood base, leaving a 3/4″ channel down the center. Place the two sheets of aluminum foil over the top surface, folding it to fit the 3/4″ channel, and attach the ground wire to the aluminum foil with a screw. Make sure the ground wire is long enough so that it can be connected to a common ground — e.g., the screw in the cover plate of an electrical outlet. Place the two pieces of asbestos over the aluminum foil, folding them to fit the 3/4″ channel. (Dampen the channel area to keep the asbestos and aluminum foil from cracking and tearing.) Staple the asbestos and aluminum foil in place along the outside edges of the two 1/4″ plywood strips.

To prevent the edges of the asbestos and foil from fraying, tape them to the sides of the 1/2″ plywood base. Place the heating element in the channel and hammer a nail 1-1/2″ from the center of each end of the plywood base. Attach the end strings of the heating element to the nails (the nails and heating element should all be in line with each other). Connect the ground wire to the common ground and plug into a 110-volt outlet when ready to use.

To bend acrylic, remove the protective paper from a sheet of the plastic. Place the acrylic on top of the strip heater and position the area to be bent directly over the heating element. Do not let the element touch the acrylic. Do not leave the plastic unattended while heating because scorching can easily occur. The plastic is ready for bending when the heated area begins to soften and become flexible. Bend the acrylic to the desired angle, with the heated side on the outside of the bend. Hold the acrylic in the desired angle until it has cooled enough to maintain its shape.

Figure 12. Important steps in making a strip heater are shown here (from top): nailing ¼″ plywood strips on a base board; adding asbestos and aluminum; and installing a heating element.

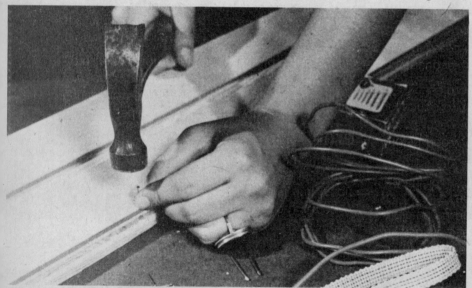

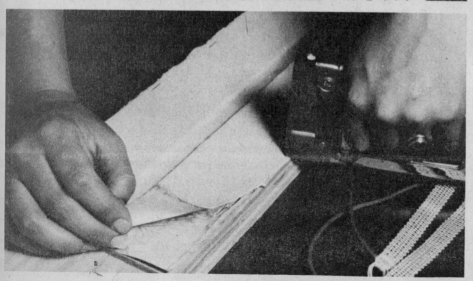

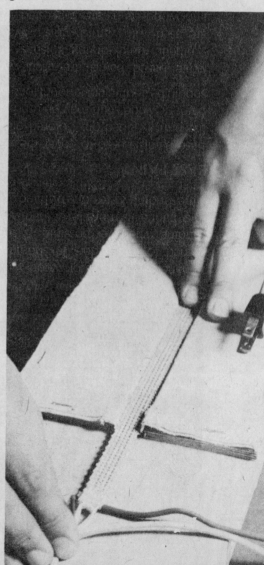

WORKING WITH THERMOSETTING PLASTICS

Because thermosetting plastic comes in a liquid form, it must undergo a chemical change in order for it to become a solid. This chemical change occurs when a catalyst is added to the plastic. Once the plastic has been changed from liquid to solid, the change is permanent.

Polyester resin is a thick liquid plastic used for casting and laminating. When a catalyst is added to it, a chemical change causes the resin to heat up and harden. Before it hardens, however, the resin first goes through a gelling stage. The process which occurs between the liquid, gelling stage, and the solid state is called curing. The length of time the curing takes depends on the amount of catalyst used — i.e., the less catalyst used, the longer the curing period; conversely, the more catalyst used, the shorter the curing period. The curing process, therefore, may take minutes, hours, or days. The amount of catalyst used is determined by the amount of resin used and whether the craftsman is casting or laminating (casting is the pouring of the resin into a mold; laminating is the building up of resin in layers). The resin can be opaque, transparent, or colored by mixing it with special pigments.

Certain preparations must be made and precautions taken before working with polyester resins. The work area should have good ventilation because the resin and catalyst give off fumes. If exposed to these chemicals for a long period of time or if working with large amounts of resin, wear a respirator with a chemical filter. Also wear protective gloves. When dry sanding, cutting, or filing the resin, wear a cloth filter mask or goggles if necessary. Store catalyst and resin in a cool, dark place and keep them away from exposed flames. Do not smoke near the chemicals. To remove resin or resin dust from the body, wash with cold water. If too much catalyst is added to the resin, it causes cracking and smoking. If this should happen, run cold water over the form.

Cover the work area with wax paper or other disposable paper. Have all equipment and supplies ready. Acetone is used to clean resin from hands, brushes, and clothes when it is still in a liquid or gelling state.

Figure 13. A careful layout of materials is just one of the precautions essential when working with polyester resins. The work surface should be covered with waxed paper or some other disposable paper.

Types of Polyester Resin

There are two basic types of polyester resins: one designed for casting and the other for laminating. When casting, use either a flexible or a rigid resin. The flexible type is preferred when embedding materials into the resin.

Coloring

Special polyester resin colors are available in liquid, powder, and paste form. Before using the catalyst, a very small amount of color is added to the resin and mixed thoroughly to prevent streaking.

Catalyst

The catalyst, which is usually in a liquid form, is usually sold with the resin. It is measured out with an eyedropper. Lamination resins require more catalyst than casting resins in order to cure. (Use the proportions given in the directions because too much heat will cause the thick resin to crack.) Mix the catalyst and resin thoroughly with a stick.

Molds

Many types of molds can be used for casting resin. Molds are available at craft centers but they can also be made at home out of plaster, wax, aluminum foil, or flexible rubber. The beginning craftsman may find it easier to work with ready-made molds and experiment later with hand-made molds.

Casting

Casting is simply the process of pouring the catalyzed casting resin into a mold. The resin remains in the mold until it has cured properly. It is removed when hard. If the exposed surface of the resin is tacky (sticky) while in the mold, brush a thin layer of highly catalyzed resin (six parts resin to one part catalyst) over the top. Wait until this mixture hardens and then remove the form from the mold.

Impregnation

Impregnation is the embedding of materials in polyester resin. To prevent the resin from

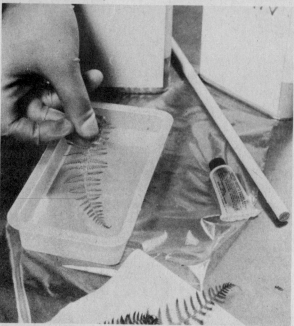

Figure 14. Casting is the process of pouring the liquid resin into the mold (top). Putting a fern or other material into the mold before it cures is called impregnation (bottom).

Figure 15. A handsome paperweight like this one can be made by casting and impregnating liquid resin. To prevent cracking, use a flexible polyester resin.

cracking while it cures, a flexible polyester resin should be used. Different types of materials can be impregnated, such as paper, burlap, canvas, cloth, dried flowers, leaves, seeds, and legumes.

Fillers

Fillers are used to strengthen the resin and make it putty-like. Materials used as fillers include wood chips, sawdust, crushed stone, metallic flakes, sand, and talc. The putty-like consistency achieved by adding fillers allows for a buildup of resins over a wire armature or over such other forms as candles or molds. Before putting the filler into the resin, Cab-O-Sil (a type of filler) can be added. This thickens the resin and prevents the filler from settling to the bottom when it is added. When using Cab-O-Sil, wear a mask. After the catalyst is added, use a putty knife to apply the resin.

Once the polyester resin has cured, it can be cut with wood or metalworking saws with sharp blades. Hand or electric drills with bits for drilling into metal may be used for drilling into cured polyester resin. When drilling, use a mild soap-and-water mixture to reduce the friction. Also, clamp down the form to be drilled.

Sanding and Polishing

When sanding, use wet or dry sandpaper, working from a coarse grit (#150), to medium grit (#220), and then a fine grit (#400). If sanding a flat edge, use a sanding block to prevent dipping. After sanding, the worked areas will be dull and marred. To polish these areas, brush over them with a highly catalyzed polyester and let cure.

Projects You Can Do

Plastics offer many opportunities to the avid craftsman. The following projects demonstrate the basic skills a craftsman must know in order to create original art forms. If the craftsman's workshop already contains basic metal and woodworking tools, this craft can be relatively inexpensive.

ACRYLIC BOOK STAND

An acrylic book stand is an attractive yet functional form that can be used to hold a cookbook and keep it clean while following a recipe. Materials needed for this project are: (1) a 1/4" thick acrylic sheet, 12" x 25"; (2) a strip heater; (3) grease pencil; (4) ruler; (5) files; and (6) wet or dry sandpaper; and (7) a 14" strip of wood.

Before starting the project, check the edges of the sheet of acrylic. If they are rough, file and sand them. After this has been done, remove the protective paper and, working lengthwise, measure 7" in from one edge. Draw a vertical line with a grease pencil and ruler from the top to the bottom of the acrylic sheet. Now turn the sheet over and measure 7" in from the first 7" line. Make another vertical line. From this line, measure 2" and draw a third vertical line. Turn the acrylic over and center the first vertical line over the channel of the strip heater. When the line is centered, gently rub it off with a soft cloth and heat the plastic to the flexible stage. Place a strip of wood along the area to be bent. Bend the heated acrylic, with the heated side on the outside of the bend, to a 90° angle. Hold in position until cooled.

Figure 16. To build up resins over a form—such as a candle—fillers are added to the liquid resin to give it a putty-like consistency. Various fillers are available.

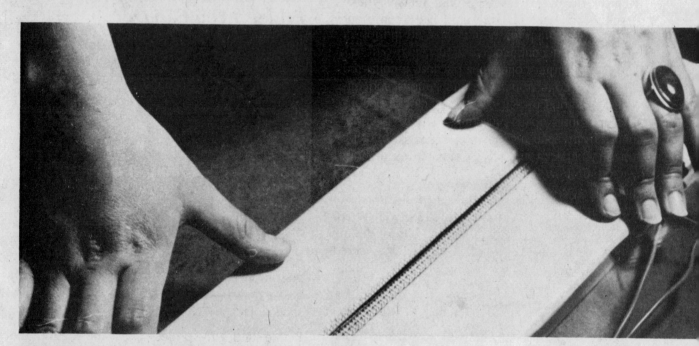

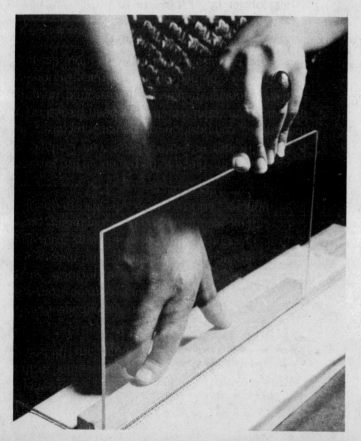

Figure 17. Directions for making an acrylic book stand include the following steps (from top): marking the surface with a grease pencil, positioning the mark over the heating channel, and bending the acrylic.

Follow this same procedure for the second and third vertical lines. Always remember that the greased line is on the surface facing the craftsman and that the heated side is on the outer side of the bend. After the third bend has cooled, clean the surface with a soft, damp cloth.

EMBEDDING CLOTH IN RESINS

The craftsman can embed any type of cloth in resin. The material should have a beauty of its own, making it worthwhile to display. Be sure, however, to follow all precautions mentioned previously.

Materials needed for this project are: (1) cloth; (2) flexible polyester resin; (3) catalyst; (4) eyedropper; (5) cellophane; (6) flat-edged piece of wood or spatula; and (7) pliable plastic bowl.

Figure 18. An acrylic book stand, most often used for holding cookbooks, is shown in completed form. Remember to sand the edges of the acrylic before beginning the bending process.

Figure 19. The steps required to embed cloth in resin include pouring the resin onto cellophane (top left), placing the cloth (top right), adding resin over the cloth (lower left), and spreading evenly (lower right).

Lay a sheet of cellophane, a little larger in size than the cloth, on a level, smooth working surface. Pour the flexible polyester resin into the plastic mixing bowl. Add the correct amount of catalyst with an eyedropper, according to the directions on the can, and mix thoroughly. Pour the resin into the center of the cellophane and let it spread evenly. Place the cloth on top of the poured resin. Then, pour another layer of resin in the center of the cloth and let it spread evenly again.

Place another piece of cellophane at one edge of the resin and, as smoothly as possible, lay the cellophane across the top of the cloth in the resin.

Figure 20. An important step in making plastic jewelry is bending the acrylic around a form of the required size (above). The finished jewelry (below) suggests avant garde design.

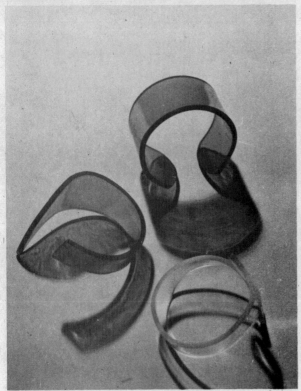

With a smooth, flat edge, gently work out air bubbles and even out the resin so it is the same thickness throughout the cloth. Let the resin cure. Remove the cellophane after the resin has solidified. The edges may be left as they are or they may be cut, sanded, and polished. If this display of fabric is to be hung, hooks can be adhered with epoxy or the fabric can be framed. Remember, use acetone to clean utensils and resin spills before the resin has time to cure.

CLEAR PLASTIC BRACELET

Contemporary plastic jewelry can be made with ease. Materials needed are: (1) a 1/16" thick sheet of acrylic, 7" x 1½"; (2) files; (3) wet or dry sandpaper; (4) oven; (5) asbestos; (6) protective gloves; and (7) circular or oval form.

Smooth out the edges of the acrylic sheet by filing and sanding. Round off the corners with a file and then sand. Edges may also be rounded if desired. Place the acrylic sheet on asbestos and put in into a preheated 275° F oven. Heat. When plastic is flexible (determined by the ease of lifting up a corner of it), remove from oven with protective gloves and wrap it around a circular or oval form. Hold until cooled (dipping in warm water helps the acrylic cool quicker). Clean with soft, damp cloth.

For Additional Reading

Newman, Day Hartley and Scott, Lee, **Plastic for the Craftsman,** Crown, 1972.

Newman, Thelma R., **Plastics as an Art Form,** Chilton, 1966.

Newman, Thelma R., **Plastic as Design Form,** Chilton, 1972.

Nordness, Lee, **Objects, U.S.A.,** Viking, 1970.

Painting, John, **Sculpture in Fiberglass,** Watson-Guptill, 1972.

Zechlin, Katharina, **Setting in Clear Plastic,** Taplinger, 1971.

Decoupage

The art of decorating with applied paper cutouts is easy to do, yet it allows the craftsman to design and produce imaginative and beautiful objects.

The origin of decoupage is historically unknown. However, there is evidence that in Siberia, as long as 3000 years ago, primitive people used cut decorations as appliqués on hangings. The Chinese cut paper for decorations 1500 years ago. Hiram Manning, a present-day decoupeur, owns a pair of Chinese pictures which date back centuries. These are composed of cuttings from silk robes which were glued on silver and placed under glass.

Decoupage, as it is known today, became popular in the eighteenth century in France and Italy. At that time, artists painted scenes and designs on furniture for nobles and wealthy people. Decoupage developed as a means of duplicating an artist's work at a fraction of the cost. In Italy, decoupage was called "l'arte del povero," or the poor man's art. Italian artists used the technique of pasting cut out prints on a surface and covering them with a transparent coating which produced a hand-painted look imitative of an artist's original creation.

Until the eighteenth century, the only reproductions available had been block prints. These were printed primarily for religious and educational purposes. Once engraving was perfected, however, a wealth of material became available.

As decoupage developed, engravers and printers began to make available good prints of original art works. The prints were colored and applied by skilled craftsmen to furniture and other small, decorative items. The decoupaged objects were so beautiful that they soon became appreciated for their own sake. Craftsmen were commissioned to use decoupage as a method of decoration, instead of hand painting.

The three main styles or periods of decoupage are eighteenth century, Victorian, and modern. Eighteenth-century decoupage was classic in feeling — hand-colored original designs and reproductions of fine art works were the basic design sources. Two artists closely associated with eighteenth-century decoupage are Jean Pillement and Francois Boucher. Pillement's work, for the most part, exhibited a Chinese influence and was very difficult to cut. Boucher's art was characterized by cherubs and garlands of flowers.

Because of greatly improved printing techniques, Victorian decoupage consisted of precolored prints, as well as embossed prints and the elaborate use of gold paper trim. Indeed, the trend of the Victorian era was toward overdecoration.

With all this activity, cutting soon became a distinct art. Probably the most famous cutters of the Victorian era were Miss Amelia Blackburn and a Mrs. Delany. Examples of their exquisite work may still be seen in the British Museum and the Victoria and Albert Museum, both in London. Queen Victoria herself was a collector of decoupage. Her collection was quite famous and differed from earlier collections because it consisted largely of a decoupage variation called "vue d'-optique," in which the designs give an illusion of depth.

Robert Sayer, a famous collector of prints of the Victorian era, collected the works of Pillement, Boucher, and many other artists. He published them in a book entitled *The Ladies Amusement Book*. Sayer's collection was very popular in the Victorian era and many of his prints are still being used today.

As the name implies, modern decoupage makes use of all the modern products derived from today's printing processes. These include such items as greeting cards, calendars, and magazines as well as printed art work. Variations from the basic cutting technique, such as dechirage, collage, montage, and repousse, are also frequently used in modern decoupage.

In dechirage, the piece to be pasted on the surface is carefully torn instead of being cut. Collage is the artistic composition of designs, pictures, or any artistic material which have been pasted on a surface. Montage makes use of assorted designs and objects combined on a flat surface; repousse makes use of "raised" or embossed cutout designs on a flat surface.

Figure 1. An elegant example of l'arte del povero, this Venetian secretary (opposite) is decorated with applied engravings, lacquer, and gold. (Courtesy, The Metropolitan Museum of Art, Fletcher Fund, 1925.)

Figure 2. This Victorian decoupage panel, "Wood Vetch," is one of the series called "Mrs. Delany's Flora." Mrs. Delany was a British decoupage artist. (Courtesy, The British Museum, London.)

Originally, all prints used in decoupage were black and white and had to be colored by hand. However, modern color printing techniques have made possible beautiful color reproduction. In view of the current interest in the art of decoupage, it is fortunate that chemists have developed fast-drying lacquer-like finishes with which to cover the cutouts. Decoupage — taken step by step — is neither difficult to learn nor hard to do. One's first project can be a beautiful and lasting object of art.

Figure 3. Supplies for decoupage include scissors, brushes, sandpaper, steel wool, glue, sealer, finish, wax, and brush cleaner. Most are easily available locally or by mail.

Common Terms Used In Decoupage

Antiquing: a technique using color, most often brown, to "age" an object.

Base Coat: opaque colored paint or wood stain used to cover the raw wood.

Bleeding Print: a print in which the colors run or blur when sealer is applied.

Brayer: a rubber roller for flattening and adhering the cutout to the surface.

Bridge: an uncut connecting strip used to support the delicate parts of a cut out print before it is applied.

Curing: a process of hardening for preservation.

Cutout: a design cut out of a print and used as decoration on the decoupaged object.

Decoupage: the art of decorating surfaces with applied paper designs.

Finish: a clear, lacquer-like liquid used to cover the cutout.

Flowing On: the method of applying finish to the surface over the glued cutout.

Plasti-tak: plastic, sticky material used to hold the cutout to the surface while creating the design.

Sealing: covering with a liquid coating to prevent bleeding or running of color.

Submerging: the process of applying repeated coats of finish to the decorated surface for proper buildup over the design.

Wet Sanding: special sandpaper and water used to smooth and level the decorated and coated surfaces of a project.

Basic Equipment And Supplies

Before starting any decoupage project it is advisable to assemble all the necessary equipment and supplies. All are craft items and are easily purchased at a local craft shop or from a mail-order craft supplier. Many of the items, such as sandpaper, brushes, glue, turpentine, and steel wool, may be obtained at a hardware or paint store. Pens, India ink, tweezers, colored pencils, and scissors may be found in various retail stores. The special paints and finishes required are best purchased from a craft shop or mail-order craft supplier as ordinary paint stores do not usually stock them.

The selection of the box or plaque to be decoupaged and the print or prints to be used as the decoration should be decided upon first. The other supplies will be governed by this selection. For example, the selection of the plaque and the print will determine what base paint to use; whether antiquing will be desirable; whether to use ornamental trim, lustre wax, or hardware; and the style and type of hardware.

For a first project it is advisable to use a commercially manufactured box or plaque since these are made of new, unfinished wood. Later projects can include beautiful and unusual old wooden boxes containers or plaques, and even furniture, any of which may be purchased at auctions and antique shows.

Design prints for a first project are also best selected from the prints available in craft shops. The possibilities for design are, of course, limitless. It is fun, for future use, to assemble a portfolio of prints, designs, and decorations. Calendars, greeting cards, post cards, illustrations from books or magazines, even wedding announcements are just a few suggestions for sources of material for a portfolio.

Following is a list of basic equipment and supplies, with explanations regarding their use.

WOOD PLAQUE OR BOX

A plaque is a flat, shaped piece of wood. The size of a particular plaque should be determined by the area of wall to be covered, the decor of the room in which the plaque will be placed, and the selection of the cutout which will be decoupaged onto the plaque surface.

Wooden boxes are probably the most popular objects for modern decoupage. Selection of a box should be determined by the way it will be used and how it is to be decorated. Boxes come in various styles, depending on whether or not they require hinges and on the type of closure.

Both first-project boxes and plaques should be of new wood, free of knots, properly kiln dried and pre-sanded to a reasonable smoothness. They should be small in size.

Figure 4. Wood plaques and boxes are popular items for beginning decoupage projects. Boxes and plaques should be small, and made of good quality new wood.

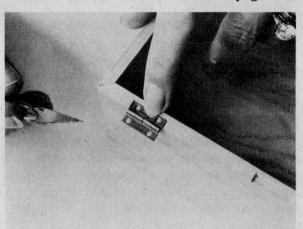

Figure 5. Hinges are a basic supply item in decoupage; notches for adding them are made with a "V"-tool. Choose the type and size of hinges at the time the box is chosen.

WOOD PUTTY

This comes as a powder and is mixed with enough water to form a stiff paste. The paste is applied to the holes and other imperfections on the plaque or box and allowed to dry. It is then sanded smooth. Do not mix more wood putty than will be used at one time. The mixture hardens quickly and cannot be reused.

HARDWARE

Hardware is the metal trim, closure devices, or clasps used on boxes; hangers for plaques; and decorative rings on the top of plaques which may be used for hanging or just as decorations.

If hinges are required with a particular type of box, they may be either concealed inside the box or applied as added decoration to the outside. Concealed hinges are usually rectangular in shape while outside hinges usually have decorative shapes. For best artistic results selection of hardware should be made at the time the box is selected.

PRINT

The "print" is the decorative paper print design or drawing which is applied to the surface being decoupaged. As previously recommended, a commercially produced, new, colored print should be used for a first project.

The thickness of a print is of great importance because it determines the number of coats of finish necessary to "submerge" the print after it has been cut out and glued to the surface. Embossed cards, post cards, and other thick paper prints should generally be avoided for first projects.

Black and white or uncolored prints may be used but also are not recommended as a first project because such prints must be hand-colored. Furthermore, some types of paper should not be used for decoupage, such as newspaper, wallpaper, and other papers where the quality of the paper and the printing ink are inferior.

ORNAMENTAL PAPER TRIM

This is an optional item on boxes and plaques. The most commonly seen trim is a gold-embossed paper, used as borders, on corners, or as the dominant design. Ornamental paper trim comes in various widths, shapes, patterns, and colors. Trim should also be selected when the design is planned.

SCISSORS

Scissors are the basic decoupage tool and should be of top quality. Be sure that they fit the hand comfortably and that a sharp, fine cut can be achieved with little effort.

Decoupage scissors are similar to cuticle scissors, having a curved blade. The curved shape and short length of blade insures a proper cut. Straight scissors — small scissors with straight blades — are also used in decoupage for preliminary cuts and for straight cuts.

HOBBY KNIFE

This is a sharp-pointed knife which can be used as a substitute for decoupage scissors. It is most effectively used to cut out the small, inaccessible inner areas of a print.

Figure 6. This selection of prints demonstrates the wide variety of subject matter available to the decoupage artist. Beginners will find it easier to use a commercially prepared print.

PLASTI-TAK

Plasti-tak is a sticky, plastic material used to hold the cutout print on the wooden object or pattern paper while creating the design. Plasti-tak will not mar the wood surface or leave sticky residues on either the wood or the paper. It can be reused and should be kept in one wad.

TWEEZERS

Tweezers are an optional, but frequently useful tool. They are used to lift delicately cut prints onto the pasted surface of an object to be decoupaged. Long-nosed tweezers are best.

SANDPAPER

Three weights of sandpaper are necessary for any project: #220, #400, and #600. The #400 and #600 must be "wet" sandpapers. One package of the three combined weights is sufficient for one project.

SANDING BLOCK

A hand-sized block of wood with a felt pad attached to the underside should be used when sanding whenever possible. A surface sanded in this manner is more level than would be possible if the sanding were done by hand alone.

BASE PAINT

Base paint is used to cover the raw wood before the print is glued on. Colored oil- or water-based paint or wood stain may be used. A two-ounce jar should be a sufficient amount for one project.

Water-based paints are used with lacquer-type synthetic, quick-drying finishes. Oil-based paints are used with varnish finish. Water-based paints and wood stains are suggested for a first project because they are quick drying, need little or no sanding and are compatible with quick-drying finishes.

BRUSHES

The average decoupage project requires three brushes: a one-inch brush for the base paint (nylon bristles for water-base, natural bristle for oil-base); a one-inch nylon brush with tapered tip for finish coats (except varnish, which requires natural bristles); and one small artist's brush for various small tasks.

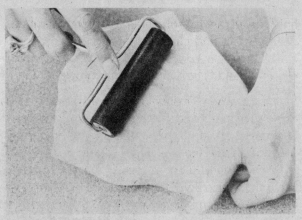

Figure 7. Use a brayer to secure the design to the surface. To protect the print, first place a clean cloth over the design, then roll the brayer back and forth briskly.

INDIA INK

This is a waterproof ink used for limning the fine lines of a design which are too difficult to cut. It can be applied with a pen or a very fine brush — the pen is easier to use. If a mistake is made the ink can be removed with a damp sponge before it is dry.

PEN

A pen is used to apply an ink signature or additional fine lines on the design. A "fine" nib is recommended.

GLUE

A white, clear-drying glue should be used for adhering print and trim to the painted or stained surface of the object to be decoupaged. One two-ounce bottle of glue is sufficient for several projects.

BRAYER

A brayer, a rubber roller attached to a handle, is used to adhere the design to the painted or stained surface by rolling it back and forth over the glued print. The brayer not only sticks the design down, it also helps to eliminate air pockets and any excess glue under the design.

A brayer should never be rolled in direct contact with the print. To do so might mar the colored surface of the design. Therefore, a clean lint-free dampened cloth is placed over the surface of the design before the brayer is used.

Figure 8. The decoupage on this box, designed by Fran Otnes, incorporates elements from many magazine illustrations and paintings. (By permission from Lithopinion #27, the graphic arts and public affairs journal of Local One, Amalgamated Lithographers of America and lithographic employers, New York. © 1973 by Local One, A.L.A. Photo by Wayne Ponton.)

SEALER

Sealer is a shellac-type coating which is used, in spray form, to seal the raw wood and prevent color variations from showing through the base paints. It is also used to seal the colors of the prints and to seal color when a project is antiqued. One can of sealer spray should be sufficient for a single project. It is advisable to purchase a sealer of the same brand as the finish and the brush cleaner to ensure that they are compatible.

FINISH

Finish is the clear, liquid coating used to "submerge" the cutout design glued to the painted surface of the wooden object being decoupaged. One quart is an adequate amount for a single project. There are two types of finish: one is a synthetic, lacquer-type finish; the other is a varnish. Because the former is quick-drying and is quicker and easier to apply than varnish, it is recommended for first projects. Finish is applied with a brush which should not be used for any other purpose. Finish should be stirred with a wooden stick so that it is always thoroughly mixed. It should never be shaken to mix.

Varnish is a natural finish. It is thinned with turpentine and one coat takes about eight to twelve hours to dry. It should be stirred, not shaken, and applied with a brush used only for this purpose.

BRUSH CLEANER

This is a special liquid used for cleaning the brushes used to apply synthetic, lacquer-type finishes. A one-pint can of brush cleaner should be sufficient for one project. For easier use, it should be stored in a small glass jar, but large enough to accommodate the brush being cleaned. The lid of the jar should be metal and tight-fitting. Brush cleaner can be used repeatedly and replaced only when it becomes too thick with excess finish.

TURPENTINE

Turpentine is used to clean varnish brushes, to thin varnish, and to mix with oil color for antiquing.

ANTIQUE COLOR

Antique color is applied after the print or prints

Figure 9. Imaginative use of decoupage on egg cups, by Fran Otnes. (By permission from Lithopinion #32, *the graphic arts and public affairs journal of Local One, Amalgamated Lithographers of America and lithographic employers, New York. © 1973 by Local One, A.L.A. Photo by Wayne Ponton.)*

have been glued on and several coats of finish have been applied. The purpose of the antique color is to yield an aged, antique look or to subdue color.

STEEL WOOL

Steel wool, #0000 weight, is used dry as a buffing agent to give sanded surfaces of a decorated object a soft patina or shine. When using the steel wool on a surface, rub with a brisk, *straight* motion so that the surface becomes warm to the touch. A hand-rubbed, soft shine is the desired effect. One small package of steel wool should be sufficient for one project.

FINISHING POWDER AND OIL

Finishing powder mixed with finishing oil is an additional and optional buffing process. It is used to add to the patina of the finish.

LUSTRE WAX

Lustre wax is a solid, decorative wax available in gold, silver, copper, and other metallic colors as well as in paint colors. It can be used instead of ornamental trim as a decoration on the edges of plaques and boxes or to adorn inside surfaces.

CLEAR WAX

Clear wax is applied to add shine and to protect the decorated surface. One two-ounce jar is sufficient to wax several projects.

COLORED PENCILS

Artists' colored pencils may be used to delineate fine lines on color prints which are too fine to cut. They may also be used to color black and white prints and to repair damage where premature or too-deep sanding has whitened or spoiled the colored surface of a print. Colored pencils are an optional item.

LINING MATERIAL

Lining material is used to line and decorate the backs of plaques and the inner parts of boxes. There is a wide choice of linings, such as velveteen, cotton, silk, or brocade. Felt is an excellent lining for the backs of plaques.

Linings for boxes should be selected to coordinate with the exterior decoration on the box, both in color and in style. These should be installed only after the outer surfaces of a box are completely finished.

Basic Procedures

After assembling all necessary supplies, the decoupeur is ready to begin. Close attention must first be given to planning the design for the project. This will display the decoupeur's creative ability.

THE DESIGN

There are several things to remember when planning a design. Be sure that the color of the base paint will complement and enhance the design. Make sure that the design dominates its area. A large expanse of plain painted wood is dull and uninteresting.

In planning a design, it is helpful to draw the exact outlines of the shape of the box or plaque to be decoupaged on a piece of plain paper. Then, with tweezers, place the cutout print on the paper. Arrange the design to fit each area. If necessary, cut the design apart, shift the cut pieces, and add or combine prints. When the design has been decided upon, the cutouts may then be held in place with plasti-tak.

In planning and laying out a design, the print or prints may extend over the slot between the edges of the base and lid of a box. The print will be slit along the opening after it has been glued and the glue has dried. Ornamental trim may be used in a similar manner.

CUTTING

The manual skills of cutting prints and designs should be practiced before starting a project. Select prints from magazines or similar sources as practice material. Attention should be paid to the shape of the subject matter being cut out. For example, blades of grass should be sharp, clouds or edges of garments should be soft and flowing. A simple way to judge a well-cut print is to reverse it and view it from the back. If the design is still pleasing, it has met the test.

Figure 10. A delicate design featuring birds was used for this decoupaged box. Decoupage is generally associated with traditional styles of interior decoration, although some artists have used the technique in innovative ways.

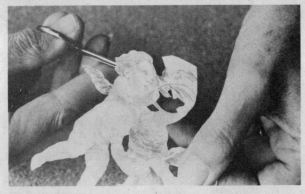

Figure 11. Cutting must be done with care and precision. Inside areas should be done first (top), leaving the outside area for last (bottom). A knife can be used for the outside cutting.

Cutting is important and must be planned. Analyze the print to determine where to make the first cut. Ordinarily, inside cuts and contained areas where cuts do not go out to the edge should be cut first. Both the decoupage scissors and hobby knife are good for such cuts. When scissors are used for inner cuts, the scissors should be held underneath the print. This exposes the cutting action. Use straight scissors to trim away any excess paper around the outside of the print. The outline of the print is always cut last, with either decoupage scissors or knife. (The procedure for cutting the outline is described later under *Essential Instructions.*)

If the outer parts of the print are intricate or delicate, "bridges" of paper should be left, to be cut last. If a print is to be torn, the outer edge should not be trimmed away. When tearing, tear the edge of the print to create an uneven edge, leaving enough plain paper around the print to enhance the design. Always tear the edge away from the print with a downward motion so that the bevelled edge projects from the top or printed side.

ESSENTIAL INSTRUCTIONS

Decoupage is not a craft to be rushed. Read the following instructions carefully to become familiar with the entire procedure. An understanding of these instructions will minimize mistakes and produce a first project of which one can be proud.

Making Surface Repairs

Examine the surface of the wooden box or plaque to be decoupaged for dents, knots or cracks. These cannot be hidden with base paints or stains. If imperfections are found, fill and repair them with wood putty. Apply the wood putty mixture with a finger or hobby knife. Work it into the imperfection on the box or plaque. Immediately smooth the place with the flat edge of a hobby knife blade. Wipe away any excess putty. Allow the wood putty to dry and sand it smooth with #220 sandpaper. If the box or plaque is to be stained with a water-based wood stain and not painted, substitute the wood stain for plain water when mixing the wood putty. The wood putty repair will then match the color of the wooden surfaces of the box or plaque once they have been stained.

Concealed Hinges

If concealed hinges are to be used, proper notches must be cut in the box base and the lid. On the edges of the base and lid (using the hinge for a pattern), mark the notch outlines with the hobby knife. Cut the notch to the marks with the knife. Make the cuts just deep enough to accommodate the thickness of the hinge. Notches in base and lid should be the same depth and at matching points.

Figure 12. Dents or cracks in the wood should be carefully filled in with wood putty. Apply the putty with a hobby knife, as shown, or with the fingertip. Smooth the surface immediately.

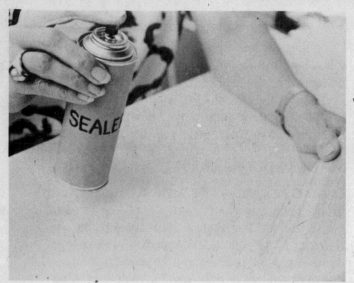

Figure 13. After the wood has been smoothed and sanded, apply sealer from a spray can. Hold the spray can about 12" from the wood, and apply a light even coat over the outside of the object.

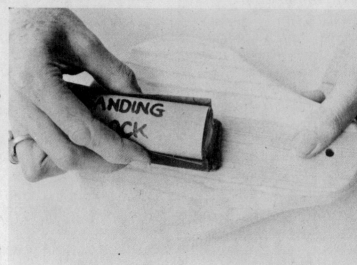

Figure 14. Use a sanding block, rather than just a sheet of sandpaper, for the sanding process. Paper is wrapped around the block and held there by pressure from the hand.

Sealing

Seal the wood object by spraying with sealer. To do this, hold the object about 12 inches from the spray can and spray three light, even coats over all outer surfaces of the object. Allow 30 minutes for each coat to dry. After the last coat of sealer has dried, sand all the sealed surfaces. Use #220 sandpaper on a sanding block.

When using a sanding block, a sheet of sandpaper four inches square is wrapped around the felt surface of the sanding block (sanding surface down). It is held on the block by finger pressure. Apply light, even pressure. The sanding block should be used both when sanding raw wood and when the surface is being leveled after the design has been submerged by the finish coats. Sand with the grain of the wood. Repeat the sanding and sealing processes twice.

If the base paint is to be a wood stain instead of a colored paint, omit the sealing process and sand surfaces smooth. Wipe sanded surfaces clean.

Applying the Base Paint

Thoroughly mix the base paint. Water-based paint is best applied with a one-inch brush in several thin coats. It can be thinned as necessary with water and mixed by shaking the jar. Apply a thin, even coat of base paint to all surfaces which are exposed or which will be coated with finish. If a

partition box is being used, remove the partitions and paint them separately.

Apply paint along the length of the grain. Wipe out any drips and runs while the paint is still wet. Suspend the painted object on a can so that the paint can dry. The number of coats of base paint necessary to cover the raw wood varies. Light-colored paints require at least two coats. Dark-colored raw wood will always need a minimum of three coats when being covered with a light-colored paint. Proper coverage with colored base paints requires a complete opacity, with no wood surface showing. Two or three coats of paint is usually sufficient to achieve this.

Water-based paint dries quickly, usually in 15 to 30 minutes. Each additional coat of paint should be applied only when the prior coat is fully dry. Water-based paint should not be sanded between coats but may be sanded after the final coat has dried 12 hours. Light hand sanding with dry #400 sandpaper should be done to eliminate runs and drips, but minor roughness need not be sanded. Clean the brush immediately after each coat so that the paint will not dry on the brush.

For decoupage work, oil-based paints should be flat enamels. They may be used as base paints only when varnish coats are used to submerge the print. Flat enamel should be used because varnish adheres to it better than to glossy enamels.

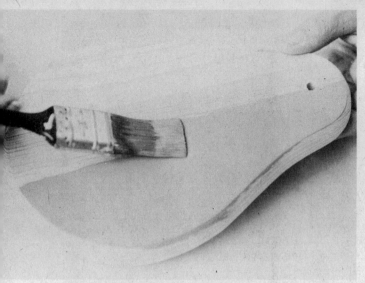

Figure 15. Apply paint with the grain of the wood, as shown. The number of coats needed will depend on a number of factors, such as the color of the paint and the darkness of the wood.

Each coat of an oil-based paint takes 6 to 12 hours to dry. Thin, light coats applied with a one-inch brush are recommended. Each coat should be lightly sanded with #400 sandpaper. Oil-based paint is thinned with turpentine and should be stirred to mix. Because oil-based paint and compatible varnish coats are slow drying, with repeated sanding necessary, they are not suggested for a first project.

Applying Wood Stain

Wood stains follow the same basic procedures for mixing and for use and cleaning of brushes as colored paints. These are used when a wood-grain background is desired. A water-based stain is recommended. The wood should not be sealed when a wood stain is used as the stain will not penetrate sealed wood.

Wood stain, which is mixed by just shaking the jar, should be applied in a thin coat with a one-inch brush and can be thinned as necessary with water. A two-ounce jar of stain is usually a sufficient quantity to do one project. Because water-based stain dries quickly (10 to 15 minutes), the stained wood should be wiped clean with paper towel immediately after the stain is applied. Repeat stain coats — wiping after every coat — until the desired shade of darkening is achieved. Allow base paint or stain to dry 12 hours before next step.

Preparing the Print

"Peeling" a print means reducing the thickness of the paper. This is done by first soaking the print in a solution of vinegar and water. Then, starting at an edge of the soaked print, split the layers of paper by peeling away the back (uncolored) part. When the print has been reduced to the desired thickness, it should be allowed to dry before cutting.

Place uncut print on sheets of newspaper and spray only the printed side with a light, even coat of sealer. If the print does not "bleed" when the sealer is applied, it is ready to be cut or torn. If the print bleeds, discard it.

If ornamental trim is to be used, the trim should be sprayed with three light coats of sealer. Let dry between coats. (Gold-embossed trim may be changed to silver by using a paper towel to rub paint-brush cleaner on the gold paper. This removes the gold finish.)

Figure 16. Wooden blocks by Fran Otnes. (By permission from Lithopinion #32, the graphic arts and public affairs journal of Local One, Amalgamated Lithographers of America and lithographic employers, New York. © 1973 by Local One, A.L.A. Photo by Wayne Ponton.)

After determining what part of the design is to be used and what part is to be cut away, cut or tear the print. The proper cut of any print used in decoupage is a bevel cut. A bevel cut means cutting the paper so that the cut edge is rounded toward the underside. To achieve a bevel cut, hold the decoupage scissors with the blades resting against the index finger. The curve of the scissor blades must be toward the back of the hand. Hold the cutting hand so that its palm is turned up enough to have the scissors cut at a slant, with the bottom blade closer to the cutting line. Hold the print loosely in the opposite hand. The paper should be turned as cutting progresses. Learn to move the paper constantly so as to cut an uneven, interesting edge. The cutting hand does not move.

If a hobby knife is used, the cutting part of the blade should be held at a 45-degree angle with the surface of the print. With smooth, even pressure guide the blade of the knife along the lines of the print which are to be cut. It is helpful to do knife cutting on a smooth, hard surface, such as masonite or plywood. When properly used, the knife makes a clean, sharp cut. Practice with scrap paper to perfect a proper cutting technique.

Next, spray two light coats of sealer on the colored side of the cut or torn print. Sprayed sealer coats on prints take about 10 minutes to dry.

Applying the Design

Using a finish brush, apply one coat of finish to the painted or stained wood. This coat of finish will be the base on which the design is glued. One brush-on coat is sufficient; it should be allowed to dry several hours.

Lay out the design on a paper outline of the box or plaque or on the box or plaque itself. When satisfied with the design, use plasti-tak to hold it in place until it can be glued. If trim is to be used, the necessary amount should be measured out at this time, but not cut.

After the finish has dried, glue on the cut out or torn print and any ornamental trim. To do so, moisten the back of the print with a damp sponge. Then, using the fingers, spread an even coating of glue on the surface where the print will go. Using tweezers if necessary, carefully place the print in position on the glued area. Press down with the

Figure 17. The design should be planned, laid out, and arranged carefully before it is applied permanently. Let the pieces dry on a model of the wood or on the wood object itself.

fingers to adhere all parts. Excess glue on the face of the print can be wiped away later.

Cover the glued print with a damp cloth and roll with the brayer to stick the print down flat. When using the brayer, start at the center of the design area and gently press and roll the entire design. Lift the cloth to determine that the design has been properly glued down and that air bubbles and excess glue under the print have been eliminated. Replace the cloth and reroll with the brayer if necessary. Stubborn air bubbles can be pricked with a pin to allow air to escape. Edges which have not stuck may be brushed with extra glue and restuck.

For ornamental trims, apply glue with a brush; glue in place and cut, miter, and remove extra pieces of trim as necessary. Brush the trim with a coat of glue to act as a sealer.

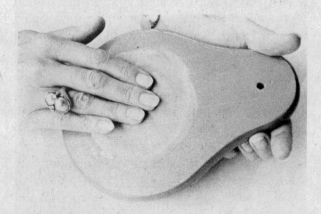

Figure 18. Spread a coat of glue on the prepared wood, using the fingers as shown. Then place the print in the proper position and smooth down with the fingers. Wipe away excess glue.

After the design is thoroughly glued but before any excess glue is dry, the painted part of the wood and the print face should be wiped clean with a damp sponge.

Now is the time to apply a signature to the project, if desired, using India ink and a pen. Any design feature which was too fine to cut, such as raindrops, butterfly antennae, or reins of horses, also can now be drawn in ink. Allow the project to dry 24 hours and reseal both the glued print and ink additions with spray sealer.

Applying Finish

Mix the finish thoroughly. Using the flow-on method, apply the proper number of finish coats to the area being decoupaged. (The flowing-on of a coat is done by first loading the brush with finish. Then, while holding the brush at a 45-degree angle, allow the finish to flow onto the surface. Do not go back and "brush smooth.") If the piece is to be antiqued, only six finish coats should be applied at this stage. If the project is a plaque with no ornamental trim and it is not being antiqued, 15 coats should be applied. If it is a box and it is not being antiqued, 20 coats should be applied. Between coats, suspend the project on a can above the work surface.

If a plaque or box has a fairly large area, each successive coat should be flowed-on at an angle 90 degrees to the direction in which the prior coat was applied. Edges of boxes and plaques not decorated by prints should not have finish flowed-on. Rather, they should be coated using a brushing action, so that the excess finish will not drip.

After each coat is applied, remove any bubbles or lint. It is not necessary to sand after each coat. After all necessary coats have been applied, let the piece cure for 24 hours.

Antiquing

If the project is to be antiqued, six coats of finish must first be applied over the print. Then spray or paint the antique color on all surfaces to be antiqued and allow to dry for only two or three minutes. Next, using paper towels, wipe to the desired degree of darkness. Allow antiquing to dry 24 hours. Seal carefully with spray sealer, using sufficient coats to cover completely. Allow sealer to dry several hours, then apply an additional 10 coats of finish. The first several coats of finish over the antiquing should be applied in the same direction as the antique streaking. Allow the project 24 hours to cure.

Sanding

Sand with #400 wet sandpaper. Using water with detergent added, wet the sandpaper and the wood surface. Carefully sand the outline made by the raised edges of the cut out print. If the cutout is not damaged by this hand-sanding, a sanding block can then be used. Sand until level. Wipe dry periodically to determine when the surface is smooth, level, and dull. When a proper surface has been achieved, wipe clean with clear water and dry.

After the first stage of sanding has been completed, apply an additional 10 coats of finish. Allow the piece to dry and cure for two to three weeks. Then, repeat the wet sanding with #400 wet sandpaper, using the sanding block on flat areas and hand-sanding on edges. Sand in the direction of the print or with the grain of the wood. Sand all surfaces until smooth and dull, leaving no low or shiny spots.

Next, repeat the wet sanding process using #600 wet sandpaper. Continue until the surface has a soft patina or shine. Wipe surface dry.

Figure 19. For antiquing, first apply six coats of finish to the object. Then brush or spray the antique color on the surfaces to be covered. Rub the color into the surface with a paper towel.

Figure 20. Trim a piece of cardboard to fit the space to be lined; then cut the lining larger than the pattern on all sides (top). The lining should fit the box snugly (bottom).

Polishing and Waxing

Polish with #0000 steel wool, rubbing briskly in the same direction as for sanding. The friction of hard rubbing makes the surface warm. This is normal. Rub until the correct soft shine is achieved. This takes time.

If more shine is desired, use finishing powder and oil. Apply with felt. Rub in the same direction as the steel wool. When the desired shine is achieved, remove excess powder and oil with a clean cloth.

Use a clear wax for decorated surfaces. Apply an even coat with a damp cloth and allow it to dry. Buff with a flannel cloth to shine.

Lining the Plaque or Box

Apply lining to back of plaque or insides of box. To cover the back of a plaque, first make a paper pattern of the plaque. Transfer the pattern to the lining material. Felt or contact paper may be glued directly in place, but velvet or other lining materials should be glued to cardboard first. Apply glue to back of plaque and position lining. Use brayer to adhere smoothly. Be sure lining on back of plaque is not visible from the front.

Box linings should be mounted on cardboard before being installed. Cut the cardboard pieces to fit sides, bottom, and lid; cut the lining material one-half inch larger on all sides than the cardboard patterns. Miter the corners by diagonally cutting off the overlap at the corners. Fold fabric back over the cardboard and glue one-half inch of material (preferably at the top edge) to the back of the cardboard patterns. Put lining pieces in place to test fit before gluing. Adjust as necessary by trimming cardboard at the bottom edge. Glue side linings in place first, bottom last.

Using Lustre Wax

If additional decoration or trim is needed, lustre wax may be used. It can be applied straight from the jar with the finger, or it can be diluted with turpentine and applied with a brush. If a mistake is made or the effect is not the one desired, the lustre wax may be removed by wiping with a paper towel dampened in turpentine. Allow to dry five minutes and buff with paper towel.

Attaching Hardware

The final step is attaching hardware. Position it on the object and mark the holes for screws with an awl. Then make holes with the awl at the places marked. Insert screws and turn in until heads are flush with the hardware surface.

Hinges are attached to the base of the box first, screws installed only half way. Then mark screw holes on lid with awl. Attach lid to base with hinge by installing screw in lid half way. Then tighten all screws. Install any other hardware items in the same manner.

Figure 21. After the box is lined, apply the hinges and hardware. Mark the screw holes with an awl, then use the awl to make the holes. Insert screws so that the heads are flush with the surface.

Projects You Can Do

Interest in a craft is stimulated by a particular project. The projects here are meant to give ideas for projects one might want to undertake. The mushroom plaque and antique trunk box projects detailed here are excellent projects for beginners. They incorporate all the basic techniques needed to learn the craft of decoupage without sacrifice of utility or beauty.

MUSHROOM PLAQUE

The necessary supplies for making a mushroom plaque are: (1) a wooden bread-board plaque; (2) a mushroom print; (3) dusk blue water-based paint; (4) one package of wet sandpaper, including #220, #400, and #600; (5) spray sealer; (6) a sanding block; (7) base paint brush; (8) scissors; (9) finish brush; (10) glue; (11) brayer; (12) one pint of synthetic lacquer finish; (13) one pint of brush cleaner; (14) #0000 steel wool; (15) clear wax; (16) lining material; and (17) hardware (a bracket for hanging).

Procedures

1. Examine wood for cracks or imperfections. Fill

Figure 22. The decoupage craftsman can create a variety of interesting gifts. These two purses (left) are good examples. The egg-shapes mounted on stands were also decoupaged (right).

with wood putty if necessary. Allow wood putty to dry.

2. Sand wood with grain, using #220 sandpaper on sanding block. Hand sand the end grain on the edge of plaque.

3. Spray-seal wood with sealer. At proper intervals, spray and seal two additional coats.

4. Apply base paint to wood by brush. Allow paint to dry 30 minutes. Add additional coats sufficient to cover. Allow base paint 12 hours to dry.

5. Stir lacquer finish. Brush one coat of lacquer finish on painted wood. Allow lacquer finish coat one hour to dry.

6. Cut out print. Spray-seal print with three coats of sealer.

7. Glue print to wood. Sign with ink. Dry 12 hours.

8. Spray-seal print and signature with sealer.

9. Apply 15 coats of lacquer finish over painted and decorated surface by brush, at one hour intervals. Use flow-on method over top surface but brush finish on edges of the wood. Rotate the direction of each coat 90 degrees. After last coat, allow to dry 24 hours.

10. Wet-sand by hand, using #400 sandpaper, until level and dull. Clean with water. Let dry.

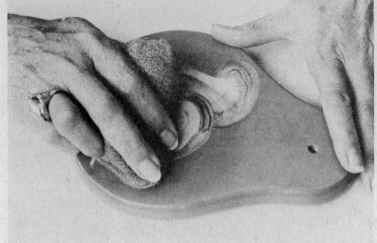

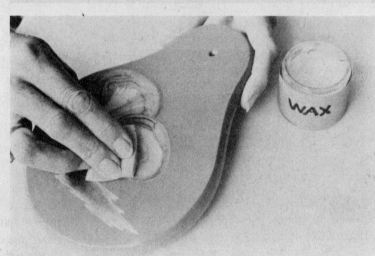

Figure 23. To finish the mushroom plaque project, coat the design with lacquer and wet-sand the dried finish (above). Later steps are buffing with steel wool and applying wax, which is buffed with a soft cloth (above right). The finished plaque (below right) makes an attractive wall decoration.

11. Apply an additional 10 coats of lacquer finish. Use procedure in step 9. Allow coats to cure for at least 48 hours. For better results, let the project cure several weeks.

12. Wet-sand with sanding block, using #400 sandpaper, until level and dull. Sand with grain, except edges.

13. Wet-sand with sanding block, using #600 sandpaper, until soft shine is achieved. Sand with grain except edges.

14. With #0000 steel wool, buff with the grain until desired shine is achieved.

15. Apply wax. Buff with soft cloth.

16. Measure, cut, and glue lining.

17. Install bracket for hanging.

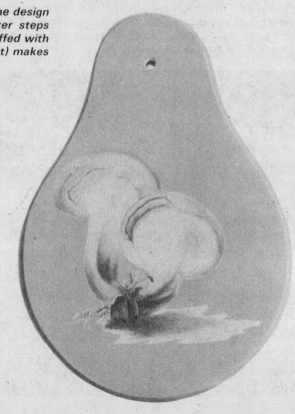

Figure 24. The second project is an antiqued trunk-shaped box. This box has been trimmed with gold embossed braid and lined with velvet. A dark shade of antiquing was used.

ANTIQUE TRUNK BOX

Necessary supplies for this project are: (1) a trunk-shaped wood box; (2) a print (antique in character); (3) rust-color water-based paint; (4) gold embossed braid; (5) plasti-tak; (6) umber spray antique; (7) concealed hinges; (8) hobby knife; (9) scissors; (10) one package of wet sandpaper, including #220, #400, and #600; (11) spray sealer; (12) sanding block; (13) base paint brush; (14) finish brush; (15) glue; (16) brayer; (17) one quart of synthetic lacquer finish; (18) one pint of brush cleaner; (19) #0000 steel wool; (20) clear wax; and (21) velvet for lining.

Procedures

1. Examine wood for cracks or imperfections. If necessary, fill with wood putty. Allow wood putty to dry.

2. Sand wood with grain, using #220 sandpaper on sanding block.

3. With knife, cut notches for hinges in both box base and box lid.

4. Spray-seal wood with sealer. At proper drying intervals, spray and seal two additional coats.

5. Apply base paint to box base and box lid by brush. Allow paint to dry 30 minutes. Add additional coats sufficient to cover. Allow base paint to dry 12 hours.

6. Stir lacquer finish and apply one coat to painted wood with a brush. Allow finish coat one hour to dry.

7. Cut out print. Spray-seal print and gold braid trim with three coats of sealer. Use plasti-tak at box corners to hold box base and box lid together. Plan design.

8. Glue print and gold braid trim to wood. Top coat gold braid trim with glue. Sign with ink. Dry 12 hours.

9. Spray-seal print and signature with sealer.

10. Using the hobby knife, slit print and gold braid extending over box opening. Remove plasti-tak from corners of box.

11. Apply with brush six coats of lacquer finish over all painted and decorated surfaces. Allow one hour drying time between coats. Use flow-on method over decorated surfaces and brush-on method on edges of box. After last coat, allow to dry 24 hours.

12. Spray antique. Wipe for streaked effect to give desired shade of darkness. Allow antiquing to dry 24 hours.

13. Spray-seal entire antiqued area.

14. Apply 15 coats of lacquer finish, by brush, over all painted and decorated surfaces. Allow one hour drying time between coats. Use flow-on method over all painted and decorated surfaces, brush-on method on edges. After last coat, allow to dry 24 hours.

15. Wet-sand by hand, using #400 sandpaper, until surface is level and dull. Clean with water. Let dry.

16. Apply an additional 10 coats of lacquer finish. Use procedure in step 14. Allow coats to cure a minimum of 48 hours. If possible, let cure several weeks for best results.

17. Wet-sand with sanding block, using #400 sandpaper, until level and dull. Sand with grain, except edges.

18. Wet-sand with sanding block, using #600 sandpaper, until soft shine is achieved. Sand with grain, except edges.

19. Using #0000 steel wool, buff with grain until desired shine is achieved.

20. Apply wax. Buff with soft cloth.

21. Measure, cut, and glue lining in box base and box lid.

22. Install hinges on box base and box lid.

Figure 25. These boxes, each very different but handsome, suggest the many design possibilities in decoupage. The shape of the box, the color of the finish, and the prints are all factors in design.

For Additional Reading

Harrower, Dorothy, **Decoupage: A Limitless World in Decoration,** M. Barrows, 1958.

Hukel, Virginia, "Exquisite Decoupage Art," **Decorating and Craft Ideas Made Easy,** Oct. 1971.

Manning, Hiram, **Manning on Decoupage,** Hearthside, 1969.

Nimock, Patricia, **Decoupage,** Scribner, 1968.

Nimock, Patricia, "Tops In Tables," **Needles and Craft for the Creative Woman,** Spring/Summer, 1974.

Robertson, Joyce, "Under Cover of Glass," **Decorating and Craft Ideas Made Easy,** Mar. 1972.

Wing, Frances S., **The Complete Book of Decoupage,** Coward-McCann, 1965-70.

Paper Crafts

Paper, one of the most versatile of the craft mediums, offers limitless opportunities for creativity and imagination.

Although the word "paper" is derived from papyrus, which is a plant used by the Egyptians as early as 2400 B.C. to make a paper-like material on which they wrote, it is not known when or by whom the process of paper-making was discovered. It is generally believed, however, to be of Asian origin. By 300 B.C. the Chinese, who attribute the discovery of paper-making to one of their ancient statesmen, were using papers made from silk wastes for painting and writing. Paper was also being used in Taiwan (Formosa) and Korea before the Christian Era.

Figure 1. The Japanese have put paper to many novel uses. Among the most familiar of these is the paper kite. (Courtesy, The Smithsonian Institution, Washington, D.C.)

Figure 2. Papyrus is one of the most ancient forms of paper-like material. This Greek fragment (above) is inscribed with Euclidean geometry. (Courtesy, Chicago Natural History Museum.)

Throughout history almost every country has used paper in many ways other than writing or communication. The fine arts of painting, watercolor, and drawing, now usually done on canvas, were mostly produced on paper. In Mexico, where festivals have always been popular, paper was used for papier-mâché pinatas, banners, flags, and often even for costumes. The Japanese, famous for the artistic use of paper through *origami* and wood block prints, have long used paper in everyday life as well as for trimmings at festivals. The walls of many Japanese homes are built of thin translucent sheets of paper stretched across bamboo and wooden frames; Japanese kites in the form of a fish or large dragon are familiar sights. Indeed, there are similar special uses of paper for every country of the world.

The modern art of quilling was first known in the fifteenth century as rolled paper work. Later, in the seventeenth century, Italian nuns meticulously rolled small bits of paper around the quill end of a bird feather to use in decorating religious pieces of manuscript and ornamental plaques. Quilling spread through France, England, and then to colonial America as a craft which often replaced embroidery or tapestry work as a pastime.

Papier-mâché, the art of molding wastepaper,

was first introduced in France and Germany to use up paper left from newspapers, handbills, and posters. These ground-up papers were mixed with a paste and fashioned into such useful and decorative articles as toys, trays, frames for mirrors or pictures, and sometimes even furniture. Often, very old (200 years or more) and fine pieces of papier-mâché can be found in museums — objects made this way are more durable than might be imagined.

Paper is a significant creative craft material because of its versatility and adaptability. It can be twisted, cut, folded, laminated, lacquered, carved, ground-up, and sculpted. It is truly the most practical of all craft media due to its unusually low price and its availablity in a variety of sizes, shapes, and textures. There are coarse grades of paper, such as cardboard or press board, as well as very fine, expensive papers. Some papers have treated or coated surfaces to allow for special printing effects. Some are decorative, such as the very expensive and famous Japanese papers which have dried flowers, leaves, and butterflies pressed right into them. The type of paper used for paper craft depends upon the project. There are papers particularly suited to specific projects and each is easily obtained.

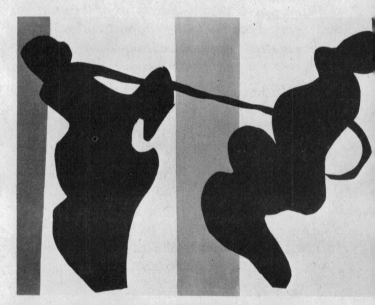

Figure 3. Henri Matisse's color stencil, "The Cowboy," demonstrates this artist's brilliant use of cut paper forms. (Courtesy, Collection, The Museum of Modern Art, New York. Gift of the Artist.)

Common Terms Used In Paper Crafts

Curl: to run paper over the straight side of a table, ruler, or edge of pair of scissors.

Expansion: the cutting and folding of paper to create expanded forms.

Grain: the direction in which the fibers of the paper run and in which the paper will roll the easiest.

Mash: the ground-up paper used in papier-mâché; can be sculpted and sanded.

Papier-Mâché: the art of working paper mixed with glue into forms and shapes.

Quill: to roll quilling paper into various shapes.

Quilling: the art of filigreed paper folding and rolling; openwork.

Score: to run across the paper with a blunt knife or dull scissors blade in order to break the top layer of the grain of the paper and achieve a crisp fold line.

Weight: the thickness of paper.

Basic Equipment And Supplies

The supplies necessary for paper crafts are easily acquired at crafts stores and often already on hand. A list of materials includes a variety of brushes for painting and applying glue; paper clips; a compass; polymer gloss medium; white craft glue; gesso, a glue and oil liquid; an X-acto knife for detailed work, a blade knife, and a dull kitchen knife for scoring; pencils; straight pins; a ruler with a metal edge; T-square; a stapler; scotch tape; and finally, of course, a variety of paper, including newspaper, medium-weight drawing paper, cardboard, colored tissue paper, quilling paper, waxed paper, and graph paper.

Basic Procedures

In order to facilitate the making of paper projects, it is best to learn at the outset some fundamental procedures in the manipulation of paper. Each of the techniques discussed here includes a small exercise to demonstrate its use, as well as to provide familiarity in working with paper. Because each new skill is based on a skill previously described, it will be to the reader's advantage to follow this section step-by-step. It would be best to use a medium-weight drawing paper for these projects; other types of paper can be used once the procedures are learned. Drawing paper can be bought in tablets of 25 or 50 sheets.

FOLDING

There are several ways to use folding as a tool in paper craft. Generally, unless the paper is quite thin, it first needs to be scored and then folded on the score mark. Therefore, draw a line where the fold is needed, then draw a dull knife or dull scissors along the line. Now erase the line and the paper should fold crisply where the score was made.

Straight Fold

As illustrated in the accompanying diagram, score and fold a 10" x 10" piece of paper (medium weight). This will produce the basic or accordion fold, which is used in most folded designs. It takes practice and patience because the paper can be

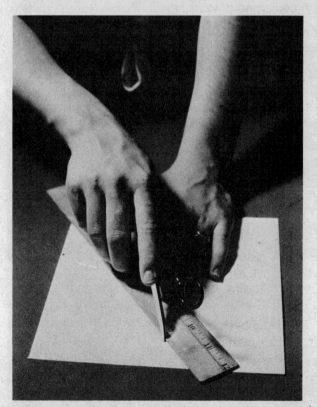

Figure 4. Use a ruler to draw a light line where a fold is needed. Then draw a dull knife or scissors along the line to score the paper for a crisp fold.

Figure 5. Accurate scoring is a necessity when preparing paper for the basic accordion fold.

easily crumpled. Do not try to bend the paper without scoring, or the paper will not form a crisp, even fold.

1. Draw the pattern onto the paper using a ruler and pencil. Make solid lines on one side and dotted lines on the other.

2. Score on the front of the sheet on the solid gray lines.

Figure 6. When the paper is properly scored and folded as shown, the accordion fold is neat and even.

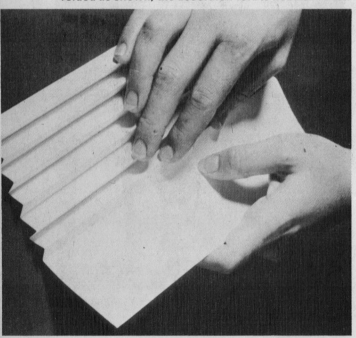

3. Score on the back of the sheet on the dotted gray lines.

4. The paper should begin to crease itself into an accordion fold.

5. Bend the paper carefully without creasing anywhere except on a scored line.

Curved Fold

This fold is slightly harder because it is done working against the grain of the paper.

1. Scale and transfer the diagram illustrated to a sheet of 10" x 10" paper. (Place a sheet of tracing paper over the diagram and trace. Place the tracing over graph paper and count how many squares run across and down the tracing covers.) On the sheet of 10" x 10" paper, draw lightly the same graph but in a larger scale — e.g., one square equals 1/2" or 1". Then, redraw the pattern, extending the lines through the larger squares that correspond to the smaller squares. Again, draw solid lines on one side of the paper and dotted lines on the other side.

2. Carefully score the solid gray lines on the front side of the paper. Then score the dotted gray lines on the back side of the paper. The paper should begin to bend into a three-dimensional surface relief of curves.

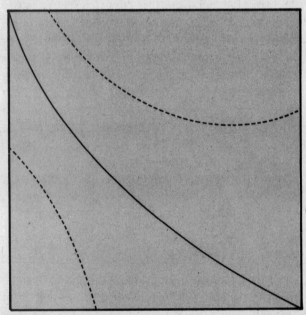

Figure 7. This curved fold pattern is worked against the grain of the paper. Make sure that solid lines are scored on the front side of the paper and dotted lines on the back side.

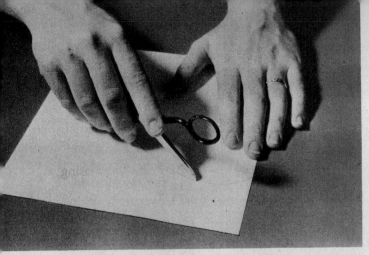

same place lightly two or three times to make the edges precise and crisp rather than press too hard with the knife, causing a rough, jagged cut.

1. On a sheet of scrap paper, with a ruler and pencil, lightly draw a line.

2. Put the ruler next to the line.

3. With the edge of the blade of the X-acto knife next to the metal edge of the ruler, cut precisely along the line.

4. On another scrap of paper, draw a curved line.

5. Without the ruler, practice cutting along curved lines with the knife.

6. Following the diagram, cut along the solid black line as evenly and as carefully as possible, being sure to cut all the way through the paper.

7. Pick up the piece of paper carefully in the center and gravity will pull it into shape, causing expansion.

Figure 8. Hold paper securely while drawing the scissors across the curved fold lines (above). The completed fold (below) was carefully worked to avoid creases in areas other than those scored.

3. Practice with different sheets of paper to see exactly how much of a curve a particular paper will take without creasing in other areas; some papers "give" or stretch better than others.

CUTTING

Cutting is mainly used to create an outer edge and should always be done with some sort of padding underneath, such as several thicknesses of newspaper or a cutting board. Cutting may also be used for decorative slits or for expansion, which is a type of alternating cutting.

Expansion

To become accustomed to working with the paper, cut through a medium sheet of drawing paper several times with an X-acto knife. Work for a precise cut. If the edges of the cut are jagged or rough, either the blade is dull or the knife is being jerked through the paper. It is better to cut the

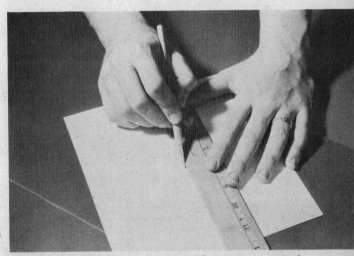

Figure 9. Draw a line on a piece of scrap paper and put the ruler next to the line. Cut along the line with an X-acto knife (above). Then draw a curved line and practice cutting without a ruler (below). Cutting surfaces should always be well padded.

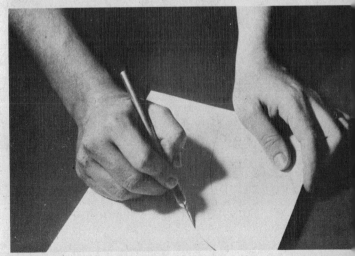

8. Trace the expansion pattern onto a 10″ x 10″ piece of paper.

9. Try more of the illustrated expansion diagrams. Cut along the solid black lines carefully and try a different type of expanded paper form each time.

Figure 10. The diagram (above) for a spiral fold should be carefully cut all the way through the paper along the solid black lines. When the paper is picked up in the center, it will fall into an interesting shape (below).

Cutting and Folding

After completing the expansion exercise, cutting should be much easier and it will be fairly simple to learn the process of cutting and folding. Familiar examples of this cutting procedure are Mexican folk art cutouts and lacy paper doilies. Because the paper is folded first, the resulting designs are almost always symmetrical.

To experiment with cutting and folding, take a piece of square paper and fold it once in half. (Practice cutting with the X-acto knife through folded scrap paper first.)

1. Transfer the pattern in one of the accompanying diagrams to the twice folded piece of paper.

2. Cut along the solid black lines, removing the negative or inner areas and leaving behind the outer form (the piece of paper is still held together).

3. Discard the small cut-out shapes and open the paper. The result will be the same design that was drawn onto the paper.

Figure 11. When paper is folded, cut designs are almost always symmetrical. This paper (below) was folded in half and the inner shapes were cut out.

Figure 12. These folded diagrams will make interesting patterns when the inner portions are cut out.

4. Experiment, using different folding methods, to create original patterns. For example, fold a sheet of paper three times and then in half once. Cut patterns as desired.

Cutting and Scoring

Creating a three-dimensional shape instead of a two-dimensional design with paper is most easily done by cutting and scoring. Each technique, when used alone, has its limits; but when combined, they produce numerous designs.

1. Transfer the diagram to a sheet of 10" x 10" paper, with a pencil.

2. Cut along the solid black lines.

3. Score on the front side along the solid gray lines.

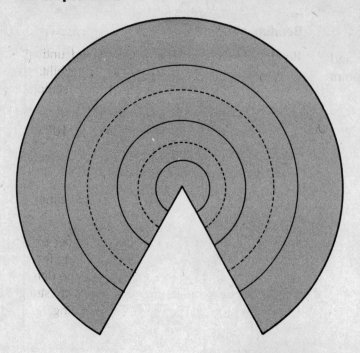

Figure 13. A three-dimensional shape may be made from this pattern (above). Cut along the black solid lines and score the gray and dotted lines (above right). Bend the scored lines, then overlap the edges and glue them together (right).

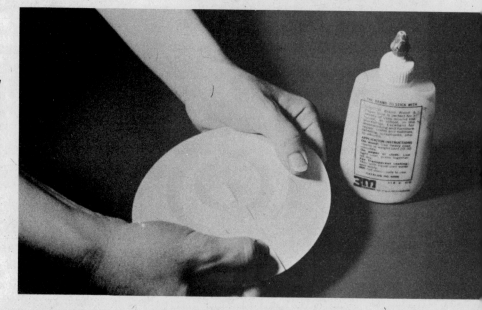

4. Score on the opposite side along the dotted gray lines.

5. Bend the shape along the scored lines carefully.

6. Bring edge A to edge B, creating a small three-dimensional relief sculpture.

7. Overlap these edges and glue them with small amounts of white craft glue (do not use too much). Several of these may be made and glued together. The diagrams offer other patterns with which to experiment.

BENDING AND CURLING

Bending and curling are primarily used to create small free-form sculptures. Working these two basic exercises will add to one's familiarity with the texture of paper and its ability to adapt to various shapes. Bending and curling are often used in making preliminary sculpture models in which the intended material, such as steel, would be too expensive with which to experiment. To do a bending test to check the direction of the grain, roll paper between hands to see which way it bends most easily — it will bend with the grain.

Bending

1. Using a 10″ x 10″ sheet of drawing paper and following the diagram, bend side A over to point C by curling or rolling the paper.

2. Staple the curl in place.

3. Bend side B under to point D and staple.

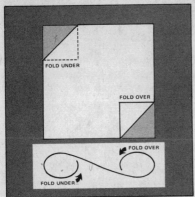

Figure 14. This is a diagram for a basic bend, a small free-form sculpture.

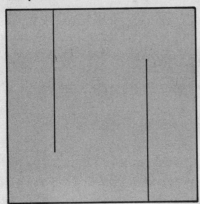

Figure 15. This diagram is for a bending and cutting exercise. Cut only the solid black lines and then bend the paper almost any way.

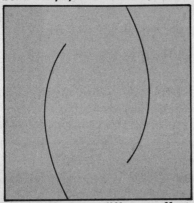

Figure 16. For a different effect, follow the curved cuts shown in this diagram.

Bending and Cutting

Bending by itself is somewhat limited until it is combined with cutting. Then, the possibilities of creating beautiful three-dimensional sculptures become limitless.

1. Transfer the diagram to a sheet of 10″ x 10″ paper. Use only straight cuts.

2. Cut along the solid black lines.

3. Bend these and staple into place either according to the diagram or at will.

4. With another 10″ x 10″ sheet of paper experiment with cutting and bending following the diagram, using only curved cuts. Notice the different effects. Now try the next exercise with straight and curved cuts and bending before scoring.

Additional Bending With Scoring

When scoring is added to bending and cutting,

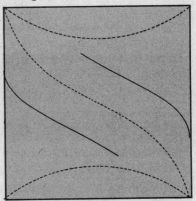

Figure 18. Another interesting design emerges as the pattern above is cut, scored, and bent.

Figure 17. These are two finished examples of cutting and bending patterns (below), created from two sheets of 10″ by 10″ paper.

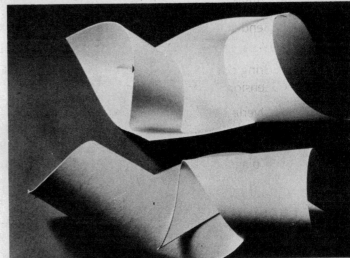

design or sculpture is further enhanced and expanded.

1. Trace the diagram onto a sheet of 10" x 10" paper.

2. Cut through the paper along the solid black lines, score along the front on the solid gray lines, and score on the opposite side along the dotted gray lines.

3. Bend the pieces indicated, letting the scored areas curve in and out naturally.

4. Staple where indicated. Try an original design — bending, scoring, and cutting. Then staple into place.

Curling

Curling the paper is almost the same as bending the paper, except that, in curling, the paper should retain its shape without glue or staples. There are many ways to curl paper — here are a few suggestions:

1. Roll a piece of paper 1" wide and 3" long tightly around a pencil. Release. Roll another piece of paper the same size around the fingers loosely, hold, then release. The difference is noticeable and will also depend on the type of paper used.

2. Pull a strip of paper over the edge of a table (only a table edge which is at a 90° angle will work), or pull the paper over the edge of a ruler. The paper will curl inward towards the side pulled over the table or ruler. Because one side of the paper has been stretched more than the other, the paper will curl. For extreme curling use the

Figure 19. These three paper forms are excellent examples of abstract designs. When bending and scoring, try to create original designs, letting the scored areas of paper curve in and out naturally.

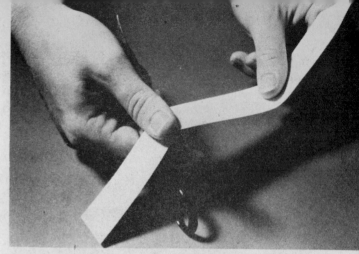

Figure 20. When curling paper, pull it over a table or ruler or across a scissors blade (above). It may also be rolled around either the finger or a pencil (below).

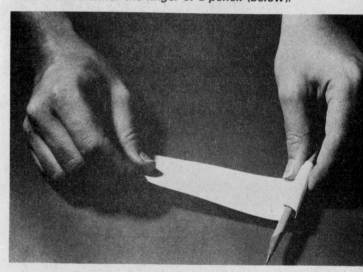

edge of a scissors and pull the paper across the blade as on the ruler. Be cautious of the scissors' edges. Curling exercises are a good introduction to the art of quilling.

QUILLING

Quilling is decorative and very lacy. Each small piece is a strip of quilling paper (available at craft stores) 1/8" wide rolled into a particular quilling shape and glued to the other pieces in a woven fashion.

Before beginning to quill, the basic rolls must be learned. Each roll is a variation on the first roll, which is called the *master* or *tight roll*. Take a strip of quilling paper and moisten one end. Bend one edge of the strip into a small fold. Insert the round end of a toothpick into the fold and begin wrapping or rolling the quilling paper around this end. Try to keep the paper tight while rolling it. By holding it as shown, the roll should remain aligned. The longer the strip of paper, the wider the roll will be. With a small amount of glue on the end of another toothpick, glue the loose end in place. Hold the roll until the glue is dry. Carefully remove the toothpick.

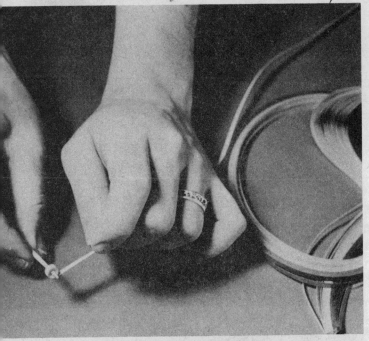

Figure 21. Begin decorative quilling by rolling a strip of quilling paper 1/8" wide (above) into such shapes as a master roll or tight roll (below).

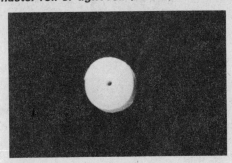

Loose Roll

Roll as for a tight roll, then let the roll unwind until the desired amount of looseness is achieved. Glue loose end as before.

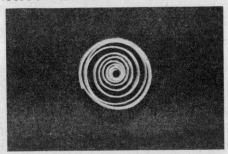

Teardrop or Leaf

Make a loose roll as above, gluing as before. Taper the glued end by pinching; leave the other end rounded.

Marquise

Make and glue a loose roll as before. Taper both the glued side and the opposite side into an eye shape, pinching it into a point.

"S" Shape

In opposite directions, make a loose roll at each end of a strip of quill paper. Do not glue. Vary the tightness of the roll or the lengths between the rolls.

Scroll Shape

Loosely roll the ends of a strip of quilling paper towards the center. Distances and tightness can be varied.

"V" Shape

Pinch the center of a small strip of paper. Roll the ends out loosely — glue if desired.

Heart Shape

Pinch the center of a small strip of quilling paper and roll the ends to form a heart shape. Do not glue. After trying all of these basic rolls, try some of the combinations of rolls and scroll as indicated in the diagrams.

Lattice

Sometimes lattice is introduced into quilling to create lacy areas with an effect different from that of a roll. To make up lattice for special effects,

Figure 22. Lattice work objects (below) introduce an effect which is different from the usual roll design of quilling. The collar is useful as a support for the center of a quilling project.

place a piece of graph paper onto a foam board. Place a piece of translucent waxed paper over the piece of graph paper. Pin both to the foam board. Line strips of quilling paper flat onto the waxed paper, using the graph paper as a guide line. Pin ends of strips into place. Lay strips in the opposite direction, gluing with very small amounts of glue at each overlap.

Corners

Corner areas may be reinforced by putting several rolls together and then lining the edge with a strip of quilling paper, as illustrated in the diagram.

Collar

A collar is used to make the reinforcement for the center of a quilled frame. It is sometimes topped with a curled or braided rope. A braided rope is made by braiding three strips of quilling paper together and gluing the ends. This is then glued carefully to the top of the collar (see diagram). To top a collar with a curled rope, wind a piece of quilling paper around and up the length of a toothpick. Glue to top of collar for both decoration and added strength.

Quilling is usually done over a pattern, not in a free-form style. Once quilling is mastered, it is fun to experiment with original designs.

The following exercise is an introduction to the easiest method of working quills together.

1. Trace the pattern.

2. Place a sheet of translucent waxed paper over the pattern.

3. Pin both of these on a sheet of cardboard, or use another material in which pins may be inserted easily.

4. Make the first quill. In the illustration of the flower coaster, the first quill should be a marquise.

5. Place a pin in the center of the quill to hold it in place on the proper pattern.

6. Make a quill (in this case another marquise) which fits next to the first quill (see diagram).

7. Dot a small amount of white craft glue on the end of a toothpick and place a small amount where the first marquise contacts the second.

Figure 23. This elaborate pattern can be transferred to paper (below left) with the quilling pinned to the pattern (below right) for accuracy.

8. Pin the second piece into place, making sure the glue touches both areas.

9. Keep working until all the quills are glued into place.

10. Let dry and unpin. With a flat knife carefully slide the quills off, using the knife where glue is stuck to the waxed paper.

11. Move onto a piece of cardboard. Glue only small edge areas down (see diagram). Spray with acrylic clear spray for permanence and stiffness.

PAPIER-MÂCHÉ

Papier-mâché is the art of sculpting, molding, and pasting together wastepaper or the stripping and gluing of sheets of paper. Once the basics have been learned, almost any project can be crafted from papier-mâché: for example, rings and bracelets, toys, figurines, ornamental plaques, masks, and even simple furniture. In varied stages of drying, the paper may be carved, smoothed, or sculpted. When dry, it may be sanded, painted, and decorated in many possible ways. To learn to work with papier-mâché, a step-by-step procedure follows for making a coaster.

Strip Papier-Mâché

This process is used for major shape definition and under-strength in making any type of object. It is usually finished over with ground paper mash or is painted as is. The strips of paper are usually used over either heavy or corrugated cardboard or wire.

1. Cut a circle of corrugated cardboard the size for a coaster. Add about 1/4″ so that the layers of papier-mâché will not make the piece too small.

2. Cut a strip of corrugated cardboard 1/2″ wide and as long as the perimeter length (circumference) of the circle (see diagram).

3. Lay the circle flat. Run the piece of cardboard around the outside edge of the circle and tape the ends together with cellophane tape. Tape bottom to sides as shown in the diagram.

4. Tear sheets of newsprint in approximately 1/2″ strips (it is easiest and quickest to tear several sheets at a time by tearing them against the edge of a ruler).

5. With a wide brush, dampen one strip of paper with water. Coat the strip liberally with wheat or wallpaper paste. (Keep the brush, when not in use, in a jar or old container filled with water so that the paste will not harden. As after any project, clean the brush thoroughly with soap and water and hang it up to dry.) Wrap the strip around the sides of the coaster form (the cardboard shape) and bend the edges of the paper over the edges of the cardboard. Parts of the paper may be cut with scissors to make them fit more evenly over the form. With the brush and extra paste, work over the strip so that there are no air pockets and the paper flatly adheres.

6. Continue tearing and coating the strips, first with water, then with paste. Apply flatly to the cardboard form until there is a three-layer buildup of strips on the form.

7. Let the form dry overnight. (It will have a tendency to warp. To avoid this, place a rubber band around the edge of the coaster form to hold it in a circular shape until thoroughly dry.)

8. When the coaster is dry, a design may be painted on it with acrylic paints or poster paint. If using poster paint, apply two coats of clear lacquer for surface durability. The coaster may also be covered with paper mash.

Papier-Mâché Mash

This is ground up paper with stiffeners and glue added. It is used over a prepared surface such as the coaster described above. The mash may be purchased or it may be made at home. For the purposes of this project, it would be easier to buy the mash. It comes in one-pound packages in dry form.

1. For this project, use the coaster already made. Paint it with a thin coat of diluted glue (half water and half white craft glue).

2. Follow the instructions on the mash package for making it moist, pliable, and ready to use (prepare only a small amount at a time so that none will be wasted).

Figure 24. To use papier-mâché mash to finish a coaster, apply the mash (above) and blot it with a paper towel. Sand the dried coaster (below) until the surface is very smooth.

Figure 25. The entire coaster is painted with gesso (above) and, when dry, sanded again to a smooth surface. Acrylic paint is used for decoration (below) and a polymer will help to waterproof it.

3. Apply the mash with an old kitchen knife. Spread it evenly onto the sides and inside of the coaster. Do not cover the bottom of the coaster.

4. Blot the excess moisture with a paper towel to shorten the drying time.

5. Place the coaster on a tin pan in a 150° F oven with the door open. In about 20 minutes, the coaster should be almost dry.

6. Take it out and flatten or scrape along the surface of the mash with the kitchen knife to smooth out the unlevel areas — do as much of this as possible because it saves work later.

7. Allow the piece to dry overnight.

8. Smooth the dried coaster with sandpaper until the surface is uniform.

9. Paint the entire coaster except the bottom with gesso (a readily available water-based primer) and let it dry. The gesso will fill in those areas of the mash which are marred or have a texture. When the coaster is dry, *lightly* sand the surface again to make sure it is smooth.

10. Decorate the coaster with the pattern in the diagram or an original pattern. Use acrylic paint. Let it dry and then paint over the design with polymer gloss medium. The polymer will seal the surface and help to make the coaster waterproof. Coat it again with polymer and let dry.

11. Glue felt to the bottom and carefully trim the edges for an attractive finished effect.

Projects You Can Do

The following are useful and creative projects which will assist the beginner in understanding the many and varied effects that can be achieved with paper. The projects are easy to complete and are given in a step-by-step format. The first project is no harder than the last but it is imperative that the section "Basic Procedures" be reviewed before these projects are begun.

STAINED GLASS WINDOW

For this project the following items are necessary: (1) the materials described above, under "Basic Equipment and Supplies"; (2) a sheet of very heavy white poster board (see guidelines below regarding the size needed); (3) a variety of colors of tissue paper for the stained glass; (4) a can of white or black spray paint; and (5) a small jar of gloss acrylic medium.

To estimate the size of the window, measure the area of the window and frame to be covered and subtract 1/2" from the length and width. The window should not be placed where it might be exposed to extreme moisture.

Figure 26. This pattern will make a very effective paper stained glass window. It can be scaled to fit the measurements of any window.

Procedures

1. Plan a design of the window including desired colors on a separate sheet of paper. This may be an original design or one that is traced.

2. Scale the design to fit the area of the glass in the window.

3. Transfer or trace the design onto the front of the large piece of poster board in pencil.

4. With a matt knife, cut away the excess board from the edges so that it is the same size as the window measurements.

5. Again using a matt knife, cut precisely every area to be filled with the tissue paper. The area left after cutting should resemble the leaded areas of an actual stained glass window.

6. Spray the entire front and inner edges of this area with either white or black spray paint. This will insure a uniform front surface.

7. With an X-acto knife, cut out a piece of tissue paper to fit into the window. This will be glued from the back. Turn over the large cut-out design.

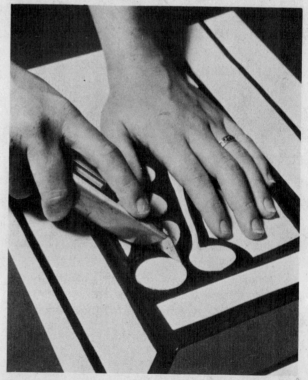

Figure 27. After tracing a design onto poster board, use a mat knife to cut away the excess board and the areas to be covered with tissue paper.

Figure 28. The tissue paper pieces are coated with gloss acrylic medium (above), which glues them to the poster board (below) and makes them translucent.

Lay the tissue paper over it and cut out a piece slightly larger than the area to be covered by that color.

8. (Practice this step first.) Lay the piece of tissue on some scrap paper and coat the front of it with gloss acrylic medium. While the piece of tissue is still wet, stretch it across the back of the major poster cut-out. The gloss medium will adhere the piece to the back of the poster board. Since tissue paper may bleed, try not to fold the tissue paper or get the bleed onto the hands while the tissue is still wet. Do not place this anywhere near the front of the window or it will transfer color onto the front. Let the piece of tissue dry and then trim away the excess edges.

9. Repeat this procedure with each additional area until the window is complete. Do not overlap colors. Let the window dry. The gloss medium should make the stained glass areas translucent. If there are places where the gloss medium on the piece of tissue is not sufficient to be transparent, repaint it from the back. Paint on the back color by color. Do not press hard with the brush while the tissue is wet because the fibers are weak and the tissue may tear.

10. Staple the window into place and touch up the staple marks. Do not glue the window into place or it will never come off. If the frame of the window is metal, tape the frame into place with double-faced tape.

The window should not be placed where it might be exposed to extreme moisture.

Figure 29. This stained glass window has been placed in a bedroom where the light filtered through the design creates a unique and pleasant effect.

PAPER-FOLDED SCULPTURAL HANGING LAMP

This sculpture should only be used as a mood lamp and not as a primary source for lighting a room. For fire safety and protection, use only a low watt light bulb in this lamp.

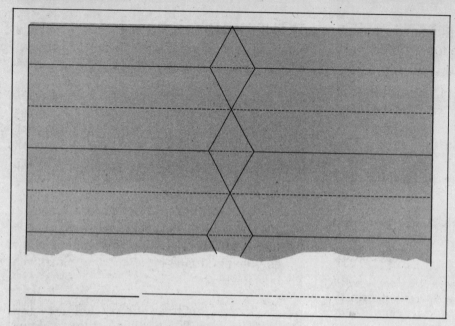

Figure 30. *This is the basic diagram for a folded paper lantern. The lamp can be scaled to fit any area.*

For this project, the following items are needed: a sheet of No. 2 white bristol paper or board or very heavy drawing paper, pencil, white craft glue, a paper punch, string or fishing line, clear spray varnish, shellac, and alcohol (or linseed oil).

Procedures

1. Transfer the diagram to the large sheet of paper. The measurements may be changed according to the desired size of the lamp.

Figure 31. *For the paper lamp project, score and fold the lines (below). Use a paper punch (top right) to make holes for string (bottom right) that gathers the top and bottom of the lamp.*

2. Score and fold on the lines indicated. Score on the solid gray lines on the front of the sheet. Score on the dotted gray lines on the back of the sheet. Fold the score lines carefully (do not fold anywhere except where the paper was scored).

3. With the paper punch, punch holes in the sides of the paper. These will then become the top and bottom of the lamp.

4. Referring to the diagram, bring side A to side B and glue carefully with white craft glue.

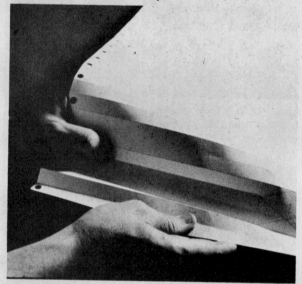

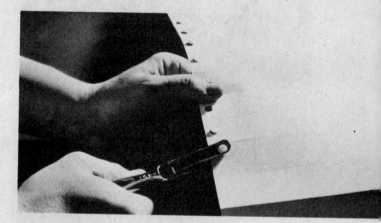

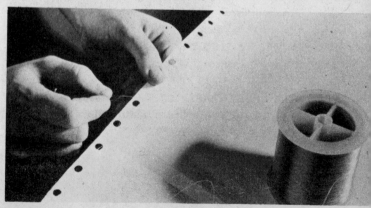

5. Running the fine string or fishing line through the punched holes, gather the top and bottom of the lamp as in the diagram.

6. To make the lamp translucent, paint it or coat it with a mixture of half shellac and half linseed oil or alcohol. Let dry (drying may require several days). Spray the lamp with clear spray varnish to provide durability. This should first be done to a small test strip of paper to make sure that it does not ruin the paper.

Either buy a lamp hanging fixture to use or make one. Never let the light bulb touch the lamp itself.

Figure 32. The finished sculptural lamp (above) makes a striking addition to any room.

TISSUE HOLDER

This project combines both quilling and papier-mâché. It may be used in a bedroom or bathroom.

Necessary supplies are: an empty tissue box, heavy corrugated cardboard, newspaper, wheat or wallpaper paste, cellophane tape, papier-mâché mash, papier-mâché tools, brush for mash, scissors, gesso, spray paint (optional), string, white craft glue, ruler and pencil, felt, acrylic paint, and sandpaper.

Procedures

1. Cut out the corrugated cardboard according to the illustration. The cardboard should be slightly larger than the tissue box — add 1/2" to each measurement.

2. Score along the fold lines as indicated.

3. Fold sides up and fasten with tape.

4. Check to see if tissue box fits loosely.

5. With a pad of newspaper under the work, begin dampening and coating layers of newspaper onto the box, alternating with water and wheat paste.

6. Cut a few sheets of newspaper large enough to completely wrap around the sides and bottom of the box.

7. Make sure to brush each time over the entire surface so that all air pockets are removed between the cardboard and the newspaper.

8. Cut pieces to finish the corners. Completely wrap the box with newspaper, inside and out.

9. Repeat until all areas of the box are covered with three coats of newspaper.

10. Cut a lid out of corrugated cardboard to fit the box. The dimensions of the lid should be slightly larger than the bottom of the box.

11. Carefully cut out an oval area from the center of the lid. (The center of the lid is easily determined by running diagonals from one corner to the opposite corner. Where the diagonals meet is the center.)

12. Make a rim 3/8" high that will run 1/4" inside the bow on the lid.

13. With paste and newspaper (which has been

ripped into strips), apply the rim to the bottom of the lid — use three coats of newspaper to secure it.

14. Put the lid on the box to make sure that it fits. Make any necessary alterations in the rim at this point because it is very difficult to change after it has dried.

15. Cut strips of newspaper as in the illustration to fit around the oval area of the lid. With other strips of newspaper, begin to cover the top and bottom of the lid with alternating layers of paste, water, and newsprint until the top, bottom, and oval edge have three coats of paper. Work around the rim on the bottom. It is a good idea to alternate the paper at the edge of the oval and the paper covering the top so there will be no bulging areas.

16. Let the pieces dry completely. To avoid warping, place small pieces of cardboard at the edges and corners of the box and then secure it tightly with string. Place the lid flat side down and weight it with small stones to keep it flat (do not place the stones on the rims).

17. Now make up 1 quart of paper mash.

18. Wet the surface of the *sides* of the holder and the *top* of the lid with a thin mixture of half glue and half water. Do not put the mash on the inside of the box, the bottom of the holder, or the bottom of the lid.

19. Press a layer of mash onto the top of the lid, along the edges of the oval cut-out and on the ends of the lid.

20. Blot excess moisture with a paper towel.

21. With a kitchen knife, apply mash to the sides of the holder; blot.

22. Put both the holder and the lid on an old tin pan and place into a 150° F oven to dry. Leave the pieces in for 20 minutes with the door open. This will remove most of the moisture but not all of it.

23. Remove both pieces from the oven. With the flat side of the kitchen knife, smooth over the lid and sides of the holder until as smooth as possible.

24. Let dry completely and sand first with coarse sandpaper, then medium, and then fine until the areas covered with mash are again as smooth as possible.

Figure 33. The newspaper covered cardboard box should have a matching top with either a rectangular or oval opening in the center. Be sure the pieces match before any further work is done.

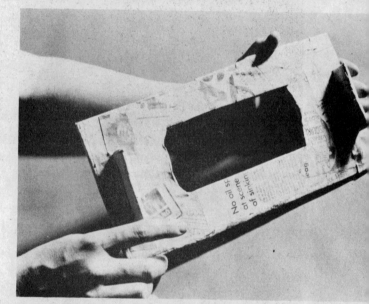

Figure 34. The cover of the tissue holder (above) has a rim that is placed on the underside, 1/4" from the edges. This will insure a good fit. The overall size of the holder should be tested with a tissue box (below) before it is finished.

Figure 35. The completed tissue holder (above) combines both quilling and papier-mache work. It is not only attractive but very durable.

25. Dust the holder and top with a dry brush to remove excess sanding mash.

26. Give the holder and the top a coat of gesso and let dry. The gesso will fill in any rough, pitted areas and should dry in several hours if the coat is not too thick.

27. Sand lightly again to insure a slick surface.

28. Paint the inside of the holder and the bottom of the lid with a brush and acrylic paint of desired color.

29. Paint the outside of the holder and the top of the lid with the same color or a contrasting color.

30. Let dry and check to see if the tissue box still fits.

For Additional Reading

Johnston, Mary Grace, **Paper Sculpture,** Davis, 1952.

Johnson, Pauline, **Creating With Paper,** Univ. of Washington Press, 1967.

Kenny, Carla, and John B., **The Art of Papier-Mâché,** Chilton, 1968.

Ogawa, Hiroshi, **Forms of Paper,** Van Nostrand Reinhold, 1971.

Wallace, Maud, **Decorative Quilling,** Craft Course Pub., 1973.

Basketry

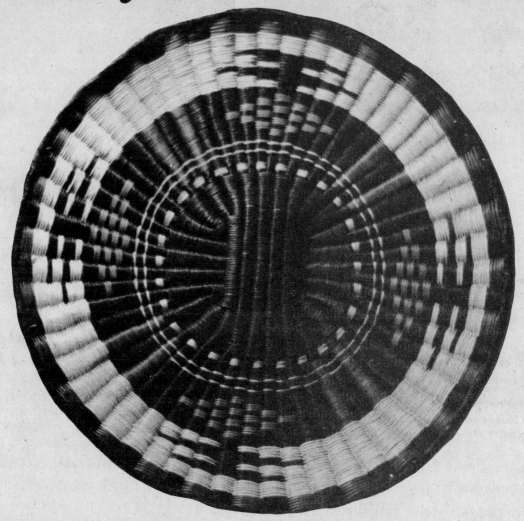

Beautiful contemporary baskets and sculptural forms can be created by using simple coiling and twining techniques.

Because the materials used in ancient basketry, such as vegetable fibers, are not preserved over long periods of time, it is difficult to establish exactly when basket making originated. Most of the prehistoric examples of basket work have been found in dry deserts and dry caves. Examples of coiled and twined baskets dating from approximately 8000 B.C. have been found in the Nile Delta region of Egypt. Specimens dating from about 7000 B.C. have been found in early American Indian graves in the Great Basin of the Rocky Mountains. Impressions of weaving patterns in mud and on pottery have been helpful in determining the existence of specific basket tech-

niques in various cultures. Such impressions reveal the existence of basketry in a late Neolithic Chinese culture (about 3000 B.C.). Twined baskets 5000 years old have been found on the coast of Peru. The first evidence of basketry in Europe was found in the area of the Swiss Lake Dwellers and dates from 2500 B.C. Bronze Age baskets dating from 2000 B.C. have been found in the British Isles in peat bogs. Indeed, basketry has been practiced by cultures at all levels of development.

Among the most intricate and sought after baskets were those created by the Pomo Indian women of northern California. The most prized of the Pomo baskets, the ceremonial feather basket, had thousands of feathers decorating the surface. In addition to the feathers, tiny flat shells, beads, or pieces of metal were often added. The size of

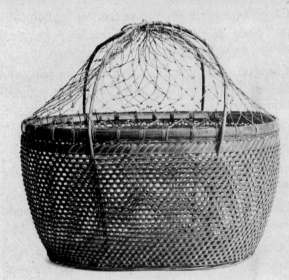

Figure 2. Contemporary adaptations of historic design are seen in a ceremonial basket with feathers (above) by Lois Granhold and in a seed pod basket (above right) by Joann Skabo. Of historic note is a bamboo carrying basket (right) from China. (Courtesy, Field Museum of Natural History.) The Egyptian basket (bottom) is about 4000 years old. (Courtesy, The Metropolitan Museum of Art.)

these ancient baskets ranges from Indian burial baskets no larger than the head of a pin to grain baskets several feet in height and diameter.

Baskets have many uses, and basketry served many needs of primitive man; one of the most important was to provide watertight containers. In fact, Hupa Indians of California made a cooking basket so closely twined that it was used for cooking soup. Other uses of basketry include construction of and adornment for walls, roofs, and doors; rugs, chairs, and hammocks; household utensils in the preparation, cooking, and storage of food; transportation items such as rush balsas, mat rafts, sails, cradles, and coffins; equipment for hunting and fishing, such as corrals, dip nets, creels, bait baskets, and traps; clothing ranging from hats, collars, skirts, and belts to footgear; shields, helmets, body armor, and other articles of war; and rattles, drums, and other musical instruments.

The fibers used in basketry were usually untwisted strands. Bones or sticks were used as tools for sewing in the same fashion as is the modern awl. Materials used by various cultures depended largely on the wild plants indigenous to the area.

Figure 1. This Hopi twined tray (opposite) is a fine example of American Indian design in basket making. Aesthetics were a consideration even in the most functional of such objects. (Photo, Don Dedera.)

Common Terms Used In Basketry

Awl: a pointed tool used for making small holes suitable for the passage of binder fibers in coiled basketry.

Binder: the material connecting one row of core elements to another row in coiled basketry.

Bird's Eye: a technique in twining in which three crossing wefts produce a design having a dot inside two curving wefts.

Butterfly: a method of winding yarn into units suitable for weaving or twining.

Cane: a plant of the rattan family mechanically processed to a uniform diameter; used for warp and weft elements in baskets.

Chevron: a "V"-like design made from two rows of double weft twining turned in the same direction.

Coil: one element or row of core strands usually bound in a circular fashion.

Core: the strand or strands of fiber forming the inner structure of a coiled basket.

Crochet: a process in which fibers are looped through each other.

Double Weft: two strands of weft or weavers passing on both sides of and twisted between warp strands; the result is a woven fabric.

Dovetail: a method of joining areas of color in tapestry weaving or twining; weft strands connect around a common warp strand.

Ghiordes Knot: the knot used to create a pile or shag surface.

Imbrication: a supplemental surface texture or decoration used on coiled baskets.

Interlocking: a method of joining weft strands to each other between areas of color in weaving or twining.

Raffia: a fiber from palm trees found in Madagascar; it is processed for use in basketry.

Reed: a tall bamboo-like grass processed to a uniform thickness for basketry.

Rod: a single fiber strand or a branch of a tree.

Slit: the openings created in slit weaving or twining.

Soumak: a technique used in weaving and twining to create surface texture.

Split: a branch or shoot of a tree which has been divided into flat strips or sections.

Spoke: used to indicate the warp or vertical elements of a basket.

Stitch: the binding of two or more core elements to each other.

Tapestry: a flat surface weft-faced weave made of isolated areas of pattern or color.

Twining: the hand process of interlacing the two elements of warp and weft to produce a fabric.

Warp: the vertical or structural strands of a woven or twined fabric.

Weaving: the process of moving a single weft strand over and under warp elements.

Weavers: another name for the weft in a twined basket.

Weft: the horizontal or fastening strands of a woven or twined fabric.

Wicker: the name applied to a basket made of willow.

Basic Equipment And Supplies

Many materials are available to the modern basket maker. The contemporary artist using basketry techniques to create sculptural forms can choose from natural and manmade yarns, cords, and fibers readily available from weaving and craft supply stores. Most yarns and cords should be at least two-ply to sustain the constant pulling required in a firm self-supporting form. Any fiber should be tested for strength and durability before it is used for basketry. Careful selection of core elements in coiling and of warp or spokes in twining is critical to achieving the desired result. Coiling binders and twining wefts or weavers need not be as large as the cores and warps but must be able to hold up under friction and tension without fraying or pulling apart.

Those who construct traditional baskets will have no difficulty locating materials. Natural materials are abundant throughout the world. Experience enables one to determine the proper type of material for a particular project. Some basketry materials grow in the backyard or along country roadsides. Others, such as cane, reeds, and raffia, which are not as readily available, can be purchased at most large craft supplies stores.

NATURAL MATERIALS

Reed

The most common commercially available natural material used in basketry is reed. Reeds are available in round sizes and splits or flat strips ranging from the smallest diameter 000 (1 millimeter, or 1 mm) to the largest diameter 16 (5 mm). Both the scale of the basket and the techniques employed help to determine the suitable reed. Small baskets require finer reeds and large baskets heavier ones. The preparation or soaking time required depends upon the size and quality of the reeds. Smaller reeds may need only to be dipped; larger sizes may need soaking for 30 minutes or more. It is important that any reed be soaked long enough so that it bends easily and does not split or break. Soaked reeds are covered with a damp cloth until used. Do not keep reeds wrapped in a damp cloth for several days as they will begin to mold.

Cane

Cane, a member of the rattan family, can be obtained from certain craft suppliers. Cane and rattan are most frequently used in larger basket work. They characteristically have a glossy deep gold surface which distinguishes them from reed. Both cane and rattan are available in round and split sizes and are soaked in the same manner as reed.

Willow

A more common basket material found in the United States is willow. More difficult to use than reed or cane, willow should not be used by the beginner.

Other Natural Materials

Basketry materials are normally categorized by the portions of the plants most suitable for basketry. Essentially, any plant material which can be made pliable through soaking is appropriate for some type of basketry work. The following list

Figure 3. A horizontal pattern was used in weaving this Apache burden basket. Natural materials were used for the basket and the decorative hanging strips. (Photo, Don Dedera.)

contains only the most common plants found in the United States.

Grasses and Stems: bulrush or cattail, cane, broom corn, Canadian blue grass, reed grass, milkweed, basket rush, and sedge.

Shoots: white birch, cottonwood, hazelnut, mulberry, poplar, three leaf sumac, willow, and weeping willow.

Fibrous Roots: alder, bracken, cedar, elm, hemlock, and black locust.

Vines: clematis, honeysuckle, English ivy, and wisteria.

Runners: grapevine and Virginia creeper.

Barks: basswood, paper birch, red and white cedar, white pine, redbud, and black walnut.

Leaves: cattail, holy grass, squaw grass, corn husks, iris, palm leaves, and yucca.

Ferns: maidenhair fern.

TOOLS

Most tools required in basketry can be found in the home or are inexpensive and available in any hardware store. These materials include: (1) an awl for piercing rods and core elements to insert new rods or for sewing of the binder fibers; (2) pruning sheers for gathering materials and trimming rods; (3) a utility knife for splitting, piercing, and cutting rods and weavers as well as for general usage; (4) round-nose pliers for bending spokes in borders and pulling through binding elements (the ends should be covered with adhesive tape so as not to bruise the fibers); (5) measuring tape; (6) cloth for covering dampened fibers; (7) large pan or basin for soaking the materials; (8) singeing lamp for singeing off the fine hairs on cane and reed; (9) large-eyed needle for sewing and binding; (10) spring-type clothespins for temporarily securing parts and handles; (11) a small hammer for pounding weavers in place; and (12) scrap cardboard.

Basic Procedures For Coiled Basketry

Coiled basketry is the oldest of the techniques employed in basketry. It is comprised of two elements: the core, consisting of a bundle of fibers coiled spirally, and the binder or sewing thread of a similar material. Natural basketry fibers such as reeds and grasses must be soaked in water for a few hours and kept damp as they are worked. The fastening of cores with binders is usually accomplished with an awl or needle. The awl is used to make a hole or opening large enough for the binder material to pass through. A large-eyed tapestry needle is used with yarns or other similar materials.

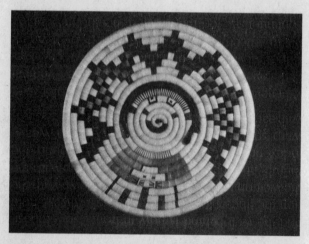

Figure 4. This Hopi coiled plaque is an example of one of the oldest techniques used in basketry. (Photo, Don Dedera.)

BEGINNING THE BASE

There are three main ways to begin the base of a coiled basket. The core elements in the first two methods of forming the center are tapered or staggered to a gradual point whether they be natural reeds, rope, or yarns. This helps to keep the starting center tight and capable of being coiled

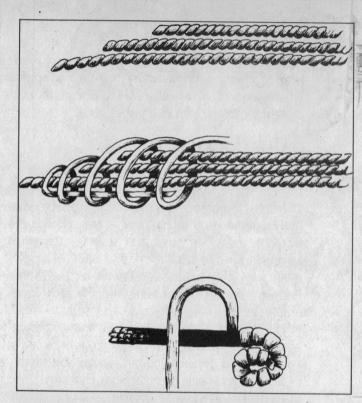

Figure 5. To begin the snail center and rosette, stagger the core elements to a gradual point (top). Then, lay the binder at the tapered end and wrap around the core elements (center). The core elements should be wrapped tightly with the binder so that the wrapped core will bend easily and coil into a spiral (bottom).

around itself. To start, lay the binder alongside the tapered core elements and wrap it around them, beginning from the farthermost point of the tapered end. Continue wrapping until the wrapped core can be bent and coiled around itself to form a spiral.

The first method, known as a snail center, radiates outward with each stitch or binder and subsequent coil. The center of the snail type remains flat and has a consistent number of stitches over the entire base. In the second method, called rosette, the first completed spiral of the core is fastened with binding stitches that pass through the center until a full revolution is made with the core. The center is thicker than the rest of the base. The third method, called four cross, is made by laying four elements of core fibers crosswise at their center to form a woven square. The fastening is begun by wrapping one of the elements with a binder and bending it sideways to meet the second element. This second element is joined with the first and wrapped together such that it includes the third and eventually the fourth ele-

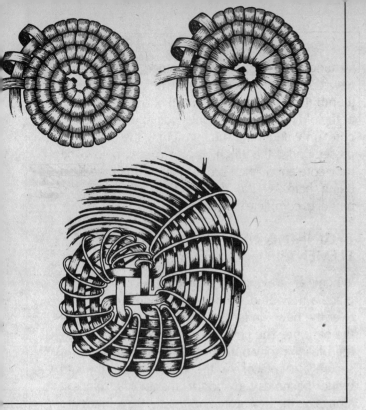

Figure 6. The snail center (top left) remains flat and the size of the stitches is the same for the entire base. The rosette center (top right) is thicker than the rest of the base because the first two core spirals are bound with stitches. The four-cross center (bottom) is formed by crossing four core elements in a sqaure and wrapping the binder.

ment. The core becomes larger as each element is added in the wrapping process. The center forms an initial square base; the actual coiling process begins with binding stitches on the side where the wrapping began.

THE STITCHES

The actual stitching of the binder can be done in several ways, depending upon the desired surface texture, design, and firmness of the form.

Figure Eight

The most common stitch is the Figure Eight or Navajo Stitch. It requires more time than most of the other stitches but gives a very firm form. The binding passes between the new and the old coil in a figure eight movement.

Lazy Squaw or Long and Short Stitch

The Lazy Squaw Stitch is made with one long stitch which goes down behind the new and the old cores, under the old core, out to the front and then up over the old and the new cores. This is fol-

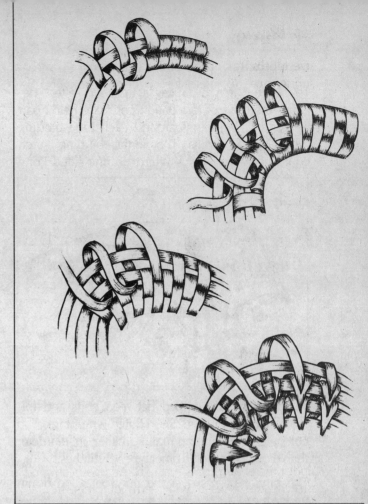

Figure 7. A variety of stitches can be used to bind the coiled elements together. Some of these binding techniques include (top to bottom) the Figure Eight Stitch, Lazy Squaw Stitch, Single Rod Coil, and Split Stitch.

lowed by one or more short stitches which wrap around the new core foundation only. The strength of the form is weakened if several short stitches are made between long stitches. As each row builds outward, the next long stitch is inserted under a short stitch of the previous row.

Single Rod Coil

The binding fiber wraps around both the new and the old coil, interlocking with stitches of the old coil as it passes under the old coil.

Split Stitch

The Split Stitch, a variation of the Single Rod Coil, is a decorative stitch. The "V" pattern can be used to create a very delicate lace-like design. Each binding stitch passes through the center of the stitch below it in the old foundation coil.

Lace Stitch

The Lace Stitch produces a light airy effect because the rows of foundation cores are held apart by vertical wrappings around each long binding stitch joining coils. The initial binding stitch could be considered similar to a one-sided Long

Stitch which is wrapped between coils and followed by one or more Short Stitch wrappings. The core elements are normally smaller in diameter than those used for the other types of stitches.

The binder passes over the new core and down under the old core, as in the Lazy Squaw. However, instead of being carried up and over the old core to the top of the new core, the binder passes between coils and wraps around the Long Stitch. Wrapping begins at the top of the old core and continues around the Long Stitch upward toward the new core. The number of times the Long Stitch is wrapped determines the distance between coils. Vertical wrappings between cores are spaced by the short wrappings between Long Stitches on the new core.

This stitch is used by the Fuegian Indians of South America. It produces a mesh-like fastening with the core elements slightly exposed. Begin by

forming a small loop with the binder on top of the new core element and hold it in place with the thumb. Pass the binder under the top of the stitch of the old core below. It does not go under the old core, only under the stitch fastening the core. As it passes under the stitch, it also passes below the new core and is then brought up through the loop being held by the thumb. Pull tightly on the binder to complete the stitch.

BEGINNING NEW BINDERS AND CORE ELEMENTS

Whenever a length of binder becomes short, place a new binder alongside the new core; bind over the new binder with the remaining length of the old one. The new binder should be bound by the old one for approximately 1 inch to fasten it securely in place. At the point where the old binder becomes too short to manipulate, place it alongside the new core and use the new binder to bind the old end along with the core. If a core element consisting of several fibers is not long enough to complete the form, add elements one by one in a staggered fashion to keep the core diameter the same throughout. Core elements of a single fiber strand are taper cut and joined to a new core length which has also been tapered at the end. The angle of the two tapered ends should be identical to avoid a lump in the core. Depending upon the fiber, glue or tape can be used to secure the two ends until they are fastened by the binder.

Figure 8. Place a new binder next to the old one (top) and bind over it. If additional fibers are needed to complete the length of the core (bottom), add them in a staggered fashion.

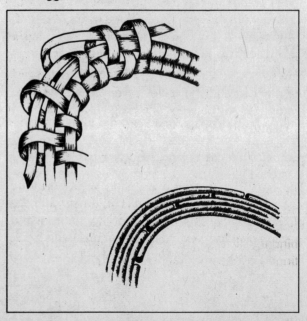

ENDING A COILED BASKET

The outermost edge of the coiled basket should be ended parallel to the point where the basket began. Cut off each core element approximately 1/4" longer than the previous one for a tapered ending. The binder is continued with the same stitch as before the cores were tapered. When only one core element remains unbound, pass the binder around this single core and the old core below. Continue binding around the two until the new core is completely covered. Insert the end of the binder under the binder that covers the core below; use a needle or an awl.

DESIGN AND COLOR IN COILED BASKETRY

Coiling techniques afford great flexibility and freedom of design and color. A mixture of any or all of the stitches within one form results in interesting textural patterns. Various sizes and types of fibers can be used as binders to create additional textures. Core elements that are exposed or change size also provide interesting variety, especially if the form is uneven or asymmetrical. Color binders are carried along with core elements in the same way as new binders are begun and ended. They exchange places with the binder and are used whenever the color changes with the design.

Shaping is controlled by the placement of the core elements. If a form is to slope inward, the new core is placed toward the inside. An outward movement places the new core toward the outer edge of the old core. Pulling tightly or relaxing the tension on the core decreases or increases the diameter of the form. Most traditional basket forms tend to be circular, with the core element making a continuous spiraling motion. Oval baskets can also be formed using coiling techniques. Begin the center base with the core element bent into a hairpin shape proportioned to the length of the oval form desired. Begin in a Figure Eight Stitch at the bend and work toward the ends to fasten the cores together. When the binding reaches the short end of the hairpin shape, the other end or new core is curved around and bound to the oval center base; use any of the binding stitches. The rest of the form can be continued in the same manner as a circular form.

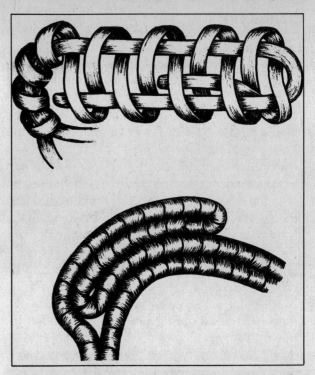

Figure 9. For an oval basket, the center base is begun with the core element bent into a hairpin shape (top). Core elements (bottom) turned back and bound on themselves establish an irregular design.

Coiling techniques can be used to create purely sculptural forms capable of supporting themselves. The strength of various fibers, the individual techniques, and both structural and decorative characteristics should be explored before sculptural form is attempted. Core elements can be turned back and bound on themselves to establish a different pattern of movement and thereby change the form itself. The core element can be wrapped with a binder and allowed to float unbound to create holes in the form. The basic techniques should be considered a point of departure in any form being created. Do not hesitate to experiment and develop original techniques. There is no right or wrong way to utilize a technique — the only limitation is whether or not the desired goal is attained.

Basic Procedures For Twined Basketry

Twining is probably the most versatile of the textile techniques. It was first used for basket forms, then became a textile technique prior to the invention of actual loom weaving. The vocabulary of twining is similar to that of weaving. The two basic elements of warp and weft produce the weave.

Twined baskets and sculptural forms are easily shaped by either increasing or decreasing the number of warps being woven. To decrease a form, join two warps. Cut off one of the two warps after it has been twined over for an inch or more. To increase the form with yarns and cords, twist the double weft and place half a double length warp strand in the open twist. Twist weft again with the other half of the warp strand placed into the opening. Follow this procedure whenever the form increases in size. Insert additional warp spokes alongside previous spokes to increase when using natural materials. Increasing can be done totally within one section to create a flaring out or bulge at that point. Gradual expansion of a form is done by adding new warps at regular intervals. Whenever a weft becomes too short to be used, the ends are placed beside a warp, and a new looped weft is begun over the same warp. Short weft ends are always carried beside a warp and twined over.

Figure 10. To increase a form (top), twist a double weft around each warp and lay it in a looped double warp. Place the weft ends along side a warp (bottom) and begin a new looped weft.

THE WEAVES

Several methods of twining are described here. It will be helpful to follow the illustrations as one reads about the techniques.

Double Weft or Single Paired Weft

A weft fiber is doubled at the center or two weft yarns are tied together to create the double weft. If yarns are used for the double weft, wind these into workable units known as butterflies. Use a long strand of yarn and loop it in the center. Working from the center, place half of the strand between the index and forefinger. From this point pass the yarn under the thumb and over the little finger. Wind on two fingers in a figure eight motion. Leave enough yarn unwound to wrap around the cross of the figure eight twice. Wrap the end around the cross once and pull the end of the yard through the loop made by the wrapping. Repeat a second time to bind securely the yarns

Figure 11. To fashion a butterfly unit (top), loop the yarn around the thumb. Wind a figure eight with the yarn (bottom). Then, wrap the point where the eights cross.

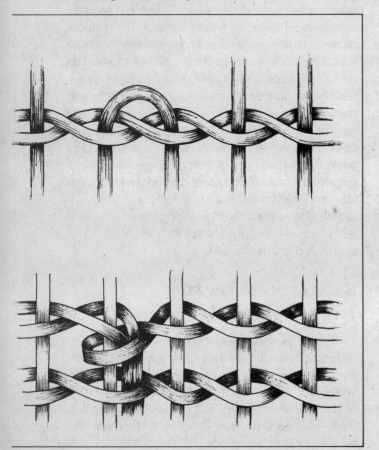

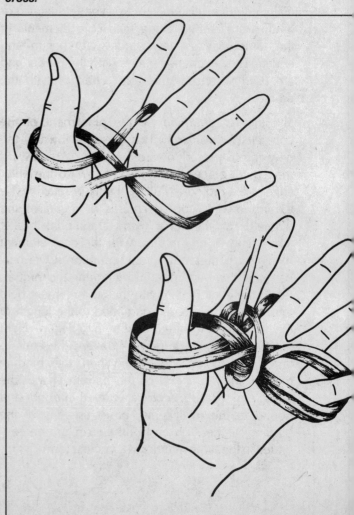

into a butterfly shape. Place the other half of the weft between the index and forefinger and wind it in the same manner. The yarn then pulls out from the center strand held between the two fingers. Place the center loop of the weft over one warp spoke.

The process of twining is that of a simple twisting motion of the weft between warp spokes. Clockwise turns of the double weft occur with each motion. The positioning of the two strands in the hand should produce an even-tensioned weave. Hold the back weft up with the index finger while the front weft is held out and down with the thumb. Join the two wefts and hold them together with the ring and little fingers; they provide tension for both wefts. As the two wefts are held in position with the fingers, pull a warp spoke in front of the down weft or through the half cross. The wefts have changed position at this point: the weft which was in front is now behind a warp,

Figure 12. When twining, the back weft is held up with the index finger, and the front weft is held out and down with the thumb (top). Hold the two wefts in position (bottom) and, with the other hand, place the warp in front of the down weft.

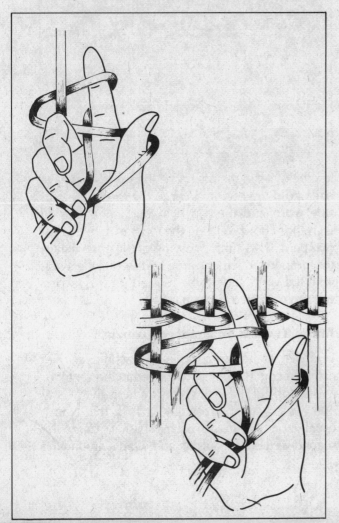

Figure 13. For a checkerboard effect, twine continuously for the desired height, thus producing stripes. Then, make a complete twist between two warp spokes to start a new row.

and the weft behind is now in front. Now reposition the fingers to repeat the process. Always hold the weft on top of the warp out and down with the thumb, and the weft behind the warp up with the index finger. Continue this process around the warp spokes of the basket to produce a weave with each weft lying at a slight diagonal.

Whenever two weft yarns of different colors are tied together to produce the weave, vertical stripes develop around the basket. A checkerboard effect can be accomplished by twining continuously for the desired height (producing stripes), then making one complete twist between two warp spokes causing two consecutive warps to have the same weft color facing the outside. This offsets the stripe sequence. Each time a full twist is made, the color sequence reverses. Full twist or complete revolutions of the two weft colors between warps keep one color constantly on the outside and another color on the inside. Half or normal twists cause the colors to appear alternately side by side.

Vary the twisting by turning the two wefts counterclockwise. Hold the wefts in the hand in the same manner as above, but roll the weft on top of the warp upward and the weft under the warp downward. This is a reverse movement from the previous method and produces a weave with the wefts laying at the reverse angle.

Open or lace-like effects are also possible in twining. The weft is usually pushed down to produce a solid weave; openings can be made by leaving spaces between rows of weft. Double twisting of the weft between two warps produces an effect known as rope twining. These double

Figure 14. To achieve the rope twining effect, make double twists of the weft fibers between two warp fibers (top). For a lace-like effect, cross pairs of warp fibers and twine two weft fibers between the split warp (bottom).

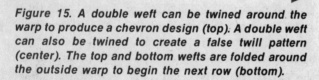

Figure 15. A double weft can be twined around the warp to produce a chevron design (top). A double weft can also be twined to create a false twill pattern (center). The top and bottom wefts are folded around the outside warp to begin the next row (bottom).

twists of the weft force the warps apart causing open spaces. Make lace-like patterns by combining or crossing warps into pairs or groups and twining over them. On the second row of twining, split the warp pairs and join them with the warps to either side to form new pairs. This splitting of warp pairs back and forth creates delicate patterns.

Whenever double weft twining is worked back and forth instead of in a circular manner, a chevron design can be produced. Make a chevron or right-angle "V" by twining clockwise from left to right across the work and clockwise going back from right to left. Make a false twill pattern with a two-color weft twined back and forth and twined clockwise in one row and coun-

terclockwise in the next row. In turning to weave back, fold the bottom over to the top of the outside warp and the top weft under the outside warp. Join both wefts on the top between the last two pairs. This simple turning of the edge makes the proper movement around the outside warp with the weft ready to be twisted for the second warp to be pulled through.

Taniko Twining or Wrapped Twining

Two weft strands are used in this technique. They can be a continuous strand looped in the center or two strands of different colors tied together. Carry one weft yarn horizontally across the warps, usually on the inside of the basket. Carry the second weft on the outside and wrap it around the

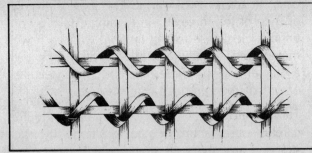

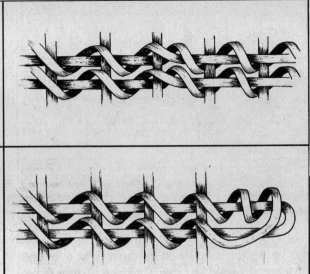

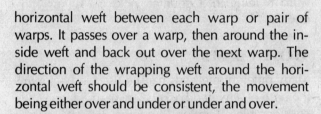

Figure 16. Two weft strands are used in Taniko twining. One weft is carried in a horizontal line and the other is looped around the horizontal weft and each warp (top left). A change in color can be made by crossing the weft under tension (top right). A flat twined piece is worked by turning the looped weft and weaving backward (right).

horizontal weft between each warp or pair of warps. It passes over a warp, then around the inside weft and back out over the next warp. The direction of the wrapping weft around the horizontal weft should be consistent, the movement being either over and under or under and over.

When the inside horizontal weft is held under tension, the outer weft wrappings incline to the right or left depending upon the direction of the weave. The inside wrappings are vertical around the horizontal weft. When the warps are closely spaced and the inside weft pulled tightly, none of the inner weft color shows on the outside. The inside of the basket has a salt and pepper effect when both weft colors show. Textural and color patterns can be made by changing the weft under tension. By carrying the outside weft horizontally under tension and wrapping with the inside weft, a mixing of the two patterns occurs. Complete reversal of the positions of the two weft colors, the outside to the inside and vice versa, creates areas of color patterns.

A flat twined piece is worked in the same manner as a circular form with the exception of turning and weaving backward. At the turning edge, carry the front wrapping weft over the last warp thread and wrap it around the bottom hroizontal weft twice. Then fold the horizontal weft back under all of the warps and place it again in a horizontal position. Carry the front weft back over the first warp and wrap it around the back horizontal weft between the first and second warps. The angle of the wrappings in weaving back will lie in an opposite direction from the previous row.

Bird's Eye Twining

Three weft fibers, usually of different colors, are used in bird's eye twining. Carry one weft horizontally on the back of the warp and two wefts on the face or top of the warp. Pull the bottom weft up into a loop between each warp. The two top warps cross as they pass through this loop. The lower color of the top becomes the high color and the high color becomes the lower color. The top two wefts continue to pass over a warp and cross each other as they move through the loop formed between warps by the back weft. Each time all three fibers are pulled tight to make an even-tensioned weave. The effect can be changed by switching one of the top wefts with the back weft.

Figure 17. In bird's eye twining, three weft fibers are used. Pull the horizontal weft into a loop between two warps; then, cross the other two wefts as they pass through the loop. Pull tight.

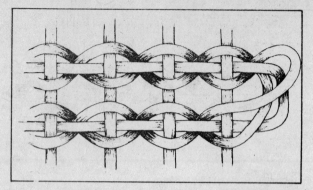

Figure 18. At the turning edge for bird's eye twining, the horizontal weft is turned in a U-shape and placed under the first warp.

The two wefts can also be carried on the back and the single horizontal weft on the top for a reversal of the weave. A decorative surface texture is created whenever the single horizontal weft is pulled tightly each time and the two wefts left slack.

In turning around on a flat twined piece, the two wefts cross beyond the last warp and under the back weft. Fold the back weft backward and place it in its horizontal position under the warp. The two top wefts turn back over the first warp and cross under the loop of the back weft, which is pulled up between the first and second warps.

Three-Strand Twining

Three weft yarns are used for this technique. The three strands are secured by taping or knotting to a warp. Place two wefts on top of the warp and one below the warp. Carry each weft over two warps and under one warp. Roll the upper of the two wefts clockwise across the next warp and behind the third warp. The lower of the two wefts moves across the first warp and behind the second warp. Bring the weft below the warp to the top between the first and second warps and

Figure 19. Three-strand twining is made by passing two wefts over the warp and one under. Only one weft goes under any one warp.

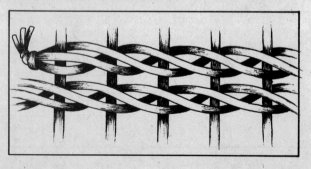

carry it across two warps. This begins the sequence of the three strand twining. Make a continuous clockwise rolling motion, with each weft moving individually over two warps and beneath a different warp. Three different colors, textures, or sizes of fibers produce an interesting weave.

Turning around on a flat woven piece requires careful observation of the positions of each strand. Carry the weft strand which has passed over the last two warps around and under the last warp. Bring the weft strand beneath the last warp back over the last two warps. Take the weft which has passed over one warp only (the last warp) under the last warp and bring it out, moving over two warps. Each weft is in position for the backward twining in a counterclockwise rolling motion.

WOVEN BASES

Many different methods can be used in beginning the base of a twined basket. The shape desired has considerable relationship to the technique chosen to begin the base. Each method forms a slightly different structure. Important is the selection of spokes or yarns large enough and sturdy enough to support the basket. Bases should be slightly domed in the center with the basket resting on the outer edge.

If a woven base is being made, an odd number of spokes must be used to create the continuous over and under weave. This odd number of spokes must be maintained as the weaving progresses and more spokes are added. Twined baskets do not require an odd number of spokes because of the nature of the technique.

The simplest round base is made of two groups of spokes or warps crossing at right angles. Each group of warps consists of four warp spokes crossing at their center. These spokes are bound together by a single weaver woven or a double weft twined three or four times around the four parts of the crossing warps. The warps are then divided into groups of two and the weft worked over the pairs three or four times. Divide the pairs and weave over each warp individually. If the base is being woven instead of twined, insert an extra or odd-numbered spoke alongside another

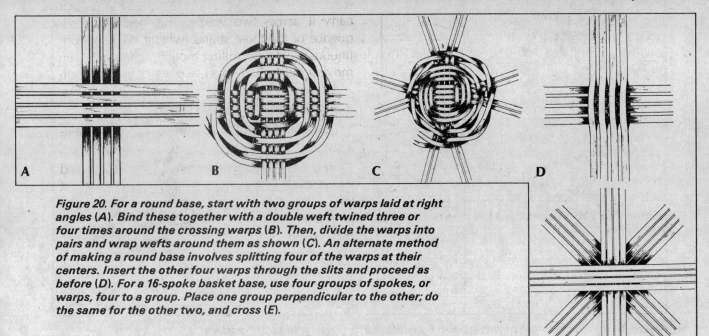

Figure 20. For a round base, start with two groups of warps laid at right angles (A). Bind these together with a double weft twined three or four times around the crossing warps (B). Then, divide the warps into pairs and wrap wefts around them as shown (C). An alternate method of making a round base involves splitting four of the warps at their centers. Insert the other four warps through the slits and proceed as before (D). For a 16-spoke basket base, use four groups of spokes, or warps, four to a group. Place one group perpendicular to the other; do the same for the other two, and cross (E).

spoke to make the weaving progress properly. Add spokes as needed to maintain a tightly woven base. An alternate method is started by piercing or splitting four rods at their centers. Insert four other rods through the split centers of the first four rods. The weaving or twining progresses as in the first method.

A 16-spoke basket base is made of four groups of spokes, each group consisting of four spokes. Place four parallel warp spokes at a right angle to four other parallel warps in the center of both. Cross the second two groups of four spokes in the same manner and place them diagonally across the center of the first two crossed groups. Hold the groups together at the center and tie them temporarily with a string to make handling easier. Weave a single weft or twine a double weft over each of the four groups three or four times. Then divide each group of four spokes into pairs. Weave over the pairs three or four times before dividing them and working them individually. It may be necessary to add more spokes for baskets with large bases. There must always be an odd number of spokes if the base is being woven.

Oval Bases

Three basic methods can be used to form an oval base. The main difference is the method used to secure the short side spokes at right angles to the

longer end spokes. Place four or more long spokes parallel to each other to form the length and ends of the basket. Place short cross spokes for the basket sides at their centers under the long spokes. Space these apart and at right angles to the long spokes. Bind with a single strand weaver. Do the first method of binding with loops which secure the short spokes to the long spokes. The weaver passes on top of the long spokes, looping around and under the right-angled short spokes twice. It passes on to each short spoke, looping around each in a continuous strand. Continue to use this single strand weaver for the base over and under each side and end spoke if the base is

Figure 21. For an oval base, lay the spokes (left). Wrap the weaver around the four spokes to secure them to the horizontal spoke (right).

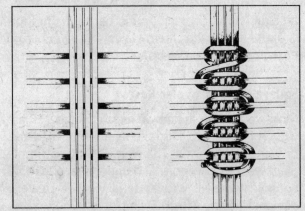

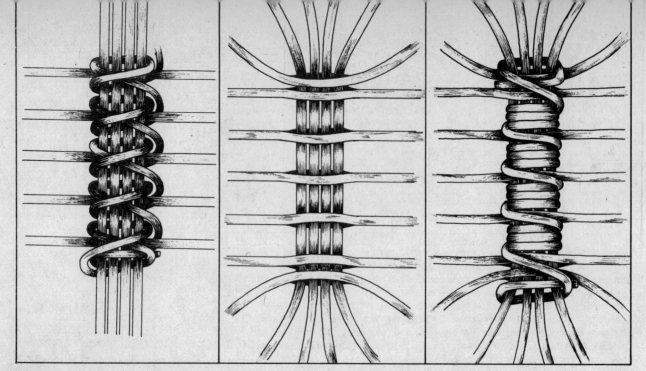

Figure 22. An oval base can be made either by wrapping the weaver in an "X" pattern (*left*) or by splitting the spokes and wrapping the weaver (*center and right*).

woven. If the base is to be twined, secure the binding weaver around the last spoke and begin the twining with a double weft.

The second method binds the spokes in place with an "X" passage of the weaver. Place the short spokes on top of the long spokes at right angles. The binder moves to the right diagonally across the short spoke, under and across the long spokes, up diagonally to the left across the short spokes, down diagonally across the back of the long spokes and on to bind the next short spoke in the same manner.

Wrapping binds the spokes to each other in the third method. Split each short spoke in the center and slide it onto the long spokes. Place two short spokes side by side for reinforcement at the ends of the long spokes. Secure the weaver at one end and wrap it over and over the long spokes. Make an equal number of wrappings between the short spokes, to space them evenly apart before crossing to the next section.

Square or Rectangular Bases

Most traditional square or rectangular bases are woven from flat splints, although round materials or yarns can be used. The weave can be a simple plain weave of over one and under one, or a more complicated twill weave. Twill weaves create a diagonal pattern effect. Examples of twill weaves

include an over two-under one movement or an over three-under one pattern. Each weft passes over a different grouping of warps, stepping one splint up with each new weft. Warp and wefts are cut long enough to form the base and sides of the basket. The two elements are interwoven in the center of both. Since the material for both is the same, warp becomes weft and weft becomes warp as they are woven over each other. The same number of vertical splints as there are horizontal splints is required to weave a square base. Rectangular bases have more vertical splints. The extending splints around the square are bent upward to form the sides of the basket. The sides can either be woven or twined.

The bases of square and rectangular baskets can be completely twined. A series of warps are placed parallel to each other. Tape them temporarily in position across one end. Using a double

Figure 23. A square or rectangular base can be made by making a simple (*left*) or a twill (*right*) weave.

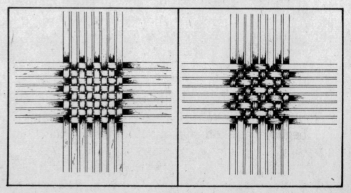

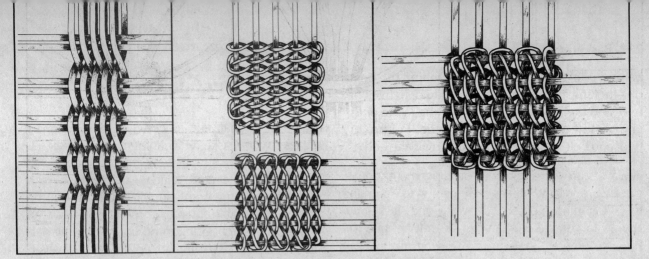

Figure 24. *The base of a rectangular basket can be completely twined by weaving a double weft through parallel warps (left). Two sections can be twined (center) and splinted together at right angles (right) for a sturdy base.*

weft, with beginning ends extending outward to form paired warps, twine across the parallel warps at a right angle. Allow enough weft beyond the last twined warp for a paired side warp. Use two new wefts for each horizontal row until the square or rectangle has been woven. Use the paired wefts which extend beyond both sides of the woven base as paired warps for a straight side or use them individually for sides slanting outward. Bend the double wefts and parallel warps up to become the warp of the sides. Weave or twine the sides of the basket.

A very sturdy base is made of two overlapping twined sections forming a double thickness. Twine a double weft back and forth across the center of vertical warps. Continue the twining to a height equal to the width of the woven vertical warps forming a square. Twine a second set of vertical warps of the same number as the first in the same way. Place the two twined sections on top of each other with the warps at right angles. Twine around all of the splints, binding the two layers into one. If the basket is to be square, bend the splints up and weave or twine the sides. For a rounded basket, draw the sides up gradually and add extra splints at the four corners to fill in the spaces.

BORDERS

Borders are used as a decorative finish to the top edge and occasionally the bottom edge or foot of a twined basket. The finish used most frequently is the track or woven border. Before the border is begun, make certain that the sides are level at the

top. Measure around the basket from the bottom to the top with a ruler or yardstick. Tap any uneven sides down with a small hammer. Make the actual border with the warp spokes. The spokes, if of natural materials, must be thoroughly dampened to prevent their splitting or cracking when bent to begin the border. Bend each warp spoke, sideways, one at a time, at a right angle directly above the last row of weaving. Once bent, the warp becomes weft, to move in and out around the warp spokes to its side.

The simplest of the track borders is begun by bending a warp spoke sideways and moving it in front of the next or first spoke and behind the second spoke. Leave the end on the inside of the basket. Bend each consecutive warp spoke sideways and pass it in the same manner in front and behind the next two spokes. The last two warp spokes follow the same movement to complete the finished edge. Use the awl to loosen the first two warps which began the border so that the last two warps can pass in sequence in front and behind. After weaving all warps around, go back and tighten the border by pulling on each end of a spoke. Then cut the ends of each spoke at an angle slightly beyond the spoke holding them to the inside. Don't make the cut too short or the border may become unwoven.

Wider track borders are made by passing each warp spoke over more warps. Various methods of movement produce slightly different borders. Examples of other methods of weaving the warp spokes around the border include: (1) behind one, in front of one, behind one, in front of one, and behind the next one tucking in the end; (2)

behind one, in front of two, and behind the next one tucking in the end; (3) behind two, in front of two, and behind the next one tucking in the end; and (4) in front of two, behind three, in front of two, and behind the next one tucking in the end.

Always carry the method of movement completely around the border with the awl to open up the beginning portion, allowing the last few spokes to complete the cycle. Do not hesitate to use an original system of weaving the warp spokes around the border. Always make sure the ends rest securely next to the last spoke of each movement as they are being cut.

If yarn is used for warp in a soft basket or sculptural form, the ends can be woven back into the fabric and no border is necessary. Two adjacent warp yarns cross positions and are woven back into the fabric with a needle. The right warp end is woven back up alongside the left warp. The left warp end is woven back up alongside the right warp.

Projects You Can Do

Many functional and decorative items can be created with basketry techniques. The beginner will discover the simplicity of the techniques and hopefully find a craft which can be done with minimal equipment and supplies. Because of the limited materials required, most projects can be carried. Those choosing to do basketry using natural materials have limited portability, however, because of the necessity for soaking fibers. For that reason, two of the three projects that follow utilize yarns and cords instead of grasses and reeds.

COILED NAPKIN RINGS

It is advisable to experiment with each of the coiling techniques before attempting a project requiring control of design and form. Each napkin ring can be a sampler of the technique as well as a

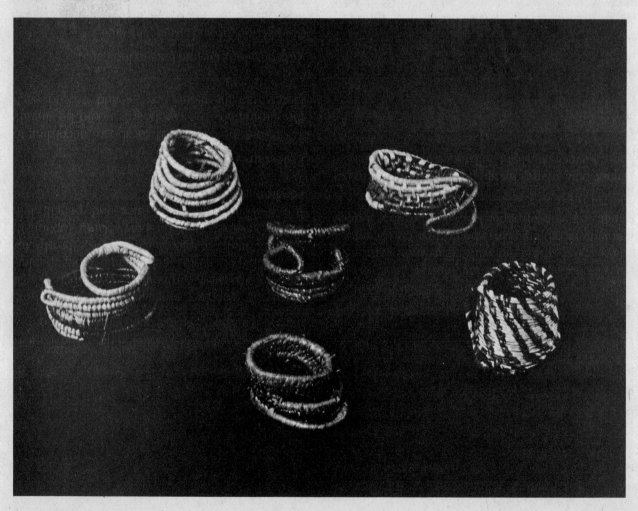

functional item. Experiment with color to create interesting designs within each ring.

Materials

The following materials are needed for this project: a reed 1 mm in size for core elements, assorted colors of raffia for binders, a large-eyed needle, and scissors. Instead of reed and raffia, a heavy 2- or 3-ply jute can be substituted for the core and yarn for the binders.

Procedures

Make six napkin rings by using a different coiling technique for each ring. Begin by wrapping six tapered 1 mm reed core elements with raffia for 6". Form the wrapped section into a circular ring and begin binding the old core to the new core. Continue coiling around the ring until the desired width has has been obtained. Cut the core elements one by one and complete the napkin ring by securing the binder thread under the binder of the old core.

COILED CHEST ORNAMENT

After the basic skills of coiling have been mastered, the designing of a particular object can be undertaken. Ideas for designs are abundant in nature and in the design motifs of various cultures. Whatever the inspiration, do not attempt to duplicate a specific form or pattern. Rather, interpret the essence of the form. Because basketry is a simple technique, many people begin with an idea and allow the materials to dictate the ultimate result. The chest ornament is constructed in pieces which are then assembled.

Materials

For this project, the following items are needed: heavy 2- or 3-ply jute for the core element, assorted metallic cords and yarns, decorative fabric trims and laces, metal rings, beads or buttons, a small plexiglass mirror, and hooks and eyes.

Procedures

Measure for fit around the neck with a tape measure. The size and approximate weight of the

Figure 25. A different coiling technique was employed to make each of the napkin rings (opposite). Assorted colors of raffia were used to create the designs and bind the core elements together.

piece should be considered when fitting the piece around the neck. The neck portion is constructed by using any of the coiling techniques. If the ornament is to be a collar form, it can be constructed in one piece. Be sure to add enough length to the neck piece so that a hook and eye can be attached. The hook and eye form the fastening device.

Figure 26. A variety of materials can be used to create unusual basketry objects. Decorative lace and a small plexiglass mirror were incorporated into the design of this coiled chest ornament.

Whenever a mirror is incorporated into the design of a body ornament, as in the one shown, set the mirror within a coiled frame. Begin the frame by forming a tight coil and working outward, keeping the disc flat. This flat disc must fit the back of the mirror to prevent scratching it. When the correct diameter is obtained, place the mirror on top of the disc and continue coiling. Gradually pull tighter on the core element, forcing it to move inward on top of the mirror. These inward rows of coiling over the edge of the mirror form a frame which secures the mirror in place. End the rows of coiling when the desired frame width has been reached.

Decorative fabric trims and laces as well as beads, buttons, or other similar objects can be worked in as the coiling progresses. Trims and laces, when carried along with the core element, create unusual and interesting areas of pattern or texture when they show between each binding stitch. Beads or buttons can be sewn onto the surface or secured in place with a binding stitch. Decorative materials should not detract from the beauty of the individual coiling stitches, however.

When connecting one portion of the ornament to another, experiment with the various coiling stitches to determine the most satisfactory one. Many other types of adornment, such as bracelets, earrings, rings, hair ornaments, and belt buckles, can be created with coiling techniques.

TWINED SCULPTURE

Twining is probably one of the oldest and most diverse of the textile techniques. Many objects woven on a loom can be twined with ease. However, the traditional loom is essentially limited to the construction of two-dimensional surfaces which, upon removal from the loom, can be manipulated into three-dimensional forms. Because twining is not restricted to the framework of a loom, it is possible to develop a form three-dimensionally. It is often easier to work on and to be able to see a form from all sides when it is being twined than to attempt to imagine a flat form on a loom in three dimensions.

Materials

Materials necessary for this project are: assorted colors and textures of yarns, cords, or rope.

Figure 27. When using the twining technique to make a three-dimensional form, it is important to choose a warp material that is strong enough to support the sculpture. Additional warp can be twined in place if the original warp element is cut too short.

Procedures

Decide upon the size of the sculptural form and select the material to be used for the warp elements. Use a warp material which will be strong enough to support the form. (A strong warp is required for any hanging or standing form.) Examine the diagrams of the various methods for beginning the base of a twined basket and decide upon a technique. Cut the warp elements longer than the required length, allowing enough extra length for take-up or shrinkage in the twining process. It is practically impossible to calculate the exact amount of additional length required because of the unique characteristics and sizes of different fibers. Large diameter fibers will require more additional length than fibers of a small diameter. After the actual twining is begun, additional warp elements will be required to increase the circumference of the form. If a warp element is too short, twine a new warp in place, and carry the old warp alongside.

The sculpture shown was begun from the top with a woven square center. Additional warp elements were twined in place at regular intervals, causing the sides of the form to expand. The three-dimensional ridges were twined by using the double weft technique. As the weft strands are turned, a warp element is pulled between the two wefts in a loop. The warp end is not pulled completely through. Each warp loop should be pulled up longer than the width of the ridge when finished. Continue pulling each warp up into a loop with each double weft turn around the entire form. Once completely around the form, twine outward on the warp loops. This outward twining on the loops forms the ridge. The ridge will be twice the fabric thickness of the rest of the form because each warp element has doubled in thickness while being looped.

Twine outward until the desired width of the ridge has been reached. At this point the twined weft must be secured to prevent it from slipping off the ends of the loops. To secure the twined weft insert the two strands of the double weft through the loop hole of each looped warp. Pass the double weft through each warp loop around the ridge. The ridge is now made firm by pulling on the end of each warp element hanging free below the inner edge of the ridge. These warp elements are

the ends which were not pulled through the double weft as each warp loop was being formed. Pulling on each warp end will draw a warp loop of the ridge tightly against the outer edge of the ridge. The tighter each warp end is pulled, the stiffer the ridge will become.

Regular twining resumes with each warp being pulled completely through the turns of the double weft. Each time a ridge is desired, the warp is pulled up in loops and the weft worked outward on the loops. When the entire form is completed, the warp ends are worked back up into the fabric with a needle or crochet hook. Each two side-by-side warp ends cross and are woven up into the fabric alongside their opposite warp. Another way to finish the warp ends is to use one of the border finishes described for baskets.

For Additional Reading

Christopher, F. J., **Basketry,** Dover, 1952.

Maynard, Barbara, **Modern Basketry from the Start**, Scribner, 1973.

Navajo School of Indian Basketry, **Indian Basket Weaving,** Dover, 1971.

Rossbach, Ed, **Baskets as Textile Art,** Van Nostrand Reinhold, 1973.

Tod, Osma Gallinger, **Earth Basketry,** Bonanza Books.

Whiteford, Andrew Hunter, **Indian Arts,** Golden Press, 1970.

Leather Craft

The oldest craft of all is still one of the most popular.

It is very likely that as long as man has eaten meat, he has used leather. Leather ranks first among the many uses for wild and domestic animals. Obtaining food was the initial reason for slaughtering animals; the items that could be made from the hide were a close second. Prehistoric people used animal skins as clothing. Later, hides were used to provide shelter in the form of tents and lodges. Many other articles were made from leather: pouches and bags for storing grain and water; foot coverings; and eventually, weapons. Prehistoric people had nothing resembling rope or string. They relied entirely on the property of leather straps to expand when wet and contract when dry to secure stone arrowheads, drills, knives, axes, and spears to wooden shafts and handles. These wet straps were also used to tie together pieces of wood used for constructing tents, carts, and sleds.

Nomadic tribes used leather for harnesses and travoises, as well as for food and water containers. Until the development of weaving and rope making, leather provided the materials for all the clothing and strapping needs of early people.

Figure 2. Note the decorative motif on the Blackfoot tipi (left). (Courtesy, Field Museum of Natural History, Chicago.) The chess set (above) was made by an eighteenth-century Spanish craftsman. (Courtesy, The Metropolitan Museum of Art, Gift of Gustavus A. Pheiffer, 1948.)

For centuries before brass and bronze were used, shields and armor were made of leather. There are accounts, during Julius Caesar's reign, of ships from Brittany with leather sails. Before the invention of paper, writing was done on parchment, which is very thin leather — similar to that used on drums. Leather has commonly been used for chair coverings and — exclusively to this day — for saddles and harnesses. Leather also has been used for jewelry, book coverings, floor tiles, window coverings, canoes, and picture frames. It has been stomped, stretched, shrunk, tooled, stitched, woven, compressed, knotted, knitted, molded, folded, polished, painted, embossed, and even gold-leafed. Even today new uses are being discovered.

The uses for leather expand as new ways of processing it are developed. Because early people did not tan their leather, it was hard, smelly, and perishable. Eventually salt came to be used as a preservative and eliminated the odor, but hides were still stiff and unsuitable for clothing. The people of some early cultures (as well as contemporary Eskimos) chewed hides to tan them. It was

Figure 1. This leather sculpture is the work of Lizbeth Wolf, who is also the author of the article on plastic crafts. Contemporary craftsmen have put leather to many imaginative uses.

discovered that tannin or tannic acid in tree bark could be used to make leather soft, pliable, strong, and odor-free. With few changes, this process was used for centuries and is still used. Known as oak tanning or vegetable tanning, it produces a leather with the right flexibility for stretching, tooling, and shaping.

It was not until the end of the nineteenth century that a process called chrome tanning was invented. This process uses chrome salts instead of tannin and was a boon to the leather industry. It not only shortens the time required to tan leather (from several weeks to several hours) but produces a leather of increased strength, resiliency, and durability. Goods such as shoes, luggage, and clothing last longer and resist scratching. Today, most leather is chrome tanned. However, such leather is not as suitable for craft projects as oak-tanned leather.

Leather craft in America (apart from the commercially manufactured leather goods) is traditionally of western style. The art of leather stamping and carving came to the west via Mexico and Spain where it is an old tradition. Leather craft has maintained its western tradition for 200 years with little change. Floral designs and mountain scenes are as popular today as they were years ago. However, in the last few years artists and craftsmen, still excited by the texture and versatility of leather, have begun to experiment with and break away from the western tradition. The result has been a widespread rebirth of interest in leather as a creative medium.

Leather has traditionally been used for practical and functional articles such as belts, purses, and billfolds. Contemporary craftsmen still make these articles but also produce items of a more decorative or unusual nature: hanging pots, sculpture, room dividers, belt buckles, jewelry, macramé, and furniture. Contemporary craftsmen are beginning to discover that creativity with leather is limited only by the imagination.

Common Terms Used In Leather Craft

Anvil: the end of a snap-setting tool used to connect the socket and button of a snap.

Back: the leather taken from the back of a steer, including the shoulder.

Belly: the two sides of a hide which covered the belly of a steer.

Bend: the part of the hide taken from the back of a steer and not including the shoulder.

Bevel: a carving term describing the flattening of one edge of a cut line.

Button: the visible part of a snap.

Eyelet: the part of a snap which holds the stud in place; the bottom piece of the snap arrangement.

Finishing: the process of covering leather to protect and preserve it.

Oak Tanning: tanning process which uses oak bark.

Ounce: the thickness of leather; 1 ounce equals 1/64".

Oxalic Acid: a mild bleaching agent used to clean leather.

Rivet: a metal fastener which has the advantage of being easy to attach and very permanent.

Set: to attach one part of a snap or rivet firmly to another part.

Shoulder: the part of a hide taken from the shoulder of a steer.

Skive: to shave down the thickness of a piece of leather.

Socket: the part of a snap which attaches to the button.

Stud: the part of a snap which fits into the socket, metal-headed nail, or rivet used as ornamental trim.

Tannin: the chemical agent in bark which cures leather.

Tanning: the process of curing leather.

Vegetable Tanning: any tanning process using tree bark.

Figure 3. Leather has long been used to cover chairs. It can be used in its natural color, as on the chair shown, or dyed. The tanned leather used today is strong, resilient, and durable.

Figure 4. Stamping and tooling devices were used to create the various decorative patterns on the leather belt shown above.

Basic Equipment And Supplies

Before making any large initial investments in supplies, the beginner should be quite serious about pursuing this craft. If interested, the following tools and other materials are those that are necessary for the leather craftsman.

TOOLS

Tools needed include: (1) an awl for piercing and widening holes for lacing and stitching; (2) ball tracer for tracing designs from paper to dampened leather; (3) circle edge slicker, a round wooden tool used for smoothing leather fibers and making a smooth, lasting edge on leather; (4) common edger, a cutting tool used to round off an edge before using an edge slicker; (5) dividers for tracing circles, spacing stitching holes, and marking lines parallel to an edge; (6) edge creaser to crimp the edge of raw leather and to add a parallel groove along that edge; (7) lacing needle, a flat needle designed to be used with leather lacing; (8) leather shears — these have a slightly serrated edge which allows for clean cutting of leather; (9) mat knife; (10) modeler, a two-ended tool for modeling, lifting, and stippling leather in the carving process; (11) one-prong thonging chisel for cutting lacing slits around corners and curves; (12) rawhide mallet for setting snaps, rivets, and other permanent fasteners as well as for striking saddle stamps; (13) rotary punch, a hole punch with several sizes arranged on a revolving wheel; (14) round drive punch, a tool available in many sizes for punching holes; (15) saddle stamps, a general term encompassing over 100 various stamping tools used in leather carvings; (16) sewing awl, a kind of hand-held sewing machine used for stitching leather; (17) skife, a tool with replaceable blades used to reduce the thickness of leather in specific areas; (18) snap setter, a small set of tools used to fasten snaps; (19) square, such as a simple carpenter's square for laying out 90° angles; (20) swivel knife, a knife unique to leather craft which is used in the carving process; (21) thonging chisel, a chisel used to cut several lacing slits at a time; (22) V-gauge, a gauge used to cut halfway through the back of leather wherever a crease is needed; and (23) X-acto knife.

1. Dyes. There are several leather coloring agents on the market and most are available in craft stores. Felt-tip pens, acrylic paint, and oil paint can also be used.

2. Finishes. There are a variety of finishes on the market which protect the surface of leather. They are available in several colors and have varying characteristics. Some soften, some age, and some harden; some are shiny and others are dull.

3. Glue. White craft glue, rubber cement, or contact cement are equally acceptable.

4. Lacing. Made from goat or calf skins and available in 1/8" or 3/32" widths, lacing is available in colors or can be dyed.

5. Thread. Used for stitching, waxed and unwaxed thread is available in nylon and linen.

Other necessary materials include: (1) eyelets; (2) rivets; and (3) snaps.

LEATHER

Because there is a large variety of leather available, it is important to check the characteristics of each type before selecting a piece for a project. For general craft purposes, vegetable-tanned calf, steerhide, or cowhide is best. Calf is a fine-grained leather, ideal for carving and for small projects. Skins are about 2 1/2 ounces in weight and 8 to 10 square feet in size. Steerhide is a heavier, coarser-grained leather ideal for carving and molding. It averages about 4 ounces in weight and skins range to 28 square feet. Cowhide is the best craft leather. It has both the fineness of calf and the heaviness of steerhide. It weighs up to 10 ounces and sizes exceed 28 square feet.

When a smooth surface or a lining is desired, chrome-tanned leather is the best buy. Consult a dealer for what is available. Usually a variety of exotic leather such as alligator, lizard, suede, and ostrich can also be found. It is important to learn what is available in order to have the best and most appropriate material for a particular project.

Leather is sold in a variety of ways — usually by whole skins, half skins, full sides, backs, bends, and shoulders. As a rule, the larger the piece, the better the price. Leather is priced by the square foot and is often available at craft stores in small cuts. When buying, consider the weight or thickness of the leather. This is referred to in ounces. One ounce equals 1/64" in thickness.

Basic Procedures

Before actually beginning work with the leather itself, design the project on paper; then, cut out and construct the object with the paper patterns. The various parts of a purse, for example, should be laid out on paper, cut to actual size, labeled, and pinned together. The pieces should be altered or recut until they fit perfectly. Cutting paper patterns prevents costly mistakes in judgment and design. If the project is to be repeated, it is advisable to cut the shapes out of cardboard once the shape of the piece is decided.

A carved, or incised, design should first be done on paper. It is a simple matter to transfer an image from paper to leather, but a difficult one to actually draw on leather.

CUTTING LEATHER

Once the parts of a project have been cut into cardboard shapes, place them on the leather with as little waste as possible. Trace around the outline of the shapes lightly in pencil, and, with a mat knife or leather shears, cut out the leather shapes. It is important that the knife be sharp and that enough pressure be exerted to cut completely through the piece in one stroke. If a straight line is to be cut, place the knife along a straight edge.

CONDITIONING LEATHER

Conditioning leather for working and tooling requires that it be uniformly damp throughout. The leather should be soaked for several minutes in warm water and then wrapped in a plastic bag. This should then stand for several hours to allow the fibers to swell and reach a uniform density. Before carving or edging, remove the piece from the bag and allow it to dry until its natural color returns. If it becomes too dry, lightly dampen it with a sponge. These conditioning and dampening procedures will keep the leather supple and workable.

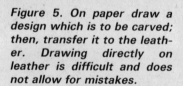

Figure 5. On paper draw a design which is to be carved; then, transfer it to the leather. Drawing directly on leather is difficult and does not allow for mistakes.

EDGING

Edging is the process of finishing off an edge so it is smooth and trim. This is done by first using a common edger to remove the surface corner of the edge. Then with an edge creaser, follow the edge with a firm, uniform pressure to crimp and groove the edge. To assure a neat, finished appearance, be certain the leather remains damp while edging is being done.

SKIVING

Skiving is the process of reducing the thickness of leather that is to be stitched, laced, or glued. The tool used is called a skife, which is like a potato peeler because only a narrow section of the blade is exposed. This helps prevent the removal of too much leather. The skife is drawn along the edge of the back, or fleshy, side of the leather several times until about half the thickness is removed. The purpose of skiving is to pare down the leather

so that the thickness of two pieces together will equal the thickness of one piece.

FOLDING

Folding is the best method for creating a finished edge. Begin by skiving away half the thickness of the leather along an area twice as wide as the part to be folded under. With a straight edge and the small end of a modeler, make a crease on the fleshy side, where the fold is to be made. This crease should be made while the leather is still damp. (See *Conditioning Leather* above.) Using a straight edge, bend the leather, fleshy sides together, along the moist crease; remove the straight edge; and fold the leather. With a mallet, gently pound the edge flat, being careful not to mar the surface. Weight the fold with books and allow the leather to dry. Once the fold is dry, lift it and apply contact cement to both surfaces. When the cement is dry, press the fold together. If desired, the edge can then be stitched for added strength.

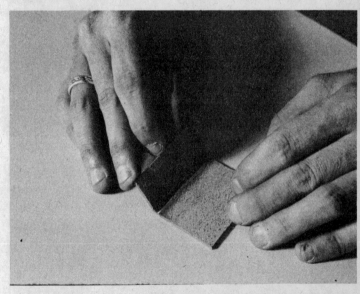

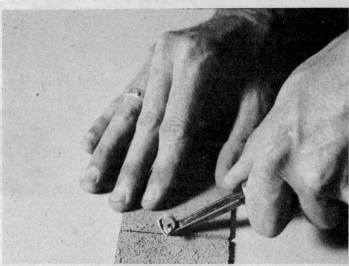

Figure 6. Skiving is an important step in leather working. A tool called a skife (below left) is used to reduce the thickness of the leather along an edge where a seam is planned. Two steps in the folding process are skiving an area twice as wide as the fold (above right) and using a modeler tool to make a crease at the fold (below right).

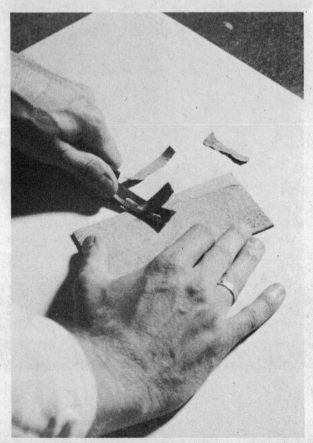

CREASING

Creasing is done when a piece is to bend in a particular spot. It is done simply by cutting a V-shaped groove on the fleshy side of the bend, halfway through the leather. The bend is made while the leather is still wet by folding over and lightly tapping the crease with a smooth mallet. The crease is then weighted with books and allowed to dry. When the leather is dry, the crease is permanent.

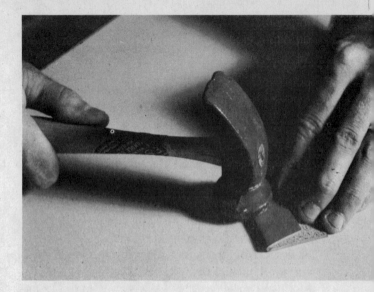

Figure 7. A hammer is used on wet leather during the creasing process. Prior to this step, a V-shaped groove was cut in the fleshy side of the bend, half way through the leather.

Lacing is the method of sewing or stitching pieces together with leather strips instead of with thread. Begin by laying the pieces together as they will be when the lacing is completed. Then, using a divider, work a line on the upper piece. The line should be parallel to and about 3/32" away from the edges to be laced. (Before the slits are stamped it may be necessary to glue the two leather pieces together to prevent slipping.) With the thonging

chisel, stamp slits along the line, going through both pieces of leather. To insure even spacing of slits, the first thong of the chisel should be placed in the last slit of the previously stamp slits.

There are three basic kinds of lacing techniques: the running stitch, the whipstitch, and the double buttonhole stitch.

Figure 8. When preparing to stitch leather with leather lace, a process called lacing, use a divider (below) to work a line 3/32" from the edge to be laced. Then, use a thonging chisel (right) to stamp slits along this line. Space the slits evenly by placing the first thong of the chisel in the last of the slits already stamped.

Skive the end of a piece of lacing, insert it into the flat needle, and tap the prongs to hold in the lace. Next, use an X-acto knife to cut a 1/8″ slit at the other end of the lace, about 1/4″ from the tip. To begin lacing, pass the needle through the first hole, from the back to the front, and then into the second hole, from the front to the back. Once through the second hole, the needle should be inserted through the slit in the end of the lace and pulled tight. This keeps the lace from coming undone. Continue passing the needle in and out of the holes. After passing through the last hole to the back, loop the lace twice around the previous stitch and pull tight.

The Whipstitch

Begin the whipstitch by inserting the needle through one piece of leather, from the fleshy side to the front. This means that as the lace comes out of the first hole, the tail end will be sandwiched between the two pieces of leather to be laced together. For the second stitch, the needle goes around the top of the seam, through the second hole (through both pieces of leather), and out the front again. Repeat the operation from back to front, going all the way around to the beginning.

Figure 10. Another basic lacing stitch is the whipstitch, which resembles a spiral binding. To finish the stitch, tie the lace off by running the needle through the back half of the first hole.

Figure 9. A basic lacing stitch, the running stitch, is similar to that used in sewing. Thread the needle through one end of the skived lacing, and cut a slit in the other end before beginning.

Tie off the lace by running the needle through the back half of the first hole so that the lace is again sandwiched between the two layers.

The Double Buttonhole Stitch

The double buttonhole stitch is begun by passing the needle from front to back through the first hole of both pieces to be laced, leaving out about 3″ of the tail end. Make a full loop of lacing around the right hand side of the tail, front to back. Insert the needle through the second hole, and pull tight.

Figure 11. For the third lacing stitch, the double buttonhole stitch, pass the needle through the first hole; leave a tail of 3″; loop lace around tail; and insert through second hole. Pull tight.

Figure 12. For a double buttonhole stitch: insert needle under "X" created by the previous loop; pull tight; put needle through next hole; pull tight.

Next, insert the needle under the "X" created by the first loop, and pull tight. Insert the needle through the third hole, from front to back, and pull tight. Then, insert the needle under the "X" created by the previous stitch and pull tight. Continue the two-part procedure: first through the hole in front; and then through the "X." At the corners of an article it is necessary to go through two of the holes twice so that the lacing will fit smoothly.

After inserting the needle through the last hole and under the last "X," pull out part of the first stitch so that the tail end can be sandwiched between the two layers of leather. To end the lacing, insert the needle down through the first loop and halfway through the first hole. Pull tight and cut off the excess. Both ends of the lace are now sandwiched between the layers of leather (see illustration).

STITCHING

Another method of joining together parts of a project is by stitching or sewing with thread. To stitch together sections of a project, begin by using a divider to mark a line parallel to the edges. Also with the divider, mark off equal distances to designate where holes are to be punched. Holes should be made with an awl or a drill because making holes with a needle is very difficult.

Leather stitching is done with two needles, one at each end of the thread. The first needle is inserted through the first hole and pulled halfway through. Both needles are then inserted through the second hole from opposite directions and pulled tight. For the third hole, the needles are again inserted through the same hole from opposite directions. This method produces an extra strong double stitch which is a necessity for leather work.

Figure 13. When stitching leather with thread, punch holes in the leather with an awl (above). Use two needles (below); insert both through the same hole but from opposite sides.

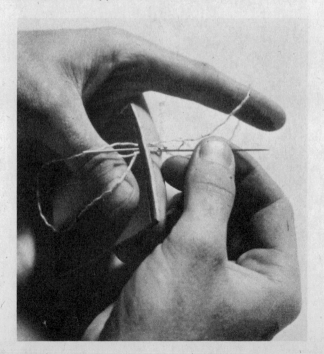

STRETCHING AND FORMING

Stretching is a process which alters the flatness of leather by stretching it over an existing form. The best forms are usually wooden, and it is often best to carve and shape the entire finished form. If, for instance, a pot is the project, it is necessary to make the entire form in wood first. To do this requires soft wood and common carpentry tools. When the wooden form is done, mark on the wood where the seams are to be located. Cut leather shapes large enough to cover the segments marked on the form, allowing enough for stretching and nailing. Immerse the leather in hot water for about 10 minutes until the leather is thoroughly wet. Begin stretching the leather and tacking it to the outside of the carved wood with small nails. Pull the leather tightly to avoid bumps, and allow it to dry for at least 48 hours. When it is dry, remove it and form each consecutive piece. Once all the pieces are formed, cut them to size according to the marks on the form and stitch them together.

Forming is a process similar to stretching, but two forms are used: one for a bottom and another slightly smaller matching shape to fit inside. Clamping the two together with wet leather between is known as forming. Forming is used for small and simple three-dimensional shapes, such as small boxes and bottles.

Begin by cutting the desired shape from a block of wood. This block is called the outside piece. The finished shape, called the inside piece, should not be any smaller than 2″. Using a divider, mark a line around the top surface of the cut-out piece of wood to indicate the thickness of the leather. Cut away this margin all the way around the piece. This is done so that the leather and the wooden form will fit back into the hole left in the outside piece. If the article is to be a smoothly rounded shape, file the edge of the inside piece, for its shape will be the shape of the finished piece. Now soak the leather in water for 10 minutes. Next, place the leather over the inside piece and set the piece on plywood. Then take the outside piece and place it firmly over the inside piece. With three or four C-clamps, tighten the outer block until it is tight against the plywood. Allow the leather to dry for 48 hours; then remove and trim to size.

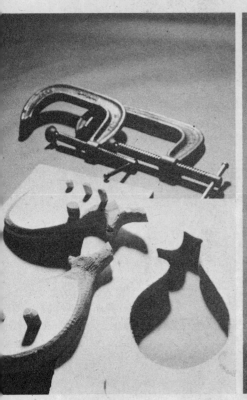

CARVING

Carving is the process of cutting and stamping a permanent design into the surface of leather. Once the leather has been conditioned (see *Conditioning* above) and the design has been traced, the next step is to cut the design into the leather. A swivel knife is used to cut a shallow groove into the surface. The first stamp used is the beveler, which slopes one side of the cut line to make some forms advance and others recede. This adds a three-dimensional quality to the design. The next stamp, a pear shader, makes gradual depres-

sions which resemble shading. The next stamp is the background tool, available in a variety of sizes and textures. Background tools are used to give an overall even texture to the leather.

The beveler, the swivel knife, the pear shader, and the background tool are the basic tools that are almost always used in carving. In addition dozens of other stamps can be used to heighten the appearance of the carving. The choice is entirely individual. The stamps add surface texture to a design — the inventive use of stamps is always rewarding.

Figure 14. After leather is conditioned, it can be carved. The first step is to cut a groove from the surface with a swivel knife (above). Use a beveler to flatten one side of the cut line (below). Beveling produces a three-dimensional effect in the design. When a shaded effect is desired, use a pear shader (top right) to make slight depressions in the leather surface. When an even texture is desired, use a background tool (bottom right) on the background of the main design.

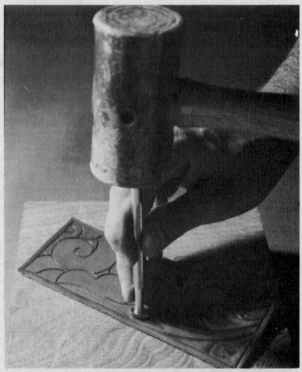

Figure 15. Two pieces of leather that are to be joined together must be cemented. Use a small piece of cardboard to spread the glue evenly on both pieces (left). When the glue is dry, press the pieces together slowly (right).

CEMENTING

Cementing is done to join two pieces of leather either for lining one piece with another, laminating, or cementing parts prior to stitching. Contact cement and rubber cement are the most effective glues, especially for lining. Do not use a glue which dries hard, as it will stiffen the leather. Begin the cementing process by cutting several small cardboard cards. These facilitate even spreading of the glue. Cut a piece of leather somewhat larger and slightly thinner than the area to be lined. Pour a small amount of glue onto the fleshy side of this piece of leather. Spread the glue evenly with one of the little cards, making sure all areas of the piece are covered. Repeat the operation on the piece to be lined. Allow both pieces to

dry. Beginning at one end, lay the thinner lining piece over the thicker main piece. Press the two pieces together gradually to avoid air pockets and wrinkles. When they are firmly together, trim off the excess lining.

For gluing pieces prior to stitching, white glue is often used in place of contact cement. It has the advantage of not dragging on the needle as it is pulled through the hole. Begin by applying a bead of white glue to one of the two sides to be joined — prior to punching any holes or slits. Join the two parts and slide them back and forth to distribute the glue evenly on both parts. Separate the two parts and let the glue dry slightly (1 to 3 minutes). Join the parts again and press them together with C-clamps for 45 minutes.

FASTENING

Snaps and rivets are handy and permanent for joining leather. They are particularly useful for straps and belts and for any item on which stitching or lacing is not practical.

Snaps

Snaps consist of four parts: the button and socket form the visible top half; the eyelet and stud form the invisible bottom half. Begin by punching a hole in the top piece of leather, making the hole large enough for the socket. Place the socket and leather on the anvil of the snap-setting tool (tool used to set in the snap). With the button over the socket and the concave end of the setting tool

Figure 16. Snaps used in leather work come in four parts. The button and socket are the visible parts, and the eyelet and the stud are the invisible components in the finished item.

over the button, strike with a mallet. One brisk blow is enough to set the snap top. For the bottom punch a hole the size of the eyelet. Insert the eyelet and place it over the opposite end of the set tool. Place the stud over the eyelet, the setting tool over the stud, and again strike with the mallet. The two halves are complete.

Figure 17. To set the snap top, use the mallet to strike the set tool one sharp blow (top). Place an anvil under the leather as shown. To set the bottom half of the snap, insert the eyelet, then the stud, and again strike the setting tool with the mallet (bottom).

Rivets

The easiest and most appropriate rivet for leather is known as a rapid rivet. It consists of two parts: the button and the base. Rivets come in several

lengths to accommodate various thicknesses. Begin by punching a hole through both pieces to be joined — the hole should be large enough to accommodate the button. Insert the base through

Figure 18. Rivets are a convenient way to join leather. The type most often used is the rapid rivet. It consists of a button and a base (right). Begin by punching a hole through the pieces to be joined (above).

the bottom of the hole, pat the surface, and, using the concave end of a snap set and a mallet, strike the button. The two parts are now permanently joined.

CLEANING

Once an article is constructed, it must be cleaned before dyeing or finishing. Dissolve 1 teaspoon of oxalic acid in 1 pint of water. Apply this solution to the leather with a clean rag and then allow the leather to dry. Oxalic acid is a mild bleaching agent and will dissolve grease and fingerprints — both of which will prevent an even dyeing.

DYEING

Dyeing is the process of coloring the leather. Dyes may be applied on small areas with a paint brush or over large areas with a sheep's-wool pad or a sponge. It is important to apply the dye evenly — this is done by applying the same amount with each stroke. Once the dye is dry, a second coat

Figure 19. Small areas of leather can be colored by applying dye with a small paint brush. Test the dye on a leather scrap before applying.

may be necessary for a uniform covering. It is often a good idea to test the dye on a leather scrap to get an idea of the result.

FINISHING

All leather should be finished to protect and preserve the surface. The best protection is leather

Figure 20. When large areas of leather are to be dyed, use a wool pad or sponge to apply the dye evenly. A second coat may be necessary.

lacquer, a clear coating which sinks deep into the leather and seals it against moisture and grease. The lacquer should be applied with a clean, lint-free rag and, if the leather is a natural color, the lacquer should be rubbed briskly into the surface. However, heavy rubbing on dyed surfaces may weaken some dyes. Once it is dry, the surface may be given a coat of paste wax or clear boot wax to heighten the shine.

Projects You Can Do

Three different items are suggested here as projects. Each involves a variety of skills, and it does not matter if a particular item is done first or last.

CARVED LEATHER BELT

1. Obtain a piece of 8-ounce cowhide which is long enough for a belt and at least 3" longer than the desired finished length.

2. Cut a straight edge through the selected piece, being careful to avoid waste. Use a mat knife and a metal straight edge.

Figure 21. To begin a leather belt, cut the leather the desired length and width using a straight edge as a guide.

3. Measure the width of the belt and, with a knife and straight edge, cut the other side of the hide. Be certain to hold the straight edge firmly and to cut through the leather in one stroke.

4. Select the front of the belt and cut the point. Usually a curved point is best for the lead end of a thin belt and rounded corners best for the lead end of a wide belt.

Figure 22. Cut the point for the front of the belt. Make a curved point for a thin belt and rounded corners for a wide one. Then soak the leather in water for several hours, allow to dry, and remove the top corner edge of the belt.

5. Soak the leather in water and place it in a plastic bag for several hours.

6. Remove the belt from the bag and allow it to dry until the natural color returns.

7. With a common edger, remove the top edge of the belt all around.

8. With an edge creaser, firmly line and crease the edge all around.

9. Draw the design to be carved on a piece of paper, using the belt itself as a template to insure that the design will be the actual size of the belt.

10. Lay the finished design over the belt and, with a ball tracer, trace the image onto the belt. The pressure from the ball leaves a mark on the leather.

11. With a sharp swivel knife, cut the design into the surface of the leather.

12. With a beveler and a mallet, bevel the back-

ground side of the cuts made. This will make the foreground areas appear to protrude.

13. With a pear shader, stamp those areas which are to be shaded.

14. With any of the various other stamping tools, create patterns to be shaded on the surface of the design. Note: The marks of each tool vary depending on the angle from which the impression is made and the strength of the blow. When in doubt, test the stamp on a damp scrap of leather.

15. The final stamp is the background tool. It may be used over the solid areas or it may feather off away from the image. Again, experiment before beginning.

16. Once the stamping is done, many craftsmen use the swivel knife to add a few small, accenting cuts or details. Do this now, if desired.

17. Once the carving is finished, dampen the edge of the leather. With a circle edge slicker, smooth and polish the edge until it appears smooth. Just before finishing with lacquer, apply an edging compound and buff.

Figure 23. After a carving is finished, smooth and polish the edges of the leather. Use a circle edge slicker for this operation. Apply an edging compound and polish again.

18. Measure and decide upon the placement of the buckle. Skive the back of the belt at the point where the belt is to fold over.

19. If a buckle with a tongue is to be used, cut a slot for the tongue by punching a hole 3/8" on either side of the center of the fold and in the center of the belt. With a knife, cut two slits from hole to hole and remove the piece between holes.

20. With the buckle in place, punch the appropriate-size holes for the rivets or snaps to be used. Snaps are preferred if buckles are to be changed.

21. If a loop is needed to hold the tongue of the belt flat, it should be inserted between snaps or rivets.

22. Set rivets or snaps according to the directions in "Basic Procedures".

23. Put on the belt and mark the spot for the hole where the belt is most comfortable; punch the hole.

24. It is wise to punch two additional holes 1/2" on either side of the center hole to allow for adjustment.

25. If any coloring or dyeing is to be done, it should be done at this point. The leather should be dry. Follow the directions in "Basic Procedures."

26. Finish the belt with a coating of clear leather lacquer applied with a soft rag. Note: Burnishing the edge with a round slicker is possible while the lacquer is wet.

Figure 24. When using a buckle with a tongue, cut a slot for the tongue by punching a hole on either side of the center of the fold; then cut two slits from hole to hole (left). When using a buckle that requires a loop to hold the tongue of the belt flat, insert the loop between snaps or rivets and set them in place (above). Punch a hole at the point at which the belt is most comfortable; punch additional holes on either side to allow for adjustment.

FORMING A HANGING POT

1. From a square piece of 1" thick plywood, cut a form from the center. This form will be the mold for half of the finished pot — two halves will be shaped from leather and sewn together. The form should be cut out with a saber saw, which is a saw that will not destroy the outer piece of plywood.

2. From around the perimeter of the hole in the plywood, cut an amount equal to the thickness of the leather to be shaped. For example, if the leather is 8 ounces thick, remove 1/8" all around the hole.

3. Select an 8-ounce, vegetable-tanned leather and cut a shape large enough to completely cover the form, allowing at least 1/2" extra for error.

4. Soak the leather in hot water until completely saturated.

5. Lay the wet leather over the hole in the plywood and force the form into the hole and the leather with it.

6. It may be necessary to weight the form in place if it has a tendency to come out.

7. This should be allowed to dry for 48 hours.

8. Remove the first piece of shaped and repeat the operation for the other half of the pot. If the pot is to be exactly symmetrical, the operation will be the same. If the pot is not to be symmetrical, the reverse side of the wooden form will be used. Otherwise, the two shapes will not match when placed together.

9. After the second piece is dry, remove and trim both pieces allowing just enough room for stitching.

10. On the top of each half-section, carefully mark off the stitching holes with a divider. Be certain that each half has the same number of holes marked.

11. With an awl, punch the holes.

12. With white glue, spot glue the two halves together, using pins to make the holes coincide. Allow 45 minutes for drying.

13. Using a long piece of linen thread with needles at both ends, begin stitching the halves together. Remember each needle carries the thread through each hole from opposite directions.

14. Choose a place on each side to stitch on loops for hanging

15. Cut two long laces to attach to the loops for hanging.

16. Finish the pot with clear lacquer.

CHROME-TANNED WALLET

1. Write down the measurements for the pieces of a wallet. (The design of the wallet can be based on one you already have.) Draw outlines of the pieces on paper and cut them out so that they may be pinned together. If the paper pieces fit together properly, take the pieces apart and smooth them out.

2. Lay out the back of the wallet on 2-ounce chrome-tanned leather. Cut it out, adding a 1/4" allowance all around for folding.

3. Cut the lining from the same leather, making certain it is the size of the back template.

4. With a skife, skive away half the thickness of the back along a margin 3/8" from all edges.

5. Apply contact cement evenly over the fleshy side of both the back and the lining.

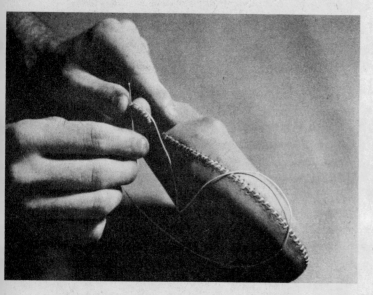

Figure 25. Linen thread is used to stitch together the two sides of a hanging pot. Remember that the thread is worked with two needles, inserted from opposite sides.

Figure 26. To begin a wallet, make a paper pattern of an old wallet. Draw and cut out a pattern for each part of the wallet, and pin the pieces together for fit.

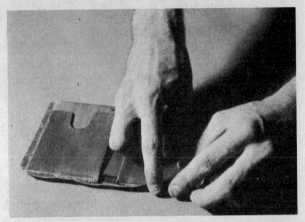

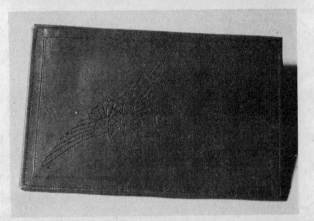

Figure 27. Steps in making a wallet include: applying the glue to the fleshy side of both the back and the lining after both pieces have been skived (above); cutting slits between the corners of the lining and those of the back to allow for folding (top right); folding the edges of the back (center right); and sewing around the edges using a sewing machine (bottom right).

6. Position the lining and lay it down slowly, removing air bubbles.

7. With a small, stiff paint brush, spread cement around the edge of the lining and allow it to dry.

8. At the four corners, cut a small slit from the corner of the lining to the corner of the back to allow for folding.

9. The divider should be cut from the same leather and be the same length as the liner, but 1/4" less in width.

10. The divider should be cemented around the two side edges and the bottom edge and then glued to the edges of the liner.

11. The inside also has glued edges. This part should be made according to individual preference — some people like flaps, some like pockets, and others like plastic folders. Readymade insides can also be purchased.

12. The side edges and the bottom edge should be attached to the divider as in step 10.

13. With the liner, the divider, and the inside glued in place around the edges, apply glue to the outer two side edges, to the bottom of the inside, and along the top edge of the liner. Allow the glue to dry.

14. Fold the edges of the back over to join the recently glued edges in step 13.

15. With the inside down, machine sew around the four sides about 3/32" from the edge.

For Additional Reading

Cherry, Raymond, **General Leathercraft,** McKnight and McKnight.
Meilach, Dona Z., **Contemporary Leather,** Regnery.
10;hide

Early American Decorative Painting

Painted designs, authentically reproduced on tin and wood by early American craftsmen, is still a popular craft.

Country painting, one technique of Early American decoration, is a folk art which originated in the United States in the eighteenth century. It is not "tole" painting, which is the French word for sheet iron, nor is it "Pennsylvania Dutch," a kind of painting stemming from German folk art. The craftsmen of this early American era simply called it "japanned ware," the proper name of the truly American craft.

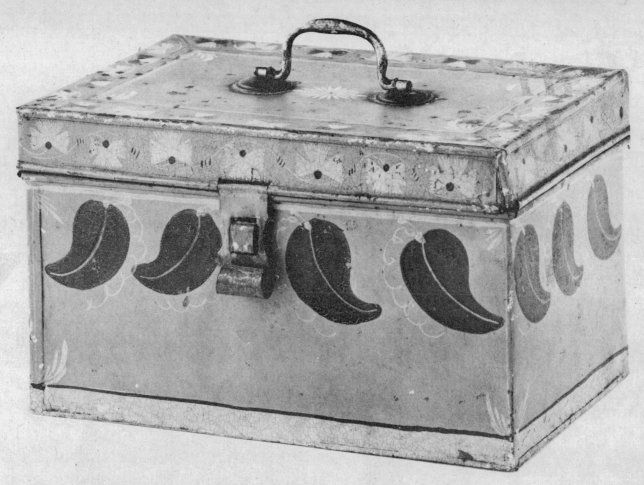

Figure 2. Leaves and flowers adorn this tin and brass box, made in the United States between 1825 and 1860. The origin of these pieces can be identified by the variations in their colors and patterns. (Courtesy, The Henry Francis du Pont Winterthur Museum.)

Edward Pattison, an immigrant from Ireland, is credited with the establishment of the tin industry in this country. He introduced the manufacture of tinware in Connecticut, trained many apprentices, and encouraged extensive peddling of tin products. He started making handmade, tin-plated kitchenware about 1750. The early pieces were left undecorated, but, near the turn of the century, the ware was japanned. This meant that the tin was given an asphaltum basecoat and dried by heat, an imitation of oriental lacquering. The pieces were then decorated or "flowered." Whole families were often involved in creating this tinware, with the women doing the decorating. Tin peddlers carried the japanned ware

Figure 1. A tin pot (opposite), suitable for coffee or tea, is dated between 1830 and 1860 and probably came from Pennsylvania. (Courtesy, The Henry Francis du Pont Winterthur Museum.)

from the northeast tin centers as far west as the Mississippi River and as far south as New Orleans.

Many shops and craftsmen clung to certain established styles in decoration so that the source of these can often be identified. One of these was Zachariah Stevens of Stevens Plains, Maine, who opened his shop in 1798; another Maine craftsman was Oliver Buckley. This tin center was, at one time, the headquarters for over a hundred peddlers. Maine designs were of a style similar to canvas painting and were on background colors of white, yellow, red, and black.

One of the best-known tin businesses was owned by Oliver Filley of Bloomfield, Connecticut. He opened branch shops in Elizabeth, New Jersey, Lansingburg, New York (near Troy), and Philadelphia, Pennsylvania; later his son opened a shop in St. Louis, Missouri. The decoration on the ja-

Figure 3. These three boxes, made of tin and brass, are decorated with painstakingly symmetrical designs. They date back to the period between 1825 and 1860. The largest is 6¼" high; the smallest, 4¾" high. (Courtesy, The Henry Francis du Pont Winterthur Museum.)

panned ware of the Filley shops was often symmetrical or characterized by white bands under designs of fruit or flowers with several fine, black brush strokes. Both types of painting often appeared on asphaltum backgrounds.

It seems logical that some of the Filley apprentice painters in Pennsylvania should have been natives of that state who adapted these Connecticut patterns to appeal to the local people. The Pennsylvania designs were more colorful and employed more blue.

Two New York tin centers were operated by men trained in Connecticut. One was Aaron Butler of Greenville whose daughters, especially Ann, are well known for their decorating. Their work can be recognized by profuse ornamentation: tulips; rosebuds; red stems; six- and eight-pointed stars;

and the design, often on a white band with many groups of tiny dots scattered throughout. The other tin center was at Fly Creek and was owned by Stephen North. Mercy North, his daughter, is known for her decorated pieces containing red and white bands with many combinations of beautifully executed brush strokes.

Much research on Early American decoration and its techniques has been done by Esther Stevens Brazer, a descendant of Zachariah Stevens of Maine. Her book, *Early American Decoration*, published in 1940, assembles the results of her research. After her death in 1945, a group of her students organized a guild in her memory. That guild is now The Historical Society of Early American Decoration, Inc., with headquarters at Cooperstown, New York.

Figure 4. This painted tray dates from the period between 1830 and 1860. (Courtesy, The Henry Francis du Pont Winterthur Museum.)

Common Terms Used In Early American Decorative Painting

Apple Tray: a square basket, originally created in 1840, with a 4" floor and four 3" curved sides.

Asphaltum: a solution of mineral asphalt mixed with varnish, which makes a dark brown varnish. When applied to bright tin, a brown finish results, the tone depending on the thickness of asphaltum applied.

Background Colors: colors applied to articles in flat enamel, giving an opaque finish.

Band: wide stripe used on boxes, trays, etc., and usually white or red.

Base Coats: the first color applied in a design, over which other colors, usually transparent, will be painted.

Border: the area within the boundary line or rim of the decorated piece.

Country Painting: brush-stroke patterns on wood and tinware.

Country Tin: tinware and utensils made by country tinsmiths of the eighteenth and early nineteenth centuries and often decorated with country painting.

Cut Corner Tray: an octagonal tray, sometimes called a coffin tray, with a 3/4" flange and usually painted with country designs.

Flat Enamel: paint which dries to a soft, opaque, dull finish.

Hard Gloss Varnish: a finishing material of gum dissolved in linseed oil, used to give a hard, protective finish.

Japan: black asphaltum varnish for coating metal which produces lacquer-like results.

Japan Colors: pigment ground in japan for an opaque look.

Medium: a liquid used with paints to give fluency.

Oil Colors: pigments ground in oil which are slow drying; some colors are transparent, others semitransparent.

Quills: soft, pliant brushes made of camel hair.

Sanding Primer: an undercoat used to prepare a metal object for painting.

Satin Finish Varnish: varnish which dries to a soft, matte finish.

Supersee: common name for frosted acetate, used for painting patterns.

Tin: thin sheet of iron coated with tin; tinplate.

Wet/Dry Sandpaper: sandpaper which can be used dry or with water.

Basic Equipment And Supplies

It is most important to use only the equipment outlined in this section. Other kinds of brushes and paints will not produce the same effects. Local art supply stores and paint and hardware stores handle most of the items and will generally order the others if requested. There are also many mail order supply houses which carry supplies specifically for Early American decoration.

1. **Brushes.** 3/4" long, square-tipped quills, #3 and #4, and handles. These are used to paint base coats, and all sizes of brush strokes. Pointed, sable watercolor brush, #2; used for making very small brush strokes and thin, fine, short lines, dots, and curliques. 1" long liner quill, #1, with handle; used for long, fine lines and strokes as in veins, and also for striping. Oxhair one-stroke 1" brush: used for background colors and for varnish coats. 1" polybrush: sponge rather than a bristle brush, used for varnish coats.

2. **Japan Paints.** Striping white, chrome yellow medium, signcraft red. Available in cans and, when mixed with varnish, used for brush strokes and base coats.

3. **Artists' Oil Colors.** Alizarin crimson, prussian blue, raw umber, burnt umber, lampblack. Mixed with varnish and used for over strokes or mixed with other colors.

4. **Background Paints.** Flat enamel. Black is used most for backgrounds, but other flat subdued colors may be used such as mustard, antique red, or bayberry green; available at hardware stores and often in antiquing kits.

5. **Varnishes.** Clear gloss varnish. Used as a medium with japan and oil colors and also for finishing and protective coats; available at paint supply stores or hardware stores. Satin finish varnish: dull, matte finish used as a final coat. Sealer: thin liquid used to seal the grain of wood. Rust preventive. This stops the rust from developing under the paint; one type is naval jelly.

Other supplies include: (1) tracing paper; (2) tracing pen; (3) supersee; (4) black shiny paper for practicing brush strokes, experimenting with colors before putting them on a pattern, or for use in back of a pattern to show up colors; (5) palette; (6) palette knife; (7) practice board — a piece of cardboard covered with shiny black paper to practice brush strokes on and which can be cleaned with turpentine and used repeatedly; (8) board — a piece of masonite, or smooth, heavy cardboard about 14" by 18", necessary for fastening on tracings and patterns for painting; (9) pure gum turpentine; (10) lard oil or olive oil for dipping brushes after use and cleaning to keep them soft; (11) tack rag, a slightly sticky cheesecloth, for dusting; (12) bottle caps, about 1" in diameter to hold varnish while painting; (13) small jar or deep bottle cap; (14) lava soap and Q-tips for removing unwanted marks; (15) wet/dry sandpaper, #600; (16) sponge; (17) masking tape; (18) white pencil for marking off measurements; and (19) lint-free rag.

Figure 5. Special supplies and materials, such as Japan paints, are needed for decorative painting. Most of the items are available at art supply stores.

Basic Procedures

The basis of all Early American decorative painting is the brush stroke. Since country painting is essentially brush stroke painting, the importance of learning this technique is obvious. After some practice, a rhythm develops and with it much satisfaction in perfecting the strokes. By following the instructions carefully and by practicing, brush strokes will soon become lovely designs for decorative painting.

HOW TO PAINT BRUSH STROKES

Sitting in a good light, place the palette to the right, and the practice board in front of you. (Note: For left-handed persons, reverse the order, as well as the directions.) Keep the lint-free rag in the lap, handy for cleaning brushes.

Pour some varnish into a clean 1" bottle cap on the palette. Also pour some turpentine (for cleaning brushes) into a larger cap or small wide-mouthed bottle. Opening a can of chrome yellow medium, dip out about 1/8 teaspoonful with a palette knife and place on the palette.

Dip the #3 quill about halfway into the varnish, then into the edge of the paint. Stroke the brush back and forth on the palette many times to load or "dress" it. The consistency of the paint should be like heavy cream.

Figure 6. Mastering the brush stroke is a key procedure in decorative painting. Practice the strokes slowly and carefully until a slow, steady rhythm is developed.

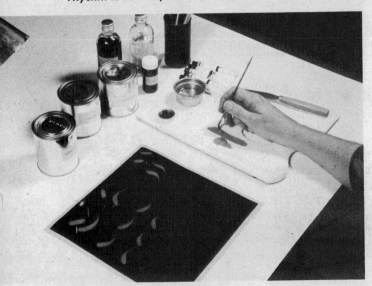

Hold the brush like a pencil; put it down until about half of the brush is on the practice board and the tip is at this angle: / . Pulling down slightly and to the right, begin lifting the brush until just the narrow edge of the brush is on the paper, making the tail of the stroke. The stroke should look like an inverted eyebrow. Do the same stroke over and over until a rhythm is achieved: down, pull, up; down, pull, up. This is a slow steady rhythm; do not try to go too fast and do try to lift the brush gradually, beginning to lift it almost as soon as it is put down. Practice one or two pages and when comfortable with the brush, try a stroke going in the opposite direction, which will look like an upright eyebrow. Start the brush at this angle: \ . Pull up and to the right and follow through as with the first stroke. After learning this stroke, try making groups of strokes. Make the middle one first, then one on each side, bringing them to the same point as the first one.

The "S" Stroke

Having stroked the brush back and forth, notice that it has a wide side and a knife-thin side. The stroke above was begun with the wide side and ended with the edge. In making the "S" stroke, place the brush with just the tip on the practice board at the / angle; pull down slightly at this angle, then, putting more pressure on the brush, pull to the right and down, lifting and pulling to the left again for a fine line.

The Straight Stroke

For this stroke, reach out a little with the brush, put it down, and lift while drawing it straight toward you until there is a point.

Circles

Trace a circle on your practice board. Make two or even three strokes around the outer edge of the circle to give a firm outline. Fill this in with broad strokes, taking as few strokes as possible. Stroke out the paint on the palette, then with the tip of the brush, smooth out any ridges with a very light touch.

Leaves

For a heart-shaped leaf, paint the outer edges with brush strokes, as with the circle, but following the

#4 QUILL

#3 QUILL

#2 POINTED BRUSH

#1 QUILL LINER

Figure 7. These are samples of brush strokes made with quills of three different sizes and with a pointed brush. Note that each implement is designed for a specific type of stroke.

outlines; then, fill in with broad strokes, and smooth out any ridges. For leaves with rounded points, start at the top, making brush strokes toward the bottom. For pointed leaves, start at the bottom, bringing strokes to a point for the pointed tips.

Dots and Curliques

Use a #2 pointed watercolor brush for these. Make a soupy mixture with the paint; dip the end of the brush into the mixture. Hold the brush straight up, not at an angle as before, and very lightly touch the brush to the board. This should make a perfectly round dot. To make the curliques using the regular paint mixture, rest the right hand on the left and, again holding the brush straight up and down, move the tip into the circular motion of the pattern.

Helpful Tips in Brush Stroking

The size of a brush stroke depends on how much pressure is put on the brush. For a large stroke, press down all the way and let the brush spread out, then begin lifting. For a smaller stroke, use only the end of the brush. Practice the strokes listed on the chart, using the brush indicated.

If strokes seem runny or weak in color, add more paint to the mixture. If strokes have ridges or a ragged end, add more varnish to make the paint flow more freely. In both cases, be sure to stroke the brush back and forth on the palette to get a proper mixture. A stroke should be smooth and without streaks. Practice to learn the right consistency for the paint.

Hold the brush correctly.

Clean the brush occasionally — both paints and varnish dry out after exposure to air.

Make a *brush stroke* — do not draw or merely fill in the tracing.

If there are puddles on the side of the strokes, the brush is overloaded.

COPYING THE PATTERN

Place a sheet of tracing paper over the design, fastening securely with clips. Trace the pattern carefully with a fine-point pen. After tracing, place the pattern on the work board. Cut a piece of supersee the same size as the tracing and place it over the tracing, dull side up. Fasten both papers to the board with masking tape. Now it is time to paint the design, following these steps:

1. Set up the palette as for brush strokes, and dip a bit of red paint from the can onto the palette. If the brush has been kept in lard oil, clean it by dipping it in turpentine. Using the brush stroke technique and the #4 square-tipped quill, paint the base coats in the design. (In some designs, the base coats may be yellow or white. In such a case, follow directions for the pattern.) Try not to just fill in the spaces, but make every stroke a brush stroke. This is very important; it makes the difference between a stiff, unnatural look, and one

Figure 8. On tracing paper that has been clipped over the design, trace the pattern with a fine-point pen (left). Paint the base coat, in this case red, with a #4 square-tipped quill. Use the brush stroke technique carefully (right) to avoid filling in broad areas.

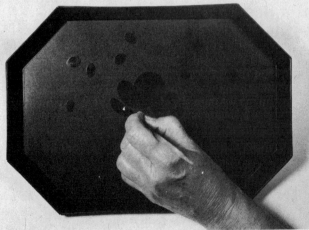

which has rhythm and feeling. *In all steps, let paint dry 24 hours.* After painting, clean brushes thoroughly in turpentine, dip in lard oil, and place in a position where they cannot be bent.

2. Squeeze out about 1/4" of paint from the tube of alizarin crimson, and about half that much of burnt umber. With a palette knife, add a touch of burnt umber to the alizarin crimson to tone it down. Mix the paint and varnish as for the first brush strokes, stroke out, and apply the strokes where shown. Since this is an oil color, the stroke will appear transparent. These strokes are the shadows and should be a medium tone — not too dark, not too light.

3. The white strokes create the highlights on the flower or fruit, and should be transparent and light. To get this mixture, add just a touch of white paint to a drop of the varnish on the palette and stroke it out many times, then test the color and texture on a piece of black paper. If the color is correct, but runny, stroke out more; if it is too white, add more varnish and stroke out. Apply white strokes where indicated. This stroke should not cover the alizarin stroke entirely; rather, it is usually half on the alizarin stroke and half on the red base coat.

4. Notice that green was not included in the list of paints. This is because the greens in country painting vary and must be matched to the pattern being copied. The most common color is a subdued green with a slight olive cast. To make green: squeeze some prussian blue on the palette, then dip out some yellow and some red in separate places. Add a small amount of blue to the yellow until a medium shade of green is acquired. Then add red, a bit at a time, to tone down the color. Use the palette knife when mixing colors. To make the green darker, add more blue; to make it lighter, add more yellow; to tone it down, add red.

5. Put some chrome yellow medium and some burnt umber on the palette. Add a touch of burnt umber to the yellow and mix with the palette knife; this is to tone it down. Here again, the yellow must be matched to the pattern, as the shade varies. Paint all yellow strokes, dots, curliques, etc., except the thin yellow color which is used as overstrokes or veins on the leaves. For this thin color, add more varnish to the paint until it is hin and transparent. Stroke paint out on the palette so it will not be runny.

6. If black veins or strokes appear in the pattern, they are generally applied now. Mix lampblack with varnish and apply as directed. Use the brush which best fits the type of stroke desired.

7. When this part of the pattern is dry, do the striping. This is done by using the #1 quill liner and pulling it toward yourself in a straight line. The width of the line will depend on the pressure on the brush. If a fine, thin line is desired, use just the tip. For a heavier line, press more on the brush.

Figure 9. Next, mix some alizarin crimson with burnt umber, according to directions, and apply accent strokes on the red base coat (left). For the white touches on the flowers (right), add a little white paint to the varnish, and apply over the base coat and alizarin strokes.

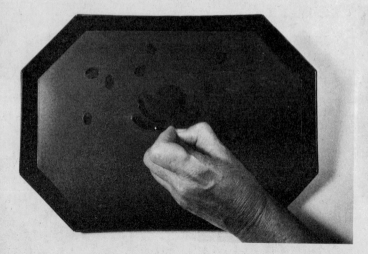

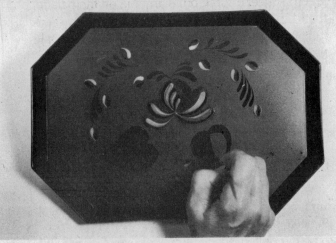 

Figure 10. Because green shades in country painting vary widely, mix green paint as instructed to match the pattern being used. Apply green for leaves and other areas (left). Yellow is applied twice: once for the strokes and dots (right); the second time, for veins on the leaves after it is mixed with varnish.

8. When the pattern is completed and dry, varnish it with the polybrush. Pour a little varnish into a small paper cup or 3″ clean jar top; dip the polybrush in about 3/4″, then stroke it out on the pattern, smoothing out the varnish. Notice that the supersee turns clear as it is varnished. When the pattern is dry, fasten it to a piece of cardboard with Scotch tape. Fasten the tracing to the other side of the board. This becomes a permanent pattern which can be used many times on several different articles.

PREPARING AN ARTICLE FOR DECORATING

To paint a piece of tin which has a coat of paint on it, remove the old paint with paint remover and rinse thoroughly. If the tin has no paint on it, clean it with detergent and water to remove any oil or dirt and let dry thoroughly. If there is any rust at all, treat the tin with a rust preventive since rusting continues, even under paint. Rusticide or naval jelly can be used for this purpose. Again clean, then sand the whole piece, where necessary, until smooth. A damp sponge is useful for cleaning the article while preparing it. Clean the surface with a tack rag to remove all dust; now it is ready for the first coat of paint.

Sanding Primer

Apply one coat of sanding primer with the 1″ background brush. Use a light touch and just the end of the brush so that there will be no ridges when the paint dries. Allow to dry for 24 hours, then sand with wet/dry sandpaper.

Sanding

Using wet/dry sandpaper, rub down the primer coat. This is done by tearing off a piece of sandpaper about 1″ x 2″, folding it, and dipping it into water. Sand until smooth. Clean with a damp sponge.

Figure 11. To prepare a tin piece for painting, remove any old paint. However, if the piece is unpainted, clean it thoroughly with detergent. If there is still any trace of rust on the tin after the piece has been prepared, apply a coat of rust preventive. Use rusticide or naval jelly.

apply two coats of a wood sealer, 24 hours apart. Sand again with wet/dry #600 sandpaper. If the wood is going to remain the natural color, give it one coat of varnish and sand. To stain the wood, apply one coat of stain after the first sanding, then apply one coat of varnish and sand again. If painting wood, give it two coats of thinned flat paint, 24 hours apart, and sand lightly.

PAINTING THE ARTICLE

Now that the piece is prepared and has a smooth surface, it is time to decorate the article. Cut a piece of tracing paper the exact size of the piece to be decorated. Place the paper over the pen and ink tracing, and, after deciding exactly where and how the design is to appear on the article, center and place it correctly. Trace the design on the paper with a pencil.

For a dark background, rub a piece of chalk over the back of the new tracing, and then with the hand, rub off as much excess powder as possible. If working on a light background, rub a pencil over the back of the tracing and rub off excess with the hand. Place this tracing on the article, fastening it in one or two places with masking tape so it will not slip. Now trace the design with a sharp pencil and the design will appear on the painted surface. If tracing a design on a wooden piece, do not bear down too hard, as it will make an indentation in the wood which cannot be removed. Remove the tracing.

Background Color

Clean the surface with a tack rag. With background brush, apply one coat of black flat enamel, or another flat color, first thinning the paint until it flows from the brush like light cream. Use the tip of the brush to smooth out the paint and beware of ridges and drips. Apply a second coat of the flat enamel and, when this is dry, sand as with the sanding primer. When the coat is smooth, it is time to do the design. (Follow the same process for the reverse side if necessary.)

If working on a light-colored background, it is best to give the article a coat of varnish to protect it from marks and smudges. Sand before decorating.

Wood Background

Sand wood smooth with a medium-coarse sandpaper. Wipe clean with a damp sponge, and

Figure 13. Trace the design to be used on the piece. First, make a tracing with pencil and paper. Then, use chalk for a light background and pencil for a dark background, as directed.

Follow directions for each pattern until it is time for striping and the brush stroke border. At this point, *before* proceeding with the striping and border, the article must be varnished so that corrections may be made more easily. Before varnishing, remove any unwanted smudges, fingerprints, or tracing marks with a sponge or Q-tip and lava soap. Clean with a damp sponge and when dry, clean surface with tack rag.

Varnishing

Use a 1" polybrush to varnish the surface. Varnish in a good light so that all areas are covered and there are no drips or dry spots. Varnish will go on more smoothly if it is at room temperature or warmed slightly (Place it in a cup of warm water a few minutes before using). It is a good idea to transfer the varnish from the can to small-topped bottles to keep it from being exposed to too much air. The article being varnished should also be at room temperature or warmed slightly. Clean polybrush in turpentine and detergent and water, or a household cleaner with grease-cutting solvents. Let dry before using again. A 1" background brush may also be used for varnishing.

Striping

Mix some burnt umber with the chome yellow medium, making a "dirty yellow." Use the liner quill for striping, and, holding it with the thumb and forefinger, place the outer fingers on the edge of the article and pull the liner toward you in a steady even line in the place to be striped. Striping is usually done along the edges of an article to accentuate the form and act as a frame for the painting.

Brush Stroke Border

Apply the brush stroke border when the striping is dry. This usually follows the line of striping and may be a line of single brush strokes, or a combination of strokes.

Finishing

When decorating is complete, and the article has been cleaned of any spots or smudges, give the article two coats of varnish, 24 hours apart, front and back. Allow it to dry for several days. When decorating a tray or another piece which will receive hard wear, rub it down with wet/dry sandpaper until smooth. Do not be alarmed if the piece appears to be gray — this will disappear when varnish or wax is applied. Give it another coat of varnish and let dry for several days. Rub this down in the same manner and, when smooth, apply a coat of spray wax, polish it, and repeat. This will give a hard, protective finish.

For an article such as a canister which will be used for decorative purposes, rub down with wet/dry sandpaper until smooth, and apply a coat of satin finish varnish. If the first coat does not cover completely, it may be necessary to apply a second coat.

Figure 14. Varnish the surface, using a 1" polybrush (left). Be sure to apply the varnish smoothly and evenly; leave no dry spots or bumps. A liner quill is used for striping (right). Striping is used to accent the edge, or border, of the piece.

Projects You Can Do

The following projects include all of the basic steps in Early American decorative painting and require a minimum of supplies. Other brushes and colors can be added later. However, these techniques are employed in all categories of decorative painting. The patterns are basic, and can be done by a beginner. Many pieces of old tin can be found in attics, flea markets, and antique shops, and there are many which lend themselves to decorating. Reproductions of early tin are also available, some with the background colors completed.

Most of these patterns are shown as they were used originally, but they can be adapted to other pieces. For instance, the cut corner tray pattern could be used on a canister, a box top, or a round tray. The coffee pot pattern could be used on a pitcher, a coal scuttle, a large canister, or even a tray. The border design on the canister could be used as a border on a box, around the bottom of a small canister, or a cut corner tray, which is where the design was used originally. The pattern on the bread board is a candle sconce pattern. Keep in mind the proportion of the piece and the pattern, and be sure it is appropriate to the piece being decorated.

Other objects which can be decorated are wastebaskets, wooden bowls, watering cans, letter holders or candle holders. Directions in "Basic Procedures" should be followed along with the step-by-step directions given with each pattern.

1. Prepare tray with black background according to directions.

Figure 15. This is the pattern for a cut corner tray. For best results on the finished piece, follow the color key carefully.

R — Red
AC — Alizarin Crimson
W — White
G — Green
Y — Yellow
TY — Thin Yellow
DY — Dirty Yellow

2. Trace design and transfer to tray.

3. Paint red base coats. If base coat does not appear to be quite solid looking, apply a second coat the next day. Always paint the entire base coat; green goes on top.

4. Paint alizarin crimson strokes.

5. Paint thin white strokes.

6. Paint all green leaves and strokes.

7. Add a touch of burnt umber to the yellow, and make yellow strokes, stems, and thin yellow veins in leaves.

8. Give tray a coat of varnish.

9. Do curliques and striping on the tray floor, and striping along edge of tray.

10. Do border brush strokes.

11. Finish as directed.

Figure 16. Apply border brush strokes to the tray (top) and finish as directed (bottom).

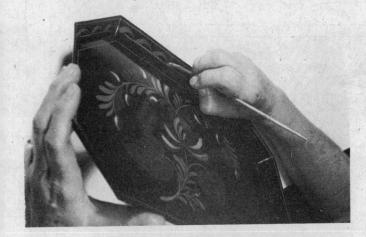

R — Red   W — White   G — Green
A — Alizarin Crimson   Y — Yellow

Figure 17. This is the pattern for a breadboard. Again, follow the color key exactly.

BREADBOARD

1. Prepare board according to directions for preparing wood.

2. Trace design and transfer it to board.

3. Paint red strokes.

4. Do alizarin strokes.

5. Do thin white strokes.

6. Paint the green strokes and do striping. (Piece was varnished in step 1 when the board was prepared.)

7. Paint yellow strokes and green border strokes.

Figure 18. The finished breadboard is a handsome object, and a functional one as well. A decorated breadboard would make an ideal gift for anyone interested in early American design.

COFFEE POT

1. Prepare coffee pot with black background.

2. Trace pattern and transfer to pot. Reverse pattern and trace on other side.

3. Paint red base coats. It will be easier on this piece to do the color on one side at a time, unless the artist is very careful not to smear the wet paint.

4. Paint alizarin strokes.

R — Red
AC— Alizarin Crimson
W — White
G — Green
Y — Yellow
TY— Thin Yellow
DY— Dirty Yellow
B — Black

Figure 19. This pattern for a coffeepot comes complete with color key. Note that the colors are coordinated to those used on the cut corner tray.

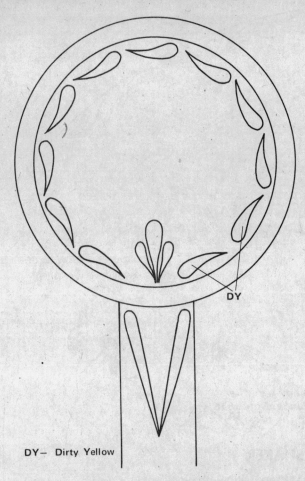

DY— Dirty Yellow

Figure 20. This is the pattern for the coffeepot lid. It is used in conjunction with the main pattern for the pot, shown on page 475. When painted a dirty yellow, this color provides a nice contrast with the black background.

Figure 21. The finished coffeepot is neat and professional looking. This project can be done easily and quickly by the inexperienced craftsman. The inspiration for this design came from nineteenth-century pots, which are now expensive antiques.

5. Paint thin white strokes.

6. Paint green strokes and leaves.

7. Paint yellow stems, strokes, and dots.

8. Paint black veins in leaves.

9. Paint thin yellow on green strokes and leaves.

10. Varnish.

11. Do striping around top, botton, and lid.

12. Do brush strokes around lid and on handle.

13. Finish as directed.

YELLOW WOODEN TRAY

1. Paint mustard yellow background on tray, preparing as directed; varnish and sand.

2. Trace design and transfer to tray.

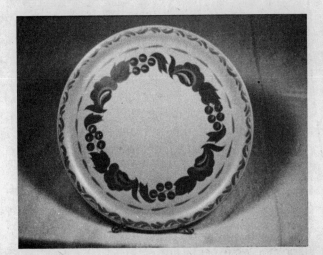

Figure 22. Making a round wooden plate is easy and rewarding. Follow the basic procedures in the text for preparing a wood object. The background color is a mustard yellow. This plate can be mounted and hung on the wall, or it can be displayed on a plate hinge.

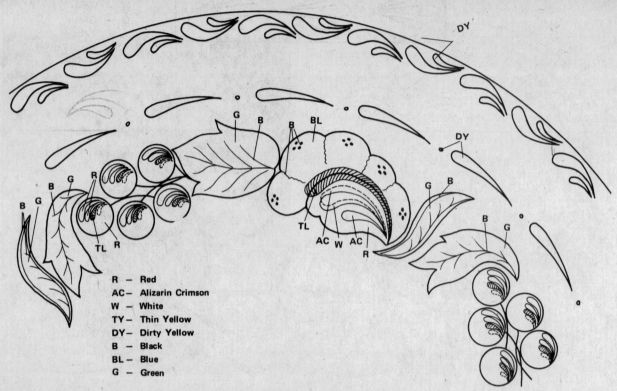

R — Red
AC— Alizarin Crimson
W — White
TY— Thin Yellow
DY— Dirty Yellow
B — Black
BL— Blue
G — Green

Figure 23. This is the basic pattern for the wooden plate shown on the opposite page. A color key is included for the artist's guidance. Note that the basic pattern is repeated four times to form a circle on the plate.

3. Paint all red, keeping cherries perfectly round.

4. Paint alizarin strokes.

5. Paint blue sections by mixing white and blue until a medium color is reached; add raw umber to tone it until there is a "dirty" blue on the palette.

6. Paint thin white strokes.

7. Paint in green leaves, making the paint a little thinner than on other patterns. This should also have just a touch more blue than used previously.

8. Add burnt umber to yellow. Do thin yellow strokes and striping. (Piece has been varnished.) Stripes may be marked around outside using a white pencil in a compass: make the pencil a little shorter than the pointed end of the compass, and hold the pointed end over the rim of the tray, the pencil in from the edge about 1/4 inch. Pull along toward you, turning the tray as you go. Cover the point with masking tape so it will not scratch. When you paint the stripe, pull the Liner Quill along the white pencil line.

9. Do black strokes and veins, using #2 brush and liner quill.

10. Do brush stroke borders.

11. Finish as directed.

SHAKER

1. Prepare tin with black background.

2. Trace pattern and transfer it to tin.

3. Paint red base coats; give second coat if necessary.

Figure 24. This shaker is another project for the ambitious craftsman. The background color is black and the flowers are mainly red.

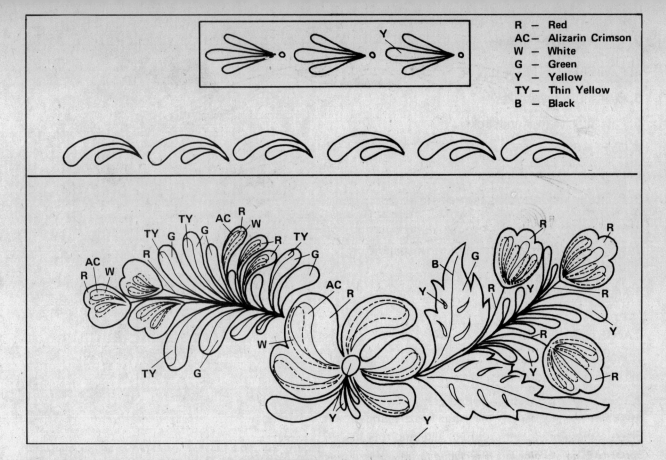

Figure 25. Two final patterns are given for decorative painting projects. One is for a shaker (above), illustrated on page 477. The other is for a canister (below), illustrated on the facing page. Color keys are supplied, as is customary.

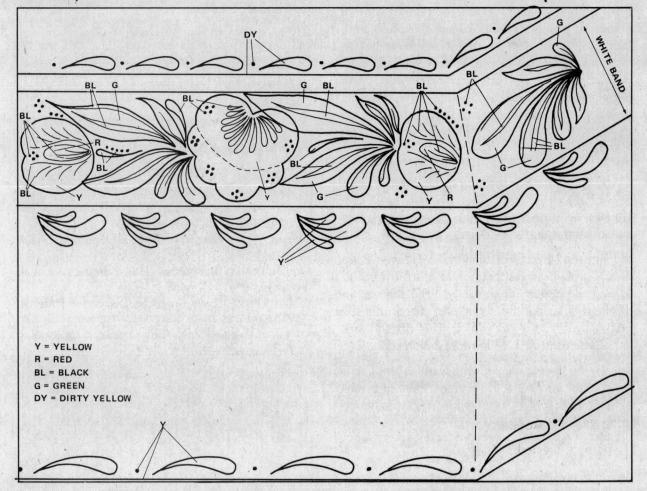

Y = YELLOW
R = RED
BL = BLACK
G = GREEN
DY = DIRTY YELLOW

4. Paint alizarin crimson strokes.

5. Paint thin white strokes.

6. Paint green leaves and strokes.

7. Paint yellow strokes.

8. Paint black veins in leaves.

9. Paint thin yellow strokes and veins in leaves.

10. Varnish and stripe.

11. Do border strokes and strokes on handle in dirty yellow.

12. Finish as directed.

CANISTER

1. Prepare background by painting with antique red flat enamel and varnish.

2. Paint white band on as follows: Measure, and mark with white pencil, 1¾" strip to be painted. Place some white paint on the palette and mix in several drops of varnish until thinned out. Add a touch of burnt umber to make it off-white, then add a few drops of turpentine. The mixture should be quite runny. With the largest quill, test the color on black paper — it should be thin without being too transparent. Stroke out the brush and, starting on the outer line, pull it along one line as far as it will go, then along the other line, making a firm edge on either side. Fill in between with broad strokes. Do one section at a time, brushing as quickly as possible because the paint sets up quickly. Do not try to go back over it. Practice on black paper first.

3. Trace pattern on white band, rubbing pencil on back of tracing.

4. Paint yellow base coats (no burnt umber); this includes the entire large flower.

5. Paint red strokes on small yellow flower. Paint brush strokes across bottom of the flower following the bottom line exactly. With the end of the finger, pat out the upper part of red until the original line does not show. The dotted lines show where the red blended area should end.

6. Mix the green; thin it with varnish until it is transparent, but still a lively color. Paint in leaves with as few strokes as possible. This should be done quickly and left to even out.

Figure 26. The finished canister is an unusual and attractive object. The background color is red, and most of the accents are yellow.

7. Do all strokes and veins in black, using #1 quill and #2 brush.

8. Give canister a coat of varnish.

9. Add umber to yellow and do striping.

10. Do brush stroke borders.

11. Finish as directed.

For Additional Reading

Brazer, Esther Stevens, **Early American Decoration,** Pond-Ekberg Co., 1940.

Coffin, Margaret, **American Country Tinware 1700-1900,** Thomas Nelson & Sons, 1968.

Lipman, Jean, **American Folk Decoration,** Dover, 1972.

Murray, Maria, **The Art of Tray Painting,** Bramhall House, 1954.

Sabine, Ellen S., **Early American Decorative Patterns,** Van Nostrand, 1962.

Slayton, Mariette Paine, **Early American Decorating Techniques,** 1972.

Collage

Figure 1. The collage "Eskimo Blue" is by Suzanne Peters, a Chicago artist. Crayons, ink, tissue, and watercolors were used to create the intriguing effect of over lapping contrasts and textures.

Collage, the gluing together of small papers and articles into a design, is a rewarding, artistic, and practical form of self-expression.

The origin of collage is attributed to both Georges Braque and Pablo Picasso. Each artist utilized the method at the turn of the century. However, prior to this, Italian portrait painters had pasted small pieces of chain, gilded paper, and sometimes real stones and jewels onto their canvasses.

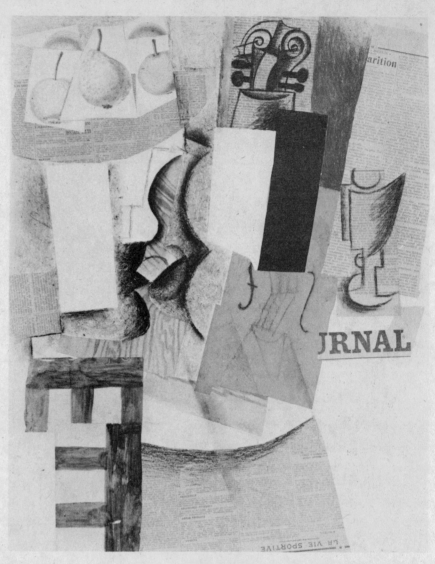

Figure 2. Artist Pablo Picasso completed this collage, "The Violin," in 1913. (Courtesy, Philadelphia Museum of Art, A.E. Gallatin Collection; photo, A.J. Wyatt, Staff Photographer.)

Both Picasso and Braque were influenced by the writings, theories, and paintings of Paul Cézanne. Along with another group, they began to paint in an abstract geometric style later referred to as analytic cubism.

In an effort to return to a more realistic form of painting, they retained the geometric format but began to incorporate such realistic materials into their work as sand, newspapers, and string. They built up areas and added texture in unorthodox ways by also including in their creations such items as hair, feathers, cloth, and even tickets and old matchbooks. Thus collage as a true art form was born as a result of the transition from analytic cubism to synthetic cubism.

However, collage did not stop at a two-dimensional level. The Dadaists used collage effectively to express their views of society by gluing together garbage and everyday items. One of their most famous works is "The Urinal" by Marcel Duchamp.

The word "collage" is taken from the French verb *caller*, which means to paste or glue. The beginning of a collage is the pasting or gluing of paper to paper, of paper to board, or of any of several materials to others.

Collage today is an accepted art form. It allows the artist the freedom to approach the medium in whatever manner is pleasing and does not restrict him to any format or material. This medium is a direct form of communication for an artist; that is, it allows the artist to work with whatever materials he chooses.

Collage is different from other art forms because it does not dictate a particular style. Style is often

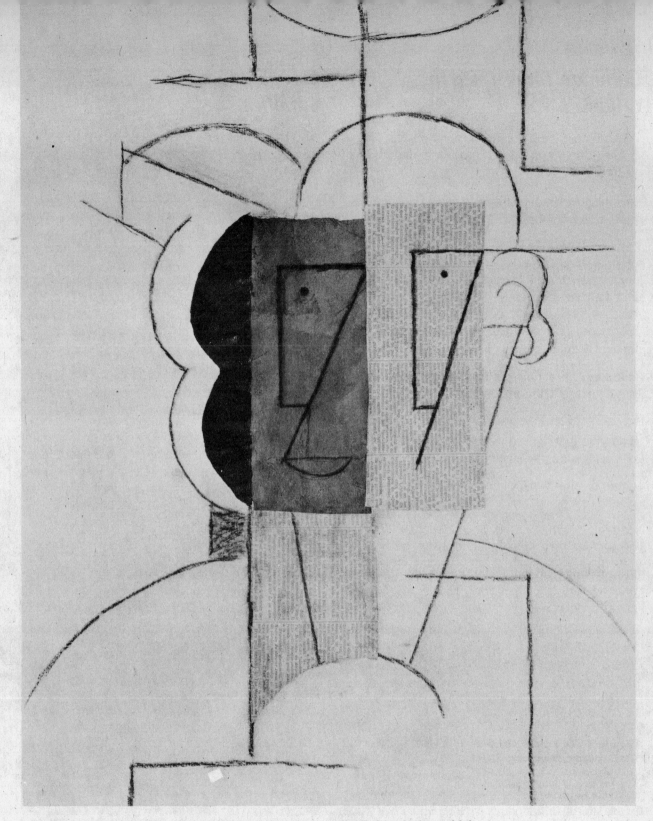

Figure 3. "Man With a Hat" is a collage by Pablo Picasso. The Cubist design, which was done in 1912, was created with charcoal, ink, and pasted paper. (Collection, The Museum of Modern Art, New York.)

controlled by materials and, because the materials are never the same for any two persons, the style of collage is always a variable. Collage is an excellent medium for both the beginner and the experienced artist. The inventiveness and creativity used in a collage usually do not result from experience but from a willingness to experiment with the basic procedures.

Common Terms Used In Collage

Assemblage: the grouping of found objects put on a three-dimensional level into a two-dimensional design.

Brayer: a roller, available in various sizes, used to press glued material flat.

Cover Stock: heavy paper used for glossy color photographs in magazines.

Dot Pattern: dots which result from the printing process for the photographs and illustrations in magazines and newspapers; used in collage for areas of texture.

Extender: an acrylic gel used either as an adhesive or to extend the amount of color or pigment.

Gesso: a mixture of lime, whiting, zinc white, and hide glue that is used as a water-based primer in preparing surfaces for collage.

Ground: the surface upon which a design is placed.

Priming: sealing the surface of a board with gesso or other sealers by the substance on the surface.

Printmaking Papers: paper especially suited to printing and excellent for collage; also called graphic papers.

Basic Equipment And Supplies

The materials listed here represent the tools needed for constructing collages. Particular papers and fabrics are discussed in detail in the "Basic Procedures" section which follows.

The essential items needed for almost any collage project are: (1) adhesives and glues; (2) background material (the board or paper to which the collage is pasted); (3) brushes for applying paint or glue (a variety of sizes is beneficial); (4) fabric and cloth; (5) found objects; (6) palette knife for applying glue and textures; (7) paper; (8) pins (plain straight pins are useful to organize or hold pieces of the collage down before gluing); (9) scissors or knife; and (10) a brayer.

Basic Procedures

Creating a collage is much like creating a painting or drawing, but collage permits more freedom for exploration. Before attempting a collage, experiment with various materials and tools to find desirable effects. Collage can be expensive or inexpensive. Several necessary materials — such as a scissors, crayons, pencil, heavy or light cardboard to use as a ground, colored papers, magazines, tissues, fabric scraps, paper tissues and napkins, string, old letters, white glue, and a small brush — are usually available in the home.

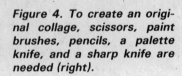

Figure 4. To create an original collage, scissors, paint brushes, pencils, a palette knife, and a sharp knife are needed (right).

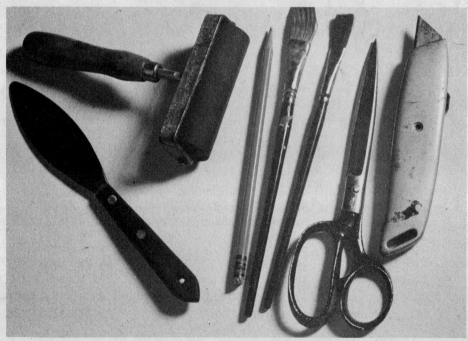

BACKGROUNDS

The first decision in collage is selecting a background. This may be anything from a piece of laundry cardboard to any of the boards described below, which can be purchased at an art store or lumber yard. The surface should be rigid because, without a strong background, there can be problems of warping, wrinkling, and cracking. All of the following papers and cardboards are different — each is best for its respective type of collage. Buy a sample of each and experiment with it.

Figure 5. The base of the collage should be a poster board, mat board, or illustration board strong enough to hold the materials pasted to it.

Bristol Board

Available in several thicknesses referred to as plys, this white board is often confused with tagboard.

Poster Board

Often called railroad board, this is a board available in several thicknesses as well as in a wide range of colors. Any collage created on this type of board may have a tendency to warp and should be mounted on something stronger when ready to frame. As the name suggests, this board is widely used for posters; it is also used for mounting photographs.

Mat Board

Very heavy board used for matting pictures and prints. It is available in a variety of colors and does not need to be backed when finished.

Illustration Board

This board, which is available in several grades of thickness and should be backed, has a drawing surface mounted onto regular cardboard. It can have either a rough or smooth finish and is particularly suitable for collage artists who combine watercolor with their work.

Watercolor or Rag Boards

These are often very expensive and only the heaviest ply will do for collage. They are high in rag content and must be backed.

Graphic Paper

Used by draftsmen, illustrators, and printmakers, graphic paper is available in a variety of types. It also must be backed.

Canvas Board

Excellent for use in collage, this is canvas which has been glued to heavy cardboard; it does not require mounting.

Hardboards

Hardboards, sometimes called particle boards, are available in a variety of thicknesses and sizes. They are made by pressing chips of wood together. Do not buy marine or tempered hardboard because it has been oiled to make it water repellent and collage materials will not adhere to it. Use the standard hardboard.

PREPARING THE SURFACE

Collage pieces adhere easily to a rough surface. Some surfaces which are either too rough or too smooth must be primed. A primer closes the pores of a surface so that the background material will not absorb too much glue or paint.

Hardwood boards, because they have been sanded, need a coat of primer to make the surface rougher. Canvas also needs a primer. Grounds which do not need priming include hard papers or cardboard which have been coated with a color, with any papers, or with a canvas board. Through experience, one quickly learns which type of background surface needs preparation and which does not. Rules to remember about priming are: (1) if the background absorbs too much water, glue, or color, it needs to be primed; and (2) if nothing will adhere to the surface properly, it is too slick and needs to be primed.

Primers

There are two types of primers: oil-based and water-based. Because water-based paints and emulsions are used in the projects described here, use a water-based primer. The most common water-based primer is *gesso*.

It is not advisable to use an oil-based paint since oil and water do not mix, nor should casein paint be used for priming because it often cracks.

Priming a Board

To prime a board, use an inexpensive 2″ wide brush or a small roller. Pour a small amount of gesso into a can or jar and add water until it is the consistency of cream. Because gesso in a can or jar will dry out quickly, keep the top tightly closed. Paint the board with the gesso — it is better to apply several thin coats of gesso rather than one or two very thick ones as they are likely to crack. Wait until each application is dry before applying another coat (usually about a half hour).

When working in collage, it is best to develop the habit of having a jar of water handy in which to keep brushes. This prevents ruining a brush with a buildup of gesso or glue and also makes cleaning the brush easier. However, never leave brushes overnight in water as they will deteriorate, become brittle, and lose bristles.

Gesso may be tinted with acrylic paints before it is applied to the ground. Simply mix the gesso with a small amount of pigment and water to make the proper color. Use pigment sparingly: the gesso serves as an extender for the pigment. To change the color, apply two coats of gesso to cover the color and then repaint.

Figure 6. To prime the background board, paint it with several thin coats of gesso. If a colored background is desired, the gesso can be tinted.

Figure 7. Tinting the gesso involves mixing it with a small amount of pigment and water until the desired color is attained.

 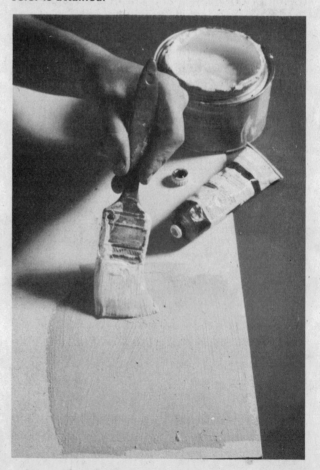

GLUES AND ADHESIVES

In some forms of art, many of the following are not categorized as glue or adhesive. However, for collage, they have particular properties which makes it advantageous to treat them as such. The following is a list of glues which are most reliable and give the best results in water-based work. It is not advisable to use children's paste or rubber cement because they are not durable enough.

White Glue

White glue is a plain adhesive which is available under many brand names. A good all-purpose craft adhesive, white glue is more economical when purchased in large quantities rather than in small bottles. The glue is thinned with water and the brush should be put in water between uses.

Polymer Mediums

In painting, polymer mediums are not referred to as adhesives. For collage, however, they are useful for both gluing and finishing a surface, especially paper or cloth. They have a plastic base, are water soluble, and dry to a clear, hard finish. Of the two types of polymer — gloss and matte — the gloss is preferable. Again, the brush should be put in water between uses.

Acrylic Gel

This is an extender which can be used as an adhesive. It gives the same effect as any polymer medium because it has a similar base. However, acrylic gel comes in a tube and is applied with a palette knife. It does not dry as hard as polymer mediums and requires more than one coat.

Modeling Paste

This acrylic product is thick, white, opaque, and dries quickly. It is used for building up layers of texture and also for adhering small objects (stones, coins, etc.) to a collage by embedding them in the paste. Modeling paste dries very quickly. The addition of gel will retard drying and allow some maneuvering, but not much. It is best to apply modeling paste, which may be sanded when dry, with a palette knife.

Epoxy

This glue is not water soluble and will bond together metal, wood, and most other substances. Available in various forms at both hardware stores and art stores, it sets up very fast. The tools used must be cleaned immediately by wiping them off because, if the epoxy dries, they will be ruined.

ASSEMBLING COLLAGE MATERIALS

After the ground and adhesive have been prepared, the collage can be assembled. The easiest way to work with the materials described here is to experiment with them. Learn to leave open spaces in a composition and do not use every material on hand.

Newspapers

Although they are flimsy, newspapers provide many types of textural and patterned materials which may be incorporated into collages. Look for large areas of light and dark grays, large dot patterns, graphs, charts of special interest, or photographs. Newspapers are generally used for textured effects on selected areas. When covered, these areas become gray tonal areas to be used as desired. Because newspaper deteriorates easily, the best adhesive is polymer medium — it will dry

Figure 8. Brush a coat of polymer over newspaper and magazine clippings that are used in a collage. Before applying the polymer, be sure that the pieces are completely flat or wrinkled, as desired.

very hard and is practically waterproof. Apply the newspaper to a collage as to any other paper, taking care to spread it over a layer of applied glue. Then work over it with a brush until the piece is completely flat or, if desired, leave some wrinkled areas in the composition. Be sure to coat the paper with polymer after it is in place to insure durability. This method can also be used for magazines, fabric, and other papers.

Magazines

Magazines are an endless source of collage materials. The quality of magazine paper is usually very high and it does not deteriorate quickly.

Figure 9. Newspapers and magazines are rich sources for collage materials. Keep a collection of interesting clippings; remember that magazine covers can also be used.

Moreover, the effects of the inks used in magazines are different from those of pigment colors. Look for differences and subtleties in both color and texture to provide a dynamic contrast in a collage.

Magazine covers, usually of heavier stock paper, often yeild interesting results. But whether using the magazine cover or the body stocks, check the other side of the page; it may bleed through when the paper is applied to the background. Also, the polymer medium will make the page so translucent that the reverse side will show up almost as well as the front side. However, this in itself can provide interesting effects.

Treated Magazines

Magazines may also be "treated" to alter the composition, color, and final appearance. One way of doing this is by "washing" a photo. Pick several photos from a magazine and experiment. Turn the water faucet on full force and run the water over one spot on the paper. The ink will run off in that area — how much ink will run is controlled by both the force of the running water and its temperature.

For a different effect, crumple the paper and then let water run into the crevices, weakening the color in those areas. Wet the paper, crumple it, run it under water again, and let it dry flat on a

Figure 10. "Treating" magazines can produce unusual appearances for collages (below). Wet the page, crumple it, and wet it again. Continued rubbing will partially remove the image (below right).

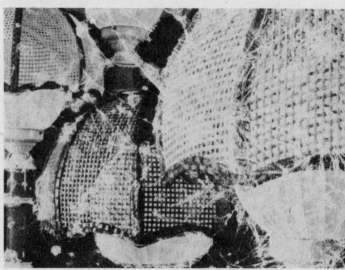

piece of newspaper. After a piece of paper is very wet, areas can be obliterated simply by rubbing the fingers over the unwanted areas. The harder the rub, the more color will be removed. Control the color by practicing with it first.

Work with the shape in addition to color. Pieces can be cut very neatly with scissors or ripped out of the magazine. Try both cutting and tearing all the edges. Also try using pinking shears. Experiment in several ways.

Printmaking, Drawing, and Drafting Paper

Although each of these papers is used for specific purposes, all can be used in collage. They are available in an almost endless variety. There are heavy white papers, thin papers, and some with rough or very smooth textures. Some of these papers absorb much water, some are shiny, and some are dull. There are also some specific pa-pers which are available in colors. These include construction paper, charcoal paper (for charcoal drawings), and watercolor papers. There are even papers which simulate cloth, such as velour paper, which is available in a variety of colors.

Oriental Papers

These handmade papers, usually of Japanese origin, and used for a variety of drawings and prints. To the collage artist they are especially useful because they are very delicate in texture but quite strong when cut or torn. Some are actually collages in themselves, with inlaid leaves or pressed flowers.

Also available are *origami* papers — dull on one side, bright on the other. Some have flecks of gold or silver in them. These papers are traditionally used for origami — the art of paper folding — but they produce excellent effects in collage.

Figure 11. Artists' papers provide a variety of colors, textures, and weights for collages. The assorted colored papers (left) have flat or shiny finishes. The deckle-edged papers (right) have an interesting texture and a soft edge that blends well with other materials.

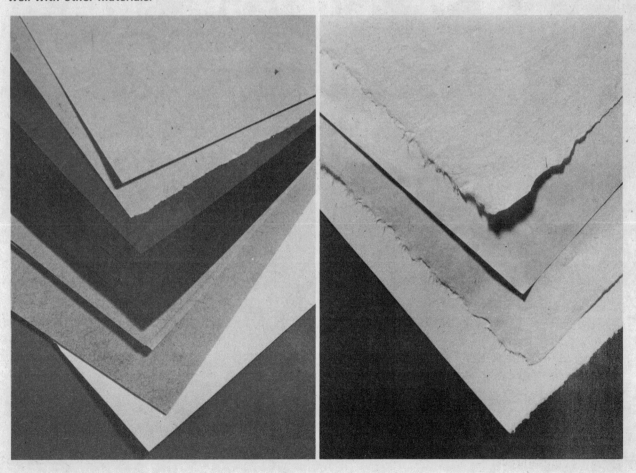

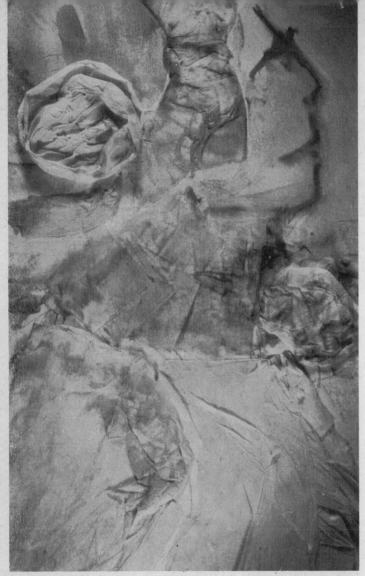

Tissue Paper

Tissue paper is the best paper for collage. It adds color and brilliance, is inexpensive, and is one of the most versatile collage mediums. It can be used directly or as a dye or stain, and it can be prepared in layers before assembling the collage. Tissue paper is easy to control and offers a wide range of colors.

By overlaying each of the three primary colors (red, yellow, and blue), the secondary colors (green, orange, and violet) are created. This is possible because of the transparency of tissue paper. Also by overlapping several strips of the same color, different shades of the color can be obtained.

A fine experiment to try when first working with tissue papers is to take all of the various paper samples on hand and cut or tear off a small piece (2" x 2") from each one. Then combine each of these pieces with a small square of tissue paper, overlapping the tissue paper onto the torn sample and adhering it with polymer medium. This will strengthen the tissue paper, just as it does newspaper. These small samples will demonstrate the possibilities which tissue paper allows.

Figure 12. In an untitled collage (top), the author used tissue paper effectively. Tissue paper is inexpensive and easily obtainable in a variety of colors (bottom). A stain can be made with wet tissue (right) by brushing the water from the paper to the surface that is to be tinted.

Also experiment by overlapping colors of tissue paper: try green on a white ground with a yellow over that; or glue the yellow down first and then the green; or, try different grounds, such as gray or foil, over doilies. The possibilities are endless.

After working with tissue paper, various sorts of odds and ends are frequently left. These should be saved and put to later use. They may be placed over areas as a color wash, for example, or used to color an area of newsprint. Pasting tissue paper over the newspaper with polymer enhances the newspaper but does not affect its readability. For scraps of tissue which seem too long or too small to be used as a wash, dampen a sheet of white paper with water and lay the pieces of tissues on the paper, arranging them in patterns. Let the paper dry and discard the tissues. The dye from the tissues will have transferred onto the paper. This can also be done with a polymer medium instead of water with one difference. If the tissue is left on the paper longer than a few minutes, it

will be bound there by the polymer. When using polymer, try to find a compatible length of time for the tissue and paper being used. This will result in colors deeper than the diluted effect achieved with water.

There is one further simple experiment to try with tissue which demonstrates the versatility of collage. Glue a piece of fabric or paper onto a white background. Take a small piece of strong colored tissue and paint one side of it with polymer. Place it into position over the other object. Now, instead of brushing the top side of the tissue with polymer as before, either run water over the tissue and let it bleed, brush water over the tissue for watercolor effects, or dip the surface of the collage several times in water by holding the collage face down and passing it across the top of the water surface. (Do not plunge the collage into water or immerse it completely.) Each should yield a different effect. Let the collage dry and then proceed to finish it.

Figure 13. An interesting effect is created when two colors of tissue paper are overlapped (below). The transparency of the tissue blends to make new colors. Water can be applied to the tissue for still another effect (below left).

Fabric

All kinds of cloths — from sheer to loose woven — can be used in collage. One of the most widely used fabrics is cheesecloth.

Figure 14. Because of their colors and textures, fabrics are excellent materials for collages. Their use is limited only by the imagination of the artist.

White glue works very well with cloth. Apply glue to the background area where the fabric is to be, then glue the wrong side of the fabric and press it into place. Roll over it with a brayer or by hand to keep it down. Of course, the fabric can be altered to suit individual taste. Paint on cloth with watercolor or acrylic, dye over it, tie dye areas of it, or batik the cloth. Often cloth is bleached to yield an old, faded look.

The fabric chosen does not have to be glued down flat — it can be gathered or pleated. Crumple or wrinkle parts of it. Once again, experiment — see how the cloth can be manipulated.

Figure 15. Wrinkled pages from magazines were used in the assembly of a collage (below) that has a multi-layered design. The details of the pictures — the bedding, the ceiling tiles, and the wood paneling — add depth to the overall design. Although a smaller number of individual pieces are used, an attractive collage (right) can still be created with an assortment of fabrics in coordinated colors. A collage that has a strong, bold design (below right) was produced by using only two different fabrics.

Figure 16. Acrylic paint, rice paper, tissue, and instant coffee were used to create this collage by Suzanne Peters. (Courtesy, Collection of Al Collins.)

Materials to Provide Texture

Anything from sand, small stones, and glass to macaroni and dried grasses can be used to create texture. The best way to determine whether or not a particular material can be used is to experiment with it — often, for example, a material will dissolve in the glue. On a small piece of ground board, spread a medium layer of white glue. Sprinkle or place the materials onto the surface. Wait a few minutes and then tip the entire board sideways to allow the excess material to fall onto a sheet of newspaper. This residue may be reused or discarded.

Figure 17. Dried corn, peas, and rice (above) are but three examples of foods that can be utilized in a collage. White glue applied to the background (below) will hold textured objects. The layer of glue should be thick enough to hold the objects securely, but thin enough to be workable. Do not forget the pantry when looking for interesting objects to use for textures (right).

The idea is to create a desired effect. Try the following experiments with sand:

1. Using glue as though it were a pen, write some letters or a name with the glue and sprinkle with sand.

2. Place a thin layer of white glue on a piece of ground, wait, then sprinkle with sand.

3. Glue down a texture material, such as macaroni shells or seeds, and allow to dry. Cover the material with glue and then sprinkle with sand. Or paint the glue only in certain areas of the texture material and then sprinkle with sand.

4. Glue a piece of fabric to a board, apply white glue, and lightly sprinkle with sand.

5. Spray the sand different colors with oil-based or water-based paint before gluing it down or paint the sand after gluing it down.

Modeling paste is a glue but also can be used as a textured material. Lay down a layer of modeling paste with a palette knife and run an old comb across the top of the layer, trying for deep and shallow effects. Add paint to color the mixture, paint it after it is dry, or glue sand to it.

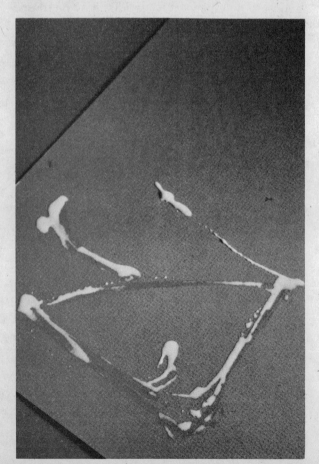

Figure 18. Spreading a thin layer of glue on cardboard (above) and sprinkling sand or beads over it (below left) creates texture for a collage. Modeling paste can also be used as texture (below). Apply a layer to the background board with a palette knife; then, experiment with combs, toothpicks, or sponges to vary the design. There are unlimited possibilities for creating textures in collages.

Figure 19. Fragments of words appear again in Suzanne Peter's "November Collage." This collage was created with crayons, rice paper, and acrylic paint.

Projects You Can Do

Working with collage is not only enjoyable but it can also become an increasingly rewarding pastime as ideas change. Following the techniques already described and trying such projects as those suggested below will help the reader to develop a sense of design and composition.

COLLAGE OF TEXTURES

Flip through magazines and find a seasonal picture of an outdoor panorama, such as snow-capped mountains in the winter. In this project the scene will be created in collage.

Transfer the picture to another sheet of paper by outlining around the major areas to indicate the boundaries of the collage. This is easily done by holding both the picture and the paper against a window, thus making them translucent. Feel free to change the size or to alter the picture in any way.

Now collect the materials which will give the textural effects desired. Possible materials for snow-caps are cracked marble, shredded styrofoam, or coconut flakes sealed with polymer. The blue of the sky can be blue paper; clouds can be made by

spraying light mists of white spray paint over the snowcaps or by using several sheets of white tissue, all glued together. Burlap or straw sprayed green are good for grasses. A dusty road could be

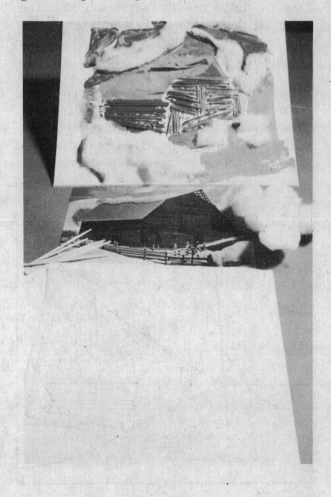

Figure 20. To begin the first project, find a photograph of a winter scene, then transfer the picture to a pattern. Assemble materials that can add texture, such as cotton balls.

made with sand and small pieces of crushed green glass for clumps of grass.

This type of collage may not be as satisfying as an original design, but the experience and practice of working only with textures is valuable. Be sure to evaluate each collage made and keep track of those which seem to generate ideas for other collages.

COLLAGE BASED ON A THEME

Many artistic collages have themes, and, although a theme is not always necessary, collage is a form of communication. Historically, collage has been used to illustrate an artist's particular thoughts and ideas on a subject. Often the materials in the collage were not only paper tissues and string but also found objects related to the subject matter.

This project will suggest four collages, each based on a different season, to illustrate how easily ideas can be generated as soon as a subject matter is decided upon.

Copy the design onto four separate boards. (Use either the design illustrated or an original one.) Decide which board is which season. For each season, rummage through available materials and choose those which seem to illustrate the feeling of a particular time of year. Decide which colors go with a season. There are, for example, many kinds of autumn: the bright, sunny yellow, gold, orange, and red autumn days of early October; the rainy, damp, dark brown, rust, and

black and gray skies of November; or the starkness of bare trees with their light brown branches and snow-flocked evergreens against threatening winter skies.

Each season need not be illustrated by weather. It can be represented by clothing, by special sports items, or by whatever else is appropriate. If mementos are collected, worked into a handsome design, and interspersed with the colors of the season, a portrait of an entire year can be created.

Figure 22. This collage project uses papers and fabrics suitable for a theme based on the four seasons.

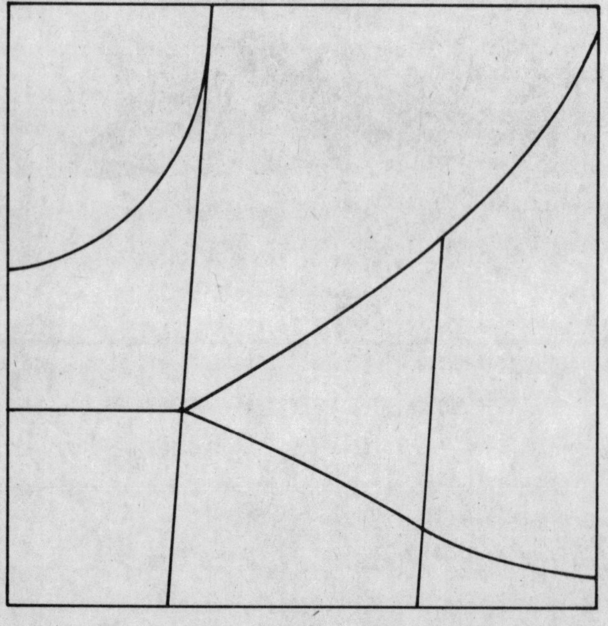

Figure 21. This diagram is a possible pattern for one of the seasons in the second collage project. Its design will be more effective if the materials overlap each other when pasted on the background.

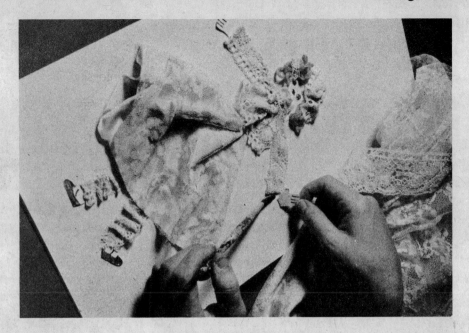

Figure 23. For the costume doll project, mark a large piece of tissue to indicate which fabrics go where. Glue wads of tissue onto the background to add dimension. After the fabric is applied, add the face, hands, and shoes.

RELIEF AND THREE-DIMENSIONAL COLLAGES

Collage can be used three-dimensionally as well as two-dimensionally. Begin by finding objects which are three-dimensional but which can be viewed two-dimensionally if placed at a different angle. A good example of such an item is a costume doll. In addition to the usual collage materials, the following items are also needed for this project: (1) drawings or cutouts of a face, hands, and shoes; (2) buttons; (3) lace, ribbons, yarns, and threads; (4) fabrics; (5) tissue paper; and (6) a large sheet of cardboard.

Prime the large sheet of cardboard with gesso. Then, using either the accompanying diagram as a guide or an original design, pencil lightly the outline of the areas to be filled in. Now, use tissue paper to indicate the material being used for the dress — in this case, taffeta. With crumpled wads of tissue and polymer medium, pad areas where a three-dimensional effect is desired. Add laces and

yarns where shown in the illustration. Paint both the dress and the skin areas of the arms. Paste head, hands, and shoes into place. Glue buttons into place. Finally, mount the board to another board to prevent warping.

It is easy to experiment further with other freeform collages. However, they must be well thought out first: there should be a theme and attention must be given to individual objects. By working and arranging the items, one can successfully create a three-dimensional collage which is communicative as well as creative.

For Additional Reading

Beaney, Jan, **Adventures With Collage,** Warne, 1970.

Brow, Francis, **Collage,** Pitman, 1963.

Hutton, Helen, **The Technique of Collage,,** Watson-Guptill, 1968.

Vanderbilt, Gloria, **The Gloria Vanderbilt Book of Collage,** Van Nostrand, 1970.

Jewelry Making

Metal casting — one of the simplest and most basic of techniques in jewelry making — has been used by almost all ancient and modern cultures.

The ancient cultures which did metal casting developed it spontaneously from the knowledge that metal became liquid and flowed when heated. Once this was discovered, the logical next step was to allow the molten metal to flow into a cavity and then cool. When the cold metal was removed, the early craftsmen found that it had taken on a cast, the texture and shape of the original cavity.

Figure 2. This bracelet was cast in bronze, using the lost wax process. It is probably the work of Benin craftsmen in Africa. (Courtesy, American Museum of Natural History.)

Among the artifacts of ancient cultures are found many intricate and beautiful cast metal pieces which indicate varied casting techniques. About 700 years ago in Africa, in what is now Nigeria, a tribe of superb craftsmen from the ancient city of Ifé cast life-sized hollow bronze portrait heads of their kings. These were first molded in wax over earthen cores. The walls of the heads were amazingly thin and uniform, indicating great skill in both modeling and casting techniques.

The craftsmen of Ifé taught casting to the people of Benin, a powerful tribe from the same area. These Benin craftsmen made many fine bronze castings (c. 1300-1700 A. D.) in a style which was more expressionistic in character than that of the Ifé, but certainly influenced by them.

Figure 1. This bronze ceremonial vessel (opposite) was metal cast during the Chou dynasty in China. (Courtesy, Collection of William Rockhill Nelson Gallery of Art, Kansas City, Missouri.)

Today, Yemi Bisiri, a Yoruba tribesman from Nigeria, still uses the ancient casting methods of his ancestors. He carves his models from beeswax over a core of hard red earth from a termite hill, and covers it with horse dung, which he packs into a ball and allows to dry and harden. Holes are made in the top and bottom of the mold with a metal tube, and a pan of water is placed under the mold. Metal is then heated, and when it becomes liquid, it is poured into the hole at the top of the mold. The molten metal melts the wax model inside. As the metal fills the cavity inside the mold, the melting wax drips out the bottom hole. The wax is caught for reuse in the pan beneath.

Other cultures which created exceptional cast metal work were the Pre-Columbian Indians of South and Central America (c. 1200 B. C. to 1500 A. D.). These people cast magnificent pieces in gold long before the discovery of the New World. Unfortunately, most of this work was stolen by the

Figure 3. This ceremonial wine vessel, cast in bronze, was made in China during the Chou dynasty. (Courtesy, Museum of Fine Arts, Boston, Anne Mitchell Richards Fund.)

Spanish Conquistadors in the 1500s, and shipped back to Europe where it was melted down for use by the Renaissance goldsmiths. The few examples which remain show exquisite detail and fine craftsmanship, such as the delicate cast wire work of the Mixtecs.

Other craftsmen in ancient India, Egypt, China, Greece, and Rome, as well as Celtic metalsmiths and American Indians, have given us rich and exciting examples of the art of casting metal. From the large bronze vessels of the Chinese to the small pieces of gold jewelry of the Pre-Columbians, one can see the tremendous range of objects, styles, and techniques used historically by man in metal casting.

The modern jewelry maker benefits from studying these examples and adapting many of the ancient methods to his own work. In this article, two different ways of casting metal will be discussed: steam casting and sand casting.

Figure 4. This silver wrist guard was designed by a Navajo craftsman to protect the wrist from the impact of the drawstring of a bow. (Courtesy, Museum of the American Indian, Heye Foundation.)

Common Terms Used In Jewelry Making

Alloy: a metal made up of two or more metals, usually to improve the strength and durability of the original metal.

Asbestos: a mineral unaffected by fire which is ground up and used to make fireproof board, cloth, and paper.

Binding Wire: in steam casting, iron binding wire (about 20 gauge) is wrapped around a tin can flask to keep it from springing out of shape.

Burnout: in steam casting, the process of melting or burning out the wax model from the investment mold.

Casting: the pouring of molten metal into a mold cavity where it cools and hardens.

Casting Sand: in sand casting, a specially treated sand which is packed into the open frames and surrounds the model to form a mold.

Cope: the horizontally placed upper part of the frame in sand casting.

Crucible: a container made of graphite or any other refractory material, in which metal is heated until it is molten.

Drag: the horizontally placed lower part of the frame in sand casting.

Flask: in steam casting, an open-ended tube of metal, usually stainless steel, in which the model is to be placed. In sand casting it is also called the frame (q.v.).

Flux: borax powder that is sprinkled on the melting metal to prevent oxidation.

Frame (also Flask): in sand casting, two parts resembling two open frames that fit together, one on top of another (the cope and the drag). The parts are usually made of cast iron, and often have one or more openings at one end for the sprue (see below). Casting sand is packed into the frame to make a mold.

Gauge: a measure of the thickness of sheet metal or the diameter of wire; also applicable to wax sheet and wire.

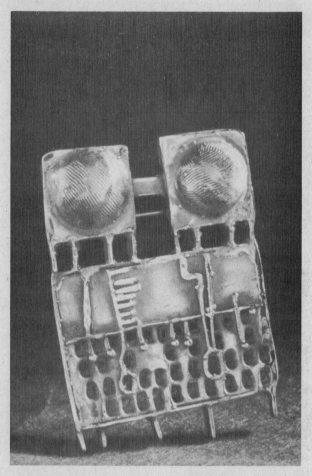

Figure 5. These stunning pins were fashioned from 14-karat gold. Note the stark contemporary designs employed by the craftsman. A turquoise was set into one of the brooches (below), which—though basically abstract—suggests the figure of a bird. Either pin can be made with a loop on the back, for hanging on a neck chain.

Investment: in steam casting, a specially formulated plaster-like substance designed to withstand high temperatures. It is mixed with water and poured into a flask that contains a model.

Karat: a unit of measure indicating the amount of pure gold in an alloy. Unalloyed gold has 24 karats; most commercial jewelry is made of 14-karat gold.

Liver Of Sulphur: a chemical compound (potassium sulfide) which, when mixed in a water solution, darkens metal, especially silver (see Oxidation).

Model: the pattern or piece to be cast. In steam casting, the model must be made of a material that will burn out easily, such as wax or styrofoam. In sand casting, it has to be of a material that can retain its own shape under pressure, such as wood or metal.

Mold: a solid form containing the cavity into which the molten metal flows to produce a casting. In steam casting, the mold is a steel tube filled with investment plaster. In sand casting, the mold is a double frame of metal packed with casting sand.

Oxidation: the natural process of metal combining with oxygen, causing impurities to form that can inhibit the flow of molten metal into the mold. In a finished piece, surface oxidation is often desired. This is achieved by using a chemical solution to darken the metal. Then, when areas are polished, there is a dramatic contrast between clean and oxidized surfaces.

Parting Powder: in sand casting, the finely ground powder that is dusted on the inside surfaces of the mold making it easier to separate the mold parts after casting.

Pickle: a 10% acid solution used to remove carbon or oxidation from the metal piece after casting.

Pumice Powder: a powder made from pumice stone, used as an abrasive to remove oxidation from metal.

Rammer: in sand casting, a wooden mallet or a piece of dowel rod used to pack casting sand into a mold frame.

Rouge: an abrasive compound used for final polishing of metal.

Sprue: the vertical channel that connects the model to the outside of the flask. Molten metal flows through this channel to the mold cavity.

Sprue Base: in steam casting, a wooden or rubber bottom that fits securely over one end of the flask, allowing the flask to be filled with investment.

Sprue Former: in steam casting, a dome-shaped piece attached to the center of the sprue base. When removed from the bottom of the finished mold, the sprue former creates a basin in the mold in which to melt the metal.

Tripoli: a coarse abrasive compound used to remove sandpaper scratches from a metal piece.

Vent: a narrow channel made in the mold that allows gases formed in casting to escape. The vents lead from the model cavity to the outside of the mold.

Basic Equipment And Supplies

Many of the supplies and equipment needed for casting can be easily made or purchased at a pharmacy or hardware store. If a local jeweler's supply house can be located, it will have everything needed for casting, including metal. Another good source of supplies is a dental supply house. One's dentist might prove helpful in giving advice on where to find needed items. Art supply stores, particularly the larger ones, or those which cater to universities where jewelry making is taught are also a possible source. Finally, there are many mail order jewelry supply houses all over the country which stock everything one could possibly need to make jewelry. These houses will send catalogues upon request. For a complete listing of these places see the book *Metal Techniques for Craftsmen* by Oppi Untracht (Doubleday, 1968, pages 467-80.)

STEAM CASTING

The first method to be considered is steam casting, a technique which uses the pressure of steam to force molten metal into a mold.

Tools and Supplies for Model Making

In order to cast, one must first make a model. For steam casting the most workable material for

Figure 6. This startlingly original ring (above) was designed and created by co-author Naomi Peck; she made the ring of silver and entitled it "Foot and Mouth Only." Co-author Lee Peck fashioned a 14-karat gold ring (below) and incorporated a jade stone in the design. Rings are especially popular with jewelry craftsmen.

model making is wax. Buy beeswax and paraffin at a pharmacy and melt them together in equal parts in a double boiler. Beeswax is soft and sticky and paraffin is hard and brittle, so a wax mixture different from the half and half combination may be achieved by varying the amounts of beeswax and paraffin. When the wax is liquid and thoroughly mixed, pour it out as evenly as possibly on a flat smooth rubber pad that has been spread with vegetable oil or sprayed with a silicone spray. When cooled, the wax can be lifted easily from the rubber pad. In this way one can make sheet wax that may be cut into shapes or narrow strips with a knife and straight edge.

Special wax for dentists and jewelers is made and sold in sheet, block, or wire form at jewelry and dental supply houses. It comes in colors which denote the softness, brittleness, or melting temperature of the particular wax.

Figure 7. The necessary tools for making a wax model for casting include a wax spatula, homemade spatula, half-round file, jeweler's saw, an alcohol lamp, and needle files.

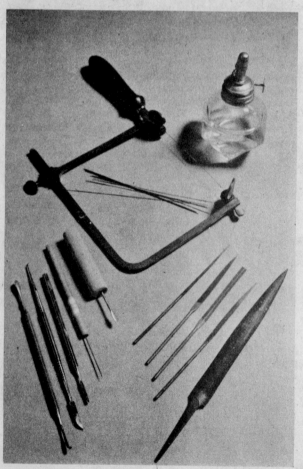

Tools are necessary to work the wax. Dental spatulas are excellent. However, wax modeling tools are easily made. Drive a nail into the end of a piece of wooden dowel rod. After the nail is firmly in place, snip off the nail head and hammer the tip of the remaining piece flat. Then, with a file, round off the edges of the flattened nail to get a small spatula-shaped tip.

Another good tool for wax modeling is a dissecting needle from a school biology kit, often sold separately from the kit. These can be made simply by glueing a heavy sewing needle eye first into the end of a piece of dowel rod. Small paring knives may also be used to work the wax.

For working on the harder File-Wax, it is a good idea to have a set of inexpensive hand files: a number 2 cut half-round file, and an assortment of different shaped needle files. Also needed are a jeweler's saw and some wax-cutting blades.

Because most waxes must be heated in order to carve or shape them, one needs an alcohol lamp and a can of denatured alcohol. The alcohol burns cleanly, and carbon does not get on the wax tools the way it does from a candle flame. Carbon should be avoided because it can work itself into the wax of a model and create a rough or porous surface on the metal casting. The lamp and denatured alcohol can usually be purchased at a hardware store.

Tools and Supplies for Mold Making

First, a flask is essential. This should be seamless and made of stainless steel which can be reused indefinitely. A good standard size is 3 inches tall by 2½ inches in diameter. Enterprising craftsmen might try to find an automobile tailpipe and cut it into sections. However, flasks can be purchased at a supply house. As an alternate, a tin can, open at both ends, may be used; but the heat from the burnout will make the tin can unusable after one casting. A good size can to use as a flask is the standard frozen orange juice can — just be sure it is metal and not cardboard. Other taller cans may be cut down in height with metal shears. It is a good idea to bind the tin can with 20-gauge iron wire to prevent the can from springing out of shape and causing the investment mold to crack during the burnout. Binding wire is not necessary with a steel flask.

Next, one must have a sprue base and a dome-shaped sprue former. These can be purchased commercially, but one can also make do with a small square of plywood or masonite board, one bar of plasticene clay, and a ping-pong ball sawed in half. The board should be two inches wider all around than the diameter of the flask.

Figure 8. A sprue former can be made by sawing a ping-pong ball in half. A sprue base can be made from a piece of plywood. The dome shape is then glued to the wood square.

Glue the ping-pong ball firmly to the center of the board, domed side up. A few pieces of specially made jeweler's wax wire, 14-gauge, will be needed for the main sprue and auxiliary sprues.

The investment plaster must be purchased. It is a special plaster mixture that is made to withstand high temperatures when ordinary plaster would break down and become powdery. This can be bought at a jewelry or dental supply store. The investment is mixed in a clean mixing bowl, preferably rubber, which is flexible and easy to clean out afterwards.

Equipment for Burning Out

Most jewelers use a kiln, a small oven which is electrically or gas powered, to burn the wax out of the investment mold. Purchasing a kiln can be an expensive undertaking, so until one decides it is worth the cost, the wax can be burned out of the flask with only a few inexpensive items.

The first item needed is an ordinary electric hot plate. Then get a large metal jar lid (larger in di-

ameter than the flask) that will rest on the coils of the hot plate and a trivet which will fit inside the jar lid. Finally, find a clay flowerpot that is wide enough and tall enough to completely cover the flask as it rests on the trivet inside the jar lid. The flowerpot must have a drain in the bottom of it and should be lined with aluminum foil with the

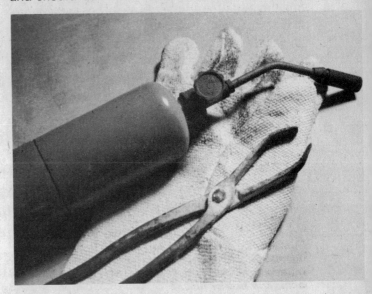

Figure 9. A propane canister-type torch can be used to burn the wax out of the flask. A pair of thongs and an asbestos glove should be used for safety reasons.

hole left open. For safety's sake, have a pair of tongs with which to grasp the flask after burnout, and an asbestos glove for lifting the flowerpot. The entire burning out process must take place in a well-ventilated room, as the wax fumes are strong and unpleasant to inhale.

Supplies and Equipment for Casting

One must have metal to begin. When buying precious metals from a supplier or a refinery, be sure to specify clean casting metal. This saves the time of cleaning the pieces before casting them, and it also saves money since sheet metal is more expensive.

If buying silver, specify sterling silver because it is harder and more durable than pure silver. If buying gold, keep in mind that most commercial jewelry is made of 14-karat gold, which is more precious than 10-karat, and less expensive and harder than 18-karat.

It is best to stay away from casting bronze or brass, as both metals give off harmful fumes when melting, and one must have a good exhaust system for cleaning the air when casting with either of these.

In order to melt the metal one needs a torch. The most inexpensive and readily available kind of torch is the propane canister type usually found in the hardware store. This type of torch is good for melting small amounts of metal, or metals that have low melting temperatures (such as pewter) because the flame is not very hot. For repeated use and a hotter, more efficient flame, an acetylene or oxygen-acetylene torch is best. (Sears, Roebuck and Co. sells a fairly inexpensive unit.)

When using the torch, always remember to keep it away from anything flammable. Be sure to have a piece of asbestos board behind and underneath the flask while the metal is being heated. Good ventilation is also necessary during the melting of any metal, as fumes are given off that are harmful if inhaled.

Figure 10. A plunging device can be made by attaching a dowel rod to a screw-type jar lid. The lid is lined with layers of wet asbestos paper and should easily fit over the top of the flask.

While melting the metal, you will need to flux it. Borax powder, found in the grocery store, is an excellent flux for casting metals like gold and silver. Pour some into a clean salt shaker and it is ready for use.

The very last item needed is the "plunger," which will create the steam needed to force the molten metal into the mold. This item must be made. Have a screw-top jar lid ready, one that fits loosely over the top of the flask (usually the lid from a large mayonnaise jar is a good size). Then a piece of wooden dowel rod, about 3/4-inch in diameter, is needed for the handle. This should be screwed to the top center of the jar lid. Finally, the inside of the lid is lined with four or five layers of wet asbestos paper (to a thickness of about 3/16-inch) and the whole device allowed to soak in a bowl of warm water until ready for use.

Have a bucket of water handy in which to quench the entire flask after casting. A plastic gallon bucket is good for this purpose.

SAND CASTING

The other method being covered here is sand casting, a process that is very direct. There is no burnout, and the metal is poured straight into the mold cavity.

Supplies and Equipment for Model Making

There are two considerations in making a model for sand casting: (1) there is no burnout because the model is removed from the frame (flask) by hand before the metal is poured into the mold, and (2) the sand is packed tightly around the model with light blows from a rammer. Therefore, the model can be made from a permanent material, and one that is strong enough to withstand the pressure exerted on it by the rammer. Models can be made from such items as wood, metal, plastic, stone, and hard File-Wax. The tools needed depend on the medium chosen. It is wise to select a medium with which one has had experience — this improves the chances for a successful model on the first try.

Supplies and Equipment for Mold Making

It is best to buy a complete sand casting kit from a jeweler's supply house. This kit should cost approximately $17.00 and usually contains the flask

Figure 11. Equipment needed for sand casting includes a flask (frames), casting sand, parting powder, borax flux, a crucible, and tongs. These items can be purchased in a kit.

(cope and drag), casting sand, parting powder, borax flux, a crucible, and tongs. Everything in it except the flux and the parting powder can be reused indefinitely.

In addition to the kit, the following items are needed: (1) two pieces of plywood cut to the outside dimensions of the flask; (2) two C-clamps; (3) a piece of ordinary screening to sift the sand through; (4) a wood or metal straight edge (used to level off the sand after it is packed into the flask); (5) a small spatula to cut the sprue channel and vents into the sand; and (6) a wooden mallet or piece of one-inch diameter dowel rod to use as a rammer.

Supplies and Equipment for Casting

Again, metal is needed to begin. Sand casting presents an excellent chance to use pewter, which has a low melting point of about 500° F and is quite soft. In fact, it is too soft to make rings

from, but does lend itself well to the making of pendants, brooches, and small sculpture. Of course, sterling silver or any of the gold alloys may also be used in sand casting.

The necessary crucible, tongs, and flux are in the kit. A torch to melt the metal (see supplies and equipment for casting under Steam Casting) and some asbestos board to put underneath and behind the flask and crucible to protect the casting area are the only other items needed.

FINISHING

When the metal has cooled and the cast piece is removed from the mold, there are still several things that must be done before it is considered a finished piece of jewelry. The metal must be cleaned, extraneous sprue wires must be removed, and areas should be smoothed and sanded. Then it is time to decide whether to give the piece a matte or shiny surface.

Supplies and Equipment for finishing the Cast Piece

When the metal casting is removed from the mold, there may be a black or brown carbon residue on it. This is normal, especially in steam casting. To eliminate this dark film from the surface of a sterling silver piece, one will need pickle — an acid sold in powder form at a jeweler's supply store. Do not pickle gold or pewter. Pickle may be made from one part sulfuric acid added to ten parts cold water. Sulfuric acid may be bought at a pharmacy. **CAUTION: always add acid to water and not vice versa**, otherwise an explosion may result. To mix the solution a glass rod and a Pyrex dish are needed. Also have ready some 18-gauge copper wire or copper tongs to lift the piece from the solution. Whenever acid is used, it is wise to have a box of baking soda handy to neutralize the acid in case it spills. Never pour acid down a drain.

The carbon residue may also be removed from gold pewter, or sterling silver by scrubbing the piece with pumice powder on a dampened toothbrush. Pumice powder is a standard hardware store item.

For removing sprue and vent wires, a jeweler's saw frame and number 2 saw blades are needed. Buy at least a dozen number 2 blades because they break easily. To hold the piece steady while sawing, use a small bench vise.

To smooth over the saw marks and remove rough edges from the piece, have ready a large half-round hand file, number 2 cut, and a small inexpensive set of needle files in assorted shapes. Finally, to remove the file marks from the piece, use emery or sand paper. Usually three grades of paper — coarse, medium, and fine — are enough to remove most file marks and give the piece a smooth surface.

To have a contrast of light and dark areas on the piece of jewelry, use a liver of sulphur solution to darken the metal. Liver of sulphur is a chemical compound that comes in dry lump form. (See the section on *Finishing* under "Basic Procedures.") It works best on pewter and silver; on gold with limited success. Most jewelry supply houses sell a specially prepared bottled gold oxidizer as well as liver of sulphur. Store the liver of sulphur in a dark airtight bottle to keep it from deteriorating.

To achieve a matte finish on a piece, rub it with fine steel wool, any grade from number 1 to number 000. Steel wool, hand files, and emery paper may be found at the hardware store.

To achieve a shiny finish, buff the casting with a felt buffing stick which has been rubbed with special abrasives. Buffing sticks are available at a jeweler's supply house, or can be made by glueing two or three layers of white felt to a flat, narrow stick.

Most supply houses sell the abrasives in solid form, either blocks or sticks. One should have a stick of the more coarse abrasive called tripoli, and a stick or red rouge for final polishing. It is important to remember not to use more than one kind of abrasive per buffing stick, so have at least two buffing sticks — one for tripoli and one for rouge. A rouge cloth is excellent for keeping jewelry shiny after it has been worn for a while.

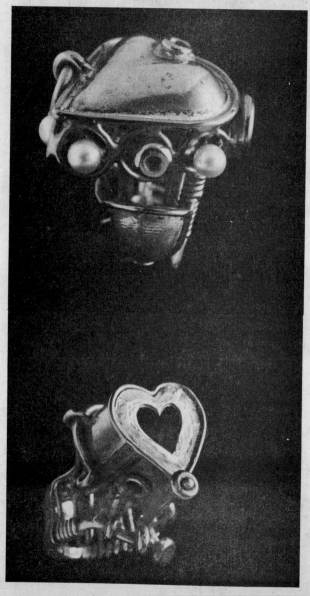

Figure 12: These three jewelry pieces were designed and made by co-author Lee Peck. A pin, or brooch, was fashioned from 14-karat gold (above). Sterling silver is the basic material for the cast ring called "Heart-On #3" (right). Another 14-karat gold ring in the same series is called "Heart-On #4" (above right). Note that "Heart-On #4" is decorated with pearls—usually associated with more traditional jewelry design, but here used effectively with a contemporary style.

Figure 13. A 14-karat gold cast pin by co-author Lee Peck incorporates a striking stone of smoky topaz (left). The 14-karat gold ring (below) was entitled "Clasped Hands" by Naomi Peck. Metal casting is an ancient art, known in many countries and in many periods. Some of the most striking pieces ever cast in gold were created in Mexico in Pre-Columbian times.

Basic Procedures

The casting processes explained here are relatively simple ones. Once all the tools and equipment are assembled, the only major concern is the creation of the model. Then, by following these instructions, step by step, make as many different kinds of jewelry pieces as time and ideas allow.

STEAM CASTING

As mentioned earlier, steam casting requires the making of a wax model. Since there are several different kinds of waxes, and as many wax modeling techniques, the discussion will be limited to the basics. And after working with the wax for a while, one begins to develop his or her own personal technique.

Wax Modeling

One manner of wax working is done with the soft beeswax/paraffin mixture, or the more pliable dental wax sheet and wire (pink or green sheet and green or blue wire). Bear in mind that it will take a little while to learn how to work with the wax. The more experience one has with the nature of wax, the better the model will be. So experiment with the wax first. Here are some suggestions:

1. Heat the tip of the wax tool over the flame of the alcohol lamp. Press the tool into a piece of wax and watch how the wax melts, puddles, then cools.

2. Take a thin strip of wax and hold it near the flame. When a droplet of wax forms on the tip, move the strip and let the droplet fall onto another piece of wax.

3. Take a small spatula and scoop up some wax. Hold the tool over the flame and allow the wax to melt. Pour the wax onto a second piece, as with the wax droplet, and build up a mound of wax.

4. With the wax tool, carve into the mound. For a sharp cut, use the tool cold. For a smoother, rounded edge, heat the tool before cutting.

5. Try pressing small shapes like nail heads, needle points, or anything else that is handy into the wax for a texture.

6. Take thin strips of wax sheet or wax wires and experiment with ways of joining them — side by side, at angles, etc.

7. Bend wax wires around such items as dowel rods or pencils to make coils.

8. Put two wax shapes together, heat the wax tool, and insert it briefly between the two edges, causing them to fuse together.

9. Roll sheet wax back and forth on itself, creating folds or wrinkles.

11. Poke the wax tool all the way through a piece of wax, making a hole. Make odd-shaped holes and holes of different diameters.

Note: If soft wax breaks while being bent, it needs to be warmed. It may be warmed in the hands, in hot water, or by passing it several times quickly over the lamp flame.

To experiment with the harder File-Wax, do the following:

1. Saw off a block of wax to the desired thickness.

2. Incise it with knives and saw blade.

3. File away parts of the block with different shaped needle files.

4. Bore a hole all the way through the block of wax with the sharp tip of a file. Change the shape of the hole by filing into it at different angles.

5. Use sand paper to smooth sharp or rough edges.

This experimentation will demonstrate that the softer wax lends itself to the making of organic shapes, while the harder File-Wax works better with more geometric designs. Remember, with any wax, the model should be kept as light as possible. Otherwise, the finished piece of jewelry will be too heavy and difficult to wear comfortably. Also keep in mind that the cast piece will look exactly like the finished model, so be certain that rough edges have been smoothed out and that the model is completely satisfactory. It is much easier to make changes in wax than it is when the piece is cast in metal. It is wise to make a small sketch before beginning work on a model.

Spruing the Model

Once the model is completed, it is time to set it up in the flask.

1. Gather together the model, some 14-gauge wax wires, and the ping-pong ball sprue former and wooden base.

2. With the wax tool, firmly attach the sprue (a 14-gauge wax wire) to the heaviest part of the model. In the case of a wax ring, attach the sprue to the ring shank opposite the ring top. If the model is large and flat, tilt the piece to allow the metal to flow easier later on. Broaden the sprue where it attaches to the model. Auxiliary sprues, also of 14-gauge wax wire, may be added to help the metal flow to the extremities of a large model.

Figure 14. Sprues are made from a 14-gauge wax wire and attached with a wax tool to the model. A single sprue is attached to the wax ring at the shank opposite the ring top.

3. Now measure out the amount of metal needed to cast the model. Take two small glasses and fill them half full of water, with exactly the same amount in each glass. In one glass submerge the model and sprues until the main sprue is one-half inch under water. In the other glass add metal until the water level is the same in both glasses. Add about a fourth more metal to allow for a complete fill of the mold.

Figure 15. The water displacement method is used to measure the metal needed to cast a model (above). Using a large, flat model (above right), attach the main sprue to the heaviest part and auxiliary sprues to the extremities. The model is attached to the sprue former and positioned inside a flask (below right). Place tape around the edges of the flask top, and use plasticene clay as a filler between the flask bottom and the sprue base.

4. Attach the sprued model to the sprue former (ping-pong ball), allowing the main sprue to be one-half inch long.

5. If casting a big piece which will need a large volume of metal, the auxiliary sprues can touch the ping-pong ball dome, but none should be closer together than 1/8 inch.

6. Paint the model and sprues with a solution of one-half liquid detergent and one-half water. This will help prevent bubbles from forming on the model during investing.

7. Place the flask over the model so that the model is centered in the flask. The model should never be more than one-half inch from the top of the flask so that gases formed during casting can escape. The model should never be less than one-quarter inch from the top or sides of the flask, or the investment may crack from the force of the metal entering the flask and break out of the mold.

8. Roll a coil of plasticene clay and use it to make a fillet between the base of the flask and the wooden sprue base.

Once the model is sprued up and the flask is in place, it is time to invest.

Investing the Model

1. Fill the prepared flask two-thirds full of luke-warm water.

2. Pour the water into a rubber mixing bowl.

3. Add investment and begin mixing it by hand. Be sure to mix the investment thoroughly, dissolving all the lumps. When the investment is the consistency of pancake batter, not watery or stiff, it is ready to be poured.

4. Tape a strip of masking tape around the top edge of the flask, allowing it to project about an inch above the top of the flask. This will allow for filling the flask entirely without having to worry about overflow.

5. Pour the investment into the flask, making certain to pour down the side of the flask and never directly on the model. In this way the investment surrounds the model without trapping large air bubbles on the underside of it. Fill the flask completely.

6. Gently agitate and/or tap the flask to release air bubbles that may be trapped around the model. Be very careful not to dislodge the model from the sprue former. (If this occurs, remove the model immediately and rinse it thoroughly. Pour investment out of the flask into a water-filled bucket, and clean the flask. When model and flask are dry, resprue and reinvest.) Note: Do not pour investment down the drain, because it will clog the pipes. Rather, pour the excess into the garbage.

7. Set the mold aside, allowing it to harden and dry for at least one hour.

8. When the investment is firm, remove the tape from the top, and the sprue former and the base from the bottom.

9. Be sure the top of the mold is flat. If not, file or sand it flat.

10. Scrape off any plasticene clay still stuck to the flask.

Burning Out the Wax

1. Place a metal jar lid on the coils of the hot plate, so that the lid will trap any melting wax.

2. Put a trivet inside the metal lid, and place the flask on the trivet, with the sprue hole at the

Figure 16. A hot plate is used to heat the flask during the investment process. A trivet holds the flask inside a metal lid resting on coils. Then, a flower pot is placed over the flask and coils.

bottom. This will allow the melting wax to drip out freely.

3. Line the flowerpot with aluminum foil, leaving the hole at the bottom open.

4. Invert the flowerpot and place it over the flask and coils of the hot plate.

5. In a well-ventilated room, plug in the hot plate and allow the wax to melt out of the mold. This should take approximately two to three hours.

6. When the flask is glowing a dull red, the mold is ready for casting. Check the color of the flask by lifting the flowerpot slightly with an asbestos glove. The interior of the pot is supposed to reach 1100° F, so if the flask is not glowing, close the hole in the pot with foil only after there is no longer any smoke coming from the hole.

Casting the Mold

1. Assemble the metal, flux, torch, asbestos board, tongs, "plunger," and water-filled bucket. If metal appears dirty or greasy, clean it according to the instruction in the later section on Finishing, steps 1-4. **CAUTION: Never use casting metal pieces that are small enough to fall into the sprue hole and clog it.**

2. Remove the flask from the hot plate using tongs.

3. Holding the flask with the sprue hole facing down, clean the sprue hole rim with small spatula. Make sure that any residue or loose investment does not fall back into mold.

4. Place the flask, sprue hole up, on the asbestos board and fill the basin with metal.

5. Sprinkle metal lightly with flux.

6. Light torch and begin melting metal. When metal is completely molten, it begins to "spin" on the surface.

7. Remove plunger from the bowl of water. *Do not remove the torch from the metal until the plunger is poised above the flask, or the metal will freeze and not flow.*

8. As one hand removes the torch, the other hand presses the plunger down *immediately* and *squarely* on the flask top. Hold the plunger in place for about 45 seconds. It is a good idea to practice placing the plunger on an uninvested flask top, just to get the feel of it.

9. Allow the flask to cool for about five minutes. With tongs, lift the flask and plunge it into the water-filled bucket. The investment will bubble and disintegrate, leaving the cast piece, which can be removed from the water by hand.

Figure 17. After removing the flask from the hot plate, place it on an asbestos board (below left). Add the metal to the basin, and sprinkle it with flux. Then, light the torch and begin the melting process. It is important that the plunger be placed over the flask (below) immediately after the torch has been removed from the metal. Hold the plunger in position for about 45 seconds.

SAND CASTING

In sand casting the most important thing to remember is that the model must be smooth and have no undercuts. Otherwise, it would be impossible to remove it from the sand without destroying the impression it made there. As in wax modeling, always keep the model as light and thin as possible, so that the finished piece is not too heavy to wear comfortably.

Procedures

1. Carve a design in wood, bone, stone, clay, metal, plastic, or hard wax. Sand and polish the model until it is smooth. (If using wood, sand it and apply three coats of shellac to the finished model to seal the grain.)

2. Place the drag, the frame without the pins, face down on the plywood molding (sprue hole facing down).

3. Center the model inside the drag, but slightly toward the lower end away from the sprue opening.

4. Sift parting powder lightly over the model and surface of the molding board.

5. Check the sand to see if it is well tempered: when broken in half by hand, it should break cleanly and not crumble. If the sand is crumbly, sprinkle some glycerine (available at a pharmacy)

Figure 18. After the model has been made, check to be sure that the surface areas are smooth. Then, position the model inside the drag, centering it at the lower end opposite the sprue.

on the sand and knead it in as one would clay or dough. New sand will not usually require this treatment.

6. Through a piece of screening, sift enough sand over the model to cover it with about one inch of sand.

7. Pack the sand firmly around the model with the fingers.

8. Sift enough sand into the drag to fill it to the top. Take the rammer and pack the sand down around the model and along the sides of the drag.

Figure 19. When using this casting technique, it is important to examine the sand to determine if it has the correct consistency. New sand is usually well tempered and should break in half without crumbling (top). Use a piece of screening to sift about an inch of sand over the model (bottom).

9. Sift more sand into the drag until it is overfilled. Again pack the sand down firmly with the rammer, and remove the excess by scraping a straight edge diagonally across the surface of the drag.

10. Place the second molding board on top of the drag and turn the entire works over. Remove the first molding board and expose the model.

11. Place cope over the drag and secure it in position with the locking pins. Dust the model and surface of the sand with parting powder.

12. Repeat steps 6 through 9.

13. Clean away excess sand from work area.

14. Carefully separate the cope from the drag and set it aside, mold cavity up.

15. Gently remove the model from the drag, taking care not to upset the surrounding sand. (Press a piece of sticky modeling wax or a wad of chewing gum to the model to help remove it from the sand.) Blow away all loose sand from the mold cavity.

16. Using a small spatula, carve a sprue channel from the model to the sprue opening in the end of

Figure 20. Continue to sift sand into the drag until it is overflowing (top left). Then, use a rammer to pack the sand firmly inside the mold (top right). Next, place the cope over the drag and scrape off excess sand (bottom left). Repeat sifting and packing processes. Separate the cope from the drag, and set aside the drag from the excess sand before attempting to remove the model (bottom right).

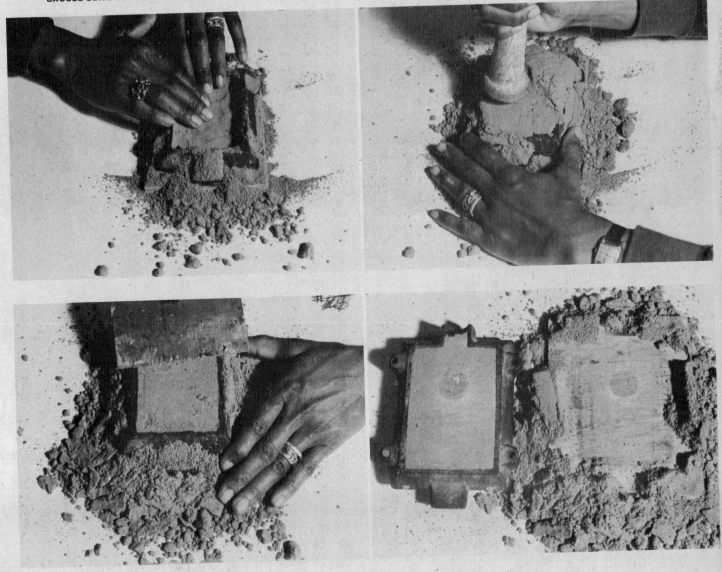

the drag. Cut a few short channels as vents radiating part way out from the model. Always cut away from the model cavity.

17. Blow away all excess sand and replace the cope on top of the drag.

18. Secure the molding boards to either side of the assembled flask (cope and drag) with two C-clamps.

19. Stand the flask on end with the sprue hole facing up.

Figure 21. Use a spatula to carve a sprue chanel from the model to the sprue opening. Carve several sprue chanels radiating out from the model (top). Use tongs to pick up the crucible containing the molten metal and pour it through the sprue hole. After the mold has cooled, separate the frame (bottom).

Figure 22. After separating the cope from the drag, remove the button and store the sand for future castings. The finished piece should be thoroughly cleaned, and any rough edges should be smoothed.

20. If using a new crucible, prepare it before filling it with metal. This is done by shaking some flux into the crucible (both halves) and heating the flux with the torch. Make about four applications of flux, heating it after each application, until a glassy surface builds up.

21. Put the metal into the crucible and sprinkle it with flux. (See measuring metal under "Basic Procedures," Steam Casting, *Spruing the Model*. Melt the metal with the torch.

22. Pick up the crucible with the tongs, keeping the torch on the metal all the time.

23. When the metal is molten (it moves easily when rocked), pour it steadily into the sprue hole. Keep the torch on the metal while pouring.

24. Allow the mold to cool (ten minutes). Separate the cope from the drag. Remove the piece. Knock the sand out of the frames with a rammer and save it for another casting.

FINISHING

Just as the term implies, "finishing" is all the things done to a casting to make it a completed piece of jewelry: sawing, filing, sanding, and so on. Finishing techniques are used on all metal castings, no matter what method was used to cast them.

Procedures.

1. Remove all investment, oxidation, and dirt by pickling the cast piece. (See *Finishing* under "Basic Equipment and Supplies.") Use pickle only with sterling silver work.

2. Place one quart of water in a Pyrex dish and add one-half cup of pickle. Or use ten parts water and add one part sulfuric acid. **REMEMBER: Add acid to water.**

3. Heat the pickle on the stove or hot plate, but do not boil.

4. Drop the piece into the solution and allow it to remain there until it is free of oxidation (about a half hour).

5. Remove the piece and rinse it. It is important never to allow anything made of iron to touch the pickle solution, or it will cause all pieces in the solution to be coated with copper. It is also possible to skip steps 1 through 4 and simply scrub the piece with a damp toothbrush that has been loaded with pumice powder. The cleaning will not be as thorough as with pickling, but it will be adequate. Use the pumice powder technique for cleaning gold and pewter pieces.

6. Brace the piece in a small bench vise. Pad the jaws of the vise with paper toweling so that the jaws do not mar the surface of the piece.

Figure 23. A bench vise and jeweler's saw are used in the finishing process. The piece of jewelry is placed between the padded jaws of the vise, and all extraneous pieces are cut off with the saw.

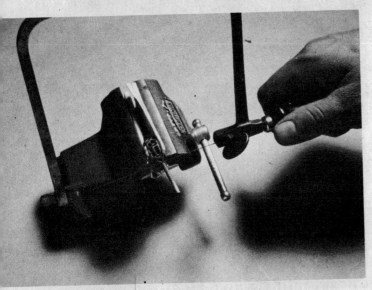

7. Insert a blade into the jeweler's saw frame so that the teeth angle down toward the handle. Tighten the top nut. Press the frame against a table edge to compress it. While it is compressed, insert the bottom of the blade into the bottom clamp and tighten it. Release the compressed frame slowly. The blade should be rigid and under tension, or it will not saw. Because these thin blades break easily, do not apply great pressure during sawing. Apply a little beeswax to lubricate the blade if it is sticking. Remember, the cutting action takes place on the downward stroke.

8. Saw off all sprues, vents, and extraneous metal pieces.

9. Take a half-round file and smooth over blade marks. For hard-to-reach areas use needle files. The correct way to file is from the tip of the file to the handle, in a forward motion. At the same time, file away all unwanted bubbles and rough surfaces from the cast piece.

10. Fold a small piece of coarse emery paper and sand away file marks from the piece. Rub in several directions so as not to make deep parallel scratches.

11. When sanded areas are smooth, change to medium and then fine grain emery paper and repeat the process.

12. Thoroughly wash and rinse the piece.

13. If planning to oxidize areas of the piece, take a small lump of liver of sulphur and dissolve it in a Pyrex dish with a few cups of water. The solution works best when heated, so place it on the stove or hot plate and heat it almost to boiling.

14. Attach a copper wire to the piece and immerse the entire piece in the solution.

15. Remove the piece to check the progress. Reimmerse it until the desired darkness is achieved. Never leave the piece in the solution too long, as a thick black coat that chips easily may result. (To darken gold it is best to use the specially prepared gold oxidizer from a supply house and follow the directions on the bottle.)

16. Rinse the piece thoroughly and dry it.

17. Dip thumb in water and then in the dry pumice powder. Rub it on the piece, removing

oxidation from the raised areas and leaving the hard-to-reach areas alone.

18. To give the piece a matte finish, rub it in one direction only with fine steel wool.

19. To achieve a shiny surface, omit the steel wool and rub the piece rapidly with a buffing stick to which tripoli has been applied.

20. Clean off the tripoli residue by scrubbing the piece with a toothbrush and some liquid detergent. Rinse and dry the piece thoroughly.

21. To give the piece a final polish, rub it rapidly with a buffing stick to which rough has been applied. Scrub again with detergent, rinse, and dry. The piece is completed.

Projects You Can Do

The following projects are all simple ones, designed to introduce both of the casting techniques covered here. Having once produced a piece in either of the methods described, it will be possible to make increasingly complicated and larger pieces or one that combines the two casting techniques. The possibilities are endless.

STEAM CASTING: BAND RING

1. Have ready a wooden dowel rod, one that is as close in size as possible to the diameter of the finger, but never larger.

2. Wrap the rod with masking tape until it is the size of the diameter of the finger.

3. Cut a coat hanger into several three-inch pieces, and file shapes into the tips.

4. With a knife and a straight edge, cut a one-half inch strip of wax and press the filed tips into the wax sheet to create a texture or pattern.

5. Bend the strip tightly around the dowel rod. Where it overlaps, make a cut.

6. Flow hot wax in the seam, joining the two ends smoothly. Continue the texture over the seam to hide it.

7. Take wax wires or narrow wax strips and work them into the pattern to echo some of the pressed-in shapes. This will yield a variation in the levels of the ring which were formed by the depressions from the coat hanger, the original surface of the sheet, and the raised edge of the wires. Do not make the wax wires stand up too high or the ring will be uncomfortable to wear.

8. To add more interest to the design, heat the tip of the filed coat hanger, and push it all the way through the wax strip, making holes. Be careful not to make too many holes or to put them too close together — this would weaken the ring and it might crack with wear.

9. Smooth out all rough edges and carefully remove the ring from the dowel rod.

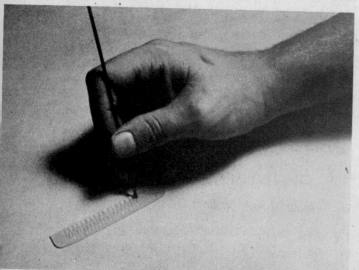

Figure 24. Cut several pieces from a wire coat hanger, and file shapes into the tips. Use a knife and straight edge to cut a wax strip. Then, press the tips into the wax to create a design.

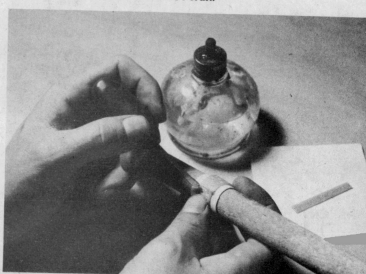

Figure 25. Wrap a wooden dowel rod with masking tape and bend the wax strip around the taped portion. Cut the strip to fit the diameter of the dowel rod and seal the seam with hot wax.

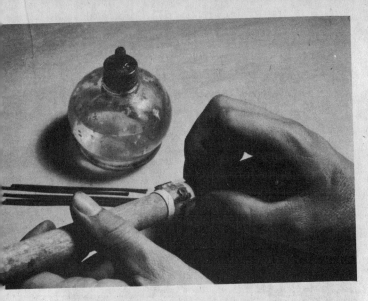

Figure 26. Narrow wax wires can be worked into the wax strip to raise the depressions formed by the pieces of coat hanger (above). After the rough edges have been smoothed, sprue the model and cast it. The addition of the wax wires creates variations in the levels of the ring design (right).

10. Check the inside of the ring for lumps that can be smoothed out with the wax tool. Flow some hot wax into the inside of the seam to fill it.

11. Sprue up the model. (See "Basic Procedures.")

STEAM CASTING: PENDANT

1. Lay out a piece of sheet wax approximately two inches square.

2. Cut strips of sheet wax of varying widths and apply them flat or on edge to the surface of the square.

3. Extend some of the strips slightly beyond the edge of the piece.

4. Pierce the surface of the wax sheet. Try out some of the techniques learned from experimenting with the wax.

Figure 27. Cut wax strips of varying widths and apply them in an irregular fashion to the surface of the piece. Pierce the top of the pendant to create an interesting effect (left). Cut two pieces of wax wire, and attach them in a U-shaped loop to the bottom of the pendant (right).

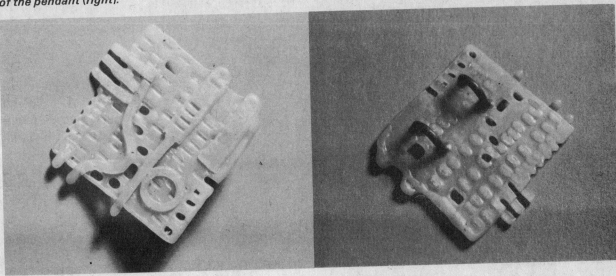

Figure 28. Half-drilled cultured pearls are inexpensive and can be purchased from a jewelry supplier. To add them to the pendant, cut a small piece of wire and attach it at a right angle to the surface (left). After the pendant has been cast, apply glue to the peg and pearl to secure the mounting (right).

5. Turn the piece over. Make two U-shaped pieces from 14-gauge wax wire, and attach them straight up and down and side by side, about one-third of the way down from the top of the piece. These loops will hold the pendant level and keep it from tipping forward when it is hung on a chain or cord. Make sure that the loop openings are at least 3/16 inch wide, so that a cord or chain can pass easily through them.

6. To mount a pearl in the pendant (optional), attach a small piece (about one-quarter inch long) of 20-gauge wax wire perpendicular to the surface of the model. After the piece is cast, the pearl will be mounted on the peg. Inexpensive cultured pearls, which are often sold at jewelry supply houses, can be ordered half drilled. Then, by applying a small amount of epoxy glue to the peg and into the half drilled hole, the pearl may be mounted in place and allowed to dry until set. Do not mount any stones or pearls, however, until the piece has been completely finished — cast, filed, snaded, oxidized, and polished. Otherwise, there is the risk of damaging the stone or pearl. Cord, clasps, and chain may all be purchased at jewelry supply stores.

SAND CASTING: BUTTON

1. Take a block of hard File-Wax and saw off a piece about 3/8-inch thick.

2. Saw the thin piece into a 1¼ inch square.

3. With a half-round hand file, file the corners away until an oval or a circle is shaped.

4. With knives and needle files begin to file and carve away areas to create the design. Remember, do not make any holes or undercuts that will make it difficult to remove the model from the sand mold later.

5. With coarse to fine sand paper, sand the model as smooth as possible.

6. After casting, drill two small holes through the piece so that it can be sewn to fabric. Remember to allow room for this in the design, or better yet,

Figure 29. After the first button is finished, the wax model or the metal button itself can be used to make a complete set. Begin by rounding out a circle from a piece of file wax, and then carve a design on the surface (left). After the piece has been cast, drill two holes through the button (right).

work the space where the holes will be into the design.

7. Cast the button in the sand mold.

8. With a hand drill and a 1/16-inch drill bit, drill two holes in the button.

9. Finish the button according to the directions in "Basic Procedures." Now, using the wax model again, or the metal button as the model, it is possible to make several buttons as a complete set for a coat or jacket.

For Additional Reading

Bovin, Murray, **Jewelry Making,** privately published, 1964.

Morton, Philip, **Contemporary Jewelry,** Holt, 1970.

Pack, Gretta, **Jewelry and Enameling,** Van Nostrand, 1961.

Untracht, Oppi, **Metal Techniques for Craftsmen,** Doubleday, 1968.

Von Neuman, Robert, **The Design and Creation of Jewelry,** Chilton, 1972.

Flower Making and Preserving

Flower making and preserving are creative activities for those interested in making artificial flowers or in preserving fresh flowers, weeds, or plants.

Throughout the world, man has tried for centuries to duplicate flowers in one form or another. One of the earliest forms of duplication were bone china flowers. The bone china composition process was discovered and developed in England around 1750. Some of the earliest forms of floral bone china, such as flower encrusted vases and figurines, can be seen in the British Museum. Today, most department stores sell bone china flowers in the form of bouquets in a basket, as separate flowers on wire stems, or as decorations on vases or other china pieces.

Another type of artificial flower is found in the Botanical Museum of Harvard University. *The Ware Collection of Glass Models* represents the artistic and scientific efforts of two German brothers, Leopold and Rudolph Blaschka, who created the flowers over a period of nearly 50 years. They were not only artists by trade, but naturalists as well. With the financial backing of Mrs. Elizabeth C. Ware and her daughter, the Blaschka brothers accepted a contract with Harvard University, and from 1887 until 1936 created thousands of glass models for display. No other museum in the world contains comparable collections.

Like the pendulum of a clock, craft trends go from one extreme to another in popularity. For instance, tissue paper was first used to make flowers as long ago as the 1880s. Until that time, wrapping had been the primary use of tissue paper. However, two sisters named Heath began to crumple it, cut it, fringe it, and flute it — with surprisingly interesting results.

Then, in 1887, crepe paper was accidentally discovered. A superintendant, walking through a tissue paper mill, came upon a heap of strangely crinkled, discarded paper. The operator explained that too much water had mistakenly gotten into the paper and as a result, crepe paper was discovered. It was first imported from England in 1892. (Crepe paper has a great advan-

Figure 1. This Victorian style arrangement (opposite) shows the colors and shapes of summer flowers, dried and preserved for year-round enjoyment. (Courtesy, Georgia Vance; photo, Kenneth Bergeron.)

Figure 2. These realistic looking orchids (above) and apple blossoms (below) are glass arrangments from the Ware collection at the Harvard Botanical Museum. (Courtesy, Shostal Associates, New York.)

tage over tissue in making realistic flowers because it can be so easily manipulated to simulate real flowers.)

The art of drying and preserving live plants and flowers was conceived centuries ago and is undoubtedly as old as civilization itself. The early Greeks and Romans decorated their banquet tables with garlands of preserved flowers. The monks in medieval times dried flowers using a "hanging" method. The early settlers in America had flowers, foliage, and plants hanging from the beams in their barns in order to preserve the summer and fall beauty through the winter months. The first straw flowers arrived in England in the sixteenth century and were cultivated into the type which exist today. Chinese lanterns also decorated many English homes at this time and many other dried pods and flowers enhanced British interiors.

Pressing live flowers can be labeled Victorian art, for as early as 1850 delicately arranged, pressed flowers and leaves were mounted for keepsakes by Victorian ladies. Seaweed was then gathered at low tide and brought home to be pressed between blotting paper in books. In 1849, the Rev. Lansborough published a book entitled "A Popular History of British Seaweeds," which guided Victorian enthusiasts in the hobby of pressing flowers and weeds for preservation.

One of the most popular uses today for pressed flowers is a floral arrangement mounted under glass and used as a picture. Modern designs can be achieved by the addition of ferns or leaves or by separating petals and forming a design or border.

Common Terms Used In Flower Making and Preserving

Cupping: the particular way of stretching crepe paper between thumb and forefinger to form a cupped shape; used for making petals.

Pressing: the placing of flowers between blotters and weighing them down.

Tinting: restoring lost color with watercolors.

Tying: binding with fine tying wire.

Wrapping: the wrapping of stem wire with floral tape.

Basic Equipment And Supplies

Following is a list of materials needed for flower making and preserving. They are easily obtainable and none are expensive.

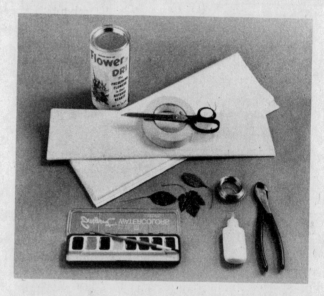

Figure 3. The supplies needed for flower making and preserving are available in craft departments.

1. Tying wire. A fine wire, usually sold in a spool. Wire sold for hanging pictures is a suitable substitute.

2. Stem wire. A stiff heavy wire should be used for large flowers which would ordinarily have a heavy stem such as large roses, dahlias, or peonies. Lightweight coat hangers may also be used for this purpose. A medium-weight wire can be used for carnations, pompon chrysanthemums, and small sprays. Fine wire, which is slightly heavier than tying wire and stands alone, can be used for stems of separate small flowers such as pansies or violets. For smaller buds and flowers which will be attached to a main stem, a fine wire such as tying wire may be used.

3. Flower centers. Most craft departments or stores carry small packages of flower centers in assorted colors and varieties. If the stamens are at each end of a bunch, they should be folded in half or cut in half and then tied with tying wire into smaller groups.

4. Leaves. Some stores will carry packages of readymade leaves in assorted shapes and sizes. Instructions for making leaves are given later in the chapter.

5. Floral tape. A green tape 1/2" wide which comes in a flat roll. It can be made either of crepe paper or of a plastic self-adhering material. The plastic floral tape requires no gluing.

6. Silica gel (or Flori Dry). A granular mixture for preserving flowers, approximately four pounds should be purchased initially. In addition to the above, other necessary items include: (1) wire cutters; (2) white glue; (3) crepe paper; (4) tissue paper; (5) blotting paper, such as the kind used for a desk blotter, for pressing flowers; (6) scissors; (7) masking tape for reinforcing the petals of dried or preserved flowers; (8) tweezers; and (9) watercolors.

Basic Procedures

For each of the techniques discussed here for working with flowers, there are a few introductory steps which should be taken. For artificial flower making, first collect all the materials necessary for making the flowers. For pressed flowers, construct a temporary press to hold the flowers and select those which seem attractive. For making pictures, leaves and foliage are important for filling in backgrounds and borders. The only materials necessary, other than the press

on the "gathering day," is a sharp knife or scissors for cutting and trimming. When flowers and foliage are completely dry, select the background and frame and have the remaining supplies ready.

To prepare for flower preserving, have air-tight containers and sufficient Silica Gel ready so that flowers may be imbedded as soon after cutting as possible. Have tying wire, stem wire, wire cutter, and scissors available. After flowers are removed from silica gel, carefully store them in a box or other container until enough have been collected for a bouquet. Have tools and supplies ready for assembling.

ARTIFICIAL FLOWERS

When cutting crepe paper petals, the grain of the paper is important because the paper will stretch in only one direction. All patterns shown here have an arrow pointing in the direction of the grain. Be sure the lines of the paper run in this direction.

Cutting Crepe Paper

Do not unfold the package unless instructed to do so. If the package has a heavy label, use it as a cutting guide; if not, measure and draw a line for the desired width and cut right through the package.

Figure 4. A mass of crimson spreads over this Chinese import bowl. The arrangement features real flowers, preserved to form a traditional creation. (Courtesy, Georgia Vance; photo, Kenneth Bergeron.)

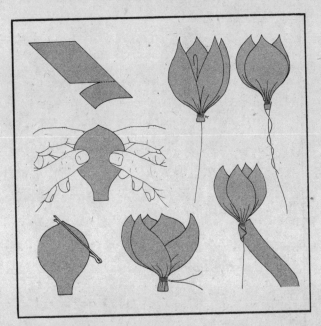

Figure 5. Several petals may be cupped at the same time. To roll the edges, place bobby pins over upper edge of petal. Roll under and remove pin. To fasten, twist wire two or three times and fold ends.

Cupping the Petals

Several petals may be cupped at the same time — be sure the grain of each petal runs in the same direction. Stretch each petal between thumbs and forefingers, pulling out slightly and stretching paper through center.

Rolling the Edges

Place a bobby pin or knitting needle over the upper edge of the petal. Roll under, then remove pin.

Fastening With Tying Wire

Cut off about 4" to 6" of wire and tie it around the base of the flower, about 1/2" from the end. Be careful to keep the tying wire high and tight enough so it will not slip off. Twist the wire tightly 2 or 3 times, then fold down ends. Do not cut wire.

Attaching Stem Wire

Some instructions call for making a small hook at the end of the stem wire and forming a flower over wire; other methods call for placing the stem next to the base of the flower and twisting the tying wire around the stem wire. A drop of glue can be dabbed on the base of the flower to strengthen the joining.

Wrapping Wire and Adding Leaves

If floral tape is not available, cut a 1/2" width of moss green crepe. Cut through the folded package.) Cut pieces of floral tape into not more than 6" to 8" lengths — shorter lengths are easier to work with. Cut the ends on the diagonal. If paper floral tape is used, place a small amount of glue on one end. Place the glued end over the base of the flower to cover and wrap tape around the stem wire on the *diagonal,* stretching the tape and twisting the wire with one hand and holding the tape with the other, keeping the tape smooth. When a leaf is to be added, place it next to the stem wire and wrap the two wires together as one. If self-adhering floral tape is used, follow the same method as above but omitting the glue.

Making Leaves

Trace a leaf pattern onto lightweight cardboard and cut out the leaves using green crepe paper. Place glue on a piece of fine wire (heavier than tying wire) and press down the center back of leaf. Hold until completely dry. If heavier leaves are desired, place another leaf over the wrong side of the first leaf and glue it in place. If desired, mark veins by drawing them with a knitting needle, using a firm stroke.

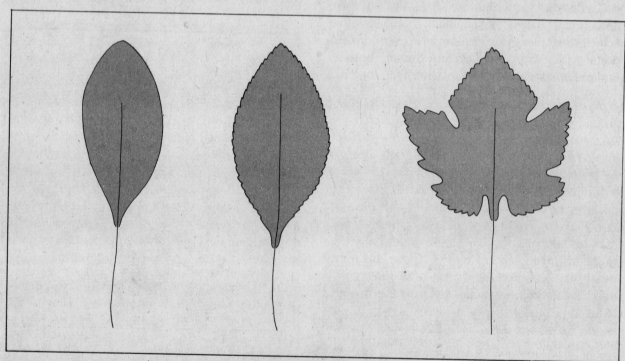

Figure 6. These basic leaf patterns may be used for most paper flower arrangements. Fine wire is glued to leaves that are cut out of green crepe paper.

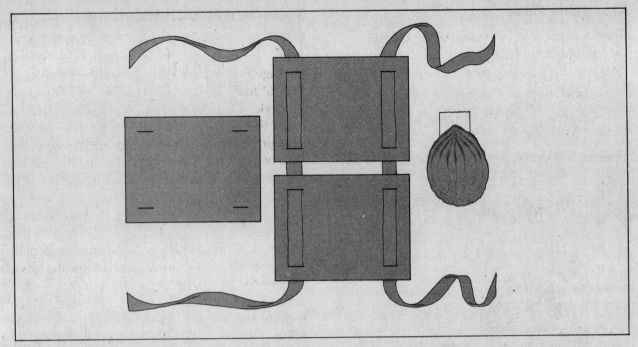

Figure 7. A temporary press can be made with heavy cardboard and ribbon. Blotters and newspaper should be placed between the two pieces of cardboard to protect the flowers. The press is most helpful while out collecting flowers. It will secure and separate the blossoms as well as begin the pressing of the flowers.

PRESSED FLOWERS

Some of the more common wildflowers which press well are buttercups, daisies, goldenrod, late purple asters, black-eyed susans, and trumpet weed. Do not try to press thick, heavy flowers such as thistle — these can be preserved in their natural state. Ferns, grass, and leaves are, of course, easy to press because they are flat.

To make a temporary press, take 2 sheets of heavy cardboard about 9" x 12" or larger and make 4 horizontal slits in each. Draw ribbon through slits. When going to collect flowers, take along a few sheets of newspaper and 2 blotters. Place a blotter over each piece of cardboard. Place the first layer of flowers on one blotter and place a double piece of newspaper over the flowers. Make additional layers with newspaper between, ending with the second blotter. Close the press and tie the ribbons. (When placing flowers between layers of newspaper, be sure the flowers are the same thickness in each layer.)

After arriving home, open the press and add fresh newspaper between each layer of flowers. If some flowers, such as daisies, have a thick center, take a few pieces of a blotter the size of the flower and

cut out a hole in the center. Place enough of these around the flower center until they are built up to the same level. Place a heavy weight, such as several books, on top and leave for several days. Check flowers and add fresh paper. Again, place weights on top of press and leave for another week. Continue this method until flowers are completely dry. This process may take anywhere from a week to a month.

After flowers are completely dry, separate those which need to have color restored. Most flowers lose some of their natural color in drying. Some of these may also need some reinforcing. If a flower is about to fall apart, remove the petals and place each petal on a piece of cellophane tape or masking tape and press in place. Carefully cut around each petal, leaving a small piece of tape at the center of the flower. Now, put the flower back together again, being careful to hide the tape.

To restore color, place a few drops of liquid detergent into a small container of water. Using water color paints, a small brush, and the detergent-water, paint color onto petals. If the flowers are completely dry, only the pigment in the paint will penetrate the petals and the color should dry quickly.

Drying Flowers, Plants, and Weeds Upside Down

Cut the stems to desired length. Remove all unnecessary parts, dead leaves, or insect eaten leaves, but do not strip them completely. Stems may be curved *before* drying by bending and tying in the direction desired.

Figure 8. To dry flowers, plants, and weeds, hang them upside down, allowing air to circulate freely on all sides. Keep them out of direct sunlight and dampness. (Courtesy, Georgia Vance; photo, Kenneth Bergeron.)

Group 3 or 4 stems together and tie them securely, or place an elastic band around them because they shrink while drying. Thick stems should be hung alone. Hang them upside down, allowing air to circulate around all sides. They can be hung on a clothes line, but should be placed in a shed, garage, cellar, or attic and, kept out of direct sunlight and dampness. After about 8 to 10 days they should be stiff to touch and the stems should snap easily when completely dry. A longer drying period may be necessary during humid weather. Weeds, pods, straw flowers, Japanese lanterns, cockscomb, and money plant are examples of plants which dry well in this manner. This method, of course, requires no extra materials or equipment.

Drying Fresh Flowers With Silica Gel

All flowers should be cut when they reach full bloom or are about to open. Cut flowers on a bright sunny day, but not after a rainfall — the least amount of moisture is desirable. Place flowers immediately into silica gel (instructions follow). If this is inconvenient, use a jar of slightly tepid water to hold the flowers until ready to use.

Figure 9. Fresh flowers are preserved in an air-tight container such as this cake tin and supported by about a two-inch layer of silica gel. (Courtesy, Georgia Vance; photo, Kenneth Bergeron.)

Choose a container such as a cake tin, plastic box, or any shallow air-tight container. Remove all but 1" or 2" of the flower's stem. Pour about 2" of silica gel into the container. Using fingers, make a small well in the center. Carefully place the fresh flower faceup in this well. Push silica gel up under petals to be sure they are supported. Fill a cup with silica gel and gently trickle the crystals onto and around the flower. It is important to slowly trickle the crystals as the petals cannot support a great amount of sudden weight. Build up the crystals slowly to keep the flower in its natural shape. Continue sprinkling the silica gel until the flower is completely covered. Several flowers can be placed in the same container, providing they do not touch each other.

Place the lid on the container and be sure it is airtight. Do not open it for at least 3 days. Dense, heavy flowers may require longer to dry. To be certain the flowers are completely dry, tilt the container and check. If the top layer is still moist, again trickle silica gel until the flower is covered and seal container.

To remove the flowers from the container, slowly pour the crystals into another container until the flowers are exposed. Using curved-nosed tweezers, pick up the flower at its base and lift it out. If any petals have loosened and dropped off, they can be secured with a drop of white glue or silicone sealer.

Figure 10. To remove flowers from the container, slowly pour crystals into another container until all the flowers are exposed. Lift out each flower base with a curved-nose tweezers. (Courtesy, Georgia Vance; photo, Kenneth Bergeron.)

Drying Fresh Flowers With Borax-Sand Mixture

To 3 parts borax, add 1 part heavy, clean, finely-sifted sand; or, to 3 parts pure white sand, add 1 part borax. As this is a less expensive method of preserving flowers, larger containers with more depth may be used. Stem wire can be attached before the flowers are dried by making a small hook at the end of the wire and inserting the straight end into the center, hooking the wire into the flower. Flowers with many petals, such as zinnias, marigolds, or carnations, may be tied together with tying wire or cellophane tape at the base of the flower to hold the petals securely while drying.

Slowly trickle sand-borax mixture onto flowers as in the silica gel method. The container need not be covered. With this mixture, flowers will take 3 weeks or longer to dry, but they may be left in sand indefinitely without harm to flowers.

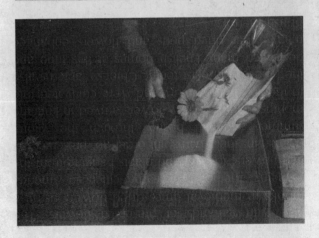

Figure 11. The sand drying method takes three weeks to dry the flowers. Gloriosa daisies (top) are dried face down while delphinium and larkspur (center) are dried in a horizontal position as sand is trickled over them. The uncovering technique (bottom) is the same as the silica gel method. (Courtesy, Georgia Vance; photo, Kenneth Bergeron.)

Making a Bouquet

Having dried sufficient flowers and foliage to make a bouquet, place flowers on stem wires by laying the wire next to the stems of the flowers and wrapping these with floral tape. Flower colors may be protected against the humidity by spraying them with a clear acrylic such as Krylon or Gard's Spra-tone. The surface will be moist, but will quickly dry without absorbing moisture.

Storing Dried Flowers for Later Use

Carefully wrap air-dried flowers in tissue paper and lay them in a box. To store silica gel dried flowers, place them in a large air-tight container with about 4 tablespoons of silica gel placed in a small tin or a pyrex custard cup. Check periodically to be sure the crystals are still blue and if necessary dry the silica gel by removing only the custard cup and placing it in a warm oven (250°)

for about 20 minutes. Reseal the container.

Choosing Colors of Flowers for Drying

Violets and purples tend to either darken too much or fade; harsh magentas, however, become a more favorable color. Yellow keeps its original color and may even become more intense. Marigolds in particular look almost fresh after drying. Blue does not retain its color too well and is not easily found. Some available blue flowers are delphiniums, larkspur, and hydrangea. Red can be preserved with a fast-drying method, such as silica gel. It is wise to choose orange-reds or deep pinks rather than blue-reds. Foliage usually dries to a soft gray-green, especially lilac and rose foliage. Remember, too, that white is important in a large, mixed bouquet. White larkspur, sweet peas, daisies, or Queen Anne's lace are some of the more attractive white flowers.

Figure 12. Flowers preserved in silica gel must be stored in an air-tight container. The flowers shown above are safely stored in a plastic bag. (Courtesy, Georgia Vance; photo, Kenneth Bergeron.)

Projects You Can Do

Because original flower pressing and preserving projects are easily decided upon, the suggestions offered here deal only with making bouquets of artificial flowers. The following material gives step-by-step procedures for making several kinds of individual flowers.

BOUQUET I: DELPHINIUMS, POMPON CHRYSANTHEMUMS, AND ROSE OF SHARON

Although this bouquet is time-consuming, the effort will be worthwhile and the results rewarding.

Delphiniums

Materials required are one package of pastel crepe paper, floral tape, yellow stamens, tying wire, stem wire, and three daisy leaves for each spray.

To begin the buds, cut through the package of crepe paper to make a 2″ width of folded paper. Cut through both ends to make separate pieces. Trace a pattern for a circle onto a light piece of cardboard and cut it out. Using the pattern, cut out circles for buds. Then, to cut the flowers, trace a pattern for the flower onto a light piece of cardboard and cut it out. Using the pattern, cut out two pieces for each flower.

Figure 13. Delphiniums, pompom chrysanthemums, and rose of sharon make a delightful paper flower arrangement.

To make the buds, place one circle over the end of a pencil and mold the bud. Remove the pencil and tie a 4" piece of tying wire around the base, being careful not to crush the buds. Make about seven or eight of these for each spray.

To make the flowers, place two flower pieces together, turning the top piece so the petals do not match. Fold two stamens in half if they are tipped at both ends or use four stamens. Make a *small* hole in the center of the flower with the end of a pair of scissors and push the ends of the stamens through it. Press flower and stamens together and tie with a 4" piece of tying wire around the base of the flower. Make about 18 flowers for each spray.

Cut several 2" pieces of floral tape to wrap flowers and buds. If paper tape is used, spread some glue onto a dish or piece of cardboard so it will be handy. Dip one end of the tape into the glue and wrap each stem of buds and flowers, covering the wire (see "Basic Procedures").

To assemble the spray, tie three buds together with tying wire, having the center bud slightly higher. Wrap as one piece. Add two or three more buds and tie these together below the first group. Tie and wrap the stems as one. Tie group of buds to a 12" piece of stem wire with tying wire. Add three flowers below the group of buds and tie and wrap for 1 inch. Continue to add a group of three flowers an inch apart down the stem until the spray is the desired length. Add the three daisy leaves which have been cut (see "Basic Procedures"), or make leaves and wrap the remainder of the stem. If the spray does not turn to one side when completed, bend wire slightly.

Pompon Chrysanthemums

Materials required are: one package each of white and moss green crepe paper, floral tape, stem wire, glue, stapler, and pliers.

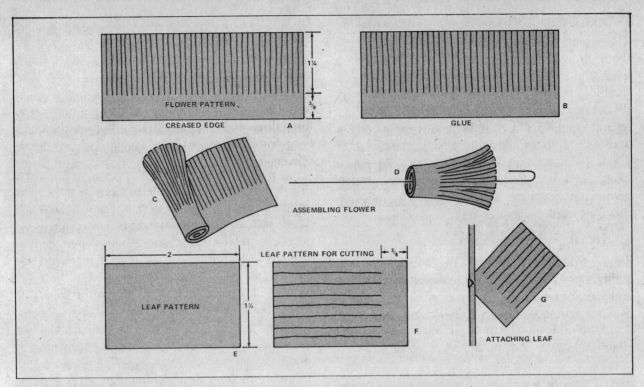

Figure 14. Pompom chrysanthemums (above) are simple to assemble, as shown in this diagram. Buds, flower centers, and flowers can be created from the diagram for delphiniums (opposite page).

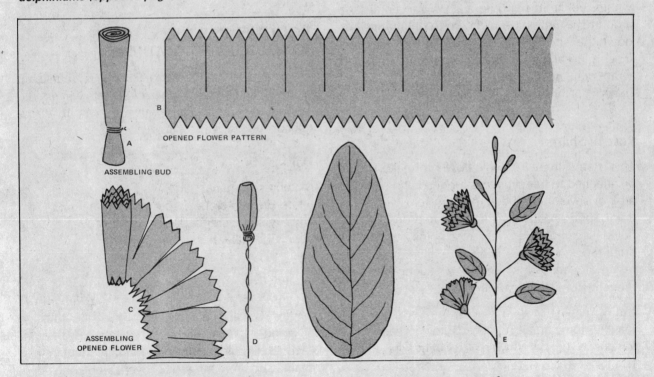

Figure 15. The rose of sharon blossom is excellent for large or small arrangements. A floral spray is assembled by placing a bud at the end of a piece of stem wire. Twist the wire several times. Alternate leaves and buds along the wire according to the directions.

Cut through the packages of crepe paper, making 2½" widths of folded paper. Unfold these and cut them into 12" lengths for each flower. Now fold each strip in half lengthwise to make a 1¼" width double strip 12" long. Crease the edge sharply. Bring ends together to make a 6" length, then fold again to make a 3" length. Even the creased edges and secure them either with 2 staples placed about 1/4" from the creased edge, or with paper clips. Cut a very fine fringe along the open edge within 3/8" from the creased edge. Carefully remove the staples, leaving the strip folded.

To make the flower, spread glue along the strip on the top side only. Starting at one end, roll the strip tightly to the end. Glue the remaining layers at the end. To assemble, make a small hook with a pair of pliers at one end of an 8" length of stem wire. Carefully push the straight end down through the center of the pompon until the hook catches.

Next, make the leaves. Cut several pieces of green crepe paper (2 for each flower) into 2" x 1-1/4" pieces. Cut one edge into 8 sections, cutting to within 3/8" from opposite edge. Wrap floral tape around the 3/8" base of flower, continuing tape down the wire for about 1 inch. Cut and glue tape. Place glue along the uncut edge of the leaf and wrap diagonally down the stem. Wrap the remainder of the wire with floral tape.

Rose of Sharon

This is an extremely simple flower to make. It can be attached to tree branches for decorating a large area or several can be placed on stem wire for a floral spray. Materials required are: one roll of fluted streamers in bright rose, pink, or fuscia; floral tape; stem wire; tying wire; glue; and daisy leaves. If the sprays are to be attached to tree branches, omit the stem wire.

Cut 6" lengths of streamers for the buds. Cut 10" lengths for partially opened flowers and 18" lengths for opened flowers. Cut tying wire into 6" lengths.

To make buds, roll a 6" length of paper and tie it with tying wire. Cut floral tape into 3" lengths. Starting at the base of a bud, wrap the bud and tying wire (see "Basic Procedures"). Set buds aside.

To make opened and partially opened flowers, cut between every third notch on one edge of a fluted strip to within 1/2" from the opposite edge. Roll approximately a 2" strip for the center of the flower, then loosely gather the remainder of the strip around the center, turning the flower while gathering. Tie with tying wire and wrap with floral tape. Carefully spread out the petals.

To assemble these for a floral spray, place a bud at the end of a 12" piece of stem wire. Twist the tying wire around the stem 2 or 3 times. Cut the floral tape into several 3" lengths and wrap the wires together. Attach 1 or 2 more buds down stem as desired. Leaving 1" of covered tying wire extended, attach a partially opened flower, then 3 or 4 opened flowers and leaves down the stem (see "Basic Procedures" for attaching leaves). To assemble the flowers for attachment to tree branches, it is not necessary to make sprays. Buds and flowers may be attached directly to the branches by tying them with tying wire or stapling them in place. Be sure to wrap the buds and flowers with floral tape before attaching.

BOUQUET II: DAISIES, TULIPS, JONQUILS, AND GLADIOLI

This is another bouquet project. It is, of course, up to the individual what kinds of flowers will go into a bouquet — they can be mixed or can be a bouquet of only one kind of flower.

Daisies

Materials required are white typing paper or white duplex crepe paper; tying wire and stem wire; yellow crepe paper; white covered tying wire; glue; daisy leaves; and floral tape.

From typing paper, cut pieces 3" x 4" for daisy petals. Cut pieces of covered wire into 2½" lengths — 12 for each daisy. Cut tying wire into 4" lengths. For the centers, cut through the package of crepe paper, making a 1" width. Cut through each end. Fold each strip in half, then in half again. Cut a fine fringe 1/2" deep, along one edge. Gather together and tie with tying wire. Spread out fringe.

To make the petals, fold a piece of white typing paper in half to make a folded piece 1½" x 4". Open up the fold and spread glue across one half

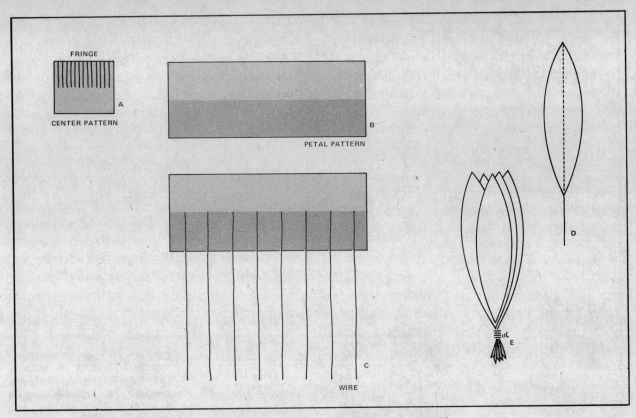

Figure 16. *White typing paper may be substituted for crepe paper when making daisies. This pattern gives the actual size of the daisy petal.*

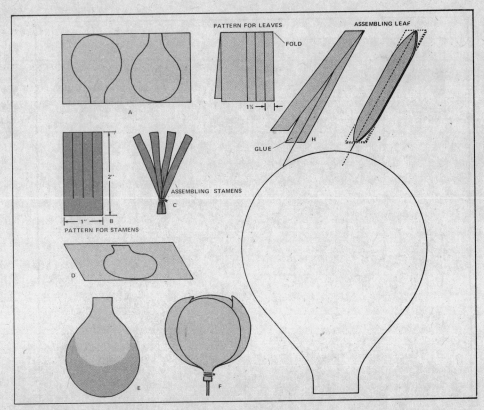

Figure 17. *Using two-tone duplex crepe paper gives more contrast to these tulips. Crayons may also be used to shade the outer portions of the petal.*

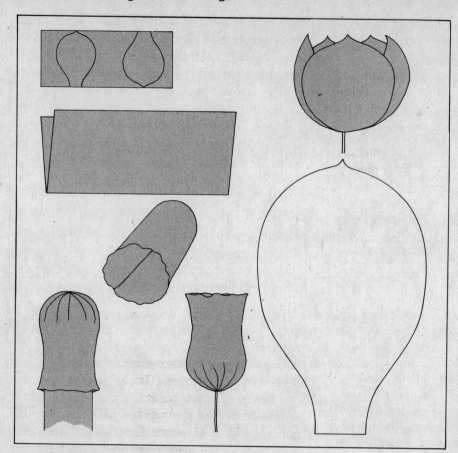

Figure 18. A broomstick handle is helpful in molding the tubular portion of the jonquil. The double petals can be attached to the rounded center.

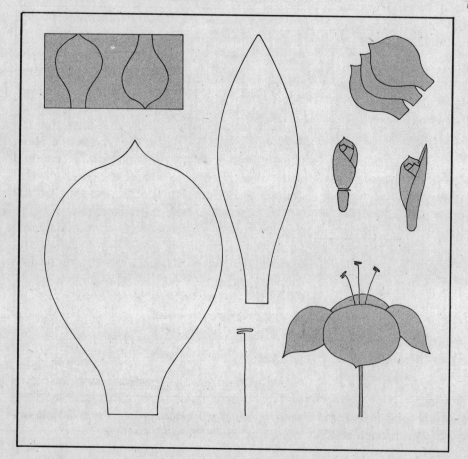

Figure 19. Gladioli are made from this basic petal pattern. Each bud requires three double petals. Gladiolus buds are most effectively used in a spray.

of paper only. Place pieces of covered wire 3/4" apart across glue, having wires end at the fold line. Fold down the other half of the paper and press together. Smooth out around the wire and cut out petals, having the wire as the center spoke. A pattern is given for the actual size but it is not necessary to draw each petal.

To assemble, place 12 petals around a center and tie these together with tying wire. Place a piece of stem wire next to the daisy and tie with tying wire, placing a drop of glue on the base of the daisy. Wrap the stem with floral tape for about 2" inches. Place a leaf next to the stem and wrap remainder of stem, adding another leaf about 1" below.

Tulips

Materials required are 1 package of 2-tone rose duplex crepe paper, 1 package each of green and black regular crepe paper, 12" lightweight stem wire for leaves, 12" medium weight stem wire, tying wire, glue, and crayons or pastels.

To cut the petals, trace the pattern for the petal onto lightweight cardboard and cut it out. Cut through the package of rose crepe paper, making a 3" width and cut through each end. Trace the pattern onto several layers and cut out 4 petals for each tulip.

To make the stamens, cut through the package of black crepe paper, making a 2" width and cut through each end. Cut a strip in half, then in half again. Cut each 1" x 2" piece into 4 sections, leaving 1/2" uncut at edge. Roll the stamens together and tie with 4" piece of tying wire.

Next, place a petal on a piece of cardboard with the wide end of the petal toward you. With crayon or pastels shade the outer part of the petal, using yellow on the light pink side or orange on the rose side. Cup petals, having shaded side away from you (see "Basic Procedures").

To assemble, tie stamens with tying wire to the medium weight wire. Place a small amount of glue on the base of the stamens to prevent the wire from slipping. Place 4 petals, shaded side out, around the stamens and tie them with tying wire. Wrap the base of the tulip and the entire stem with floral tape.

To make the leaves, cut off several folds from the package of green paper (do not cut through this package). Fold piece in half to make a 10" depth. Now cut folded piece into 1¼" widths. Apply glue down 10" of the inside of strip. Place a piece of lightweight stem wire down the center, leaving 2 inches extending. Press the other half of the strip in place to make a two-layered leaf with wire between. Taper each end. Place leaf next to the stem of the tulip and wrap the 2" extension of the leaf wire together with the stem wire. Make one leaf for each tulip.

Jonquils

Materials required are 1 package each of yellow and moss green crepe paper, 12" lengths of green covered medium weight stem wire, 12" lengths of uncovered lightweight stem wire, glue, and tying wire.

For the petals, cut through the package of yellow paper making a 3" width of folded paper. Cut through each end. Trace pattern onto lightweight cardboard and cut it out. Trace pattern onto several pieces of yellow paper and cut out the petals. For the centers, cut through the package of yellow paper, making a 4" width. Cut through each end. Fold a strip in half lengthwise and crease sharply. Then ruffle the folded edge by stretching the paper.

To make the jonquil, place glue on one edge of a 4½" folded strip and glue together, overlapping 1/4". Place tubular piece over a broomstick with ruffled edge down. Press the paper over the end of the broomstick to round it off and then glue the folds in place. Allow this to dry completely. Next, make a small hook at the end of the green covered wire with pliers and place the hooked end through the center. Place a drop of glue on the end of the hook to hold it in place. Glue 2 petals together to make double petals; make 5 double petals for each jonquil. Hold flower center and wire upside down. Glue 5 petals around the rounded end of the center, overlapping the petals. For leaves, follow the instructions for tulip leaves, making one for each flower.

Gladioli

Materials required are 1 package each of orchid and moss green crepe paper, white covered tying wire, glue, black marking pen, and 14" heavy stem wire.

Figure 20. The brilliant poppies spill over a lustrous bowl. The texture of the crepe paper gives the flowers a realistic appearance. (Courtesy, Dennison Co.)

Cut through the package of orchid paper making a 3″ width of folded paper. Cut through each end. Trace pattern for petal onto lightweight cardboard and cut it out. Using pattern, cut out petals: each flower requires 4 double petals (two placed together but not glued). Each bud requires 3 double petals.

To make the calyx, cut through the package of green paper, making a 3″ width. Cut through each end. Trace the pattern for the calyx and cut it out — 1 for each flower and 1 for each bud. To make the stamens, cut the white covered wire into 3″ lengths. Bend one end of wire into 2 small folds about 1/4″ long and squeeze these together. With the marking pen, blacken the folded end. Make 3 stamens for each flower.

For buds, roll 3 double petals together, overlapping 3/4 of the petals and tying these together (see illustration). Place glue along the long edge of the calyx and wrap around bud. Wrap the remainder of the bud with floral tape. Make 3 or 4 buds for each spray.

For flowers, tie 3 stamens together with tying wire. Cup each double petal and place 4 of them around the stamens with the petals cupping out. Tie with tying wire. Glue a calyx over the base of the flower, as on the bud. Wrap the remainder of the stem with floral tape. Make about 7 flowers for each spray.

Finally, tie one bud to the end of the 14″ wire. Wrap this with floral tape for 1 inch. Tie on another bud and wrap for 1 inch. Add 1 or 2 more buds 1″ apart, then add flowers 1″ apart. Wrap the remainder of the stem with floral tape. For leaves, follow the instructions for tulip leaves. Make 1 or 2 for each spray.

For Additional Reading

Beautiful Flowers 'n Things, Craft Course, 1970.

Dennison Flower Book, Dennison Manufacturing Co., 1963.

Hamel, Esther Veramae, **Creative Designs With Dried and Contrived Flowers,** Simon and Schuster, 1971.

McDowall, Pamela, **Pressed Flower Pictures,** Scribner, 1969.

Pantz, Phillis, **Decorating With Plants and Natural Materials,** Doubleday, 1971.

Squires, Mabel, **The Art of Drying Plants and Flowers,** Bonanza Books, 1958.

Dough Art

The popular folk art of making decorative objects from various kinds of edible and inedible bread dough owes its beginnings to ancient bakers who first began to sculpt and mold the pliable substance while preparing the "daily bread."

The knowledge of bread making is as old as recorded history; bread is also man's first formulated food. Since the first baker pushed his fist into a soft mound of dough and gave a brief thought to the resulting shape, bread dough has been explored as an artistic medium as well as a nutritional one.

The earliest evidences of bread making come from the Neolithic Age. Ancient graves, dating from 6000 B.C., were found to contain small fragments of bread-like material. The first breads were probably made of crushed grain mixed with water and formed into paddies which were left to dry in the hot sun. Later, the grain was crudely milled, resulting in a slightly finer product.

Figure 2. The stylistic Madonna and Child on this "baked Christmas card" was designed by Ray Ameijide. (By permission from Lithopinion 32, *the graphic arts and public affairs journal of Local One, Amalgamated Lithographers of America and lithographic employers, New York, © 1973 by Local One, A.L.A.)*

The Egyptians are credited with the discovery of a leavening agent and, in time, they also invented the first baking ovens. Wheat is believed to have been raised first in ancient Abyssinia. The grain was carried by boat down the Nile to Egypt. The

Figure 1. This quaint house was made from baker's clay. Dough art is sometimes called "poor man's ceramic" because no expensive equipment is required to create decorative objects.

archeological explorations at Deir-el-Bahari have turned up ancient loaves of bread, either round or triangular in shape, which had been baked in ovens and which represented the finest bread product of that period.

Bread became an important factor in the success of Egyptian civilization and a symbol of its bounty. Bread was ceremoniously cast upon the waters of the Nile in tribute to the gods and has been discovered in Egyptian tombs, where it was placed to sustain the departed spirits of the dead. Often bread was used for money. At the end of a work day, laborers were paid their due in bread.

The developing Greek civilization borrowed much from the Egyptian culture, including the secret of leavened bread. Realizing the importance of bread, the Greeks came to worship it much as the Egyptians had done. Demeter was named "Goddess of Bread," and the "Celebration of Bread" became one of the more important Greek festivals. Eventually, the Greeks began to use bread dough for decorative as well as for religious and ceremonial purposes.

The circular millstones for grinding grain were invented by the Romans, who also saw the practicality of enlarged baking ovens where bread could be prepared on a commercial level. Roman bakers, in business by 168 B.C., were careful to mark each loaf with their own personal sign. Loaves of bread, left baking in beehive-shaped ovens at the time of the catastrophic eruption of Mt. Vesuvius in 79 A.D., have been found in the ruins of Pompeii.

As European cultures developed during the Middle Ages, bakers' guilds were formed. Substances other than bread dough were developed for decorative and artistic baking purposes during this time. One of the more successful ones, marzipan — a sweet, pliable material — was made from crushed almonds and pressed into molds or freely sculptured. While too expensive at first for widespread use by the common people, this new, highly popular substance triggered the production of a vast variety of molds for candy and breads.

Various kinds of fancy baked goods became traditional fare for market places, village fairs, and large festivals. Individual regions featured their own specific design, often commemorating some locally famous event or story. Large honey biscuits and delicate honey cookies, decorated with biblical parables, family coats of arms, historical captions, sayings, and tales, were proudly displayed before being consumed.

Inedible forms of bread dough evolved along with the edible, probably appearing first in Yugoslavia and later in other parts of Europe. South America

Figure 3. These intricately detailed ornaments of bread dough illustrate the skill developed by Ecuadorian craftsmen.

and Mexico developed a highly decorative form of bread dough art, utilizing brilliant color and minute detail. The folk art of Ecuador included highly ornamented mirrors, picture frames, figurines, and nativity scenes as well as a wide variety of jewelry made from bread dough which has the lasting power of ceramics. Today, the tourist in Bolivia, Peru, Columbia, Ecuador, and Mexico will be dazzled by the vast array of designs in both utilitarian and decorative baked objects produced by local craftsmen.

In the United States, the contemporary movement is back to nature, back to harmonious, organic living, and back to the more simple pleasures of folk art. The bread dough medium, in all of its varieties, represents a fundamental link with man's earliest beginnings.

Figure 4. Mushrooms, molded of bread dough, were combined with tree bark, strawflowers, and a pine cone in this decorative wall plaque.

Common Terms Used In Dough Art

Acrylic: an odorless, quick drying, water-based paint made from plastic polymers; also acts as a strong adhesive.

Baker's Clay: a clay-like material made of salt, water, and flour; must be baked in order to become hard.

Bread Dough: a substance made with bread, white glue, and a small amount of glycerin or liquid detergent; hardens without baking.

Creative Clay: a mixture of cornstarch, baking soda, and water which is cooked briefly to form a pliable material.

Dough Appliqué: the process of applying several layers of dough over a foundation layer.

Glazing: the brushing of the surface of a baker's clay item with mayonnaise, canned milk, or egg yolk before it is baked. By glazing, a surface may be made to appear smooth, glossy, crackled, or browned and antiqued.

Sealer: a clear acrylic or shellac applied in several light coats over any finished dough project to prevent the absorption of moisture and to add a protective, glossy, or matte coating to the surface; may be sprayed on or painted with a brush.

Tempera: an inexpensive type of water-based paint which can be used to tint the uncooked dough or to decorate the finished product.

Basic Equipment And Supplies

One of the greatest appeals of this medium is that it is relatively inexpensive. Most of the varying dough recipes, both edible and inedible, use reasonably priced ingredients from the grocery store; many of the shaping tools and extra equipment may be found in an ordinary kitchen. Sometimes referred to as a "poor man's ceramic," dough art requires none of the expense of clay, potter's wheel, kiln, and glazes as does actual ceramic work. Yet the dough material has the plasticity of clay, the lasting quality of ceramics or porcelain, is nontoxic, and displays a warmth and beauty all its own.

THE DOUGH

There are a variety of dough recipes, each one calling for slightly different ingredients and techniques of preparation. One recipe may be suitable for very tiny, fragile items while another is best for larger, sturdier projects. Some types of inedible doughs will not be longlasting while others will hold up for years. Various doughs can be stored in plastic bags in the refrigerator and used over a period of weeks while others must be used within hours of preparation. While guidelines for the handling of various doughs will be given during the course of this article, personal experimentation is highly recommended.

Flour

The flour called for in some of the recipes can be of nearly any kind as long as it is white. It does not need to be "self-rising" or "enriched" and does not require sifting before use. Generally, the least expensive flour available is perfectly satisfactory.

Salt

The salt, which does not have to be iodized, can be any brand available as long as it is of the table salt variety.

Water

Comfortably warm water from the faucet is recommended for those doughs requiring kneading. The warm water gives the dough a pleasant feel and seems to speed up the kneading process. It appears to make no difference if the water is "hard" or "soft."

Baker's Clay Mix

A ready-made dry mix of salt and flour may be available at craft stores for those who do not care to make their own. However, the water must still be added in correct proportions and the dough kneaded until the desired consistency is attained, so very little time and effort are saved by buying the mix.

Bread

Several recipes call for the use of white bread. Generally, fresh bread is preferable but older bread, when placed in the freezer for several days and then thawed, is also adequate.

Glue

Any brand of general-purpose white glue can be used. Several recipes call for the glue to be mixed with pieces of bread; this causes the bread to change back into a doughy substance. When kneaded properly, the bread and glue mixture will not be sticky. White glue, which is colorless when dry, is often mixed with water to give a porcelain-like surface to the finished project.

Glycerin

Easily purchased at any drugstore, glycerin is added to the bread and glue recipes to improve the plasticity of the dough. It is also helpful to moisten the hands with glycerin periodically while working with the dough. A few drops of liquid detergent may be tried as a substitute for the glycerin, and hand lotion can be used to keep the hands from drying.

Whitening Agent

Several additives may be used to enhance the whiteness of the dough. Small amounts of white acrylic paints, white tempera, or tube watercolors are recommended.

Cornstarch

Several recipes use cornstarch as a basic ingredient rather than flour or bread. Often the cornstarch recipe, containing baking soda, is used as "play dough" in nursery schools and kindergartens. It is safe for small children, is easily made and worked, and stores well for long periods of time.

Most of the equipment required for the basic dough recipes is readily available in well-stocked kitchens, with only a few special items needed from a hardware or paint store. The following supplies are not required for all dough recipes, nor are they necessary for all projects.

Garlic Press

A garlic press, while not necessary, is a handy gadget to use with dough. Such items as string-like hair, manes, and tails can be produced from the long, thin, "noodles" of dough squeezed through a press. A garlic press can be purchased chased at hardware or department stores containing a section for gourmet cooking ware.

Shaping Tools

The kitchen drawer is the first place to look for dough tools. A small paring knife is probably the most versatile tool available and may be the only one needed. Other tools might be a rolling pin, melon-ball shaper, potato ricer, pastry wheel, vegetable peeler, ice pick, pieces of dinner ware, or a nut cracker. Check the "stray items" drawer for pencils, toothpicks, popsicle sticks, bottle lids, golf tees, manicure scissors, or anything else with which to jab, poke, prod, or pinch. Cookie cutters are excellent tools for cutting and shaping, while a child's toy box may yield various tools and molds for play dough. A wide variety of wood, plastic, or metal specialty tools for clay and dough sculpting are also available at craft and hobby supply stores.

Figure 5. Although a variety of special tools are available, practically all of the equipment necessary for dough art can be found in the home. A paring knife is almost indispensable. Other utensils that might be useful include a pastry wheel, tweezers, and cookie cutters.

Other Household Equipment

Aluminum foil is indispensable for projects using dough which must be baked. When making several small projects, it is easiest to form each one on a separate piece of foil, then slide the foil onto a cookie sheet and place in the oven. Wax paper may be employed as a surface on which to work when using the materials which are dried in air.

Several of the doughs respond well to being pressed into molds. Antique and Jell-O molds as well as candy, cookie, and marzipan molds might be considered. A variety of molds for plaster, resin, and candles are offered by local craft shops. Stoneware cookie molds pressed into small rounds of dough make interesting imprints, as do ornamental metal and wooden buttons and costume jewelry with interesting surfaces. Some materials, such as metal buttons, hard seeds and nuts, some pasta products, odds and ends of old jewelry, beads, and chains, can be pressed into the soft dough and baked in.

Color Additives

Color may be added to the various doughs either before using or after, depending upon the type of dough prepared and the particular project being attempted. Baker's clay, after being baked in an oven, turns delicately brown and closely resembles an edible dough. The natural coloring of this type of dough is one of its charming qualities. However, the addition of some color to a project after baking is quite acceptable. Tempera paint is most easily handled — it is applied with a small brush — and can be used by anyone. Acrylic paint is somewhat more expensive but perfectly satisfactory. Felt-tip markers may be used, but the surface of the baked dough is often so uneven that the color from such markers is not satisfactory. Vegetable dyes may be employed, added either before the dough is used, during the mixing process, or afterward. The same is also possible with a variety of other commercial dyes.

Dough made from bread and glue is often colored before use, generally by the addition of small amounts of tempera paint or tube watercolors. Projects made from bread dough can be decorated with pigment after completion as well. Other dough recipes should be experimented

Figure 6. Commonly used cooking ingredients, such as Worcestershire sauce, canned milk, egg yolk, and mayonnaise, provide a variety of finishes when brushed over the unbaked dough. Such pre-bake glazing is not essential, however.

with by adding color either before or after baking or drying in order to arrive at the most satisfying results.

Wire

Dough material lends itself to the making of hanging ornaments. A light grade of wire, cut into 1- or 2-inch lengths and then twisted around a pencil, makes a good hanger for an ornament. A non-rust steel or aluminum alloy wire is recommended. The wire loop (or paper clip, bobby pin, etc.) should be inserted while the dough is soft.

Another type of wire, #9 green-covered wire, is ideal for use with bread dough when designing small flowers requiring stems. Heavier wire or a fine grade of chicken wire or wire mesh can be used for support when larger, heavy projects are undertaken.

Sealer

All dough art work will last longer and look better if it is protected by a sealer. The dough containing salt absolutely requires sealing to avoid softening and crumbling. Depending upon the product used, a nearly invisible matte finish is possible, as is one of high gloss. Clear acrylic and shellac come in spray-type containers and are easily handled. Craft shops carry a variety of other types of transparent sealants as well. In some instances, shellac or lacquer can be applied by brush. All surfaces, front and back, should be sealed.

Basic Procedures

Working in dough is a pleasant pastime for everyone. It is an ideal project for children of all ages and for various clubs, organizations, and fund-raising groups.

Generally speaking, the resulting objects improve in quality as one's skill increases, but the medium does not require great expense, concentration, time, or special ability. Moreover, the craft imparts a satisfying feeling of achievement regardless of the artistic worth of the end product.

Of the half-dozen or more dough recipes found in craft magazines, two of them are the most satisfactory. Other recipes appear to be simply variations of these basic two, but all should be tried if one is interested in achieving unusual results or is seeking some quality not present in the master recipes.

Baker's clay, made with flour and salt, is an inedible, nontoxic dough which closely resembles edible dough when baked. It smells pleasant while baking and puffs up slightly, softening edges and details, and turns light brown. If it is baked too long, it becomes dark and will catch on fire if forgotten in a hot oven. If coated with a matte finish sealant after baking, the dough will continue to resemble any regular cookie or bread dough product. This type of dough is excellent for all projects with the exception of the most delicate. It is extremely longlasting but subject to breakage, as is any ceramic or porcelain item. However, the unused dough does not save well and begins to deteriorate within hours of being prepared.

Bread dough, consisting of white bread and glue, works particularly well for small projects requiring minute detail and fragile edges. It is used primarily for making small, delicate flowers because the material is highly pliable and elastic; it can be pressed and gently pulled until very thin. The finished products are sturdy and longlasting. The unused dough can be successfully stored in a sealed, plastic bag in the refrigerator for several weeks.

BAKER'S CLAY

Baker's clay is most satisfactory if used right after preparation and baked as soon as each project is completed. When the dough is allowed to remain unbaked for an hour or more it begins to get sticky; covering the dough in a container will not remedy this problem. Often, more flour can be kneaded into the softening dough. However, such treated dough has a greater tendency to expand and crack while baking, often distorting pertinent details of the design.

Preparation of the Dough

The very first step in working with baker's clay is to allow time enough for the dough preparation, the creative process, and the baking of the finished piece. The master recipe calls for 4 cups of flour, 1 cup of salt, and 1½ cups of water.

Mix the flour and salt together in a flat-bottomed plastic bowl. A spatula or wooden spoon may be used for mixing, but the hands are best. Wear plastic gloves to protect the hands from excessive drying. Add warm water slowly, stirring constantly. As soon as the dough has formed enough to pull away from the sides of the bowl, turn it out onto a floured counter. Knead it vigorously, adding more flour if it becomes too sticky or more water if it is dry and crumbly. Continue to knead for seven to ten minutes or until the dough resembles heavy, thick clay with a smooth, elastic surface. (If salt granules show, the dough is too dry. If there is any tendency for the dough to stick to the fingers or counter, it is too wet.) Place the material immediately in a covered, plastic container or bag and remove only small pieces at a time while working with the dough.

Working the Dough

Baker's clay may be rolled out with a rolling pin and cut into shapes with cookie cutters. Like clay, it may be handled and shaped into sculptured figures and built up on chicken wire foundations or, for larger projects, on a metal armature. Or, it can be formed over crushed balls of aluminum foil. It can be molded into forms and have forms molded into it. It can be squeezed, pinched, stretched, or cut. One piece can be sealed to another by lightly wetting the two surfaces.

Figure 7. Baker's clay consists of flour, salt, and water. Use a wooden spoon and a large bowl to mix the correct amount of each ingredient (above left). When the mixture pulls away from the sides of the bowl, turn it out onto a floured surface (above right). Then, knead the dough (below left) until its surface is smooth and elastic (below right).

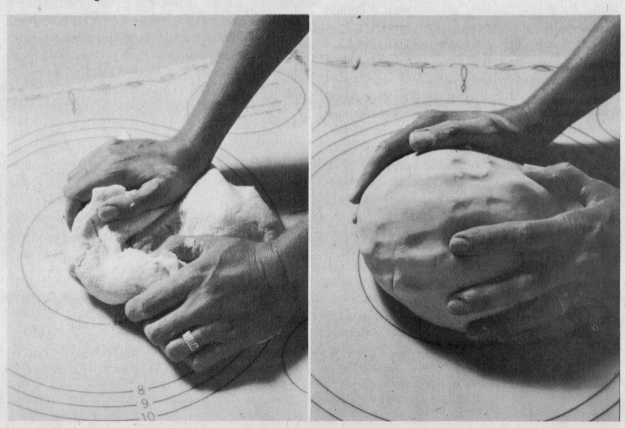

A variety of surface effects can be achieved by coating the dough with a number of substances before or during baking. Mayonnaise applied several times during the baking process will result in a crackled, rich, warm brown color. A canned milk coating causes a deep brown, semigloss surface which can be utilized for highlighting. Other colors and textures are created by using egg yolk, egg white, weak solutions of tea or coffee, lemon juice, and shoe polish. Before using, the dough can be colored with vegetable or powdered dyes; generally, however, color is added after baking.

Baker's clay cannot be attached to other surfaces before baking. As a general rule, the dough will not cook well if parts of it are more than several inches thick. Dough which is too soft may enlarge and crack during baking, and dough which is too dry may develop an unpleasant granular surface.

Baking the Dough

The purpose of baking this material is two-fold: (1) to "set" the dough, driving out the moisture and leaving a hard, sturdy substance; and (2) to achieve the color and appearance of a real dough product. When the dough creation is relatively thin — under 1/2" in thickness, for example — the dough browns as it dries and becomes evenly hardened. When items to be baked vary in thickness or are 1 to 3 or more inches thick, problems can arise. Generally, the larger or thicker the item, the longer it must bake and at a slower temperature.

Most small projects such as ornaments the size of cookies, which are relatively thin, can be cooked in a 350° oven for approximately 30 minutes. Figures or constructions from 1/2 to 2 inches thick will probably require an hour or more and should be baked at 300° or 325°. Larger projects require longer baking. A baker's clay project is done when it has baked through completely and is rock hard. If items must be cooked for long periods of time, it is sometimes helpful to lightly cover the item with aluminum foil. The foil reduces the speed of browning so that an item which must cook three hours or more will not come out of the oven too dark to be attractive.

Figures with long legs, arms, hair, or shapes made of several thicknesses of dough tend to warp during baking. This problem can be offset to some degree by placing the item, before baking, on the surface of the stove after the surface has been warmed by the oven. The warm metal of the stove seems to dry out the underneath surface of the dough creation and, in most cases, helps in cutting down or eliminating the tendency to warp.

Thin areas or the uppermost surfaces on dough projects will brown faster than the main body. Sometimes, as in the mane and tail of a lion design or the fur on a dog, this is desirable. However, this early browning can be controlled by careful placement of small pieces of aluminum foil, covering only those areas which are darkening too rapidly.

All projects should be constructed on aluminum foil and baked on cookie sheets or other large, flat metal pans.

Finishing the Dough Project

After the dough piece has thoroughly baked, been removed from the oven, and cooled, it can be finished in a variety of ways. If the surface color is entirely satisfactory and attractive, perhaps nothing more should be done to enhance it. In this case, several coats of a matte finish sealer will protect the item, yet will be scarcely visible as a coating over the surface.

Color can be applied at this time, either as a highlight or as a covering of the entire surface. Tempera is inexpensive and easily used. Any of the other coloring agents previously mentioned deserve experimentation. All pieces must be sealed as a final step.

An interesting surface can be achieved by antiquing a finished piece. After completely sealing a project with several coats of clear, acrylic spray, brush on a coat of wood stain, such as oak, walnut, or teak. Then, after letting the piece dry briefly, rub the stain off with a soft cloth. Several more coats of sealant will bring back a slight gloss to the finished product.

Dough sculptures can be mounted on wooden plaques, driftwood, barn siding, cork board or used in ecology boxes and miniature scenes. A dependable adhesive is epoxy glue, particularly the quick-set type. Once set, the glue will hold indefinitely, and there is no danger of the dough creation coming loose from its wooden backing.

BREAD DOUGH

Made primarily of bread and glue, this dough can be successfully formulated from several recipes. It stores well when placed in a sealed container and refrigerated, and can be used over a period of several weeks.

Preparation of the Dough

The master recipe for bread dough calls for 6 slices of white bread (if extremely soft, allow to dry in air for several hours); 2 tablespoons of white glue; and 2 teaspoons of glycerin (or liquid detergent). Other additives include 6 drops of lemon juice and 6 drops of white paint (tempera or tube watercolor) or white shoe polish.

Remove crusts from the bread and tear or cut the bread slices into small pieces. Mix the crumbs and glue together in a small bowl, kneading the mixture with the hands until a small, pasty ball is formed. Work in the remaining ingredients and continue working the material with the hands until the dough is firm, smooth, and not sticky. If it seems too sticky, add more bread crumbs; if too dry, mix in more glue. Place the dough in a plastic bag and store until needed.

Figure 8. When making bread dough, first remove the crusts from slices of white bread and tear the bread into small pieces (below). Next, mix in some white glue (top right) and form a ball of dough. Blend in glycerin, lemon juice, and paint (center right), and knead until the dough is firm and smooth. If the dough is too sticky (bottom right), add more bread. If the dough is too dry, add more glue. Store the dough in a plastic bag.

Coloring the Dough

Color may be added to the dough either before use or after a project is completed. Probably the easiest method of tinting is to mix the individual colors desired into the fresh dough, later adding more color to the completed project if necessary. Tempera paint or vegetable colors are best to use when tinting fresh dough. Color only small amounts of material at a time unless planning a very large project containing only one or two major colors.

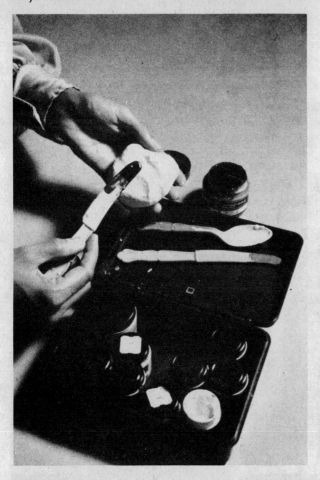

Figure 9. When coloring bread dough with tempera paint, flatten a small ball of fresh dough and add the paint. Work the paint into the dough by kneading and squeezing; mix thoroughly.

Make a ball about 1" in diameter and flatten it on a on a piece of paper. Apply tempera color with a popsicle stick or brush, or carefully add vegetable color drop by drop. Work the color into the dough by kneading and squeezing, taking care to mix it thoroughly. If the color develops darker than desired, add uncolored, white dough to lighten the shade. Repeat this process with each color and store each ball of dough in a separate sealed container. Marbleized dough may be created by partially mixing balls of different tints together.

Working the Dough

Anytime the dough is being worked for the first time or has just been taken from the refrigerator, it is helpful to knead it for several minutes to render it pliable and to bring it approximately to room temperature. Keep a container of hand lotion or glycerin handy and occasionally put a few drops on the hands to keep them moist. When one piece of dough is to be added to another, it must be glued. Merely sticking the damp ends together will not result in a permanent seal. To adhere the surfaces, the same white glue used in the preparation of the dough may be employed. If, however, the dough creation will receive hard wear and tear, as in the case of rings, pins, and brooches, a regular cement must be used to join surfaces.

A bread dough project cannot be hurried. When it consists of many separate, assembled pieces, such as the petals of a rose or decorations or an ornament, it must be allowed to dry thoroughly between steps. Work on wax paper so that the dough object may be carefully laid down to dry without the problem of sticking to surfaces. Often a block of styrofoam can be used as a base and the wire stems of flowers placed in it as the flowers dry.

Occasionally, bread dough will shrink and crack as it dries, especially if the dough was too dry to begin with. It may be helpful to brush a light coat of equal parts water and white glue over each object when the design is completed and the drying process ready to begin. This procedure will give a glossy finish to the creation as well as retard cracking.

Finishing the Project

After a project has been completed and allowed to air-dry entirely, the finishing touches can be added. Color may be applied by using tempera, acrylic, or oil paints or by using vegetable and commercial dyes. Wood stains and shoe polish may be used to give an antiqued finish. All dough pieces should be sealed with a lacquer or shellac as a final step.

Projects You Can Do

Four projects are suggested here, each using either baker's clay or bread dough. Although the last project is the most detailed, none is difficult and each should be fun.

BAKER'S CLAY ORNAMENTS

Probably the easiest project for someone new to the art of working in dough is making cookie-cutter ornaments, either as Christmas decorations or as jewelry to be worn. The ornaments are easily decorated with tempera paint or felt-tip pens, just as one might use frosting on real cookies.

The materials needed are prepared baker's clay dough, an assortment of cookie cutters, rolling pin, thin wire cut into 1½" lengths and twisted to form small loops, cookie sheet, tempera paint (or other paint) in a variety of colors, small brushes or magic markers, and spray sealant.

Start with about 1/3 of the prepared dough, forming a ball and then flattening it slightly with the hands. Using a rolling pin, roll the dough out on a slightly floured counter to about 1/4" thick. Cut the dough with the cookie cutters, dipping each cutter into flour occasionally to prevent the dough from sticking. Before placing each shape on a cookie sheet, insert a wire loop in the soft dough, taking care that the wire ends do not protrude.

Bake the cookies in a 350° oven for 20 to 30 minutes or until the cookies are rock hard and the desired shade of brown. Some shapes tend to expand and puff up slightly, making the resulting ornament either more attractive or unusable.

Figure 10. Before beginning baker's clay ornaments, make hangers for them from short lengths of wire that have been twisted around a pencil to form loops (top left). Prepare the baker's clay and roll out one-third of it (top right). Use cookie cutters to cut the dough, place the pieces on a cookie sheet, and insert a hanger in each piece (bottom left). Bake the ornaments and then paint them if desired (bottom right).

Sometimes a light covering of aluminum foil while baking helps prevent excessive puffing of the dough and produces a flatter cookie.

The cookie ornaments can be decorated after they have cooled. They may be completely covered with paint or merely outlined and only slightly decorated. Because the natural color of the dough is part of its charm, leaving part of the natural surface exposed will result in a finished ornament which more closely resembles a real cookie.

The final step is that of applying several light coats of spray sealer to both sides of the baked dough — allowing 15 to 30 minutes drying time between coats, depending on the brand and type of spray used.

plaque, driftwood, barn siding, tree bark, pressed cork or other mounting material; and a strong adhesive.

The dough to be pressed into molds should be on the stiff side without being crumbly. When making the dough, knead in extra flour and work the material ten minutes or longer to achieve a stiff, smooth, yet pliable substance.

Lightly sprinkle the mold with cornstarch to prevent sticking, shaking out excessive, loose cornstarch before applying the dough. Press a ball of

Figure 12. Baker's clay can be pressed into molds. When used in this way, the dough should be slightly stiff. First, dust the mold with cornstarch so that the dough does not stick (top). Note that the dough is kept in a plastic bag until needed. Firmly press a ball of the stiff dough into the mold (bottom). The choice of molds is limited only by the imagination of the craftsman.

Figure 11. These Christmas tree ornaments were cut out of baker's clay. Paint was used to add decorative touches.

USING A MOLD WITH BAKER'S CLAY

Materials needed are prepared bread dough; white glue; paint (tempera or watercolor in tubes); brush; floral tape; stiff wire (#9 green-covered wire if available); shaping tools; toothpicks; knife; cuticle or découpage scissors; and sealer, either matte or gloss finish.

Materials needed are prepared baker's clay dough; mold; cornstarch; kitchen paring knife; various substances for glazing, if desired (see discussion of glazing in section on common terms); cookie sheet; paint or stain; sealant; wooden

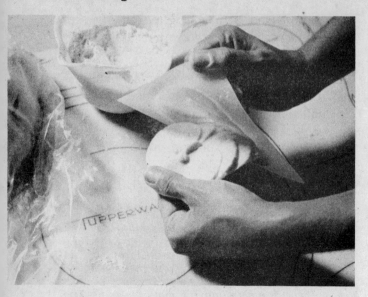

Figure 13. The baker's clay must be removed from the mold very carefully: start at one edge and gently pull back the dough (above). Place the molded dough on a flat surface and examine it; trim off any excess dough and reshape any distorted areas. With the mold on a piece of foil or a cookie sheet, apply a pre-bake glaze (right). Bake, cool, and paint the molded dough.

Figure 14. The molded dough, painted or stained if desired, must be sealed. Brush on several coats of shellac or clear acrylic. Mount the object on a wooden plaque, a scrap of lumber, a slab of tree bark, or some other material; use a strong adhesive.

dough firmly into the mold, filling all corners and crevices. Lift out the dough gently, starting at one edge and carefully pulling back. Thicker dough may be tapped out or a dough ball may be pressed into the back of the molded dough and used as a handle.

Examine the molded dough carefully, trimming off excess dough with the fingers or paring knife and gently reshaping if necessary. Thick dough may be inconspicuously pierced in several places with a pin to help prevent distortion and warping during baking.

Now is the time to apply a prebake glaze, if desired. Place the object on a cookie sheet and bake at 300° to 325° until done. Rapid browning can be slowed by a covering of aluminum foil. After the molded form has cooled, it may be painted, stained, antiqued, or left its natural color. As with all dough projects, the item must be sealed with a shellac or clear acrylic.

Many molded items are especially attractive when mounted on a background. Wooden plaques, available at hardware stores and craft shops, can be stained, painted, antiqued, or covered with material such as burlap. Weathered siding or lumber scraps along with tree sections, slabs of firm tree bark, or pressed cork are examples of other material with potential as background mountings. A strong adhesive is necessary to permanently glue the dough design to the background material. Various types of wood glue or quick-set epoxy glue are recommended.

MAKING A BASKET OF DOUGH

Lovely and unusual baskets that can be made from this versatile material are occasionally found for purchase in the more expensive gift shops; however, they can be made at home quite easily. The basket, which is woven, baked, and covered with sealant, can be used in flower arrangements, as an Easter basket for holding decorated eggs, or as a container for real bread and rolls. It is longlasting when stored in a dry place and can even be cleaned with a slightly damp cloth.

Materials needed are prepared baker's clay dough, a metal bowl to be used as a mold, rolling pin, ruler, sharp knife, orange shellac, gloss varnish, and a small brush.

Prepare the dough by working it until warm, soft, and smooth. Using approximately 1/2 of the dough, roll it out on a slightly floured surface until about 1/4" thick. Cut the dough into strips of equal width and long enough to fit over the bowl. Strips may be extended by attaching two or more together at the ends, moistening and gluing each contact surface.

Cover the outside surface of the bowl with aluminum foil, tucking the edges over the rim. Invert the bowl on the cookie sheet. Lay the dough strips over the bowl, in one direction, spaced evenly. Weave in an equal number of strips at right angles, moistening and gluing the strips at each junction. Trim away all excess dough around the rim of the inverted bowl.

Bake the construction (still supported on the bowl) in a 300° to 325° oven for 1 to 1½ hours or until cooked through. The basket may be covered with aluminum foil if it darkens too rapidly. Cool completely before gently inverting the metal bowl and sliding the basket off.

A decorative rim can be made by twisting the remaining strips of uncooked dough together and attaching them to the basket by moistening and gluing all the adjoining surfaces. Place the dough

Figure 15. Use baker's clay for a woven basket. Cut strips from the dough (top left). Twist some strips to make a rim and weave the others, shaping them over an inverted bowl (top right). Join the rim and woven strips with toothpicks (bottom left). Remove bowl after dough cools (bottom right).

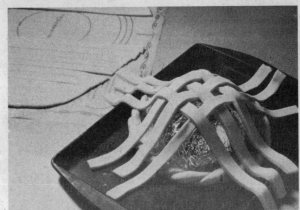
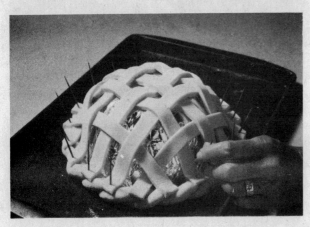

basket in a loose wrapping of aluminum foil, leaving the rim and interior of the basket exposed. Put the basket with its foil protection back into the oven, baking just long enough to brown and set the rim.

The completed basket must be sealed with more care than the previous projects if it is to be used and expected to last. Equal amounts of orange shellac and gloss varnish can be mixed and carefully brushed on the basket; allow complete drying between coats. Do not allow drips to harden. Cover completely with a final coat of pure varnish for a high-gloss effect.

Although the basket can be cleaned with a damp cloth, do not allow it to remain damp for any length of time and do not set it down on a wet counter surface. Store the dough basket in a dry, cool place.

FLOWERS FROM BREAD DOUGH

Bread dough is particularly suited for small, delicate projects although it may be used successfully for larger ones. However, a full loaf of bread does not produce a large quantity of dough and, when large projects are contemplated, the other dough recipes will probably be more satisfactory. Bread dough cannot be surpassed for making small doll house-sized miniatures, jewelry, picture frame and mirror decorations, and flowers, all of which have the appearance of a porcelain material.

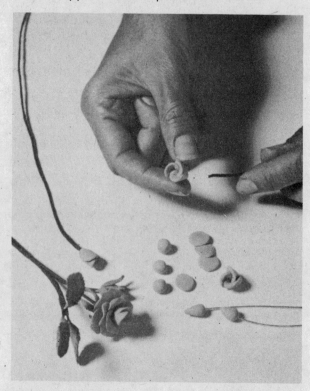

Figure 16. These baker's clay baskets have been sealed with several coats of a mixture of orange shellac and gloss varnish. Clean dough baskets with a damp cloth and store these versatile pieces in a cool, dry place.

Figure 17. To make the center of a rose from bread dough, flatten and form several small balls of dough into a petal shape. Then roll together three of these pieces (top). Use either a real rose leaf or a plastic one as a mold (bottom).

Figure 18. The rose center should be completely dry before petals are added. Shape each petal so that it resembles one from a real flower.

Before beginning a project of making flowers, it is advisable to consult a good flower book with many clear color plates. These pictures can serve as guides to shape, tint, and relative size of numerous flowers and will help in achieving a natural looking dough design.

Materials needed are prepared bread dough; white glue; paint (tempera or watercolor in tubes); brush; floral tape; stiff wire (#9 green-covered wire if available); shaping tools; toothpicks; knife; cuticle or découpage scissors; and sealer, either matte or gloss finish.

A rose is a good flower for the beginner because it is easily made, each petal being pressed from a small ball of dough and then wrapped around the stem. The first step is to color the dough. Divide the dough into walnut-sized pieces, add color to each, then work the ball until the desired shade is evenly mixed throughout.

Work with small amounts of dough at a time, keeping the remaining material covered in a plastic bag. Roll a number of small, pea-sized balls of dough and flatten each one, forming a petal shape and making sure the edges are particularly thin. Overlap three petals using a small amount of white glue to form a seal. (Because this dough does not adhere to itself well, all joints must be glued.) Roll the petals together, forming the center of the rose. Cut a length of #9 wire or cover a piece of wire with green floral tape and gently insert one end into the base of the rose cen-

ter, pinching the dough around the stem and sealing with a small dab of glue. The glue in the center must dry for 12 hours before more petals are added. A small drinking glass, a lump of clay, or a styrofoam block can be used to hold the stem and rose upright while it is drying.

The petals are added in rows of three, with each row having petals which are slightly larger and broader than the previous one. Apply a small amount of glue to the base of the rose and add the first petal, allowing it to flair slightly. Lightly curl back the upper edge, copying an actual rose or a picture of one in order to approximate a natural look. Attach the remaining two petals. Start on the second row of petals in the same manner, using glue to attach them and curling and waving each one. Alternate the second row of petals with the first row, as one finds in nature. Allow the glue in each row of petals to dry before attaching the next row.

A third row of five petals finishes the rose, which will now measure about 1" in diameter. Natural color gradation can be achieved by adding small amounts of white dough to the basic color as each row of petals is made, causing the rose to become deeper in color towards the center.

A calyx is a small collar of green leaf segments arranged around the base of a blossom. One may be devised for the rose by forming a small, flattened teardrop of green dough and cutting it, from the smaller end, into five, tapering segments. Do not cut the dough completely through to the far end. Roll the teardrop between the fingers and gently separate and flair each section, cutting tiny nicks along the edges with cuticle scissors. Slide the calyx up the stem of the rose and attach it to the base of the flower with white glue.

Leaves may be formed by using either a real rose leaf or a plastic one as a mold. Form a small amount of green dough into the general size and shape of the desired leaf. Press it onto the underside of the leaf chosen to serve as a mold. Squeeze out and thin the edges of the dough to conform to the appearance of the real leaf. The dough material will pick up the natural vein pattern of the leaf and appear quite realistic. Peel the dough leaf off carefully and glue the base to a length of green wire, pressing the base slightly around the wire. Cut teeth into each leaf with scissors.

Figure 19. It is difficult to distinguish the real rose (top) from the bread dough one (bottom). Always study natural flowers — size, color, etc. — before attempting to make them from dough.

After the finished flower has dried completely, seal it either with a spray gloss or matte lacquer or brush on several coats of glue mixed with equal parts water. A gloss is produced by placing the item in a 350° oven for a few minutes after applying the final coating of glue and water.

The leaves of a rose are assembled in threes, using floral tape. The three-leaf sections are then attached to the rose stem with the same tape. Cut away excess wire when assembling the leaves to avoid an overly thick, bulky stem.

All types of flowers can be designed with bread dough, either following the basic directions given for the rose, by adding each petal separately, or by cutting the flower petals from a single, flattened round of dough. An oxeye daisy, black-eyed susan, or any other flower with numerous, similar petals can easily be constructed by cutting a whorl of petals from a single piece of dough. Interesting centers for such flowers are made by pushing the dough into a tiny mesh such as netting or nylon stockings. For each flower attempted, always return to nature and observe the form, size, shape, color, and arrangement of the petals, calyx, leaves, and stems.

Bread dough flowers look elegant when arranged in small baskets, antique china dishes, sugar bowls, and vases. They may be placed on brooches, pins, and earrings or even serve as place-card holders for fancy dinner parties. Flowers, mushrooms, small animals, and insects — all from bread dough — can be attached to plaques, jewelry boxes, mirrors, frames, and shadow-box pictures.

For Additional Reading

Andreas, Liza, "Bread Basket," **Family Circle,** May 1974.

Chernoff, Goldie Taub, **Clay-Dough, Play-Dough,** Scholastic Book Services, 1974.

Du Pont, Ana, **Bread Dough Artistry,** Craft Course, 1968.

Gerhard, Mae, "Balthasar," **Life Magazine,** Dec. 15, 1972.

Johnson, Ilse, "Cookies and Cathedrals Glazed with Good-to-Eat Glass," **Life Magazine,** Dec. 15, 1972.

Lanier, Ruth Asawa, "Christmas Claybake," **Ladies Home Journal,** Dec. 1964.

Mergeler, Karen, **Too Good to Eat: The Art of Dough Sculpture,** Folk Art Publications, 1972.

Sommer, Elyse, **The Bread Dough Craft Book,** Lothrop, Lee and Shepard, 1972.

Weber, Elizabeth, **From Bread to Flowers in the Palm of Your Hand,** Cunningham Art Products, 1972.

Williams, Greta, **Bread Dough Miniatures,** Craft Course, 1973.

Antiquing

Using paints, glazes, and finishes to produce an antique look can provide a creative approach to furniture decoration.

When paint was first used to decorate and brighten the gloom of the family cave is a fact lost in the history of man. However, it is known that paint made its first appearance as a means of decorating furniture among the Egyptians and, not long afterwards, among the classical Greeks and Romans.

Following the time of the Crusades, the walls of medieval halls and castles were brightened by painted decoration. The prosperity of the late medieval churches, however, enabled them to hire artists who were highly skilled. These artists became famous for their work in gold leaf and their ability to create illusions with the paint brush.

Constant observation of lovely painted church furniture led the common people to desire aesthetically pleasing furniture in their own homes. France and Italy became flourishing centers of painted decoration, and knowledge of this craft eventually spread throughout the other European countries.

Whereas the furniture of the royal palaces in seventeenth-century France depended heavily on gilding (see "Common Terms"), people of the upper nobility used furniture that was painted white and embellished only with gold trim. This furniture, after it had been polished for generations, developed a delightful patina and an off-white look of age. It is this effect which "French antiquing" strives for.

Another step in the seventeenth-century development of painted finishes came with the sudden desire of European people to own Chinese lacquer furniture, which was becoming extremely popular and quite scarce. Europeans soon became skillful in simulating lacquer finishes and used these to tastefully complement the graceful Queen Anne furniture produced in the first half of the 1700s.

Among all the Europeans, however, it was the French who became leaders in the art of decorative furniture. French upholsterers, cabinetmakers, and finishers reached almost perfect harmony in their combined skills: finishers were able to make their work harmonize with upholstery fabrics by using colored varnishes and, at the same time, to enhance the design of the cabinetmakers. These combined skills peaked at the time of the French Revolution, and never again was such perfection reached. Indeed, the furniture pieces remaining from this period now command the highest prices on the antique market.

The next major development in the art of decorating furniture occurred in the United States. Throughout the American colonial period, decorated furniture had been imported from Europe. However, in the early 1800s, native craftsmen began to furnish many homes, often traveling from house to house to do their work.

These pieces were, for the most part, excellent copies of the European formal pieces. Then, about 1815, a native style of decoration was developed. This style was mainly restricted to chairs referred to as "Hitchcock" chairs, or "Fancy Chairs." The method of decoration was to apply a base coat of a reddish color and, after this had dried, to apply a black or brown coat. The second coat was then partly wiped away, giving the wood a resemblance to rosewood.

In addition to this basic decoration technique, many of the ring turnings on the chairs were striped with gold or other metallic colors. The larger cross slats of the chair backs were embellished with elaborate stenciled designs in various colors. From these great traditions evolved the modern craft of antiquing — the application of a painted finish and glaze, both of which are covered with a protective finish, to create an antique look.

Common Terms Used In Antiquing

Bleeding: a showing, or "bleeding," of dye through the base coat.

Distressing: depositing flecks and spots of the glazing medium by snapping a partly loaded brush a short distance from the piece.

Flow: the tendency of paint and varnish to flatten or flow over the brush marks and hide them, causing the finished surface to be smooth.

Gilding: decorating by gold bronzing or gold leafing.

Grain: the direction in which the most prominent lines run in a piece of wood; also the direction in which a piece of wood will split.

Highlighting: bringing some areas of a piece into prominence by removing particular areas of glaze.

Runs: lumps of paint caused by using a brush that contains too much paint.

Scuff Sanding: a light sanding with a relatively fine paper (220 to 500 grit).

Teeth: a very fine scratching produced in a glossy finish by scuff sanding; allows for better adhesion between coats.

Basic Equipment And Supplies

When considering the purchase of supplies, one

Figure 1. *Some of the supplies needed for antiquing include sandpaper and a sanding block, steel wool, brushes, a tack cloth, cheesecloth, and a trial board to experiment with the base and glaze coats.*

may either buy an antiquing kit or buy supplies separately. Either alternative is available in paint stores, hardware stores, and some department stores. The kits usually contain the following items: one can of low-gloss enamel or latex base coat; one can of antiquing glaze; cheesecloth or burlap; #120 and #220 grit sandpaper; and, of course, instructions.

For the beginner, the kits offer certain advantages: the materials are all compatible and the cost is the same or only slightly higher than buying the ingredients separately. The disadvantages are the unavailability of "custom" colors and the necessity of buying certain quantities and items that may not be needed.

Following is a list of necessary supplies if one chooses not to purchase a kit:

1. Bronzing liquid. This is either a slow-drying lacquer or varnish which is used as a base for bronzing powder.

2. Bronzing powder. This is used with the bronzing liquid to tone or stripe the furniture item with gold.

3. Brushes. 1- or 2-inch sizes of average quality are adequate. For especially good varnishing results, purchase a quality varnish brush that is tapered.

4. Cheesecloth. This is an open-weave, lint-free cloth used for wiping the glaze coat.

5. Clean cloth. This cloth can be either open or close weave, and should be free from all grease and dirt and, preferably, lint-free. Cloths that have been washed many times usually do not have any lint.

6. Cleaning solution. Any commercial cleaner that will remove wax and dirt will do. Or a mixture of 1/2 gallon of water, 1/4 cup of detergent, and 1/4 cup of household ammonia will work. The solution is used to clean the object before antiquing, regardless of

whether the furniture has a clear finish, is painted, or is unfinished.

7. Coarse woven burlap. This should be a burlap with a weave comparable to that of burlap bags. Obtainable in upholstery or fabric shops, it is used to wipe and texture the glaze coat. The textured effect is accomplished by pressing the burlap directly onto the glaze coat.

8. Drop cloth. In order to protect the floor or carpet, place old newspapers or cheap material about 10 feet square under the piece being antiqued.

9. Excelsior. These are curled shavings used to create certain effects on the glaze coat. They can be obtained at no charge from places that unpack furniture and appliances.

10. Glaze. This is a pigmented slow-drying varnish or lacquer with other additives; it is used to cover the base coat. When partly dry, it may be wiped to achieve different effects.

11. Latex base coat. This paint is for the first coat applied.

12. Mixing stick. This is a broad, flat piece of wood for mixing paint and is obtainable free at paint stores. It is preferable, however, to have the paint mixed at the store in a mechanical shaker.

13. Paint can opener. This small device for opening paint cans is available free at most paint stores.

14. Plastic wood. This is a filling material available clear or in colors.

15. Putty knife. This blunt knife, which has a broad, thin surface and shape, is used for transferring such soft materials as putty and plastic wood from their containers to the places to be filled. It can then be used to level and pack in the fillers.

16. Safety glasses. This hard-plastic eye protection will protect the eyes from sharp objects and spilled liquids.

17. Sandpaper. Beige-colored adalox is recommended, either #120 or #220 grit. The sandpaper is used to smooth the old surface and to produce "teeth" in a varnish coat for correct

adhesion of the antiquing base coat.

18. Satin varnish. This nonglossy type of hard varnish protects the somewhat delicate finish of the glaze coat. The low luster of the varnish also enhances the depth of the finish.

19. Sealer. This enamel primer is available in cans or as a spray; used to prevent "bleeding."

20. Semigloss enamel base coat. This is an oil-based paint which can be used as the base coat. It requires a cleanup with turpentine.

21. Spackling paste. This powder can be purchased in most paint stores. When mixed, it is used to fill small dents and scratches.

22. Tack cloth. This commercially available sticky cloth, also called tack rag, is saturated with varnish and turpentine and then squeezed out. It is purchased in a plastic con-

Figure 2. This table was stripped to the bare wood because it had been painted several times and the surface was in poor condition.

tainer and, when not in use, must be kept in a clean, airtight jar.

23. Trial board. This is any piece of board used for experimenting with glaze coats.

24. Varnish. This hard, clear, protective finish seals wood and the antiqued finish.

Basic Procedures

Antiquing is not only one of the easiest crafts to learn but also one of the most helpful in developing several basic skills in a gradual and interesting way. None of the skills is difficult; each is useful in the everyday care of furniture. Basically, what will be explained here are the techniques for using paint and varnish brushes.

CLEANING THE OLD FINISH

One advantage of antiquing is that it is not necessary to remove the old finish — it is, however, necessary to clean the old finish. Dirt and wax must be removed or the antiquing base coat will not adhere.

Wear rubber gloves; dip a clean rag, sponge, or scrubbing brush into a cleaning solution. Then, with a scrubbing motion, go over one section of the piece at a time. As soon as one section is completed, dry it with a clean rag. Use a turning and mopping motion — the cleaner only loosens the dirt and wax; the clean cloth removes it from the surface. (*Note:* If there is veneered wood on the piece, use lukewarm water and only a slightly damp sponge or rag. Quickly wipe dry.) Let the piece dry several hours if necessary.

Look the piece over carefully for runs or sags from the previously applied varnish or paint. These can be removed with a sharp knife or by sanding (first with #120 sandpaper and then #220). If there are several dents and scratches, decide whether to fill all, some, or none.

FILLING DAMAGED AREAS

Open a can of clear plastic wood and, using a putty knife to remove a small amount from the can, press the plastic wood down in the spot to be filled. It is best to make the fill a little higher than the wood surface as the plastic wood tends to shrink as it dries. If the spots are rather small,

Figure 3. After the surface area has been cleaned, the damaged areas should be filled with plastic wood or spackling paste. Use the flat side of a putty knife to smooth the filler (left). Some of the dents and scratches can be left to create a distressed appearance. For those areas that are to be filled, apply the filler so that it is slightly higher than the wood surface (right).

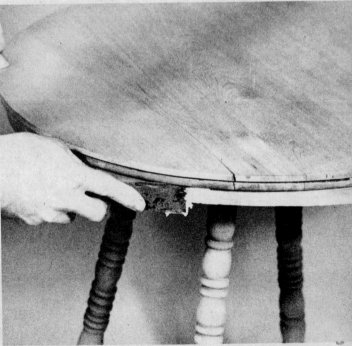

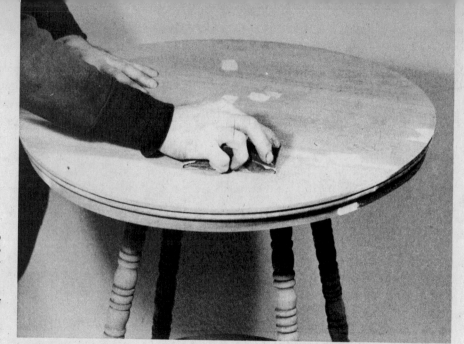

Figure 4. Allow the filler to dry before sanding. Put the sandpaper in a sanding block and smooth the filled areas. Then, smooth the entire surface. Use a small piece of sandpaper for hard-to-reach places.

spackling paste may work better. The only disadvantage in using the latter is that it must be mixed; plastic wood comes premixed.

Allow whatever drying time is recommended on the package. Refill the spots if the fills have shrunk below the wood surface. Wait the proper time, then sand the fill level with the surface.

SANDING THE OLD FINISH

After sanding the fills, go over the entire piece with #220 sandpaper held in a sanding block. In hard-to-reach places, the sandpaper may be folded four ways and used without the block. The purpose of sanding the old finish is to create "teeth," a slight scratching of the previous surface for better adhesion between coats.

APPLICATION OF THE BASE COAT

Before beginning, it is a good idea to experiment with the base coat paint on a trial board. A great deal more is learned by experimenting than merely by reading directions. Be sure that the paint is well mixed. At this point the paint can be transferred with an old ladle or tablespoon from the can to a more convenient container. Check the directions on the base coat can to see if the paint should be diluted. Before starting to apply the paint, however, dust off the piece with a brush that will get into crevices, then with a clean cloth, and finally with the tack cloth.

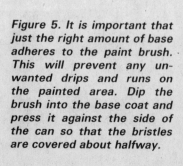

Figure 5. It is important that just the right amount of base adheres to the paint brush. This will prevent any unwanted drips and runs on the painted area. Dip the brush into the base coat and press it against the side of the can so that the bristles are covered about halfway.

Figure 6. Use a 2-inch brush to apply the base coat to large surface areas. Smaller areas, such as the table rim and legs, require a smaller brush. Finish brushing in the direction of the wood grain.

Next, dip the bristles of the brush about halfway into the paint; remove any excess paint by pressing the brush against the side of the paint container. If using a latex base coat, keep a water-dampened rag handy; if using an enamel base paint, the rag should be dampened with turpentine.

Start the application of the base coat paint on the trial board. This gives the paint a chance to work evenly into the bristles of the brush. A second tip is to start on the side of the piece least exposed to view. In this way there is time to perfect the brushing technique before doing the front sections.

If working on a chair, turn it upside down and use something to support it in this position. Paint all parts that are reachable in this position and then paint the outside of the chair (if the outside were done first, it would have to dry completely before the inside could be done).

If working on a chest of drawers, take out the drawers, remove all the hardware, and use masking tape to cover brass or other areas not to be painted. Prop the chest up so the bottom can be easily reached.

If the piece has a large panel, start the brush strokes in the middle and brush toward an edge. Then brush toward the opposite side from the middle, overlapping the thicker paint on the previous brush stroke. At this point it is permissible to brush crossways or in any other direction, but always finish in the direction of the grain and with progressively lighter strokes. Always check for runs and sags on the edges or carvings — these can be removed with the dampened cloth and then recoated. Continue to inspect the piece as work progresses.

A 2-inch brush will suffice for most of the work, but a 1-inch brush may be necessary for small places. Keep watching for any sign of bleeding. If there is any indication of discoloration, wipe the spot off with the damp cloth and then spray or brush on enamel sealer. In fact, the sealer can be used as a first coat to insure against all possibility of bleeding.

Let the base coat dry according to directions and clean the brushes. If, after it has dried, the base coat does not entirely conceal the color of the original finish, it is necessary to recoat the piece. This often happens when a light color is used over a dark old finish. Scuff sand the base coat with #220 sandpaper before applying the second coat.

APPLICATION OF THE GLAZE

Stir the glaze mixture thoroughly and dip a clean, dry brush about halfway up the bristles. Remove any excess glaze by pressing the brush against the side of the container. Brush a liberal coat of the glazing material on the trial board, then wipe the wet glaze with a soft, lint-free cloth. Work the cloth in circles and scrub a little. Finally, using a clean cheescloth, wipe the glaze all one way, following the original grain direction.

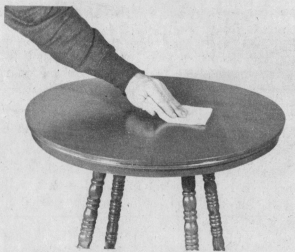

Figure 7. After the base coat has dried, brush the glaze on the wood surface (above left). When the glaze has partially dried, it can be wiped with steel wool to produce the desired texture (above right). A tack cloth is used to wipe the surface areas after the glaze has dried (right).

Recoat the trial board with glaze several times and experiment with burlap, excelsior, and dry brushes for a wood grain effect. Pressing a sponge on the surface can also create unusual patterns. To try a new technique, recoat with the glaze. It can always be wiped off.

Once a glaze effect has been selected, coat a section of the piece with glaze, wipe off the excess with the lint-free cloth, and texture the glaze as desired (cheesecloth is probably the favorite medium for this purpose). Remember to clean the brush when you are finished.

APPLICATION OF GILDING

There are three methods of applying gilding to furniture: (1) brushing on prepared gold paint, which is cheap in cost; (2) using bronzing liquid plus bronzing powder; or (3) doing traditional gold leaf work. The last two give excellent results. Gold leafing, however, is expensive and not recommended for beginners.

Bronzing liquid is a slow-drying liquid with a varnish-type base. It is applied like any varnish, but only to those areas that are to be covered with bronzing powder.

Pour some bronzing powder onto a piece of soft, dark cloth that is about 4" to 6" square. Slip a small piece of the same cloth over a fingertip. Use the cloth-covered fingertip to transfer the gold or bronze powder from the large cloth to the areas that have been covered with bronzing liquid. The powder may be tapped on or rubbed on. It may be rubbed partly off by using another cloth over the fingertip. After the bronzing liquid has set the powder, use a small syringe or a tapping motion to dislodge any excess powder. Clean all containers when you are finished.

APPLICATION OF SATIN VARNISH

After having created the desired glaze effect and perhaps having applied some gilding, add a protective hard finish over the rather delicate glazes. It is also important to use a varnish that is not shiny: satin varnish has that property and also has the added advantage of not showing fingerprints very clearly.

In many of today's homes, the temperatures are slightly lower than is advisable for good varnishing. To offset these lower temperatures, the following procedure is suggested. Select a clean 8-ounce jar, preferably one that is calibrated in ounces. Before pouring or handling varnish or turpentine, it is wise to put on safety glasses. Transfer the varnish from the original can to the container by means of an old spoon or ladle. Add turpentine or mineral spirits if directed. These two solvents are usually interchangeable but not always; it is safer to follow the directions exactly. Then, to offset the cool house temperature, immerse the jar in a saucepan of warm water, covering about half the jar. The water should be replaced as it cools.

The piece to be varnished should be elevated, if possible, so that its surface is not chilly and it is easier to reach. Go over the surface with a tack rag; then dip the brush into the varnish mixture about halfway up the bristles. Press the brush against the side of the container in order to eliminate any excess varnish. Make a few trial strokes on an old newspaper in order to work the varnish into the brush and to get the feel of the brush. It is a good idea to apply some varnish strokes on the trial board, starting in the middle and drawing the brush toward one edge. Next, start from the middle and brush to the opposite edge, overlapping the previous stroke where the varnish is thicker.

Use very light pressure on the brush — varnish should be flowed on rather than brushed on. Finish by using progressively lighter pressure. A light stroke can be acquired by holding the brush so that the fingers touch the metal clasp (the *ferrule*) around the bristles.

Figure 8. Transfer the varnish from its original container into a clean glass jar and add turpentine or mineral spirits. With light brush strokes, apply the varnish in the direction of the original wood grain so that the previous coats are not disturbed.

Figure 9. Base and glaze coats were applied to the natural wood to create an antiqued finish. The glaze was worked into certain areas to produce highlights and a wood-grained appearance.

The varnish is applied, in the direction of the original wood grain, of course. Because this same direction was followed in the application of the base and glaze coats, there is little risk that the coat of varnish will disturb the previous coats. Always check for runs and sags on the edges. These can either be brushed out or rubbed out with a turpentine rag. Remember to clean brushes and utensils in turpentine when you are through using them.

Projects You Can Do

The following projects can be done with a minimum of expense and time. They include examples of antiquing unfinished furniture; antiquing over clear, varnished finishes; and antiquing over painted finishes. All projects are illustrated step-by-step, enabling the beginner to develop the basic skills necessary for achieving satisfactory results.

ANTIQUING A PAINTED CHAIR

Almost every home has old wooden chairs which, in many cases, have been relegated to the attic or basement because of their shabby appearance. Most contain several coats of paint.

Preparation for Antiquing

First, check the item carefully for any loose parts, rough chips knocked out of the previously painted surface, or nails and screws showing plainly through the old paint cover. Unscrew the latter, if any, and remove the surface under them by drilling. Screw them back in, cover the holes

Figure 10. Use an appropriate sized brush to apply the base coat (left). After the base has dried, brush on a coating of glaze. Then, work in the glaze with a cloth until the desired effect is achieved (below).

Figure 11. It is necessary to thoroughly clean the surface of the chair before the finish is applied (above). The antiqued effect was achieved by sealing the base and glaze coats with a satin varnish (right).

with plastic wood, and, after it dries, sand the fill so that it is level with the wood surface.

Sand any chipped edges with #120 sandpaper. Then apply enamel primer to these spots to prevent poor adhesion and to help make the level of the chipped out spots even with the main surface. Finally, fix any loose pieces with glue, wash the chair with cleaning solution, and let it dry for several hours.

Brushing on the Base Coat

After stirring the base coat thoroughly, follow the application method described under "Basic Procedures." (Note particularly the explanation of how to apply the base coat when working on a chair.) Allow the chair to dry for about four hours. Clean brushes and containers. Inspect the base coat after it has dried. If it has completely concealed the previous coat, it is time to glaze.

Brushing on the Glaze

Brush on the glaze coat. Use a clean, dry, lint-free cloth to wipe off the excess glaze, and then use a cheesecloth to achieve a misty effect if desired. Let the chair dry overnight.

Brushing on the Satin Varnish

Prop the chair in the upside-down position and start applying the varnish. Do the inside, then set the chair right side up and varnish the outside. It is especially important to clean the varnish brush with turpentine when you are finished.

ANTIQUING AN UNFINISHED STOOL

Begin by sanding the surface, first with #120 sandpaper and then #220. Go over the surface with a damp sponge to raise any fuzzy grain fibers that might later come up in the base coat. Then resand with #220 sandpaper and wipe the surface with the tack rag.

Apply the base coat as described for the preceding project. Let it dry for at least four hours. When drying is complete, check the piece for skips and runs. Clean brushes and utensils.

Figure 12. Check the stool for damaged areas (top); then, sand the wood until it is smooth (below left). The varnish is applied after the base and glaze coats have dried completely (below right).

Next, brush on the glaze coat in the usual manner, wipe off the excess, and use a dry brush to simulate the grain of the wood. Leave to dry overnight. Finally, apply the satin varnish coat as described above.

ANTIQUING AND GILDING A PICTURE FRAME

Picture frames are sold in many colors and finishes, but it is often difficult to find one that is exactly the right color. Antiquing not only solves the color problem but also allows for creativity.

Wash the frame with the cleaning solution. If the surface has a high sheen, dull it down with #220 sandpaper. Apply the base coat as detailed in "Basic Procedures," remembering to clean brushes and utensils. Apply the glaze coat in the usual manner and let dry. Again, clean brushes when you are finished.

Apply the gilding as follows. Cut two pieces of soft material, one about 5 inches square, the other about 2 inches square. Next, apply the bronzing liquid according to directions on container, and only to those areas to be gilded. When the bronzing liquid reaches the stage where it is no longer wet but sticky, pour some bronzing powder on the large piece of fabric and put the small piece over a fingertip. Dip the fingertip into the powder and tap or rub the powder gently on the areas where there is bronzing liquid.

When the desired effect is achieved, blow away any excess powder and allow the piece to dry for several hours. Finally, apply the satin varnish. Let dry under as dust-free conditions as possible.

Figure 13. After the base coat has dried, use a soft cloth to work in the bronzing liquid. Apply the liquid only to those areas that are to be gilded (left). Gilding lends a rich finish and adds highlights to the grain of the wood (right).

For Additional Reading

Cennini, Cennino, **The Craftsman's Handbook,** Dover, 1933.

Johnstone, James B., and the Sunset Editorial Staff, **Furniture Finishing,** Lane Books.

Kuhn, H. W., **How to Refinish Furniture,** Fawcett-Haynes.

O'Neil, Isabel, **The Art of the Painted Finish for Furniture and Decoration,** William Morrow, 1971.

Wright, Florence E., **How to Stencil Chairs,** Cornell Univ. Press.

Pottery and Clay Modeling

Making pottery and molding clay by the technique of wheel throwing is one of the most difficult of all craft skills to learn. Yet, it is one of the most satisfying.

Much of man's knowledge of early civilizations has been derived from studying remaining clay artifacts. Fired clay is an almost indestructible historical record — objects break but the shards remain as evidence of man's past actions and ideas.

Pottery formed without the use of a spinning wheel was made as early as 5000 B.C. in eastern Mediterranean areas. A thousand years passed before a wheel was used to assist the potter in the forming process. It was then discovered that shaping a symmetrical (or nearly symmetrical) form was easier while turning the clay on a platform supported by a rotating vertical axis. At first man used the wheel only to scrape and refine a form that had previously been hand-built. By 3000 B.C., however, Middle Eastern pots were formed by applying pressure with the hands to clay that was spinning on a fast-turning wheel.

Figure 1. *This piece of pottery was unearthed by archaeologists in the Nazca Valley in Peru. (Courtesy, Field Museum of Natural History, Chicago.)*

Almost all ancient civilizations have made pottery. While some cultures learned the craft independent of others, most cultures learned about pottery making from migrating people or from tradesmen. As already mentioned, the earliest pottery originated in the Middle East about 5000 B.C., reaching southeastern Europe by 2500 B.C. Pottery making in China began approximately 3500 B.C.

The development of pottery in the New World was entirely free of any influence from the rest of the world. Although the potter's wheel was not known to early New World civilizations, their work in clay was very sophisticated. The earliest pottery (2500 B.C.) in the Americas has been found in Central and South America.

The forming and firing of clay forms has been going on all over the world for thousands of years because of the availability, the functionality, and the plasticity of the material. Clay, which is found everywhere in the world, was used by primitive agrarian societies in making storage containers and cooking vessels. While the initial reason for interest in pottery was a practical one, the lasting fascination and love of clay forms developed through a sense of the aesthetic possibilities of this plastic material. Clay is a medium for the expression of ideas: clay forms are concrete extensions of the hands and the mind.

In the United States, since the beginning of the second half of the twentieth century, extraordinary attention has been given to the making of pottery. University classes in ceramics are overflowing with students. Even elementary and secondary schools are offering courses in pottery

Figure 2. An 18th-century Wedgewood chocolate set (below) exemplifies English skill in relief pottery. (Courtesy, The Metropolitan Museum of Art, Gift of Ferdinand Hermann, 1912.)

making. More and more adults are seeking instruction in pottery making at art centers and evening schools. There is an unprecendented interest in all crafts. People want to make useful, beautiful objects with their own hands. They want and need a connection between themselves and their work — a connection that starts with an idea and continues to the finished product.

Common Terms Used In Pottery and Clay Modeling

Bisque Fire: the firing prior to the glaze fire. Although the bisque fire hardens the object, it is still porous enough for the glaze to adhere.

Black Hard: a stage in the drying process after leather hard (see below); lacks sufficient moisture to maintain a cohesive bond between two joined pieces of clay.

Ceramics: the art and technology of making forms of clay or glass treated by fire.

Clay Body: a mixture of clay (or clays) and water into a workable consistency for use in pottery.

Earthenware: the lowest fired ware of the three categories of pottery (see also porcelain and stoneware); fired below pyrometric Orton cone 6 (2246° F).

Grog: fired clay that has been crushed and ground to various particle sizes and added to the clay for porosity.

Handbuilding: forming clay forms by hand without the use of the potter's wheel.

Kiln: a firing chamber for pottery.

Knuckle Pull: the process of lifting the clay wall in the forming process called throwing.

Leather Hard: a stage in the drying process of clay when there is sufficient moisture content to bond clay to clay.

Plasticity: the quality of clay that allows it to be manipulated and to maintain its shape.

Porcelain: the highest fired ware of the three categories of pottery; fired above pyrometric Orton cone 10 (2381° F).

Porosity: the openness of the clay body; also refers to the hardness and vitrification (see below) of the clay.

Pyrometric Cone: a small (1⅛″ or 2⅝″ in height) tetrahedral cone composed of ceramic materials compounded to bend at a given amount of work heat when placed in a kiln, thus enabling the potter to determine when to complete the firing.

Scoring: scratching the surface of the clay before joining clay to clay.

Sherd or Shard: a broken piece of fired pottery.

Slip: a combination of clay and water.

Stoneware: the middle fired ware of the three categories of pottery; fired between pyrometric Orton cone 6 and 10.

Throwing: forming on the potter's wheel.

Turning, Trimming, or Tooling: the technique of removing excess of support clay from wet clay forms.

Vitrification: fire hardening of ceramic materials.

Wedging or Kneading: the hand mixing of clay into a homogenous mass free of air pockets.

Wheelhead: the wheel on which clay is formed; part of a potter's wheel.

Wheel Wedging: the centering technique of forcing the clay up and down on the wheelhead.

Basic Equipment And Supplies

For the purposes of this discussion, attention will be restricted to the clay and potter's wheel. Discussion of decoration, firing, and other forming techniques are too comprehensive for the limitations of this article. The purpose here will be to introduce the new craftsman to one aspect of ceramics — throwing on the potter's wheel. For additional information, please refer to the reading list at the end of the article.

CLAY BODY

Clay is mixed with other clays to form a body suited to the manner in which it will be molded. The potter may wish to handbuild instead of throw, or to work with stoneware rather than earthenware or porcelain. In each case, the composition of the clay body is different. For throwing purposes, it is essential that the clay body be plastic (meaning that it will maintain the given shape). In addition to categorizing by use, clay bodies are classified according to the temperature range at which they mature into a hard, rock-like state. There are three such categories: (1) porcelain, the highest temperature range; (2) stoneware, a temperature range not as high as porcelain; and (3) earthenware, a relatively low temperature range. Categorization is also determined by the purity of the clay bodies — porcelain being the purest (free of metallic oxides) and earthenware being the least pure. Porcelain is always white in color while stoneware and earthenware may vary from white to dark earth tones. The novice should avoid porcelain as a throwing body because it is difficult to manipulate on the wheel.

Once the beginner is aware of the categories of clay, it will be possible for him to select the correct type for a given project. The determination of clay body should be based on the firing limitations of an available kiln. If the kiln will only fire to an earthenware temperature range (2000° F), it would be foolish to model stoneware or porcelain.

PURCHASED CLAY

Clays may be purchased dry from large refractory companies throughout the United States. But, it is usually sold in one ton or more loads and then must be mixed. It is suggested that the novice begin by purchasing a premixed clay body. Check with a nearby university ceramics department or a professional potter to find out where quality premixed clay can be purchased inexpensively (one should not pay more than $0.15 per pound plus shipping).

FOUND CLAY

Many sites contain found clay, which will be most likely suitable for throwing earthenware. Found clay should be free of humus (organic impurities) and coarse particles of stone. The unwanted particles can be eliminated by liquifying the clay with water and then pouring it through an old screen. The water may then be eliminated by placing the slip (liquified clay) in a large shallow container under the sun. If cracking results in the drying or firing, the clay particles may be too fine. An addition of 10 percent of 20-mesh grog should eliminate the problem. Grog can be made by pulverizing bisque fired pots or it may be purchased from refractory companies or ceramic supply dealers. The term "mesh" refers to the number of holes per inch in a screen. The greater the mesh number, the finer the particle. Firing tests must be made to determine the maturation temperature range. Put a small amount of clay in a kiln, fire to a given pyrometric cone, and see what happens. Does the clay harden or does it melt? If it does not harden, it was not fired at a temperature high enough. On the other hand, if it melts, the temperature was too high. Start low (2000° F) and work higher through a series of tests.

THE POTTER'S WHEEL

In the Western world, three types of potter's wheels are used: the treadle wheel, the kick wheel, and the electric wheel. The treadle wheel, as the name implies, is a horizontally moving treadle propelled by foot. This is connected to a crank shaft which supports the wheelhead. The

Figure 3. The kick wheel is operated by pushing the bottom of the foot against the large flywheel. This motion turns the vertical shaft which moves the wheelhead.

kick wheel is propelled by kicking or shoving the bottom of the foot against a heavy horizontal fly wheel. This moves a vertical shaft which supports the wheelhead. The electric wheel has a wheelhead driven either by a belt or by a gear; the source of power is an electric motor.

Each type of wheel has an advantage and a disadvantage when compared to the other types. The treadle and kick wheels cost less and have fewer maintenance problems than the electric wheel. After years of use, the bearings are the only parts that need to be replaced. A good electric wheel, costing over $400, is the easiest on which to throw large forms. An excellent kick wheel may be purchased for under $200, while a treadle ranges in cost between $200 and $300. The mechanisms of the treadle wheel provide the potter with direct control: the potter's foot controls the speed of the wheelhead. The action of the kick wheel is a bit smoother with less vibration. But the control is not as direct because the potter first kicks the flywheel, then begins to throw on the wheel. The clay turns on the wheelhead until the momentum falls off. The electric wheel should have a variable speed range from 0 rpm to approximately 180 rpm. Those electric wheels with a switch from low to high speed should be avoided.

When considering the purchase of any type wheel, get several opinions from knowledgeable potters. And, of course, use personal judgment when evaluating craftsmanship of the construction and quality of products.

THROWING TOOLS

The preference and number of tools used in throwing varies, but certain tools are very helpful to the beginner.

1. Water bowl: a flat-bottomed container (approximately one quart) used to hold water necessary for lubricating clay during the throwing process.

2. Elephant ear sponge: used to apply and remove water and to smooth the rims of thrown forms; may be purchased at ceramic supply houses.

3. Clean-up sponge: a foam-rubber sponge placed beside the wheelhead while throwing

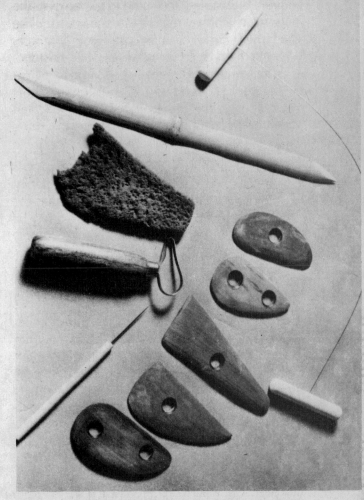

Figure 4. Among the throwing tools a beginning potter needs are a dowel rod and needle, a pear pitter, an elephant ear sponge, a bamboo stick, a wire cutter, and an assortment of ribs.

to catch the slip thrown off by centrifugal force; sponge should be approximately 10" x 6" x 2".

4. Needle: serves as a cutting tool to level or shorten a thrown cylinder. Actually, it is a 6" length of 3/8" or 1/4" wooden dowel rod with a sewing machine needle forced into one end.

5. Rib: a hardwood shaping tool that pushes positive and negative curves into a clay wall while throwing.

6. Bamboo and cutting wire: used to cut a 45° bevel in the circumference of the outside bottom of a pot after throwing is complete. The cutting away of this area removes excess clay and also provides a gripping groove

which enables the potter to remove the thrown form from the wheelhead. The thrown form must be cut away from the wheelhead by cutting wire. This stranded, stainless steel wire about 1/32" in diameter is secured between two 1/2" x 4" dowel rods. A source for the proper wire, called lead out wire, is model airplane hobby shops.

7. Pear pitter: a trimming tool for removing excess support clay. (Trimming or turning is described in detail later.) The pear pitter or trimming tool — as well as the needle, the ribs, the bamboo, and cutting wire — may be purchased from a good ceramic supply house. A paring knife, which may be substituted for the bamboo, can be purchased at any dime store.

Basic Procedures

There are prevailing myths about throwing on the potter's wheel that should be dispelled. It is believed by some that an inherent talent is required to learn the technique — this is not so. Any reasonably coordinated person can learn this skill. What is required is self-tolerance, patience, and tenacity during the early stages of development. One must be willing to spend many hours of practice over a long period of time to acquire the skill. The rate of development varies with the individual. After much practice, the novice should be able to begin to make rudimentary cylinder and bowl forms — a feeling of freedom and confidence arrives only after a great deal of experience in working with the material.

PREPARATION FOR THROWING — WEDGING THE CLAY

Before the throwing process begins, it is necessary to wedge the clay. Wedging or kneading is a technique for mixing the clay into a homogeneous mass free of air pockets. Any trapped air will become an annoying bubble in the clay wall while throwing. The clay should have an equal moisture content throughout and the consistency should be soft, but not sticky.

Find a strong table on which to do the wedging. The table should be about 6" above the knee cap. A good surface for the tabletop is one that is hard and slightly absorbent. Asbestos board, transite, and prepoured concrete slabs work very well and are usually available at lumber yards. Canvas or plaster surfaces are not recommended.

The two most effective wedging methods are known as the European wedge and the Oriental screw wedge. The European wedge is the easiest to learn but the least effective. This method, as shown in the accompanying illustrations, is much like the technique used for kneading bread dough. Take a large ball of clay (15 to 20 pounds) and force the top of the mass into the center with the heels of the hands. Use the entire body weight as a pushing force. Keep the arms stiff from the shoulders down. Now recover by reaching the extended fingers over the top and again forcing the top into the center. The body moves in a rocking, rhythmic motion. When the clay forms an elongated loaf, stand the loaf up vertically and fold the top into the center. Continue until the clay is well mixed.

Figure 5. Using the European wedge method, fold and push the outer clay into the center.

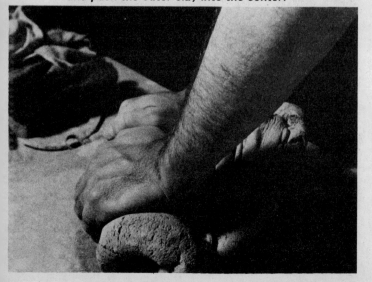

Figure 6. After folding and pushing, the clay mixture becomes smooth and fairly soft (below).

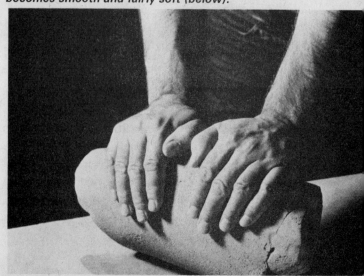

Figure 7. This photograph (above) shows the correct body position for wedging the clay. Keep the arms stiff from the shoulders down when kneading.

Since the Oriental screw wedge is much more difficult to master, use the European technique as a working method while gradually learning the other. The Oriental is similar to the European technique except that the top of the clay is rolled into the center with a very slight clockwise twist, with the left hand exerting a little more pressure than the right. It is necessary to maintain a ball shape at the top of the mass in order to correctly effect the kneading action. The recovery, after forcing the clay into the center of the mass, is to position the right hand behind the top right of the ball while the left hand is positioned on the left side of the top ball. The kneading should continue

Figure 8. In preparing clay by the Oriental wedge method, first lift the top of the clay from the center (A), then push it back down with a twisting motion (B). Maintain the ball shape during kneading (C), and, finally, slap the clay into shape (D).

for about five minutes once the wedging techniques have been mastered.

The only true test to determine if the clay has been wedged well is to throw with the kneaded clay. If air bubbles are trapped in the clay, they will be felt when pulling up the clay wall. There is a quick test to give some indication as to the condition of the clay: cut through a wedged loaf of clay with the cutting wire and examine the cross sections. If the clay appears to be well mixed, with no air pockets visible, it is probably ready to throw.

POSITION AT THE WHEEL

As a general rule of thumb, the height of the seat should be adjusted to about the same height as the wheelhead. A simple four-legged stool will suffice. One should be able to bend comfortably over the clay. Brace the elbows on the thighs near the groin. This method of bracing applies only when working with the electric and kick wheels. Many potters, using an electric wheel, will elevate their left foot on a block. This places the left arm in a more advantageous position for bracing. The height of the block depends on the size of the thrower—average height is from 6" to 8".

When sitting on the treadle wheel, brace the wrists on the top box rim that surrounds the wheelhead. The assumed position should be a comfortable one. Try to keep the back straight and do not roll the shoulders forward into a slouch. Many potters over the age of 40 have back problems due largely to lifting incorrectly when loading and unloading kilns. Another cause of back trouble stems from assuming an incorrect position while throwing at the wheel.

TURNING THE WHEEL

Now it is time to begin throwing. The kick wheel must be kicked in a counterclockwise direction. Using the bottom of the right foot, push the heavy flywheel away from yourself. Continue a shoving kind of kick to achieve a maximum speed for centering (approximately 150-200 rpm). Some potters use a kicking and pawing method. This requires a simultaneous pushing out against the flywheel with the right foot (a kick) and a pulling in toward oneself with the left foot (a paw). It may be necessary to grasp the seat in order to kick with more vigor.

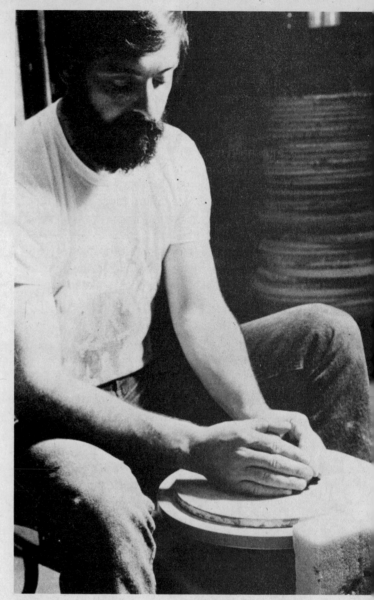

Figure 9. When using an elecric wheel, elevate the left foot on a block and brace the elbows on the thighs. The stool and the wheelhead should be the same height.

The treadle wheel also requires a start in the right direction, as the wheel is capable of turning in either direction. The direction of the wheel determines the side on which form finger pressure will be exerted while throwing. (In the western world, traditionally, the wheel turns in a counterclockwise direction and therefore throwing is accomplished on the right side of the clay form.)

The electric wheel turns in a counterclockwise direction, except for those manufactured in the Orient, which are capable of turning in either direction.

WHEEL WEDGING — A PRELUDE TO CENTERING

Wheel wedging is the process of forcing the clay in and upward, then down and outward by exerting hand pressure against the clay while the wheel is turning. This process leads to centering. Not all potters begin by wheel wedging — many go directly to centering. However, wheel wedging is a good way of becoming familiar with the clay and its workable characteristics. Wheel wedging also helps to align the clay particles, making the centering and forming process easier.

Start with six balls of clay about the size of a softball. Cover all except one ball of clay with a thin film of plastic (dry-cleaning bags) to keep the clay from drying out. Beginners should use a softer consistency of clay for learning to center.

Forcing the Clay up

Set the water bowl next to the wheelhead at the farthest point from you. Place a moistened clean-up sponge next to the bowl and against the wheelhead. Thus, it will absorb the slip flying off. Force the clay down on the center of the wheelhead. Begin turning the wheelhead at high speed. When using the kick wheel, kick the flywheel to high speed. Then, rest the feet while making contact with the clay. Do not kick and throw at the same time. On the other hand, when using the treadle wheel, one does treadle and throw simultaneously.

Moisten the hands by dipping them in the water bowl. Then place them on the turning clay — the left hand first and the right thumb over the left as illustrated. Force the clay down hard enough to insure its adherence to the wheelhead. If either the wheelhead or the clay ball has a film of water on it, the clay will not adhere.

Next, with the muscle part of the thumb and heel part of the left hand, push the ball of clay toward the center of the wheelhead. With the lower right hand, pull the clay toward the center. Move the clay up to a height of about 4" or 5". Always release the clay gradually by moving the hands to the outside. Beginners usually release so quickly that the clay adheres slightly to the hands, causing it to move in an elliptical path off center. As the clay moves upward, force the hands closer to-

Figure 10. When forcing the clay up on the wheelhead (top) and applying downward pressure (center), the hands should be positioned as shown. The clay will adhere to the pressure points on the hands (bottom).

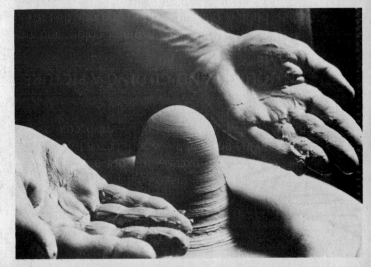

ward the center, thereby forming a cone shape. If a hollow forms in the center of the clay, it must be squeezed out using the inward pressure. If allowed to remain, the hollow will cause weaknesses and air pockets in the clay wall. For the beginner using the kick wheel, it may be necessary to rekick the wheel before forcing the clay down. As one becomes more experienced, it is not necessary to kick the wheel as frequently during the wheel wedging process.

Downward Pressure on Clay

The downward pressure on the clay is a more critical maneuver than forcing the clay up. The hand position is basically the same but the emphasis given to particular pressure points along the hands changes. Begin with the left hand. Apply the muscular pad at the base of the thumb on top of the clay. Try to keep the fingers as vertical as possible while wrapped around the top of the cone of clay. The right thumb pad is placed over the left and the fingers of the right hand are wrapped over those of the left hand. If using an electric or kick wheel, keep the forearms braced on the legs (the wrists braced on a treadle wheel) while applying pressure downward on the clay.

As the cone flattens out, continue to maintain pressure with the fingers along the vertical wall of the clay while applying a downward pressure with the muscular base of the thumbs. The hands will open up as the base of the clay becomes wider. The movements of the hands should be gradual and fluid without quick readjustments in position. Hold the downward pressure of the thumbs and the inward pressure of the fingers for a few turns of the wheel after feeling the clay coming into center. One senses this only after many hours of practice. Force the clay up and down approximately three times, or until the clay flows smoothly, then center the clay on the third downward motion. Remember to release the clay gradually. The centered clay need not be absolutely true, but it should not have a visible wobble.

POSITION OF HANDS

There are several different hand positions that potters use for throwing. For a starting point, only one basic position will be explained here. As one

becomes more experienced, a variation of this position may be more comfortable for your hands. Take the position by first making the letter C with the thumb and the first finger of the left hand. The thumb should be pointing down. Then tuck the entire right hand (right thumb first) into the hollow formed by the C. Point the fingers away from yourself. The C clasps the right hand as shown in the accompanying illustrations. Next, rotate the right wrist clockwise slightly and bring the right thumb up between the first two fingers of the left hand. Now roll the right fingers into a fist. Lastly, project the knuckle of the first finger of the right hand away from yourself.

If these instructions seem a bit complex, perhaps an explanation of the position's function is in order. When two hands are braced together, each has more stability — thus the clasping C of the thumb and finger of the left hand. The right thumb braced next to it provides added strength. When lifting the clay wall (knuckle pull), the tip of the middle finger of the left hand is on one side of the wall and and the first knuckle of the first finger of the right hand is on the opposite side of the wall. These two points are the pressure areas of the fingers that do the throwing.

OPENING A CYLINDER

When learning to throw, it is best to practice developing one simple form before attempting another. The basic short cylinder (often referred to as the dog dish) is a good introductory form. The clay is first centered. Now, with the wheel turning at high speed, brace the forearms on the thighs, lean over the clay, and take the hand position. The knuckle of the first finger of the right hand should ride along the right outside wall of the turning centered clay. With the tip of the middle finger of the left hand, make contact with the center of the clay and force an opening into the clay. Do not point the fingers into the clay, thereby causing the forearms to be lifted from the thighs. Rather, pivot the fingers from the wrists. It is much easier to maintain a center if one pulls slightly toward oneself with the opening fingers.

Allow the third and little fingers of the left hand to follow the middle finger into the opening, thus forming an inverted cone well. (If a wobble in the clay results, use the cutting wire to remove the clay and start centering again with a new ball of

A

B

Figure 11. *Begin throwing the clay by forcing an opening into the center (A), then deepening it to ¼" from the bottom (B) and widening it to ¾" across the base (C). The walls are then carefully lifted (D).*

C

D

clay.) Open the clay to approximately 4" from the bottom — simply estimate the depth of the opening. Look down over the clay and compare the depth of the wheelhead with the depth of the opening. Another method is to gauge the depth with the needle. Once the proper depth is reached, widen the opening by exerting pressure on the bottom of the opening toward the right pressure point (first knuckle of the first finger of the right hand). Attempt to maintain an equal thickness across the bottom.

When the opening has reached three-quarters across the base of the centered clay, begin to exert an equal pressure at the left pressure point, thereby squeezing the clay up into a wall. Now the speed of the wheel should be decreased to about half the speed used for centering. If the squeezing pressure is too great, the wall will weaken and eventually tear away from the base. If this happens, begin again.

As the wall is lifted again, the motion should be deliberate and fluid. Do not hesitate and do not allow the hands and forearms to pivot from the elbows. Keep the elbows braced on the thighs.

The beginner will have a tendency to widen the form while lifting the wall. This is a mistake. Since it is much easier to widen than to close the form, it is wise to maintain a closed form when throwing a cylinder.

While lifting the wall, lean the pressure points toward the center of the opening so that the top

Figure 12. *A knuckle pull (below) is used to make final adjustments on the clay. The index fingers of both hands apply pressure to the outside wall, while the fingers of the left hand exert force on the inside walls.*

374 / **Pottery and Clay Modeling**

A

B

C

Figure 13. The right thumb is positioned on the rim (A) and the other fingers on the walls (B), as shown. The first knuckle pull strengthens and controls the shape (C).

will be narrower than the bottom. When near the top of the wall, do not continue to squeeze — just maintain the space between the left and right pressure points. Hold this position for a few turns of the wheel, allowing the clay to adjust itself.

The final touch of the first pull is to level out the top of the wall with the underside of the first joint

of the right thumb as illustrated. These three pressure points strengthen and control the top of the clay wall.

SECOND KNUCKLE PULL

The second knuckle pull is executed to further thin and heighten the clay wall. (A thrown form

Figure 14. In the second knuckle pull, the thumb action (below) levels the top.

Figure 15. As the thumb evens out the top, the fingers apply pressure to heighten the wall (below).

Figure 16. The knuckle pull is repeated to further lift and thin the wall (above).

Figure 17. Pressure is also applied to smooth the bulge that forms (above).

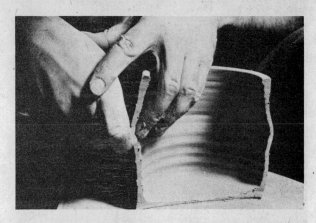

Figure 18. This pulling action creates uniformly thin walls (right).

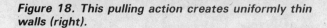

with a thin wall is usually one indication of a well-crafted piece.) With the left pressure point, exert force on the inside bottom corner. A bulge will form on the outside wall. Just below that bulge, press in with the right pressure point. Hold this squeezing action for two complete turns of the wheel, then lift with a fluid motion. A collar of clay should precede the pressure points if the clay is being lifted properly.

More pressure must be exerted at the bottom of the wall. Then, as the lifting action rises, the pressure points should relax gradually. The top is again finished with the assistance of the thumb, as mentioned previously. The knuckle pull is re-peated until the wall is thin enough (approximately 1/4" thick for a small pot).

The clay wall may be straightened by using the vertical rib. Hold the rib in the right hand and gently press the flat side of the rib against the outside clay wall. With the left pressure point, apply pressure to the bottom corner of the cylinder. Push the clay into the rib and slowly move the left pressure point up along the inside wall of the cylinder — bottom to top. Upon reaching the top, reach over with the left thumb and hold it against the top of the rib as a brace. Hold this position for a few revolutions, then release gradually. This should straighten the cylinder wall.

Figure 19. A vertical rib is held against the outside to straighten the walls (left). The left thumb braces the top of the rib as the cylinder completes a few rotations (right).

EVALUATING ONE'S WORK

The basic cylinder is usually considered an exercise in learning the throwing technique. Further development is required to complete the form. Instead of drying and firing the cylinder, it makes more sense to evaluate one's progress by carefully examining this work. Take the cutting wire and cut between the bottom of the cylinder and the wheelhead. Then slice the cylinder in half vertically and check the cross section. Look for a uniform wall thickness throughout. It is normal for the wall to be thicker in the bottom corner. Beginners may find it necessary to trim excess clay away from the bottom wall with the pear pitter. As skill increases, less trimming or tooling is required.

REMOVING CYLINDER FROM THE WHEELHEAD

To remove the cylinder from the wheelhead, first cut a 45° bevel with the bamboo as illustrated. Hold the bamboo in the right hand as holding a pencil. Turn the sharp edge near the point into the clay so that it is actually cutting the clay away. Place the needle under the cut-away clay as the wheel revolves. Remove the excess clay from the wheelhead. Cut across the bottom of the pot, using the cutting wire as the pot turns one revolution. Then remove the pot as shown — i.e., the right hand closest to you; the pot between the thumb and first finger; and, the left hand on the opposite side of the pot with the heel of the hand and little finger gripping the cut-away bevel. Give the pot a slight twist and lift. Place the pot on a board to dry.

TRIMMING, TOOLING, OR TURNING

The potter should strive to throw a thin clay wall so that only a minimum amount of trimming is necessary. Some small functional forms, such as pitchers and mugs, should be thrown so that absolutely no tooling is required. As mentioned earlier, the beginner may need to trim excess clay from the bottom of a cylinder in order to achieve a thin, even-walled form. The pot must also reach a drying stage called leather hard in order to be handled without distorting. At this point the pot has dried so that the surface is firm enough to be picked up without leaving fingerprints. If the pot

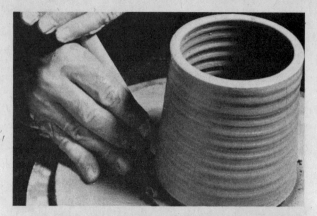

Figure 20. To trim the piece, hold the bamboo at a 45° angle and cut a bevel at the base with the sharp edge (top). The needle is then placed under the cut-away piece to remove the excess clay (bottom).

dries to the point that the clay is no longer pliable, it has reached a stage called black hard. At this stage the pot is too dry for trimming or for adding moist clay parts like handles to the thrown form.

The leather hard form is placed on a moist wheelhead. If a thin film of water is rubbed on first, the pot will adhere to the wheelhead after a short

Figure 21. Grasp the handles of the cutting wire and slide it under the bottom of the clay pot. As the wheel makes one final revolution, cut the cylinder away from the base of the wheelhead.

drying period. (If the pot is not sticking properly, use a small coil of clay around the base of the form.) The pot is again centered by rhythmically tapping the left side of the form with the left fingertips as the pot turns slowly on the wheel. This technique requires further practice.

After the pot is centered and adhered to the wheelhead, grasp the handle of the pear pitter in the right hand and push the thumb against the cutting loop of the tool. The trimming is done on the right side of the pot; the fingers of the left hand support the left side of the pot, with the left thumb placed against the right thumb as an additional brace. Brace the elbows as in throwing. Begin cutting the clay with the loop of the tool, moving slowly down along the bottom side of the pot. Repeat the process until the clay wall appears to be an equal thickness throughout.

Projects You Can Do

All thrown forms are based on an understanding of how to throw the basic forms — the plate, the bowl, and the cylinder. The cylinder is usually the starting point. Once the basic cylinder is mastered, the bowl and plate forms are much easier to learn. Many beautiful and useful objects can be made from a simple cylinder form.

FLOWER POT

Throw two cylinders that are approximately the same size. Dry them to leather hard and trim if necessary. Cover the cylinders with plastic to keep them from further drying.

A

B

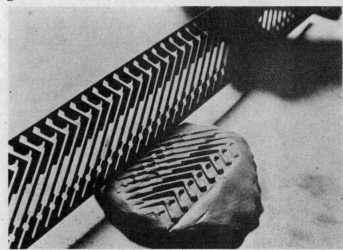

Figure 22. To begin the flower pot project, flatten clay between the hands (A), then press a textured object into it (B), and stretch the slab by pulling and slapping it (C).

C

A B

Figure 23. When the slab has dried to the leather hard stage, score the surface by scratching the areas to be joined (A), then apply slip to the scored areas of the base and top (B). Place the slab and cylinder together and tap in place (C). Cut an opening in the finished flower pot (D).

C D

Now take a ball of clay the size of an orange and flatten it out with the heel of the hand. Texture the flattened ball with anything that has the possibility of developing an interesting pattern in clay — everything from fingernails to the bottom of tennis shoes. Press a texture into the clay or press the clay onto a textured surface. Experiment. After pressing the texture, stretch the clay out by pulling the slab toward you while slapping it down on an absorbent surface. Pick up the clay by gently moving both hands under the slab. Give the slab a quarter turn and repeat the slapping technique. Repeat the whole process until the slab is nearly 3/8" thick. If the slab is sticking to the surface, the clay is being slapped too hard or directly downward. The stretching action, which comes from pulling the clay toward you while slapping it down, transforms a texture that is often very rigid and sterile into a lively, organic surface. Next, allow the stretched slab to dry to the leather hard stage. Then join a portion of the stretched slab to the top of one of the thrown cylinders. It is necessary to score and cover with slip those areas of clay that are to be joined. (Scoring is the process of scratching into the surface of the clay. Slip is formed by combining water with clay that is in a liquid state and stirring.) Score and apply slip to the rim of the cylinder. Tear off from the stretched slab a section that is larger than the opening of the cylinder. The actual size and configuration of the slab are personal decisions. Place the slab over the cylinder. The wet slip on the rim of the cylinder will indicate where to score and apply slip to the underside of the slab. Join the slab to the cylinder with a gentle tapping of a paddle (any flat-sided object held in the hand will function as a paddle). Cut a large opening or a number of small openings in the slab. Soften any sharp edges caused by cutting or tearing. Repeat the technique for the second cylinder. Decorate and fire the pieces and then arrange them together.

Figure 24. The finished flower pots use a cylindrical base. The shape of the tops may be varied. Dried flowers or weeds look attractive in these pieces.

Figure 25. A fired clay cylinder and a flat disc or clapper (above) are the pottery segments of the wind chimes. When several of these pieces are assembled with appropriate connecting materials, they make a striking room accent (right).

WIND CHIMES

Throw four cylinders of any size. When leather hard, poke a small hole through the center of the bottom of each cylinder. The hole must be large enough for the tether or rope that will hold the clapper of the chime. Using small balls of clay, pinch out the clay into flat discs with diameters slightly smaller than the opening of the cylinders.

Poke holes of the same size through the centers of the discs in the same manner as the cylinders. Fire the discs or clappers — then assemble after firing. Tie the clappers into the cylinders as shown. The sails that catch the wind and the tether should be made up of materials that are related to the clay. A plastic sail and a chrome chain tether would not be appropriate. Dry, decorate, and fire.

A MUG

Throw a cylinder about 20 percent larger than the desired size of the finished mug. Make an effort to throw the wall thin, keeping in mind that the function of the mug is to hold a heavy liquid. Smooth the rim by draping the elephant-ear sponge around the rim. Flare the rim outward so the form will be more comfortable to drink from. Allow the cylinder to dry to the leather hard stage and trim if necessary. Use coils to form a handle. Experiment and attempt to make a unique handle based on a coil technique. Roll out several small coils, then roll the small coils together into a larger one while preserving the resulting texture. Score and apply slip to areas where the handle will be attached. Dry, decorate, and fire.

For Additional Reading

Cardew, Michael, **Pioneer Pottery,** St. Martin's Press, 1969.

Leach, Bernard, **A Potter's Book,** Transatlantic Arts, Second Edition, 1967.

Nelson, Glen C., **Ceramics: A Potter's Handbook,** Holt, Third Edition, 1971.

Rhodes, Daniel, **Kilns: Design, Construction, and Operation,** Chilton, 1968.

Mobiles

One of man's newest art forms, mobiles reflect the energy and vibration of everyday living and can be an added feature to any home or office.

The original idea for mobiles is attributed to a well-known contemporary artist, Alexander Calder. Prior to Calder's innovations, little had been attempted in changing the form or content of sculpture. Anything that was not solid was not considered sculpture.

The Impressionists and Post-Impressionists both experimented with new artistic methods, primarily in painting, as a rebuttal against the redundancy of nineteenth-century work. As a result, they inspired a group known as the Futurists, who in turn renounced everything that did not move or vibrate. The Futurists created paintings and drawings which were solely of such moving objects as speeding cars and people in motion. They wanted to portray the idea that nothing ever stands still — man is set in motion and progress will not stop.

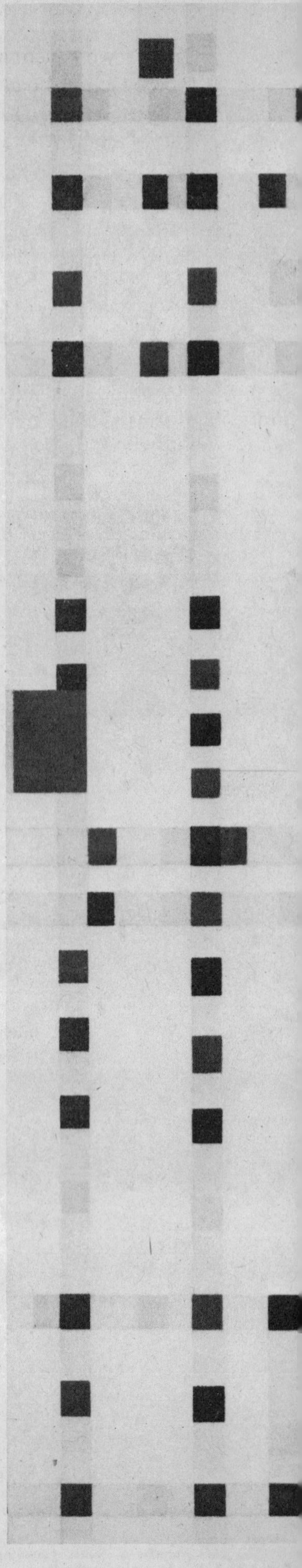

Figure 1. Mobile-maker Alexander Calder's interest in geometric shapes and primary colors was partly inspired by paintings like "Broadway Boogie-Woogie" (detail) by Piet Mondrian. (Courtesy, Collection, The Museum of Modern Art, New York.)

Calder's work stemmed from the relief sculptures and collages generated by the Cubists. Their new and fresh approach to pure form and "pure" (primary) color encouraged Calder to work in geometric shapes and colors. Calder's first small sculptures were inspired by puppet circuses. These small, animated people and animals seemed alive and full of motion. Made from small scraps of cork and wire, the figures were skillfully pulled together to create an impression of circus performers. The more Calder strived for motion in the figures, the more he became entranced with motion alone. Finally, after a visit with Mondrian, whose paintings were of primary colors and black and white, Calder was inspired to make his first attempt at moving sculpture. By using only geometric shapes and primary colors, he created the first true mobile, a sculpture in which each part moves independently of the other parts.

Mobiles today are used for many purposes: some are purely decorative to delight a child or enhance the home; others are used for such educational purposes as representing the solar system. Mobiles can be created by everyone and can symbolize any subject or can be abstract. They are improvisational, delightful, and easy to make. When completed, a mobile adds life and motion to a room, not only by its movement but also by the shadows it casts and the light that radiates from it.

Figure 2. Sheet metal and brass wire were used by Alexander Calder in his lively 1951 mobile "Streetcar." (Courtesy of The Art Institute of Chicago, Gift of Mr. and Mrs. Samuel A. Marx.)

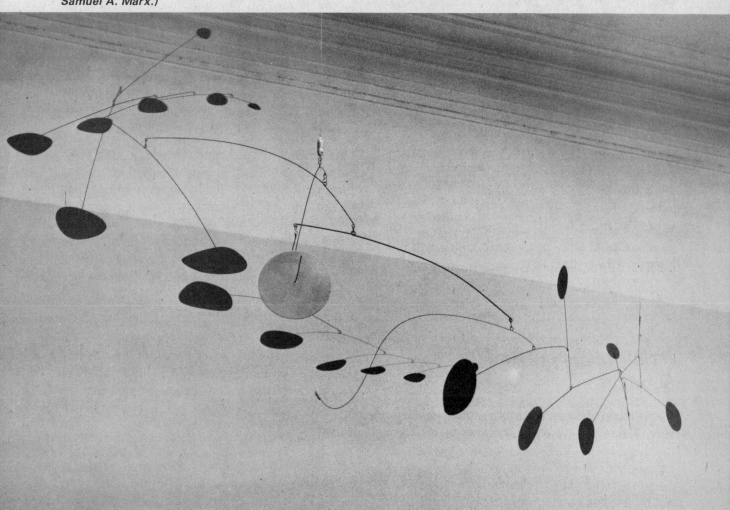

Common Terms Used In Making Mobiles

Arms: the lengths of wire used to suspend objects in air; keeps them swinging and moving without hitting each other.

Attachment Methods: the various ways of attaching pieces to the arms of a mobile (see also *Construction* under "Basic Procedures").

Balance: to hang a mobile so that the sides are level.

Balance Loop: the loop made in the arm of a mobile at the determined balance point.

Laminate: to glue veneer wood to other pieces of wood.

Mobile: a hanging, moving sculpture.

Smoothing an Arc: the process of running a hand over the arc arms of a mobile to make them bend down at the ends of the arc.

Stabile: a static sculpture which has the appearance of being mobile or moving.

Static: characteristic of a composition which is lifeless and uninteresting, but may be used for special effects.

Symmetrical: being the same on both sides, as if an imaginary line were drawn down the center; the mirrored equal sides will contain the same parts.

Table Mobile: a mobile suspended from a small sculpture on a table or the floor rather than one hung from the ceiling.

Basic Equipment And Supplies

Many materials can be used in mobiles. However, before one attempts the construction of a mobile, it is best to consider materials which are easily handled and then experiment as desired. There is also a range of materials which should not be used since they can cause complications. Such materials include very light papers, such as tissue paper, and very heavy items, such as huge chunks of wood.

CARDBOARD

Cardboard is extremely versatile: it can be cut in any desired shape and painted. Things can be glued to it; it can be covered with wrapping paper, ribbons, bows, or fabric.

One type of commercial cardboard is known as illustration board. This is available in several thicknesses and is made from layers of gray cardboard glued together with a layer of white drawing paper on top. The drawing paper is excellent for pencil drawings, draftings, or watercolors. Try to find the double thickness weight. This is durable and will not warp.

Another type of board to look for is poster board or railroad board. A lightweight board which has a medium-texture surface, poster board is usually less expensive and more porous than illustration board. Because it is more porous, poster board will accept spray paint readily and is more suitable for one-color shapes that are either brush or spray painted. Railroad board is often just a colored poster board, but it is available only in a limited selection of colors. Therefore, it is usually better to paint the mobile's shapes. The choice of color is greater and the cost is considerably less.

One other cardboard which should be mentioned is matt board, which is generally used for matting pictures. It is of high quality, strong, durable, and comes in two surfaces, deckled and smooth. Available in different weights, matt board also comes in single and double thicknesses as well as in several colors — sometimes with a different color on each side, which can add interest to a mobile's twirling parts.

METAL

Although there are many types of tins readily available for mobiles, there is usually a variety of tin on hand. A large coffee can, flattened out and cut into shapes, works well; as do flat pieces such as the lids and bottoms of ham tins or sardine cans.

Metal in the form of a thin sheet of galvanized iron (tagger's tin) is available at hardware stores. The best gauges to use for mobiles are 0.006 and 0.012. These are lightweight and can be as easily cut by metal shears as paper is cut with a scissors. The same metal is also available in heavier gauges, which can be used in making very large mobiles or floor stabiles.

PLASTIC

Plastic, which is available in a variety of sizes, shapes, and weights, may be fused together and molded. Tubular plastic can be bent into any shape; plastic sheets can be sawed into desired shapes and then decorated for special effects.

One of the first types of plastic to experiment with is dipping plastic. This plastic, which is available in a variety of colors, adheres to the wires and stretches across the area in between. With this technique, one can construct many different shapes which are easy to manipulate. When finished, this type of mobile can be placed in an area where it can be moved by the wind. Being very light in weight, the mobile will revolve endlessly, throwing sparkling, colored shadows on wall surfaces.

PLASTER OF PARIS

Plaster of Paris may be used in mobiles to achieve more sculptured effects. It can be used alone in a mobile made solely of small flat or three-dimensional decorative shapes; or, it may be combined with other hanging objects to add weight. Plaster is often used as the focal point in a mobile made from a variety of materials. Because plaster can be a weight problem in counterbalancing, it is often used specifically for this physical characteristic.

A word of caution about plaster: always mix it in a rubber bucket. Then, when any leftover plaster dries, it can be easily removed by twisting and bending the bucket. Also, never pour liquid plaster down any type of drain. It will harden in the drain and, needless to say, cause irreparable damage because nothing will remove it. It is best to leave any remaining plaster in the bucket, then break it out when it is dry. Or, pour it into an empty wax carton and use it later to make small hand sculptures.

Figure 3. Immerse bent wire into dipping plastic, which is available in a variety of colors (above). Place the completed lightweight mobile so that the wind will cause it to move (below).

Plaster Molds

When added to water, plaster becomes a thick paste which may be used in two ways. It is generally poured into molds and allowed to "set" — that is, to go through hardening stages. The plaster first becomes very warm, then very cool, and finally bone dry. Because it will set very quickly, the plaster should be poured almost immediately after being mixed. It can be put into a variety of molds made especially for plaster; or, it can be poured into cut down, empty waxed milk cartons. After the plaster has set, the carton can be stripped away. The block or blocks may then be shaped and carved with small knives and files, and finally sanded into the desired shapes. (To start with a cylindrical shape, use a waxed paper cup.)

Figure 4. When plaster is mixed with water, a thick paste forms which can be poured into molds (below). The resulting blocks can be carved and sanded into desired shapes (right).

Dipping in Plaster

The second method of using plaster, although not the easiest, is dipping. Bend several pipe cleaners into the shapes to be used, such as letters to spell a name. Do not make up too much plaster because it will only harden and be wasted. Place the letters on an "S" hook; quickly dip each letter or shape into the plaster, coating it well, and then hang up the "S" hook to allow the letter to dry. The shapes may be dipped repeatedly, but it is advisable to let them dry fairly well before redipping. When dry, the shapes may be sanded and then spray painted, painted with a brush, or simply left plaster white.

GLASS

Glass is one of the most widely used materials for mobiles. The luminous qualities of glass are a delight when used alone or when combined with other materials — it adds sparkle and tinkling transparency to any mobile. Generally, glass is not used by the beginning mobile craftsman. This is not because glass is difficult to work with, but because a beginning craftsman must first learn balance and proportion, which are more easily attained with cardboard or paper. Once one is able to judge weight and its relationship to balance, glass becomes a highly desirable medium with which to experiment.

Glass has characteristics not found in plastic. Unfortunately, however, cutting glass is usually a problem until the technique is mastered. Glass must be cut with a glass cutter. This is a small diamond-tipped wheel which produces a "scratch" across the surface of the pane. While holding the edge of the pane with one hand, make a line on the glass. Tap along the line on the opposite side of the glass with the other end of the glass cutter. The pane should then crack along the inscribed line. Often, until one becomes experienced in glass cutting, the glass crack will deviate from the original line. Although there are also cutters made especially for circles, it is advisable to use only straight-line geometric shapes until an agility with glass is developed.

Glass is available at both glass outlets and craft centers and may be obtained in a variety of colors. Colored glass is generally thicker and often has a decorative surface. Moreover, parts of the glass may be slightly marbleized because of impurities. Although each of these features helps to create natural and decorative additions for a mobile, they are also the same features that cause glass to fracture and make it difficult to cut.

In some craft stores, glass is available in precut shapes. One may wish to experiment with these before creating original pieces. The precut shapes are those commonly made up for Tiffany lamps and other types of shades.

One other special characteristic of glass is that it is difficult to drill. This can cause problems in hanging glass pieces on a mobile. To circumvent this, merely wrap the piece of glass securely with thin wire as shown in the illustrations. Use the loose end of wire for hanging and for attaching the piece onto the mobile.

Figure 5. This illustration shows colored glass in a variety of shapes. Glass can be purchased in precut shapes at craft stores.

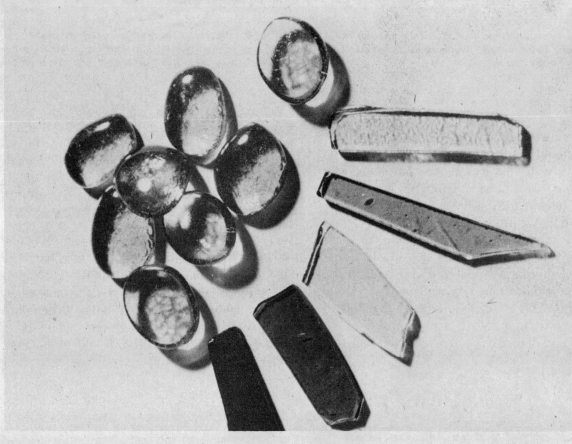

Figure 7. Experienced woodworkers can experiment with original designs. This piece was cut from two kinds of wood, glued together and varnished.

Figure 6. Inexperienced woodworkers should use a lightweight balsa wood, which is available in craft stores or hobby shops.

Figure 8. Veneers, sometimes used to make mobiles, are easily twisted and can be glued together or glued to some other surface to provide a wood-texture.

WOOD

Because there are many types of wood available, wood should be dealt with in two distinct ways. For those with little experience in working with wood, the best is balsa wood, which is easily obtainable at any craft store or hobby shop. Balsa comes in thin sheets, which can be cut in various shapes with a razor blade or an X-acto knife and painted, varnished, or glazed. Because it is extremely light, balsa wood can be used to make small three-dimensional constructions or large, flat shapes. This wood also comes in a variety of block-type shapes, which can be used as is; painted and decorated; or, carved into small statues, figures, or animals.

For those experienced with woods, a wooden mobile should be easy to construct. In addition to designing and building an original one of different types of wood, experiment with various shapes. Consider contrasts of wood: try gluing two or more kinds of wood together; cut out a shape and put a clear or honey maple varnish on it.

Veneers are also used in mobiles. Available at lumber yards and sometimes through mail-order catalogs, veneers bend extremely easily and may be twisted and glued together. They should be held in place until the piece dries. Veneers can also be used as decoration by gluing them onto other surfaces, such as cardboard or plain, inexpensive woods.

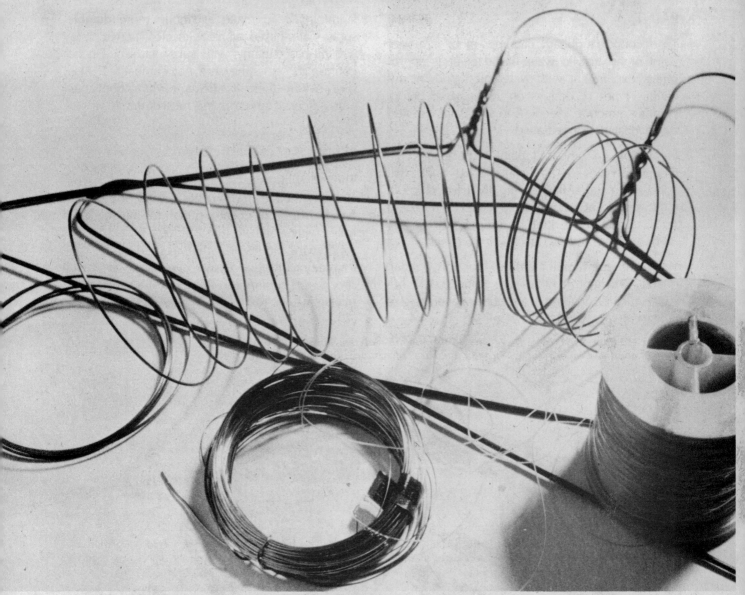

Figure 9. Of the various types of wire available (above), galvanized iron wire is best for holding the hanging pieces of a mobile. This wire can be purchased or can be appropriated from household coat hangers. Finer wire is used for attaching mobile pieces to the iron structure.

WIRE

The best wire for holding the hanging pieces in a mobile is galvanized iron wire. Although this wire will hold just about anything, one should always test first to see if it is strong enough. Obtainable at practically any hardware store, the best gauge to work with is the 12, 14, 16, or 18, depending on the weight of the materials. (The gauges refer to how thick or thin the wire is — the lower the number, the thicker the wire.) Sometimes this kind of wire is called "fencing wire" because this is its usual use. Other types of wires are also avail-able. Brass or copper wires are usually too soft and too easy to break when bending, and they are more expensive than iron wire.

THREADS

The parts of a mobile should be suspended by some sort of thread. Many people use nylon thread, but thin nylon fishing line is better. Neither of these is overbearing in appearance and will not detract from the mobile. Try to avoid using heavy sewing thread because it breaks easily and wears out quickly.

PAINT

To decorate cardboard or paper mobiles, poster paint or an acrylic water-based paint is appropriate. Experiment with watercolors and try out various types of designs on scrap paper before painting a mobile. Needless to say, paint can add a great deal to its appearance.

For metal, an oil-based paint is necessary. Although acrylics or any water-based paint will adhere to metal at first, eventually it will chip off. Oil-based paint can produce either a flat or a shiny surface. Turpentine is used as a thinner for oil-based paint and also for cleaning brushes.

Whatever type of paint is used, buy only a small quantity. Large quantities are unnecessary because the area covered in a mobile of average size is minimal. To make a mobile more durable, spray water-based paints with clear acrylic spray and oil-based paints with spray varnish. Do not confuse these — they are not compatible. Also, spray where there is adequate ventilation at all times — spraying outdoors is most desirable.

TOOLS

The following is a list of basic tools used in constructing mobiles: (1) brushes — two or three soft hair brushes; (2) a center punch for making small holes with which to band pieces; (3) a compass for drawing circles or partial arcs; (4) a matt knife for cutting through heavy cardboard; (5) metal shears for cutting tin shapes; (6) needle-nosed pliers; (7) ruler; (8) scissors; and (9) tape measure.

Figure 10. Shown are basic tools needed for making mobiles. They include center punch, compass, ruler, mat knife, tape measure, pliers, brushes, scissors, and metal shears.

Basic Procedures

There are no set rules for building mobiles. Rather, mobiles should be a composition of parts which move within themselves and share a spatial relationship with each other. Also, there is no limit to the kinds of materials which are used for mobiles. However, some materials are more easily manipulated at first. Others may give the desired visual effect, but may not be heavy enough to work efficiently. In such cases, the materials must be weighted with small pieces of metal.

BALANCE

Balance is the mainstem of a mobile. It creates the "give" of the mobile which allows it the freedom to spin and twirl endlessly in the air. In other words, balance gives a mobile the bounce that it needs — it allows the members of the mobile to circulate within themselves freely and without obstruction.

Symmetrical Balance

There are two types of balance: one is symmetrical, the other is asymmetrical. Symmetrical balance produces very little play and is rather static. While a symmetrically balanced mobile will swing around in a circle when suspended from a point, it does not "give" enough to allow the smaller members to move easily. Symmetrical mobiles generally move as a whole rather than as individual moving parts.

Asymmetrical Balance

Asymmetrical balance allows more play within the structure. It generally consists of a counterbalance construction, such as one large ball counterbalancing two small balls. In such a construction, however, one end of the mobile will have a tendency to hang slightly lower than the other end. If the mobile hangs too low at one end, it can be balanced by moving the wires holding the objects either closer together or farther apart. One of the most important points to remember is that the play in a mobile is what gives it life and movement. This should be an important factor when designing and planning mobiles.

Figure 11. Symmetrical mobiles (left) are static and swing in a circle. Asymmetrical mobiles (right) show a great deal of movement within the counterbalanced structure.

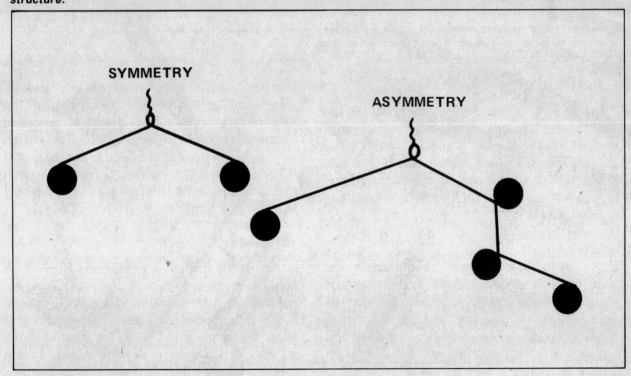

SYMMETRY

ASYMMETRY

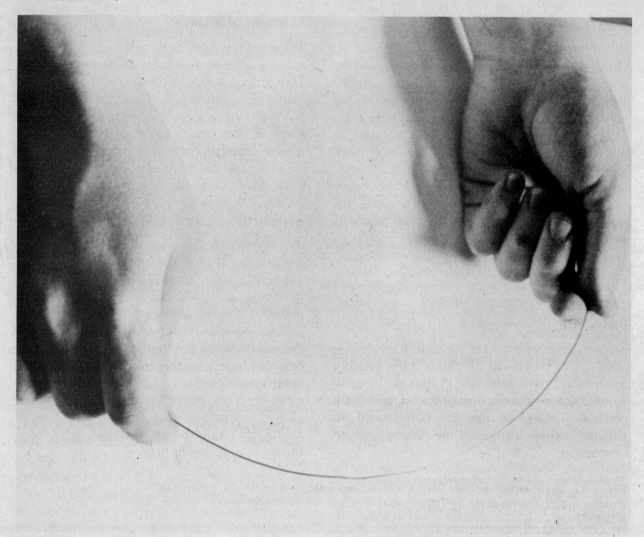

Figure 12. Most major structural arms of a mobile are curved downward, making them conducive to movement when the mobile is hung.

CONSTRUCTION

Although it is undoubtedly easier to follow instructions for a specific mobile than it is to simply read about how to make a mobile, the following general tips on making mobiles will be helpful. When ready to construct a mobile, consult the first project at the end of this article for step-by-step procedures.

Essentially, all mobiles are constructed in the same manner. Success depends upon the design and the ability to create a good balance. As mentioned previously, there are two types of mobiles: the kind which is suspended from the ceiling and the kind which is suspended independently from a small platform on a table or on the floor.

It is best to begin with two-dimensional mobiles rather than large three-dimensional shapes. The former tend to show more of a sense of movement by turning from a broad to a thin side and by having a flat surface for the wind to play against. It is also wise to start by making a completely geometric mobile: it will be much easier to grasp how to work with balance and with floating shapes.

Wire Arms

Generally the large, major structural arms which hold the mobile's parts away from each other are not straight. A gentle curve which slopes slightly down at each end gives the mobile more of a sense of play when it is hung. The hanging or the general tendency to slope down adds to the overall movement of a mobile.

Figure 13. To attach a mobile piece to the arm, punch two holes in the piece and run the end of a wire through the outer holes (above).

Figure 14. Wire is attached to another piece of a different shape (above) by the same method.

Piece Attachment

There are three ways to attach a piece of the mobile to the arm:

1. Attachment at end of arm (vertical). From the end of the curved arm bend 1/2" back toward the curve. Punch two holes in the piece to be at-

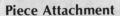

Figure 15. To attach a glass piece, wrap flexible, fine wire around it, then twist and secure at top with a small ring.

tached. Run the end of wire through the outer hole and push the bent end up through the inner hole. Bend the end flatly over onto the piece to hold it in place.

2. Attachment at end of arm (horizontal). Bend a 2" length of wire in half. Bend one piece up into a right angle 1/4" from the bent end. On the other piece, at the open end, also bend 1/4" up. Punch a balance hole through the piece to be attached. Punch a second hole 1/2" away. Slip the ends through the holes, with the long end through the balance hole. Bend the long end into a hook. Bend the short end back towards the hook.

3. Attachment for glass. Wrap flexible, fine wire around the piece of glass, twisting and securing it at the top with a small ring. This may be done at the bottom of the glass as well. An attachment for plastic is the same as for glass, except that small holes may be drilled into the plastic and connected with rings.

Hanging Mobiles

One way of hanging mobiles from the ceiling is from a light fixture. If this does not work, drill a hole in the ceiling and insert a lead or plastic plug which will expand to hold a screw. There is a flange or wing-type plug that works even better. Drill a hole about the size of the plug and insert the outside casing into the hole. Then screw the inner bolt into the plug to extend the flanges or wings. Do not tape or nail the mobile to the ceiling because it will eventually fall.

Projects You Can Do

The following are simple and varied projects. Read through them first, noting the step-by-step procedures and the illustrations accompanying them.

GEOMETRIC MOBILE

Out of cardboard, cut two 6″ circles, two 4″ circles, one 7″ circle, and one 5″ square. Paint each circle or pair of circles the same color. Paint the square the opposite color. Also needed is 16 or 18 gauge wire: two lengths of 12″ each, two lengths of 16″ each, and one length of 18″. Remember that mobiles are always started from the bottom.

1. Take one length of 16″ wire and smooth it into an arc by running the hand over the length of it several times until it is slightly arched (it is best to add 2″ to the desired length of an arm to allow for the curvature). Connect one 2″ circle at one end with a vertical connection and one 7″ circle at the

Figure 16. Free-hanging geometric mobiles are especially attractive when they use a variety of shapes and brilliant primary colors.

other end, also with a vertical connection. Find the balance point by holding the wire arm with pliers until it is level. Construct a balance loop at that point.

2. Smooth the 18″ wire arm into an arc and loop it from the end to the balance loop just made. Vertically connect one 4″ circle to the other end. Find the balance points and loop.

3. Smooth a 12″ arm to an arc and connect it at the last balance point with a loop. At the other end, connect the 5″ square with the horizontal connection method. Find the new balance point and loop.

4. Smooth the other 16″ length of wire to an arc and connect it to the last balance point. Connect the 2″ circle to the other end, find the balance point, and loop.

5. Using the second 12″ arm, smooth it to an arc, loop, and connect to the last balance point. Add the 4″ circle at the other end, find the balance point, and loop. Run fine fishing line from the ceiling to the loop and connect the two with rings. Let the mobile hang.

VACATION MOBILE

While on vacation, people often collect small cards, sea shells, souvenirs, road maps, and snapshots. Then, when they arrive home, they have nothing to do with them except put them in a drawer and eventually throw them out. These items can be made into a very attractive mobile. One may glue snapshots to metal if other objects are heavy, or use cardboard and place one picture on each side. The same can obviously be done with sections of a road map, table napkins, or small items which need backing. Sometimes an agate or special stone can be attached by the method used for glass.

The best way to organize this kind of mobile is to first lay the materials on a table and arrange them as desired. Then determine the distance of the arcs so that each piece will have room to move after it is hung. Connect each item either vertically or horizontally or hang from fishing line, as in step 5 of the previous project. Remember, start at the bottom and work up. Continue to balance the mobile as work proceeds.

Figure 17. Many items collected while on a vacation will serve as eye-catching parts for a mobile. Shown is such a group of objects, including snapshots and various stones.

Figure 18. To make wire and glass mobile chimes, cut out pieces of glass in the shapes and sizes shown in the diagram on the right, or use an original design of your choice.

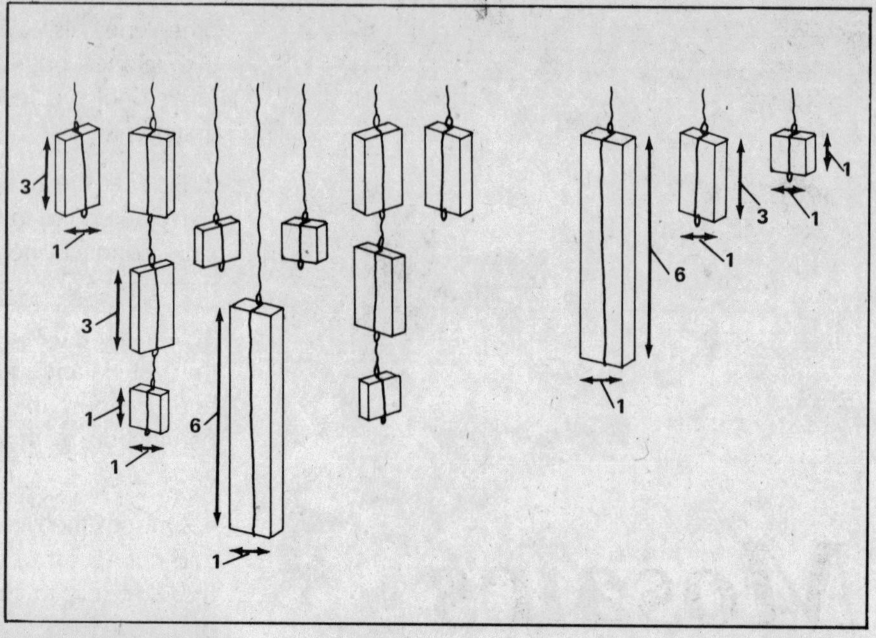

Figure 19. The completed project (below) combines movement, a variety of shimmering shapes, and a lovely, musical sound.

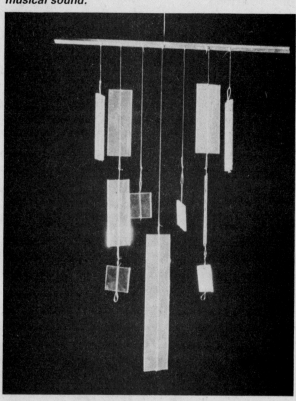

WIRE AND GLASS MOBILE CHIMES

There are several ways of approaching this type of mobile. First become familiar with the colors and shapes of available precut glass.

Using the design in the diagram or an original design, set out the pieces of glass that will be needed. Arrange a 16-gauge wire frame for the glass. Wrap thin wire around each glass and connect all units with rings, as shown in the diagram. Connect the glass chains to the proper wire. Suspend wire construction A from wire construction B. Hang the chimes on a porch or near a window.

For Additional Reading

Arnason, H. H., **Calder,** Van Nostrand.

Bland, William, **Mobiles,** Museum Press Limited, London.

Lynch, John, **How to Make Mobiles,** Viking.

Lynch, John, **Mobile Design,** Crowell.

Schegger, T. M., **Make Your Own Mobiles,** Oak Tree Press and Sterling Publishing Co.

Mosaics

The art of creating a decorative surface by placing together small pieces of various materials is as old as time and as new as tomorrow.

Mosaics, one of the oldest and most enduring of art forms, began more than 5000 years ago. It was not confined to a single area or period, but was used by many ancient peoples as a means of artistic expression.

The Sumerians of Babylonia adorned their buildings with cones of fired clay. Later they decorated various objects with silhouetted figures, cut from conch shells, set against a mosaic background of semiprecious stones. The Egyptians, Greeks, and Romans used mosaic primarily for architectural decoration, paving walks, walls, and ceilings with small stones and tiny cubes, or tesserae, of variously colored marble.

It was during the Byzantine Period in the Middle East — paralleled by the Early Christian period in Southern Italy — that mosaic art reached its height. This period is often referred to as the Golden Age of Mosaic. With Emperor Constantine's conversion to Christianity, mosaic emerged as one of the church's great mediums of expression. Artists were sent out from Constantinople to decorate the walls of great cathedrals. These artists both designed and executed their own work. Using the direct method, they worked "on location," embedding individual tesserae (cubes) of marble, precious and semiprecious stones and metals, and brilliantly colored glass into a bonding base of cement, mortar, or plaster. Their mosaic decorations, which caught reflected light, were especially appropriate for dimly lighted church interiors and for surfaces with curves, such as the curves of an apse. A radiance of vibrant, broken color seemed to emanate from the uneven surface. This new monumental style, with its religious themes, was in marked contrast to earlier symbolic art.

Through the fourth, fifth, and sixth centuries, Constantinople, Ravenna, Venice, and Rome became centers of great mosaic art. San Vitale, the Tomb of Galla Placidia at Ravenna, and the Hagia Sophia at Constantinople were built during this period. During the Middle Ages a more rigid, formalized mosaic style evolved out of strictly enforced rules designed to inspire reverence and

Figure 1. This detail is from the magnificent mosaic "Empress Theodora and Retinue," a sixth-century Byzantine work located in the basilica of San Vitale, at Ravenna, Italy. (Hirmer Fotoarchiv.)

meditation. This tendency towards abstraction and broad, simple treatment of subject matter was well suited to the technique of mosaic.

With the dawning of the Italian Renaissance in the fourteenth century, mosaic art began a decline that was to last for centuries. The indirect method, in which a "cartoon" or sketch was enlarged from the artist's drawing and copied on paper, was first used during this period. Students or assistants then glued tesserae onto the paper and transported the paper sections to the work site where they were pressed into place. The result of the indirect method was a flat, perfectly even mosaic surface; missing was all the sensitivity, directness, and originality of the old direct method.

During this period, the independent art of mosaic was gradually submerged by the dominating in-

Figure 2. This section of an intricate Roman mosaic pavement dates back to the second century A.D. (Courtesy, The Metropolitan Museum of Art, Anonymous Gift, 1945.)

fluence of painting. Mosaicists strove to imitate the methods and appearance of painting. Thus, whereas only a few strong colors were used in the best early mosaics work, color gradations increased to the point where the Vatican Studio boasted of over 28,000 different shades and tones. Moreover, the tesserae were fitted together more closely and polished smooth, eliminating the texture that is the very essence of mosaic. The art eventually deteriorated to the actual copying of well-known paintings, particularly portraits, in order to preserve them.

As economic conditions changed, less expensive frescoes replaced mosaics in architectural decoration. Mosaic art continued, but mainly in the form known as "comesso," or Florentine mosaic, fostered by the Medici family in Florence. This technique used ground and polished surfaces of natural, precious and semiprecious stones which were cut and so closely set that no spaces were evident between the tesserae. This style enjoyed wide popularity into the eighteenth century. It was not until after World War II, when mosaicists joined other twentieth-century artists in breaking with tradition, that mosaic art was again envi-

sioned as an independent and vital medium for truly creative expression. Outstanding mosaicists, such as Gino Severini and Juan O'Gorman, were keenly aware of the inherent qualities of their special medium and thought and expressed themselves in that medium. Not only did mosaic art become an integral part of architecture, but it was now viewed with interest as secular decoration and applied to such movable objects as sculpture, decorative accessories, and portable wall panels.

The mosaic artist today is no longer confined to specific materials used in rigidly prescribed methods. There is, at times, an almost indistinguishable line between mosaic, collage, construction, and assemblage. The concern of the contemporary mosaicist is not with labels, but with creative expression and the quality of that expression. Almost anything can be used to create mosaics: pebbles, sea shells, tiles, nails, glass, wood, and even the scrap of today's technological society The mosaic artist's choice of materials is as limitless as his imagination.

Common Terms Used In Mosaics

Buttering: the process of applying adhesive to the back of a tile or tessera before setting it in place.

Direct Method: the method in which individual tesserae are buttered and set by hand onto a base; or, set into a setting bed of adhesive, mortar, or cement in order to create a surface design. A sketch or color plan may be followed, but an experienced craftsman often works from spontaneous ideas.

Grout: the mortar-like material that is used to fill the spaces between the tesserae after they are set into place.

Grouting: the technique used in filling the spaces between mosaic tesserae with a mortar, cement, or other substance after setting is completed.

Indirect Method: the method in which a design is first drawn on paper onto which the tesserae are temporarily glued facedown into position. The paper, with tesserae attached, is then lowered paper side up and pressed into place on a prepared setting bed. After the mastic or mortar of the bed has hardened somewhat, the paper is moistened and peeled off. This method results in a design that is in reverse of the original drawing, unless the original drawing was sketched in reverse.

Marme: small cubes of marble; one of the oldest of mosaic materials.

Mastic: a thick, putty-like, waterproof adhesive used for setting mosaic materials.

Mosaic: the term given to a finished piece of work created by placing together small pieces of various materials which form a decorative surface or design.

Setting Bed: the layer of adhesive (*i.e.,* "white glue" or mastic), cement, plaster, or mortar into which tesserae are embedded by the direct or indirect method; also called bonding base.

Smalti: tiles cut by hand from slabs of opaque glass. Their irregular surfaces produce a highly reflective and varied mosaic surface. Also known as Byzantine tiles, Smalti are regarded as the "King of Mosaics."

Tessera: a tile or little cube of variously colored marble, glass, enamel, and ceramic used to make a mosaic. Because contemporary mosaics incorporate almost any material that can be adhered, the "little cube" definition is no longer adequate. To cover the great variety of both natural and manmade materials used by the mosaic artist today, a tessera should be defined as a fragment or piece of material used to create a mosaic.

Basic Equipment And Supplies

Most mosaic equipment and supplies can be obtained at craft and hobby departments of stores or at some art supply shops. Wood, hardware, and certain other materials can be found at lumber

Figure 3. "Moses and the Daughters of the Pharoah" is a centuries-old mosaic from the famous church of Santa Maria Maggiore in Rome, Italy. (Scala—New York/Florence.)

yards, building supply or hardware stores. Starter kits, containing everything necessary to make simple mosaic projects, are available at craft and hobby shops or at some art supply stores.

Work should be done in a well-lighted area and on a sturdy work surface. There should be adequate storage space for materials and tools. The use and limitations of the materials selected must be considered when planning a mosaic. For instance, some porous or fragile materials are not suitable for an outdoor project.

For the beginner, a great deal of elaborate equipment is not needed, but there are a few necessary basic items. These are described below.

Figure 4. The three most commonly used types of tesserae are glazed ceramic tile (left), Byzantine or Smalti title (center), and Venetian or glass tile (right).

TESSERAE

A mosaic can be made by using almost any material that can be cut and/or formed into a design and then applied or embedded onto a base. Tile has been the traditional mosaic material for thousands of years. Tiles are sold in various forms: mounted on paper with the back of the tiles covered; on a web-mesh backing that can be soaked off or glued (with the tiles still on) to a base; or loose in bulk packages. Tiles on the web-mesh backing can be cut with scissors into desired pieces or shapes; glue is then applied to the backing; and the entire area is pressed into place on a base. There are several different types of tiles available.

Ceramic Tiles

Ceramic tiles are most popular with beginners. They are the least expensive and the most easily obtained. They come in a wide range of colors in 3/4″ squares, with either a glossy or matte (dull) finish. They are relatively easy to cut and lend themselves to a variety of projects. Porous ceramic tiles should be soaked in water and dried before use or they may absorb moisture from the embedding material and come loose.

Glass or Venetian Tiles

These tiles are economical (as well as beautiful), all-purpose materials suitable for floors, walls, panels, and small art objects. They come in 3/4″ squares with beveled edges that catch and reflect light.

Smalti or Byzantine Tiles

These are the most beautiful and the most expensive mosaic materials, and are preferred by professional traditional mosaicists. They are rectangular in shape, hand-cut from slabs of jewel-toned opaque glass, and have irregular sizes and surfaces.

Marme or Marble Tesserae

These are expensive, subtly colored cubes of marble — one of the oldest of mosaic materials.

Other Tesserae Materials

Depending on its form (sheets, cullet or nuggets, dalles or thick slabs, fragments of bottles, etc.), stained, colored, or clear glass may be cut and adhered as tile. It may also be embedded or cast. Furthermore, materials found in nature (i.e., beach pebbles, shells, driftwood, wood, dried seeds, other foodstuffs, etc.) and man-made objects selected for their interesting shape, texture, or pattern make exciting mosaic tesserae.

TOOLS FOR CUTTING AND SHAPING TESSERAE

Only a few tools are necessary for mosaic work.

Tile Cutters or Nippers

These are the basic and most widely used tools for cutting and shaping commercially prepared tiles. They are mechanically similar to a pair of pliers, with a working end consisting of two vertically aligned blades that open and close. They are

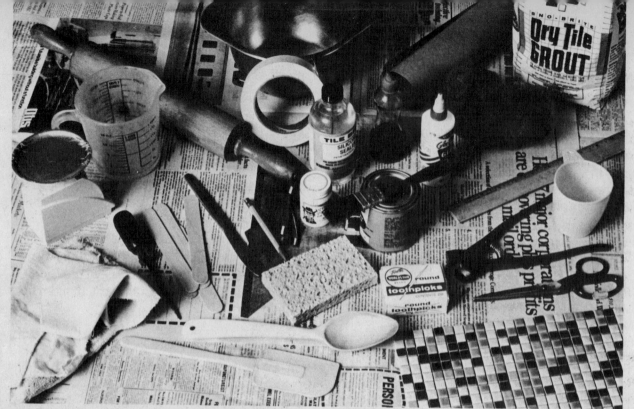

Figure 5. Basic supplies for the mosaics craftsman include tesserae materials, tile clippers, and grout. Other supplies include such common household items as sponges and toothpicks.

available at craft, hobby, and art supply stores that carry mosaic supplies and at some hardware stores. The best quality cutters are those with carbide or carboloid-tipped cutting edges, long cushioned handles, and a spring return which automatically reopens the cutting jaws.

Glass Cutter

A good ball-end glass cutter can be useful for cutting glass and thinner tiles. (It is a good idea to wear thick gloves when cutting stained glass.)

Hammer

Where size and shape of the pieces of tesserae are not important, the tesserae can be placed between several sheets of newspaper and then broken with an ordinary hammer.

ADHESIVE OR SETTING MATERIALS

In choosing an adhesive, consider the type of materials used (i.e., porous or nonporous, transparent or opaque): the function of the piece (i.e., table or tray top, purely decorative wall panel); and whether the piece will come in contact with the elements or with liquids.

Casein-Based Glues

These so-called "white glues" are versatile adhesives that set up quickly, are transparent when dry, easy to apply, and popular with beginners. They are water resistant but not waterproof.

Polyvinyl Glues

These are another type of the "white glues." They are similar to the casein-based glues and work best on porous materials. "Elmer's Glue-All" is a polyvinyl glue.

Mastic

When a strong, waterproof bond is desired, rubber-based mastic is recommended. It can be used in both direct and indirect methods. Putty-like in consistency, mastic spreads easily. It can be applied directly to the base and materials pressed into it, or each separate piece of material can be buttered on the back and then pressed firmly in place. There are two additional advantages of mastic: (1) because it does not dry as quickly as "white glue," changes are easier to make; and (2) because of its "tackiness," it can be used effectively on vertical or curved surfaces as well as on horizontal surfaces without "running." Mastic is available in beige, brown, and black tones as well as white.

Modeling Paste

A relatively expensive acrylic adhesive, modeling paste is useful for specific problems, such as small projects or adhering heavy or irregularly shaped materials. It resembles thick white putty; is easily spread with a spatula, palette knife, or tongue depressor; sets up quickly; and will adhere to practically all materials. It also works equally well on horizontal, vertical, or curved surfaces. Modeling paste may be colored by the addition of water-soluble paint. Sand, gravel, or crushed stone can be sprinkled over and pressed into the top layer for surface texture. It is conveniently water soluble in paste form but is water proof when dry.

Cement

Ready-mixed cements are best for the beginner because they are readily available at building supply and hardware stores and need only the addition of water.

Magnesite Cement

This versatile, but expensive, cement is the one preferred by many professional mosaicists. It can be used in both the direct and indirect methods. A variety of "unlike" materials can be embedded in it. And, it can be applied in thick or thin layers.

Temporary Water-Soluble Adhesives

For adhering tesserae to paper in the indirect method, it is important to use a temporary glue or paste that is strong enough to hold the tesserae in place but also easily soluble in water. A satisfactory flour-and-water paste can be made from one part flour mixed with eight parts water, boiled for five minutes, and strained.

New and Improved Adhesives

New and improved adhesives, such as latex cements, epoxy, and polyester resins, have made possible many new mosaic techniques, particularly involving the processes of casting, fusing, and laminating.

A BASE OR SUPPORT

Almost any rigid, durable surface can be used as a base for a mosaic if it is properly prepared beforehand. The surface should be dry, firm, and smooth with all bumps, lumps, grease, and dust removed.

Bases, with and without framing or edging, can be purchased at hobby, craft, or art supply stores. If making the base, consider using plywood or masonite; pottery, plates, pans; or three-dimensional sculptured forms. It is advisable to make or select a base before purchasing tesserae, adhesive, etc. After transferring the design onto the base, or onto paper the size and shape of the base, the proper amount of materials needed can be more accurately determined.

GROUT

Grout is the mortar-like substance which is worked into the spaces between tesserae after setting is completed. It is necessary for smooth functional surfaces, such as table tops and trays, and is added protection for outdoor projects.

A ready-mixed grout, which may be purchased in craft and hobby shops and some art supply and hardware stores, is good for beginners. Grout may be left white or it can be colored with dry colors available at the same stores where grout is sold.

FINISHING MATERIALS

To clean a mosaic, the following are necessary: soft rags, sponges, clear water (never use a detergent), steel wool or copper pads, sandpaper, plastic scraper, and tweezers for the stubborn bits of dried grout. Most mosaics require little or no "finishing" other than cleaning or, possibly, polishing, which enhances the natural qualities of the material. The grouted surface can be made stainproof or waterproof by coating it with a silicone polish or sealer. For pieces that are exposed to the elements or come in contact with liquids, the sealer should be renewed periodically.

FRAMING MATERIALS

Most mosaic designs, particularly wall panels, look best when left unframed. However, a frame or edging may be required for functional pieces, such as counter or table tops, or desired on a wall panel. Several ready-made frames are available in hobby and craft stores. When any framing or edging is attached it should be protected with masking tape before adhesives or cement and mosaic material are applied.

RELATED EQUIPMENT AND SUPPLIES

1. Eye goggles for protection against flying pieces of materials when cutting.

2. Spatula, palette knife or putty knife to spread mastic or cement, butter tiles, apply grout, scrape away dried grout and cement, and do many other jobs.

3. Plastic scraper, similar to a windshield ice scraper, for scraping excess dried grout or cement without scratching tiles.

4. Trowel for applying and smoothing large areas of cement or mortar.

5. Tongue depressor or "popsicle" stick for mixing and spreading.

6. Tweezers for holding and placing small tesserae.

7. Toothpicks for getting out tiny, hard-to-finish areas.

8. Screwdriver or penknife for removing any mistakes after glue, mastic, or cement has dried.

9. Buckets and plastic bowls for mixing.

10. Containers and boxes for storing loose materials.

11. Rolling pin for rolling and pressing when using the indirect method.

12. Drawing, "kraft," and tracing papers for planning and transferring designs when using the direct or indirect method.

13. Brushes for such odd jobs as grouting, sealing, weatherproofing, toning, and finishing.

14. Waxed paper, wax, grease, or oil for easy removal of cement or mortar bed.

15. Nails for nailing edging or framing.

16. Hardware cloth (also called metal builder's cloth) for reinforcing cement or mortar.

Basic Procedures

There are two traditional methods of working with mosaic materials: the direct method and the indirect — or reverse — method. For both of these methods, one must first create or adapt a design (to be transferred to a base or to a piece of heavy paper); prepare a base, support, or setting bed; cut and shape selected tesserae to carry out the design; and grout, clean, and seal the completed mosaic surface. In planning a design, simplicity should be the primary consideration. Initially, it is a good idea to stay away from complicated details and any design with rounded areas, such as a

Figure 6. These three basic designs all make use of the square. A checkerboard effect (left) is a popular favorite. Rows of squares are staggered for another design (center). For another basic design, four small squares form a larger square, which is then duplicated in rows (right).

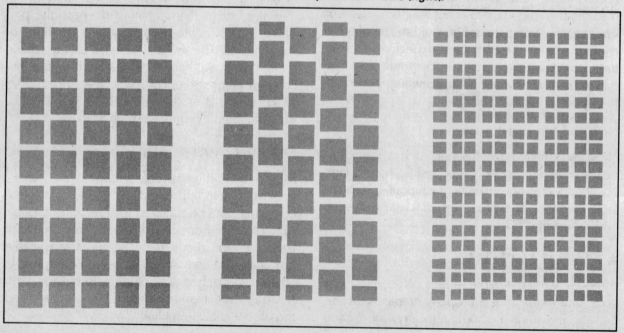

Figure 7. This is one of the basic designs for mosaic work. Note the gentle curve; it is prudent to avoid circular shapes or rounded areas when working with tiles.

Figure 8. Another basic design for mosaics resembles an abstract painting. Again, the rectangle is the geometric shape that is chosen. Several colors can be used in this design.

flower petal or the human form. Mosaic designs may be realistic representations. They can also be completely abstract or nonobjective designs developed from interwoven geometric or free-form lines and shapes. They are most successful when conceived as two-dimensional patterns, without an attempt to create illusions of depth.

The basic skills required for these procedures should not be difficult for the beginner to develop. With a little practice and experience, they can be performed with ease and confidence.

THE DIRECT METHOD

The direct method is basically the simplest mosaic method and is easier and faster than the indirect for beginners. In this method, mosaic tesserae are (1) either buttered with adhesive and set individually onto a base or support, or (2) they are embedded individually onto a base spread with adhesive or into a setting bed of cement or mortar. If desired, grout can then be used to fill in any spaces between the tesserae.

Although a rough sketch and/or color plan may be followed, the direct method is most effective for working spontaneously from an original idea. The tesserae are placed right side up, which permits the artist to see the design immediately. Moreover, mosaic tesserae of varying thicknesses, weights, shapes, and textures may be used to create a more interesting surface. An uneven surface quality and control of light reflection, resulting in a more vibrant piece, is easily obtained by the depth and angle of placement of the tesserae.

THE INDIRECT METHOD

The indirect method is also called the reverse method because a design is first drawn or painted on heavy paper (such as "kraft" paper) onto which tesserae are then temporarily pasted or glued face down. An advantage of the indirect method is that mistakes in design are easily corrected on the paper before the tesserae are embedded or adhered. The paper with the tiles attached is then lowered, paper side up, onto a prepared base of adhesive or a setting bed of mortar. Thus the design is reversed from the original drawing. The paper is then rolled or pressed to embed the mosaic tesserae securely and evenly into the ad-

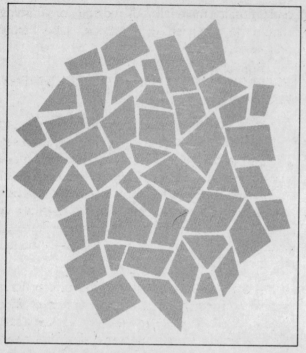

Figure 9. A variety of geometric shapes are utilized in this basic design (above), which resembles a stained-glass window. Note that the spaces between the tiles are very irregular.

hesive or mortar bed. After the mortar or adhesive has begun to harden, the paper backing is removed by wetting it thoroughly with a cloth or sponge and peeling it away from the tesserae.

A characteristic of the indirect method is that the mosaic surface that is revealed is level and flat, which is desirable for such utilitarian surfaces as table tops and trays. The indirect method is also used extensively in making large surface mosaics, such as murals and walls, where tesserae are put on in sections.

There are certain important things to remember when working indirectly. First, the paper on which the design has been drawn and to which the tesserae are to be pasted must be the same size as the base or setting bed to which the design will be transferred and embedded. Second, the adhesive should not only be strong enough to hold the

Figure 10. The indirect method (below) makes use of heavy paper. Glue the tiles to the marked paper; then place the paper, tile side down, onto the adhesive base or mortar bed.

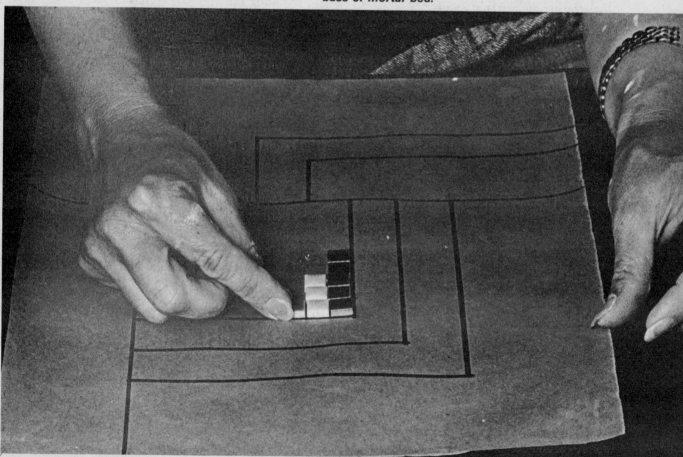

tesserae in place but easily soluble in water. Finally, if tesserae are of uneven thicknesses, the mastic, cement, or mortar should be thick enough for the thickest tile to be deeply embedded.

TRANSFERRING A DESIGN

When using the direct method, designs may be outlined directly on a base or drawn with a sharp tool or stick in a setting bed. To trace a design of the same size as the final mosaic design onto a base surface, use carbon paper or coat the underside of the sketch with heavy pencil or chalk. Then, place paper — right side up — onto the base. Tape the paper at the corners to prevent it from sliding out of position. Go over the entire design with a sharp pencil, ballpoint pen, or stylus. Remove paper, study the transferred design carefully, and select colors. Color the transferred design or mark the areas of color on the design, in order to easily follow the color plan. If freehand sketching is difficult and a design needs to be enlarged, rule off squares on the design. Mark off an equal number of larger squares on the project surface, and enlarge the design by drawing in one square at a time.

When using the indirect method, the design should be outlined on heavy paper (such as "kraft" paper) to which tesserae will be adhered. Be sure that this paper is the same size as the base to which the design will be transferred and embedded. If the design is not to be reversed when embedded, it must be drawn in reverse on the paper.

PREPARING A BASE

The surface of a mosaic base should be clean, dry, and smooth. (The one exception to a smooth surface is an especially "slick" one, such as plastic, which needs to be "roughed up" in order to provide a better adhering surface.) If the base is porous, a coat of shellac or waterproof silicone sealer should be applied to both sides of the base and let dry. This reduces the chance of warpage and also prevents moisture in the adhesive from being absorbed by the porous surface. (Loss of moisture causes the adhesive to crack and fall off.)

Hardware for hanging or installation should be attached to the base before applying adhesive and mosaic material. All edging or framing should be protected with masking tape before adhesive is applied.

PREPARING A SETTING BED OF CEMENT OR MORTAR

A setting bed of cement or mortar serves as an adhesive and as a base at the same time. For a setting bed, a box or wood form and a work surface should be prepared into which the cement or mortar will be poured. A form is a bottomless box or frame that may be loosely nailed together, or one corner may be hinged and another fastened with a hook-type latch for easy removal. About 3 to 4 inches is a good depth for a form.

If this framing-in is temporary, the box or form should be rubbed with a separating film of wax, grease, or oil. Thus, when the form is taken apart, the hardened cement or mortar slab will easily separate from it. The form should be placed on a work surface, such as a piece of plywood, covered with heavy waxed paper so that the mortar also does not adhere to it. To keep the form from sliding out of position, nails can be hammered a short distance into the work surface.

Mix the cement or mortar with water until it is the consistency of thick batter. Cement color may be added at this time to color the mixture. It is advisable to use a disposable container, such as a cleaned, cut-off plastic bleach bottle that can be thrown away afterwards. (Leftover plaster or mortar should never be poured down the sink drain.) Pour the cement mixture into the form or box to half the depth desired for the finished slab. Tap the sides of the box or form to level the mixture and to force air bubbles to the surface, where they can be broken.

To reinforce the cement slab, cut metal hardware or builder's cloth about 1 inch smaller than the base and press it into the wet mortar. Pour the second (and final) layer of mortar over the hardware cloth, tapping the sides again to level. Smooth the surface with a trowel or spatula and proceed with setting tesserae directly or indirectly into the mortar. (A design to be followed can be traced into the mortar with a sharp tool or stick, if desired.) After the cement or mortar has hardened and dried for a few days, the box or frame may be dismantled.

CUTTING AND SHAPING TESSERAE

The basic technique of cutting and shaping is the same for all types of tesserae. Hold the tessera to be cut between thumb and side of forefinger, with thumb on top for a firm grip. In the other hand, hold tile cutter or nipper far back on the handles. Hook thumb around the top handle; manipulate the bottom handle with other fingers. Open cutter and place cutting edges 1/16" to 1/8" over the edge of the tessera, away from the hand holding the tessera. The cutter edges will be at a right angle to the tessera edge and directly in its middle. Grip the tessera firmly within the cutter edges by squeezing the handles of the cutter. Give a sharp snip and the tessera will break, leaving the two pieces still held firmly between thumb and forefinger. These two pieces can then be cut to form smaller pieces.

Tesserae can be cut in any size and shape. When the cutter is used correctly, a fracture line is formed in the exact direction in which the cutter

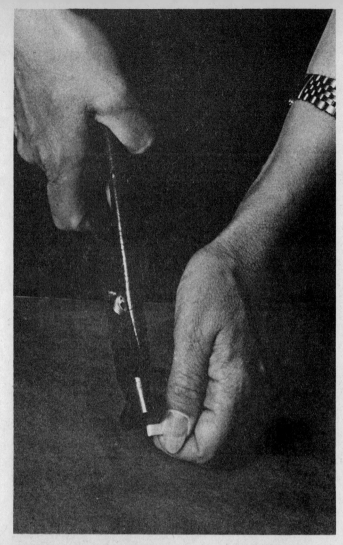

Figure 11. The basic cutting procedure is the same for all kinds of tesserae. Grip the tesserae firmly between the thumb and forefinger, as shown (above). Hold the cutter at the end of the handles.

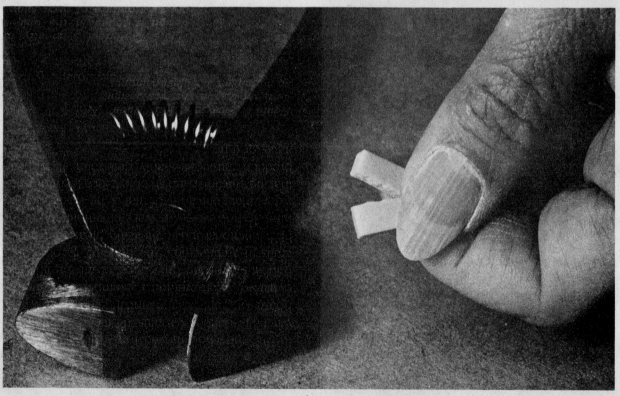

edge is aimed. For instance, placing the cutters diagonally will produce triangular cuts. Keep in mind that some tiles are easier to cut than others (e.g., ceramic tiles are easier to cut than glass tiles) and that smaller bits are more difficult to shape and handle. Therefore, small tiles are best avoided by the beginner.

GROUTING

Some artists prefer not to grout at all, feeling that the spaces between the tesserae have an interest of their own. Actually, grouting is undesirable in designs where a variety of unlike materials has been used. These are usually set in mastic or cement-type adhesives, which work their way up slightly between the tesserae.

Applying Grout

Cover all exposed wood or metal trim with masking tape. Gradually add dry grout powder to water and mix in a clean, grease-free container until the mixture reaches the consistency of heavy cream or thin batter. If colored grout is desired, add grout coloring until grout is a shade darker than desired because it will dry to a lighter color. Spread grout over the tesserae with the hand, rubber spatula, or palette knife. Make sure to

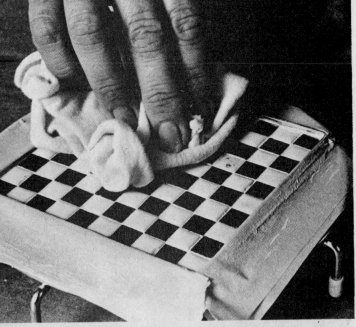

Figure 12. A soft cloth or sponge can be used (below) for cleaning grout. Steel wool is used for problem spots (lower left). Oil paint and turpentine are used to tone down grout (lower right).

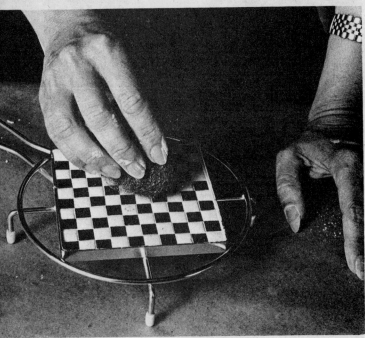

Figure 13. Grout and water should be measured carefully (above left) to insure the correct proportions. Mix the grout and water (above right) until the mixture has the consistency of batter (right).

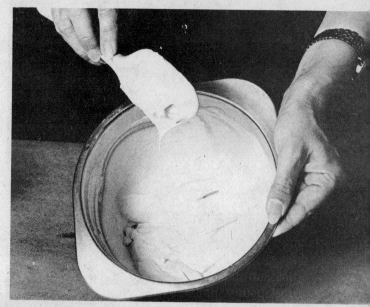

work it into all cracks and spaces. (When all cracks are filled, "tap" the project by raising it up 1 or 2 inches and gently dropping it down, thereby forcing out all air bubbles.)

Cleaning

Scrape excess grout off with hands, spatula, or dampened cloth or sponge. (Always use clear water; never add a detergent.) Set project aside to dry for about a half hour. Then wipe mosaic surface carefully with a damp sponge or cloth — this will leave a fine film of grout — and allow to set again for about 1 hour. With a soft, wet rag or moist hand, go over tesserae again with a circular motion and smooth grout between tesserae with wet fingertips. Let set another hour and then polish with a dry, soft cloth. (The drying process should never be rushed because grout that sets too quickly will become brittle and crack.) Steel wool or a copper pad, plastic scraper, and tweezers are useful for removing stubborn bits of dried grout. Dried grout can be "toned down" by brushing on and wiping off an oil stain made by adding oil paint to turpentine.

Sealing

The grout between tesserae or the entire grouted surface can be made stainproof or waterproof by coating it with a silicone or another waterproof sealer. Pieces that are used or displayed outdoors or that come in contact with liquids should be recoated with sealer periodically. The sealer can be applied with a dry, lint-free cloth or brush or simply poured onto a finished project. Let stand for a few seconds and pour off any excess. Allow to dry for about 2 hours and finally buff with a soft, dry cloth.

Projects You Can Do

Starting with a small project, such as an ashtray, trivet, or wall plaque, gives the beginner an opportunity — with a minimum investment in equipment and supplies — to become familiar with mosaic materials, to explore possibilities of basic techniques, and, to produce an interesting and satisfying mosaic piece in a relatively short time.

This simple project, using the direct method, may also be used as a coaster, paperweight, or decorative wall plaque.

Equipment and Supplies

For this project, the following items are needed: (1) one metal trivet frame 4¼" square, or four pieces of angle-shaped wood picture molding, mitered at the ends; (2) a square of 1/8" thick masonite or pressed board, cut to fit the frame; (3) 100 ceramic tiles (for example, 50 white and 50 black ceramic tiles); (4) mosaic adhesive such as white glue or mastic (approximately 2 ounces); (5) spatula, palette knife, putty knife, or tongue depressor for spreading adhesive and grout; (6) 1/2 pound of grout; (7) silicone polish or sealer; (8) 4 strips of sheet cork or felt backing if necessary; (9) masking tape 1" wide; (10) soft cloth or sponge; (11) steel wool or copper scouring pad; and (12) mixing bowl and newspaper.

Procedures

Spread newspaper on work area. If using picture molding, glue the pieces together with white glue or some other carpenter's adhesive and allow several hours to dry. (This is best done the day before doing the mosaic project.) Apply a coat of silicone sealer to both sides of the masonite square and let dry.

Put masking tape around edges of the frame to protect it from adhesive or grout stains. Then apply a ribbon of mosaic adhesive around the inside bottom of the frame. Place the masonite square into the frame, smooth side up.

If necessary, soak tesserae loose from paper backing. Soak in warm water and wipe dry.

Apply a ribbon of mosaic adhesive onto the ma-

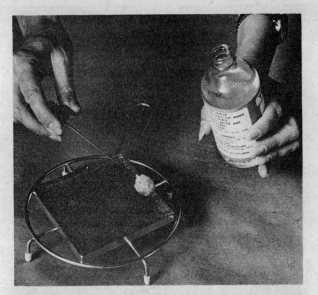

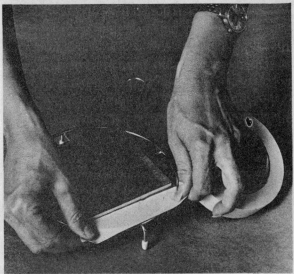

Figure 14. To make a hot plate or trivet, the first steps are applying silicone sealer to the masonite square (top), and then placing masking tape around the four edges of the frame (bottom).

sonite along the left edge, working down from the top left corner. For example, place a black tile, ridged side down, into the adhesive at upper left corner. Next to it, along the left edge, place a white tile; then black, white, black, etc. Space the tiles in the first row by moving gently with forefinger or a toothpick.

Apply a ribbon of adhesive into the next row. Place tiles, starting with a white one at the top. Space as above. Repeat process until all 100 tiles are glued into place.

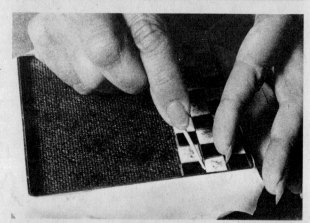

Figure 15. The next steps, shown above, are to soak the tesserae off the backing and dry the tiles. Next place a ribbon of mosaic adhesive on the masonite. The right-hand column of pictures shows the procedure for placing individual tiles, row by row, adding a ribbon of adhesive when a new row is begun. The tiles must be spaced carefully for a neat final result using the forefingers or a toothpick as shown.

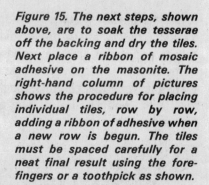

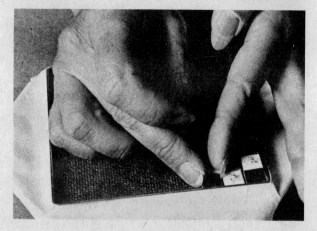

Figure 16. After the tiles have been allowed to dry properly, mix and apply grout (top row). Be sure to spread the grout thoroughly to reach all areas. Follow proper steps for cleaning grout and the result is a handsome, finished hot plate (bottom row).

Wait 8 to 20 hours (depending upon humidity or dampness) until the adhesive is dry and firmly holding the tiles. Test by trying to move the tiles with the finger. When adhesive is dry, prepare grout. Put it in a mixing bowl and add water, by pouring it down the side of the bowl, a little at a time, while stirring slowly with a spoon or by hand. Mix until grout is smooth and the consistency of heavy batter. With the hand or a rubber spatula, rub the grout over the mosaic, working it into the spaces between the tiles. Clean the grout off the surface of the tiles with a damp cloth. Be careful not to scoop out any of the grout from between the tiles. Let dry for about 30 minutes.

Then wipe again with a damp cloth and, if necessary, smooth grout between tesserae with a wet fingertip. Leave to set for about 1 hour. Then polish with a dry, soft cloth.

With a sponge or cloth, clean the trivet top and edges. If necessary, scrub top with steel wool or a copper scouring pad and scrape any excess grout from the top of the mosaic with a plastic scraper, penknife, or palette knife. To waterproof the grout, rub mosaic with silicone polish or sealer. If trivet frame does not have feet, glue four thin strips of sheet cork or felt backing to the bottom of the trivet or at the four corners.

SMALL TABLE

This is a simple project, using the indirect method, that results in an attractive and useful table.

Equipment and Supplies

To make this table, you will need the following: (1) a 12″ square of 1/2″ to 3/4″ plywood; (2) a square foot of ceramic tesserae, pasted face down on paper; (3) adhesive such as white glue or mastic; (4) 3/4 to 1 pound of grout or mosaic cement; (5) spatula, putty knife, palette knife, or tongue depressor for spreading adhesive, grout, or cement; (6) mixing bowl; (7) masking tape, 1″ wide; (8) sponge, cloth, and newspaper; (9) shellac and brush; (10) silicone polish or sealer; (11) lighter fluid for clean-up, if necessary; and (12) 4 screw-on legs.

Procedures

Spread newspapers on floor beneath table frame. Shellac plywood square on both sides and let dry. Nail metal edging to plywood. Then screw legs into plywood base. Place masking tape around metal edging to protect it while working.

Check the sheet of tesserae to see that all pieces are attached to the paper and are facedown. If any have come loose, glue them back in place with a water-soluble glue or a water solvent flour paste. With the paper side down (bottom side of the tesserae up), wet tesserae with a sponge until they are thoroughly dampened.

Put grout or cement in a bowl. Add water, pouring it down side of bowl, a little at a time, while stirring slowly with a spoon or by hand. Mix until grout is smooth and is the consistency of heavy pancake batter. Pour three-fourths of the grout or cement evenly over the entire surface of the plywood.

Redampen bottom side of the tesserae. Place the entire sheet, paper side up (bottom side of the tesserae down) into the wet grout or cement. Push the paper and tesserae around until the paper is evenly spaced on the base. Push down firmly with the hand until the paper surface is level with the table top edge. Starting in the center, and using the flat of the hand, rub out to the edges of the

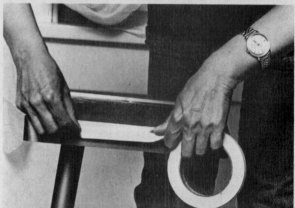

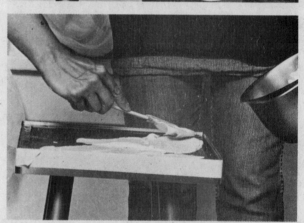

Figure 17. To prepare the table frame for this project, first shellac the wood (top). Mask the edges of the table (center) to protect them from grout; then apply grout, as shown (bottom).

paper sheet. Squeeze any excess grout or cement out over the edges. Continue until the top is perfectly level. (A flat board or rolling pin can be used for pressing and leveling.)

Let the cement or grout set for a few minutes. With a wet cloth or sponge, thoroughly dampen the paper holding the tesserae together. Let paper soak for a few minutes. Then, holding one edge of the paper between thumb and forefinger, pull it up and remove it in one piece, if possible, or in long strips. If paper continues to adhere to the tesserae, sponge it again. But, do not dilute the grout or cement with too much water, as this may weaken its consistency. If individual pieces pull up with the paper, push them down into place after removing the paper.

Straighten any pieces that are out of line. Equalize surface around any that are pushed down too far by gently rubbing hand over area around tesserae. If this does not level the surface, pry up the piece, place a bit more grout or cement into the area, and replace. Fill in any areas between tesserae with more grout or cement, redampening it if necessary, until cracks between are filled level with tesserae. Place a matting of dampened newspaper over the entire top and let the grout or cement dry gradually, usually 8 to 10 hours. The matting prevents the cement from drying too quickly and becoming brittle or powdery.

When the cement is dry, wipe off the chalky film surface with a damp cloth or sponge. If cement or grout spots remain on the tesserae, dampen surface thoroughly and rub with fine steel wool. Clean off and wipe dry. Waterproof the cement or grout between tesserae with silicone polish or sealer. Remove masking tape from the edging. Clean off any adhesive or foreign matter with lighter fluid.

Note: If desired, a mosaic of original design can be applied indirectly to the top of the table. The top can be made from personally selected tesserae rather than a square foot of ceramic tesserae.

In this case, soak tesserae in warm water for 10 to 20 minutes to loosen backing paper. Peel off paper, and dry tesserae with cloth or towel. Separate into piles by color shades. When shellac on plywood square has dried, place a sheet of heavy paper (kraft paper) on the surface. Trace outline of top and cut it out. (Cut-out shape should fit exactly the table top and barely miss touching edging.) Draw the design on the paper (backwards, if it is not to be reversed on the table top). Spread water-soluble glue (e.g., Duco cement) or a flour/water paste mixture on small areas of the design and apply individual tesserae face down on the paper. Depending upon the design, it may be necessary to shape and cut the tesserae with a mosaic cutter or tile nipper before pasting them down. After all tesserae are pasted onto the paper and dry, proceed as above.

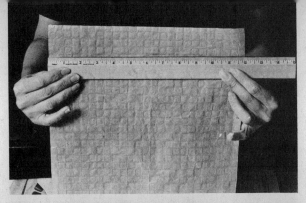

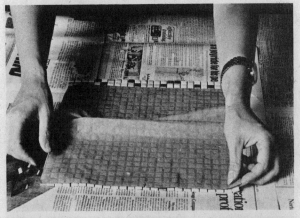

Figure 18. For a small table project, begin by (from top) measuring a 12" square on a sheet of tesserae, pasting down any loose tesserae, checking the firmness of the sheet of tesserae, and wetting the backing of the tesserae with a sponge.

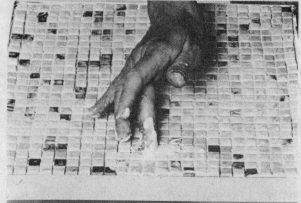

Figure 20. In the final stages of the table project (from top) press down tiles if needed. Also, apply additional grout if needed. The finished table has been carefully cleaned.

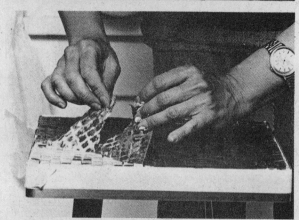

Figure 19. The next steps (from top) are to place the sheet of tesserae carefully on the table frame. Push down firmly with the fingers; then press and level with a rolling pin. Use a sponge to wet the paper backing of the tesserae sheet and then carefully remove the backing.

For Additional Reading

Aller, Doris and Diane, **Mosaics,** Lane (Sunset Craft Books), 1959.

Hendrickson, Edwin, **Mosaics: Hobby and Arts**, Hill and Wang, 1957.

Lovoos, Janice, and Paramore, Felice, **Modern Mosaic Techniques,** Waston-Guptill.

Timmons, Virginia Gayheart, **Designing and Making Mosaics,** Davis, 1971.

Williamson, Robert, **Mosaics: Design, Construction and Assembly**, Hearthside Press, 1963.

Young, Joseph, **Mosaics: Principles and Practices**, Reinhold, 1963.

Design In Crafts

Design is the underlying groundwork and foundation for organizing all crafts and their materials.

Design is order, and to find pleasure in design is a universal human response to the language of art and to the order that is in nature. Design is also, in arts and crafts, the cornerstone of the creative process.

The design of a work is an arrangement of space, forms, and colors in a pattern that is both aesthetically pleasing and, when necessary, functional. Today, for example, we tend to think of the Parthenon only as a work of art, as an architectural form that pleases the eye.

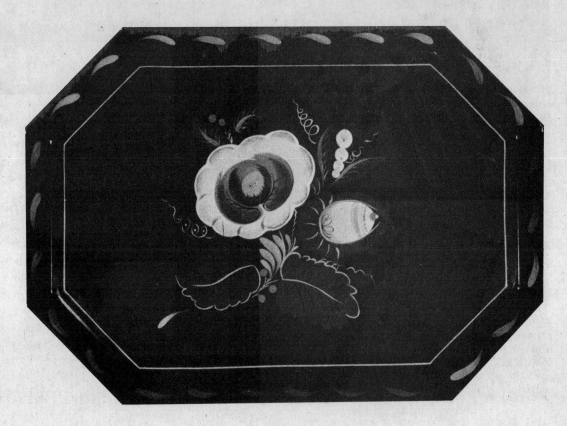

Figure 2. The classical beauty of the Acropolis in Athens, which reaches its height in the Parthenon, exemplifies symmetrical design and harmony.

The ancient Greeks who built it, however, thought of the Parthenon not only as an aesthetically pleasing and satisfying architectural form but also, and perhaps first and foremost, as a functional building. They *used* it. In it they worshipped their gods. The Parthenon was not only beautiful, but useful. This was so because of its design — a *good* architectural design, since it incorporated both the aesthetically pleasing and the functional.

Figure 1. In every area of crafts, the artist must combine the principles of good design and composition with his own creative imagination and his skill in working with materials.

In the visual arts and crafts — which include architecture, painting, and sculpture, or combinations of all three — it is chiefly in architecture and in crafts that design is called upon to furnish aesthetic pleasure and at the same time serve a human purpose. From his study of architectural forms from ancient times, Louis Sullivan, the renowned Chicago architect of the late nineteenth and early twentieth century, gave his profession the concept that a building's design should express its use, often stated in the dictum "form follows function." Of course, in painting and in sculpture, as opposed to architecture, the chief and sometimes only function of the completed work is to please the senses.

The English work "design" comes from the Latin *designare*, which means "to mark out." Used as a verb, the English word means to make a plan or pattern for a unified and coherent whole. Used as a noun, the word means the manifestation of that plan or pattern in the completed whole.

All design begins in nature. Every snowflake, for example, has its own unique pattern. And when the basic elements of human design are investigated, it is found that all of them originate in models from nature such as a snowflake, or a leaf, or an egg, or even the stripes of a zebra. Why this is so is not known, but it is generally agreed that derivations from natural models are intrinsically satisfying to humans. They are both aesthetically pleasing and, when they must be functional.

Thus, there is no proper history of human design. There are and have been many different "schools" of design, but all of them throughout history have relied upon one or more aspects of elemental, natural design. What we today label as Egyptian, Greek, Etruscan, or Roman art, or as the Byzantine or Romanesque or Italian Renaissance or Flemish schools of painting, sculpture, or architecture, or as Impressionism or Cubism or any one of a score of more recent movements in the arts, all have their basis in elemental, natural design.

It does happen, however, that for a time some specific school or movement will achieve prominence and exert a strong influence on artists and craftsmen. One of these in fairly recent times was Art Nouveau, which flourished at the end of the last century and the beginning of this one. Its principles enjoyed a wide revival in the United States and Europe in the 1960s, this more recent influence extending to advertising, fabric design, illustration, and interior decorating.

Figure 3. Natural design is found everywhere, waiting for the careful observer who can see the patterns of dandelion seeds or the veining of a leaf. (Courtesy, The Volume Library.)

Figure 4. Sand sculptured by the wind creates a panorama of curved, three-dimensional forms and patterns. (Courtesy, The Volume Library.)

Preceded by and influenced by the Pre-Raphaelites (one of whose artistic principles was "to study nature attentively"), Art Nouveau emphasized flowing linear patterns related to natural forms together with flat color patterns. The lamps designed by Louis Tiffany are Art Nouveau, for example, as are the architecture of the Spaniard Gaudí and the exotic, sensual illustrations of the Englishman Aubrey Beardsley. Traces of the movement's influence can be found in the works of such artists as Pierre Bonnard, Paul Gauguin, Edvard Munch, and Henri de Toulouse-Lautrec, to name only a few. Its influence can also be seen in the intricately embellished decorative work done by Louis Sullivan for the buildings he designed.

The turn of the twentieth century, in fact, was a period of great excitement in design and crafts. Closely related to Art Nouveau and to the Pre-Raphaelites, William Morris's "arts and crafts movement" flourished in England. It was both a social and an aesthetic movement, emphasizing handwork in opposition to the late-Victorian ugliness of mass-produced factory items. Morris's work had a tremendous impact throughout Europe. It led to the establishment of the Wiener Werkstätten, an influential organization of craftsmen and designers, at Vienna in 1903. The ideas of the movement were adapted by the Bauhaus and, still later, by contemporary Scandinavian designers.

The Bauhaus was a more recent but extremely influential school of design. It was an actual school — that is, students attended classes there — founded by Walter Gropius at Weimar, Germany, in 1919. The Bauhaus attempted to do away with distinctions between "fine" art and "applied" art and to combine in its instruction both the accepted

Figure 5. The intricate designs and flowing lines of Art Nouveau style are shown perfectly in Beardsley's pen drawing for an edition of "Le Morte d'Arthur."

THE LADY OF THE LAKE TELLETH ARTHVR OF THE SWORD EXCALIBVR

principles of art through the ages and the concepts introduced by twentieth-century technology. One of these concepts was that the twentieth-century artist is actually a craftsman who must satisfy a specific need — a principle that would surely have been endorsed by pyramid makers, Gothic cathedral builders, Renaissance painters, and followers of Morris as well. Another principle of the Bauhaus was that the artist should have practical training in craftwork to acquaint himself with materials and processes. To this end the school offered courses in ceramics, weaving, and stained-glass design.

In 1925 the school moved from Weimar to Dessau, where its founder, Gropius, designed a building to house it, an asymmetrical structure whose dynamic composition exemplified another Bauhaus aim: the unification of all the arts and crafts in architecture. The building is, of course, both functional and aesthetically pleasing. Gropius himself, however, was wary of simplifying to the extent that Sullivan had; that is, he would not say that the function of an art object (or a technological product) must necessarily determine its appearance, or form.

Figure 6. Picasso's 1910 "Nude" (left) shows the abstract design so prominent in Cubist painting.

Figure 7. Perfect symmetry of design is found in the unique crystal structure of each snowflake.

The Bauhaus closed when Hitler came to power in Germany in the early 1930s, but many of its teachers came to the United States and taught and designed here, including Gropius and Ludwig Mies van der Rohe. Their influence on contemporary urban architecture and design has been tremendous — it can be seen not only in stark glass and steel buildings throughout the country, but also in such diverse fields as typography and tableware design, and, in general, the contemporary approach to art education.

The basic, elemental aspects of all good design are symmetry, or the lack of it (asymmetry), balance, line, rhythm, and repetition — in sum, the arrangement of form and mass and colors in space. The human eye perceives design in mountains and in shorelines, and in grains of sand and snowflakes. The artist understands these perceptions and utilizes them in his creations. The two wings of a butterfly, for example, which duplicate each other in reverse and balance each other more or less perfectly, have the quality known as symmetry, a quality that is thought to give humans a feeling of security. The eye follows the flow of the wings' pattern and returns to its beginning reassured by it. In their works, creative artists and craftsmen often utilize this element of design to enhance the impression their finished work will make upon the viewer.

The blossoms on the stem of a flower, on the other hand, are usually asymmetrically balanced. That is, they may not duplicate each other in reverse but overall they *will* balance, perhaps with two small blossoms on one side of the stem and a larger blossom on the other side. In the same manner, the leaves on a tree limb may be asymmetrically placed, but balanced overall. Moreover, they will repeat each other rhythmically around the limb. This is their natural design. In man-made designs, artists often try to convey this same quality.

In nature, of course, we see everything as lines — diagonal, horizontal, perpendicular, circular.

Figure 8. In his "organic" plan for houses like Fallingwater, architect Frank Lloyd Wright integrated architectural style with the natural forms of the setting. (Courtesy, The Volume Library.)

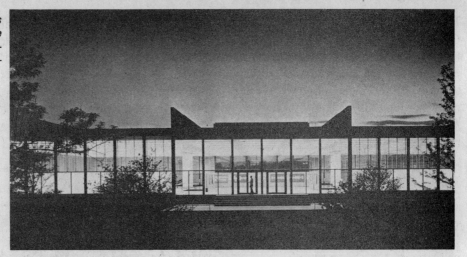

Figure 9. Mies van der Rohe's buildings utilize the pure form of typical Bauhaus design. (Courtesy, Illinois Institute of Technology.)

Figure 10. An aerial view reveals intricate geometric patterns on the landscape. (Courtesy, Canadian Government Travel Bureau.)

Whatever his medium, the artist must also use lines: horizontals for their quality of calmness, perhaps, diagonals for tension, and so forth, with different types of lines combined and opposed to achieve different effects. Combinations of lines — combinations that are usually repeated rhythmically, sometimes with slight variations to add interest — are used especially by designers in the decorative arts and crafts.

A final element of design is a harmonious relationship between parts, that is, an overall pattern. The bell tower of St. Mark's, Venice, for example, exhibits a harmonious relationship between all of its parts. So, too, do Michelangelo's *David*, da Vinci's *Mona Lisa*, Rembrandt's *The Night Watch*, and Picasso's *Les Demoiselles d'Avignon*. So, too, do a patchwork quilt, an Oriental rug, a windmill, a Grecian urn — as well as a stalk of corn, a snowflake, and the body of a butterfly. The bell tower of St. Mark's, incidentally, was begun in the ninth century but not finished until the sixteenth, when the belfry and spire were added. So harmonious is the relationship of the tower's parts, however, that even though it was built over a period of almost seven centuries, it still gives viewers the impression of a unified and coherent whole.

Design, then, is the ordering of space, forms, and colors so that human beings feel comfortable with the arrangement. Design is, however, only one element in a visual or craft object. Such objects have at their source not only the ordering of space so that humans feel at ease with the arrangement but also so that, in the finest art, they feel lifted out of themselves to a higher plane of feeling, just as they often are by what they discover in nature.

Figure 11. *An intricate four-layer woven design, shown in a natural setting, displays harmony in form and color.*

Common Terms Used In Design in Crafts

Asymmetry: a form of composition that lacks symmetry because one side is generally different from the other; the design, however, is still usually balanced.

Balance: the harmonious relationship or arrangement of the elements in a design so that they are in proper proportion to each other.

Composition: the arrangement of elements in the design for an object that is being created.

Design Feasibility: the determination of whether an object can actually be made from the proposed design.

Dynamic: in design, a composition that appears to be moving, stimulating, and generally of a rather exciting nature.

Grid: the underlying pattern that provides the format or arrangement for a design.

Harmony: the rhythmic cohesiveness in a composition so that all parts form a unified whole without any element of discord.

Inversion: in symmetry, the 180° displacement of a unit.

Mirroring: in symmetry, the creation of a mirror image of a design element.

Modular System: in design, a system of organization comprised of identical units called modules.

Module: a unit in a design that is exactly the same as every other unit in that design.

Proportion: the balanced unity of all elements in a design.

Regularity: the repetitive aspect of a design in which proportions and modules are all the same.

Rotation: in symmetry, the moving of a design unit around a center point with the same part of the unit always facing toward the center.

Static: a design characterized by elements that appear to be fixed or stationary.

Symmetry: a form of composition in which all parts correspond in size, form, and arrangement on opposite sides of a plane, line, or point.

Translation: in symmetry, the repetition of the basic elements along a line of design so that they are all oriented in the same direction.

Basic Equipment And Supplies

The word "design," as used in history and in present-day arts and crafts, refers to the basic elements and principles of composition — the orderly plan that determines the aesthetic effectiveness of an artistic object. Design does not affect the physical properties of materials themselves, but the way in which materials are arranged, ordered, and combined to create a work of art. When working with clay, for instance, design affects the form of the pottery, not the clay itself.

The designer/artist/craftsman must, of course, consider his or her chosen material when thinking of the design. The material disciplines the artist's design concept. For instance, an artist would not choose to make a large table of clay, but would use a material more appropriate to the object's function, such as wood, metal, or plastic. Each material has certain possibilities and limitations. The inherent characteristics of a material — its strength or fragility, its rigidity or malleability, its durability or delicacy — define how far the designer can go in experimenting in terms of design.

This principle of *design feasibility* or practicability is based on determining the function of an object and then relating the design concept to an appropriate and suitable material. In making a wind chime, for instance, the choice of that particular object determines the function; then the design is conceived, and finally the construction materials are selected. If the design includes tubular shapes, such materials as hollow wood (bamboo), thrown clay forms, metal tubing, or all three could be used. If the design concept calls for flat or varied shapes,

materials that might be selected include plastic discs, sea shells, fired clay, or found objects such as juice-can lids.

To design an object efficiently, first work out the formal concept of what the object is and what it is to look like; then see which material best suits the design. The process of determining design feasibility begins with the design idea, which is sketched and then studied carefully. Next to the sketch, make notations indicating essential ideas: color, texture, how and where the object will be used. The attentive craftsman will then put the initial design aside and return to it later to restudy the concept and revise or add to his original idea.

When a composition has been conceived and the materials chosen, the design should be analyzed to discover what is good about it or what should be changed to improve it. Compositional sense — at least good compositional sense — is not something that is learned overnight. It is usually acquired by practice and experience. The craftsman discovers by trial and error which combinations will help him to achieve the effect he wants. It is best to begin by following known paths — the work of other designers, the principles established in great paintings and sculpture.

Follow known paths, too, in learning to work with a given material. Work and practice step by step until the correct sequence is mastered. Once the physical processes of handling the chosen materials have been mastered, it is time to be creative and try out original designs. Within the limitations of the material and his skill in working with it, the craftsman's aim is to achieve a design that is aesthetically pleasing. There are several ways of organizing materials to do this.

Figure 12. Choosing materials that are suitable for the design concept is an important step, whether the craft be pottery making or crewel work.

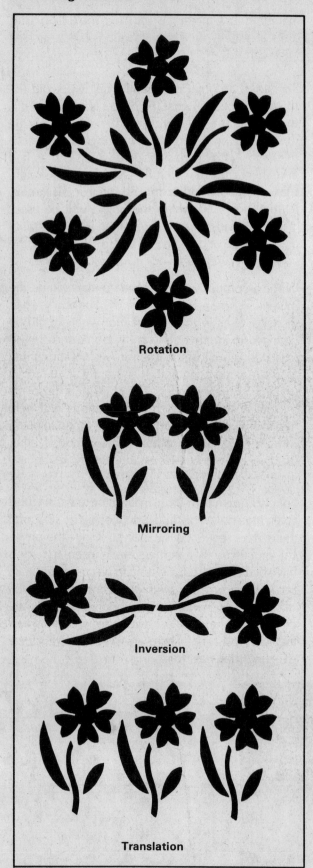

Figure 13. Symmetry Operations

Rotation

Mirroring

Inversion

Translation

SYMMETRY

The easiest, most common, and most obvious form of visual organization is *symmetry*. The principle of symmetry is easy to learn and to apply because it has its own set of rules. When these rules are followed, the composition will always work in a certain way. Symmetry is a sort of "fail-safe" system of composition, but it is useful both as a system of design and as a learning tool.

There are four "rules" of symmetry, called symmetry operations. They are mirroring, rotation, inversion, and translation. In each operation, the space relationships between the elements change to achieve a different effect, a different "feel." Each one results in a different basic pattern of organization. It is important to bear in mind, however, that although these operations are described as distinct processes, they are most effective and most frequently used in combination.

The first operation is mirroring. This operation is exactly what it says: the creation of a mirror image. To experiment with the simplest example of mirroring, take a sheet of paper and draw a line down the middle. Now, on one side of the median line, draw any simple pattern. Then hold a pocket mirror along the line so that it reflects the pattern. The pattern is, of course, exactly reversed — right becomes left and vice versa.

Rotation is another of the symmetry operations. As the name implies, it refers to moving an element of

Figure 14. Design elements are repeated along a line in this ancient frieze, a detail from the Treasury of Atreus at Mycenae, built about 1500 B.C. (Courtesy, The Metropolitan Museum of Art; original in the British Museum.)

design around in a circular motion. The same side of the shape or form must always face the inside of the imaginary circle that is the basis of this design. Rotation might typically be used for the center of a mosaic, for example, because it is an interest-drawing focal point. One can use partial rotation or complete the operation, whichever better suits the purpose of the design. Rotation can be the starting point for many intricate designs.

Inversion is the third symmetry operation: turning the basic design element upside down and back-wards. It is just as controlled as any of the other operations. In fact, it can be expressed very pre-cisely as a 180° displacement from the standard position. Inversion is unique in the symmetry oper-ations, however, because the relationship between the initial position and the inverted one is quite unlike the others.

The last symmetry operation is translation. Transla-tion is merely the theoretical term for repeating the basic elements in a line so that they are all oriented in the same direction.

Symmetrical organization appears in many natural forms. A tall stand of cattails growing for miles around a lake shore can be seen as an example of translation. Their reflection in the water creates a mirror image. Rotation appears, for instance, in the arrangement of flower petals around the center of a flower or in the arrangement of clover leaves around the stem.

In each case, note that the combining elements are all the same — a cattail stalk, a flower petal. This is also true when the symmetry operations are ap-plied to many basic patterns in crafts. In a mosaic table top, for example, the simplest design element, a square, is used. Each tile is exactly the same. Even when the design is inverted, or mirrored, or other-wise altered, the basic element remains the same. And underlying each design using the basic square is a basic format — the checkerboard.

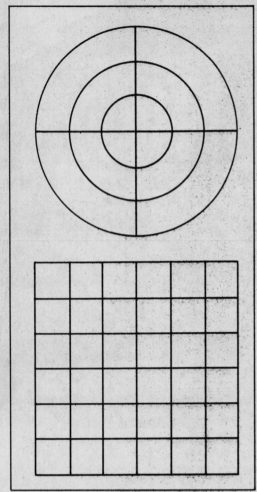

Figure 15. Grids (above) reveal the underlying format of a design. Each stitch in a needlepoint pattern (right) can be planned on a grid.

Grids

In the case of a pattern using edge-to-edge squares, the basic underlying format is the checkerboard grid. In all cases, a grid is the underlying format that relates similar design units. The designer chooses units that are the same in shape, size, and weight. The grid simply reinforces the basic arrangement. It demonstrates each element's relationship to other parts of the composition.

The checkerboard grid is a familiar one. It can be used as the underlying format in ways as varied as laying out the streets of a city, planning the design of a rug, or working out an intricate Scandinavian sweater pattern. It is, of course, not the only possible grid that the designer can use.

Modular Systems

In the symmetry operations and in using the grid, the design units consistently utilized are identical. Each unit is the same, and all are interchangeable within the design framework. The units are called *modules*. A module is a unit that is exactly the same as every other unit in its system.

Modular systems are not new, but they are peculiarly typical of contemporary design thinking. There are several reasons for this: modular units can be mass-produced, making them inexpensive. They are easy to use. And they are flexible in their application, which makes them appropriate in a mobile, changing society.

In furniture, modular units provide a choice of arrangements and a flexibility in the number and placement of the units. Modular systems are widely used in contemporary construction, notably in prefabricated housing units, in identical units put together in skyscrapers, and even in entire housing complexes such as Habitat. Bricklaying illustrates

Figure 16. Modular construction is the key concept in Habitat, the innovative, 158-unit housing complex built for Expo '67 in Montreal. (Courtesy, Wide World Photos.)

an ancient modular system; steel-beam construction involves modules also.

Fresh and creative design ideas within the modular concept are an important aspect of contemporary design. But the module is by no means the only design element with which the designer and craftsman can work.

Variations From Symmetry

A symmetrical organization, by its very nature, is regular. The proportions are all the same, the design units (or modules) all the same. This regularity sometimes may be too repetitive for the designer's taste, or it may not work in the piece being created. Before leaving symmetry altogether, try making some progressive changes within the established system.

For instance, if the grid that constitutes the basic format is made up of 2" squares, try using a few 4" squares as a variation. A 4" square will fit into the same modular system (taking the place of four smaller squares), but it will effectively break the monotony and add a pleasing variation to the design. One can use the larger squares in regular or irregular ways: they can be inserted in a regular pattern or interspersed more or less at random throughout the design.

Remember that when irregularity is introduced, it may be hard to control. Be careful where nonconforming elements are placed. Unless one adheres

to design judgments and basic principles already described, the nonconforming elements will not appear as pleasing variations, but as intruders in the design.

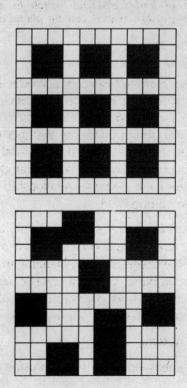

Figure 17. Although both these basketry designs are symmetrical, they also show the interesting spatial relationships that make a composition dynamic.

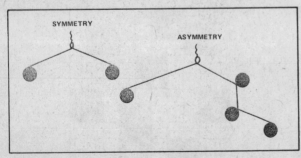

Figure 19.

One of the criticisms often made of compositions based on symmetry is that they are too static. In fact, symmetrical compositions may be quite dynamic. These two design factors do not have a one-to-one correspondence.

Simply, static compositions tend to sit in one place visually. There is little eye movement involved in looking at them. In a dynamic composition, on the other hand, the eye moves through the composition discovering spatial relationships between areas. If this latter type of composition is desired, then the eye plan should be fluid. It should not stop. There must always be a path for the eye to follow.

A dynamic composition is not necessarily "better" or "worse" than a static one; it is merely planned differently. The designer should decide which type of composition — static or dynamic — will best fulfill his expectations and wishes for the object he is creating and the effects he wants to achieve.

ASYMMETRY

In a symmetrical composition, one half of the composition matches the other in a predetermined way. Its obvious opposite is asymmetry.

Neither symmetry nor assymetry is necessarily static or dynamic, balanced or unbalanced. These are all separate factors that operate independently. Symmetrical compositions, as already mentioned, can be either static or dynamic, but they are always balanced within the harmonious nature of symmetry. Asymmetrical compositions are often dynamic, although they too may be static if the designer wants them to be. But an asymmetrical composition should also be balanced.

Harmony in Composition

Is an asymmetrical composition "harmonic"? Harmony in composition is the result of good proportions, of well-defined relationships between areas, and of balance. Some combinations create harmony; others create discord. Therefore, an asymmetrical composition can be harmonic or not, depending on how the basic relationships are handled.

To achieve harmonic compositions, consider the relationships between the parts. Such relationships can be definite and obvious, or subtle and ambiguous. Beginning designers and craftsmen may feel more comfortable if they begin working toward clear and definite relationships, trying the ambiguous ones when they have had more practice.

First, look at the space relationships within the design. Are the elements of the composition so close together that the eye cannot appreciate each shape, or are they so far apart that they have no relationship at all? Does the design continue throughout the entire composition? Are the spatial relationships monotonous? Perhaps they should be varied.

JUDGING AN ORIGINAL DESIGN

At the beginning, try each concept one step at a time. First try symmetry. Then try changing to asymmetry. Strive for good spatial relationships; work on achieving balance and harmony.

Always draw out a plan first. Then decide on a material that is suitable and feasible for both the design and one's budget. Try to be imaginative and to put ingenuity to work in design concepts. The craftsman should apply his own sense of design and his own taste in design when planning a project.

Once a design is completed, put it away for a while before reviewing it critically. Then ask these questions:

Does the design have good proportion?

Is the composition too repetitive?

Is there too much going on?

Could the parts be better related to one another?

Are the spatial relationships well organized?

Does one side balance visually with the other? (To test this, imagine the work suspended from the center by a string. Does one side seem or feel as though it would hang lower than the other? If so, the composition is out of balance.)

Finally, is the design the best you can do?

Then begin your project and enjoy it. When it is finished, ask the same questions that were asked about the design. Planning and revising designs are only half the game. Making the piece is the other half.

Figure 18. A well-designed mobile tests the craftsman's ability to combine asymmetrical design with good balanced composition.

Figure 19. In this pattern, negative and positive areas can be arranged and experimented with for interesting visual effects.

Projects You Can Do

Each of the following projects should be considered as an exercise in applying the design principles discussed earlier. They will provide practice in creating and manipulating compositional forms, bridging the gap between theory and working with the materials chosen.

EXERCISE ONE

With a sheet of black construction paper, cut out a pattern similar to the one in the illustration. Use a knife to cut the patterns carefully, leaving the positive and negative sections intact. Then fasten each section with glue or tape to a light-colored (preferably white) board. Which seems stronger — the negative shape design or the positive one? What kind of result could be achieved by placing parts of the negative design in with the positive design? Do some of the shapes or areas lose their definition?

By working with two sets of the pattern, one can develop an awareness of shape definition. A white figure (positive) on a dark background (negative) is often more powerful than a dark figure on a light ground. In thinking about why this is so, consider another idea: in writing dark ink is used on white paper; the eye is also accustomed to reading dark type on light paper. The dark element is always the figure, the lighter color the ground. By reversing this pattern and placing the white figure on a dark background, the ordinary is changed into an unusual perceptual phenomenon.

Through such reversals of the ordinary and the expected, many unusual designs can be created. However, the aim is not just to be different, but to find out what effect an unusual compositional handling will have on a design that might otherwise be ordinary.

Color reversal is only one example of the factors that can give designs an unusual viewpoint. The more distinctly personal an artist makes his work — so that it is unique to his way of working — the closer he is to creating and developing his own style, one that sets his work apart from others in the same field. This personal style is the outstanding characteristic of a creative artist/craftsman.

Figure 20. An unusual and striking variation on the basic square has been achieved in these fabric-covered cubes designed by Mary Ellen Savage.

EXERCISE TWO

From magazine illustrations, cut out textures and colors that seem to be similar or related in some way. Look for large areas of solid colors or close-ups of textures such as woods, autumn leaves, snow, fabrics, and the like. Cut these areas into 1" squares.

On a piece of cardboard, draw a simple checkerboard grid of eight 1" squares by eight 1" squares. (Correctly sized graph paper can also be used.) Begin to place the cut-out squares on the grid, working them into patterns. Try several versions of this project. Vary the grid or the colors; use the symmetry operations (mirroring, inversion, etc.) to vary the pattern. For instance, perhaps the squares include many shades and textures of blue. Using only blue tones, from very pale to navy, will hold the composition together, no matter how sporadic the design. The color is the unifying factor. Then try a two-color design, perhaps yellow and brown. By patterning these colors in a definite order, all sorts of design and pattern relationships can be created.

Variations

How can this exercise be applied in original work? Consider a construction using squares of clear and smoked plastic, or a needlepoint design for a jacket, or stained wood squares glued together to make a cheese board or trivet.

As an alternative, vary the size. For instance, use tiny squares (say, ⅛") of silver and brass soldered or enameled together to make a medallion. Or, to go in the opposite direction, try huge squares of poured concrete alternating with bricks grouped in squares for an unusual patio floor.

Don't overlook any possibility for variations on this same theme. For example, combine large squares of cork with mirrored tiles to personalize a small wall at home; or cut and lead stained glass in alternating colors, then frame them to use as a window covering.

All these ideas were generated from one simple square grid. Use other grid patterns and try to devise some original ideas. While doing so, experiment with various shapes and with shapes grouped differently over the grid. Look for unusual patterns that are interesting and that seem to have a practical application in your craft.

Whatever the project, be meticulous. Ask yourself if all the possibilities have been explored. Can one or two particular designs be developed even further? Then return to the same questions that were asked earlier about the design. Each time the design is reviewed and revised, it will be reshaped and clarified. The better the artist becomes at clarifying his designs, the better the end product will be.

EXERCISE THREE

The last exercise involves exploring other variations on a basic theme to generate design possibilities from a basic compositional idea. This exercise concentrates on using imagination in terms of materials. Take a piece of jewelry as an example: a band necklace from which a small medallion is suspended. In the original concept, imagine that the band necklace is silver; the medallion is a silver crescent backed with rosewood and decorated with two small pearls. The piece, then, has four components and three different materials — silver, rosewood, and pearls.

The first variation could be in the band necklace itself: make it of copper or bronze or even leather. Or replace it with a gold or silver chain. The second piece, the silver crescent, could be made of bronze, copper, or wood. Next, the pearls could be replaced with agates or other semiprecious stones or even small beads. Finally, the rosewood could be replaced by any other decorative wood, by several kinds of metal, or even by clear or smoked plastic. From the same basic design, at least 20 different necklaces could be generated.

This imaginative way of thinking can be applied to nearly any kind of craft material. All one needs to do is draw the design on paper and then substitute materials that seem compatible with it. Thus, one compositional design can be the starting point for any number of creative, unusual works.

For Additional Reading

Kepes, Gyorgy, **The Language of Vision,** Theobald, 1945.

Moholy-Nagy, Laszlo, **Vision in Motion,** Theobald, 1947.

Naylor, Gillian, **The Bauhaus,** Dutton Studio Vista.

Neumann, Eckhard, **Bauhaus and Bauhaus People,** Van Nostrand Reinhold, 1970.

Papanek, Victor, **Design for the Real World,** Pantheon, 1971.

Pevsner, Nikolaus, **The Sources of Modern Architecture and Design,** Praeger, 1968.

Thomas, Richard K., **Three Dimensional Design,** Van Nostrand Reinhold, 1969.

Wong, Wucius, **Two Dimensional Design.**

Figure 21. These examples of the potter's and the weaver's crafts illustrate how the basic principles of good design can be applied in varied kinds of work.

Candlemaking

When the invention of electricity replaced candles as the prime source of light, candle making became a beautiful and creative art.

Candles date back to the first civilizations. Egyptians placed candles in their tombs, and their drawings depicted cone-shaped candles held aloft in dishlike holders. The Greeks left many candlesticks in Crete which date from about 3000 B.C.

The Romans had both tallow and wax candles. Tallow candles were called "dips"; the tallow was rendered from beef or mutton suet. The process of making dips was simple, but tedious. Several strands of yarn, serving as the wick, were dipped into the melted fat and allowed to cool. The dipping and cooling processes were repeated alternately until the desired thickness was reached. Wax candles or "tapers," made of beeswax, were produced by repeatedly pouring melted beeswax over a suspended wick and removing any unevenness in the finished candle by rolling it over a hard surface. Beeswax tapers were so costly that only the wealthy could afford them. Thus, dips made of tallow were the most common source of lighting. The common folk used a rushlight, consisting of a reed stripped to the pith and dipped in oil.

Figure 1. This tin and wood candle mold (opposite) is from a nineteenth-century Shaker community in Canterbury, New Hampshire. (Courtesy, The Henry Francis du Pont Winterthur Museum.)

Figure 2. Large candle molds such as this were useful during the mid-1800s when candles where the main source of lighting. (Courtesy, The Henry Francis du Pont Winterthur Museum.)

Candle making was exclusively a domestic project for many years, but, with the growth of medieval town life, it became a specialized craft. In the large cities of Europe, guilds of chandlers — one for tallow and one for wax — were set up in the thirteenth century. These were designed to maintain the distinction between the two candle types. The chandlers went from house to house making candles. In the fifteenth century, a Monsieur de Brez of Paris invented the candle mold. This was important only to tallow chandlers because beeswax could not be molded satisfactorily.

The emergence of modern candles began in the nineteenth century. The first improvement was by a French chemist, M. E. Chevreul, who proved that fats were composed of fatty acids and glycerin. These components, when separated under pressure, produce palmitic and stearic acids, the substance of the superior stearin candle. From this beginning, new processes for producing pure candle stock appeared in rapid succession. The next important ingredient was spermaceti, which was derived from the oil in the head cavity of the sperm whale. This produced a candle with superior illuminating power, but the candle was extremely brittle. This brittleness was corrected by the addition of beeswax.

The successful production of paraffin wax in 1850 was of great importance. By 1855, paraffin was being profitably produced in England, Europe, and the United States. Discovery of petro-

Figure 3. Tapers were made in this tin candle mold, which dates back to the mid-nineteenth century. (Courtesy, The Henry Francis du Pont Winterthur Museum.)

leum in the United States in 1859 made possible the economical production of paraffin. Its disadvantage — a low melting point — was overcome by combining it with stearic acid. This composite material was soon used in most candle production.

The modern candle-making machine evolved from Joseph Morgan's machine of 1834. This was the first which permitted continuous wicking and ejection of molded candles by movable pistons. These machines can produce up to 1500 candles an hour. For certain specialized purposes, tallow "dips" are still produced. Beeswax and taper candles are still produced in the same way as they were in the fifth century, the major difference being that a machine now dips thousands of candles at a time instead of two by hand.

Candles have always been popular in both spiritual ceremonies and aesthetic functions. Though candles no longer are needed for illumination, they are valued for their soft light and beauty.

Basic Equipment And Supplies

The relatively few materials needed to begin candle making are readily available from a variety of sources. For the best selection and the newest ideas, the hobby craft store is a good place to start. Most major department stores have a craft section which includes candle supplies, as well as a large variety of kits to choose from. Large craft stores which have a mail-order service are also a good source. A complete kit can also be found in a large drug store, dime store, discount variety store, or toy store.

WAX

The first item to obtain is the wax. Always use slab wax which has been produced for candle-making purposes. This is sold in 11-pound blocks and will make approximately four quart-sized candles. Do not use grocery store paraffin because the melting point is too low.

The differences in wax are the hardness and the melting temperature. (The latter is the temperature at which the finished candle will melt while burning.) Low-grade wax will melt at temperatures of 125° F to 133° F. This type of wax has a limited use, such as candles for glass containers. Medium-grade wax melts at 136° F to 148° F. This is the most easily obtained type and is ideal for molded candles, sand candles, and novelty candles. The highest grade of wax melts at 155° F and is used for sculpting and hot wax baths.

The uniqueness of a candle begins with three basic items — the individual design, the scent, and the dye — which can be mixed together in hundreds of combinations. Stearic acid is used to improve the quality of the candle.

DYES

There are many types of candle dyes. The easiest to find and to use are liquid color or concentrated and colored cubes of wax. As a last resort, crayons can be used, but they tend to settle, re-

Figure 4. Supplies should be systematically arranged before work is begun. A block of wax, glass molds, wicks, and various oils, chemicals, and perfumes are among the supplies shown here.

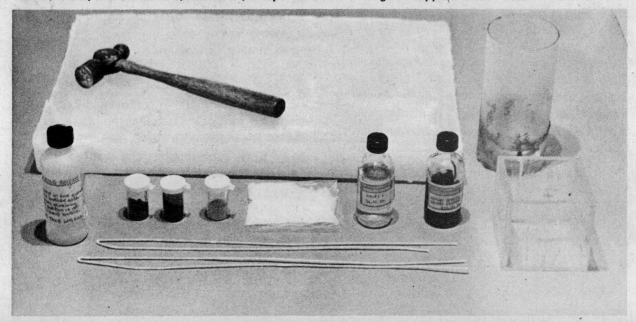

sulting in a candle of various shades. They also may smoke and sputter while burning. Do not use food coloring because it will not mix with the wax. When using cubes, start with one cube, drop it into the melted wax, and stir. Test the color by dropping a small amount of colored wax into a small dish of cold water. If liquid dye is used, add a few drops to the hot wax, stir, and test the color in the same way.

Interesting effects can be obtained by mixing colors for candles. By keeping in mind a few simple rules and by using the accompanying color chart, and endless variety of colors can be achieved for candle designs.

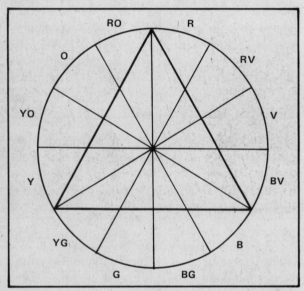

Figure 5. Color chart key: R—red, RV—red violet, V—violet, BV—blue violet, B—blue, BG—blue green, G—green, YG—yellow green, Y—yellow, YO—yellow orange, O—orange, RO—red orange.

Remember that color can always be added but that it cannot be removed. Begin, therefore, by adding just a little of the darker color; then, obtain the desired shade by adding additional color a little at a time. To tone down a color, add a tiny amount of the color that is opposite the one being used on the color chart. Again, remember to work very slowly, adding only very small amounts of color at a time.

To use the color chart, find the shade the candle is to be. For example, blue and red make purple. If, however, the candle is to be red-violet, begin adding a little more red until the desired shade is achieved.

SCENT

Candle scent, available in both liquid and tablet form, has an oil base, and mixes well with wax. Perfume can also be used so long as it has an oil base. A half ounce of scent is adequate for 2 to 3 pounds of wax.

There are two ways the scent may be added: either to the melted wax just before pouring or by soaking the wick in the scent. For a stronger scent, use both methods.

STEARIC ACID

Stearic acid increases the melting point of the candle and makes it harder. This is obviously beneficial in hot weather when candles tend to droop or bend. The acid also makes the candle more opaque and intensifies the color. Stearine or stearic acid is added to the melted wax — use about three tablespoons per pound of wax. Never use stearine in glow candles (candles in glass containers) or hot wax baths because its opaque quality will keep light from shining through.

WICK

The wick must fit the candle: a wick too small will sink into the candle and burn out; a wick too large will smoke and drip excessively. The larger the diameter of the candle, the larger the wick has to be. A woven cotton wick is the type used in all candles. When the wick is to be inserted from the top of a finished candle, the wick must first be dipped in melted wax several times until stiff. Then, heat an ice pick and make a hole down the center of the candle. Insert the stiffened wick into the hole and then fill it with melted wax. A small-sized wick is essential for thin candles up to 1¼" in diameter, a large size is for candles 1¼" to 4" in diameter. Several wicks may be inserted in oversized candles, such as sand candles.

MOLDS

Candles can be made in commercially produced molds or from objects around the house. Candle molds are made from metal, plastic, or rubber. Metal is the most durable, and many classic designs are available. Plastic comes in many novelty shapes, and in two halves which have to be clamped together. Rubber comes in one piece with a slit in the side that is sealed before pouring. Other molds which may be used are: ceramic plaster, milk and cream cartons, juice cartons, any prewaxed cartons or hard plastic containers, gelatin molds, and sherbet or drinking glasses. All of these molds should be first treated with a mold release such as a spray silicone. Pouring temperatures of wax also vary according to the type of mold that is being used: metal mold, 190° F to 200° F; plastic and rubber, 145° F to 150° F; cardboard, 145° F; and glass, 170° F.

MELTING EQUIPMENT

A few pieces of simple equipment and a stack of newspaper are all that is necessary to create a candle. Most of the necessary equipment is around the house. Begin by assembling the following items: (1) double boiler or melting pot and a pan; (2) candy thermometer; (3) pouring container (an old seamless coffee pot is perfect); (4) hobby knife or paring knife; (5) ice pick; (6) long knitting needle; (7) pencil; (8) pot holders; (9) electric hot plate (or the stove); (10) cookie sheet or aluminum foil; (11) stirring spoon with a long handle; and (12) floral clay.

Basic Procedures

The art of candle making is very easy to learn. Once the basic steps are mastered, experimentation and variation are endless. Each candle is an original because the craftsman selects the color, shape, scent, and decoration. Making the first candle from a slab of white wax is a new, exciting art form to be tried by every hobbyist. If any attempt proves unsatisfactory, just melt the candle down and start over again. There is no need for costly mistakes in candle making.

Begin by covering the work area with newspaper. Assemble all the required equipment and supplies.

PREPARING THE WAX

Break the slab of wax into small pieces by placing the wax in a sack such as a pillowcase and hitting it with a hammer. Melt the wax in a pot over boiling water to the temperature required for the mold being used. Do not get water in the wax. Check the temperature of the wax with a candy thermometer. When the wax has reached the correct melting temperature, add stearic acid (if desired). Stir this with a wooden spoon or dowel.

Figure 6. The slab of wax is broken into smaller pieces with a hammer and then added slowly to the melting pot (above). The mold to be used determines the temperature, which should be measured with a candy thermometer (below).

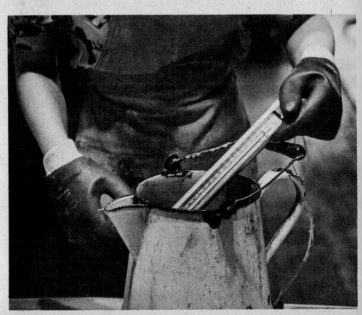

Figure 7. When the wax is melted, transfer it to another pot for mixing (above left). Stearine or stearic acid, which comes in powdered form, can then be added as a hardener. Add stearine to the liquid wax and mix well (above right).

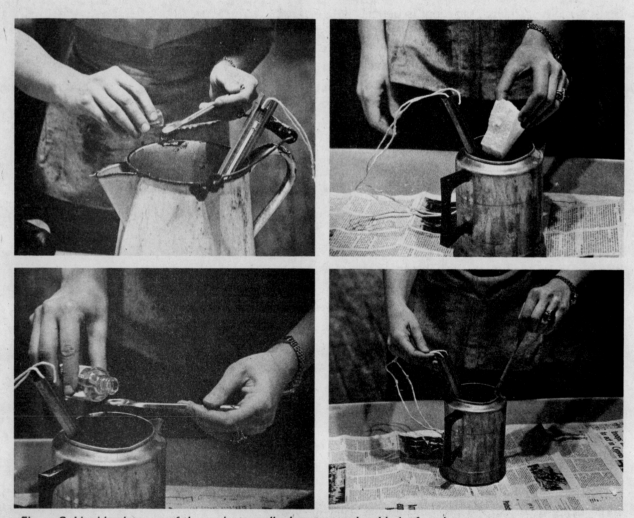

Figure 8. Liquid color, one of the easiest candle dyes to use, is added a few drops at a time (top left). Test the color by dropping a chunk of wax in cold water (top right). Scent can be added to the liquid wax (below left); or used to saturate the wick, or both. Mix it thoroughly with the liquid wax (below right).

Add color dye and add scent. Bring wax to correct temperature before pouring.

PREPARING THE MOLD

Be sure the mold is clean. Use the appropriate mold release and wipe away the excess. Thread the wick through the closed end of the mold. Cut the wick, making sure there is plenty of extra at both ends. Pull the wick taut and, with floral clay, seal over the wick and around the hole on the outside of the mold. This will prevent the hot wax from seeping out. Be sure that the mold sealer is flat enough to allow the mold to rest evenly. Turn the mold right side up. Pull the wick taut and tie it around a pencil lying across the top of the mold. Make sure the wick is in the center of the mold.

POURING THE WAX

Place the mold on a cookie sheet or similar item. Pour about 1/4" of wax at the correct temperature to seal the wick hole. Let this set for a half hour. Hold the mold at an angle and, using a pot holder,

Figure 9. The first step in preparing the mold is to clean the inside thoroughly and spray on silicone mold release (above left). The mold release is needed so that the candle can be removed from the mold in one piece. Cut the wick to fit the mold, but leave an extra allowance at either end (above right). Thread the wick through the bottom of the mold; then pull it taut and wrap around a stick or pencil (below left). To prevent wax seepage, seal the base of the mold (below right) around the hole made for the wick.

Figure 10. Pour wax into the mold. Begin with a layer about ¼" thick to seal the wick hole. After that layer sets, hold the mold at an angle and pour the wax slowly down the side.

pour the wax into the mold slowly and carefully. Let the wax slide down the sides of the mold so that no air bubbles form. Fill the mold to the desired height and save at least one cup of wax to fill the cavity left by shrinkage. Make sure the mold is perfectly level while the wax cools.

FILLING THE WELL

After approximately one hour the wax on top of the mold will begin to cool and cloud to the correct color. This is the time to start filling the well.

Insert a knitting needle into the warm candle near the wick two or three times to relieve pressure caused by wax shrinkage. Be careful not to insert the needle all the way to the bottom of the mold. Reheat the left-over wax and pour it into the cavity which has formed. Do not fill the well beyond the first pouring, or it will stick to the sides and be difficult to remove from the mold. Left-over wax should be poured into a separate container to cool because it can be used again. Never leave it to harden in the melting pot.

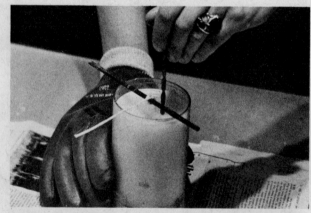

Figure 11. When the candle has partially cooled, use a long, narrow object to make a hole, or well, near the wick (top left). Then fill the well with reheated wax (below left). To save the leftover wax for reuse, pour it into a separate container (above). Do not allow it to harden in the pot.

MATURING THE CANDLE

Let the candle cool for at least eight hours at room temperature. Remove the floral clay and loosen the wick on both ends of the mold. Turn the mold upside down and let the candle slide out. If it does not slip out of the mold, place it in the freezer for 15 to 30 minutes. Do not strike the mold because this dents it for any further use.

Figure 12. Untie the wick from the stick or pencil after the candle has thoroughly hardened (left). Then cut off the wick to the desired length (right).

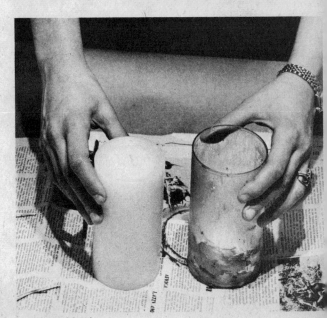

Figure 13. Remove the candle from the mold with care: turn the mold upside down and let the candle ease out (left), so that the two pieces are separated without damaging either (right).

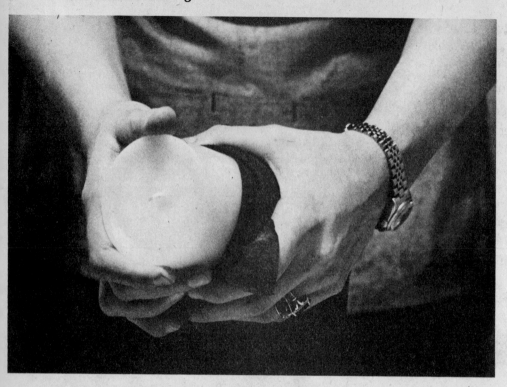

Figure 14. The final step is to remove seam lines from the candle by cutting them away with a knife and then polishing the candle with a cloth.

Figure 15. This charming "gingerbread house" candle illustrates one of the many variations possible with molded, dyed candles. (Courtesy, Lee Wards.)

FINISHING TOUCHES

Remove the seam lines from the candle with a hobby knife or paring knife. A nylon stocking is excellent for polishing the seam line and removing blemishes. Cut the wick to the desired length, and the candle is ready to use or decorate further.

SAFETY PRECAUTIONS AND OTHER HELPFUL HINTS

Candle wax is very similar to cooking oil. It is flammable but, with certain precautions, accidents need not occur.

1. Always melt wax over boiling water either in a melting pot placed in a water-filled pan or in a double boiler. Heating wax directly over an open flame is hazardous. If wax is heated over water, the temperature will not exceed 212° F and no problems will develop. Wax will not boil but will start to smoke if it is too hot.

2. Do not exceed 260° F when melting candle wax. This will cause the wax to burn, will ruin the mold, and will cause the color to be uneven.

3. Never pour wax directly over an open flame.

4. Never pour wax over or in the sink because it will clog the plumbing.

5. When pouring a candle, always place the mold on foil or on an old pan in case the mold should leak. Place this on a newspapered surface.

6. Never leave hot wax unattended.

7. Hot wax can cause burns on the skin. If this happens, run cold water over the burned area so the wax will harden and peel off. Treat as a regular burn.

8. **NEVER** pour water on a wax fire, as it will cause the fire to spread. To extinguish a fire in a pan, turn off the heat and cover the pan with its lid. Always keep baking soda handy, as it will extinguish a wax fire. Do not move pan or lift lid until pan is cold to the touch.

9. Always slip chunks of wax into hot wax — never drop them.

10. Always pour left-over wax from the melting pot into shallow pans. Then clean the pot with paper towels.

11. Always use a candy thermometer to check the temperature of the wax.

12. Pour wax at 175° F. If the temperature is lower, the candle will look dull and pitted because air bubbles do not have a chance to escape. Pouring wax higher than 175° F will create steam bubbles.

13. Mold seams can be removed with a spatula and buffed with a nylon stocking.

Figure 16. The interesting effects achieved in the ice cube candle explain why this technique has become so popular with home craftsmen.

Projects You Can Do

The fulfillment in candle making is achieved by using the imagination to create a unique candle. The basic process of making a candle is relatively easy. The various candles described in this section can be made with a minimum investment of work, time, and money. Keep in mind that these projects are just starting points for an endless assortment which can be designed and made.

ICE CUBE CANDLES

1. Make a pillar candle 2" x 7" with a metal mold as described in "Basic Procedures." Make sure that the wick will burn only up to 2" in diameter. This will allow the ice cube decoration to remain intact. Additional materials that are needed are cracked ice cubes and a metal mold, 4" x 7", square or cylindrical.

2. Prepare the work area.

3. Prepare the wax as described earlier.

4. Prepare the mold. Then place the 2" x 7" candle in the center of it. Its wick will serve as the wick for the entire candle.

5. Pour a small amount of wax (1/2") in the bottom of the mold to secure the center core candle.

6. Place cracked ice cubes around the center core to a depth of approximately 3".

7. Pour hot wax to within 1/2" of the top of the ice. After waiting a minute for the wax to harden slightly, continue placing ice and pouring wax until reaching the top.

8. Let the candle cool at room temperature for at least three hours.

9. After removing the candle from the mold, turn it on all sides so that all the water escapes. It may

be necessary to use a knitting needle to release some of the trapped water.

10. Be sure to dry the mold thoroughly so that it will not rust.

Variations of the Ice Cube Candle

1. Use a tapered candle the same height as the candle, instead of the 2" x 7" center core suggested above. (The tapered candle will allow the ice cube design to burn; the 2" x 7" will not.)

2. Instead of ice cubes, fill the outside of the mold for the basic 2" x 7" candle with sea shells or beads. If, when the candle is removed from the mold, the shells or beads are embedded too far in the wax, run a butane torch over the outside of the candle until the desired effect is achieved. Be sure to work on a surface that is covered with many layers of newspaper.

Figure 17. This candle was decorated in three stages with seashells. Note that the shells on top were placed first. Wax overlaps the shells to some extent to hold them in place; excess wax is removed when the candle is thoroughly dry.

SAND CANDLES

In addition to the basic equipment, a fairly large box filled with at least 8″ of clean, damp sand is needed. For a thick crust of sand on the finished candle, pour the wax at 200° F. For a thinner crust of sand, pour the wax at 150° F. For larger candles, embed driftwood or branches into the sand before pouring the wax.

1. Prepare work area.

2. Prepare the wax: break it into small pieces and melt it to the desired temperature (150° F or 200° F).

3. Add stearic acid, dye, and scent, following directions in "Basic Procedures."

4. Prepare the sand mold. First, spoon out the sand to the desired shape (vases, pots, or bowls may also be pressed into the sand). Then, press three holes of equal depth into the bottom of the sand to form a footed candle. Use fingers or an article such as an ice pick handle. Do not go through to the bottom of the box.

5. To pour the wax, hold a tablespoon near the bottom of the sand mold and slowly pour the wax into the spoon until the bottom of the mold is covered. This will prevent an indentation in the bottom of the sand.

6. After the candle has set for an hour, reheat the wax to the melting point and fill the well following the directions in "Basic Procedures."

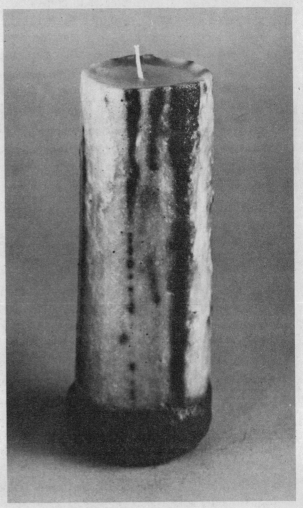

Figure 18. This sand candle can be made in a variety of sizes and shapes, and the sand crust can be made in varying thicknesses. The project calls for a large box filled with a minimum of 8″ of sand.

7. Heat an ice pick and insert the wick or wicks in position after the candle has matured for at least an hour (an additional hour after the filling of the well).

8. The candle chould be left to mature at least eight hours at room temperature.

9. With *great* care, lift the candle from the sand. Wash off the excess sand with cold water. (Note: It is a good idea to wash the candle outside to avoid getting sand all over the house or down the drain.)

Variations of the Sand Candle

1. Add small pebbles or small sea shells to the sand and pour the wax at the higher (200° F) melting point.

2. After the candle has matured, add chips of dye to the top of the candle. Shave off extremely small parts of the color dye chips — either the same color or various colors. Place the shavings on top of the candle and, with a butane torch, very lightly melt them into the wax just enough so that the color starts to bleed.

3. Make clusters of candles. Instead of one indentation in the sand, make connecting indentations. This type of sand candle makes an excellent hanging candle.

4. Make stepping stone candles. Make the indentations at various levels and connect them. Try using driftwood and tree branches to connect the various levels.

5. Trim the candle around the edges with dried flowers or small ceramic animals. These will look like miniature wildlife scenes, reflecting pools, or whatever else the craftsman wishes to create.

For Additional Reading

Feder, Carol, **The Candlemaking Design Book,** Watts, 1974.

Newman, Thelma R., **Creative Candlemaking,** Crown, 1972.

Schutz, Walter E., **Getting Started in Candlemaking,** Collier Books, 1972.

Strouse, Susanne, **Candlemaking,** Sterling, 1968.
+1

6. Place a piece of aluminum in the sand mold and pour the melted wax into the aluminum foil. This will produce a very glossy candle. For a more interesting candle, try using different colors of wax. If using different colors, make sure that each layer hardens completely before pouring or the colors will run together.

BABY ANIMAL CANDLES

For this project, the following materials are needed: (1) plastic molds (hollow toys will do); (2) one medium block of wax; (3) candle color or box of child's wax crayons; (4) scent (optional); (5) wick — height of mold plus 1½"; (6) masking tape; and (7) melting pan, knife, and nylon stocking.

1. Prepare the mold by first cutting a hole in the bottom to allow for pouring.

2. Lay the wick across the center of the mold and secure at the bottom with a piece of masking tape.

3. Close the mold and tape along all sides to insure tight closure.

4. Set the mold upside down in a secure position. One easy way to hold a mold in place is to fill a small box with sand and push the mold in it until it will stay upright.

5. Place the wax, a small amount of the color desired — shaving or chipping makes it melt more easily — and the scent, if desired; in the melting pan. Place the melting pan in heated water until the wax and color are melted and are ready to pour. **Do not** leave the hot wax unattended and do not exceed 200°F.

6. Pour the wax into the mold and allow to cool. During the cooling process the wax may shrink, and it may become necessary to add a small amount of molten wax to completely fill the mold.

7. When using more than one color, remember to allow each color layer to harden before pouring the next color.

8. When the wax is completely cool, remove the candle from the mold. If necessary, trim excess wax with the knife from the line where the mold was joined together. Using the nylon stocking, polish the candle until it has a smooth, shiny surface.

9. Trim the wick, if necessary.

Scrap Art

Scrap art is a delightful way of transforming trash into treasures.

For hundreds of years man has used worn-out materials in various ways. Completely worn-out garments, for example, were cut into pieces and woven into rugs or made into the beautiful patchwork quilts which are seen today in many museums. Modern technology has resulted in the development of many new products for the home. Trash cans often contain such items as ice-cream sticks, colored or clear glass bottles, plastic containers, cigar boxes, tin cans, odds and ends of fabric, ribbon, paint, and nail polish. All of these things can be used in scrap craft.

Church groups, clubs, and camps hold bazaars and sell such handmade items as pot holders, neckties, and aprons made from scraps of fabric; toys and dolls from old containers or socks; Christmas tree ornaments from scraps of felt; and rugs, quilts, and pillows from worn-out garments. Articles utilizing plastic, including wreaths and toys made from plastic bags and toys and plant holders made from plastic containers, are also sold.

Many craftsmen have created original works of art from attractive boxes or containers. And bags, banks, toys, and vases are but a few examples of the items that can be made from discarded plastic.

The ancient art of mosaic is usually not thought of in relation to scrap art. However, today, mosaic designs are made from many materials, including such food items as croutons, beans, and rice. The appearance of an ordinary box or bottle top can be transformed into an attractive gift simply by covering it with a mosaic design.

Scrap, of course, also includes much of the material discarded from factories. Many of these materials, such as scraps of metal, fabric, and wood can be purchased or obtained from metal companies, fabric mills, or lumber mills.

Common Terms Used In Scrap Art

Baste: to sew long, temporary stitches.

Curl: to curl the edges of tin with long-nosed pliers.

Invisible Stitches: small stitches, made as inconspicuously as possible.

Liquid Lead: used in making Tiffany glass items and available in tubes at most craft departments or stores. It gives a raised effect.

Long-Nosed Pliers: sold primarily for craft work and available in most hardware or craft stores. The long, narrow end (nose) makes it easy to get into small areas.

Score: to make a line impression, using a ruler and the back edge of scissors.

Basic Equipment And Supplies

The equipment needed for making tin flowers or cans are long-nosed pliers, tin shears, a hammer, nails, coat hangers or heavy wire, tying wire, heavy work gloves, masking tape, and glue. For creating mosaic designs, necessary materials include rice, watercolor or tempera paints, a small brush, glue, toothpicks, and clear and colored nail polish. For miscellaneous crafts, assemble such items as glue, scissors, a ruler, a pencil, needle and thread, masking or cellophane tape, watercolors, a small brush, straight pins, toothpicks, heavy cardboard, manicuring scissors, nail polish, polish remover, liquid lead, and wire.

Each of the projects described below includes a list of the materials needed.

Basic Procedures

For tin craft, assemble materials. Wear heavy work gloves to prevent cuts.

For other scrap crafts in this article, assemble materials and prepare working area. When articles are to be painted, it is helpful to have water and paper towels handy to clean brushes and a few small dishes or bottle tops for mixing colors.

Before making the bureau boxes described in this article, gather scraps of trim, beads, and odds and ends of fabric. The same applies to the barrel-back chair pin cushion and various items made from plastic bottles. Otherwise, follow the step-by-step procedures for each project.

Projects You Can Do

Scrap materials usually bring to mind items due for discard, unusable materials, or empty containers. The dictionary describes scrap as "small pieces, fragments, leftovers, discards, junk." Junk may be a true description in some cases, but these projects will demonstrate how scrap material can be recycled into usable and desirable items at little, if any, cost.

BARREL-BACK CHAIR PIN CUSHION

Materials

Materials needed for this project are: (1) one round cylinder-type container with bottom, such as an oatmeal or salt box; (2) styrofoam ball or large wad of steel wool; (3) glue; (4) scissors; (5) scraps of fabric, preferably with a small print; (6) 2 yards of contrasting or matching yarn; (7) cellophane or masking tape; and (8) needle and thread.

Cutting

Enlarge the pattern (see the accompanying illustration) to size. Place it on the fold of a piece of typing paper and cut it out. Make several copies for additional chairs. Tape the pattern to the container in several places, placing the lower edge around the bottom of the container. If more or less length or width is needed, make the necessary adjustments in the pattern. Discard the container top. With sharp scissors, knife, or razor, cut out

Figure 1. A piece of scrap fabric with a small pattern should be used for this barrel-back chair pin cushion, made from an oatmeal container or a salt box.

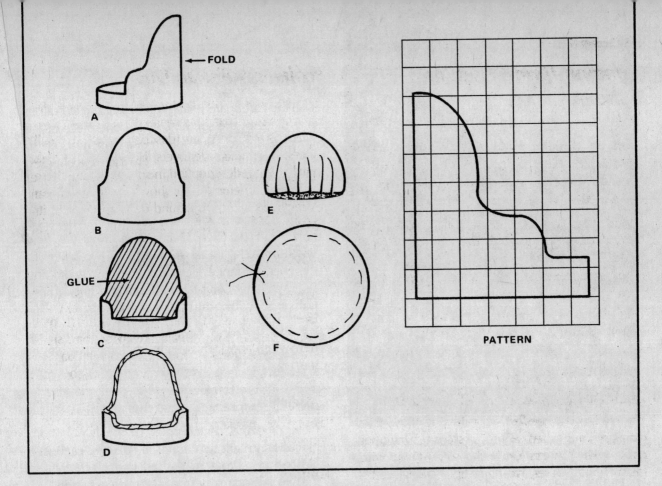

Figure 2. Tape the pattern in several places to the outside of the container (A). The lower edge of the pattern should be placed on the bottom of the container (B). Make any adjustments in the pattern size, and cut out the chair form. Pin the pattern to the fabric, cut the material, and glue on (C). After covering the inside and outside, glue on yarn around the edge (D). To cover the seat, cut a circle from the fabric. To cover a styrofoam ball, make slits around the edges of the circle (E); to cover a wad of steel wool, sew a running stitch around the edges (F).

container around pattern, leaving the bottom in place.

Pin the pattern on the fold of the material, centering the design. Cut out fabric for the inside of the container. Cut an identical piece for the outside of the container.

Assembling

Spread glue around the sides and back of the inside of the container; do not spread glue on bottom. Place one of the fabric pieces, right side out, over the glue and press it in place. Spread glue around the outside of the container and press the second piece of fabric in place. Be sure all edges are glued securely. When the chair is completely dry, trim all the loose threads. Then, spread glue around all the edges and press the yarn in place.

If a styrofoam ball is used for the inside of the

chair, cut a small section off the bottom so that it will lie flat. If stuffing such as steel wool is used, use a wad large enough to fit the inside of the chair.

To cover a styrofoam ball, cut out an 8" circle of fabric. Spread glue over the top of the ball and center the fabric on the ball. Press in place. Make slits around the fabric, leaving about 3½" uncut across the center. Glue the slit pieces in place to cover the ball.

To cover a wad of steel wool or other stuffing material, cut out a 10" circle of fabric. With needle and thread, sew a running stitch 1/4" from the edges, leaving 4" ends of thread. Place the wad inside the circle and draw the ends together making a pillow. Tie the ends securely.

Spread some glue inside the chair across the bottom. Place the ball or pillow inside the chair and press it in place.

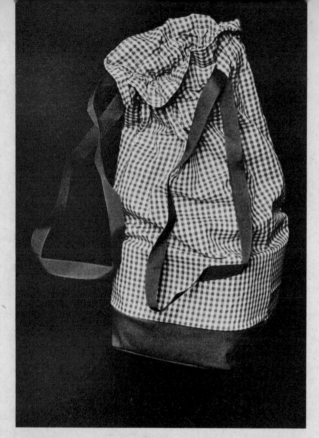

Figure 3. A plastic gallon container, fabric, and ribbon were used to make this drawstring bag. It makes a useful carryall for beach gear, hair rollers, or sewing supplies.

DRAWSTRING BAG

Materials

Materials for this project are: (1) plastic gallon container, such as is used for milk or bleach; (2) 1/2 yard solid and 1/2 yard checked material; (3) needle and thread; (4) lightweight cardboard; (5) safety pin; and (6) 2 yards of 3/4" gros-grain ribbon.

Cutting

If the plastic container has a handle, cut around the container below the handle with scissors or a sharp knife. If there is no handle, cut the container to a depth of about 10" or 12".

Making Pattern

Place the container on a piece of cardboard. Draw a line around the bottom to make the pattern. Cut out the cardboard, allowing an extra 1/2" *outside* the line. This 1/2" allowance will be the seam. Measure around the outside of the container to determine its perimeter. Write the value for the measurement on the pattern.

Cutting Fabric

Use the cardboard pattern of the bottom to cut out one piece of the solid color and one piece of the checked fabric. The solid color will be used to cover the outside bottom of the bag; the checked fabric will be the bottom lining.

Divide the perimeter measurement in half and add 1" for seams; this is the new width. From solid color, cut out two pieces measuring the new width and 2½" in length. Next, cut two pieces of the checked fabric measuring the new width and 14½" in length (cut fabric on pattern line). These four pieces will be the outer sides of the bag.

Cut two pieces of checked fabric measuring the new width and 16" in length for lining the sides of the bag.

Assembling

Determine the center point of the two bottom pieces and mark two opposite edges of each (see illustration). These marks indicate placement of the two side seams. Set the bottom pieces aside.

With right sides together, join one of the checked pieces for the outside (measuring the new width and 14½" in length) to a solid piece (measuring the new width and 2½" in length) along the width in a 1/2" seam (see illustration). Do the same thing with the other outside pieces. Press all seams flat. With right sides together, join the sides of the two sections using 1/2" seams: start at the solid color and stitch to within 3" of the top (see illustration). Do not stitch the ends. Knot the threads to secure both ends of each seam. Starting at the top edge, stitch a 1/2" seam for 1¾". Knot the threads as before, and press the seams flat. The 1¼" opening that remains will be the casing for the drawstring (or ribbon).

Turn the completed side section wrong side out. Match the two side seams with the two marks made previously on the solid color bottom section (it should also be wrong side out). Baste the side section to the bottom; stitch the bottom to the side section with a 1/2" seam. Turn the bag right side out and place it over the plastic container.

With right sides together stitch the remaining two pieces of checked fabric with 1/2" seams. *Do not leave an opening.* Knot threads and press seams flat. Turn the completed lining section wrong side out. Match the two side seams with the two marks on the remaining bottom section (also wrong side out). Baste as before and stitch the bottom to the side section with a 1/2" seam. Place the lining inside the container, matching seams of lining and those of the outside of the bag.

Turn under the upper edge of the outside of the bag 1/2"; do the same with the upper edge of the lining. Pin the lining to the outside of the bag,

baste, and stitch 1/8" from the edge. Sew another seam 1" below, and a third seam 1½" below that (stitch across the pattern line).

Cut the ribbon into two one-yard lengths. Attach a safety pin to the end of one length and thread it into the casing and around the bag. Stitch the ends of the ribbon and arrange it so that the stitching does not show. Do the same thing with the other length or ribbon at the opposite opening. Pull both ribbons to close.

Figure 4. To begin the drawstring bag, make a pattern for the bottom pieces 1½" larger than the container (A). Mark opposite sides of these pieces for seam placement (B). Measure the perimeter of the container and cut out the side pieces of the bag (C). Sew together pieces of solid and checked fabric for the outside (D). Repeat, then sew the two outsides together, starting at the bottom and ending 3" from the top (E). Now make the ribbon casing by stitching down 1¾" from the top (F). Attach the bottom (G). Make the lining, then sew it to the outside pieces and make seams for the ribbon casing. Use a safety pin to thread the ribbon through the casing (H). Sew ribbon ends together and pull the seam to the opposite side (I). Repeat for the second ribbon (J).

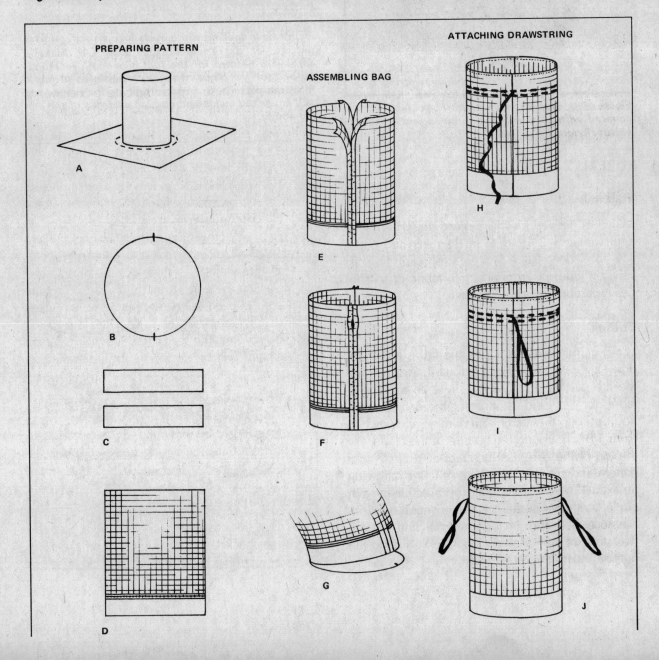

Figure 5. This finished bureau box (above) was covered with corduroy and trimmed with braid and velvet ribbon.

BUREAU BOXES

Materials

Materials needed for this project are: (1) any can approximately 3¼" to 4" in diameter and about 1½" to 2" deep (such as a tuna fish can); (2) scissors; (3) glue; (4) trimmings; (5) fabric or felt; (6) heavy cardboard; and (7) a pencil.

Cutting

Wash can thoroughly. Using the lid as a pattern, draw a circle on heavy cardboard. Again using the lid as a pattern, draw a circle on a piece of fabric for the inside bottom of the can. Discard lid. Cut out the cardboard circle, allowing an extra 1/8" all around the *outside* of the circle. For the top of the can, use the cardboard circle as a pattern and cut out two circles of fabric, allowing an extra 1" by 1¼" for a hinge on one side of each circle, as shown in the accompanying illustration. Measure the depth of the container and cut out two strips of fabric long enough to fit around the outside and inside of the can.

Assembling

Spread glue on the inside bottom of the can. Place the first fabric circle (same size as lid) over the glue and press in place. Place glue around the inside of can and press a strip of fabric in place, trimming it to fit. Set second strip aside.

For the cover, spread glue on each side of the cardboard circle and press the two fabric circles in place, matching the hinges. Glue the hinges together. Place the lid on the top of the container and glue the hinge to the side of the can. Allow the hinge to dry in place. Glue the second strip around the outside of the can, placing the strip over the hinge.

Trim the can with braid, sequins, beads, or as desired. Loose covers can be made by omitting the hinge or cans can be left uncovered.

Figure 6. In making the bureau box, use a can as a pattern for the inside bottom lining (A). Make a cardboard pattern for the top, allowing a rectangular end for the hinge, then cut two pieces of fabric from the pattern (B). After attaching the hinged top (C), cover the inside and outside surfaces of the can (D) and E).

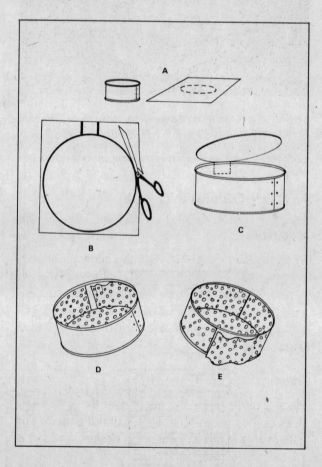

Figure 7. These decorated cans are handy containers for jewellery, coins, or paper clips. They can be left open (left) or covered with a loose lid (center). The outside can be trimmed with fancy braids, ribbons, beads, and sequins (right).

Figure 8. A plastic half-gallon container for ice cream was used to create a container for buttons or sewing equipment (above). The sides and top are decorated with cut-out fabric floral motifs and satin ribbon.

BUTTON OR SEWING BOX

Materials

Materials needed are: (1) a half-gallon plastic ice cream container with cover; (2) glue; (3) tracing paper; (4) pencil; (5) manicuring scissors; (6) 1/4-yard print cotton fabric or chintz; (7) 1 yard of 5/8" satin ribbon; (8) needle and thread; and (9) damp paper towels.

Cutting

Place a piece of tracing paper over the cover and sides of the cover and trace it. Cut out pattern. Pin pattern to the fabric, center the design, and cut it out. Cut out enough motifs or flowers from the fabric to cover most of container.

Assembling

Before gluing, spread glue on the back of a scrap of fabric and allow it to dry. The glue should saturate the fabric but not stain it.

Spread glue on the cover and press the round piece of fabric in place, using a damp paper towel. Spread glue on the backs of the motifs and press them in place around the container.

Trimming

Measure the circumference of the container below the cover and cut the ribbon 1/2" longer. Place a small amount of glue on the ribbon at the ends and at the center; press the ribbon in place around the container.

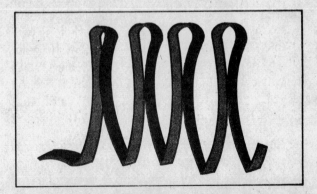

Figure 10. Make a candy ribbon bow to decorate the box by cutting ribbon ends on the diagonal, arranging the ribbon in four equal loops, and gathering them with a thread.

Figure 9. This striking wall hanging was made by covering a board with wood grain contact paper and mounting pieces of tin, wire and buttons. Old tin can lids can be cut and curled to make flower petals.

SCULPTURED WALL HANGING

Materials

Materials needed for this project are: (1) tin can lids in various sizes and colors (silver, gold, or bronze) for flowers; (2) tin shears; (3) heavy work gloves; (4) tying wire; (5) coat hangers or heavy wire; (6) pliers; (7) masking tape; (8) buttons with shanks for flower centers — preferably gold, silver or bronze; (9) long-nosed pliers; (10) hammer; (11) thin nail; (12) aluminum foil or foil pie plate; (13) wood, plywood, heavy cardboard, or fiber board for background; and (14) 1 yard of contact paper in simulated wood tone (if heavy cardboard or fiberboard is used).

Cutting Flowers

Remove lids from cans (use an electric can opener if possible), opening the end of can which is without imprinted markings. Place a lid on a board, and, using the hammer and the thin nail, punch two holes in the center of each lid approximately 3/8" apart.

There are many ways by which lids can be cut with tin shears to form flowers. Invent designs or try the following.

1. Cut a lid into four sections to within 3/8" of the center. Then divide the lid into eight sections by cutting between quarters. There should be about 3/4" left at the center (see accompanying illustration).

2. Cut a lid into two sections; cut to within 3/8" of center. Then divide each half into three sections. There should be about 3/4" left at the center.

3. Cut a lid into eight sections as above, then cut between each section again, making cuts slightly shorter than the previous ones.

4. Make four cuts on a slant (see illustration), cutting into a lid about 3/4". Then make two more cuts in each section, turning the lid and keeping the cuts on a slant.

5. Cut a lid into four sections.

6. Cut a lid into 16 sections, then cut again between each section. The last cuts should be slightly shorter than the original ones.

7. Cut a lid into 4, 8, 16, or 32 sections, but cut only 1" into lid.

Curling Edges of Flowers

Using gloves, place long-nosed pliers over one edge of a cut section and roll the edge toward the center on a diagonal (see illustration). Roll opposite edge. Edges may also be rolled under, of course, or one edge over and one edge under.

Assembling Flowers

Use two or three lids for each flower. Draw a double strand of tying wire through the shank of a button (see illustration), then draw one end through a hole in the top lid and through the corresponding hole of the second and third lids. Draw the other end of the wire through the remaining holes. Twist wire tightly to fasten. Assemble the other flowers in the same manner.

For leaves, cut large ovals from aluminum foil or from a foil pie plate.

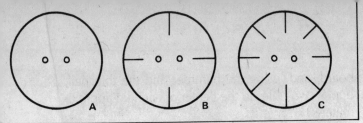

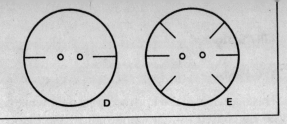

Figure 10. To make a "flower" from a tin can lid: punch two holes about 3/8" apart in the center (A). Cut the lid into four sections (B). Divide each quarter in half to make eight equal parts (C).

Figure 11. Another type of "flower" can be made as follows: cut twice across the diameter of the lid to within 3/8" of the center (D). Then divide each section into three parts, a total of six cuttings (E).

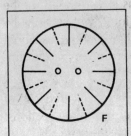

Figure 12. For a third type of "flower" (F), divide the lid into quarters, then into eighths, and finally into sixteen equal segments. The last eight cuttings should be slightly shorter than the others.

Figure 13. Start a "flower" by making four 3/4" slanted cuts into the lid (G). Turn the lid and make eight additional slanted cuts (H). Be certain that the slanted cuts are all made in the same direction.

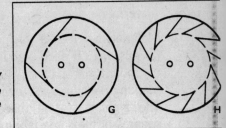

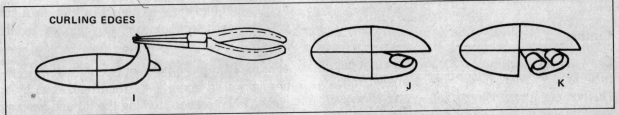

CURLING EDGES

Figure 14. To curl the edges of the "flowers" place pliers over the edge of one of the sections (I). Roll the pliers on a diagonal to curl the tin (J). Place the pliers on the other edge and curl in the opposite direction (K).

Figure 15. To attach the button center to the flower, draw a strand of tying wire through the button shank (L). Then thread the wire through the holes in the lids (M) and secure the wire.

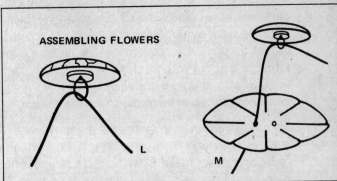

ASSEMBLING FLOWERS

Assembling Wall Hanging

Select wood, plywood, heavy cardboard, or pressed fiber board for the background, and cut it to the desired size. Smooth all rough edges. If a wooden board is used, stain it the desired color and shellac or varnish. If plywood, cardboard, or pressed fiber board is used, cover carefully with the contact paper.

Cut several lengths of heavy wire from coat hangers; bend and curve as shown in the illustration. Place one of the wires on the board for a stem. Mark the board at the points at which the wire is to be attached (two points for each stem). With a hammer and the fine nail, make the holes in the board. Twist tying wire around the coat hanger, insert both ends of tying wire through the punched holes, and tape to back.

After several stems are attached to the board, attach flowers as follows: make a hole at the top of a stem or where desired and bring both ends of tying wire from flower to the back of the board. Tape the ends. Glue leaves where desired.

Make a loop by cutting a length of wire and folding it in half. Attach picture hanging hooks on opposite sides and run wire through them.

To make a floral arrangement with tin flowers, assemble flowers and leaves on stems and arrange the assembled flowers in a low bowl. Cut the stems to different lengths and use glue to attach the leaves to the stems.

AFGHAN

This afghan is made from scrap fake fur which can be purchased from a fabric mill by the bag or in short lengths. Other usable fabrics include scrap corduroy and woolen or other warm fabric. The finished size of the afghan will be 56" by 72".

Materials

Materials needed for this project are: (1) fake fur; (2) scissors; (3) needle and thread; (4) lightweight cardboard for pattern; (5) colored pencils or marking pens; and (6) sewing machine (optional). The afghan can be made reversible by using squares of the same fabric, a lightweight blanket, or any other warm material as a backing.

Cutting

Draw an 8" square on cardboard and cut it out. If material is in small pieces, use a smaller square. Do not cut fur into too small pieces, however, because it will be difficult to work with. Using the pattern and a colored pencil, draw an 8" square onto the back of fabric and cut it out. It is not necessary to place the pattern on the grain of the fabric: a bias cut will not show or make any difference in assembling. If corduroy is used, however, be sure to place pattern on the line of the fabric.

The afghan shown requires 63 squares; it is 7 squares wide and 9 squares long. If the afghan is to be reversible, make 126 squares. Colors should blend.

Assembling

Sort squares according to color. (Afghan can be made with a different color combination on each side if desired.)

Select nine squares for the first row. Baste them together on the wrong side about 1/2" from the edge. (An alternate method is to place the squares side by side and cross stitch them together.) Use a pencil or marking pen to write 1T on the wrong side of the first square in this row. On the floor, lay out squares for the next row. Be sure that the colors blend and that the same colors are not next to each other. Baste the squares as before and write 2T on the wrong side of the top square. Make five more rows, each time selecting colors

Figure 16. This afghan was made from different colored squares of fake fur. Any type of fabric and color combination can be used. The afghan can be backed with a blanket if it is to be reversible.

that complement the previous row; mark the top square of each row on the wrong side.

Sewing

Stitch the squares of the first row together, taking about a 1/2" seam. Remove basting. Sew the remaining rows. Baste row 1T to row 2T. Sew the two rows together. Lay the seam open to prevent too much bulk. Baste row 3 to row 2 with 3T at the top; join the remaining rows.

If the afghan is to have a backing of the same fabric as the front, repeat the sewing steps above. If backing of a different fabric is to be used, cut the fabric to the same size as the afghan. To join front and back, place right sides together, baste, then sew around three sides and half the fourth, leaving an opening for turning. Turn right side out. Turn under the seam allowance on the open edges and pin. Using a strong double thread, sew the opening together using tiny stitches.

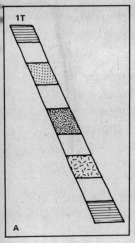
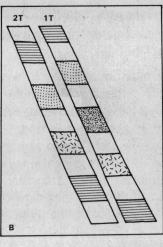
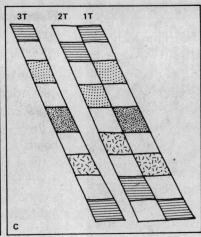

Figure 17. To assemble the afghan, use a cardboard pattern to cut squares of material, and stack the pieces according to color. Baste together nine squares of material (left). Mark the top of the strips, and alternate the colors in the next row of squares (center). Assemble the rows so that the same colors are not placed side by side (right).

Figure 18. The plastic pin box and pieces of old jewelry were decorated with rice for a mosaic effect. The rice was glued to the surface areas and arranged with a toothpick. Then the design was painted.

MOSAIC BOX AND JEWELRY

Materials

Materials for this project are: (1) old earrings, bracelets, rings, or pins with missing stones (for the jewelry project); (2) any small box of plastic or cardboard (for the box project); (3) short-grained rice (do not use minute rice or wild rice); (4) glue; (5) toothpicks; (6) clear nail polish; (7) watercolors or tempera paint; and (8) a small brush.

Covering a Box

Spread a small amount of glue, about the size of a penny, on the center of the top. Drop a few grains of rice onto the glue. Using a toothpick, arrange the grains of rice into the shape of a small flower. Make a second flower close to the first. Add additional flowers and glue, placing the grains of rice so as to fill in the space within each flower as much as possible. Make as many flowers as desired. Glue a few grains of rice around the flowers for leaves. Allow the design to dry for about 10 minutes. Carefully paint the flowers and leaves. (Flowers that are to be white need not be painted.) When the flowers are dry, add a background by spreading a small area with glue and pushing rice as close as possible around design until the entire top of the box is covered. Cover the sides of the box top with glue and rice in the same manner.

Allow rice and glue to dry for a few minutes, then paint the background, pushing paint around rice to cover. Allow the paint to dry for at least one hour. Paint the mosaic design with a coat of clear nail polish, being careful not to disturb the paint. Wait 10 minutes and then add a second coat.

Making Mosaic Jewelry

Use old jewelry with missing stones — preferably with an area about the size of a dime or penny. Fill in the spaces with glue and rice or remove additional stones and make a completely new design. Paint rice as desired, then brush with two coats of clear nail polish.

Figure 19. An assortment of gift boxes can be made with shirt cardboard and wrapping. The boxes can be constructed to the desired size and covered with paper.

GIFT BOXES

Materials

Materials needed for this project are: (1) shirt cardboards, 8″ x 14″; (2) cellophane or masking tape; (3) rubber cement; (4) gift wrapping paper; and (5) scissors.

Making the Pattern

Determine the box size by following these rules: (1) all sides of the box must be the same depth; (2) the top of the box should be 1/16″ larger on all sides than the bottom; and (3) the sides of the top are usually shorter than those of the bottom.

The following are instructions for the top and bottom of a box, the bottom of whose measurements are 3½″ x 5½″ x 1¼″. For the bottom, draw a line across the 8″ dimension of the cardboard 1¼″ from the lower edge (see accompanying illustration). Measure and draw another line 3½″ above the first, then a third line 1¼″ above the second. Cut the cardboard across the last marked line. Measure and mark a vertical line 1¼″ from the edges of the right and left sides — the width between these lines should be 5½″ (see illustration).

Using the back of a pair of scissors and a ruler, score all lines by pressing the scissors lightly over them. The impression or groove left in the card-board makes it easy to fold. Take care not to cut or scratch the cardboard. The scored side will be the wrong side of the box.

For the top, measure and draw a line across the 8″ dimension of cardboard, 1″ from the lower edge. Draw another line 3⅝″ above the first, then draw a third line 1″ above the second. Cut the cardboard across the last marked line. Now draw a vertical line 1″ from the right edge and another line 5⅝″ from the first and another 1″ from the second. Cut off the remaining cardboard. Cut out the corners marked X on the illustration for both top and bottom. Score all lines. Do not assemble the box at this time; use it as a pattern for the wrapping paper.

To measure for the wrapping, place the bottom of the box on the wrong side of a piece of wrapping paper; with a pencil, lightly draw a pattern around the box, remove the box. Now measure and mark a 1/2″ margin around the outside of the pattern on the wrapping paper. Carefully cut out the paper on these last lines. Clip the corners and cut out each corner marked X on the illustration. Repeat this procedure for the top.

Turn up the sides of the bottom and the top of the box along the scored lines. With masking or cellophane tape, join the corners on the outside of the box.

Wrapping the Box

Place the wrapping paper over the bottom of the box and glue the 1/2″ margin at the top of two sides opposite each other. Glue the notched pieces at these sides to the outside of the box. Now, fold back the notched pieces of wrapping paper of the remaining two sides and tuck them in. Glue the remaining 1/2″ margins to the inside of the box. Cover the top of the box in the same way.

Diagrams are given for two other boxes: (1) a 4″ x 4″ x 1/2″ box requires one sheet of cardboard 8″ x 14″; (2) a 5″ x 11″ x 1½″ box requires two sheets of cardboard 8″ x 14″.

Figure 20. These Tiffany style vases are inexpensive to make. Paint small section with different colors of nail polish, and outline the areas with liquid lead (left) or a black marking pen (right).

TIFFANY VASES

Materials

Materials needed are: (1) plastic liquid detergent bottles; (2) various shades of nail polish; (3) liquid lead; (4) permanent black marking pen; (5) sharp scissors or knife; (6) cotton swabs; and (7) nail polish remover.

Preparing Bottle

Be sure the outside of the bottle is completely clean. Use the marking pen to draw a line around the bottle at the desired height. Cut out a hole in the top of the bottle and widen it until the line is reached. Carefully cut along line.

To Make a Vase Having a Large Pattern

With the permanent marking pen, outline large areas on the bottle as shown. Use different shades of nail polish (colors can be mixed) to fill in the areas. If the polish is thick, it should cover the bottle with one coat. If thin, allow the bottle to dry completely, then apply a second coat. Blot any runovers with a cotton swab dipped in nail polish remover.

With liquid lead, carefully outline each area and across the top and bottom of the bottle.

To Make a Vase Having a Small Pattern

With the permanent black marking pen, outline small areas around the bottle. Start at the bottom and fill in each area with different shades of nail

polish, using two coats if necessary. Cover an area 1" wide around the bottle at a time. Allow it to dry completely and then go over every outline again. Be careful to make the lines as even as possible and to completely fill in the corners. Fill in areas for another inch and repeat procedure. Continue to the top of bottle, ending with a solid line of black at the upper edge.

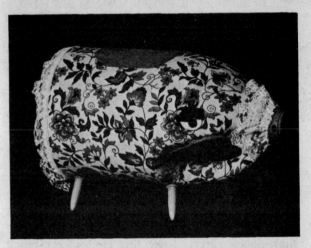

Figure 21. The finished piggy bank is supported by plastic corn cob holders. When the bank is filled, the coins can be removed by unscrewing the bottle cap.

PIGGY BANK

Materials

Materials needed for this project are: (1) bleach or fabric softener bottle; (2) 1/2 yard of print fabric; (3) 1 yard of lace; (4) scraps of white, black, and gold felt; (5) glue; (6) four corn holders; and (7) thin wire.

Preparing Bottle

Wash and dry bottle thoroughly; replace cap. Place handle down. With scissors or knife make a 2" slit on the top back of the bottle (see accompanying illustration).

Cutting Fabric

Cut a 13" x 20" piece of print fabric. If the circumference of the bottle is more or less than 20", cut fabric accordingly.

Assembling

Place glue along the long edges of the fabric. Start at the slit and wrap the fabric around the container, ending at the slit; 1" of fabric should extend over the rounded end (bottom of the bottle). Slit the 1" extension, about every inch, and glue the slits so that they overlap and are flat.

Cut 4" slits in the fabric at the neck end of the bottle about every 2" and glue so that they overlap and are flat. Glue the fabric under the handle as well as possible; it will be covered later. Cut a strip of fabric the length of the handle and wide enough to completely cover it; glue the strip in place. Glue strips of fabric to cover any bare spots. From the print fabric, cut out a circle 7" in diameter and glue it to the rounded end (bottom) of the bottle.

Cut out a piece of gold felt 5" x 3½". Round off each corner and glue the felt to the indentation above the handle.

For the snout, cut out a 1¾" circle of felt and glue it over the cap. Slit the edges, fit, and glue flat. Cut out a 3/4" strip of gold felt and glue it around the sides of the cap. Cut two tiny circles from black felt and glue these to the front of the snout for nostrils.

Assemble the eyes as follows: cut out two 1" circles from white felt. From black felt, cut out two small circles for pupils and glue them to the white circles, slightly off center. Then cut a 3/4" strip of black felt 1¼" long. Cut fringe at one side. Glue one eye to each side of the bottle about 3" from the snout and 1/2" up from gold section. Glue fringe for eyelashes over eyes.

To make the ruffles, cut two pieces of lace, each about 12" long. With needle and thread, gather the straight edge and place it around the face about 1/2" from the snout; tie the threads under the handle. Gather and tie a second ruffle around the snout. Glue another piece of ruffle (without gathering) around the bottom of the bottle as shown.

Cut out a piece of gold felt and round off the corners. Cut a 2" slit in the center. Glue the felt over the slit at top of back.

For the tail, cut two pieces of gold felt each 3/4" x 5" in length. Sew the two pieces together by hand 1/4" from one long edge. Cut thread and fasten. Sew by hand 1/4" from first seam. Trim edges slightly. Draw a 10" piece of medium-weight wire through the remaining 1/4". Punch a small hole in the back of the bottle and push the uncovered end of the wire into the hole. Twist wire to curl. Insert the corn holders as legs.

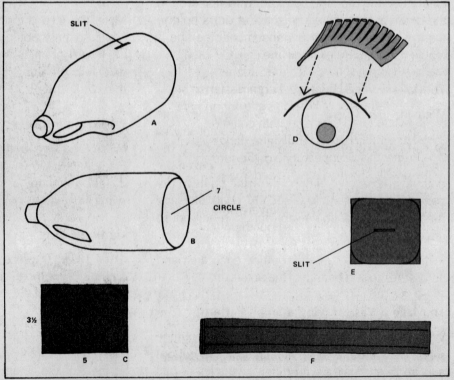

Figure 22. To make a piggy bank, cut a slit on the side of a bottle (A). After the sides of the bottle are in place, glue a circle of print fabric to the bottom (B). A rounded piece of felt is glued above the handle (C). Make each eye from a circle of white felt. Cut small circles from black felt for the pupils (D). Cut a rounded piece of gold felt with a slit in the center (E), and place the felt over the slit in the bottle. Use two pieces of felt and wire for the tail (F).

Boutiquing

**Boutiquing is a craft which deals with
a wide array of decorative elements, such
as painted eggs, styrofoam, and beads.**

The egg is one of the oldest symbols known to
man. Throughout history, men have used it to
represent the universe, and practically all
cultures have put the egg to decorative and
ornamental use. In 988 A.D., the Europeans
developed a batik method — a wax resist
technique — for decorating eggs. As the wax
resist was applied, the egg was dipped into
various dyes. The wax was then removed and
the dyed design remained on the egg. Unusual
beaded eggs originated with the Sudanese in
Africa, and jeweled eggs were commissioned by
a one-time emperor of Russia as gifts for his wife.
The Russians filled their eggs with colored
crystal to symbolize day and night: darker jewels
to represent the disappearance of the sun; and
lighter jewels, the daylight. Indeed, many ornate
pieces which decorated the boudoirs of wealthy
European and Russian noblemen are now
displayed in museums throughout the world.

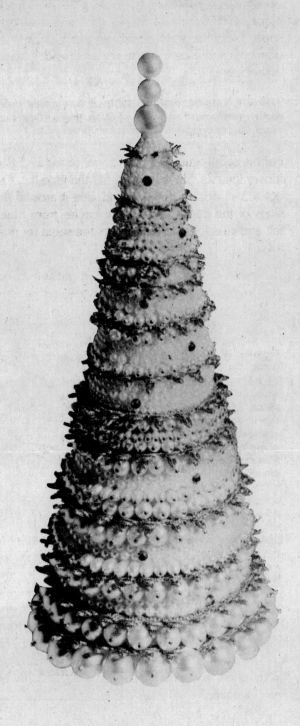

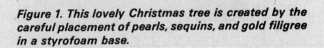

*Figure 1. This lovely Christmas tree is created by the
careful placement of pearls, sequins, and gold filigree
in a styrofoam base.*

Figure 2. This beaded bag (above) was made by an Indian craftsman, probably a Plains Indian. (Courtesy, Field Museum of Natural History, Chicago.)

Figure 3. Two creations of the 19th-century jeweler Carl Fabergé are the Kelch Hen Egg (below left) and the Chanticleer Egg (below right). (Courtesy, the FORBES Magazine Collection, New York.)

The egg is also a symbol of rebirth and fertility. Easter eggs represent the new life that returns to nature in the spring. The custom of exchanging eggs was established in ancient times: the early Christians of Mesopotamia were the first to use eggs as gifts for Easter. According to legend, the Persians believed that the earth was hatched from a giant egg. Thus, they painted eggs in spring colors, as did the Egyptians. These ornamental eggs were often given as gifts and were considered very valuable.

Beadcraft, another aspect of boutiquing, is almost as old as civilization itself. Ancient usage of the bead can almost be used to chart the ages of man. Beads, identified as belonging to the Neolithic period, have been discovered by archaeologists. Egyptian artisans were using beads as early as 4000 B.C. American Indians used beads for money as well as for ornaments on clothing, belts, moccasins, and tomahawks. Today there is a fascinating variety of round, square, convex, concave, and carved beads.

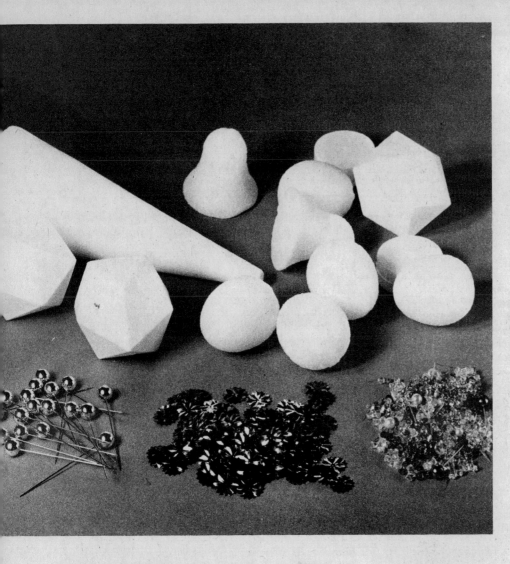

Figure 4. Styrofoam, which may be bought in many shapes, can be imaginatively adorned with pin-in decorations and "jewels."

Basic Equipment And Supplies

Following are separate lists of materials for eggery, styrofoam crafts, and beadcraft.

EGGERY

Several kinds of eggs can be used for boutiquing. Obviously, the most common are chicken eggs. Double-yolk chicken eggs and duck, goose, and turkey eggs may also be used — these are available from hatcheries or farms. Other suggested materials, depending upon the type of project undertaken, are: (1) diamond dust for adding sparkly effects to surfaces; (2) white or cement glue; (3) gold braid, gold paper lace, and gold leaf (available in sheets); (4) hinges, available in various sizes, for holding egg pieces together; (5) miniature ornaments such as pearls, beads, ribbons, and sequins; (6) acrylic paints; (7) straight pins; (8) sharp knife or single-edge razor blade for scoring eggshell; (9) manicure scissors; (10) darning needle and thread; (11) toothpicks; (12) colored pencils; (13) plaster of Paris; (14) paint brushes; (15) masking tape; (16) shellac; (17) egg cartons; and (18) paper towels.

STYROFOAM CRAFTS

Styrofoam is a widely used craft material. Lightweight and waterproof, it is available in almost any shape, from cones and blocks to sheets.

Styrofoam can be cut with a sharp knife or punctured with a pencil point or soldering iron. Pieces can be joined with glue, pins, or toothpicks.

Supplies necessary for working with styrofoam are: jewels, fabric, sequins, straight pins, braid, and ribbons for decorating the ornaments; and

Figure 5. This eye-catching anniversary "egg tree" utilizes twig branches, plastic grass, and a plastic goblet or dish. Photographs are mounted on styrofoam backings and hung from the branches.

scissors, pencil, paper, brush, and glue for tracing patterns. For flocked ornaments made with styrofoam balls, the following additional materials are suggested: designer yarns, tinsel, and gold and silver thread.

BEADCRAFT

Part of the fun of beadcraft lies in collecting interesting beads. Thrift and antique shops can be valuable sources; old costume jewelry can be dismantled and the parts used in new and original ways. Of course, beads can always be purchased. There are several kinds available including cut, faceted, flower, lined, opaque, translucent, seed, spacer, and vertebrae beads.

Other supplies necessary for beadcraft are beadcraft thread and wire, bead pins, dental floss, elastic yarn, flower wire, glue, pliers, ruler, and T-pins.

Basic Procedures

The procedures for the three crafts discussed here will be described separately.

EGGERY

Use large white eggs. Carefully wash and dry the eggs, and allow them to warm to room temperature.

Emptying the Eggshell

Hold an egg in one hand over a bowl. At one end of the egg make a small hole, approximately 1/4" in diameter, with a hat pin and take away the small pieces of shell right around the hole. Make a second hole a bit larger at the opposite end. Place the mouth over the small hole and blow the contents of the egg out of the larger hole into the bowl. (The contents can be cooked and eaten.)

Rinse the inside of the eggshell with water; then blow again to remove the water. Set the eggshell, small end down, in an egg carton to drain and dry. Eggshells should be thoroughly dry before they are cut to prevent warping and formation of mildew.

Cutting the Egg

The egg has two layers. The outside layer is hard like porcelain; the inside, soft like chalk. To keep the egg from cracking while cutting, paint the entire shell with white glue and let dry.

Cutting a Hole for a Figure. (1) With a pencil, sketch an opening of the desired size on the eggshell. The hole must be large enough to allow a small figure to be placed inside the egg. (2) Use small manicure scissors to cut an opening along the pencil line. (3) Cut around the pencil line, taking small cuts with the middle part of the scissors.

Don't worry about jagged edges — they can be covered. If the egg cracks, apply one coat of white glue to both the inside and the outside of the shell.

Cutting an Eggshell in Half. An eggshell can be cut horizontally or vertically in half. Score lines gently with a razor blade and cut through.

Cutting a Door and Placing Hinges. (1) With a pencil, sketch an opening of the desired size on the eggshell. Use a razor blade to cut out this "door." (2) Place the hinge on the door so that the ridge at which the hinge bends is along the edge of the door. Trace around the hinge and along the edge at the bend of the hinge (this will be a notch). (3) Place the hinge on the egg so that the ridge is along the edge of the hole (or "doorway"). Trace around the hinge and along the edge at the bend of the hinge as before. (4) Cut out rectangular notches in the door and the egg for the hinge. Use manicure scissors and snip into the edge of the shell. (5) Place the hinge into the notch on the egg. Glue hinge to egg with cement glue (epoxy) and allow to dry for several hours. Avoid getting glue into hinge. Glue hinge to door and allow to dry for several hours.

Trimming the Egg

Gather trim — pearls, jewels, sequins, gold-silver braids (preferably with adhesive backing), velvet, or scraps of lace. Some braid has loops which can be filled with small beads. To fill braid with beads, apply a bit of glue to each loop and, using tweezer, place a pearl on each loop. Then, place a line of glue next to the beads for another type of braid. Place the ends of the braid at the top or the bottom of the egg so they are not noticeable. Beads which have already been strung are particularly easy to apply. Allow the glue to dry.

Miniature figures can be placed inside the egg. They can either be glued or attached to a small piece of white styrofoam which has been placed inside the egg. Grass or angel hair can be used to cover the styrofoam. The figures can be used to create scenes which tell a story or depict an historical event. These are particularly apropos for holiday gifts and displays.

Decorated eggs may be mounted on a base. This base can be plain or decorated with many of the same ornaments used for the egg.

STYROFOAM CRAFTS

Rather than discussing general procedures for working with styrofoam, the reader is referred to the "Projects You Can Do" section of this article. Several specific methods of working with styrofoam are described.

BEADCRAFT EMBROIDERY

Embroidery with beads involves threading the beads on cord or string and holding the beads together as a design. Use a needle to fasten the beads to a prepared backing. Embroidering on loosely woven fabric is easier than on closely woven material.

The threads or lines in the fabric act as a guide for keeping the stitches straight. If using plain material with no guides, add lightly colored chalk lines. Use beads with large holes in case the thread must pass through the hole several times. The type of bead is very important; on projects which will be laundered, use only glass, plastic, or ceramic beads — never wooden ones. Detergent will cause the wood finish to flake. Use thick wool yarn.

Learning the Stitches

The *running stitch* is the basic stitch. Thread a needle with a polyester thread and knot one end.

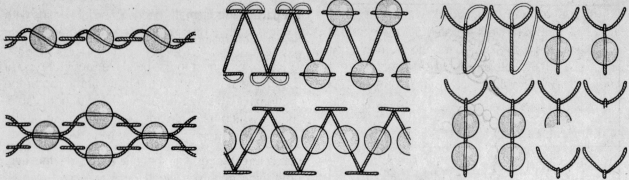

Figure 6. The basic stitch in beadcraft embroidery is the running stitch (left). Use a winding thread under each stitch to hold the bead. A chevron stitch (center) can be done with one thread, doubled back halfway on the underside running stitches. A Y-stitch (right) begins with a loose, arc-like stitch, fastened by a stitch from underneath for the tail.

Bring the needle from the wrong side of the fabric backing to the right side. Slip a bead onto the needle and go back through the wrong side again, pulling the thread until the bead lies flat. This is one running stitch. The stitches should be neat and evenly spaced, but space between stitches can be longer or shorter than the stitches themselves. The beads will not slide around on the thread if the running stitches are close together and the beads are large enough to fill in the spaces.

The chevron stitch looks like two parallel rows of running stitches with a third thread winding between rows. The stitch is made with one thread on two parallel lines (see illustration). Practice a few times using embroidery floss, then string some beads to determine the desired placement.

The Y-stitch looks like the letter "Y" and is very easy to make. Variations of this stitch depend upon the length of the stem of the Y. Follow the diagram to learn the stitch. The Y-stitch makes an interesting border.

Projects You Can Do

PLASTER OF PARIS EASTER EGGS

Materials

The materials needed are: dry, empty eggshells; plaster of Paris; small brushes; acrylic paints; masking tape; clear shellac; needle; and bottle caps or disposable plastic cups to use as egg holders.

Making and Painting Plaster Eggs

Chip out a small hole at both ends of each of sev-

eral eggs, and blow out the contents of the eggs into a bowl (see under "Basic Procedures"). Then wash out and dry the shells. Enlarge one of the holes in each egg by chipping away some of the shell. Place the eggshells in the egg cups with the chipped-out holes facing up. Mix plaster to a creamy consistency, following the manufacturer's directions. Pour the plaster slowly and carefully through the chipped-out hole in each eggshell.

Fill the shells to the top and allow a few days for drying. When the plaster is set, gently tap the egg against a hard surface and peel the shell away. If necessary, sand the plaster egg until it develops a smooth surface. Paint the eggs. Apply two or three coats of a light color, allowing each coat to dry before applying the next. After paint is dry, apply two or three coats of shellac.

JEWEL-LIKE MOSAIC EGG

Materials

The materials for this project are: dry, empty eggshells; six or eight colors of enamel paint; small brushes; colored sequins; round, colored 1/16" beads on thread; match sticks; egg carton; large needle; and white glue.

Preparation of Eggs

With a darning needle, pierce a small hole in the small end of each egg and a larger hole at the opposite end. Blow out the contents of each egg, then wash out and dry the shells (see under "Basic Procedures").

Work with the smaller end of the egg up. Copy

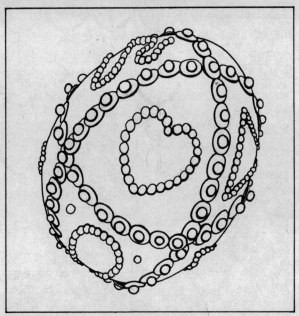

Figure 7. Pictured above is the finished mosaic egg project, ready for display.

symmetrical designs quarter by quarter: first on the front of the egg, then on the back, joining the lines at the sides. Use bright colors for filling in one-color areas on the top and bottom of each egg. Let each color dry before starting another. Use eight colors on each egg. When drying the egg, place a match stick in one of the holes and push the other end of the match stick into the lid of the egg carton. After half of the egg has been enameled and is dry, repeat the process on the other half.

Using a large needle, draw a line with clear-drying glue on an area where threaded beads are to go. Lay the beads on the glued lines, and hold them in place so that they do not slip while the glue dries. Cut off any excess threaded bead and glue the last bead to the egg. Place glue over all beaded areas to make sure they are secure. Glue sequins on the design lines and over the holes of both eggs. Glue a single bead in the center of each sequin.

LACQUERED EGGS

Materials

Materials needed for this project include: dry, empty eggshells; dried moss; small, dried flowers; delicate fern fronds; clear glue; acrylic paints and soft brushes; small sponge; bowl; egg carton; and paper towels.

Preparing the Eggs

Select such materials as dried flowers, moss, and fern fronds. Create a design and lightly trace it onto the egg. Brush glue on eggshells to fit design. Moisten fingers to pick up materials; place them on the glue. Place all petals and cover the holes at each end of the egg. Moisten a sponge and squeeze it in a paper towel until the towel is damp. Press the towel gently against the materials until they are affixed to the shell; remove excess glue. Place the egg in the egg carton until the glue dries. Repeat the steps to attach any remaining materials to the shell. Let the design dry for several days.

Coat the egg with an acrylic varnish, applying it to half the egg at a time. Apply three coats, brushing each coat in a different direction.

Figure 8. This lacquered egg (above) is decorated with dried flowers, leaves, and moss. These materials should be thoroughly dried before they are glued to the egg.

Figure 9. For the styrofoam balls project, use fabric, sequins, ribbons, and beads for decoration. Fabric and ribbon are glued to the ball, then the beads and sequins are secured with pins.

STYROFOAM BALLS

Materials

Materials needed for this project include: styrofoam balls; pencil and paper; scissors; fabric; clear-drying glue; pins; braid; and jewels, sequins, and beads.

Decorating the Ball

Trace a pattern of a section of the ball on paper, cut out the pattern, and pin it to the fabric. Cut out the fabric around the pattern and glue the fabric section to the ball. After the material is glued, pin each end of the section to the ball with a straight pin to secure it. Repeat the procedure, adding fabric sections all around the ball. (The ball will have alternating areas of styrofoam and fabric.) Then, glue thin braid at the edges of each fabric section. Fill in areas of the braid with sequins and beads, using pins to attach them. Designs can be added between the fabric sections using sequins, pins, pearls, or jewels. Finally, cut a piece of braid for hanging the ball. Overlap the ends to form a loop. Glue the ends together and pin them into the braid and ball.

STYROFOAM CENTERPIECE

The centerpiece — consisting of a snow scene with several buildings, a small girl, and small artificial evergreen trees — is constructed of styrofoam, cardboard, and various trims.

Materials

The materials needed for this project are: one styrofoam circle 17" in diameter; one styrofoam circle 13" in diameter; one styrofoam block 5" x 5" x 3"; one styrofoam ball 5" in diameter for the arch at the top of the block; one square styrofoam column about 6" tall; one styrofoam cylinder about 5" tall; styrofoam slabs; two styrofoam balls from which onion-shaped domes will be made; a small styrofoam ball for head; cardboard; wrapping paper; scissors; knife; spoon; felt-tip pens; clear-drying glue; trims; artificial snow; and tiny evergreen trees.

Constructing the Centerpiece

Glue the 13" circle on top of the 17" one for the base. Glue the 5" x 5" x 3" block of styrofoam to the center of the base. Cut the 5" ball in half and scoop it out to form arches (see illustration); glue this piece to the top of the square block. Glue the square styrofoam pillar behind the arched structure. For the top of the pillar, cut four triangles measuring 2" on each side from cardboard and glue them together (see illustration). Glue this piece to the top of the square pillar. To the left of the arched structure, glue the 5" cylindrical pillar. Using a knife, fashion two onion-shaped domes from the two styrofoam balls (see illustration). Glue one dome to the top of the cylinder. For the remaining building, cut and glue styrofoam slabs as shown in the illustration. Glue the remaining onion-shaped dome top to this building. Trim the pillars, buildings, and domes with braids and beads as desired.

To make the little girl, cut a circle about 5" in diameter from wrapping paper. Fold the circle in half and roll it into a cone. Glue the ends together to make the dress. Make the sleeves the same way using circles 3" in diameter. Glue the sleeves to the dress. Glue a small foam ball to the top of the dress for a head; paint in facial features. For the hat, roll several strips of wrapping paper, glue together, and trim with scissors to a point; glue feathers made with colored felt pens to the hat. Glue the girl to the base.

Add artificial snow and tiny evergreen trees to complete the scene.

STYROFOAM FLOCKED ORNAMENTS

Materials

Materials required for this project include: styrofoam ball, designer yarn in several colors, thin cord, gold and silver braid, white glue, straight pins, pencil, and tinsel.

Preparation of Ornament

Make an outline of the desired design on the foam ball. Glue gold and silver cord over the lines.

Cut the various colors of yarn into 1" lengths, keeping the colors separated. Spread glue over the part of the ball which is to be flocked with one of the colors. Paste the 1" pieces of yarn to the glued area of the ball, covering it completely. Repeat the procedure with the other colors.

To enhance the appearance of the ornament, make the following tassel.

1. Cut a piece of cardboard 4" x 2" and wrap tinsel or yarn around the 4" side about 30 times.

2. Put a 7" thread under the wrap (see illustration) at one end and tie a knot to hold the wrap together. This end will be the top of the tassel.

3. At the other end, cut the wrap free from the cardboard. Trim the bottom if necessary.

4. Cut a 12" piece of yarn. Wrap this length tightly around the top of the tassel several times. Tie the ends and clip off the extra yarn.

5. Pin the top of the tassel to the ornament.

STYROFOAM EASTER EGG

Materials

Materials required for this project are: (1) a styrofoam egg; (2) sequins; (3) clusters of tiny artificial flowers; (4) single tiny artificial flowers; (5) small oat pearls; (6) small faceted beads; (7) appliqué flowers; (8) bunny or some other Easter figure; (9) narrow velvet ribbon; (10) straight pins; (11) hatpin; (12) scissors; (13) knife; and (14) white glue.

Cutting the Egg

Cut the egg lengthwise with the knife so that one piece is larger than the other. Using the knife, scoop out a cavity in the larger piece big enough for the figure. The smaller piece will be used for the base.

Decorating the Egg

1. Begin decorating the egg by placing sequins and small faceted beads around the cavity. However, leave some space between the cavity and the sequins and beads for the placement of flowers. Use straight pins to position the sequins and beads.

2. Insert clusters of tiny flowers into the egg between the cavity and the sequins and beads and also inside the cavity.

3. Place the figure inside the cavity. If the figure cannot be inserted into the styrofoam, glue it in place.

4. Fill in any empty spots around and inside the cavity with the single tiny flowers.

5. Cut a length of the velvet ribbon for a bow. Glue a faceted bead on a straight pin, and pin the bow to the top of the egg.

6. Cut a length of velvet ribbon for around the front of the egg, and pin it in place. For a more decorative effect, glue an oat pearl on the head of each pin before inserting it through the ribbon.

Decorating the Base

1. Arrange appliqué flowers around the base about halfway between the top and the bottom. (Leave enough space at the center of the top for the egg.) Secure the flowers by inserting a straight pin with an oat pearl attached through the center of each flower.

2. Cut a length of velvet ribbon for around the bottom of the base. Pin it in place with straight pins to which oat pearls have been attached.

3. Insert clusters of tiny flowers around the base, and fill in empty spots with single flowers.

4. Insert the hatpin into the flat part of the base and out the top. To make the base level, push the end of the hatpin into the styrofoam.

5. Press the egg onto the protruding end of the hatpin. To make the decoration more stable, place glue on the hatpin and at the points where the egg will touch the base before pressing the egg onto the hatpin.

EMBROIDERED LEATHER HANDBAG

A plain handbag or change purse can benefit from an embroidered and beaded design. Use an old leather handbag at home for practice, or buy one with no decoration. Use a smooth leather rather

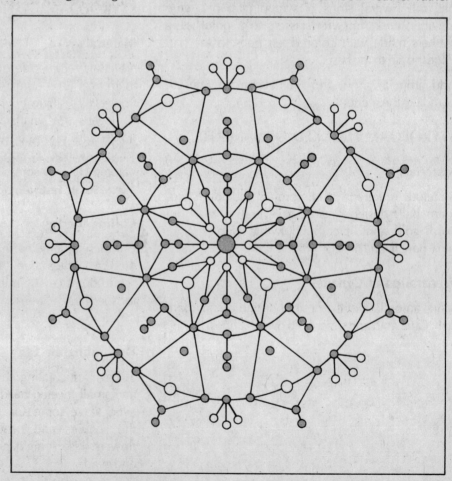

Figure 10. On the right is the pattern for a beaded and embroidered handbag. Be sure to use a thick needle for sewing on leather.

**Figure 11. Embroidered beadwork decorates this handsome evening bag (above).
The embroidery for this bag is time-consuming but well worth the effort,
considering the price of a purchased bag of this type.**

than suede. Sewing on leather requires a heavy-duty needle with a large eye. When the needle goes through the leather, the eye will make a hole larger than the thread, and the thread will go through without any problem. Use buttonhole twist when sewing on the leather. It is strong, has a sheen, and comes in a variety of colors.

To make embroidered decorations, follow the steps suggested in *Beadcraft Embroidery* under "Basic Procedures." For leather decorations, use a sharp knife and carefully cut out leather circles of the desired size. Glue and stitch the desired pattern.

For Additional Reading

Barth, Edna, **Lillies, Rabbits, and Painted Eggs,** Random House, 1962.

Glick, James E., **Boutique Eggs and Ornaments,** Mission Viego, California, 1973.

Hofsimde, Robert, **Indian Beadwork,** 1958.

Newall, Venetia, **An Egg at Easter,** Indiana Univ. Press, 1971.

Purdy, Susan, **Festivals,** Lippincott, 1969.